list of exhibits

has no a priori evaluative significance (in the sense of preferability); further, it has no specific content or referent. When the concept acquires an evaluative significance (e.g., that there is more magic in the number 2 than the number 1, or that two heads are better than one), it begins to approximate an attitude. In this sense, an attitude might be said to be an evaluative concept which has been applied to a specific referent (Harvey et al., 1961; Rhine, 1958).

Attitudes are similar to *motives* in that both terms refer to the directionality of behavior but not to behavior itself. As Newcomb (1950) points out, the construct attitude differs from that of motive in at least two ways: First, an attitude is not characterized by an existing drive state, but only refers to the probability that a given motive (and its accompanying drive) may be elicited. Therefore, attitudes may be considered drive producing (Doob, 1947). Second, an attitude is labelled by its object and may be considered object specific, whereas motives are labelled by their goals and are goal specific.

In social psychology, opinion and value are constructs which have been used in a manner similar to attitude. At times they have been carelessly used as though they were synonymous with the term. Definitions of the term *value* are scarce and imprecise. English and English (1958, p. 576) define value as "degree of worth ascribed to an object or activity (or class thereof)." Generally, this degree of worth is ascribed by the possessor of the attitude on the basis of the instrumentality of the object for the facilitation or inhibition of goal achievement (Woodruff and Di Vesta, 1948; Rosenberg, 1953). As we have defined the term, attitude would include the affective reactions which characterize this valuing process and which give rise to or are accompanied by motive arousal (as when the affective reaction of frustration occurs upon blocking of goal-directed activity and gives rise to an aggressive motive).

Opinion is similar to both attitude and belief. English and English (1958, p. 358) define this term as "a belief that one holds to be without emotional commitment or desire, and to be open to reevaluation since the evidence is not affirmed to be convincing." This definition denies to opinion the affective reaction which typifies attitude. Hovland et al. (1953) make the following other differentiations between opinion and attitude: Opinions are verbalizable, while attitudes are sometimes mediated by nonverbal processes or are "unconscious," and opinions are responses, while attitudes are response predispositions. These differentiations seem compatible with the definition of attitude advanced in this book.

Attitude differs from the constructs of set, habit, and trait in the following ways. *Set* and *habit* reflect an action tendency. Set emphasizes motor readiness. Habit indicates a somewhat stronger action tendency than set and a more complex, enduring structure. Both set and habit are acquired as are attitudes, but neither reflects an affective or evaluative reaction. A *trait* may be defined as a more or less stable and consistent disposition of the individual to respond in a certain way which differentiates him from other individuals. Attitudes differ from traits primarily in that attitudes have a specific referent, whereas traits are nonspecific, generalized orientations of the individual. An attitude is revealed in generalized behavior toward a specific object (referent), whereas a trait is reflected in either a specific or a general behavior toward a wide variety of objects (generality of the behavior depending upon whether it is a cardinal or secondary trait).

Dimensions of Attitudes

In addition to being predispositions to respond to social objects, attitudes have been said to possess the following general characteristics (Hovland et al., 1953; Krech et al., 1962; Sherif and Cantril, 1945; Sherif and Sherif, 1956):

1. *Attitudes are based upon evaluative concepts regarding characteristics of the referent object and give rise to motivated behavior* (Anderson and Fishbein, 1965; Doob, 1947; Osgood et al., 1957). Attitudes are evaluative, affective reactions which are based upon application of evaluative concepts and which give rise to motivation. By "affective" is meant the state of the organism under conditions in which the animal is goal oriented and succeeds or fails, perceives that it is succeeding or failing, or anticipates that it will succeed or fail in goal striving. These conditions are characterized by such affective reactions as frustration, deprivation, and gratification. A special condition is the lack of goal clarity which is characterized by anxiety. These states in turn give rise to such motives as aggression, affiliation, avoidance, and so forth. Thus, attitudes are not motives, but they produce motives(and accompanying drive states). These motives, in interaction with situational and other dispositional characteristics, determine overt behavior.

It is clear that the arousal of attitude is dependent upon the existence of some drive state which is reflected in the goal orientation of the frustrated or gratified animal. It is also clear that the scales used in assessment of attitudes measure only one dimension of the affective or "feeling" reaction which we are referring to as attitude: the positive-negative evaluation of the object.

As the attitudinal referent is conceived to be goal facilitating, it will be evaluated positively; it is evaluated negatively to the extent that it is conceived as inhibiting or interfering with goal attainment. When there is a larger number of concepts or beliefs regarding the inhibition or facilitation of goal attainment by the object, the attitude toward the object will be stronger. This affective, evaluative reaction will be more intense as the goal is more important to the conceiver.

As affective reactions, attitudes are implicit responses which serve as producers of motives. The nature of this implicit response is evaluative and based upon the conception of the object by the individual holding the attitude. As previously pointed out, conception is essentially the act of placing two or more psychological entities in some relationship with one another. In this instance, it is the act of placing the object of the attitude in some relationship with the goals of the conceiver. The relationship formed in a concept may be any one (e.g., taller than, greener than, congruent with, identical to, etc.). However, the concepts which underlie attitudes are evaluative in nature and specify some degree of preferability (e.g., better than, cleaner than, more vicious than, etc.). The precise nature of the preferability depends upon the goal orientations of the conceiver.

Questions of consciousness always arise in conjunction with consideration of cognitive variables. In this regard, attitudes vary in the degree to which the possessor can verbalize or otherwise indicate his awareness of possession of such a predisposition. Hovland et al. (1953) distinguish between attitudes and opinions partly on this basis: Opinions are verbal responses which are always accessible to awareness, whereas attitudes are verbal and nonverbal response predispositions which may or may not be available to awareness.

The behavioral consequents of attitudes include such diverse behaviors as running, blushing, changing body stance, and verbalization. There are four general categories of behavior which may be described: positive approach (e.g., friendliness, wooing, etc.), negative approach (e.g., attack), negative avoidance (e.g., repulsion or fear), and positive avoidance (e.g., allowing others privacy when they are stressed). These categories of behavior correspond to hypothetical categories of affective reaction. However, attitude scales do not measure the approach-avoidance dimension of this category system; they measure only the positive-negative dimension.

2. *Attitudes are construed as varying in quality and intensity* (*or strength*) *on a continuum from positive through neutral to negative* (Krech et al., 1962; McGrath, 1964; Newcomb, Turner, and Converse, 1965). Qualitative variation of the attitude is represented by the valence (positive or negative), which reflects the evaluation of the object in relation to goal attainment. The strength or intensity of the attitude is represented by the extremity of the position occupied on the continuum, becoming stronger as one goes outward from a neutral position. This intensity reflects the strength of the affective reaction. The strength of the elicited motive is expected to correspond to the strength of this reaction. Attitudes on one side of such a continuum indicate negative affective reactions which arouse responses of negative approach and avoidance such as attack and repulsion, respectively. Attitudes on the other side of the continuum indicate positive affective reactions which result in responses of positive approach and avoidance.

Guttman (1954) posits involution as another scale component which bears a relationship to this continuum. Involution, or the degree to which the person is actively concerned about the matter in question, is curvilinearly related to either half of this continuum. As one goes out from neutral toward either an extremely positive or negative position on the continuum, involution increases up to a point, beyond which it decreases for more extreme attitudes. According to this formulation, there is some optimum degree of extremity of an attitude at which the person is most actively concerned with the issue.

The neutral point of the attitude continuum poses a problem of interpretation, to which several alternative solutions have been proposed. First, one may consider the statement that an attitude is neutral to be self-contradictory, indicating the presence of a response predisposition on the one hand and the lack of a predisposition on the other. From this viewpoint, the neutral position on the attitude continuum represents *no* attitude toward the object in question. A second, alternative interpretation which may be given to the neutral point is that it represents the point of balance in positive-negative evaluative conflict, thereby reflecting an ambivalent attitude. Guttman's approach (1954) would suggest that where ambivalence is the case, it is because the questions in the scale are not measuring a unidimensional attitude for that population of persons. Thus the universe of content cannot be represented by a single variable.

With regard to ambivalence, this term seems best reserved to refer to two or more attitudes. Then ambivalence is used to indicate the existence of two or more attitudes toward the same referent or several referents possessing some degree of similarity of stimulus value and being grouped as a referent class.

A third interpretation is based on neutral range scores achieved by inconsistent responses. It is that the subjects possessing such scores do not have integrated, clearly defined attitudes regarding the object (Walter, 1951). Freeman and Haer (1951, p. 474) offer a methodology for testing this interpretation, and, on the basis of their empirical study, reject such an interpretation as "neither empirically nor theoretically feasible in the field of opinion and attitude research." (See Chapter 2 for a discussion of methodological considerations relative to the zero point of attitude scales.)

3. *Attitudes are learned, rather than being innate or a result of constitutional development and maturation* (Sherif and Sherif, 1956; McGrath, 1964). Attitudes are learned through interaction with social objects and in social events or situations. Since they are learned, attitudes demonstrate the same properties as other learned reactions such as latency and threshold, and they are subject to further change through thinking, inhibition, extinction, fatigue, etc. (Gallenbech and Smith, 1950). Thus attitudes are subject to alteration, maintenance, and breakdown through manipulation of the same order of variables as those producing their original acquisition. All forms of learning (classical and instrumental forms of conditioning, etc.) conceivably provide bases for the acquisition of attitudes.

4. *Attitudes have specific social referents, or specific classes thereof* (Sherif and Sherif, 1956; Newcomb et al., 1965). These referents need not be concrete objects, but include such abstract referents as political issues, world problems, and Godhead. That they possess social referents reflects the social context in which they are learned. These learning experiences may be the result of direct contact with the object or situation or the result of indirect contact with them through direct contact with other persons. Indirect-contact effects include all the processes of norm inculcation and selective transmission of information occurring in social groups.

Attitudes possess varying degrees of definitiveness and scope with regard to the number and kinds of objects encompassed as referents. Krech et al. (1962) use the term *multiplexity* to refer to the scope of the attitude. A multiplex attitude is one possessing a large number or a heterogeneous group of objects in its referent class. Definitiveness refers it is a consequence of the attitude. Behavior is determined by a complex set of forces, so that the effect of any one determinant is contingent upon the number and strength of other determinants operating at any given time. Therefore, it is possible that two persons holding opposite attitudes toward a given object will behave in identical ways (outwardly, at least) toward that object. For example, two members of an industrial organization may attend a dinner honoring the president upon the occasion of his retirement. Both may speak glowingly of his accomplishments, although one has a very favorable and the other a very unfavorable attitude toward him. The attitude makes it more likely, but does not ensure, that the behavior will take a particular form.

In summary, we believe that attitude is best viewed as a set of affective reactions toward the attitude object, derived from the concepts or beliefs that the individual has concerning the object, and predisposing the individual to behave in a certain manner toward the attitude object. Although intimately related to attitude, neither the propositions that the individual accepts about the object (beliefs) nor the action tendencies are a part of the attitude itself.

Our conception rejects the notion that attitudes are composed of three components. Rather, the affective reactions specified by the traditional analysis constitute the attitude; the traditional cognitive component provides the basis for an evaluation and, thereby, for the attitude; and the attitude predisposes the individual to act in a certain manner toward the attitude object. We accept the other characteristics of attitude as traditionally described. That is, attitudes are learned; they are relatively stable; they have a specific referent (or class thereof); they vary in direction and intensity; and they possess varying degrees of interrelatedness and of scope. We would add that they possess varying degrees of definitiveness.

If the above conceptualization of attitude is correct, we would expect attitude change to occur when the individual is induced to accept concepts in the form of propositions that incorporate new and different evaluations. If one wishes to change an attitude in an unfavorable (favorable) direction, an attempt would be made to bring about acceptance of the proposition that the attitude object possesses negatively (positively) valued attributes. This is the approach usually taken by investigators who attempt to change attitudes through communications (Hovland et al., 1953). A direct attack on the evaluation should be effective only to the extent that associated concepts are changed or that the evaluation reflected by existing (and especially the more central) concepts are altered.

Relation of this Construct of Attitude to Measurement Techniques

The most frequently used methods of measuring attitude (Thurstone, 1929, 1931; Likert, 1932; Guttman, 1944) require subjects to indicate their agreement or disagreement with a set of statements about the attitude object. Generally, these statements attribute to the object characteristics that are positively or negatively evaluated and rarely neutral. In the Thurstone method of scale construction (see Chapter 2), the statements are scaled for the degree to which the statement expresses a favorable or unfavorable attitude, based upon the consensus of judges. In other methods, the scale constructor writes items that express positively or negatively evaluative propositions regarding the object. In short, the typical attitude scale measures the acceptance of evaluative statements about the attitude object. The attitude toward the object is inferred from the statements endorsed by the subject, based upon the consensual evaluation of the nature of the characteristics attributed to the object by the acceptance of these statements. Such scales measure only the positivity-negativity of the affective reaction.

It is clear that our conception of attitude is implicit in the techniques of attitude measurement. The only inferential step involved is the assumption that the evaluations of the persons involved in scale construction correspond to those of the individuals whose attitudes are being measured. This may or may not be true for specific items, but the error should be small for the total set of statements.

SUMMARY

In this chapter, we have surveyed traditional conceptualizations of the construct attitude and have attempted to present a conceptualization which integrates these approaches. Our reason for adding still another definition of attitude to the already existing multitude of such definitions is to relate the construct more closely to its operation, thereby providing some unity of approach to the research areas. For, as Campbell (1950) has observed, the disagreement about the construct implicit in the tremendous diversity of conceptual definitions is in strong contrast to the agreement implicit in the rather universal acceptance of the operational definition of the term.

We have attempted to explicate this conception of attitude by comparing it with other, similar constructs, by examining the various dimensions of the construct, and by discussing the measurement procedures in relation to the construct.

As was noted in the introduction to this chapter, the study of attitudes has occupied and continues to occupy a central place in social-psychological research. Knowledge of attitudes and their functioning is of interest both theoretically and practically. No theory of social behavior can be complete without incorporation of attitude functioning, and it is doubtful that complex social behavior can be predicted without a knowledge of attitude. To study attitudes requires that they be measured. Consequently, the major purpose of this book is to present and describe scales for the measurement of attitudes. Chapter 2 presents a description of the major procedures whereby such scales are constructed, and subsequent chapters present the scales themselves.

CHAPTER **2**

methods of scale construction

Measurement is the assignment of numerals to objects or events according to a rule or a set of rules (Campbell, 1940; Stevens, 1951). When we attempt to measure attitudes, we assign numerals to persons according to a set of rules that are intended to create an isomorphism between the assigned numeral and the person's attitude toward the object in question. Since an attitude is a hypothetical, or latent, variable rather than an immediately observable variable (Green, 1954), attitude measurement consists of the assessment of an individual's responses to a set of situations. The set of situations is usually a set of statements (items) about the attitude object, to which the individual responds with a set of specified response categories, e.g., "agree" and "disagree." The value assigned to an individual's response to a given item is called an item score, and the number derived from his item scores represents his position on the latent attitude variable. We will refer to a set of items, along with the item scores, as an attitude scale, although some writers (e.g., Green, 1954) use the term to refer to the set of scores obtained from the set of items.

In this chapter, we will discuss: (1) the properties of attitude scales and some of the problems associated with the determination of these properties, (2) the standard methods of constructing attitude scales, and (3) some special methods of attitude measurement. Our purpose is to provide the reader with the necessary background for understanding the descriptions of the scales in subsequent chapters, rather than to provide sufficient information for scale construction. We have included some methods that have not been used for scales given in this book in order to familiarize the reader with these techniques and to encourage exploitation of these methods in future scale constructions.

PROPERTIES OF ATTITUDE SCALES

The usefulness of an attitude scale depends upon its properties. At minimum, a useful scale must be reliable (yield consistent results) and valid (measure what it is purported to measure). Other characteristics of an attitude scale that often are desirable include equality of units, unidimensionality, and a zero point.

Reliability

The concept of reliability is a complex one. The simplest definition of reliability is the degree to which a scale yields consistent scores when the attitude is measured a number of times. (For a more detailed consideration of the concept and problems of reliability, see Ghiselli, 1964.) In general, there are three empirical methods of estimating the reliability of an attitude scale: the correlation between scores on the same test given at different times (the test-retest method), the correlation between two comparable forms of the same scale (the equivalent-forms method), and the correlation between comparable parts of the same scale (the split-half method).

The Test-Retest Method. This method corresponds most closely to the conceptual notion of reliability, and the procedure is simple. The attitude scale is administered to the same group of persons at two different times, and the correlation between the two sets of scores is computed. This coefficient, usually the Pearson r, is the reliability estimate. If the test is given more than twice, the average of the intercorrelations among the various scores may be taken as the reliability estimate.

The test-retest method has the advantage of holding constant the items used, thus eliminating unreliability due to differences between items, which occurs in the equivalent-forms method. It also has the advantage of requiring only a single scale; no additional forms are needed.

The test-retest method has several disadvantages. First, the fact that the subject has been tested on one occasion may influence his attitude score on subsequent measurements. The most likely effect is that the individual may remember the specific items and simply respond the same way as on the first administration, thus yielding a spuriously high reliability estimate. It is also possible that responding to an attitude scale will change the individual's attitude, or that events will have occurred during the test interval which will change his attitude. To complicate matters further, all these effects may be different for different items chosen are those nearest the individual's position on the attitude continuum. Since direction is ignored, it is as if the respondent had folded the scale over, using his position as the folding point. The resulting scale (called a J scale) represents a joint distribution having both items and individuals on it. The following figure illustrates this. The letters, *A*, *B*, *C*, and *D*, represent items along the underlying attitude continuum; the

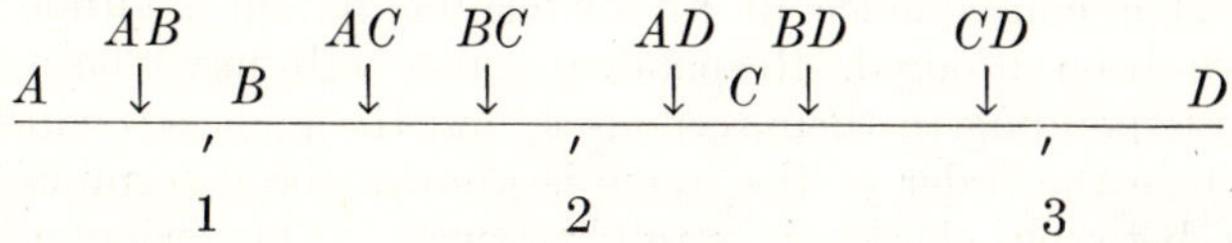

Hypothetical J scale. Letters represent items, numbers represent individuals, and arrows indicate midpoints between pairs of items.

numerals, 1, 2, and 3, represent individuals; and the arrows represent the midpoints between pairs of items. Suppose that respondent number 1 is asked to pick the two items that he is most willing to endorse. According to the assumption that such choices reflect the individual's relative distance from the items, his choices should be items *A* and *B*. It is evident, then, that all individuals to the left of midpoint *AC* will choose items *A* and *B*; those to the left of midpoint *BC* but to the right of midpoint *AC* will choose items *B* and *C*; and so on. The respondent's choices thus reveal something about his position on the underlying attitude dimension.

For data collected by the pick-two procedure, Coombs suggested a weak form of analysis called the parallelogram technique. A matrix is constructed with items as columns and individuals as rows. If an individual endorses an item, a check is entered in the cell at the intersection of the respective arrays. Rows and columns in the matrix are permuted in an attempt to arrange them so that the entries form a diagonal band from top left to bottom right, with entries in every row and every column adjacent. If this is accomplished, responses of individuals can be described simply by the order of columns representing the ordinal position of items and the order of rows representing the ordinal position of individuals on the attitude continuum.

A stronger form of analysis is possible when the respondent is asked to order items with respect to his willingness to endorse. For simplicity, we consider only data collected by order-*k* procedures. Analysis proceeds the same as in the parallelogram procedure, except that the entries in the cells of the matrix are the numbers 1 and 2, which indicate the order of choices. Permutation of rows and columns is continued until a matrix is obtained that satisfies certain conditions or until it is determined that no such matrix exists. These conditions are as follows (from Coombs, 1953):

1 Entries in each row and in each column must be adjacent with no blanks.
2 Entries in the first row and the first column must monotonically increase from left to right and from top to bottom, respectively.

3 Entries in the last row and the last column must monotonically decrease from left to right and from top to bottom.
4 Entries in all other columns must monotonically decrease and then increase from top to bottom.

If these conditions are satisfied, the responses of individuals may be regarded as a consequence of an underlying latent attitude on which items have been ordered. Respondents also will have been placed in classes corresponding to their responses, and these classes will have been ordered. Once the order of the items is known, the determination of the midpoints between classes is straightforward. The orders of adjacent classes of respondents differ only by the interchange in rank of two adjacent items; thus, the boundary between the two adjacent classes is the midpoint of the two items interchanged. (See Torgerson, 1958, for a detailed discussion of analytical procedures.)

Although the main purpose of the unfolding technique is to discover latent attributes, it can be used to construct an ordinal attitude scale by the procedures outlined above. As mentioned earlier, procedures designed specifically for attitude scale construction have been derived from the basic unfolding theory. One of these is described below.

Method of Unfolded Partial Rank Order

This technique (abbreviated UPRO) was suggested by Banta (1961) who used it in a study comparing scales developed by this procedure with standard Thurstone and Likert scales. As in other procedures, the technique begins with a set of items about the object of the attitude. Respondents are asked to respond to items using a five-category response system, ranging from "much too unfavorable for me," through "my own feelings," to "much too favorable for me." Thus the respondent provides a partial rank ordering of the items, unfolded from his own position.

Item scale values are determined by assigning integral weights to each response category and computing the mean response for each item over all respondents. Using these scale values, three UPRO respondent scores may be computed: (1) a mean agree score, computed as the mean scale value of all items the respondent checks as "my own feelings," (2) a summated rating score, computed as the mean response to all items, (3) a summated psychometric score, computed as the percent of items considered by the respondent to be either too unfavorable or with which he agrees. Banta reports intercorrelations among these scores ranging from .75 to .95 for specific referents (President Eisenhower; college fraternities) and from .05 to .84 for a generalized referent (people in general).

The characteristics of scales developed by this technique have not been clearly established. Beyond the intercorrelations among scores reported above, Banta provides no evidence concerning reliability. Validity appears acceptably high as estimated from correlations with Thurstone and Likert scales (.67 to .96). UPRO's chief advantage over the other methods is that item scale values and respondent attitude scores can be obtained from a single administration of the items. This tech-

scales for the measurement of attitudes

McGraw-Hill Series in Psychology

Consulting Editors

NORMAN GARMEZY
HARRY F. HARLOW
LYLE V. JONES
HAROLD W. STEVENSON

Beach, Hebb, Morgan, and Nissen The Neuropsychology of Lashley
Von Békésy Experiments in Hearing
Berkowitz Aggression: A Social Psychological Analysis
Berlyne Conflict, Arousal, and Curiosity
Blum Psychoanalytic Theories of Personality
Brown The Motivation of Behavior
Brown and Ghiselli Scientific Method in Psychology
Buckner and McGrath Vigilance: A Symposium
Cofer Verbal Learning and Verbal Behavior
Cofer and Musgrave Verbal Behavior and Learning: Problems and Processes
Crafts, Schneirla, Robinson, and Gilbert Recent Experiments in Psychology
Davitz The Communication of Emotional Meaning
Deese and Hulse The Psychology of Learning
Dollard and Miller Personality and Psychotherapy
Ellis Handbook of Mental Deficiency
Epstein Varieties of Perceptual Learning
Ferguson Statistical Analysis in Psychology and Education
Forgus Perception: The Basic Process in Cognitive Development
Ghiselli Theory of Psychological Measurement
Ghiselli and Brown Personnel and Industrial Psychology
Gilmer Industrial Psychology
Gray Psychology Applied to Human Affairs
Guilford Fundamental Statistics in Psychology and Education
Guilford The Nature of Human Intelligence
Guilford Personality
Guilford Psychometric Methods
Guion Personnel Testing
Haire Psychology in Management
Hirsch Behavior Genetic Analysis
Hirsh The Measurement of Hearing
Hurlock Adolescent Development
Hurlock Child Development
Hurlock Developmental Psychology
Jackson and Messick Problems in Human Assessment
Karn and Gilmer Readings in Industrial and Business Psychology
Krech, Crutchfield, and Ballachey Individual in Society
Lazarus Adjustment and Personality
Lazarus Psychological Stress and the Coping Process
Lewin A Dynamic Theory of Personality
Lewin Principles of Topological Psychology
Maher Principles of Psychopathology

Marx and Hillix Systems and Theories in Psychology
Messick and Brayfield Decision and Choice: Contributions of Sidney Siegel
Miller Language and Communication
Morgan Physiological Psychology
Nunnally Psychometric Theory
Rethlingshafer Motivation as Related to Personality
Robinson and Robinson The Mentally Retarded Child
Scherer and Wertheimer A Psycholinguistic Experiment on Foreign Language Teaching
Shaw and Wright Scales for the Measurement of Attitudes
Sidowski Experimental Methods and Instrumentation in Psychology
Siegel Nonparametric Statistics for the Behavioral Sciences
Stagner Psychology of Personality
Townsend Introduction to Experimental Methods for Psychology and the Social Sciences
Vinacke The Psychology of Thinking
Wallen Clinical Psychology: The Study of Persons
Warren and Akert The Frontal Granular Cortex and Behavior
Waters, Rethlingshafer, and Caldwell Principles of Comparative Psychology
Winer Statistical Principles in Experimental Design
Zubek and Solberg Human Development

scales for the measurement of attitudes

MARVIN E. SHAW
JACK M. WRIGHT

Professors of Psychology, The University of Florida

McGRAW-HILL BOOK COMPANY

New York St. Louis San Francisco
Toronto London Sydney

Scales for the Measurement of Attitudes

Library of Congress Catalog Card Number 66-22791

56498

1 2 3 4 5 6 7 8 9 0 M P 7 3 2 1 0 6 9 8 7 6

TO LMS AND LMW

preface

Attitude research continues to occupy a central position in social psychology. Considerable work has been done investigating the variables influencing attitude formation and change and the effects of attitudes on individual behavior. The contributions of this research are great, and their significance for theory and practice cannot be denied. And yet we cannot avoid the impression that much effort has been wasted and that the contributions might have been even greater if research had been more cumulative in nature. Nowhere is this more evident than in relation to the instruments used in the measurement of attitudes. A very common statement in research reports is that "since no suitable instrument was available, a scale [questionnaire, test, etc.] was developed. . . ." This has led to two unfortunate circumstances. First, the research that has been done by different investigators often is not directly comparable. Second, the quality of the measuring instruments often is poorer than it would have been if existing scales had been used and improved. Far too often the researcher is not sufficiently careful in selecting the tools used to test his hypotheses. Consequently, little standardization is undertaken. Sometimes the report contains no information about the scale beyond the statement that "a scale was used." In addition, there is a very practical difficulty: The researcher spends a considerable amount of time searching for a suitable scale and/or developing his own scale. This time probably could be spent more profitably on the research itself.

In summary, it seemed to us that attitude research has been hindered by the inaccessability of existing attitude scales, resulting in less-than-optimum advances in the scientific analysis of attitudes. The purpose of this volume is to bring together a number of attitude scales that have at least minimal reliability and validity. In addition to these minimal criteria, we have considered the method of construction, the population from which the subjects were drawn for the development and evaluation, and the appropriateness of the items to the current *Zeitgeist*. We have not restricted the selection to formal scales, either in the sense of Guttman's definition (1954) or in the sense of tests developed by more standard scale construction techniques. We have included a number of scales which are well known with regard to their functional characteristics and which enjoy wide usage, although they do not meet the formal definition of a scale. In this regard, we have attempted to include those scales which should prove most useful in meeting the current research needs and in providing a common base of instrumentation for the purpose of comparing research results.

At the beginning of this project we had the grandiose idea that we would make an exhaustive review of the literature and assemble *all* scales that met our criteria. It soon became obvious that this ideal could not be realized. Hence, we make no pretense that we have considered all relevant scales. Nevertheless, we hope that in some small way the scales which we have included will lead to more cumulative research and so advance the understanding of the nature and influence of attitudes.

A few words concerning the organization of the book may be helpful to the reader. Chapters 1 and 2 consider the general nature of attitudes and methods of measurement; Chapters 3 through 10 present the attitude scales and information about their characteristics; and Chapter 11 attempts an evaluation and offers suggestions for improvement. The chapters presenting the attitude scales are the heart of the book; the other chapters merely provide background and supporting information. The attitude scales have been arranged into chapters according to their referents. Thus Chapter 3 includes scales for measuring attitudes toward social practices; Chapter 4 includes scales for measuring attitudes toward social issues and problems; and so on. At the beginning of each of these chapters there is a brief description of the category subsumed in that chapter. Each chapter is further broken down into sections, each labelled with an appropriate rubric. The following information is given for each scale to the extent that it is known: method of construction, reliability, validity, population sample on which the scale was developed, number and type of items, and any noteworthy advantages and disadvantages of the scale. Each attitude scale is given in an exhibit which includes the title of the scale, source, items, directions, and, where appropriate, item scale values and/or response alternatives. When the same response alternatives are used for all items, they are given only for the first item in the scale, although in practice these alternatives would be provided for each item.

At the end of the book is a bibliography which includes references to instruments not included in this volume and also permits cross references with regard to scales presented in Chapters 3 through 10.

We have not attempted to address ourselves to any particular audience; hence we have presented some ideas that will appear "old hat" to the sophisticated reader and some that will seem abstruse to the uninitiated. We have tried, however, to make even the more complex ideas understandable to the average reader.

Last, but certainly not least, the authors are greatly indebted to the many persons who contributed to this volume. Our greatest debt is to Dr. Shirley Nickols, who did the major portion of the review of the literature. In addition, we wish to express our sincere appreciation to J. Michael Blum, Morgan Worthy, and Paul Caron, who also assisted with the literature survey, and to the publishers who generously gave us permission to reproduce the scales in this book. We are especially appreciative of the degree of cooperation demonstrated by scale constructors and other researchers whose work is cited herein. Their consideration for the work has been, at the least, impressive.

Marvin E. Shaw
Jack M. Wright

NOTICE

The attitude scales in this book are recommended for research purposes and for group testing. We believe that the available information and supporting research does not warrant the application of many of these scales as measures of individual attitude for the purpose of diagnosis or personnel selection or for any other individual assessment process.

contents

CHAPTER 1

the nature of attitudes

A large number of latent variables has been posited in psychology. These hypothesized variables serve the purposes of accounting for observed consistencies in behavior and of homogenizing or uniting otherwise seemingly discrete data. The construct attitude is one such variable which is often invoked to account for consistency in social behavior.

Attitudes, the end products of the socialization process, significantly influence man's responses to cultural products, to other persons, and to groups of persons. If the attitude of a person toward a given object, or class of objects, is known, it can be used in conjunction with situational and other dispositional variables to predict and explain reactions of the person to that class of objects. To the extent that principles governing the change of attitudes are known, they may be used to manipulate the individual's reactions to relevant objects (as is exemplified in psychotherapy, education, and propaganda). It is not surprising, then, that the study of attitudes has occupied a central place in social psychology during the past fifty years.

The task of this chapter is to survey existing conceptions of the construct attitude, to provide a conceptualization which is maximally relevant to both the theory and the measurement of attitude, and to differentiate the construct from other similar constructs as clearly as possible.

THE PROBLEM OF DEFINITION

Professional use and definition of the term *attitude* range widely, from the operationally bound to the metatheoretical. Despite the variation in the definition of the term, the existing definitions agree upon one common characteristic: Attitude entails an existing predisposition to respond to social objects which, in interaction with situational and other dispositional variables, guides and directs the overt behavior of the individual (Cardno, 1955).

Variation in Definition

Much of the variance in definitions of the term attitude may be attributed to the epistemological issue of specificity versus generality in the determination of behavior. In this context, the issue concerns the degree to which attitudes may be considered to have a specific referent. Some theorists (Eysenck, 1947; Rokeach, 1960) tend to make attitudes a generalized and pervasive disposition of the person. Other theorists (Hovland, Janis, and Kelley, 1953; Krech, Crutchfield, and Ballachey, 1962; Sherif and Cantril, 1945) consider attitudes to have a specific referent, or a specific class of referents. A review of the literature indicates the latter to be the more common point of view. Further, this viewpoint appears to have the advantage of preventing the construct from becoming so generic as to be valueless.

A second source of variation in definition of the term attitude results from the tendency to generalize the construct to include any predisposition to respond. As we use the term, it involves only predispositions to respond to social aspects of the environment. This delineation of the social from the nonsocial is critical and somewhat arbitrary. It is generally considered to include interactions with persons and person-produced objects, events, and situations. Eventually, however, this distinction between social and physical objects seems to rest upon the nature of the dispositional characteristics inferred as pertaining to the objects. Interaction with an object may be said to be social when such dispositional characteristics as motive, wish, intent, and desire are attributed to it. By contrast, the dispositional characteristics attributed to physical objects are of the order: "It will conduct electricity; it will roll; or it is heavy" (Heider, 1958).

Since one may possess an attitude only when the referent object or event is of a social nature, the referent object or event must be perceived by the possessor as having purpose or being the result of purposive behavior of some persons. One may, then, be said to entertain an attitude toward a certain type of art when the artistic product is seen as the result of purposive (motivated) behavior on the part of another human being or when the product is anthropomorphized.

A third source of variance in definitions of the construct attitude lies in the theoretical conception of the composition of an attitude. Some writers (Krech et al., 1962; Secord and Backman, 1964) conceptualized attitude as consisting of three components: an affective component, a cognitive component, and a behavioral component. Triandis (1964b) suggested that the term attitude subsumes evaluations, behavioral intentions, and opinions. We prefer to limit the theoretical construct of attitude to an affective component which is based upon cognitive processes and is an antecedent of behavior; i.e., we consider an attitude to be an evaluative reaction based upon evaluative concepts which are closely related to other cognitions and to overt behavior (Harvey, Hunt, and Schroder, 1961; Rhine, 1958). This conception of attitude is very similar to that which was advanced by Osgood, Suci, and Tannenbaum (1957) and Anderson and Fishbein (1965). Restricting the concept to evaluative reactions based upon cognitive processes has the advantage of relating the theoretical construct most closely with the operations (in the form of attitude scales) provided in this book. The scales are composed of statements of varying degrees of positivity and negativity regarding the attitudinal referent, and endorsement of the statement serves as the basis for inferring the existence of positive or negative evaluations on the part of the endorser. As more extreme evaluative statements are endorsed, a more extreme evaluative reaction is inferred to exist. It should be noted that this evaluative reaction is affective in nature. Bogardus (1933, p. 270) referred to it as a "feeling reaction."

Formal Definitions of Attitude

There are a number of traditional definitions of attitude that may be cited as illustrative of common usage of the term:

"An enduring learned predisposition to behave in a consistent way toward a given class of objects" (English and English, 1958, p. 50).

"An enduring system of positive or negative evaluations, emotional feelings, and pro or con action tendencies with respect to a social object" (Krech et al., 1962, p. 177).

"A mental and neural state of readiness, organized through experience, exerting a directive or dynamic influence upon the individual's response to all objects and situations with which it is related" (Allport, 1954, p. 45).

"An individual's social attitude is a syndrome of response consistency with regard to social objects" (Campbell, 1950, p. 31).

Anderson and Fishbein (1965) define attitude as the evaluative dimension of a concept, after Osgood et al. (1957). They further suggest that the attitude toward an object is the sum of the strength of beliefs about the object and the evaluative aspect of these beliefs. By "evaluative" is meant some order of preferability-nonpreferability (good-bad, clean-dirty, etc.) regarding the characteristics of the object. Extracting as much as possible the commonalities of the above definitions and attempting to relate the construct as closely as possible to the operation, we offer the following definition of the term attitude:

A relatively enduring system of evaluative, affective reactions based upon and reflecting the evaluative concepts or beliefs which have been learned about the characteristics of a social object or class of social objects.

The implications of this definition and its relations to other constructs will be explored in the following sections of this chapter.

TRADITIONAL CONCEPTUALIZATIONS OF ATTITUDE

To further clarify our conceptualization of attitude, it seems valuable to differentiate the term from similar constructs and to review the dimensions traditionally ascribed to attitude.

Attitudes and Similar Theoretical Constructs

To the extent that attitudes are considered to fall within the realm of personality, they are differentiated from other personality constructs on several bases. First, attitudes are relational, and, second, their referents are specific. That is, an attitude is a characteristic which implies a type of relationship between the person and specific aspects of his environment. Third, attitudes differ from many other personality constructs in their possession of an evaluative function. Fourth, attitudes, rather than being overt responses, serve as predispositions to respond overtly. Therefore, as with any mediating variable, it is necessary to measure them indirectly.

We especially wish to differentiate attitudes from such other similar constructs in social psychology as opinion, belief, and value, and from such constructs in general psychology as habit, cognition, motivation, set, and trait. Of these, it is most important to discriminate between attitude and the constructs of concept, belief, and motive.

The term *belief* emphasizes some level of acceptance of a proposition regarding the characteristics of an object or event. Anderson and Fishbein (1965) define belief as follows: Belief *in* something is acceptance at some level of probability that the thing exists, while belief *about* a thing is defined as the probability that specific relations exist between the concept and some other object, concept, value, or goal. These beliefs may have an evaluative quality regarding preferability of the characteristics or the existence of an object. This concept of belief is similar to that advanced by other authors. English and English (1958, p. 64) define belief as "the emotional acceptance of a proposition or doctrine on what one considers to be adequate grounds." As Rokeach uses the term, belief involves any expectancy, set, or proposition which the individual accepts as true of the object or event. If we accept these definitions, a belief becomes an attitude when it is accompanied by an affective component which reflects the evaluation of the preferability of the characteristics or existence of the object. The attitude would be the sum of such beliefs about the object. A belief that something does not exist would be attitudinal in nature when its nonexistence was considered preferable or nonpreferable to some degree.

Concept is a more generic term than attitude and, as a cognitive process, provides the basis for the formation of evaluations. Conception is essentially the act of placing any two or more experientially demarcated entities or events into some relationship (Harvey et al., 1961; Kelly, 1955). The relations occurring in conception may, but need not, have any evaluative connotation. Thus the concept that 2 is greater than 1 to the precision with which members of the referent class are defined. It may be seen that a small number of objects or a highly homogeneous group of objects may be defined more precisely than a large number or a heterogeneous group. Thus, simplex attitudes should be more definitive. It is also expected that as attitudes become more definitive they will become more extreme and intense. This quality of definitiveness is referred to as the "latitude of acceptance" by Hovland et al. (1957). Central attitudes tend to be stronger than peripheral ones. Therefore, central attitudes should be more definitive and possibly less multiplex. Attitudes toward one's self are among the most central attitudes and should demonstrate these characteristics.

5. *Attitudes possess varying degrees of interrelatedness to one another* (Krech et al., 1962; McGrath, 1964). Attitudes are interrelated to the extent that they possess similar referents or similar valences (by virtue of application of common evaluative concepts). Attitudes which are highly interrelated form clusters or subsystems. These subsystems are interrelated with one another to form the total attitudinal system of the individual. The interrelatedness occurs because of similarity in the referents and referent classes. They may also be interrelated through similarity in the evaluative conception applied (e.g., all the things which the person loves or hates). These relationships between an individual's attitudes need not be logical or consistent. Lower degrees of interrelatedness between attitudes lend themselves to compartmentalization which may be expected to lead to logical inconsistency and to a degree of rigidity and perseverance in behavior. With regard to degree of interrelatedness, attitudes occupy varying positions of centrality or peripherality in the subsystem into which they have been integrated. More central attitudes possess a higher degree of interrelatedness, which causes them to be maximally resistant to change. Resistance to change (or stability) of these central attitudes occurs on two bases: (1) To change one central attitude is to involve many peripheral attitudes in alteration and breakdown, the result being a certain inertia on the part of central attitudes; (2) more central attitudes possess greater value or importance to the individual behaviorally. It may be assumed that the more central attitudes are those that have been more highly learned because of more efficient reinforcement schedules. Such attitudes have lower thresholds of arousal and show greater consistency than do attitudes which are less central. The improvement in consistency is due to increased selectivity on the part of the conceptual processes upon which the attitudes are based. Such increased selectivity reflects the greater importance to the individual of the goals involved in the evaluation of the object.

6. *Attitudes are relatively stable and enduring* (Newcomb et al., 1965; Sherif and Sherif, 1956). Affective predispositions change slowly. In addition to the bases of stability discussed above, inertia and more effective reinforcement, there is a further basis in the achievement of perceptual closure. Since the more central attitudes are more definitive, they offer a higher degree of perceptual closure. To the extent that an assumption is warranted that all persons strive for at least some minimum degree of closure, these central attitudes should tend to be maintained unchanged on this basis alone. Generally, as attitudes vary with regard

to centrality, they will also vary in the ease with which they can be altered.

Both the formation and maintenance of an attitude occur in a motivational context; the goal orientation which is being fulfilled or frustrated at the point of arousal of the affective response reflects the existence of some motivated state. Sarnoff and Katz (1954) have classified these motivational contexts into three major categories: hedonic, rational, and ego defensive. To these, a fourth category might be added: the affiliative context. Although these categories are not entirely discrete or mutually exclusive, they may be characterized as follows: The informational context implies the operation of a motive such as knowing the world or seeking closure and structure. The hedonic context indicates that such primary motives as hunger and escape from pain are operative. The ego-defensive context seems to indicate that more secondary motives such as dominance and succorance are operative. Of such secondary motives, one which is of prime importance is the affiliative motive, which leads to formation of interpersonal ties and to group development. It is to be expected that many attitudes are taken on by the individual as the price of admission into the group, or as the mechanism of enhancement of status in the group.

In summary, the major sources of stability in attitudes are the interrelatedness of the attitudes, the history of reinforcement in the learning of the attitudes, and active resistance to change by the possessor of the attitude when confronted with a potential or actual thwarting of his motives or disruption of his perceptual closure.

COMPARISON OF THE PRESENT CONCEPTUALIZATION OF ATTITUDE WITH TRADITIONAL CONCEPTUALIZATIONS

The conceptual formulations of attitude that we have reviewed are largely adequate in their descriptions of attitude structure. They do not, however, explicate the process by which attitudes are formed and changed, nor do they relate in any simple theoretical way to techniques of measurement. The conceptualization that we have adopted attempts to ameliorate both of these difficulties. Many of the ideas incorporated in our analysis are not new. Indeed, we have attempted to abstract commonalities from, and to integrate, existing formulations. The result must be eclectic. We accept the usual analysis of attitude structure as involving affective, behavioral, and cognitive components, but we believe that these components are related in a manner different from that described in some former approaches.

Our Definition of Attitude

We have defined attitude as a relatively enduring system of affective, evaluative reactions based upon and reflecting the evaluative concepts or beliefs which have been learned about the characteristics of a social object or class of social objects. As an affective reaction, it is a covert or implicit response. We have suggested that it is a drive-producing response which elicits motives and thus gives rise to overt behavior. The evaluative reaction is based upon conception of the referent in terms of facilitation or inhibition of attainment of already-existing goals. Attitude scales measure only one dimension of the affective reactions: positivity-negativity.

The definition we have advanced is similar to other definitions that we have considered. It differs from the Krech et al. (1962) definition, for example, in only one minor and one major respect. It excludes from the "enduring system" the evaluative concepts and the action tendencies. The exclusion of the evaluative concepts is a minor consideration in that it is our contention that the affective reactions which form the attitude are based upon these evaluative concepts, since they pertain to goal facilitation and inhibition by the referent; their addition to the construct attitude, per se, would be redundant.

The second variation, the exclusion of action tendencies as a part of the enduring system, has more important implications. First, it should be made clear that we are not denying the existence of action tendencies in relation to attitude; we are merely treating them as something apart from the enduring system that we are calling attitude. In short, the difference between the view we are expressing and the more traditional view has to do with the relations among the conceptual, affective, and action components identified by former analyses. Whereas many former theorists have treated these components as different elements of the same system, which they called attitude, we are treating them as separate (albeit closely related) systems, or elements, only one of which is labelled attitude.

There are several reasons for this differentiation. First, we believe that it is theoretically sound; that is, that this view more adequately describes the true state of affairs. Secondly, we believe that the question of the relation of attitude to behavior other than evaluative behavior is an empirical question that should not be prejudiced by the definition of the attitude. Finally, we believe that our view of attitude more nearly coincides with the definition of attitude that is implicit in most, if not all, procedures for measuring attitudes. In the following section, our view of the structure of attitude is explicated more fully, and the relations of attitude to concepts and action tendencies are considered in greater detail.

The Structure of Attitude

The affective reactions that constitute the attitude toward a given object derive from the underlying cognitive structure relevant to that object. In the course of the individual's experiences with the object, he formulates a set of evaluative concepts or beliefs about it. These beliefs may arise from direct experience with the object or through indirect experiences in interaction with other persons. The beliefs thus formed are relevant to the goal striving of the individual and partially determine what further beliefs may be formed regarding the object. As the individual encounters the object, evaluative concepts regarding the relationship of the object to his goal attainment are formed or elicited. These perceived or anticipated effects upon goal attainment result in such affective reactions as anxiety or frustration, which in turn produce such motives as aggression or affiliation. The ultimate overt behavior will be contingent upon situational factors such as potential punishment or a closed behavioral field, and upon such other dispositional characteristics as low energy level or restricted intellect. It is to the positive-negative dimension of the motive-producing, affective reaction that the term attitude applies.

Existing beliefs regarding the object determine what further beliefs may be formed. For example, an individual may come to conceive that most politicians are dishonest and that politicians have the capacity to alter his outcomes. To the extent that dishonesty in politicians will adversely affect his outcomes, he will form conceptual evaluations about politicians which are negative and based upon the perceived dishonesty of politicians. Since concepts tend toward consistency or balance (Harvey et al. 1961; Heider, 1958; Festinger, 1957; Osgood, 1960), it is then easier for the person to accept other negatively valued concepts about politicians, e.g., that they are lazy, stupid, liars, etc. These concepts about the negatively valued characteristics of politicians are goal relevant and lead to the affective reaction, perhaps, of frustration and to an aggressive motive which may then occur in overt behavior in the form of disparagement.

Some individuals may be able to tolerate inconsistency and accept some conceptual relations about the same object that are evaluated positively and some that are evaluated negatively. In fact, we believe that this is true for most persons to some extent, but there is considerable variability in the amount of inconsistency that can be tolerated. The set of beliefs that the individual holds about the object and the associated evaluations determine the individual's attitude toward that object. They lead to an enduring system of affective reactions regarding that object. The nature and strength of this system is determined by the number and strength of the evaluative concepts or beliefs formed.

Not all such concepts or beliefs are positively or negatively evaluated. If the set of beliefs about a given object are nonevaluative, then there is no attitude toward the object unless its nonexistence bears some degree of preferability. It is theoretically possible, but extremely unlikely, that there exists an individual all of whose concepts are nonevaluative. It is also theoretically possible for the concepts or beliefs that are positively evaluative to equal those that are negatively evaluative, which would lead to two equally strong, antithetical attitudes toward the same object and to a condition of ambivalence. This seems to be the situation in certain types of pathology. This state is, however, unbalanced, and the expectation is that the individual will perceive situations in a manner that will lead him to accept new concepts which will move him from this unstable position. For socially significant objects, at least, we believe that most individuals will hold concepts that are predominantly either positively or negatively evaluative. This does not resolve the issue; it only states our position on it.

When a person holds a particular attitude toward an object, he is predisposed to act in a certain way toward that object. As we have said before, the motive which is elicited is not a part of the attitude; rather, individuals. The consequences of these latter effects will be a spuriously low estimate of reliability. There is no sure way of overcoming these difficulties, but they can be reduced by selecting an interval between tests long enough to minimize the effects of memory, but short enough to minimize the effects of other variables. Unfortunately, this theoretically ideal interval is unknown, but most investigators use intervals ranging from two to six weeks.

The Equivalent-forms Method. This method of estimating reliability requires two forms that may be considered equivalent. These two forms are then administered to a group of subjects, and the two sets of scores are correlated to obtain an estimate of reliability. Again, if more than two forms are available, the average of the intercorrelations among the forms may be taken as the estimate of reliability. The major disadvantages of this method are that at least two forms are necessary and that the correlation coefficient reflects not only consistency of measurement, but also the degree to which the two forms actually do measure the same attitude. Therefore, the acceptability of this estimate of reliability depends upon the degree of equivalence of the two forms.

The major advantage of this method is that the effects of time interval and of responding to one scale upon the response to the other are minimized, although spuriously high reliability may be obtained because of general response modes and attitudes toward the testing situation.

The Split-half Method. This method estimates reliability by treating each of two or more parts of the attitude scale as a separate scale. We have chosen to use the label "split-half method" to refer to this procedure, although the scales may be selected by treating odd-numbered items as one scale and even-numbered items as another, by randomly selecting items to constitute the subscales, or even by treating each item as a separate scale. Regardless of the method of choosing the subscales, the reliability estimate is the correlation between the scores of the separate scales. The Spearman-Brown prophecy formula (Spearman, 1910; Brown, 1910) is applied to the obtained correlation to estimate the reliability of the total scale.

When the method is carried to its logical extreme of treating each item as a scale, special computational methods are employed to reduce the work that would be required to determine the average correlation among all items. The Kuder-Richardson formula 20 (K-R 20) is the formula most often used for this purpose (Kuder and Richardson, 1937).

The split-half method has the same advantages as the equivalent-forms method, in addition to which it requires only one scale. It should be noted, however, that this is essentially a measure of internal consistency of items composing the scale and provides no measure of temporal consistency.

Validity

The concept of validity is also complicated. In its simplest form, validity is the degree to which the scale measures what it is supposed to measure. There are four general procedures for estimating the validity of psychological tests (APA Committee, 1954; Cronbach and Meehl, 1955): predictive validity, concurrent validity, content validity, and construct validity.

Predictive Validity. Predictive validity is estimated by showing how accurately we can guess some future performance on an external criterion from a knowledge of the attitude score. For example, we might wish to predict church attendance from attitude toward the church. Or we may wish to predict a person's response to a related set of items at some future date. The usual procedure is to measure the attitude and predict the future behavior on the basis of these scores. The future behavior is then measured at an appropriate time and the obtained scores correlated (or otherwise compared) with the predicted scores. The degree of correspondence is taken as the estimate of validity.

Concurrent Validity. Concurrent validity differs from predictive validity primarily with regard to the time at which the criterion measure is obtained. If the criterion measure and the attitude scale are administered at approximately the same point in time, the procedure is called concurrent validation; if the attitude score is obtained first and the criterion score at some future date, it is called predictive validation.

In estimating concurrent validity, there is the danger that one data collection operation will influence the other, thus yielding a spuriously high estimate of validity.

Content Validity. Content validity is evaluated by determining the degree to which the items of the scale sample the content of the attitude domain, i.e., the degree to which the content of the attitude scale corresponds to the content of the attitude system. This should not be confused with so-called face validity, which refers to the superficial appearance of the items. In practice, the evaluation of content validity is usually a subjective, judgmental procedure. If the items of a scale designed to measure attitude toward the church, for example, are statements about the church, then the *items* may be said to have content validity. But content validity of items does not ensure that the *scale* has content validity. In fact there are two judgments that must be made before one can say that the scale as a whole has content validity. It is necessary to judge, first, whether and to what degree the content of each item pertains to the attitude object, and, second, the degree to which the set of items represents all aspects of the attitude object. It is possible to have a set of items that have content validity but represent only one part of the attitude continuum (e.g., positive attitude), in which case the scale would not validly measure the attitude.

Some of the methods of scale construction described in the following section (for example, the method of equal-appearing intervals) involve procedures which include consensual judgments about the relation of the items to the attitude continuum. Almost always, the scale constructor chooses items that seem to him to have content validity.

Construct Validity. The notion of construct validity is more complex than other types of validity and probably is more meaningful for theoretical purposes. Construct validity is evaluated by a determination of the relationships between the attitude score and other aspects of the personality. The theoretical notions that we have about the attitude lead us to postulate various kinds and degrees of relationships between the attitude and other specified variables. In order to demonstrate construct validity of an attitude scale, we must show that these relationships do in fact hold (Ghiselli, 1964). This calls for investigation of the psychological qualities which the scale measures and a demonstration that certain explanatory constructs account to some degree for the attitude scores (Cronbach and Meehl, 1955).

There are several methods of estimating construct validity, but in each case it is the point of view that is important rather than the particular procedures that are carried out. Perhaps the most familiar approach is the known-groups technique. If our definition of the underlying attitude leads us to expect that two or more groups should hold different attitudes toward a given object, it follows that a valid scale to measure the attitude in question should yield different scores for these groups. Thus, one might validate a scale to measure attitude toward Sunday observance by showing that Baptists score higher (reveal a more favorable attitude toward Sunday observance) than do Seventh Day Adventists. Thurstone and Chave's uses of churchgoers and nonchurchgoers to validate a scale for measuring attitude toward the church is another example of this approach. Only a rough correspondence between the attitude scale scores and the known-groups is expected. In fact, too great a correspondence might lead one to question the validity of the scale, since members of the groups are expected to overlap on the scale (Cronbach and Meehl, 1955).

A variation of the known-groups approach is stimulus-group validity (Axelrod and Eisendorfer, 1961). The question asked by this method is whether respondents discriminate among groups to which attitudinal statements may be applied. For example, if one wishes to validate a scale to measure attitude toward Negroes, subjects would be asked to respond to the statements with several ethnic groups as the referent, including Negroes. If the scale is a valid measure of attitudes toward Negroes, the attitude scores should vary with the stimulus group in theoretically expected ways.

A second approach involves correlation matrices. This procedure is exemplified most clearly by the multitrait-multimethod matrix technique proposed by Campbell and Fiske (1959). The general assumption is that different methods of measuring the same trait (or attitude) should yield similar results, whereas different traits should yield different scores regardless of the method of measurement. Thus, correlations among scores for a given attitude measured by different attitude scales should be higher than correlations among different attitudes measured by different scales. One problem in the application of this method is that the different attitudes must be selected so that correlations among them would not be expected on theoretical grounds. If two attitudes should covary, theoretically, then *failure* to find a significant correlation might indicate lack of validity. Of course, perfect or extremely high correlations would lead one to question the distinctiveness of the attitudes being measured.

In some cases, internal consistency measures may be evidence of validity (Cronbach and Meehl, 1955). If the underlying theory of the attitude being measured suggests high item intercorrelations, then measures of internal consistency may be interpreted as evidence of construct validity. Note, however, that it is the theory that leads to the interpretation of the correlations as an indication of validity; some theories might suggest that high internal consistency indicates low validity.

Finally, the stability (test-retest reliability) of attitude scores may be important for construct validation. This is particularly true when the retest is given after intervening experimental manipulations. If the intervening experience produces theoretically expected changes in attitude scores, this fact may be taken as evidence of construct validity. This approach is exemplified by Thurstone's studies of the effects of movies on attitude.

In the following chapters, we have cited many instances of the kinds of evidence described above, although we may not have labelled it "construct validity."

Equality of Units

That equality of units is a desirable property of a scale would seem to be obvious. One would like to be able to say with confidence that the difference between scores of 8 and 10, for example, is equal to the difference between scores of 12 and 14. This would enable us to average the scores for a given individual derived from different scales, to compare the amount of change produced by an experimental treatment in individuals who fall at different points on the attitude continuum, to compare scores of one person with scores of another on the same scale, etc. As we shall see, the attitude scales in this book have not been shown to have equal units, although the units of some scales approximate equality more closely than others.

Unidimensionality

When we say that an attitude scale is unidimensional we mean that it measures a single attitude. A person's attitude score therefore reflects only his position on the underlying attitude continuum, and two or more persons who have the same attitude score will be at the same position on the latent continuum. If the attitude scale is not unidimensional, it means that more than one attitude (or other characteristic) is being measured by the scale. In this case, individuals having the same score may have widely different attitudes toward the particular attitude object in question. Suppose that a scale designed to measure attitude toward Americans actually measures attitudes toward Americans and internationalism. Then a person who has very favorable attitudes toward Americans and very unfavorable attitudes toward internationalism might earn the same attitude score as a person whose attitudes toward these two objects were exactly reversed. Such multidimensional scales are useful only to the extent that the contributions of the various attitudes to the total score are known and separable. (Detailed procedures for multidimensional scaling are given by Kruskal, 1964*a*,*b*; Shepard, 1962*a*,*b*; and Torgerson, 1952.)

The Zero Point

In Chapter 1 we suggested that attitudes vary in quality from highly positive to highly negative. This implies that there is a point on the attitude continuum at which the quality of the attitude changes from positive to negative (or vice versa), that is, that there is a point of neutrality or a zero point. The identification of such a point has important implications for attitude measurement. For instance, one could more readily answer such questions as whether it is easier to move a person from a moderate to an extreme position (either positive or negative) than from a slightly positive to a slightly negative position (or vice versa), whether being neutral predisposes or deters an individual from conforming to the attitudes of group members, and so on.

This is a problem in attitude measurement that has not been solved, either theoretically or practically. In fact, some theorists (e.g., Krech and Crutchfield, 1948) suggest that attitudes always have either a positive or negative sign; if they have no sign (i.e., are neutral or at the zero point) they cannot be called attitudes at all. We have adopted a similar position in Chapter 1.

TECHNIQUES FOR SCALE CONSTRUCTION

In this section we will consider various techniques that have been developed for constructing attitude scales. A brief description of each method will be given, followed by a discussion of experimental evidence relating to reliability and validity and to other properties of scales.

Method of Equal-appearing Intervals

Thurstone's (1929, 1931) judgmental procedure probably has been more widely used than any other method of scale construction. This procedure requires a large number of nonmonotone items related to the attitude object, i.e., items that will be disagreed with by persons both below and above the position on the latent attitude variable reflected by the item (Green, 1954). The steps involved in constructing a scale by this method are as follows: (1) A large number of items concerning the object of the attitude in question are formulated; (2) these items are sorted by a sizable number of judges into 11 piles or categories which appear to the judges to be equally spaced in terms of the degree to which agreement with the item reflects the underlying attitude; (3) the piles are numbered from 1 to 11, and a scale value is computed for each item, taken as the median of the position given the item by the group of judges; (4) the interquartile range, or Q value, is computed as a measure of interjudge variability, and all items for which there is much disagreement are rejected; and (5) a small number of items for the final scale are selected so that they are spread more or less evenly along the attitude continuum.

In using the scale, the respondent is asked to check each item with which he agrees. His score is the median of the scale values of all the items checked. Theoretically, an individual should agree with only a few contiguous items near his true position on the attitude continuum. If a large proportion of the respondents checks noncontiguous items, this may be taken as an indication of multidimensionality of the scale.

The reliability of scales developed by this procedure is usually satisfactory (.75 or better). Validity depends largely upon the attitude being measured and the skill of the person who formulates the items; in general, however, valid scales can be constructed using this technique. The sorting procedure was designed to yield an equal-interval scale, but there is reason to believe that this goal has not been achieved (Hevner, 1930). This is apparently because of the end-point effect. If judgments are normally distributed about the "true" value, the end category distributions are curtailed, thus displacing scale values toward the middle of the category range. Intervals at the extremes are compressed relative to intervals near the middle of the scale. The only provision for ensuring unidimensionality lies in the formulation and selection of items; however, a low Q value would seem to indicate unidimensionality. Thurstone (1929) made some attempt to determine a zero point by providing a neutral or middle category for the judges who sorted items; however, this zero point is really a range of values and hinges upon the perceptions of the judges who sort the items. Thurstone did not assume it represented a true zero point. To summarize, the method of equal-appearing intervals permits (but does not ensure) the construction of reliable and valid scales but is largely unsuccessful in producing scales having other desirable characteristics.

There have been numerous studies of the effects of various procedures upon the scales constructed by Thurstone's method. A review of the results of these studies has been prepared by Webb (1955). In general, these results indicate that item scale values are not greatly influenced by: (1) method of collecting judgments (sortings versus ratings, provision of sample item, etc.), (2) method of computing scale values (mean versus median), (3) number of judges, and (4) number of intervals or categories. Irregularities in sortings of judges, such as the judges' attitudes, judges putting too many items in one category, etc., may shift the scale value but not the ordering of the items. Failure to include items at one extreme also shifts scale values of items adjacent to this extreme.

Method of Graded Dichotomies

The method of paired comparisons (Thurstone, 1927) avoids some of the difficulties inherent in the method of equal-appearing intervals but becomes cumbersome when more than a few items are to be scaled. The method of graded dichotomies was designed by Thurstone (first reported by Saffir, 1937) to avoid these difficulties when the method of paired comparisons is not feasible. This method has been described under different labels by several writers: "method of successive intervals" (Saffir, 1937; Edwards, 1952); "equal discriminability scale" (Garner and Hake, 1951); and "method of graded dichotomies" (Attneave, 1949). Attneave's term and description will be used in the following discussion.

As in the method of equal-appearing intervals, a large number of items are collected, and judges are asked to sort them into a fixed number of categories spaced along a favorableness continuum. However, there is no assumption regarding the relative distances between categories. In fact, the mathematical model treats the categories as contiguous segments of the attitude continuum, separated by boundaries (Green, 1954). The method of computing item scale values may be outlined as follows: (1) A table is prepared with rows representing items and columns representing rating-scale categories, showing the percentage of ratings falling into each category. (2) From this table a second table is prepared with $k - 1$ columns, showing for each item the percentage of ratings falling above each category boundary. (3) Using a table of the normal curve, the percentages in the second table are converted into normal deviates (x/σ units). These units are called X values. They are given a positive sign when the percentage above the category boundary is more than 50 and a negative sign when the percentage is less than 50. (4) For each pair of adjacent categories (dichotomies), the difference between the X values of items represented in both is determined. This difference is taken as the magnitude of the intervals separating the two categories. (5) The X values are then added to the sum of all the intervals below that category. (6) Each item now has one or more X values, the mean of which is taken as the best estimate of its position on the attitude continuum, i.e., its scale value.

The advantages of this procedure over the method of equal-appearing intervals are as follows: (*a*) No assumption is made regarding the widths of the intervals; the only requirement is that each successive interval represent some additional amount of the attitude. (*b*) Scale values obtained by this method are linearly related to those obtained by the method of paired comparisons. (*c*) The method provides its own internal consistency check upon the assumptions that are made. In addition, Attneave (1949) believed that the method rationally avoids the end-point effect observed in equal-appearing interval scales (Hevner, 1930). When a number of judges rate a given item, ratings tend to distribute themselves normally about the hypothetically "true" rating. However, when the "true" rating falls at the end of the psychological continuum, it can vary in only one direction, and therefore the distribution will be skewed toward the middle of the scale. This distortion yields scale values too close to the center of the scale. The method of graded dichotomies avoids this distortion, but at a cost: Items that are placed in a given category more than 95 percent of the time cannot be scaled by this technique.

In terms of desirable characteristics, scales developed by the method of graded dichotomies are little different from those developed by the method of equal-appearing intervals with respect to reliability, validity, unidimensionality, and a zero point. However, the attempt to determine equality of units is based upon an analysis of subject responses rather than upon their subjective judgment concerning equality of intervals; hence, the assumption of equal units has a somewhat stronger rational basis.

Method of Summated Ratings

Likert's (1932) scaling technique requires a large number of monotone items, i.e., items having the characteristic that the more favorable the individual's attitude toward the attitude object, the higher his expected score for the item. These items are then given to a sample of the target population, and respondents indicate their reaction to the items by means of a five-category rating system: strongly approve, approve, undecided, disapprove, and strongly disapprove. Categories are scored by assigning values of 5, 4, 3, 2, and 1, respectively. This scoring is reversed for negatively worded items. Item scores are then correlated with total score (the sum of item scores), and items that correlate highly with the total score are selected for the final scale. [Another widely used index of item discriminability is the critical ratio based upon the means and variances of the upper and lower 25 percent (or 27 percent) of the distribution of total scores.]

The intercorrelations of the items are assumed to be due to a single common factor to which all the items are mutually related (Green, 1954). The item score is assumed to be the weighted sum of this common factor and a factor specific to the item. The common factor, of course, is the general attitude variable that we are trying to measure, and the item factor is considered error. Since the linear correlation of the total score with the general attitude factor approaches unity as the number of items increases, there is some justification for the scoring procedure. In practice, then, the respondent uses the five-point rating scale to respond to the items in the final scale, and his score is computed as the sum of his individual item scores.

The Likert procedure yields moderately reliable scales, but again validity depends upon the particular scale under consideration. No attempt is made to ensure equality of units. Unidimensionality is sometimes inferred from high item correlations with the total score, but this is not necessarily so. The high correlations could result from two or more equally potent factors. The "undecided" category is often considered as a zero or neutral point of an item, and, by analogy, the zero point of a scale might be taken as the attitude score corresponding to the score that would be obtained if the individual checked "undecided" for every item in the scale. However, this interpretation is ambiguous, since such a score could be achieved by checking the undecided category for all items, by checking "strongly agree" for half of the items and "strongly disagree" for the other half, or through some similar combination of agree-disagree responses. Thus, Likert-type scales are often reliable and valid, but they probably should be treated as ordinal scales.

It is important to remember that the interpretation of Likert scores is based upon the distribution of sample scores, i.e., a score has meaning only in relation to scores earned by others in the sample. The scale should always be standardized on a sample drawn from the target population.

Scalogram Analysis

Guttman (1944, 1947) proposed a nonmetric method for scaling attitude items. This method is based upon the idea that items can be arranged in an order such that an individual who responds positively to any particular item also responds positively to all other items having a lower rank.* If items can be arranged in this manner, they are said to be scalable. In developing an attitude scale, a number of monotone items about the attitude object are formulated, the set of items is administered to a group of subjects, and their response patterns are analyzed to determine whether or not they are scalable. With N items requiring only agreement or disagreement, there are 2^N response patterns that might occur; if the items are scalable, only $N + 1$ of these patterns will be obtained. The relative nonoccurrence of deviant patterns allows the computation of a coefficient of reproducibility:

$$\text{Rep} = 1 - \frac{\text{total number of errors}}{\text{total number of responses}}$$

where an error is any deviation from an ideal pattern. Theoretically, Rep is equal to the proportion of responses to items that can be correctly reproduced from the knowledge of an individual's score. If Rep is .90 or better, the items are said to be scalable.

Several difficulties in evaluating Rep have been discovered: (1) Rep is equal to the average of individual item reproducibilities; (2) the reproducibility of an item cannot be smaller than the proportion of S's in its largest category; and (3) the expected value of Rep often is high, especially when the total number of categories is small (Festinger, 1947; Green, 1954). Therefore, in evaluating Rep account must be taken of number of items, number of categories per item, and proportion of S's in the largest category for each item. Green (1954) suggested the following auxiliary criteria for evaluating Rep to ensure that the obtained value is not spuriously high: (1) There should be a good spread of item marginals, although most item marginals should fall between .2 and .8; (2) each response category should have more nonerror than error; (3) at least 10 items should be used when items are dichotomous; and (4) errors should be random. Problems associated with Rep are also discussed by Edwards (1957), who suggested an alternative method for computing Rep. Schuessler (1961) has suggested tests of the hypothesis that an observed configuration of responses might have arisen by chance.

* The Bogardus (1925) social distance scale was based upon this notion, but the approach was not developed into a general method of scale construction.

Although Rep is sometimes considered to be a measure of reliability, it is important to remember that it is really a test of scalability of items in the Guttman sense. In fact, Rep is more precisely a measure of unidimensionability; hence, these scales are more likely to be unidimensional than scales constructed by other procedures. The scalogram method usually yields scales that are reliable and valid according to the usual estimates of these attributes. There is no attempt to ensure equality of units or to establish a zero point; however, if an independent measure of intensity is available (see Chapter 1) a zero point may be defined as that attitude score for which the intensity is minimum.

Since a given set of items may be scalable for one population but not for another, scalability should always be checked before Guttman scales are used with a population other than the one used for development.

Scale Discrimination Technique

Edwards and Kilpatrick (1948*a*,*b*) outlined a method of scale construction that is basically a synthesis of the Thurstone, Likert, and Guttman procedures. The steps in their technique are as follows: (1) Follow the method of equal-appearing intervals to select a set of acceptable items by Thurstone's criteria; (2) administer these items to a sample drawn from the target population, following the Likert method of item selection, i.e., by means of an item analysis; (3) plot item discriminatory power against the Thurstone scale values; (4) select with each scale interval the two or three items with the greatest discriminatory power; and (5) subject the selected items to a scalogram analysis.

This procedure seems not to have been applied very extensively, and its strong and weak points have not been clearly established. However, since the Thurstone procedure requires nonmonotone items whereas the Likert and Guttman techniques require monotone items, it is clear that the underlying assumptions of one or more of the methods are being violated. One obvious consequence of applying item analysis to nonmonotone items is that items in the middle of the scale will be eliminated, since they will not discriminate between high and low groups.

Unfolding Technique

The unfolding technique (Coombs, 1950, 1953) is a method of discovering and isolating a latent attitude (or other attribute) underlying the preferences of a group of individuals. Coombs appears not to have worked out practical methods of assigning scale values to items, but at least one method based upon Coombs's theory has been suggested (Banta, 1961). The general theory will be described, followed by a discussion of Banta's technique.

The unfolding technique begins with a set of statements that are presumed to be related to the underlying attitude dimension. Respondents are then asked to choose items that they are most willing to endorse. The number they are asked to choose may vary from two to $n-1$ (labelled "pick two" and "pick $n-1$," respectively). It is assumed that the

nique has not been widely used, and more detailed evaluation is not possible at this time.

Latent Structure Analysis

Lazarsfeld's (1950, 1954, 1959) approach is more general than most of the procedures discussed thus far. He is concerned with attitude structure and measurement only as part of the broader issue of relations between concept formation and empirical research in the behavioral sciences. The method assumes a unidimensional attitude continuum along which persons are distributed according to some unknown probability distribution. Statements about the object of the attitude are formulated and administered to a group of individuals with the idea of using the obtained responses to say something about the underlying attitude continuum. It is assumed that the items are intercorrelated only because of their common correlation with the underlying attitude variable. Using these assumptions, a general latent structure model is developed that is applicable to any manifest variable.

Latent class analysis, derived from the general latent structure model, is based upon the untested assumption that items will be intercorrelated only because of their mutual correlation with the underlying attitude. Thus, persons concentrated at a given point on the underlying continuum form a latent class. Items are assumed to be independent within each latent class. Thus this analysis is actually a method of dividing a population of subjects into a number of classes or types. As Green (1954) pointed out, the latent class model implies a nominal attitude scale. If the data fit the model, we know that they behave as if there were a number of latent classes with stated properties, but we do not know whether the population of respondents can be partitioned into groups having these properties. The computational procedures are moderately complicated; the interested reader is referred to Green (1951) and Anderson (1954).

The *latent distance scale,* also derived from the general latent structure model, is a technique for scalogram analysis based on a probability model. This method has been described in detail by Hays and Borgatta (1954). Its advantage over the Guttman procedure is that perfect and imperfect scales can be represented equally well, and, since it is based upon a probability model, most of the criteria for the Guttman scale become unnecessary. The attributes of scales constructed by this procedure are similar to those of scales constructed by the method of scalogram analysis.

SPECIALIZED PROCEDURES

The Semantic Differential

The semantic differential (Osgood and Suci, 1955; Osgood et al., 1957) is really more a method for measuring attitudes than a method for constructing attitude scales. In fact, it may be thought of as an attitude scale, although the particular items included in the scale may vary. Osgood and his associates describe it as a method for measuring the meaning of an object to an individual; its use as an attitude scale thus represents a special application of the technique.

In applying the method, the respondent is asked to rate the attitude object on a series of seven-point bipolar scales. Each item appears as follows:

kind : : : : : : cruel

The respondent is asked to put a check mark in the position indicating both the direction and intensity of his feeling toward the object. Scores may be derived by assigning integral weights to each position on the rating scale.

Osgood and Suci (1955), using factor-analytic procedures, established three general factors of meaning measured by the semantic differential technique: an evaluative factor, a potency factor, and an activity factor. Since Osgood and Suci conceive of attitude as an evaluation, the evaluative factor seems to measure the direction and intensity of an individual's attitude toward the object being rated. The bipolar scales having high loadings on this factor (.75 or better) are: good-bad, beautiful-ugly, sweet-sour, clean-dirty, tasty-distasteful, valuable-worthless, kind-cruel, pleasant-unpleasant, bitter-sweet, happy-sad, sacred-profane, nice-awful, fragrant-foul, honest-dishonest, and fair-unfair. In actual practice, the number of bipolar items used varies from all 15 listed above to a few (three to five) of the most clearly evaluative pairs. For greater reliability, the attitude score may be computed as the sum or average of the ratings on all scales used.

Relative to other attitude scales, the attributes of the semantic differential appear acceptable. Using five items, Osgood and his colleagues (1957) reported test-retest reliabilities ranging from .83 to .91. Jenkins, Russell, and Suci (1957) reported an average test-retest reliability of .97 for $N = 30$. Osgood et al. (1957) also present evidence of validity as estimated by correlations with other scales. Correlations with Thurstone scales ranged from .74 to .82; Guttman scale scores toward crop rotation correlated .79 with scores obtained from a three-item semantic differential scale. However, one study suggests caution in accepting the semantic differential as equivalent to other forms of attitude measurement. Nickols and Shaw (1964) found high correlations between semantic differential scores and scores on Thurstone scales only when the attitude was not salient to the subjects.

Disguised Techniques

Procedures discussed thus far have been concerned with scales that are more or less direct in approach—the purpose of each scale is fairly obvious to the respondent. It has often been argued that respondents hesitate to answer freely either from fear of disapproval, because they feel their privacy is being invaded, or for a variety of other reasons. To try to overcome this supposed reluctance, many techniques have been proposed to hide or disguise the purpose of the measuring device.* Generally speaking, these are specific techniques for measuring attitudes rather than methods of scale construction. Several of the more common procedures are discussed here for the purpose of rounding out the coverage of various types of attitude measuring instruments. However, in the following chapters, we have generally excluded sentence-completion and pictorial techniques. The interested reader may wish to consider a procedure outlined by Thistlethwaite (1950).

The Error-choice Technique. This procedure, introduced by Hammond (1948), requires a number of statements about the attitude object, each having two equally erroneous response alternatives—one in the favorable and one in the unfavorable direction with respect to the attitude object. The respondent is thus required to choose between errors; the direction of this choice is taken as an indication of his attitude toward the attitude object. The scoring is largely based upon "hunch," but item analysis is sometimes used. Weschler (1950*b*) reported test-retest reliability of .62 and equivalent forms reliability of .48 for a scale designed to measure attitudes toward labor and management. Validity was estimated by showing that error-choice scales discriminated between members of labor unions and business groups (Hammond, 1948; Weschler, 1950*a*). There is no evidence concerning such other desirable attributes as a zero point, equality of units, or unidimensionality.

Sentence-completion Techniques. The sentence-completion technique consists of a series of sentence stubs which the respondent is asked to complete, either freely or by choosing among a list of alternatives. For example, Kerr (1943) used sentence beginnings such as "The trouble with America is . . ." to study national stereotypes held by English people. Getzels and Walsh (1958) outlined a method called paired direct and projective questionnaires (PDPQ). Their procedure requires first- and third-person incomplete statements describing situations related to the attitude object, worded so that the sentence can be completed by manifesting a reaction to the situation. Items must (1) facilitate dichotomous classification of responses, (2) be free of affect-laden words that might unduly influence the response, and (3) if possible, concern behavior situations. The set of third-person statements is given as a speed test; the first-person items, as a personal questionnaire. Scores are based upon negative responses. Three scores are computed: number of negative responses on direct (first-person) items, number of negative on projective (third-person) items, and proportion of negative responses on projective that are reversed on the direct items. Reported interscore reliabilities range from .91 to .98. Validity is inferred only indirectly from successful prediction of experimental results.

Story- and argument-completion techniques (Murray and Morgan, 1945; Weitz and Nuckols, 1953) are similar to the sentence-completion

* Campbell (1950) critically reviewed the literature on the disguised methods of attitude assessment and concluded that there is no evidence that the disguised is more valid than the more direct approaches. He also found that the more direct instruments uniformly have higher reliabilities than the disguised.

techniques except that incomplete stories or arguments are substituted for the incomplete sentences.

In general, the attributes of these techniques have not been evaluated or described. Our expectation would be that the quality of instrument attributes is highly specific to the particular instrument in question.

Pictorial Techniques. Pictorial techniques include all those procedures that use pictures or ambiguous visual forms as stimuli. Many of these are taken directly from clinical procedures. For example, the Thematic Apperception Test (TAT) has been widely used as an attitude-measuring instrument (Adorno, Frenkel-Brunswik, Levinson, and Sanford, 1950; Proshansky, 1943; Smith, 1954). Brown's (1947) use of the Rosensweig Picture-frustration Test to study ethnic attitudes is another example of a clinical tool adapted to attitude measurement. Ethnic pictures (Cook, 1950), political cartoons (Fromme, 1941), drawings of "zoot suiters" (Adorno et al., 1950), etc., are other examples of stimuli used in this approach. As a rule, respondents are shown a picture and asked to tell a story about it, to indicate what they think it represents, or to choose among alternative interpretations. Scoring is usually subjective, relying heavily on the interpretative skill of the scorer. Usually, too, there is no attempt to scale items or to establish reliability and validity.

SUMMARY

In this chapter we have described several approaches to the measurement of attitudes. The methods described range from rigorous attempts to construct attitude scales with known characteristics to highly subjective approaches that make no attempt to construct scales. In general, the more rigorous methods of scale construction yield scales whose attributes more nearly correspond to the ideal than do the less rigorous techniques, although no scale fits the ideal perfectly. Reliable and valid scales can be constructed by the methods developed by Thurstone, Likert, Guttman, Coombs, and Lazarsfeld, and by variations of these methods. All strive for unidimensionality, most for equality of units, and a few for a zero point. However, each scale listed in the following chapters should be evaluated on its own merits.

CHAPTER 3

social practices

Every culture necessarily develops ways of handling relationships among its members in a multitude of situations. We have designated these procedures *social practices*. Often there are several ways of conducting oneself in a given social situation or of dealing with a given social problem, so the approved practice may vary from individual to individual and from group to group within a culture. This means, of course, that the attitudes of individuals within a culture toward any particular practice may vary along a favorable-unfavorable continuum.

Scales for measuring attitudes toward a variety of social practices are available. In this chapter we have grouped these scales according to general classes of attitude objects and have included a section on generalized scales designed to measure attitudes toward any one of several social practices.

ATTITUDES TOWARD FAMILY-RELATED PRACTICES

In this section we present attitude scales designed to measure attitudes toward child-rearing practices, parental discipline, child guidance, and family relations. One widely used scale, the Parental Attitude Research Instrument (Schaefer and Bell, 1958), was not included because of reservations expressed by its authors. The interested reader is referred to the following studies which have used this scale: Costin (1961), Heilbrun (1960*a*,*b*), Kitano (1961), Nichols (1962), Zuckerman (1959), and Zuckerman, Norton, and Sprague (1958). The University of Southern

California Attitude Survey (Shoben, 1949) was omitted for similar reasons. Finally, a scale by Wiley (1955) was omitted because scoring instructions were not available. Additional data relevant to the latter two scales may be found in Walters and Fisher (1958) and Walters (1959).

A survey of opinions regarding the bringing up of children EXHIBIT 3-1

Description. This is one of several scales developed by Itkin (1952) to measure intrafamily attitudes. Other scales in the battery are: (1) A Survey of Opinions Regarding the Discipline of Children, (2) Attitudes toward Discipline Exercised by Parents, (3) Parents' Judgment Regarding a Particular Child, and (4) Attitudes toward Parents. The first two scales are described in the following sections of this chapter. The other two scales are described in Chapter 9 (see Exhibits 9-3 and 9-4).

These scales were developed by the Likert summated ratings procedure, although the form of some of the items deviates from the usual Likert format. The items in the final scales were selected by item analysis, but the number of items in the original pool was not given in the report. The final scale to measure attitude toward the bringing up of children consisted of 30 statements about various aspects of parental treatment of children. The first 26 items are standard Likert items; the last 4 are multiple-choice items (see Exhibit 3-1).

Subjects. The subjects for the major part of the study were students and parents of students in psychology and sociology classes at Wright, Wilson, Herzl, and Schurz City Junior Colleges, Chicago, Illinois. More than 400 subjects were drawn from these populations. For a pilot study, 83 students at Northwestern University were used.

Response Mode. The Likert-type items use the following five-alternative response mode: strongly agree, agree, uncertain, disagree, strongly disagree. The subject responds to each item by underlining the chosen alternative. For the multiple-choice items, the subject responds by checking one of the several alternatives provided.

Scoring. Each item alternative is assigned a weight ranging from 1 to 5. For items 1 through 26, a weight of 5 is assigned to "strongly agree" for positive statements and to "strongly disagree" for negative statements. The item weights are given beside each alternative in Exhibit 3-1 for the last 4 items. The attitude score is the sum of the item scores. The theoretical range is from 30 to 150, with the higher score indicating the more favorable attitude toward acceptant, positive treatment of children.

Reliability. Reliability was estimated by the split-half method and found to be .85 (corrected to .91) for a sample of 429 parents.

Validity. Little evidence of validity is available. Self-ratings of 70 parents correlated only .23 with scores on this scale.

Comments. The greatest weakness of this scale is the dearth of information concerning the validity of the scale. The item analysis data provides some evidence of validity, but the low correlations between self-ratings and attitude scores offers no basis for optimism. The interested reader may also wish to refer to a later study by the same author (Itkin, 1955).

EXHIBIT 3-1

A SURVEY OF OPINIONS REGARDING THE BRINGING UP OF CHILDREN

Following is a list of statements regarding what should or should not be done in the bringing up of children. If you strongly agree with a statement as it stands, please *draw a line under* the words "Strongly Agree"; if you strongly disagree with the statement, underline the words "Strongly Disagree," and so on, for "Agree," "Uncertain," and "Disagree."

Since this is a survey of opinions, it is desired that you indicate *your own personal opinions* regarding these questions, regardless of whether you think other people might agree or disagree with you. There are no "right" or "wrong" answers to these statements. This is a study of *personal opinions,* and of *personal opinions only.* Please fill these forms out independently.

1 A parent should look after his (or her) young child both at school and at play.
   * Strongly Agree   Agree   Uncertain   Disagree   Strongly Disagree

2 A parent should praise his (or her) child liberally in private.

† 3 If one child in a family is less quick to learn than another, his parents should spur him on by constantly pointing out the superiority of the other.

† 4 If parents can afford to do so, they should send a child to a military or boarding school, where he (or she) could obtain the proper training with the least inconvenience to the parents.

† 5 Surprise parties, birthday parties, and the giving of presents to children are likely to spoil them, and should be avoided.

6 Parents should take their children with them on trips and vacations.

7 Parents should encourage their children to bring their friends home and should help them to entertain their friends.

8 Parents should, if necessary, make almost any sacrifices of their own money or comfort in order to make their children happy.

† 9 If a three-year-old child tells wild stories which are obviously untrue, he should be punished severely for lying.

* The same response alternatives are used for items 1 through 26.
† Items marked with a dagger are negative items.

Reference: W. Itkin. Some relationships between intra-family attitudes and pre-parental attitudes toward children. *J. genet. Psychol.,* 1952, 80, 221–252. Items obtained from author and published with his permission.

†10 A parent should **never** "give in" to a child.
11 A parent should spend as much time as possible with his (or her) child.
†12 Children should be trained to do things for themselves as early in life as possible.
13 A parent should be perfectly frank with his (or her) child on the subject of sex.
14 Parents should give children of elementary school age or older reasons for any requests made of them.
†15 If a family is able to afford to do so, the training of the children should be handled by a servant or a nurse.
†16 Children should **not** be allowed to interfere with the social or recreational activities of their parents.
†17 Children of high school age should earn all of their own spending money.
18 A family should move out of an unwholesome neighborhood for the sake of the children even if such a move would make it necessary for the father to travel farther to work.
†19 A child who sucks his thumb often should be made to feel ashamed of himself.
20 Parents should praise and make much of their children in the presence of outsiders.
21 Parents should show their love and affection for their children outwardly by praise and expressions of affection.
†22 Whenever a child deserves a scolding, he (or she) should be scolded then and there, whether strangers are present or not.
†23 Parents should discourage their children from asking them intimate questions.
24 Children should **not** be teased.
†25 Young people should obey their parents because they are their parents.
26 It is **not** possible to show too much love for a child.

In each of the following you are given a statement which can be completed in any one of several ways. Please place a check in front of whichever of the alternative choices most nearly resembles your own opinion.

27 In general, a child may be expected to act like an adult at . . . .
1 (a) Seven years of age
2 (b) Ten years of age
3 (c) Thirteen years of age
4 (d) Sixteen years of age
5 (e) Nineteen years of age

28 Children should **not** be given allowances until they are . . . .
5 (a) Seven years of age
4 (b) Nine years of age
3 (c) Eleven years of age
2 (d) Thirteen years of age
1 (e) Fifteen years of age
1 (f) Children should not be given allowances **at all**
5 (g) Children may be given regular allowances even before age seven

29 Children who talk back to their parents should be . . . .
5 (a) Given a quiet talking to

4	(b) Told that another such offense would be punished
3	(c) Severely scolded
2	(d) Sent to bed without food
1	(e) Whipped severely
5	(f) Given a less severe punishment than any mentioned above

30 Children who repeatedly disobey their parents should be . . . .

5	(a) Given a heart-to-heart or man-to-man talk
4	(b) Threatened with punishment
3	(c) Scolded severely
2	(d) Spanked
1	(e) Whipped severely
1	(f) Locked into a closet
1	(g) Punished **more** severely than in any of the above choices
5	(h) Punished **less** severely than in any of the above choices

A survey of opinions regarding the discipline of children *EXHIBIT 3-2*

Description. This is one of the scales developed by Itkin (1952) to measure intrafamily attitudes. It was developed by the same procedures as the scale described above. It consists of 31 Likert-type items and 4 multiple-choice items.

Subjects. The subjects used in developing this scale were the same as those used in connection with the scale described in the preceding section.

Response Mode. The first 31 items use the following five alternatives: strongly agree, agree, uncertain, disagree, strongly disagree. The subject responds to each item by underlining the chosen alternative. The subject responds to each of the 4 multiple-choice items by checking one of the several alternatives provided.

Scoring. Weights from 1 to 5 are assigned to each response alternative. For items 31 through 61 a weight of 5 is assigned to "strongly agree" for items expressing a favorable attitude toward strict control and to "strongly disagree" for items expressing the opposite view. Scoring weights are given in Exhibit 3-2 for the last 4 items. The attitude score is the sum of the item scores. The theoretical range of scores is from 35 to 175, with the higher score indicating an attitude favoring a more strict control of children's activities.

Reliability. Split-half reliability was reported to be .95 (corrected to .97) for a sample of 423 parents.

Validity. Evidence of validity is limited to item analysis data and the correlation between attitude scores and self-ratings of 70 parents. This correlation was only .26.

Comments. More evidence of the validity of the scale is badly needed. The potential reader is referred to Itkin (1955) for further studies using this scale.

EXHIBIT 3-2

A SURVEY OF OPINIONS REGARDING THE DISCIPLINE OF CHILDREN

Following is a list of statements regarding what should or should not be done in respect to the control or discipline of children. If you strongly agree with a statement as it stands, please *draw a line* under the words "Strongly Agree"; if you strongly disagree with the statement, *underline* the words "Strongly Disagree," and so on, for "Agree," "Uncertain," and "Disagree."

These statements apply to a child of either sex unless they specifically refer to a child as a boy or a girl. There are no right or wrong answers to these statements. This is simply a survey of *opinions*. Please do not be concerned as to whether other people may agree or disagree with you, and say exactly what you feel. Please fill these forms out independently.

31 Violation of household rules should **never** be overlooked.
*Strongly Agree Agree Uncertain Disagree Strongly Disagree
32 Parents should help their children with their homework if they need help.
†33 Parents should allow their children to make up their own minds as to what they will be when they grow up without trying to influence their decisions.
†34 A child should be encouraged but **not** required to say "Please" whenever he makes a request.
35 Parents should allow children of less than fifteen years of age to see only those movies of which they approve.
36 Children should be trained to pay **immediate** obedience to their parents.
37 Parents should insist upon complete obedience from their children.
38 Children should be expected to obey commands instantly and without question.
39 An older child should be expected to take care of younger brothers and sisters.
†40 Children should be allowed to do as they please.
†41 A child should **never** be forced to eat anything against his will.
†42 A child should **never** be forced to do a thing he does not wish to do.
43 The social activities of a boy or girl of high school age should be closely supervised by the parents.
†44 Parents should **not** dictate to high school students as to when and how much they should study.
45 Children should be expected to obey commands without being given reasons for them.
46 Whenever a young child fails to come home from school promptly, his parents should question him as to where he had been.
47 Before a child of high school age goes out of the house, he should **always** be required to tell his parents where he is going and what he is going to do.

* The same response alternatives are used for items 31 through 61.

† Items marked with a dagger express an unfavorable attitude toward strict control of children's activities.

Reference: W. Itkin. Some relationships between intra-family attitudes and pre-parental attitudes toward children. *J. genet. Psychol.*, 1952, 80, 221–252. Items obtained from author and published with his permission.

48 Parents should closely supervise all of the after-school activities of their children of high school age or younger.
49 Children of high school age or younger should be allowed to go only with those friends of whom their parents approve.
50 A child should be required to say "Please" whenever he makes a request.
51 If a parent threatens a child with punishment, this punishment should be carried out without exception.
52 If parents refrain from punishing a child, they will spoil him.
53 Parents should watch their young children to see that no harm comes to them.
†54 A young person of high school age should be free to come and go as he pleases without interference from his parents.
55 A child should **never** be allowed to contradict or talk back to his parents.
†56 Young children should be allowed to choose their own playmates without any interference on the part of their parents.
†57 A child should be allowed to spend his money or allowances as he wishes.
†58 If a child wants to destroy his own playthings, he should be allowed to do so.
†59 A child's liberty should be restricted in danger situations only.
60 A parent should always insist that every one of his (or her) commands be obeyed, even if he realizes after making a command that it was an unreasonable one.
61 If one parent refuses a child's request, the other parent should refuse it also.

In each of the following you are given a statement which can be completed in any one of several ways. Place a check in front of whichever of the alternative choices most nearly resembles your own opinion.

62 Parents may allow their daughters to have "dates" beginning at . . .
1 ______ **(a)** Age 10 or younger
2 ______ **(b)** Age 12
3 ______ **(c)** Age 14
4 ______ **(d)** Age 16
5 ______ **(e)** Age 18
5 ______ **(f)** Age 20

63 Children under fourteen years of age may be allowed to go out alone in the evenings to play . . .
1 ______ **(a)** At any time they desire
2 ______ **(b)** Several times a week
3 ______ **(c)** About once a week
4 ______ **(d)** About once every two weeks
5 ______ **(e)** Less than once a month, or never at all

64 Children who misbehave should have their privileges taken away . . .
1 ______ **(a)** Never
2 ______ **(b)** Seldom
3 ______ **(c)** Sometimes
4 ______ **(d)** Often
5 ______ **(e)** Every time they misbehave

65 Girls of less than sixteen years of age should be required to be home every evening (with only a few reasonable exceptions) by . . .
5 ______ **(a)** Nine o'clock or earlier
4 ______ **(b)** Ten o'clock

3 (c) Eleven o'clock
2 (d) Twelve o'clock
1 (e) No special time in the evening

Attitude toward discipline exercised by parents *EXHIBIT 3-3*

Description. This is Scale V in the Itkin (1952) intrafamily attitude series. It consists of two forms, one for measuring attitude toward discipline by the father (Form F) and one for measuring attitude toward discipline by the mother (Form M). The statements in the two forms are identical except that they refer to the father in one form and the mother in the other. The 37 items in Form F are given in Exhibit 3-3.

Subjects. The samples used in the development of this scale were the same as those used in developing the Survey of Opinions Regarding the Bringing Up of Children (Exhibit 3-1).

Response Mode. Each item in the discipline scale has three response alternatives: good, fair, and poor. The subject responds to each item by circling the appropriate alternative.

Scoring. Each alternative is given a score of 4 for a response of "good" (indicating a favorable attitude toward strict discipline), a 3 for a "fair" response, and a 2 for a "poor" response (indicating an unfavorable attitude toward strict discipline). The last two items were designed to indicate inconsistency of parental discipline and are not scored for measuring attitude. The attitude score is the sum of the item scores on the remaining 35 items. The theoretical scores thus range from 70 to 140, with the higher score indicating a more favorable attitude toward strict discipline by parents.

Reliability. Split-half reliability for Form F was found to be .91 (corrected to .96) for a sample of 262 students, and for Form M reliability was .92 (corrected to .96) for a sample of 274 students.

Validity. Scores on Form F correlated .63 with self-ratings, and scores on Form M correlated .67 with self-ratings, based upon a sample of 57 students in each case.

Comments. The limited evidence of validity is somewhat stronger for this scale than for the Itkin scales described in preceding sections, but further evidence would be desirable. (See Itkin, 1955, for further data on this scale.)

EXHIBIT 3-3

ATTITUDE TOWARD DISCIPLINE EXERCISED BY PARENTS

Please indicate *your judgment* regarding the discipline or control exercised by your father in the following manner: If you consider your

Reference: W. Itkin. Some relationships between intra-family attitudes and pre-parental attitudes toward children. *J. genet. Psychol.*, **1952, 80, 221–252. Items obtained from author and published with his permission.**

father's *actual practice* in regard to the particular supervisory or control activity discussed in a statement to be an example of *Good Supervision* on the part of your father, please *encircle* the word *"Good"* in the column to the right of the statements; if you consider *your father's practice* an example of *fairly Good Supervision,* encircle the word *"Fair";* and if an example of *Poor Supervision,* encircle the word *"Poor"* in the column to the right of the statements. Please note that *your judgments* as to whether your parent's supervisory practice was good, fair, or poor should refer to your parent's actual *practice,* and *not* to the statement as it stands.

1	My father **never** punished me for misbehavior.	**Good**	**Fair**	**Poor**
2	My father tried to direct all my activities.	**Good**	**Fair**	**Poor**
3	My father permitted me to make my own decisions.	**Good**	**Fair**	**Poor**
4	My father permitted me to do things on my own responsibility.	**Good**	**Fair**	**Poor**
5	Requests refused by my mother were usually granted by my father.	**Good**	**Fair**	**Poor**
6	My father insisted upon choosing my friends for me.	**Good**	**Fair**	**Poor**
7	My father would not let me spend my money as I pleased.	**Good**	**Fair**	**Poor**
8	My father constantly urged me to study harder.	**Good**	**Fair**	**Poor**
9	My father gave me a great deal of freedom.	**Good**	**Fair**	**Poor**
10	My father **never** punished me for disobeying his commands.	**Good**	**Fair**	**Poor**
11	My father let me solve my own problems in difficult situations.	**Good**	**Fair**	**Poor**
12	My father let me do anything I pleased.	**Good**	**Fair**	**Poor**
13	When I came home, my father often wanted to know where I had been.	**Good**	**Fair**	**Poor**
14	My father frequently gave in to me whether I was right or wrong.	**Good**	**Fair**	**Poor**
15	My father closely supervised the out-of-school activities of his children.	**Good**	**Fair**	**Poor**
16	My father always let me have my own way.	**Good**	**Fair**	**Poor**
17	My father would not allow me to decide important things for myself.	**Good**	**Fair**	**Poor**
18	My father always required me to tell him where I was going and what I was about to do.	**Good**	**Fair**	**Poor**
19	My father too closely supervised my play activities.	**Good**	**Fair**	**Poor**
20	My father would not let his children go out often enough.	**Good**	**Fair**	**Poor**
21	My father required his children to go to bed too early.	**Good**	**Fair**	**Poor**
22	My father scolded his children too often.	**Good**	**Fair**	**Poor**
23	My father too often refused reasonable requests made by his children.	**Good**	**Fair**	**Poor**
24	My father made me do too many chores around the house.	**Good**	**Fair**	**Poor**
25	My father gave his children everything they wanted.	**Good**	**Fair**	**Poor**
26	My father used too lax discipline upon his children.	**Good**	**Fair**	**Poor**
27	My father made me come home too early in the evening.	**Good**	**Fair**	**Poor**

28	My father often gave me unreasonable commands which he always insisted that I carry out.	**Good**	**Fair**	**Poor**
29	My father expected too much of his children.	**Good**	**Fair**	**Poor**
30	My father forced his children to do too many things against their will.	**Good**	**Fair**	**Poor**
31	My father used too strict discipline upon his children.	**Good**	**Fair**	**Poor**
32	My father was too strict in not allowing his children ever to talk back to him.	**Good**	**Fair**	**Poor**
33	My father was too easy a disciplinarian, and left the discipline of his children entirely to his wife.	**Good**	**Fair**	**Poor**
34	My father too often insisted upon my doing things his way.	**Good**	**Fair**	**Poor**
35	My father nagged me too much.	**Good**	**Fair**	**Poor**
36	Sometimes my father was too strict and sometimes he was too lenient.	**Good**	**Fair**	**Poor**
37	My father was too inconsistent in his discipline, sometimes permitting his children to do things which he at other times expressly forbade.	**Good**	**Fair**	**Poor**

Attitude toward the freedom of children EXHIBIT 3-4

Description. The Attitude toward the Freedom of Children Scale was developed by Koch, Dentler, Dysart, and Streit (1934) using the Thurstone method of equal-appearing intervals. Two forms of the scale were developed, each consisting of 33 items.

The items in the final scale were selected from a pool of 123 items. The sorting of the items by the usual Thurstone procedure was done by 200 judges, most of whom were college-trained. Items were selected to have low Q values, ranging from .53 to 3.01, and to represent the entire attitude continuum. Exhibit 3-4 gives the items and the scale values for the two forms of the scale.

Subjects. The subjects were 359 adults from widely scattered parts of the country, although Chicago provided the largest number. Of the 232 women and 127 men, 135 were 29 years of age or younger; 118 were between 30 and 39 years of age; and 106 were 40 years of age or older. The two-forms reliability coefficient was based upon the scores of 233 adults from "a rather heterogeneous population."

Response Mode. Subjects respond to each item by placing beside each statement either a check mark to indicate agreement or a cross to indicate disagreement.

Scoring. The attitude score is the median of the scale values of items with which the subject agrees. A low score indicates a more liberal attitude toward freedom of children.

Reliability. The correlation between the two forms of the scale was .68, based on the scores of 233 adults. Reliability of the scale values was determined by comparing the scale values obtained from two groups of 100 judges each. The two sets of scale values correlated .97.

Validity. In addition to the validity implied by the judging procedure, it was shown that females scored lower than males (i.e., were more liberal), that the more highly educated scored lower than less well-educated persons, and that the closer the contact with children, the lower the score obtained on this scale.

Comments. Unlike most scales that we have encountered, the validity of the Attitude toward the Freedom of Children Scale appears to be relatively well established. The correlation between the two forms is minimal, but may be acceptable for research purposes. The scale has been used with some success by McKeachie (1954).

EXHIBIT 3-4

ATTITUDE TOWARD THE FREEDOM OF CHILDREN

Following you will find thirty-three statements expressing different attitudes toward the question of children's rights and liberties.

Put a check mark (√) if you **agree** with the statement.
Put a cross (×) if you **disagree** with the statement.

If you cannot decide about a statement, you may mark it with a question mark. This is not an examination. People differ in their opinions about what is right and wrong in this issue.

Scale Values

Scale I

7.09	1	A young child must be disciplined until he has learned not to touch those objects in his environment which he cannot handle without damaging.
2.56	2	When a child's wants and those of an adult are in conflict, the child should receive the more consideration.
6.00	3	Parents should feel called upon to give reasons to the young child for the restrictions imposed, only when he is capable of understanding.
10.43	4	A pre-school child should never be allowed to have his own way.
4.87	5	A child who is entangled in a disciplinary problem should be allowed to explain his point of view.
3.10	6	A child should be restricted only when he is infringing upon the rights of others.
1.62	7	Adults should give no suggestions which will influence the form of a child's play constructs.
.74	8	Play activities should never be supervised.

Scale Values		
9.65	9	Implicit obedience is always desirable.
4.39	10	Leniency in restricting the liberties of a child is better than too much severity.
9.76	11	A child's whims and impulsive desires should never be humored.
4.24	12	Children should be given reasons for the restrictions placed upon them.
5.95	13	It is necessary to teach a child that he cannot always have his own way.
2.48	14	A pre-school child should, from the time he shows any inclination to do so, be allowed to choose the dress or suit he is to wear.
7.83	15	Children are being allowed too much freedom.
3.36	16	The wishes of the child should usually be respected.
6.64	17	I would have the child ask permission before engaging in activities that are new or strange.
2.72	18	A pre-school child should be allowed freedom of action except in matters pertaining to his health and physical safety.
10.03	19	A child should be forced to obey if he does not do immediately as he is told.
1.98	20	I would place no restriction on the child's activity except in times of grave danger to himself or others.
.63	21	A child should be given anything he wants to eat.
1.14	22	The child should be allowed free choice in the matter of associates.
5.27	23	Matters of conduct should be decided by the parent and child together.
8.04	24	A child should be required to say "please" whenever he makes a request.
8.22	25	When a child's wants and those of an adult are in conflict, the adult should be given the more consideration.
3.93	26	Restrictions should not be imposed when they will discourage the child's spontaneous efforts.
10.30	27	A child should be taught to obey an adult unquestioningly.
5.44	28	The parent should choose the group with which the child is to associate, but the child should be allowed free choice with respect to his companions within the group.
9.85	29	A child should obey his parents because they are his parents.
.55	30	The parent should comply with every demand of the child.
7.32	31	A child should be required to obey immediately in matters pertaining to health and physical routine.
6.75	32	Children's activities, when they seem to an adult to be destructive or wasteful, should be restricted.
8.51	33	A child's playthings are not his to do with as he pleases.

Scale II

Scale Values		
2.59	1	Except in danger situations, a child should never be expected to obey without being given an adequate reason.
7.72	2	The child should be taught to respect the wishes of his elders.
5.25	3	When imposing restrictions upon a child, a parent should have well considered reasons and should be willing to give them.
10.01	4	A child should be required to eat everything that is set before him.
.67	5	A child should never be forced to do a thing he does not wish to do.
9.44	6	Rigid training for obedience should be started in infancy.

Scale Values		
5.75	**7**	I believe in placing upon young children but few restrictions and enforcing these strictly.
8.77	**8**	In all quarrels between young children adults should arbitrate.
.91	**9**	A child should never be required to say "please."
9.81	**10**	The will of the parent should be dominant over the will of the child.
8.16	**11**	In his explorations of property the child should always be under close supervision.
3.95	**12**	A child should be given more than one chance to obey.
5.62	**13**	It is the parents' task to make the child want to do what is good for him.
2.32	**14**	A child's liberty should be restricted in danger situations only.
4.24	**15**	When a child is absorbed in his own immediate affairs, a parent should consider the fact before making a demand.
1.27	**16**	Natural forces, not individuals, should discipline the young child.
7.61	**17**	Little children should be forced to obey, but the control of older children should be less exacting.
3.38	**18**	Within the limits of justice and safety, a young child in his play should be free from adult interference.
4.41	**19**	The older pre-school child should be allowed a certain amount of freedom in making decisions and assuming the consequences.
.54	**20**	A child should be allowed to do as he wishes in all things.
2.14	**21**	A child should be given a choice in every matter possible.
8.41	**22**	A child should always be supervised by his parents in his work activities.
3.79	**23**	From a selection of foods chosen by an adult as suitable for the young child, the child should be allowed to choose freely.
10.29	**24**	The "Puritan" method of bringing up children is the best method.
7.81	**25**	If a child does not comply at once with a request in matters pertaining to health, he should be forced to.
1.54	**26**	The child's own limitations in relation to his physical environment should be all that should restrict him in his play activities.
10.28	**27**	The whims of the child should be repressed at all times.
5.01	**28**	Within certain selected situations, a child should be allowed to assert his personal likes and dislikes.
1.81	**29**	A child should be permitted to do as he wishes with his own playthings.
9.36	**30**	A child should never be allowed openly to disagree with his parents.
6.24	**31**	In the face of an emergency situation the immediate obedience of the child should be required.
4.63	**32**	A child should be encouraged but not required to say "please" when he makes a request.
7.17	**33**	A child should not be allowed to destroy or abuse his own playthings.

Attitude toward parental control of children's activities
EXHIBIT 3-5

Description. This scale was developed by Stott (1940). It is a 30-item scale designed to measure permissive-nonpermissive attitudes toward control of children's activities. Half of the items stress parental authority and control, and half stress freedom for children. The items were not selected from a longer list by any statistical procedure. The judged meaning of the item was the only criterion for selection.

Subjects. The subjects were 48 women students at the University of Nebraska and their parents.

Response Mode. Subjects respond to each item by circling one of five response alternatives: A, complete and thorough agreement; a, agree but not completely; ?, undecided; d, disagree but not completely; D, complete and thorough disagreement. It should be noted that the response alternatives were listed incorrectly in the published report (Stott, private communication, 1964).

Scoring. Scoring values range from 0 for strong disagreement with permissive items and strong agreement with nonpermissive items to 4 for strong agreement with permissive and strong disagreement with nonpermissive items. The attitude score is the sum of the item scores. The theoretical range was therefore from 0 to 120; the higher the score, the more liberal or permissive the parent's attitude.

Reliability. Corrected split-half reliability was reported to be .86, based upon the responses of 186 adults.

Validity. The scale appears to have content validity, and the method of selecting items supports this supposition. In addition, differences in mean scores were found among selected groups. Parents were classified according to place of residence. The mean scores of fathers were 46.0 for those living on the farm, 44.7 for those living in small towns, and 65.2 for those living in the city. Comparable scores for mothers were 49.2, 57.2, and 56.5, respectively. With some ambiguity relative to town residents, these differences are in the expected direction. College students scored significantly higher ($p < .01$) than did their parents.

Comments. The evidence concerning the characteristics of this scale is very limited. It is recommended that additional evidence of reliability and validity be obtained before the scale is used for any purpose other than exploratory research.

EXHIBIT 3-5

ATTITUDE TOWARD PARENTAL CONTROL OF CHILDREN'S ACTIVITIES

Please indicate your agreement or disagreement with each of the statements by circling the appropriate letter according to the following code:

A—Complete and thorough agreement
a—Agree but not completely
?—Undecided
d—Disagree but not completely
D—Complete and thorough disagreement

1 Young people should be trained to recognize the authority of their parents. A a ? d D

Reprinted with permission from Stott, L. H. Parental attitudes of farm, town, and city parents in relation to certain personality adjustments in their children. *J. soc. Psychol.*, 1940, 11, 325–339. Copyright 1940 by The Journal Press, Provincetown, Mass.

2	Training in obedience to one's parents is fine preparation for later life for any young person.	A	a	?	d	D
3	Young people should be allowed to do as they please without interference from their parents.	A	a	?	d	D
4	Obedience to parents is one of the finest virtues.	A	a	?	d	D
5	Young people should be allowed freedom in selecting their own friends and companions.	A	a	?	d	D
6	Parents should maintain authority over their children until they are "of age" or until they get married.	A	a	?	d	D
7	Young people should not be forced to do things they do not want to do.	A	a	?	d	D
8	Young people should be allowed freedom in choosing their recreational activities.	A	a	?	d	D
9	Young people should not have to ask permission to "go out" at night.	A	a	?	d	D
10	Young people of high school age should have learned to obey their parents.	A	a	?	d	D
11	Young people should be allowed to use their leisure time as they please.	A	a	?	d	D
12	Natural forces, not individuals, should discipline young people.	A	a	?	d	D
13	Parents should tell their children of high school age where they may or may not go for amusement and recreation.	A	a	?	d	D
14	The social activities of a boy or girl of high school age should be closely supervised and controlled by the parents.	A	a	?	d	D
15	The liberty of young people should be restricted in danger situations only.	A	a	?	d	D
16	The whims and impulsive desires of young people should not be humored.	A	a	?	d	D
17	Parents nowadays are allowing their children too much freedom.	A	a	?	d	D
18	A young person should be restricted only when he is infringing upon the rights of others.	A	a	?	d	D
19	Parents should not dictate to high school students as to when and how much they must study.	A	a	?	d	D
20	When young people do not do as their parents tell them they should be forced to do so.	A	a	?	d	D
21	Children should know enough by the time they reach high school to do as their elders tell them.	A	a	?	d	D
22	Young people should obey their parents because they are their parents.	A	a	?	d	D
23	Parents should allow their children of high school age to stay out at night as late as they wish.	A	a	?	d	D
24	Young people who have had rigid training in obedience in the home make the best citizens.	A	a	?	d	D
25	Regardless of the wishes of the parents, no restriction should be placed upon a young person's freedom to do as he wishes except in cases of grave danger to himself or others.	A	a	?	d	D
26	Parents should not make their children feel that they must obey them.	A	a	?	d	D

27	Training in obedience to the authority of parents hinders the development of self-reliance in young people.	A a ? d D
28	Young people should be trained in obedience to their parents in regard to helping with the daily tasks about the home.	A a ? d D
29	Parents should demand obedience of their children.	A a ? d D
30	A young person of high school age should be free to come and go as he pleases without interference from his parents.	A a ? d D

Attitude toward self-reliance EXHIBIT 3-6

Description. This is really a set of scales developed by Ojemann (1934) to measure attitudes toward self-reliance of parents having children at different age levels. The set includes two forms for use with parents of preschool children and one form each for use with parents of elementary school children and with parents of high school children. Since all the scales were constructed as a set, all are discussed together. The items of the various scales given in Exhibit 3-6 are numbered as they were in Ojemann's report.

The procedure followed in constructing these scales is unlike that of any of the standard methods described in Chapter 2, although it resembles the Thurstone procedure. The first step consisted of a compilation of a list of 124 children's activities involving acceptance of responsibility by the child. These were then used to write items in a form such that the statement could be completed by the insertion of an age (in either years or months). Ten judges criticized these items and offered suggestions for improvement. Items that could not be written in an acceptable form were discarded. The remaining items were divided into three groups corresponding to age levels: birth to eight years for the preschool scales, three years to fifteen years for the elementary scale, and above seven years for the high school scale.

Subjects. The subjects were 119 parents of preschool children, 89 parents of elementary school children, and 42 parents of high school children.

Response Mode. The subject responds to each item by writing in the age at which the average child should be able to perform the activity described by the item.

Scoring. A scoring key was developed by asking 20 trained judges to designate three responses to each item; one representing an attitude so highly favorable that it could be given a rating of 1 on an 11-point scale, another so unfavorable as to merit a rating of 11, and a third that could be rated neutral. The ages for these three points on each item were plotted on a cumulative frequency graph and the median taken as the location of the corresponding scale points. Other points were located by interpolation. The age values corresponding to the scale scores are given below each item in Exhibit 3-6, with the age to the extreme left corresponding to a score of 11, the next one to the right to a score of 10, and so on to the extreme right, which corresponds to a score of 1. Each item is given a score corresponding to the scale value of the age nearest to the estimate of the subject. The attitude score is the average of the item scores. The theoretical range is thus from 1 to 11, with the higher score indicating a more unfavorable attitude toward self-reliance.

Reliability. Chance-half reliabilities, corrected by the Spearman-Brown prophecy formula, were as follows: preschool scale, .93 (N = 119); elementary scale, .89 (N = 89); and high school scale, .73 (N = 42). Forms 1 and 2 of the preschool scale were found to yield almost identical mean scores of the sample of 119 parents.

Validity. Ojemann maintained that *a priori* reasons for selecting the items indicated their validity, but he also reported a "close relationship" between the attitude score obtained by personal interview and that obtained by the scales.

Comments. These self-reliance scales were developed by a rather unusual procedure, but the evidence indicates that they are at least minimally reliable and valid. Since the scale values were determined several years ago, the prospective user should check these values using present-day judges.

EXHIBIT 3-6

ATTITUDE TOWARD SELF - RELIANCE

The following pages contain a list of items such as this:

I think that a child should be able to brush his teeth daily without being told to do so by the age of ________

We want you to read an item, then think of children who are neither high nor low in intelligence, physical development, etc., but near the average. Then mark in the blank the age at which anyone of these "near-average" children should be able to perform this task.

For example, if you think that the average child should be able to brush his teeth daily without being told to do so by the age of five years, place the figure 5 in the blank, like this:

I think that a child should be able to brush his teeth daily without being told to do so by the age of 5

In some cases you may wish to put down the age in months rather than years. In such cases write "mos." after the figure, like this: 2 mos.

We want your *own* opinion on each item.

Reprinted with permission from Ojemann, R. H. The measurement of self-reliance. *Univer. of Iowa Studies in Child Welfare,* **1934, 10, 103–111.**

Form 1 for Parents of Preschool Children

1 I feel that a child should carry food with a spoon from a dish to the mouth **without spilling** (does not imply never spilling), through an entire meal, by the age of ______

3.25 3.05 2.85 2.65 2.45 2.25 2.10 1.95 1.80 1.65 1.50

3 I think a child should be able to cut his own meat (if reasonably tender) with a knife by the age of ______

7.75 7.35 6.95 6.55 6.15 5.75 5.35 4.95 4.55 4.15 3.75

5 I think a child is capable of answering the doorbell and calling the person desired by the age of ______

6.00 5.60 5.20 4.80 4.40 4.00 3.70 3.40 3.10 2.80 2.50

7 I think a child should be able to **help** set the table for a family meal (e.g., place silverware and dishes on the table after an adult has given them to him and has shown him where to place them) by the age of ______

4.50 4.35 4.20 4.05 3.90 3.75 3.50 3.25 3.00 2.75 2.50

9 I think a child has the ability to take a message over the telephone to relay correctly to another member of the family by the age of ______

7.75 7.35 6.95 6.55 6.15 5.75 5.35 4.95 4.55 4.15 3.75

11 I feel that a child should be taught to manage expenditure of an allowance which includes money for a few articles of clothing (e.g., hose, handkerchiefs) by the age of ______

11.50 11.00 10.50 10.00 9.50 9.00 8.60 8.20 7.80 7.40 7.00

13 I feel that a child is capable of undressing and going to bed alone after being told it is time to go to bed by the age of ______

7.75 7.45 7.15 6.85 6.55 6.25 5.75 5.25 4.75 4.25 3.75

15 I feel that a child should be allowed to ride a kiddie kar or other mobile toy around the home block (assuming there are no hidden driveways and but two alleys, which are not often used) without being accompanied by an adult at the age of ______

5.25 5.00 4.75 4.50 4.25 4.00 3.75 3.50 3.25 3.00 2.75

17 I think a child should be able to remove all his indoor clothing when it has been unfastened for him by the age of ______

4.25 3.95 3.65 3.35 3.05 2.75 2.55 2.35 2.15 1.95 1.75

19 I think a child should be able to unbutton one-half inch buttons when in **front position** by the age of ______

4.00 3.85 3.70 3.55 3.40 3.25 3.10 2.95 2.80 2.65 2.50

21 I think a child should be able to fasten medium sized hooks and eyes when in **front position** by the age of ______

6.50 6.10 5.70 5.30 4.90 4.50 4.30 4.10 3.90 3.70 3.50

23 I feel that a child should be able to take responsibility for urination (e.g., indicate his need) by the age of ______

2.50 2.40 2.30 2.20 2.10 2.00 1.90 1.80 1.70 1.60 1.50

25 I think a child should be able to hold and drink from a cup or glass (one-half full of liquid) **without spilling** (does not imply **never** spilling) by the age of ______

2.00 1.90 1.80 1.70 1.60 1.50 1.40 1.30 1.20 1.10 1.00

27 I think that a child should be able to endure ordinary small hurts (e.g., falling from a kiddie kar) without crying by the age of ______

2.75 2.60 2.45 2.30 2.15 2.00 1.85 1.70 1.55 1.40 1.25

29 I believe a child should be permitted to play in his own unfenced yard without the immediate presence of an adult by the age of ______

3.50 3.35 3.20 3.05 2.90 2.75 2.55 2.35 2.15 1.95 1.75

31 I think a child should be able to share voluntarily toys with any child with whom he is playing by the age of ______

5.50 5.25 5.00 4.75 4.50 4.25 3.95 3.65 3.35 3.05 2.75

33 I believe a child should be able to **help** with the weekly cleaning (e.g., run the vacuum cleaner, empty wastebaskets) by the age of ______

7.50 7.25 7.00 6.75 6.50 6.25 5.85 5.45 5.05 4.65 4.25

35 I think a child should be able to dry the dishes (not scald them) after a family meal by the age of ______

6.75 6.45 6.15 5.85 5.55 5.25 4.95 4.65 4.25 4.05 3.75

37 I think a child should be permitted to run errands about the neighborhood (e.g., take a neighbor some flowers or borrow something for his mother) by the age of ______

5.50 5.30 5.10 4.90 4.70 4.50 4.20 3.90 3.60 3.30 3.00

39 I think a child should be able to bathe himself with adult supervision by the age of ______

5.75 5.50 5.25 5.00 4.75 4.50 4.25 4.00 3.75 3.50 3.25

41 I think a child should be able to remove all his own indoor clothing, including unfastening, **without help,** by the age of ______

6.00 5.70 5.40 5.10 4.80 4.50 4.20 3.90 3.60 3.30 3.00

43 I think a child should be able to dress himself when his clothes are handed to him in the proper position and are fastened for him by the age of ______

3.75 3.55 3.35 3.15 2.95 2.75 2.55 2.35 2.15 1.95 1.75

45 I think a child should be able to fasten medium sized snaps when in **front position** by the age of ______

4.75 4.55 4.35 4.15 3.95 3.75 3.50 3.25 3.00 2.75 2.50

47 I feel that a child should be able to make his own bed daily (excepting when sheets are changed) **without help** by the age of ______

9.25 8.90 8.55 8.20 7.85 7.50 7.10 6.70 6.30 5.90 5.50

49 I feel that a child should be able to assist in preparing food for the family meal (e.g., wash vegetables) by the age of ______

6.00 5.80 5.60 5.40 5.20 5.00 4.70 4.40 4.10 3.80 3.50

51 I think that a child should go to school alone a distance of two miles or less, when it is necessary to cross several heavy traffic streets, by the age of ______

9.50 9.20 8.90 8.60 8.30 8.00 7.65 7.30 6.95 6.60 6.25

Form 2 for Parents of Preschool Children

2 I think that a child should be able to use a fork to carry solid food from a dish to the mouth **without spilling** (does not imply **never** spilling), throughout an entire meal, by the age of ______

5.25 5.00 4.75 4.50 4.25 4.00 3.60 3.20 2.80 2.40 2.00

4 I believe that a child can be taught to make a good selection of his own meal when dining in a hotel or restaurant by the age of ______

11.50 10.90 10.30 9.70 9.10 8.50 7.95 7.40 6.85 6.30 5.75

6 I think a child should be able to **help** make his own bed (e.g., the child on one side of the bed smoothing covers and an adult on the other) by the age of ______

7.00 6.55 6.10 5.65 5.20 4.75 4.35 3.95 3.55 3.15 2.75

8 I believe that a child can run errands about the home (e.g., fetch a book for a parent) by the age of ______

4.50 4.15 3.80 3.45 3.10 2.75 2.55 2.35 2.15 1.95 1.75

10 I feel that a child should be able to **help** with daily cleaning about the home (e.g., pick up newspapers, straighten small rugs, empty ash trays) by the age of ______

5.75 5.30 4.85 4.40 3.95 3.50 3.30 3.10 2.90 2.70 2.50

12 I believe that a child should be put in his bed while awake and should go to sleep of his own accord by the age of ______

.50 .417 .333 .20 .166 .083 .066 .049 .033 .016 0

14 I think a child should be able to take turns with another child at using some toy or piece of play apparatus, without suggestion from an adult, by the age of ______

5.75 5.35 4.95 4.55 4.15 3.75 3.55 3.35 3.15 2.95 2.75

16 I think that a child should be able to go to school alone, a distance of one mile or less, when it is not necessary to cross heavy traffic streets, by the age of ______

7.25 6.95 6.65 6.35 6.05 5.75 5.55 5.35 5.15 4.95 4.75

18 I think a child should be able to dress himself entirely **without help** by the age of ______

7.50 7.15 6.80 6.45 6.10 5.75 5.35 4.95 4.55 4.15 3.75

20 I think a child can unfasten snaps regardless of the position or size by the age of ______

4.75 4.55 4.35 4.15 3.95 3.75 3.55 3.35 3.15 2.95 2.75

22 I feel that a child should be able to take responsibility for his bowel movements (e.g., indicate his need) by the age of ______

2.25 2.10 1.95 1.80 1.65 1.50 1.40 1.30 1.20 1.10 1.00

24 I believe that a child should be able to wash and dry his hands and face, insuring cleanliness, **without** adult supervision by the age of ______

5.00 4.85 4.70 4.55 4.40 4.25 3.95 3.65 3.35 3.05 2.75

26 I feel that a child should be able to choose his own play activities from material available about the home by the age of ______

3.00 2.70 2.40 2.10 1.90 1.50 1.40 1.30 1.20 1.10 1.00

28 I think a child should **help** put his toys away at the end of a play period after suggestion from an adult by the age of ______

3.50 3.20 2.90 2.60 2.30 2.00 1.95 1.90 1.85 1.80 1.75

30 I think a child should be able to settle minor difficulties (e.g., a struggle over a toy) with a child his own age by the age of ______

3.50 3.45 3.40 3.35 3.30 3.25 3.05 2.85 2.65 2.45 2.25

32 I think a child is capable of answering the telephone and calling the person desired by the age of ______

5.00 4.80 4.60 4.40 4.20 4.00 3.90 3.80 3.70 3.60 3.50

34 I think a child should be able to set the table for a family meal with dishes and silverware **without help** from an adult by the age of ______

7.50 7.25 7.00 6.75 6.50 6.25 5.85 5.45 5.05 4.65 4.25

36 I feel that a child should be able to hang up his own wraps, providing hooks are within his reach and near at hand, **without suggestion** from an adult, by the age of ______

4.75 4.50 4.25 4.00 3.75 3.50 3.25 3.00 2.75 2.50 2.25

38 I think that a child should be able to wash and dry his hands and face, reasonably clean, **with** adult suggestion and supervision by the age of ______

3.75 3.55 3.35 3.15 2.95 2.75 2.50 2.25 2.00 1.75 1.50

40 I feel that a child should be able to brush his teeth **without** adult supervision by the age of ______

5.50 5.35 5.20 5.05 4.90 4.75 4.45 4.15 3.85 3.55 3.25

42 I think a child should be able to put his own shoes on the correct foot and **lace** and **tie** them **without help** by the age of ______

6.50 6.35 6.20 6.05 5.90 5.75 5.30 4.85 4.40 3.95 3.50

44 I think a child should be able to button one-half inch buttons when in **front position** by the age of

4.50 4.25 4.00 3.75 3.50 3.25 3.10 2.95 2.80 2.65 2.50

46 I feel that a child should be allowed to make a choice of clothing to be worn from a few selected by an adult by the age of

5.25 5.00 4.75 4.50 4.25 4.00 3.75 3.50 3.25 3.00 2.75

48 I believe that a child should be able to **help** set the table for a family meal (e.g., assist another person) by the age of

4.75 4.60 4.45 4.30 4.15 4.00 3.70 3.40 3.10 2.80 2.50

50 I believe a child should be able to choose his own books to read from a library list of books suitable for his age by the age of

10.00 9.60 9.20 8.80 8.40 8.00 7.60 7.20 6.80 6.40 6.00

52 I believe that a child should be able to get to school on time **without being reminded** by the age of

9.25 9.00 8.75 8.50 8.25 8.00 7.65 7.30 6.95 6.60 6.25

Scale for Parents of Elementary School Children

1 I think that a child should be able to use a fork to carry solid food from a dish to the mouth **without spilling** (does not imply never spilling) throughout an entire meal by the age of

5.25 5.00 4.75 4.50 4.25 4.00 3.60 3.20 2.80 2.40 2.00

2 I think a child should be able to cut his own meat (if reasonably tender) with a knife by the age of

7.75 7.35 6.95 6.55 6.15 5.75 5.35 4.95 4.55 4.15 3.75

3 I believe that a child can be taught to make a good selection of his own meal when dining in a hotel or restaurant by the age of

11.50 10.90 10.30 9.70 9.10 8.50 7.95 7.40 6.85 6.30 5.75

4 I think a child is capable of answering the doorbell and calling the person desired by the age of

6.00 5.60 5.20 4.80 4.40 4.00 3.70 3.40 3.10 2.80 2.50

5 I think a child should be able to **help** make his own bed (e.g., the child on one side of the bed smoothing covers and the adult on the other) by the age of

7.00 6.55 6.10 5.65 5.20 4.75 4.35 3.95 3.55 3.15 2.75

6 I think a child has the ability to take a message over the telephone to relay correctly to another member of the family by the age of

7.75 7.35 6.95 6.55 6.15 5.75 5.35 4.95 4.55 4.15 3.75

7 I feel that a child should be able to help with daily cleaning about the home (e.g., pick up newspapers, straighten small rugs, empty ash trays) by the age of

5.75 5.30 4.85 4.40 3.95 3.50 3.30 3.10 2.90 2.70 2.50

8 I feel that a child has the ability to prepare a simple family dinner without assistance after it has been planned by the mother by the age of

14.25 13.75 13.25 12.75 12.25 11.75 11.05 10.35 9.65 8.95 8.25

9 I feel that a child is competent to play about the yard or house alone in the daytime when the parents are away for a period of two or three hours (assuming that there are neighbors within a block who can be called upon, if needed) by the age of

7.25 6.90 6.55 6.20 5.85 5.50 5.35 5.20 5.05 4.90 4.75

10 (Disregard legal age when marking this item.)
I feel that a child has the ability to drive the family car when adults are in the car by the age of

15.75 15.50 15.25 15.00 14.75 14.50 13.95 13.40 12.85 12.30 11.75

11 I feel that a child should be taught to manage expenditure of an allowance which includes money for a few articles of clothing (e.g., hose, handkerchiefs) by the age of

11.50 11.00 10.50 10.00 9.50 9.00 8.60 8.20 7.80 7.40 7.00

12 I think that a child can be left alone, in charge of the household, with younger members of the family (not more than three children and none younger than three years and assuming that the father is home at night) by the age of

16.00 15.60 15.20 14.80 14.40 14.00 13.60 13.20 12.80 12.40 12.00

13 I believe that a child should be taught to buy his own clothing **without help** from an adult by the age of

18.25 18.00 17.75 17.50 17.25 17.00 16.20 15.40 14.60 13.80 13.00

14 I think that a child should be taught how to obtain his own answers to his questions such as "How is silk made?" or "Where does rubber come from?" by the age of

11.75 11.50 11.25 11.00 10.75 10.50 10.05 9.60 9.15 8.70 8.25

15 I feel that a child is capable of undressing and going to bed alone after being told it is time to go to bed by the age of

7.75 7.45 7.15 6.85 6.55 6.25 5.75 5.25 4.75 4.25 3.75

16 I think a child should be able to take turns with another child at using some toy or piece of play apparatus, without suggestion from an adult, by the age of

5.75 5.35 4.95 4.55 4.15 3.75 3.55 3.35 3.15 2.95 2.75

17 I feel that a child should be allowed to ride a kiddie kar or other mobile toy around the home block (assuming there are not hidden

driveways and but two alleys which are not often used) by the age of

5.25 5.00 4.75 4.50 4.25 4.00 3.75 3.50 3.25 3.00 2.75

18 I think a child should go to school alone, a distance of one mile or less, when it is not necessary to cross heavy traffic streets by the age of

7.25 6.95 6.55 6.35 6.05 5.75 5.55 5.35 5.15 4.95 4.75

19 I think a child should be able to dress himself entirely **without help** by the age of

7.50 7.15 6.80 6.45 6.10 5.75 5.35 4.95 4.55 4.15 3.75

20 I think a child should be able to fasten medium sized hooks and eyes when in **front position** by the age of

6.50 6.10 5.70 5.30 4.90 4.50 4.30 4.10 3.90 3.70 3.50

21 I think a child is capable of taking entire care of his hair (i.e., wash, comb, decide how it is to be worn, when it is to be cut, etc.) by the age of

12.75 12.35 11.95 11.55 11.15 10.75 10.30 9.85 9.40 8.95 8.50

22 I think a child should be able to share voluntarily toys with any child with whom he is playing by the age of

5.50 5.25 5.00 4.75 4.50 4.25 3.95 3.65 3.35 3.05 2.75

23 I think a child is capable of answering the telephone and calling the person desired by the age of

5.00 4.80 4.60 4.40 4.20 4.00 3.90 3.80 3.70 3.60 3.50

24 I believe a child should be able to **help** with the weekly cleaning (e.g., run the vacuum cleaner, empty wastebaskets) by the age of

7.50 7.25 7.00 6.75 6.50 6.25 5.85 5.45 5.05 4.65 4.25

25 I think a child should be able to dry the dishes (not scald them) after a family meal by the age of

6.75 6.45 6.15 5.85 5.55 5.25 4.95 4.65 4.25 4.05 3.75

26 I think a child should be able to bathe himself with adult supervision by the age of

5.75 5.50 5.25 5.00 4.75 4.50 4.25 4.00 3.75 3.50 3.25

27 I think a child should be able to put his own shoes on the correct foot and **lace** and **tie** them **without help** by the age of

6.50 6.35 6.20 6.05 5.90 5.75 5.30 4.85 4.40 3.95 3.50

28 I think a child should be able to fasten medium sized snaps when in **front position** by the age of

4.75 4.55 4.35 4.15 3.95 3.75 3.50 3.25 3.00 2.75 2.50

29 I feel that a child should be allowed to make a choice of clothing to be worn from a few selected by an adult by the age of ______

5.25 5.00 4.75 4.50 4.25 4.00 3.75 3.50 3.25 3.00 2.75

30 I feel that a child should be able to make his own bed daily (excepting when sheets are changed) **without help** by the age of ______

9.25 8.90 8.55 8.20 7.85 7.50 7.10 6.70 6.30 5.90 5.50

31 I feel that a child should be able to plan and prepare a simple family dinner (e.g., meat, potatoes, vegetable, and dessert) by the age of ______

14.25 14.05 13.85 13.65 13.45 13.25 12.60 11.95 11.30 10.65 10.00

32 I believe a child should be able to choose his own books to read from a library list of books suitable to his age by the age of ______

10.00 9.60 9.20 8.80 8.40 8.00 7.60 7.20 6.80 6.40 6.00

33 I think that a child should go to school alone a distance of two miles or less when it is necessary to cross several heavy traffic streets by the age of ______

9.50 9.20 8.90 8.60 8.30 8.00 7.65 7.30 6.95 6.60 6.25

34 I believe that a child should be able to get to school on time **without being reminded** by the age of ______

9.25 9.00 8.75 8.50 8.25 8.00 7.65 7.30 6.95 6.60 6.25

35 I think that a child should be able to choose his own reading matter, including books, magazines, and newspapers, by the age of ______

14.75 14.40 14.05 13.70 13.35 13.00 12.65 12.30 11.95 11.60 11.25

36 I think that a child should be allowed to leave the parental home for a period of time (e.g., to a six weeks camp) by the age of ______

13.00 12.60 12.20 11.80 11.40 11.00 10.60 10.20 9.80 9.40 9.00

37 I think that a child should be able to make a desirable choice from his wardrobe of clothing to be worn, without suggestions from an adult, by the age of ______

14.00 13.50 13.00 12.50 12.00 11.50 10.80 10.10 9.40 8.70 8.00

Scale for Parents of High School Children

1 I believe that a child can be taught to make a good selection of his own meal when dining in a hotel or restaurant by the age of ______

11.50 10.90 10.30 9.70 9.10 8.50 7.95 7.40 6.85 6.30 5.75

2 I believe that a child should be able to wash, scald, and dry the dishes after a family meal by the age of ______

12.50 12.00 11.50 11.00 10.50 10.00 9.45 8.90 8.35 7.80 7.25

3 I feel that a child should be able to prepare a simple family dinner without assistance after it has been planned by the mother by the age of ____

14.25 13.75 13.25 12.75 12.25 11.75 11.05 10.35 9.65 8.95 8.25

4 (Disregard legal age when marking this item.)
I feel that a child should be able to drive the family car when adults are in the car by the age of ____

15.75 15.50 15.25 15.00 14.75 14.50 13.95 13.40 12.85 12.30 11.75

5 I believe that a child should be able to help care for the furnace or heating stove (e.g., carry ashes out-of-doors, put a shovel of coal on when asked to by parent) by the age of ____

13.00 12.40 11.80 11.20 10.60 10.00 9.60 9.20 8.80 8.40 8.00

6 I think that a child should be able to take responsibility for keeping at least one room clean throughout the week (assuming he has help in one regular weekly cleaning) by the age of ____

12.00 11.60 11.20 10.80 10.40 10.00 9.60 9.20 8.80 8.40 8.00

7 I think that a child can be left in charge of the household with younger members of the family (not more than three children and none younger than three years and assuming that the father is home at night) by the age of ____

16.00 15.60 15.20 14.80 14.40 14.00 13.60 13.20 12.80 12.40 12.00

8 I believe that a child should be taught to buy his own clothing without help from an adult by the age of ____

18.25 18.00 17.75 17.50 17.25 17.00 16.20 15.40 14.60 13.80 13.00

9 I think that a child should be taught how to obtain his own answers to his questions such as "How is silk made?" and "Where does rubber come from?" by the age of ____

11.75 11.50 11.25 11.00 10.75 10.50 10.05 9.60 9.15 8.70 8.25

10 (In marking this item disregard legal age.)
I feel that a child who lives in a city of 50,000 population should share in the use of the family car for his own enjoyment and the entertainment of his friends (this includes day or night trips to cities not larger than 50,000 and not over fifty miles distant from the home town) by the age of ____

18.50 18.20 17.90 17.60 17.30 17.00 16.65 16.30 15.95 15.60 15.25

11 I believe that a child should be able to take the entire responsibility for his school "home work" (i.e., complete it without parental reminder or supervision) by the age of ______

14.50 13.90 13.30 12.70 12.10 11.50 10.95 10.40 9.85 9.30 8.75

12 I think a child is capable of taking entire care of his hair (i.e., wash, comb, decide how it is to be worn, when it is to be cut, etc.) by the age of ______

12.75 12.35 11.95 11.55 11.15 10.75 10.30 9.85 9.40 8.95 8.50

13 I feel that a child should be able to make his own bed daily (excepting when sheets are changed) **without help** by the age of ______

9.25 8.90 8.55 8.20 7.85 7.50 7.10 6.70 6.30 5.90 5.50

14 I feel that a child should be able to plan and prepare a simple family dinner (e.g., meat, potatoes, vegetable, and dessert) by the age of ______

14.25 14.05 13.85 13.65 13.45 13.25 12.60 11.95 11.30 10.65 10.00

15 I think that a child should be included in some family discussions (e.g., on expenditures of money), his opinions being considered along with the opinions of older members of the family, by the age of ______

11.00 10.60 10.20 9.80 9.40 9.00 8.60 8.20 7.80 7.40 7.00

16 I think a child should be able to choose the movies he wishes to attend by the age of ______

15.25 14.75 14.25 13.75 13.25 12.75 12.35 11.95 11.55 11.15 10.75

17 I think a child should be able to partake in extra-curricular activities, being guided by his parents in his choice of activities (e.g., orchestra, school chorus, football, basketball) by the age of ______

13.00 12.80 12.60 12.40 12.20 12.00 11.45 10.90 10.35 9.80 9.25

18 I think that a child should be able to choose his own reading matter, including books, magazines, and newspapers, by the age of ______

14.75 14.40 14.05 13.70 13.35 13.00 12.65 12.30 11.95 11.60 11.25

19 I think that a child should be allowed to leave the parental home for a period of time (e.g., to a six weeks camp) by the age of ______

13.00 12.60 12.20 11.80 11.40 11.00 10.60 10.20 9.80 9.40 9.00

20 I think that a child should be able to make a desirable choice from his wardrobe of clothing to be worn, without suggestions from an adult, by the age of ______

14.00 13.50 13.00 12.50 12.00 11.50 10.80 10.10 9.40 8.70 8.00

21 I think that a child should be able to plan and give a simple afternoon party for his immediate friends by the age of ______

12.50 12.10 11.70 11.30 10.90 10.50 10.05 9.60 9.15 8.70 8.25

22 I think that a child should be able to buy suitable Christmas gifts for the immediate family after he has been restricted as to the amount of money to be spent for each gift by the age of ______

10.25 9.85 9.45 9.05 8.65 8.25 7.75 7.25 6.75 6.25 5.75

23 I think that a child should be able to prepare and serve lunch to the younger members of the family when the parents are away for lunch by the age of ______

14.00 13.45 12.90 12.35 11.80 11.25 10.85 10.45 10.05 9.65 9.25

24 I think that a child should be able to take the responsibility for paying one monthly bill for the family (e.g., obtain the money from his parents, pay the bill on the date it is due or before, get receipt for the payment—this refers to bills such as light, gas, or water bills) by the age of ______

12.25 12.05 11.85 11.65 11.45 11.25 10.75 10.25 9.75 9.25 8.75

25 I think that a child should be able to make his own arrangements about going to an evening party, when it means taking a street car or bus a distance of three miles or less, by the age of (This refers to a party which begins at seven o'clock and ends at ten o'clock and includes making decisions as to what time to go, whom to go with, how to meet companions, etc.) ______

15.00 14.40 13.80 13.20 12.60 12.00 11.60 11.20 10.80 10.40 10.00

Attitude toward the use of fear as a means of controlling the behavior of children EXHIBIT 3-7

Description. This is one of several scales developed by Ackerley (1934) to measure parents' attitudes toward children. The other attitude scales in this series are described in the next two sections of this chapter. The items were scaled by the Thurstone method, using 60 judges. Q values ranged from 0.6 to 2.2. The 32 items in the final scale and their scale values are given in Exhibit 3-7.

Subjects. The subjects were 160 fathers and 221 mothers, obtained from widely separated rural communities and towns in Iowa. This population was fairly heterogeneous with respect to age, education, occupational status, family size, and age of children.

Response Mode. The subject is asked to check each item he endorses.

Scoring. The attitude score is the median of the scale values of items endorsed. A high score indicates an unfavorable attitude toward the use of fear as a means of controlling the behavior of children.

Reliability. Reliability of the scale values was determined by the method suggested by Thurstone. The probable error of the scale value was found to be .09 of a scale unit, which was judged to be satisfactory for scale values recorded to one decimal.

Validity. Ackerley suggested that validity is indicated by the method used for selecting items and the agreement of experts regarding the approved response to each item.

Comments. This is an old scale, but the content of the items still seems appropriate for use today. The reliability and validity data are less extensive than desirable, however. The potential user should note especially that the probable error refers to the scale value of the items, rather than to the scale as a whole.

EXHIBIT 3-7

ATTITUDE TOWARD THE USE OF FEAR AS A MEANS OF CONTROLLING THE BEHAVIOR OF CHILDREN

Endorse the statements which express your opinion regarding the use of fear as a means of controlling the behavior of children. Place a check mark beside each statement you wish to endorse.

Scale Value		
3.5	1	I feel that scaring a child now and then by a promise of a whipping doesn't hurt the child in any way.
2.9	2	I feel that to tell my child that the policeman or the boogey man will get him if he doesn't mind is one of the best methods for controlling my child.
3.2	3	I feel that children should be frightened away from things which will do them bodily injury.
0.3	4	I believe that fear is the most desirable method to use in controlling the behavior of children.
2.6	5	I believe that parents should raise their children to be afraid of breaking the law.
3.1	6	I feel that children should be taught by parents to be afraid of overstepping social conventions.
5.6	7	I believe that fear as a means of controlling children has an equal chance for aiding and for harming the child's normal development.
1.2	8	Since fear is so powerful as a means of control it is the best method to use with children.
9.0	9	I feel that scaring children to control their behavior always makes cowards of them.

Scale Value		
1.9	10	I believe that fear is a good, easy method for controlling children.
9.2	11	I feel that the use of fear as a means of controlling children always inhibits their ability to think clearly.
10.0	12	I feel that the use of fear to control the child invariably has unlimited possibilities for injuring the normal development of the child.
3.2	13	I believe that the use of fear is desirable in incidents where immediate response to a situation is important.
0.5	14	I believe that fear is the only effective means that you can use to control children.
10.3	15	I feel that fear is a vicious method to use in controlling the behavior of children.
2.2	16	I believe in using fear to control children as it operates all through life in some form or other.
5.5	17	I believe that fear of social consequences is desirable in controlling children while fear of physical consequences is undesirable.
1.9	18	I feel that it is impossible to control children without the use of fear.
2.6	19	I believe that children should be raised in the fear of God.
7.9	20	I believe that using fear to control children will prevent their developing the ability to meet emergencies.
6.7	21	An excessive use of fear to control the behavior of a child might be damaging to the child's personality.
7.0	22	I feel that scaring children to control their behavior sometimes makes cowards of them.
5.0	23	I believe that fear should be used only in extreme cases to control the behavior of a child.
5.2	24	I believe that fear should be used only after other methods of controlling the child have failed.
8.6	25	I feel that an excessive use of fear to control a child often destroys potential possibilities which the child may have for leadership.
7.0	26	I feel that the use of fear as a means of control is sometimes injurious to the child's personality.
8.4	27	I feel that it is a poor practice to tell a child too often that if he doesn't do "thus and so" he will become ill.
8.8	28	I feel that it is undesirable for parents to frighten children by telling them they won't be loved if they fail to comply with the parent's wishes.
4.2	29	I believe that a judicious use of fear to control children is not objectionable.
10.2	30	I believe that the use of fear in any form is an objectionable method for controlling the behavior of children.
4.0	31	I believe that an occasional use of fear to control children is not objectionable.
10.0	32	I believe that fear as a means of controlling children is highly objectionable.

Attitude toward parents giving sex information to children between the ages of six and twelve EXHIBIT 3-8

Description. This is the second of three scales developed by Ackerley (1934). Like the preceding scale, it consists of 32 items scaled by the

Thurstone procedure. Fifty-five judges were used for sorting the items. Q values ranged from 0.3 to 3.6, with most of them being less than 2.0. Exhibit 3-8 gives the items and the scale values of the final scale.

Subjects. The subjects were the same as those described in the preceding section.

Response Mode. Each subject is asked to check each item with which he agrees.

Scoring. The attitude score is the median of the scale value of items endorsed. A high score indicates an unfavorable and a low score a favorable attitude toward giving children sex information.

Reliability. The reliability of the scale values was found to be .09 of a scale value.

Validity. Item content and the method of selecting items provide the primary basis for assessing validity of this scale.

Comments. As in the preceding discussion, the items of this scale seem still to be appropriate for the general population, but evidence of reliability and validity is less than adequate.

EXHIBIT 3-8

ATTITUDE TOWARD PARENTS GIVING SEX INFORMATION TO CHILDREN BETWEEN THE AGES OF SIX AND TWELVE

Endorse the statements which express your opinion regarding the giving of sex information to children. Place a check mark beside each statement you wish to endorse.

Scale Value		
1.9	1	I feel that much unhappiness in adult life is caused by parents failing to give their children adequate sex information.
2.1	2	I feel that parents should give their children correct sex information to protect them from false and harmful teaching.
7.5	3	I feel that if parents give children help in controlling other habits, sex will take care of itself.
8.7	4	I feel that parents can preserve their children's innocence by withholding sex information.
9.5	5	I feel that if parents give children sex information it will encourage them to try premature sex experiments.
6.6	6	I feel that parents may wait to give their children sex information until the age of thirteen.
8.1	7	I believe that children will acquire sex information soon enough without their parents giving it to them.

Scale Value		
3.9	8	I feel that parents should give their children sex information only if they are careful to avoid over-emphasis.
7.0	9	I believe that if parents feel an inhibition about sex, they should refrain from discussing sex matters with their children.
4.7	10	I feel that parents should have books on sex education accessible to the child.
4.4	11	I feel that a parent should give only very conservative answers to a child's sex questions.
3.3	12	I believe that parents should talk about sex to the child only if he asks questions.
1.6	13	I feel that parents should take the initiative and give information about sex before the child asks for it.
6.0	14	I feel that parents may give only such information as is based on a study of plants and flowers.
7.0	15	I feel that only parents who are emotional about sex should not give their children sex information.
10.5	16	I feel that under no consideration should a parent give a child sex information.
5.6	17	I feel that information which the parents give the child on sex has an equal chance for injuring and for aiding the normal development of the child.
7.4	19	I believe that if parents teach children the right moral principles, sex information is unnecessary.
10.3	20	I feel that it is highly undesirable for parents to talk to their children about sex.
0.6	21	I feel that it is highly desirable for parents to give children all the information that the parents have about sex.
4.0	22	I believe that parents might as well give their children sex information as they will find it out any way.
7.8	23	I feel that parental attempts to give the child sex information only serves to confuse the child.
9.7	24	I believe that the risk of giving children sex information is great enough to make it an undesirable practice for parents.
2.4	25	I feel that it is desirable for parents to give truthful answers to their children's sex questions.
5.1	26	I feel that parents may give children sex information only if they are sure that they will not discuss it with other children.
9.0	27	I feel that it makes children bold for the parents to give them sex information.
2.2	28	I feel that the home is preferable to the alley as a source of sex information.
2.9	29	I feel that parents are the only ones who can give their children the right attitude regarding sex information.
0.6	30	I feel that parents might as well refuse their children food as to refuse them sex information.
1.2	31	I feel that sex education is an important duty of parenthood.
1.6	32	I feel that parents should tell their child anything he wants to know about sex.
1.4	33	I feel that parents should give their children sex information regardless of the neighbors' attitude.

Attitude toward older children telling lies EXHIBIT 3-9

Description. This is the third and final scale in the Ackerley (1934) series. It is a nine-item, Thurstone-type scale, developed using only 20 judges. Q values ranged from 0.7 to 1.9. The items of the scale and the scale values are given in Exhibit 3-9.

Subjects. Data were obtained from the same 160 fathers and 221 mothers that were described in connection with Exhibit 3-7.

Response Mode. The subject responds by checking each item with which he agrees.

Scoring. The attitude score is the median of the scale values of the items endorsed by the subject. A high score indicates an unfavorable attitude toward the telling of lies by older children.

Reliability. The reliability of the scale values was again computed to be .09 of a scale value.

Validity. As in the case of other scales in this series, the only evidence of validity is the content of the items and the consensual validity indicated by the scaling procedure.

Comments. This very brief scale is easy to administer and score, but we are less inclined to endorse its usage than we are the longer scales in this series. One may expect that the reliability of the scale, as opposed to the reliability of the scale values, will be lower than for the longer scales.

EXHIBIT 3-9

ATTITUDE TOWARD OLDER CHILDREN TELLING LIES

Endorse the statements which express your opinion regarding the lies of other children. A lie is a deliberate attempt to deceive. These statements concern children eight to twelve years of age. Place a check mark beside each statement you wish to endorse.

Scale Value		
10.1	1	I feel that lying is dishonorable, never justifiable, and detrimental to the child.
10.4	2	I feel that a child's lie is an unforgivable sin.
0.7	3	I want my child to become a skilled liar as it shows superior intelligence to be able to lie without getting caught.
5.6	4	I feel that truth is a desirable ideal but that it is only attainable part of the time.

Scale Value		
1.4	5	I feel that the ability to lie is an asset and can be developed to the child's advantage.
2.0	6	I feel that lying furnishes a child with an excellent means for escaping difficulties without much harm to his personality.
6.7	7	I feel that a child should learn that truth pays in about 90 per cent of the cases.
4.3	8	I feel that there are times when it is more honorable for a child to lie than to tell the truth.
7.3	9	I feel that lying breeds distrust and results in disrespect of child's associates.

The traditional family ideology (TFI) scale EXHIBIT 3-10

Description. The TFI scale (Levinson and Huffman, 1955) is a multidimensional scale which purports to measure attitudes toward: (1) parent-child relationships, (2) husband and wife roles and relationships, (3) general male-female relationships and concepts of masculinity and femininity, and (4) general values and aims. However, a total score is computed which is taken as a global, admittedly crude measure of "democratic" attitudes toward family relations. The Likert method of scale construction was used. The discriminatory power (DP) of each item was computed as the difference between the mean score earned by the upper and lower 25 percent of total scores. Only 5 of the 40 items failed to discriminate between the high and low scorers at the 5 percent level or better. These were items 2, 3, 43, 51, and 52. In Exhibit 3-10 items are grouped according to family-life issues and numbered as they were in the original questionnaire.

An abbreviated, 12-item form of the TFI was also developed. This form was found to be almost as reliable and valid as the longer form. The items forming the short form are marked with a dagger in Exhibit 3-10.

Subjects. The sample used in constructing the longer scale consisted of 109 adults in evening psychology classes at Cleveland College, Ohio. The sample was relatively heterogeneous with respect to age, occupation, religion, and marital status. There were 67 men and 42 women, ranging in age from about 20 to 40. The subjects for the short form were 84 Harvard summer session students, 236 Boston University sophomores, 76 Boston University freshmen, 46 registered nurses, and 65 student nurses.

Response Mode. Subjects respond to each item by entering in the space provided a number from +3 to —3 according to the following scale: +3, strongly agree; +2, mildly agree; +1, agree; —1, disagree; —2, mildly disagree; —3, strongly disagree.

Scoring. Responses are converted into scores as follows: For "democratic" items a response of —3 is given a score of 7; —2, a score of 6;

−1, a score of 5; +1, a score of 3; +2, a score of 2; and +3, a score of 1. A score of 4 is assigned to any item to which the subject does not respond. For "autocratic" items the scoring is reversed. The attitude score is the sum of the item scores. The total score falls between 40 and 280 points, with higher scores indicating the more democratic attitude toward family relations. For convenience, Levinson and Huffman divided the total score by 40 and multiplied the result by 10, giving a possible range of 10 to 70 points.

Reliability. For the longer scale, split-half reliability was found to be .84 when corrected by the Spearman-Brown formula. For the 12-item form, corrected split-half reliability was .92, and test-retest reliability after a six-week interval was .93.

Validity. Validity of the longer form was evaluated by comparing religious groups "known" to differ in family ideology and by correlating TFI scores with scores on the California E and F scales. It was shown that the TFI discriminates between various religious groups in the expected direction; correlations with E and F scores were .65 and .73, respectively.

Average correlations between scores on the short form and E and F scores were .64 and .67, respectively.

Comments. There is some question regarding just what attitude is being measured by the TFI scale. It seems to be very similar to the E and F scales, raising the question as to whether "traditional family ideology" is just one aspect of a larger syndrome of autocratic ideology, as the authors suggest, or whether the TFI scale measures the same thing as the F scale. In any case, the evidence suggests that the 12-item form is as reliable and valid as the longer form. Hence, there seems to be little advantage in using the longer form.

EXHIBIT 3-10

THE TRADITIONAL FAMILY IDEOLOGY (TFI) SCALE

This is a study of what the general public thinks about a number of social questions. The best answer to each statement below is *your personal opinion.* We have tried to cover many different points of view. You may find yourself agreeing strongly with some of the statements, disagreeing just as strongly with others, and perhaps uncertain about others. Whether you agree or disagree with any statement, you can be sure that many other people feel the same way that you do.

Mark each statement in the left margin according to how much you agree or disagree with it. Please mark every one. Write in +1, +2, +3, or −1, −2, −3, depending on how you feel in each case.

+1: I agree a little	−1: I disagree a little
+2: I agree pretty much	−2: I disagree pretty much
+3: I agree very much	−3: I disagree very much

A. Parent-child relationships; child-rearing techniques

†39 A child should not be allowed to talk back to his parents, or else he will lose respect for them.

†40 There is a lot of evidence such as the Kinsey Report which shows us we have to crack down harder on young people to save our moral standards.

†58 There is hardly anything lower than a person who does not feel a great love, gratitude, and respect for his parents.

33 A well-raised child is one who doesn't have to be told twice to do something.

†56 A woman whose children are messy or rowdy has failed in her duties as a mother.

15 It isn't healthy for a child to like to be alone, and he should be discouraged from playing by himself.

†22 If children are told too much about sex, they are likely to go too far in experimenting with it.

†57 A child who is unusual in any way should be encouraged to be more like other children.

45 The saying "Mother knows best" still has more than a grain of truth.

9 Whatever some educators may say, "Spare the rod and spoil the child" still holds, even in these modern times.

21 It helps the child in the long run if he is made to conform to his parents' ideas.

*3 A teen-ager should be allowed to decide most things for himself.

*27 In making family decisions, parents ought to take the opinions of children into account.

51 It is important to teach the child as early as possible the manners and morals of his society.

*52 A lot of the sex problems of married couples arise because their parents have been too strict with them about sex.

B. Husband and wife roles and relationships

†31 Women who want to remove the word **obey** from the marriage service don't understand what it means to be a wife.

†20 Some equality in marriage is a good thing, but by and large the husband ought to have the main say-so in family matters.

38 A man who doesn't provide well for his family ought to consider himself pretty much a failure as husband and father.

14 Faithlessness is the worst fault a husband could have.

44 In choosing a husband, a woman will do well to put ambition at the top of her list of desirable qualities.

7 A wife does better to vote the way her husband does, because he probably knows more about such things.

8 It is a reflection on a husband's manhood if his wife works.

*43 Women should take an active interest in politics and community problems as well as in their families.

† Items marked with a dagger constitute the short form of the scale.
* Agreement with these items is given a low score, disagreement a high score.

C. General male-female relationships; concepts of masculinity and femininity

†46 A man can scarcely maintain respect for his fiancee if they have sexual relations before they are married.
†50 It goes against nature to place women in positions of authority over men.
37 It is woman's job more than a man's to uphold our moral code, especially in sexual matters.
49 The unmarried mother is morally a greater failure than the unmarried father.
†26 The most important qualities of a real man are strength of will and determined ambition.
25 Women can be too bright for their own good.
*10 Women have as much right as men to sow wild oats.
16 Petting is something a nice girl wouldn't want to do.
13 Women think less clearly than men and are more emotional.
1 Almost any woman is better off in the home than in a job or profession.
32 It doesn't seem quite right for a man to be a visionary; dreaming should be left to women.
*19 Even today women live under unfair restrictions that ought to be done away with.
2 It's a pretty feeble sort of man who can't get ahead in the world.

D. General values and aims

†55 The family is a sacred institution, divinely ordained.
28 One of the worst problems in our society today is "free love," because it mars the true value of sex relations.
34 It is only natural and right for each person to think that his family is better than any other.
4 A marriage should not be made unless the couple plans to have children.

ATTITUDES RELATED TO EDUCATIONAL PRACTICES

This category includes scales to measure attitudes toward teaching, the educational process, and child-centered practices. These scales are generally inadequately standardized and often appear to be multidimensional. From the data presented by the authors it is often difficult to determine whether the scale is designed to measure attitude toward teaching, toward teachers (see Chapter 9), or toward the educational process. In the following sections we have presented the scales that we judged to be most acceptable. We excluded, for example, the widely used Minnesota Teacher Attitude Inventory (Cook, Leeds, and Callis, 1951) because it appears to be a test for selecting "good" teachers rather than an attitude scale. We also excluded an "opinionnaire" formulated by Peckham (1962) to measure attitudes toward teaching, because the characteristics of the scale are unknown.

Attitude toward teaching *EXHIBIT 3-11*

Description. This scale was constructed by Miller (1934) for the purpose of validating a generalized scale to measure attitude toward any occupation (see Exhibit 3-34). Two 45-item forms were developed by the method of equal-appearing intervals. Items were selected so that no item had a Q value greater than 3.0, and the items in the two forms were approximately matched for scale values.

Subjects. The subjects for this study were 140 instructors and students at Purdue University.

Response Mode. Subjects are asked to place a check beside all statements with which they agree and a cross by all statements with which they disagree.

Scoring. The attitude score is the median of the scale values of all items checked for agreement. A high score indicates a favorable attitude toward teaching.

Reliability. Reliability was estimated by the method outlined by Thurstone, which takes the probable error of the median as an estimate of reliability of the scale values. This was found to be .11 for both Form A and Form B. It should be noted that this is not an estimate of the reliability of the scale in the usual sense.

Validity. In addition to the validity implied by the item selection procedure, the Attitude toward Teaching Scale correlated .437 with a generalized scale to measure attitude toward any occupation.

Comments. The evidence concerning reliability and validity is quite limited, but the scale could be very useful if properly evaluated. Since the scale values of items were determined more than thirty years ago, the prospective user would be well advised to rescale the items.

EXHIBIT 3-11

ATTITUDE TOWARD TEACHING

Put a check mark (✓) if you **agree** with the statement.
Put a cross (×) if you **disagree** with the statement.

Form A

Scale Value		
10.7	1	To strive to teach well is to pattern after Christ, who was the Master Teacher. There can be no higher calling.
10.2	2	Teaching is one of the most necessary of the professions.
10.0	3	Teachers are the nation's leaders.
9.8	4	The teaching profession has the best chance to develop good citizens.
9.7	5	Teaching develops the mind.
9.7	6	Teaching increases one's ability to meet people socially and intellectually.

Scale Value		
9.7	**7**	I believe that teaching is the most interesting of the professions.
9.5	**8**	Dealing with youth tends to keep a teacher young, alert, and active.
9.4	**9**	Teachers determine the moral standard of a nation.
9.1	**10**	Teaching is inspirational.
9.0	**11**	Teaching develops leadership.
8.9	**12**	Teaching requires more intelligence than most professions.
8.8	**13**	Teaching furnishes a chance for self-expression.
8.8	**14**	Teaching experience is valuable as an opening to broader and more advanced positions.
8.7	**15**	Teachers are the molders of society.
6.7	**16**	Teachers do very well considering the small amount of co-operation they get from school boards.
5.8	**17**	The best teachers are those recruited from the industries.
5.8	**18**	The most effective teaching is by private tutoring.
5.2	**19**	Teachers are for the most part just average college students.
5.1	**20**	Too many teachers do other work on the side.
5.0	**21**	Teachers should not be taken too seriously.
5.0	**22**	Students would learn more if the teacher followed the textbook more closely.
4.9	**23**	Teachers depend too much on textbooks.
4.6	**24**	Teaching is too often used by women merely as a stepping stone to marriage.
4.2	**25**	Teaching does not draw persons with a practical turn of mind.
4.1	**26**	Most teachers have exalted ideas of their own importance.
3.9	**27**	Too many instructors show no interest in subjects they teach.
3.7	**28**	The importance of teaching is overestimated.
3.6	**29**	Teaching is an occupation requiring only mediocre ability.
3.5	**30**	Teachers are exceedingly egotistical.
3.3	**31**	Teaching is merely a routine job.
3.2	**32**	Most teachers get by on sheer bluff rather than knowledge.
3.0	**33**	Teaching is just another means of existing.
3.0	**34**	I believe that teaching tends to get one in a rut.
2.9	**35**	Teaching develops a cynical attitude toward life.
2.7	**36**	Most teachers have one-track minds.
2.6	**37**	The teaching profession is twenty years behind the times in their methods.
2.4	**38**	Teachers are overbearing and boresome.
2.4	**39**	Teaching is a dull, uneventful life.
2.3	**40**	Teaching is a short cut to old age.
2.3	**41**	Most teachers are so careless in their dress that they look like bums.
2.0	**42**	Teachers are social business misfits.
2.0	**43**	Teaching is a lazy man's job.
1.8	**44**	Teaching leads to insanity more often than other kinds of work.
1.3	**45**	Teachers are parasites.

Form B

10.5	**1**	Teaching is one of the best means of serving humanity.
10.3	**2**	Teaching has more influence on a nation than any other profession.
10.1	**3**	The teaching profession performs more actual good for mankind than any other.
9.8	**4**	Teaching develops personality and character.

Scale Value		
9.6	5	Teaching is one of the greatest stimulants to mental activity.
9.6	6	The intellectual standards of a country depend upon its teachers.
9.5	7	Teaching develops independence and a sense of responsibility.
9.4	8	Teaching school is an education for the teacher as well as the pupil.
9.3	9	Teaching requires more than mere knowledge.
9.2	10	Teaching offers exceptional opportunities for making friends.
9.1	11	Teaching is a genteel and cultured profession.
9.0	12	The teaching profession ranks high socially.
8.9	13	Teaching is the oldest and most honored profession.
8.8	14	Teaching is the best means of self-expression.
8.6	15	Much self-satisfaction can be derived from teaching.
6.8	16	Teaching is fairly well paid for the training required.
6.1	17	Good pupils make the good teachers.
5.8	18	Women make the best teachers.
5.2	19	Teachers expect too much of the students.
5.1	20	Too many teachers like to teach, but can't.
5.0	21	Teachers are too prone to give their own ideas and not enough facts.
4.9	22	Most teachers do not understand their pupils.
4.9	23	Teachers are too idealistic.
4.7	24	Teachers take themselves too seriously.
4.3	25	Teachers have too much of a superiority complex.
4.2	26	Teaching is not often done whole-heartedly.
4.1	27	Teachers do not take enough interest in their jobs.
3.8	28	Teaching offers few opportunities for advancement.
3.8	29	Teachers do not consider the opinions of others.
3.5	30	Teachers get into a rut quicker than persons in other professions.
3.4	31	Teaching becomes boresome in a short time.
3.3	32	Most teachers are unfit for such a responsible position.
3.0	33	Teaching is not a healthful profession.
2.9	34	Teaching isolates a person from the rest of the world.
2.8	35	Teaching is a monotonous occupation.
2.6	36	Teaching routine is drudgery.
2.5	37	Teaching stifles ambition.
2.5	38	Modern methods of teaching require nursemaids, not teachers.
2.4	39	Modern teaching is inferior to that of twenty years ago.
2.3	40	Teaching has no future.
2.2	41	People teach only when they can find nothing else to do.
2.0	42	The moral standard of the teaching profession is very low.
1.9	43	The intellectual level of modern teachers is very low.
1.8	44	Failures in other lines of business usually become teachers.
1.3	45	The teaching profession as a whole is untruthful and unreliable.

Attitude toward teaching as a career EXHIBIT 3-12

Description. This is an 11-item Likert scale designed to measure attitude toward teaching as a career. It was constructed by Merwin and Di Vesta (Di Vesta and Merwin, 1960; Merwin and Di Vesta, 1959) in connection with a study of attitude structure. Items were written to have maximum affective content and minimum cognitive content. Four of the items are stated in an unfavorable direction and seven in a favorable direction with regard to attitude toward teaching. No item analysis data are reported.

Subjects. The subjects were 218 college freshmen enrolled in the College of Liberal Arts at Syracuse University, 300 additional freshmen from the same institution, 87 students from the School of Education, and 155 high school upperclassmen.

Response Mode. Six response categories are provided for each item: strongly agree, moderately agree, slightly agree, slightly disagree, moderately disagree, strongly disagree. Subjects are required to answer all items.

Scoring. Before the attitude score is computed, the direction of item scores is reversed for unfavorable items so that a response of "strongly agree" is given a value of 6; "moderately agree," a value of 5; and so on. The attitude score is then computed as the sum of the item scores. The theoretical range is from 11 to 66, with lower scores indicating a more favorable attitude toward teaching as a career.

Reliability. Corrected split-half reliability based upon the responses of 300 college freshmen was .71. Test-retest reliability was .79 for a group of 218 college freshmen retested after a four-month interval.

Validity. In addition to the usual content validity, the scale was shown to differentiate between a group of subjects who had chosen teaching as a career and a group who had not so chosen. The mean scores earned by the teaching group ($N = 67$) on two tests were 26.57 and 26.30 as compared with mean scores of 41.85 and 40.49 earned by the nonteaching group ($N = 151$). Differences between mean scores of teachers and nonteachers were significant at better than the 1 percent level of confidence in each case.

Comments. This brief scale appears to have reasonably acceptable reliability and validity for the purposes for which it was designed. The authors have stated that the scale grew out of a study of attitude structure and change and that its use is more meaningful within the framework of that study (Di Vesta and Merwin, 1960; Merwin and Di Vesta, 1959). It is recommended that the reader familiarize himself with this research before using the scale.

EXHIBIT 3-12

ATTITUDE TOWARD TEACHING AS A CAREER

Directions:

Here are some different kinds of statements. They will help you to tell how YOU, personally, FEEL about teaching as a career for YOU. For

References: J. C. Merwin and F. J. Di Vesta. A Study of need theory and career choice. *J. Counsel. Psychol.,* **1959, 6, 302–308; F. J. Di Vesta and J. C. Merwin. The effects of need-oriented communications on attitude change.** *J. abnorm. soc. Psychol.,* **1960, 60, 80–85. Items obtained from authors and published with their permission.**

each statement write in the appropriate space on your answer sheet the number which best describes your agreement or disagreement according to this code:

CODE

1—Strongly agree
2—Moderately agree
3—Slightly agree
4—Slightly disagree
5—Moderately disagree
6—Strongly disagree

1 Teaching is about the best job that I can think of.
2 There are a lot of advantages to teaching.
*3 I wouldn't care for the work of a teacher.
4 Teaching would be a wonderful occupation for anyone.
*5 Teaching may be all right for some people but not for me.
*6 I am not convinced of the importance of a teaching career.
*7 Teaching, as a career, is not worth the sacrifice of going to college, the long hours of work and the low pay.
8 I am sure I would enjoy teaching.
9 Teaching is as good a job as any.
10 There are more advantages than disadvantages to teaching as a career.
11 I would be willing to take any job related to teaching.

* Items marked with an asterisk are unfavorable toward teaching as a career.

Attitude toward physical education as a career for women EXHIBIT 3-13

Description. The Attitude toward Physical Education as a Career for Women Scale (Drinkwater, 1960) consists of statements related to the profession of physical education in terms of program objectives, personal characteristics of women in the profession, opinions of others regarding the profession, and academic requirements for a degree in physical education. From an original list of 88 items, 72 items were selected by item analysis and a measure of ambiguity. The item analysis was based upon the upper and lower 27 percent of scores earned by all subjects, and any item with a discriminating power score of less than .30 was dropped. Any item having a Q value greater than 2.25 was also eliminated. The 72 remaining items were then grouped under the specific areas of physical education with which they were concerned and divided into two matched forms of 36 items each.

Subjects. The subjects used in developing this scale were 208 high school girls drawn from two city and one county school in the Indianapolis area.

Response Mode. Subjects respond to each item by choosing one of the following alternatives: I strongly agree, I agree, I am undecided, I disagree, I strongly disagree.

Scoring. Each response alternative is assigned a value ranging from 5 for the answer most strongly in favor of physical education as a career for women to 1 for the least favorable alternative. That is, for the positive items in Exhibit 3-13 a value of 5 is assigned to "I strongly agree," a value of 4 to "I agree," and so on, whereas for negative items the value of 5 is assigned to "I strongly disagree," a 4 to "I disagree," etc. The individual's attitude score is the sum of the item scores. A high score represents a favorable attitude toward physical education as a career for women.

Reliability. Split-half reliability was found to be .93 (corrected to .96). The two-forms reliability was .87.

Validity. Validity is evidenced only by item content and by the results of the item analysis, which showed that the scale discriminated between high and low scorers at better than the .01 level of confidence.

Comments. This scale promises to be a very good scale for research purposes. Its reliability is high, and the limited evidence concerning validity is favorable. However, data are limited to the responses of the single group of 208 subjects. Cross validation is necessary before the data presented above can be accepted without question. We should also raise a question about the use of the Q value as a measure of ambiguity. Drinkwater computed the Q values from the responses of the subjects when they were asked to express their own attitude, whereas Thurstone had based his measures upon the judgments of subjects concerning the meaning of responses to the items. It is not clear that the two procedures can be used interchangeably.

EXHIBIT 3-13

ATTITUDE TOWARD PHYSICAL EDUCATION AS A CAREER FOR WOMEN

Following are some statements concerning physical education as a career for women. Please indicate your agreement or disagreement with each statement by entering a number from 1 to 5, according to the following code:

1—I strongly agree
2—I agree
3—I am undecided
4—I disagree
5—I strongly disagree

Form A

*1 Salaries of physical education teachers should not be as high as the salaries of those who teach academic courses.
2 Skills learned in physical education classes are essential in social life.
3 Physical education should be one of the first courses taken from the curriculum if a cut is necessary.
*4 Teaching physical education is considered "unfeminine" for a woman.
5 A curriculum which does not include physical education does not offer a complete education.
*6 Physical education cannot be considered a profession.
*7 Academic requirements for majors in physical education are not as difficult as those for other college students.
8 Girls look forward to their physical education classes with enthusiasm.
*9 Physical education offers little of importance in the education of young women today.
10 Physical education teachers show a sympathetic interest in the problems of their students.
11 Physical education classes provide excellent opportunities for making friends.
12 Physical education activities develop socially desirable standards of conduct.
*13 Physical education teachers are only concerned with muscle building.
14 Physical education makes important contributions to mental health.
*15 Physical education should be elective rather than required.
16 Physical education for leisure is as important as education for work.
*17 Most parents would not approve of their daughters' majoring in physical education.
*18 Physical education classes are not fitted to the individual student's interest.
19 Physical education teachers have pleasing personalities.
*20 Physical education is one of the "fads" and "frills" of modern-day education.
21 There are many opportunities in the physical education program for the character development of the students.
*22 Physical education teachers are not given the same respect by the public that other teachers receive.
*23 Girls who excel in sports are not as intellectual as other girls.
*24 By the time a girl reaches high school age she no longer needs physical exercise.
*25 It should not be necessary for a woman to be a college graduate to teach physical education.
26 Physical education credit should be required for graduation from high school.
27 Teaching physical education would be a rewarding profession.
*28 Intelligence is not as necessary as athletic skill for a teacher of physical education.
29 Women who teach physical education are well-groomed and attractive.
*30 Competitive sports should be eliminated from the physical education curriculum.
31 Physical education contributes to the physical and mental development of the girls.
*32 It is silly for high school girls to waste time playing games.
33 Physical education helps to develop poise.
*34 Competition brings out the worst qualities in a person.

* Items marked with an asterisk express an unfavorable attitude toward physical education as a career for women.

*35 Grades in physical education are not fair to the non-athlete in comparison to the "natural athlete."
*36 Girls do not require exercise in order to maintain organic health and vigor.

Form B

1 Physical education offers training for leadership.
*2 Informal recreation periods during the day would eliminate the need for required physical education classes.
*3 Other members of the faculty consider the physical education teacher intellectually inferior.
*4 "A strong back and a weak mind" are characteristics of physical education teachers.
5 Learning to play effectively together toward common goals is a major contribution of physical education.
*6 There is no need to be concerned over the present shortage of women physical education teachers.
*7 The expenditure of funds for "exercise" and "play" is unnecessary and wasteful.
8 There are many opportunities for the development of moral and ethical conduct in physical education.
*9 Physical education is not worth the trouble involved in dressing for class.
10 Physical education activities provide opportunities for satisfying social experiences.
*11 Participation in physical education is likely to result in accidents.
*12 I would never want a daughter of mine to major in physical education.
*13 Physical education contributes nothing of value to our culture.
*14 Physical education affects the physical but not the mental development of the student.
15 Physical education should be a requirement from elementary school through high school.
16 Physical education provides an outlet for suppressed emotions.
*17 Only girls who play well are wanted on intramural teams.
18 Every girl should develop to her greatest physical capacity.
*19 Most girls do not enjoy physical education classes.
*20 Girls with good grades in academic subjects should not be required to take physical education.
*21 Educated people rarely take part in physical activities.
*22 Women who teach physical education are not popular socially.
23 Physical education contributes to the total education of each student.
24 There is a large variety of interesting activities offered in the physical education program.
25 If physical education were an elective, I would elect it.
26 Everyone should keep physically fit through a regular program of exercise.
27 Physical education classes are fun.
*28 Physical education contributes nothing of value to a student's general education.
*29 Only two years of college should be required for physical education teachers.
*30 Sportsmanship is no longer emphasized in physical education.
31 Physical education teachers are understanding and interested in their students as individuals.
32 There are many opportunities to make friends in a physical education class.
33 Good health habits are learned in physical education classes.

34 Physical education activities make a significant contribution to the development of an individual's personality.

35 Competitive sports provide opportunities for learning and practicing democratic behavior.

36 All girls should have the opportunity to develop some type of active recreational skills.

Attitude toward education *Exhibit 3-14*

Description. The Attitude toward Education Scale (Mitchell, 1941) was intended to measure attitudes toward education, school, and school practices. No specific technique of scale construction was employed, but we decided to include the scale here because it has at least minimal reliability and validity. One form of the scale, Scale A, was formulated by writing 34 statements about practices in school. Items that suggested more serious, difficult, and rigid practices were given odd numbers, and those which suggested easing the pupil's task were given even numbers. Scale B consisted of the same items, but arranged in a different order so that retest scores would be influenced less by carry-over from the first administration. Exhibit 3-14 lists the items for Scale A.

Subjects. The subjects used in Mitchell's study were 382 students at West Newton High School, Pennsylvania.

Response Mode. Subjects check each item with which they agree.

Scoring. The attitude score is the difference between the number of statements checked which indicated more rigorous attitudes and those checked that indicated less rigorous attitudes. If this score is positive, the score is interpreted as revealing a favorable attitude toward strict, rigorous school practices; if it is negative, the attitude is presumed to be favorable toward less strict, less rigorous school practices.

Reliability. Reliability was estimated by correlating the scores earned on Scale A and those earned on Scale B administered twelve weeks later. This test-retest reliability was found to be .71. The relatively long test-retest interval and the fact that the items were rearranged for the second administration suggest that this may be a minimal estimate of the scale's reliability.

Validity. The scale was validated by correlating the attitude scores with class grades. The assumption was that students who hold favorable attitudes toward stricter discipline and more rigorous requirements by the school should apply themselves more diligently to their studies and therefore earn higher classroom grades than those pupils who have unfavorable attitudes toward such practices. These expectations were borne out by the .73 correlation between attitude and class grades.

Comments. As far as we are able to determine, this scale has not been used in any study other than that by Mitchell. Furthermore, there was no attempt to select more discriminating items or to extend validation beyond the one correlational study described above. The evidence that is available, however, is encouraging, and further research should be undertaken to more fully determine the scale's characteristics.

EXHIBIT 3-14

ATTITUDE TOWARD EDUCATION

Check those statements with which you agree.

I think or believe that:

*1 Discipline in schools should be stricter.
2 Pupils should be allowed more freedom to do as they please.
3 Pupils should be required to do more studying.
4 Lessons should be made easier and plainer.
5 Teachers should not do so much talking and explaining to the class.
6 Teachers should do more explaining of the difficult problems.
7 Home work should be assigned for about two hours each evening.
8 There should be no home work assigned.
9 Courses should be so conducted that all those who do not do their best would be left out at the end of first six weeks.
10 Courses should be made so easy that very few would fail them.
11 Pupils must learn to do difficult tasks in high school if they expect to do college work and succeed in after life.
12 People will be able to do the difficult tasks in life when they meet them, no matter whether they have had any practice in school or not.
13 Most high school students have too easy a time of it and do not learn to do real work.
14 Most high school students are overworked and should be relieved of some of it.
15 Pupils learn to study only by doing some real hard studying.
16 Pupils can study without learning how to do it after they once select the work they like.
17 Information gained in high school is essential for any kind of work we may wish to pursue.
18 Knowledge and information change so rapidly that the information gained in school is not so valuable since it is soon out of date.
19 Certain facts and knowledge are necessary for the study of all subjects and these facts do not change very much.
20 Pupils should study only those subjects that they like.
21 Pupils should study some subjects that do not interest them, because they may be necessary, since we do not know when we may need them.
22 Pupils should study only subjects that they feel they will need in after life.
23 In most cases those pupils who fail in college are those who have not learned how to work in high school.
24 When pupils fail in college it is their own fault and the high school should not be blamed for it.

* Odd-numbered items suggest a more rigorous, strict attitude toward educational policies and practices, whereas even-numbered items suggest less rigorous attitudes.

Reprinted with permission from Mitchell, C. Do scales for measuring attitudes have any significance? *J. educ. Res.*, 1941, 34, 444–452.

25 Pupils who fail to prepare their lessons daily should be kept after school to make this preparation.
26 When pupils fail to prepare their lessons they should not be kept after school because they are wasting their own time.
27 Discipline in high schools should be more like that of the Army.
28 Discipline in high school should be left almost entirely to the pupil himself, since he should be old enough to know why he is in school.
29 Teachers should not help pupils in their difficult problems until the pupil asks for help.
30 Teachers should explain all difficult problems to pupils before they work on them too long and become discouraged.
31 Pupils who are tardy should be compelled to make up time so as to learn the habit of being on time when they grow older.
32 Pupils should not be compelled to make up time for being tardy since they do not lose any money by it.
33 Pupils who miss a day of school should be required to make up the back work so that they do not lose anything.
34 Pupils who miss school should not be compelled to make up the work because they are missing their own time and no one else need worry about it.

Opinionnaire on attitudes toward education *EXHIBIT 3-15*

Description. This is a 50-item scale constructed by Lindgren and Patton (1958) to measure attitude toward child-centered policies and practices in education. The statements are concerned with the desirability of understanding the behavior of students, the desirability of the teacher's using authoritarian methods as a means of controlling the behavior of students, and the desirability of subject-matter–centeredness as contrasted with learner- or child-centeredness. About half of the items were taken from an earlier study by Kelley (1941).

The scale was developed by the Likert technique, but the number of original items and item discrimination data were not given.

Subjects. The samples were drawn from students in 14 in-service teacher education courses offered by San Francisco State College. There were 63 male and 98 female elementary and junior high school teachers and 45 male and 10 female high school teachers.

Response Mode. The subject responds to each item by circling A for agreement and D for disagreement.

Scoring. The attitude score is the number of positive items agreed with plus the number of negative items disagreed with, where positive items are favorable toward child-centered practices. The theoretical range of scores is from 0 to 50, with the higher score indicating more favorable attitudes toward child-centered policies and practices in education.

Reliability. The corrected split-half reliability was .82.

Validity. Validation consisted of a demonstration that elementary teachers scored higher than high school teachers and that women scored higher than men. Further evidence of validity derives from later studies by Lindgren (1961, 1962) who reported negative correlations with the F scale (—.28 for 81 nonacademic men; —.51 for 69 nonacademic women) and positive correlations with Barron's (1953) "independence" scale (.36 for men and .57 for women). It should be noted, however, that these correlations were based upon a 30-item version of the scale, constructed by eliminating the 20 items that had the lowest correlation with the total score on the original scale. This form had a corrected split-half reliability of only .64.

Comments. Less detailed information regarding the characteristics of the scale is available than is desirable, but that which is available is favorable.

Normative scores are available from the authors for kindergarten through twelfth grade.

EXHIBIT 3-15

OPINIONNAIRE ON ATTITUDES TOWARD EDUCATION

Below are a number of statements about which teachers may have different opinions. As you read through each statement, please make a circle around "A" if you are *more or less in agreement* with the statement, and make a circle around "D" if you are *more or less in disagreement* with it. *Please answer all questions.*

A D 1 Boys and girls who are delinquent are, when all is said and done, basically good.

A D 2 If boys and girls are to do an adequate job of learning in school, their needs for love must be met.

A D *3 It is appropriate for teachers to require an additional assignment from a pupil who misbehaves in class.

A D 4 How a student feels about what he learns is as important as what he learns.

A D *5 The way to handle a pupil who tells lies is to threaten to punish him.

A D *6 The high school pupil who is not interested in having dates should be commended.

A D 7 Education has failed unless it has helped boys and girls to understand and express their own feelings and experiences.

A D *8 You should tell a child who masturbates that it leads to ruined health.

A D 9 The classroom experiences that are most helpful to boys and girls are the ones wherein they can express themselves creatively.

A D *10 All children should be encouraged to aim at the highest academic goals.

* Items marked with an asterisk are scored negatively.

Reference: H. C. Lindgren and G. M. Patton. Attitudes of high school and other teachers toward children and current educational methodology. *Calif. J. educ. Res.*, 1958, 9, 80–85. Items obtained from authors and published with their permission.

A D *11 The child who bites his nails should be shamed.
A D *12 Children outgrow early emotional experiences as they do shoes and clothes.
A D 13 What boys and girls become as adults is more closely related to the experiences they have with each other than it is to mastery of specific subject matter.
A D 14 It is more important for students to learn to work together cooperatively than it is for them to learn how to compete.
A D *15 Some pupils are just naturally stubborn.
A D 16 Students should be permitted to disagree with the teacher.
A D *17 It is better for a girl to be shy and timid than "boy crazy."
A D 18 Boys and girls should learn that most of life's problems have several possible solutions and not just one "correct" one.
A D *19 The first signs of delinquency in a pupil should be received by a tightening of discipline and more restrictions.
A D *20 The newer methods of education tend to standardize children's behavior.
A D 21 Most boys and girls who present extreme cases of "problem behavior" are doing the best they can to get along with other people.
A D *22 An activity to be educationally valuable should train reasoning and memory in general.
A D 23 It is more important for a child to have faith in himself than it is for him to be obedient.
A D 24 Being grouped according to ability damages the self confidence of many boys and girls.
A D *25 Criticism of children by teachers is more effective for obtaining the desired behavior than criticism of children by others their own age.
A D 26 All questions a student asks should be recognized and considered.
A D *27 The pupil who isn't making good grades should be told to study harder.
A D *28 Children should not be permitted to talk without the permission of the teacher.
A D 29 A student who will not do his work should be helped in every way possible.
A D 30 Boys and girls in the elementary school should be promoted regardless of whether they have completed the work for their grade or not.
A D *31 The teacher should lower grades for misconduct in class.
A D 32 A teacher should permit a great deal of latitude in the way he permits boys and girls to address him.
A D *33 It is a good idea to tell a pupil that he can succeed in any type of work if he works hard.
A D 34 Students will tolerate errors and even occasional injustices in a teacher who, they feel, likes and understands them.
A D 35 A teacher should accept the deficiencies and shortcomings of a student, as well as his good points.
A D *36 Each time a pupil lies his punishment should be increased.
A D 37 Boys and girls can learn proper discipline only if they are given sufficient freedom.
A D *38 If a teacher keeps school conditions exactly the same and gives all pupils an equal opportunity to respond, he has done all he can do.
A D *39 If a pupil constantly performs for attention, the teacher should see to it that he gets no attention.

A D *40 Dishonesty is a more serious personality characteristic than unsocialness.
A D 41 A great deal of misbehavior problem behavior results from fear and guilt.
A D *42 The teacher's first responsibility in all cases of misconduct is to locate and punish the offender.
A D 43 It is better for boys and girls to talk about the things that bother them than to try to forget them.
A D *44 Most pupils need some of the natural meanness taken out of them.
A D 45 It is more important for boys and girls to be liked and accepted by their friends than it is for them to get along with their teachers.
A D 46 Teachers should answer children's questions about sex frankly and, if possible, without show of embarrassment.
A D *47 When a pupil obeys all the rules of the school, one can be sure he is developing moral character.
A D 48 When a teacher is told something in confidence by a child, he should keep the matter just as confidential as though it were entrusted to him by an adult.
A D *49 Since a person memorizes best during childhood, that period should be regarded as a time to store up facts for later use.
A D 50 Students should play a very active part in formulating rules for the classroom and the school.

Education scale EXHIBIT 3-16

Description. The Education Scale was developed by Kerlinger and Kaya (1959*a*). They first attempted to isolate the major dimensions of educational attitudes through the use of Q methodology. This resulted in two dimensions: progressivism and traditionalism. Forty Likert-type items were then written and administered to a sample of approximately 200 subjects, and the results were item-analyzed. The 10 progressive and the 10 traditional items which had the highest factor saturations (based on a factor analysis) and the highest discriminatory power were selected for the final scale. The scale appears to measure attitudes varying from very favorable toward progressive educational practices to very favorable toward traditional educational practices.

Subjects. The approximately 200 subjects used for the original item analysis were not described in detail, but most of the standardization data were reported in a subsequent report (Kerlinger and Kaya, 1959*b*). These later samples consisted of 157 graduate and 136 undergraduate education students and 305 persons from a nonuniversity population (including Kiwanis Club members, medical doctors, army officers, housewives, Sunday school teachers, etc.).

Response Mode. Subjects respond to each item by entering a number from —3 to +3 according to the following code: +3, agree very strongly; +2, agree strongly; +1, agree; —1, disagree; —2, disagree strongly; —3, disagree very strongly.

Scoring. Each item response is scored as follows: +3, 7; +2, 6; +1, 5; no response, 4; —1, 3; —2, 2; —3, 1. The attitude score may be computed separately for progressive and traditional attitudes toward education, or together as a total score. For the separate scales, the attitude score is the sum of the item scores for the 10 items constituting each scale. The total score may then be computed by subtracting the traditional score from the progressive score. The subscale scores can range from 10 to 70, and the total scale score from —60 to +60. A high score on the progressive scale means a favorable attitude toward progressive educational practices, and a high score on the traditional scale implies a favorable attitude toward traditional practices in education. Similarly, a positive total score implies progressive attitudes, and a negative total score implies traditional attitudes toward education.

Reliability. Corrected split-half reliabilities for the progressive scale ranged from .54 to .77, with a value of .75 for all samples combined. For the traditional scale, reliabilities ranged from .68 to .79, with a value of .83 for all samples. Total scale reliabilities ranged from .68 to .81, with a value of .83 for overall scales and samples. Test-retest reliability coefficients obtained from a sample of 106 students in education after a delay of three to four months were as follows: progressive scale, .70; traditional scale, .71; and total scale, .76.

Validity. Validity was estimated by demonstrating that education students revealed more progressive attitudes than did noneducational respondents ($p < .001$). Additional studies based on samples of 131 undergraduates, 93 graduates, and 229 noncollege subjects yielded similar validity estimates. However, Wheeler (1960) analyzed responses item by item and concluded that differences among groups are not as great as indicated by the total score.

Comments. The Education Scale has reasonably satisfactory estimates of reliability and validity, and the authors may be correct in stating that the scale can be used in both research and administrative situations. It seems to us, however, that the scale is measuring a single continuum ranging from highly favorable to highly unfavorable attitudes toward progressive practices in education, or conversely, highly unfavorable to highly favorable attitudes toward traditional practices in education. If so, considering each end of the continuum as a separate attitude may be misleading. We would recommend the scale for research purposes only.

EXHIBIT 3-16

EDUCATION SCALE

Instructions: Given below are 20 statements on educational ideas and problems about which we all have beliefs, opinions, and attitudes. We

Reference: F. N. Kerlinger and E. Kaya. The construction and factor analytic validation of scales to measure attitudes toward education. *Educ. and psychol. Measmt.*, **1959, 19, 13–29. Items obtained from authors and published with their permission.**

all think differently about such matters, and this scale is an attempt to let you express your beliefs and opinions. Respond to each of the items as follows:

Agree Very Strongly:	+3	Disagree Very Strongly:	−3
Agree Strongly:	+2	Disagree Strongly.	−2
Agree:	+1	Disagree:	−1

For example, if you *agree very strongly* with a statement, you would write +3 on the short line preceding the statement, but if you should happen to disagree with it, you would put —1 in front of it. Respond to each statement as best you can. Go rapidly but carefully. Do not spend too much time on any one statement; try to respond and then go on.

_______ *1 The goals of education should be dictated by children's interests and needs, as well as by the larger demands of society.

_______ *2 No subject is more important than the personalities of the pupils.

_______ 3 Schools of today are neglecting the three R's.

_______ 4 The pupil-teacher relationship is the relationship between a child who needs direction, guidance, and control and a teacher who is an expert supplying direction, guidance, and control.

_______ *5 Teachers, like university professors, should have academic freedom—freedom to teach what they think is right and best.

_______ 6 The backbone of the school curriculum is subject matter; activities are useful mainly to facilitate the learning of subject matter.

_______ *7 Teachers should encourage pupils to study and criticize our own and other economic systems and practices.

_______ *8 The traditional moral standards of our children should not just be accepted; they should be examined and tested in solving the present problems of students.

_______ *9 Learning is experimental; the child should be taught to test alternatives before accepting any of them.

_______ 10 The curriculum consists of subject matter to be learned and skills to be acquired.

_______ 11 The true view of education is so arranging learning that the child gradually builds up a store house of knowledge that he can use in the future.

_______ 12 One of the big difficulties with modern schools is that discipline is often sacrificed to the interests of children.

_______ 13 The curriculum should contain an orderly arrangement of subjects that represent the best of our cultural heritage.

_______ 14 Discipline should be governed by long-range interests and well-established standards.

_______ *15 Education and educational institutions must be sources of new social ideas; education must be a social program undergoing continual reconstruction.

_______ *16 Right from the very first grade, teachers must teach the child at his own level and not at the level of the grade he is in.

* Items marked with an asterisk constitute the progressive subscale; other items make up the traditional subscale.

______ *17 Children should be allowed more freedom than they usually get in the execution of learning activities.

______ 18 Children need and should have more supervision and discipline than they usually get.

______ 19 Learning is essentially a process of increasing one's store of information about the various fields of knowledge.

______ *20 In a democracy, teachers should help students understand not only the meaning of democracy but also the meaning of the ideologies of other political systems.

Attitude toward intensive competition in team games
EXHIBIT 3-17

Description. This scale (McCue, 1953) attempts to measure attitude toward competition with reference to seven areas: personality (29 items), recreation (6 items), physical development (6 items), skill (6 items), safety (5 items), human relationships (17 items), and public relations (8 items). The scale was developed by a procedure best described as a combination of modified Likert and Thurstone techniques. A group of 47 judges from physical education departments first judged 145 items on a five-point scale for degree of favorability toward competition and then indicated their own opinion by means of the same five-point scale. Of the 145 items, 77 unambiguous items (as indicated by judgments of favorability) were selected to represent the entire range of favorability.

Subjects. The subjects in this study were 11 graduate students and 14 teachers in the woman's physical education department at the State University of Iowa, and 5 instructors, 5 coaches, and 12 graduate students in the men's physical education department at the same institution.

Response Mode. Each item is responded to by means of the following code: a, strongly agree; b, agree; c, neutral or indifferent; d, disagree; e, strongly disagree.

Scoring. A five-point scoring system ranging from +2 to —2 is used, with the plus value for favorable responses. Thus for items stating a favorable (positive) attitude toward intensive competition, an "a" response is given a score of +2; a "b" response, a score of +1; a "c" response, a score of 0; a "d" response, a score of —1; and an "e" response, a score of —2. For those stating an unfavorable attitude (marked with an asterisk in Exhibit 3-17) these scores are reversed. The attitude score is the sum of the item scores. The theoretical range is from —154 to +154, with the higher score reflecting the more favorable attitude.

Reliability. Test-retest reliability for a group of 25 women students retested after a delay of ten to thirteen weeks was .70.

Validity. The only evidence of validity is that evidenced by the content of the items and the agreement among judges regarding the degree of favorability of the items.

Comments. The greatest shortcoming of this scale is the relative lack of evidence of validity. It has not been used in other studies as far as we have been able to determine, so its usefulness in research has yet to be demonstrated. Nevertheless we believe that it merits further study.

McCue suggested a simplified scoring system in which all position responses are given a +1; all negative responses, a −1; and neutral responses, a 0. This system yielded scores which correlated .93 with those computed by means of the five-point system. The simplified system is worthy of consideration in any future studies.

EXHIBIT 3-17

ATTITUDE TOWARD INTENSIVE COMPETITION IN TEAM GAMES

Consider how strongly you personally agree or disagree with the following statements of opinion. Consider each statement in turn and record your opinion by using the following code based on letters a through e:

Strongly Agree	Agree	Neutral or Indifferent	Disagree	Strongly Disagree
a	b	c	d	e

1 This type of competition generally promotes community spirit.
2 Participation develops physical fitness in most individuals.
3 Participation gives most individuals self-assurance.
4 Winning and losing in this type of participation helps to prepare most individuals for the competition they meet in daily living.
5 Participation helps to train most individuals to face the problems of life.
6 This type of participation enables most individuals to work off emotional tensions.
*7 Participation in this type of competition often leads to acceptance of the fact that one must play "rough" if the opponents are rough.
8 The public is so interested in this type of competition that it judges school administrators by the success or failure of their athletic teams.
9 Participation gives most individuals a high sense of self-respect.
*10 Participation tends to put most individuals in a state of emotional upset for a long period of time.
11 Participation gives most individuals an appreciation for a job which is well done.
12 The experience of this type of participation develops many individuals as leaders.
13 Most participants learn to respect any individual who has skill, whether opponent or teammate.

* Items marked with an asterisk expess negative (unfavorable) attitudes toward intensive competition.

*14 The excitement of the spectators is an emotional strain for many of the participants in this type of competition.
*15 Most high schools cannot afford the equipment necessary to make participation in this type of competition relatively safe for their players.
16 Participation gives most individuals mental relaxation after the pressure of a game is over.
17 After individuals have participated in this type of competition, they are more likely to want to participate in sports for the rest of their lives.
18 Participation gives most individuals a sense of good sportsmanship.
19 The skilled person needs this type of participation in order to stimulate him to develop his physical skill still further.
20 Participation in this type of competition helps to train most individuals to form realistic outlooks and aims.
*21 Some coaches will take the chance of playing a player even if previous injury has made it unsafe for him.
*22 Participation leads most players to expect better grades than if they were not on the team.
*23 Participation gives most players the feeling that they are doing a job for which they should be paid.
24 The ingenuity of most individuals is increased through participation.
25 Participation presents no greater danger of accidents than other phases of daily living.
26 Through participation most individuals gain in mental alertness.
27 Participation makes most people feel that they are accepted by society.
*28 Most players have limited opportunity to show initiative in the game situation.
29 Participation in this type of competition gives most individuals an enjoyment of participating in activity.
30 Most participants are happier and better adjusted individuals than nonparticipants.
31 Participation gives most individuals the ability to be at ease before the public.
32 Participation helps most individuals acquire good manners which carry over into phases of everyday living.
33 Participation helps most individuals to discover what is needed to improve their own physical skill.
34 Through participation many players learn to evade the rules of the game.
*35 This type of competition seldom promotes any interest in all the rest of the school's class program.
36 Participation trains most individuals to profit from criticism.
37 Most individuals are aided in strengthening their ethical code by participation.
*38 Most spectators get some enjoyment from humiliating their opponents through overwhelming defeat.
*39 Participation often leads to unnecessary injury.
*40 Participants tend to value accomplishment only if it is recognized publicly with prizes and similar awards.
41 Participation teaches most individuals to work for what they get.
42 Participation teaches most individuals to win without boasting.
43 This type of participation usually trains one in good health habits.
*44 Many spectators of this type of contest do some betting on the outcome of the game.
*45 Participation gives many individuals a feeling of inferiority if beaten often.
46 Participation teaches most individuals how to behave in social situations.

*47 Many spectators of this type of competition express feelings of antagonism toward the opposing side.
*48 Danger of injury is one of the principal drawbacks to this type of activity.
49 Participation teaches most individuals to respect the rights of others.
50 Participation teaches most individuals to carry through in face of hardships.
*51 This type of competition generally results in spectator control of sports.
52 This type of competition promotes a desire for greater athletic skill in younger boys who admire the success of well-known players.
53 This type of competition teaches most participants how to build up their own good physical condition.
*54 Many participants learn to say they are amateurs although they actually do get large or small financial gains from their playing skill.
*55 This type of participation does little toward equipping a person with recreation skills for later life.
*56 Participation places an undue amount of physical strain on many individuals.
*57 Many people who have entered into this type of competition do not enjoy athletics unless they can play before a crowd.
58 Participation is an effective way to get acquainted with people from other communities.
59 This type of participation enables most individuals to develop reserve physical strength for emergencies.
*60 This type of competition seldom helps to promote the whole program of physical education.
*61 This type of competition trains most individuals to consider their opponents as their enemies.
62 Participation helps most individuals to set a goal and follow it.
*63 Developing the greater strength needed for this type of participation "burns" most individuals out physically after they retire from the activity.
64 Participation teaches most individuals to get along with people in the game situation and in many other aspects of life.
*65 Participation gives many individuals an exaggerated idea of the value of their skills.
66 Through participation most individuals learn to control their temper.
67 Most highly skilled individuals get more fun from this participation than from any other type of physical activity.
68 This type of participation stimulates most individuals to give their best possible performance.
*69 Most people who reach the skill level necessary for this type of participation are not willing to participate in any other athletics in which they do not already excel.
70 Participation teaches most individuals to be modest.
71 Most participants improve their skill in getting acquainted with strangers.
*72 To develop the great degree of athletic skill required by such competition takes more time than most students can afford to spare.
73 Participation trains most individuals to make quick decisions and responses when movement is called for.
*74 This type of competition often causes a disregard for the rules of the game.
*75 Many participants of this type of competition express feelings of antagonism toward the opposing side.
76 Participation helps to train most individuals in accepting the rule of the majority.
*77 Many players get some enjoyment from humiliating their opponents through overwhelming defeat.

Attitude toward intensive athletic competition for high school girls EXHIBIT 3-18

Description. This scale (McGee, 1956) is patterned after the McCue scale described above, but with the content of the items relevant to girls. It was developed by the same procedure and involves the same seven content areas. McGee describes "intensive athletic competition" as involving crowds, intense excitement, publicity, gate receipts, and local community involvement. Eighty-two items were given to ninety-four subjects who rated each item on a five-point scale for degree of favorability toward intensive competition. If 70 percent of the subjects agreed on the favorability rating, the item was retained. Of the original items, 12 were dropped, leaving 70 items in the final scale.

Subjects. The study population consisted of 102 communities randomly selected from a list of 300 communities in Iowa and Illinois. The samples consisted of the individuals in the study population who returned mailed questionnaires. Three groups were represented: members of the Iowa High School Athletic Union, nonunion members in Iowa, and nonunion members in Illinois. The total sample consisted of 1,349 subjects: 652 in the union group, 350 in the Iowa nonunion group, and 347 in the Illinois nonunion group. Samples were heterogeneous, including administrators and teachers in high schools as well as parents of high school children.

Response Mode. Subjects respond to each item by marking an answer sheet using the following system: 1, strongly agree; 2, agree; 3, neutral or indifferent; 4, disagree; 5, strongly disagree.

Scoring. McGee used the simplified three-point scoring system suggested by McCue (1953). Responses to items stating an unfavorable attitude toward intensive competition are reversed before scoring. Then any item response of 4 or 5 is given a score of +1; an item response of 3 is given a score of 0; and an item response of 1 or 2, a score of −1. The attitude score is the sum of the item scores. The theoretical range is therefore from −70 to +70, with the positive scores indicating a favorable attitude toward intensive competition.

Reliability. Test-retest reliability was reported to be .95, based upon the responses of 94 graduate students who were retested after a two-week delay.

Validity. The scale was shown to discriminate between union members and nonmembers in the expected direction. Iowa union members earned a mean score of 20.86; Iowa nonmembers, a mean score of 11.93; and Illinois nonmembers, a mean score of 12.26. Differences between the means for member and nonmember groups were significant ($p < .01$) in each case.

Comments. There is rather limited evidence concerning the characteristics of this scale, but the available evidence is favorable. Our most serious criticism is that the scale measures a somewhat esoteric attitude and, hence, may not be generally useful.

EXHIBIT 3-18

ATTITUDE TOWARD INTENSIVE COMPETITION FOR HIGH SCHOOL GIRLS

In recent years a growing number of comments regarding athletic programs for high school girls have been expressed by the public. Parents, school administrators, and teachers are interested in athletic competition. It seems to us very worthwhile to attempt to determine what these people think about the participation of high school girls in team sports involving intensive competition. Your response to the statements attached will help us to get data on your attitudes concerning this topic.

Your identity will remain unknown but some information about you is needed for grouping the data in various ways. Therefore, it will be necessary for you to fill in and check *all* of the blanks that apply to you *on the back of the answer sheet.*

By "intensive competition" for high school girls we mean those team games comparable to tournament basketball games and which involve crowds, intensive excitement, publicity, and gate receipts.

We should like to have your personal reaction to each statement as it is presented. Do you agree or disagree with the statement? Even if the girls in your town have never participated in intensive competition what do you think the effects would be? Indicate your *own* opinion of the statement by making a heavy mark between the dotted lines opposite the item number of the answer sheet. The attitude items are in sections. Be sure to place your answers in the corresponding sections on the answer sheet. The numbers represent the following code:

Strongly Agree	Agree	Neutral or Indifferent	Disagree	Strongly Disagree
1	2	3	4	5

Section A: Personality Development

1 Participation in intensive competition develops leadership.

*2 There is a display of excessive emotion during and after girls' participation in intensive competition.

3 Participation in intensive competition trains individuals to face the problems of every day living.

*4 The publicity used in intensive competition disturbs a player's sense of values which will have lasting effects for the future.

5 Participation in interscholastic contests develops mental alertness.

*6 Tournament basketball develops such intensity of feeling that most girls playing cannot control their own emotional responses.

7 Interscholastic participation promotes a well-balanced outlook on life's values.

* Items marked with an asterisk are unfavorable statements; scoring is reversed.

*8 Since the coach must make the decisions in interscholastic competition, players lose the opportunity to plan their own plays and strategy.

9 Participation in intensive competition assists players to control their emotions.

*10 Girls who participate in intensely competitive programs tend to develop masculine mannerisms and attitudes rather than feminine reactions.

11 Participation in intensive competition enhances the ego of shy individuals.

12 Intensely competitive participation creates a sense of achievement in the girl.

13 Intensive competition builds self-respect in the girl who participates.

Section B: Recreation

1 Girls should have the same opportunity as boys to enjoy the combative struggle of interscholastic basketball.

*2 A high school girl who participates in interscholastic athletics specializes in them and so does not learn individual sports which she could play later in life.

3 Intensive competition at the interscholastic level is necessary for real enjoyment of the game.

4 The average American girl wants intensive athletic competition.

5 Participation in intensive competition enables girls to acquire a love for activity.

*6 Most high schools do not have enough time or facilities to provide both for interscholastic team sports and recreational individual sports.

7 Intensive competitive participation in high school results in girls leading an active life in later years.

*8 Participation in intensive competition does not provide relief from the stress and strain of modern living.

*9 Membership on interscholastic teams limits the girl's interest in other school activities.

Section C: Physical Development

*1 A season of scheduled contests makes undue physical demands on girls.

2 Most coaches are primarily interested in developing and maintaining the physical welfare of the girls participating.

3 One of the best ways to build strength for the functions of womanhood is to engage in athletic contests.

4 Intense competition in active sports promotes better physical condition while participating.

*5 Most girls playing interscholastic basketball games play beyond the stage of moderate fatigue to the point of exhaustion.

*6 Intense athletic competition is more suited to the physical make up of high school boys than high school girls.

7 Girls in fit physical condition do not have abnormal emotional reactions.

*8 Practice periods as well as games leave most girls on the school team over fatigued.

9 Intense competition in active sports promotes better physical condition in the years following participation.

*10 Travel to and from distant games is excessively tiring to the players.

*11 Participation during the menstrual period causes fatigue unnoticed until it has exceeded the ordinary limits.

Section D: Public Relations

*1 Participating in intensive competition before crowds of excited spectators makes too much emotional strain for most girls.

2 Participation in intensely competitive team events provides a very desirable outlet for a high level of energy.
*3 The development of a girls' team is usually done at the cost of slighting the entire physical education program for the majority of girls.
*4 Many secondary schools use their girls' athletic teams as a means of advertising.
*5 The values received by high school girls from intensive interscholastic competition are insufficient to warrant large expenditures for equipment, travel, etc.
6 Interscholastic competitive games for girls stimulate school spirit more than inter-class games.
7 A community derives prestige from the success of its girls' teams in inter-city contests.
8 Girls' interscholastic athletic contests are the most effective device for girls to use to create community interest in the school.
9 Newspaper and radio reports on girls' contests increase support of the diversified physical education program for girls.
10 Most coaches find it desirable to do everything possible to get their teams to win.
11 Interscholastic competition gives girls equal opportunity with the boys to receive public recognition.

Section E: Safety

1 Travel arrangements used by most teams are completely adequate for the safety and health of the team.
2 Most girls who play tournament ball are taught to maintain standards of practice that will increase their health and protect their safety.
*3 Intensive participation presents greater danger of accidents than other phases of daily living.
*4 The rules used in tournament games fail to consider the physical capabilities of girls.
5 Most coaches adhere to entirely adequate safety codes for their teams.
6 Adequate protective equipment is worn by the majority of interscholastic participants.
7 Most coaches are qualified to develop health and character as well as skill.
*8 Most girls participating in intensive competition lack regular and adequate medical supervision.

Section F: Skill

*1 Training girls to make quick decisions and responses can be gained more rapidly from the more general physical education program than from the interscholastic type of competition.
*2 The participant is usually trained to view athletics primarily in relation to the winning of individual records and team championships.
3 Participation in intensive competition teaches respect for the skilled player whether teammate or opponent.
4 Intensive competition meets the challenge of highly skilled players.
*5 Intensive competition for girls places too much importance on trophies and awards.
6 Sufficient skill to satisfy the average individual is developed only through competitive interscholastic participation.

Section G: Relationships

1 Interscholastic participation develops responses useful in situations of emergency.

*2 Participation in intensive competition makes girls less considerate for the rights of others.
3 Competitive athletic participation creates more loyalty to the school than does participation in other school activities.
4 Interscholastic participation teaches girls to win without boasting in public.
*5 A girl receives few advantages from identification with an interscholastic team.
*6 Membership on athletic teams prevents girls from associating with their normal social crowd.
*7 Our society needs less competitive drive in girls and women than in boys and men.
*8 Playing on an inter-class team develops more ability to cooperate than playing on a team competing intensively.
9 Participation in intensive competition teaches girls poise when meeting new people.
10 Participants in intensive competition develop respect for officials.
*11 Emphasis on winning in intensive competition causes most players to forget the rights of their opponents.
12 Participation in competitive contests helps the participant adjust to others of her own age.

The competitive attitude (Ca) scale EXHIBIT 3-19

Description. The Competitive Attitude Scale was developed by Lakie (1964) for the purpose of revealing the degree to which various groups subscribe to the "win-at-any-cost" philosophy of athletics. Fifty-five items were selected from a variety of sources: books, popular magazines, personal observations, professional journals, and situations reported by others. This set of 55 items was administered to 60 college students, and their responses were used for item analysis. Each item and the results of the item analysis were then evaluated by the chairman of a university department of physical education, a college physical education teacher and coach, an educational psychologist, and a curriculum director of a junior college. After items that seemed questionable by the item analysis and decisions of the judges were discarded, the 22 items in the final scale remained.

Subjects. Several samples of subjects were used in various phases of scale development and research. The subjects for the item analysis were 60 college students in physical education. Reliability estimates were based upon the responses of 25 upperclassmen participating in varsity athletics at the University of California, Davis, 16 graduate students at Los Angeles State College, and a sample of 80 subjects drawn from a larger group of 228 varsity athletes, who were used as subjects in a study comparing the attitudes of various groups selected on the basis of kind of school attended and the kind of sport they were participating in.

Response Mode. Subjects are asked to respond to each item by circling a number from 1 to 5 according to the following system: 1, strongly approve; 2, approve; 3, undecided; 4, disapprove; 5, strongly disapprove.

Scoring. For items 6, 13, and 18, 5 points are given for "strongly approve," 4 for "approve," 3 for "undecided," 2 for "disapprove," and 1 for "strongly disapprove." For all other items, the number of points are given in reverse order. The attitude score is the sum of the points assigned to each item response. Thus the scoring range is from 22 to 90. The higher the attitude score, the more closely the subject subscribes to the "win-at-any-cost" philosophy, i.e., the more competitive his attitude toward athletics.

Reliability. Test-retest scores obtained three months apart yielded a Pearson r of .61 ($N = 25$), and similar scores obtained six weeks apart resulted in an r of .64 ($N = 16$). Internal consistency was estimated using the Lord modification of the K-R 21 formula, yielding a reliability coefficient of .81 ($N = 80$).

Validity. The author suggests that the validity of the Ca scale is based upon the thoroughness and comprehensiveness of the item analysis and the advice of the judges. The items appear to have high content validity, and the content domain is adequately sampled. Lakie (1964) found that the scale did not discriminate among groups of subjects classified according to kind of school attended and kind of sports in which they participated, but there seems to be no a priori reason to expect such groups to hold different attitudes toward competition.

Comments. The Ca scale was developed by the Likert procedure, but the items are different from the usual Likert type. Each item describes a situation and an action, rather than simply stating a proposition. The reliability of the scale is satisfactory for group discrimination but is probably unsatisfactory for the study of individual attitude. More evidence of validity is badly needed.

EXHIBIT 3-19

THE COMPETITIVE ATTITUDE (CA) SCALE

The following situations describe behavior demonstrated in sports. Circle the category that indicates your feeling towards the behavior described in each of the situations.

1. Strongly Approve 2. Approve 3. Undecided 4. Disapprove 5. Strongly Disapprove

1 2 3 4 5 1 During a football game team A has the ball on its own 45-yard line, fourth down and 1 yard to go for a first down. The coach of team A signals to the quaterback the play that he wants the team to run.

1 2 3 4 5 **2** Team A is the visiting basketball team and each time a member of the team is given a free shot the home crowd sets up a continual din of noise until the shot has been taken.

1 2 3 4 5 **3** Tennis player A frequently calls out, throws up his arms, or otherwise tries to indicate that his opponent's serve is out of bounds when it is questionable.

1 2 3 4 5 **4** In a track meet, team A enters a man in the mile run who is to set a fast pace for the first half of the race and then drop out.

1 2 3 4 5 **5** In a football game, team B's quarterback was tackled repeatedly after handing off and after he was out of the play.

1 2 3 4 5 **6** Sam, playing golf with his friends, hit a drive into the rough. He accidentally moved the ball with his foot, although not improving his position he added a penalty stroke to his score.

1 2 3 4 5 **7** A basketball player was caught out of position on defense and rather than allow his opponent to attempt a field goal he fouled him.

1 2 3 4 5 **8** Player A during a golf match made quick noises and movements when player B was getting ready to make a shot.

1 2 3 4 5 **9** School A has a powerful but quite slow football team. The night before playing a smaller but faster team, they allowed the field sprinkling system to remain on, causing the field to be heavy and slow.

1 2 3 4 5 **10** A basketball team used player A to draw the opponent's high scorer into fouling situations.

1 2 3 4 5 **11** The alumni of College A pressured the Board of Trustees to lower the admission and eligibility requirements for athletes.

1 2 3 4 5 **12** Team A, by use of fake injuries, was able to stop the clock long enough to get off the play that resulted in the winning touchdown.

1 2 3 4 5 **13** A tennis player was given the advantage of a bad call in a close match. He then "evened up" the call by intentionally hitting the ball out of bounds.

1 2 3 4 5 **14** The coach of basketball team A removed his team from the floor in protest of an official's decision.

1 2 3 4 5 **15** Between seasons a coach moved from College A to College B and he then persuaded three of College A's athletes to transfer to College B.

1 2 3 4 5 **16** After losing a close football game the coach of the losing team publicly accused the game officials of favoritism when the game movies showed that the winning touchdown had been scored by using an illegal maneuver.

1 2 3 4 5 **17** College C lowered the admission requirements for boys awarded athletic scholarships.

1 2 3 4 5 **18** Team A's safety man returned a punt for a touchdown. Unseen by the officials he had stepped out of bounds in front of his team's bench. His coach notified the officials of this fact.

1 2 3 4 5 **19** A college with very few athletic scholarships to offer, gives athletes preference on all types of campus jobs.

1 2 3 4 5 **20** Several wealthy alumni of College C make a monthly gift to several athletes who are in need of financial assistance.

1 2 3 4 5 **21** College K has a policy of not allowing any member of a varsity squad to associate with the visiting team until the contest or meet is completed.

1 2 3 4 5 **22** The Board of Trustees at College C fired the football coach and gave as the reason for his dismissal his failure to win a conference championship during the past five years.

ATTITUDES RELATED TO RELIGIOUS PRACTICES

Although there are many scales designed to measure religious attitudes (see Chapter 7), very few scales have been constructed to measure attitudes toward religious practices. Only two scales were found that clearly fall into this category: a scale to measure attitudes toward Sunday observance and one to measure attitudes toward church and religious practice. A scale developed by Hardy (1949) to measure attitudes of Latter-day Saints toward their church and its practices is presented in Chapter 10.

Attitude toward Sunday observance *EXHIBIT 3-20*

Description. The Attitude toward Sunday Observance Scale is scale number 26 in the Thurstone series (Thurstone, 1929–1934). The usual method of equal-appearing intervals was used to select items for two 22-item forms matched for scale values.

Subjects. No data concerning the subjects used in constructing this scale are available.

Response Mode. Subjects respond to each item by checking for agreement or placing a cross by the statement to indicate disagreement.

Scoring. The attitude score is the median of the scale values of the statements checked to indicate agreement. A high score is interpreted as indicating that the respondent is in favor of strict religious observance of Sunday, a low score that he is entirely opposed to religious observance of Sunday.

Reliability. Evidence of reliability is taken from a study by Lorge (1939), who reported correlations between the two forms ranging from .73 to .83.

Validity. In addition to the validity implied by the method used to select items, the scale has been shown to discriminate in the expected direction between Seventh Day Adventists and other denominational groups.

Comments. The Attitude toward Sunday Observance Scale has not been used as extensively as many of Thurstone's scales, and the data concerning its characteristics are therefore more limited. If we can assume that it functions much as do other, more extensively used Thurstone scales, we can recommend its use for research purposes without reservation.

EXHIBIT 3-20

ATTITUDE TOWARD SUNDAY OBSERVANCE

Put a check mark (✓) if you agree with the statement.
Put a cross (×) if you disagree with the statement.

Form A

Scale Value		
5.2	1	Conduct on Sunday should be entirely up to the individual.
8.2	2	Dancing should be prohibited on Sunday.
0.4	3	There should be no restriction whatever on Sunday activities.
7.4	4	We should not work for pay on Sunday.
6.6	5	I believe in observing the Sabbath but no one should be forced to.
2.4	6	There is nothing sacred about Sunday that calls for solemn observance.
10.2	7	We should spend Sunday only in worshipping God.
3.6	8	It should be my own free choice whether to play golf or go to church on Sunday morning.
8.6	9	Everyone should go to church on Sunday.
5.4	10	The question of Sunday observance is unimportant.
1.3	11	No one has the right to interfere with my freedom on Sunday.
6.9	12	Only cultural activities should be allowed on Sundays.
5.6	13	I do not care whether there are Sunday blue laws or not.
8.1	14	It is wrong to play cards on Sunday.
4.2	15	Since Sunday observance is a religious practice, it should not be forced upon anyone.
9.4	16	All public places of amusement should be closed on Sunday.
1.9	17	Sunday observance is mere superstition.
7.2	18	Sunday observance is desirable for keeping people out of mischief.
0.3	19	Only narrow-minded fools believe in observing the Sabbath.
2.8	20	Theaters should be open Sundays as on other days.
10.1	21	Sunday observance is a commandment we must obey.
3.4	22	People who are busy during the week need Sunday for play.

Form B

Scale Value		
5.3	1	People should observe Sunday or not, as they see fit.
9.8	2	It is contrary to the will of God to work on Sunday.
3.4	3	Sunday baseball should be allowed.
8.3	4	Places of amusement should be closed on Sunday because they keep people from church.
1.1	5	People who advocate Sunday observance are religious fanatics.
7.5	6	Theaters should be closed during the hours of church service.
5.5	7	It makes little difference to me whether we observe the Sabbath.
10.1	8	Forgetting that the Sabbath is holy invokes the wrath of God.
4.8	9	People who want to observe Sunday can do so without restricting other people.
1.4	10	Sunday blue laws are ridiculous in an enlightened society.

9.2	11	The purpose of Sunday is to glorify God.
3.1	12	It is perfectly legitimate to spend Sunday for play.
7.9	13	Whatever else a person does on Sunday, he should go to church.
2.2	14	What is proper for week days is proper for Sunday.
6.7	15	I favor certain restrictions on Sunday activities.
0.7	16	Sunday blue laws are an outrage against individual freedom.
10.9	17	Sunday blue laws should be strictly enforced everywhere.
2.8	18	Golf, tennis, and movies should be allowed at all hours on Sunday.
4.1	19	Sunday observance is merely a religious custom.
8.7	20	Sunday blue laws safeguard the morals of young people.
0.2	21	I am unequivocally against any regulation of Sunday activity.
6.2	22	Even though Sunday observance is desirable, it should not be compulsory.

An attitude scale toward church and religious practices EXHIBIT 3-21

Description. This scale (Dynes, 1955) is a 24-item Likert scale concerned primarily with practices within the church. Thirty-five items were written to reflect either a sectarian or a church viewpoint. The church orientation is one which accepts and integrates existing cultural definitions and the social order into the church, whereas the sectarian orientation rejects the existing social order and states rigid requirements for members of the church. The 35 items were administered to a sample of 55 persons. Their responses were used in an item analysis which resulted in the elimination of 11 items which did not discriminate between high and low scorers. The remaining 24 items consisted of 4 church items and 20 sectarian items.

Subjects. The pretest sample consisted of 55 persons drawn from a large Protestant church in Columbus, Ohio. The final sample consisted of 100 subjects from the same population.

Response Mode. Subjects react to each item by entering a number from 1 to 5 according to the following code: 1 for "strongly agree," 2 for "agree," 3 for "undecided," 4 for "disagree," and 5 for "strongly disagree."

Scoring. Before scoring, the responses to the church items (items 2, 6, 7, and 10 in Exhibit 3-21) are reversed so that a response of 5 is changed to 1, a response of 4 to 2, and so on. The attitude score is then computed as the sum of the responses to each item. The theoretical range is therefore from 24 to 120, with the higher scores indicating a more favorable attitude toward the church-orientation and related religious practices.

Reliability. For the pretest sample of 55 persons, the split-half reliability was .86 (corrected to .92); for a sample of 100 persons, the final scale split-half reliability was .70 (corrected to .82).

Validity. Validity was evaluated in two ways. First, 10 judges from several denominations (Methodist, Congregational, Jewish, Lutheran,

Baptist, and Disciples of Christ) judged the polarity of each item. Level of agreement was 98 percent. Secondly, groups identified as "church" type (Episcopalians and Presbyterians) and as "sect" type (Holiness, Pentecostal, Church of God, Church of Nazarene, and Baptist) were compared. The church group had a mean score on the attitude scale of 76.1, whereas the sect group earned a mean score of 58.1 ($p < .001$). Since this difference was as expected on theoretical grounds, it was taken as evidence of scale validity.

Comments. Although the nature of the referent of this scale is somewhat ambiguous, it has been used with some success by Garrison (1962) in his study of the attitudes of college students. The reliability is about average for scales constructed by the Likert procedure. Validity is closely related to the church-sect typology; hence the acceptability of the validating evidence depends upon the acceptability of the theoretical analysis.

EXHIBIT 3-21

AN ATTITUDE SCALE TOWARD CHURCH AND RELIGIOUS PRACTICES

Directions: Put a 1 before those statements with which you strongly agree, a 2 before those statements with which you mildly agree, a 3 before those statements toward which you are neutral, a 4 before those with which you mildly disagree, and a 5 before those with which you strongly disagree.

1 I think a minister should preach without expecting to get paid for it.
*2 I think it is more important to live a good life now than to be bothered about life after death.
3 I think a person who is not willing to follow **all** the rules of the church should not be allowed to belong.
4 I think that we should emphasize education in religion and not conversion.
5 Testifying about one's religious experience should be a part of regular church service.
*6 I think that there is practically no difference between what the different Protestant churches believe.
*7 I feel that a congregation should encourage the minister during his sermon by saying **amen.**
8 I think a person should make a testimony about his religion before he joins a church.
9 In church, I would rather sing the hymns myself than hear the choir sing.
*10 I think being a success in one's job is one mark of a good Christian.
11 A minister who is "called" is better than one who is "trained."
12 I like the "old-time" religion.
13 I think churches should have more revivals.

* Items marked with an asterisk state a "church" orientation.

Reprinted with permission from Dynes, R. R. Church-sect typology and socio-economic status. *Amer. Social. Rev.*, 1955, 20, 555–660.

14 I think it would be wrong for a church member to have a job as a bartender.
15 I think a person should feel his religion before he joins a church.
16 I like to sing the old gospel songs rather than the new hymns.
17 I don't believe churches do enough about saving souls.
18 Heaven and Hell are very real to me.
19 All the miracles in the Bible are true.
20 Children should not become members of the church until they are old enough to understand about it.
21 I think it is more important to go to church than to be active in politics.
22 I wish ministers would preach more on the Bible and less on politics.
23 I think it is more serious to break God's law than to break man's law.
24 I think every family should have family prayers or say grace before meals.

ATTITUDES TOWARD HETEROSEXUAL PRACTICES

Attitudes toward practices involving relationships between the sexes are obviously important for understanding interactions between males and females, but surprisingly few attempts have been made to measure these attitudes. Available scales in this category are intended to measure attitudes toward dating behavior, premarital intimacy, and divorce.

A dating scale EXHIBIT 3-22

Description. Bardis (1962) developed this scale to measure attitudes toward dating behavior. It is a 25-item Likert scale. The items were selected by item analysis from a pool of 180 items. All items in the final scale had discriminatory indices over 3.0.

Subjects. The pretest sample consisted of 450 high school, college, and noncollege adults and adolescents. Both sexes were represented, and all were residents of the Midwest. For a follow-up study, a sample of 100 persons from the same population was used.

Response Mode. The following code is used in responding to each item: 0, strongly disagree; 1, disagree; 2, undecided; 3, agree; 4, strongly agree. The subjects respond by entering the appropriate number in the space provided.

Scoring. The numbers entered beside each statement are added to obtain the attitude score. The scores may range from 0 to 100. A high score is interpreted as reflecting a liberal attitude toward dating behavior, and a low score a conservative attitude.

Reliability. Corrected split-half reliabilities were reported as follows: .93 for a sample of 32 male undergraduates; .79 for 32 female undergraduates; .89 for 30 adults and adolescents born in Greece but living in the United States; and .86 for 34 American adults.

A test-retest reliability of .83 was reported for a sample of 31 male and female undergraduates at a Midwestern university.

Validity. In addition to content validity, it was shown that males have significantly higher scores on the Dating Scale than females and that Americans have higher scores than persons born in Greece. Since these scores are as expected from the "known" attitudes of these groups, these findings may be considered evidence of validity.

Comments. This is a short, easily administered scale with adequate reliability and minimal evidence of validity. All the items are stated in the direction of agreement indicating more liberal attitudes; hence, response bias may be suspected.

EXHIBIT 3-22

A DATING SCALE

Below is a list of issues concerning dating. Please read *all* statements very *carefully* and respond to *all* of them on the basis of *your own true* beliefs *without* consulting any other persons. Do this by reading each statement and then writing, in the space provided at its left, *only one* of the following numbers: 0, 1, 2, 3, 4. The meaning of each of these figures is:

0: Strongly disagree.
1: Disagree.
2: Undecided.
3: Agree.
4: Strongly agree.

Keep in mind that by dating we mean the casual association between a male and a female who are not seriously contemplating marriage. The purpose of dating is to have a pleasant time with a member of the opposite sex.
(For research purposes, you must consider all statements as they are, without modifying any of them in any way.)

_____ 1 Every person should be allowed to choose his or her dating partner freely and independently.
_____ 2 Girls should be allowed to ask boys for dates.
_____ 3 Boys and girls between 14 and 16 should be allowed to date without any adult supervision.
_____ 4 It is all right to kiss on the first date.
_____ 5 Boys of 12 should be allowed to date.
_____ 6 Boys of 14 should be allowed to date.
_____ 7 Girls of 12 should be allowed to date.
_____ 8 Going on blind dates is all right.

________	9	It is all right for dating partners to talk about sex.
________	10	Adult supervision for first dates between 12 and 14 is unnecesary.
________	11	Even when a girl is below 18, it is unnecessary for her parents to meet her boy friend before she first goes out with him.
________	12	Boys of 14 should be allowed to go steady if they wish.
________	13	Boys of 16 should be allowed to go steady if they wish.
________	14	Girls of 12 should be allowed to go steady if they wish.
________	15	Girls of 14 should be allowed to go steady if they wish.
________	16	Young people should make as much love on a date as they wish.
________	17	It is not important for a person to remain pure until marriage.
________	18	It is all right for a young dating couple to park on a lonely road.
________	19	It is all right for a dating couple to kiss in public.
________	20	Persons between 15 and 18 do not have to inform their parents where they will be while dating.
________	21	It is all right for a boy to invite a girl to his home when no one is there.
________	22	It is all right for a girl to invite a boy to her home when no one is there.
________	23	When two young people are serious about each other, it is all right for them to make any kind of love.
________	24	It is all right for a girl to wait for her date in a public place.
________	25	Dating couples between 18 and 20 should be allowed to stay out as late as they wish.

An intimacy permissiveness scale EXHIBIT 3-23

Description. Constructed by Christensen and Carpenter (1962), the Intimacy Permissiveness Scale is a 10-item, Guttman-type scale. The authors began with 21 items, but only 10 remained after tests for unidimensionality were made. The scale is designed to measure attitudes ranging from highly permissive to highly restrictive attitudes toward premarital sexual intimacy.

Subjects. The standardization sample included 149 males and 86 females from a Danish community, 213 males and 142 females from a Midwestern United States university, and 94 males and 74 females from an Intermountain United States university. Of the Intermountain sample 79 percent were Latter-Day Saint in religious affiliation.

Response Mode. The subject checks each item with which he agrees.

Scoring. The attitude score is the number of items checked. The range of possible scores is therefore from 0 to 10. Since all items are stated in terms of permissiveness, the higher the score, the more favorable the subject's attitude toward premarital intimacy.

Reliability. Tests of reproducibility were applied separately to each male and female group in each culture, and to the total sample. Obtained reproducibility coefficients ranged from .90 to .96, which meet the usual

Guttman standards. (See Chapter 2 for a discussion of reproducibility as a measure of reliability.)

Validity. Validity was demonstrated in several ways. First, the mean intimacy permissiveness scores were 8.3 for the Danish sample, 4.1 for the Midwestern sample, and 2.4 for the Intermountain sample. Thus, attitude scores corresponded to the "known" attitudes of these groups. Second, males were found to have higher scores than females in all three samples, again corresponding to "known" differences in attitude. Third, the higher the intimacy permissiveness score, the larger the percent having had premarital coitus. This statistically significant relationship held in all three cultures.

Comments. The Intimacy Permissiveness Scale appears to be relatively unidimensional; evidence of validity is better than average; and reproducibility is acceptable. The prospective user should remember, however, that items that are scalable for one population or sample will not necessarily scale in a different population. Tests of unidimensionality should be made for the particular population sampled.

EXHIBIT 3-23

AN INTIMACY PERMISSIVENESS SCALE

Please place a check mark beside each item with which you agree.

1 I would prefer marrying a non-virgin.
2 I would prefer not marrying a virgin.
3 I approve petting any time before marriage for myself.
4 I approve petting any time before marriage for my daughter.
5 I approve coitus any time before marriage for my daughter.
6 I approve of coitus on random or casual dates.
7 I approve of coitus when a couple is in love and going steady.
8 I approve of coitus when a couple is in love and formally engaged to be married.
9 Premarital pregnancy is nothing to be ashamed of or to hide providing the couple is in love and later gets married.
10 It is best not to try to prohibit erotic and obscene literature and pictures by law, but rather to leave people free to follow their judgments and tastes in such matters.

Attitude toward divorce EXHIBIT 3-24

Description. The Attitude toward Divorce Scale was prepared by Ellickson under the editorship of Thurstone. It is scale number 32 in the

Thurstone series (Thurstone, 1929–1934). The usual method of equal-appearing intervals was used in its construction, but the original scale and Q values were not given in the Thurstone report. The present authors rescaled the items, and these are the scale values given in Exhibit 3-24. Q values ranged from 0.7 for item 11 to 3.2 for item 7.

Subjects. Presumably, the scale was originally developed on a sample of students at the University of Chicago. The new scale values given in Exhibit 3-24 were obtained from a sample of 26 graduate students in social psychology courses at the University of Florida.

Response Mode. Subjects respond to each statement by placing a check beside those items with which they agree and a cross beside items with which they disagree.

Scoring. The score is the median of the scale values of items checked to indicate agreement. A high score indicates a favorable attitude toward divorce.

Reliability. Test-retest reliability was estimated to be .86.

Validity. No evidence of validity is available beyond that indicated by content and the method of selecting the items.

Comments. There is relatively little information available concerning the characteristics of this scale. Also the investigator may wish to rescale the items before using, since the values given in Exhibit 3-24 were obtained from only 26 judges, although it has been shown that reliable scale values can be computed with as few as 20 judges (Webb, 1955).

EXHIBIT 3-24

ATTITUDE TOWARD DIVORCE

The following statements express opinions about divorce. Please indicate your agreement or disagreement with each of the statements by marking them as follows:

(✓) Mark with a check mark if you agree with the statement.
(X) Mark with an X if you disagree with the statement.

*Scale Value		
3.7	1	Divorce is justifiable only after all efforts to mend the union have failed.
6.6	2	Present divorce conditions are not as discreditable as they appear.
8.5	3	If marriage is to be based on mutual affection, divorce must be easy to obtain.
1.6	4	Divorce lowers the standard of morality.

* Scale values were computed by the authors of this book.

Scale Value		
0.5	5	Divorce is disgraceful.
8.4	6	Divorce is desirable for adjusting errors in marriage.
4.8	7	Divorce is a necessary evil.
9.8	8	Divorce should be granted for the asking.
6.2	9	A divorce is justifiable or not, depending on the wants of the persons involved.
10.1	10	A person should have the right to marry and divorce as often as he chooses.
0.5	11	Divorce is never justifiable.
8.8	12	Easy divorce leads to a more intelligent understanding of marriage.
3.3	13	Divorce should be discouraged in order to stabilize society.
5.8	14	The evils of divorce should not prevent us from seeing its benefits.
9.4	15	The marriage contract should be as easily broken as made.
0.8	16	The best solution of the divorce problem is never to grant divorce.
1.2	17	Lenient divorce is equivalent to polygamy.
7.1	18	Divorce should be permitted so long as the rights of all parties are insured.
4.2	19	Divorce should be discouraged but not forbidden.
0.8	20	Divorce is legalized adultery.
3.8	21	Long and careful investigation should precede the granting of every divorce.
8.1	22	Permanence in marriage is unnecessary for social stability.

A divorce opinionnaire EXHIBIT 3-25

Description. This scale was constructed by Hardy (1957). It consists of 12 items dealing with various aspects of divorce, such as the nature of the marital contract, divorce as a solution to an unhappy marriage, the effects of divorce upon children and society, the degree of abuse of divorce, and the obligation partners should feel to remain married. Half of the items express a liberal attitude (i.e., favorable toward divorce) and half a conservative, unfavorable attitude. Although the scale is cast in the Likert format, there is no record of formal item selection procedures.

Subjects. Hardy presented no evidence of reliability or validity, but since the opinionnaire appeared promising, the present authors administered it to a sample of 12 women and 24 men undergraduates at the University of Florida.

Response Mode. Subjects respond to each item by means of the following code: ++, I strongly agree with this statement; +, I mildly agree with the statement; 0, I am more or less neutral or indifferent about it; —, I mildly disagree with the statement; and ——, I strongly disagree with the statement.

Scoring. Hardy was interested only in change of attitude; hence he merely scored differences in item responses. However, an overall attitude score may be computed by assigning scores from 1 to 5 to the various response alternatives, with the higher score indicating a more favorable attitude toward divorce. Thus a 5 is assigned to a ++ response for favorable statements and to a –– response for negative statements, a score of 4 to a + response for favorable and to a — response for unfavorable items, etc. The attitude score is the sum of the item scores, with the more favorable attitude indicated by the higher scores. Theoretical range of scores is from 12 to 60.

Reliability. The only reliability estimate is the one derived from the administration referred to above. Split-half reliability was found to be .74, corrected by the Spearman-Brown formula to .85.

Validity. The scale appears to have content validity, but Hardy reported no other evidence. The present authors found a mean score for women of 31.3 as compared with a mean score of 38.0 for men. Assuming that men in our culture have more favorable attitudes toward divorce than women, this finding may be taken as minimal evidence of validity.

Comments. The characteristics of a Divorce Opinionnaire have not been determined with any degree of adequacy. Therefore, this scale cannot be recommended for any use other than exploratory research until further standardization studies have been completed.

EXHIBIT 3-25

A DIVORCE OPINIONNAIRE

Read each of the following statements concerning marriage and divorce. Then write in the space provided the notation which best represents your own feeling about the statement:

++ means "I strongly agree with this statement"
+ means "I mildly agree. . . ."
0 means "I am more or less neutral or indifferent about it"
– means "I mildly disagree with the statement"
–– means "I strongly disagree. . . ."

______ 1 I feel that divorce is a sensible solution to many unhappy marriages.

______ *2 Marriage is a sacred covenant which should be broken only under the most drastic circumstances.

______ 3 Children are better off living with one parent rather than with two who cannot get along well together.

______ *4 Most divorces are a farce and ought to be stopped.

* Items marked with an asterisk state unfavorable attitudes toward divorce.

Reference: K. R. Hardy. Determinants of conformity and attitude change. *J. Abnorm. soc. Psychol.*, 1957, 54, 289–294. Items obtained from author and published with his permission.

______	*5	It is better for a couple to stay together, to struggle along together if necessary, than to break up a home by getting a divorce.
______	6	Divorce is a fine social institution since it alleviates much misery and unhappiness.
______	7	Although some people abuse the divorce privilege, it is fundamentally a good thing.
______	8	Marriage is essentially an agreement between two interested parties, and if they wish to conclude that agreement they should be permitted to do so.
______	*9	Divorce is no real solution to an unhappy marriage.
______	*10	Children need a home with both a father and a mother even though the parents are not especially suited to one another.
______	*11	Divorce is one of our greatest social evils.
______	12	If a couple find getting along with each other a real struggle then they should not feel obligated to remain married.

ATTITUDES RELATED TO HEALTH PRACTICES

Several aspects of practices related to health are considered in this section. Greatest interest in recent years has been centered around attitudes toward psychotherapy and counseling practices. Two scales for measuring attitudes toward these practices are discussed. One scale for measuring attitude toward chemotherapy is presented and described. One study of attitudes toward counseling (Chase, 1946) having 180 statements about counseling practices, was considered but was excluded because no attempt had been made to determine the characteristics of the items.

The custodial mental illness ideology (*CMI*) *scale* *EXHIBIT 3-26*

Description. The CMI scale was developed by Gilbert and Levinson (1956) to measure attitudes toward the treatment of the mentally ill, with special reference to "humanistic" versus "custodial" orientations. Custodialism refers to traditional practices in mental hospitals which are modeled after prisons and place emphasis upon the detention and safekeeping of inmates. The humanistic orientation, on the other hand, emphasizes the individuality and the human needs of both patients and personnel.

The CMI scale consists of 20 items selected by the Likert procedure. The items in Exhibit 3-26 are numbered as they were in the questionnaire, which contained other scales and questions. Discriminatory powers for individual items ranged from —.2 to 4.4, computed as the difference between the means of the upper and lower 25 percent on the total scale. All DPs were positive except the —.2 for item 23, and all except items 18 and 23 reach the .05 level of significance. The nondiscriminating items have been omitted in subsequent research.

Subjects. Initial development was based upon a sample of 335 staff members in three mental hospitals in Massachusetts. Staff members included aides, nurses, student nurses, and psychiatrists. Hospital C was an 1,800-bed hospital for chronic patients; hospital T was a Veterans Administration hospital of about the same size as hospital C; and hospital H was a 120-bed state hospital which provided short-term, active treatment.

Response Mode. Subjects are instructed to respond to each item by entering a number from +3 to —3 according to the following code: +3, strongly agree; +2, mildly agree; +1, agree; —1, disagree; —2, mildly disagree; —3, strongly disagree.

Scoring. Responses are converted to scores by means of a seven-point scale. For custodial items, 7 points are given for a +3 response, 6 points for a +2 response, 5 points for a +1 response; 4 points for no response, 3 points for a —1 response, 2 points for a —2 response, and 1 point for a —3 response. For the humanistic items the scoring is reversed. The attitude score is the average of the item scores, multiplied by 10 for convenience in comparing scores from different scales. The theoretical range is from 10 to 70, with the higher score representing a favorable attitude toward the more traditional practices in mental hospitals.

Reliability. Corrected split-half reliability was reported to be .85, based upon the scores of 335 subjects. Test-retest correlations based on several small samples "were of similar magnitude."

Validity. Validation was first determined by the known-groups method. Ten administrators of hospital H known for the advocacy of humanistic policies earned a mean CMI score of 18.1 with a SD of 6.1. A second group from Belmont Hospital, England, was also expected to receive low CMI scores. Their mean score was 22.9 with a SD of 6.7. Correlations between CMI scores and a measure of custodialism in role performance ranged from .5 to .8. Correlations with the F scale ranged from .67 to .79, and with the TFI scale (Exhibit 3-10) they ranged from .56 to .77. These correlations may be taken as evidence of construct validity (see Chapter 2).

Comments. This scale is relatively well researched (see also Greenblatt, Levinson, and Williams, 1957). Since items 18 and 23 did not discriminate between high and low scorers, they should be eliminated when using the scale, as suggested by the authors. Since these items were two of the three items that stated a humanistic position, this would leave all items save one stated in the same direction. This raises the question of response bias more seriously than scales that have pro and con items more evenly matched in number.

EXHIBIT 3-26

THE CUSTODIAL MENTAL ILLNESS IDEOLOGY (CMI) SCALE

This is part of a larger study by the Russell Sage Foundation. We are interested in the various ways of thinking about mental illness and some related social problems. We are trying to get answers from various groups in different parts of the country. The groups will include the general public as well as those of you who have had direct experience with hospitalized patients, i.e., nurses, attendants, and doctors.

The best answer to each statement below is your *personal opinion.* We have tried to cover many different points of view. You may find yourself agreeing strongly with some of the statements, disagreeing just as strongly with others.

Mark each statement in the left margin according to how much you agree or disagree with it. *Please mark every one.* Write in +1, +2, +3, or —1, —2, —3, depending on how you feel in each case.

+1	I AGREE A LITTLE	—1	I DISAGREE A LITTLE
+2	I AGREE PRETTY MUCH	—2	I DISAGREE PRETTY MUCH
+3	I AGREE VERY MUCH	—3	I DISAGREE VERY MUCH

1 Only persons with considerable psychiatric training should be allowed to form close relationships with patients.

2 It is best to prevent the more disturbed patients from mixing with those who are less sick.

3 As soon as a person shows signs of mental disturbance he should be hospitalized.

*4 Mental illness is an illness like any other.

5 Close association with mentally ill people is liable to make even a normal person break down.

6 We can make some improvements, but by and large the conditions of mental hospital wards are about as good as can be considering the type of disturbed patient living there.

7 We should be sympathetic with mental patients, but we cannot expect to understand their odd behavior.

8 One of the main causes of mental illness is lack of moral strength.

*9 When a patient is discharged from a hospital, he can be expected to carry out his responsibilities as a citizen.

10 Abnormal people are ruled by their emotions; normal people by their reason.

11 A mental patient is in no position to make decisions about even everyday living problems.

*12 Patients are often kept in the hospital long after they are well enough to get along in the community.

13 There is nothing about mentally ill people that makes it easy to tell them from normal people.

* Items marked with an asterisk are "humanistic"; others are "custodial."

14 Few, if any, patients are capable of real friendliness.
15 There is hardly a mental patient who isn't liable to attack you unless you take extreme precautions.
16 Patients who fail to recover have only themselves to blame; in most cases they have just not tried hard enough.
17 "Once a schizophrenic, always a schizophrenic."
18 Patients need the same kind of control and discipline as an untrained child.
19 With few exceptions most patients haven't the ability to tell right from wrong.
20 In experimenting with new methods of ward treatment, hospitals must consider first and foremost, the safety of patients and personnel.

The psychotherapy-sociotherapy ideology (PSI) scale EXHIBIT 3-27

Description. The PSI scale was developed in connection with the CMI scale described above (Sharaf and Levinson, 1957). It is a 12-item Likert scale. Four items are said to measure medical-nonmedical relations and eight, treatment-therapy emphasis. Item discriminatory powers (DPs) were computed as the difference between the means of the upper and lower 25 percent of scorers on the total scale. The DPs ranged from 1.6 to 3.8. Item-total correlations ranged from .39 to .69.

Five of the items express a socio position, which emphasizes the social responsibility of the therapist, whereas seven items express the psychological position, which emphasizes psychotherapy as a method of treatment.

Subjects. The subjects were 31 staff members at a psychiatric hospital. The sample consisted of 9 second-year residents, 8 third-year residents, 10 inpatient administrators, and 4 psychiatrists from the outpatient department.

Response Mode. Subjects are directed to indicate agreement or disagreement with each item according to the following key: +3, strongly agree; +2, mildly agree; +1, agree; —1, disagree; —2, mildly disagree; —3, strongly disagree.

Scoring. Responses are converted to scores according to the following scheme: For the items reflecting a psychotherapeutic orientation, 7 points are assigned for a +3 response, 6 for a +2 response, 5 for a +1 response, 3 for a —1 response, 2 for a —2 response, and 1 for a —3 response. For items stating a sociotherapeutic orientation, the direction of scoring is reversed. Thus, a high score represents a favorable attitude toward psychotherapy, whereas a low score indicates a favorable attitude toward sociotherapy. The attitude score is the mean of the item scores, multiplied by 10. The possible range of scores is thus from 10 to 70.

Reliability. The corrected split-half reliability was found to be .75.

Validity. The authors were able to show that the pattern of scores among members of the hospital staff were in accord with theoretical expectations. Also, the PSI scale correlated .33 with the CMI scale and .19 with the F scale.

Comments. Sharaf and Levinson (1957) state that the PSI scale was developed as a crude index of degree of preference for either the psychotherapeutic or the sociotherapeutic approach. It seems to meet this goal satisfactorily, since the scale has adequate internal consistency, and the limited evidence of validity is promising.

EXHIBIT 3-27

THE PSYCHOTHERAPY-SOCIOTHERAPY IDEOLOGY (PSI) SCALE

We are interested in the various ways of thinking about mental illness and some related social problems. We are trying to get answers from various groups in different parts of the country. The groups will include the general public as well as those of you who have had direct experience with hospitalized patients, i.e., nurses, attendants, and doctors.

The best answer to each statement below is your *personal opinion.* We have tried to cover many different points of view. You may find yourself agreeing strongly with some of the statements, disagreeing just as strongly with others.

Mark each statement in the left margin according to how much you agree or disagree with it. Please mark every one. Write +1, +2, +3, or —1, —2, —3, depending on how you feel in each case.

+1	I AGREE A LITTLE	—1	I DISAGREE A LITTLE
+2	I AGREE PRETTY MUCH	—2	I DISAGREE PRETTY MUCH
+3	I AGREE VERY MUCH	—3	I DISAGREE VERY MUCH

I. Medical-Nonmedical Relations

*1 Staff meetings devoted to clinical case presentations should be open to all nonmedical as well as medical personnel.

2 Psychodynamic interpretations to hospital patients by nonpsychiatric personnel are likely to do more harm than good.

*3 A good deal needs to be done to decrease the status differences that exist in this hospital.

*4 A medical degree should not be a necessary prerequisite for practising intensive psychotherapy.

II. Treatment-therapy Emphasis

5 A personal psychoanalysis is by far the most valuable part of a psychiatrist's training.

* Items marked with an asterisk affirm the sociotherapy position; others affirm the psychotherapy position.

6 The use of the social milieu without specific treatments may help to get the patient over an acute episode, but it rarely effects any lasting improvement in the patient.

7 Those who take a mainly social milieu approach to hospital treatment of patients are for the most part unable to recognize and deal effectively with the deeper levels of personality.

8 The mental hospital psychiatrist should try to avoid informal social relations with his patients.

*9 The psychiatrist's treatment of hospital patients would be greatly improved if he spent more time than he now does learning to utilize the hospital as a therapeutic influence and less time on individual psychotherapy.

10 If a hospital like this one had to choose between somatic and psychotherapeutic treatments, it would do well to choose psychotherapy.

11 The most important consideration in administering a hospital like this one is to make sure that patients get enough psychotherapy.

*12 A psychoanalyst who devotes himself primarily to intensive, long-term analysis of a few is failing to meet his social responsibilities.

Medication attitudes EXHIBIT 3-28

Description. This scale was adapted from the Sherman (1960) sentence-completion scale by Gorham and Sherman (1961). The Sherman scale was designed to measure attitudes toward medication and is recommended by Gorham and Sherman for intensive study of attitudes of individual subjects. The adaptation is a 14-item, multiple-choice form which is regarded as more generally useful. We have chosen to include it rather than the original sentence-completion form because it is objectively scorable and should be more easily used by the nonexpert.

Each item consists of a stem, followed by four completing statements, one of which expresses a positive attitude toward taking medicine, one a negative attitude, one a neutral attitude, and one a statement concerning a side effect. A factor analysis of the 14 items showed that most of the variance was accounted for by the first centroid factor. Each of the items had a high correlation with this factor, with 13 coefficients exceeding .90.

Subjects. The pretest sample consisted of 76 patients at Waco and Perry Point VA hospitals. About 80 percent were able to complete the scale. The main test group consisted of 369 patients.

Response Mode. Subjects are instructed to respond to each statement by placing a check mark next to the one alternative that more nearly agrees with their feelings about medication.

Scoring. Positive choices are assigned 3 points; neutral and side effects choices, 2 points each; and negative effects, 1 point. The attitude score is the sum of the item scores. The theoretical range is from 14 to 42, with the higher score indicating the more favorable attitude toward medication.

Reliability. Test-retest reliability on a sample of 45 patients was reported to be .79.

Validity. The authors considered the high correlations between items and the first centroid factor as evidence that the total score on the scale is a valid single index of the patient's belief that medication will improve his condition. This conclusion, of course, rests upon the content of the items. The hypothesis that the attitude of patients toward medication has an important effect on treatment outcome was not upheld for chronic, apathetic schizophrenics but was significantly related to symptoms tending to characterize paranoid schizophrenics. The more paranoid the patient, the less favorable his attitude toward medication.

Comments. This is a potentially useful scale for the study of attitudes toward medication. However, it has not been used with normal persons and may not stand up for such populations. Gorham and Lasky (1962) used it with some success in a study of depressives in 32 hospitals, although a significant relationship was found between attitude and treatment effect only for the placebo group. Further studies are badly needed.

EXHIBIT 3-28

MEDICATION ATTITUDES

Instructions: On these pages are the beginnings of sentences and four possible ways you can finish each sentence. They all concern medication you and other patients have been receiving. Please read each sentence and place a check mark next to the *one* statement that most nearly agrees with the way you feel about medication. Although more than one statement may apply, check only the *one* that is closest to your feelings about medication.

Complete the following example and then continue:

Medication
______ A. has something to do with sports.
______ B. means getting medicine.
______ C. is a term used in law.
______ D. is the same as education.

1 Since I started taking medication
______ A. I have been getting pills. *(I)
______ B. I feel sleepy. (S)
______ C. I feel worse. (N)
______ D. This is a hospital. (I)

* Numbers in parentheses after each alternative indicate the type of attitude expressed. P indicates a positive response; N, a negative response; I, an indifferent or neutral response; and S, an expression of side effects.

Reference: D. R. Gorham and L. J. Sherman. The relation of attitude toward medication to treatment outcomes in chemotherapy. *Amer. J. Psychiat.*, 1961, 117, 830–832. Items obtained from authors and published with their permission.

2 I take medicine because

_______ A. I am forced to take it. (N)

_______ B. I want to get well. (P)

_______ C. I want to increase weight. (S)

_______ D. This is a hospital. (I)

3 Sometimes medication

_______ A. makes me sicker. (N)

_______ B. needs water to get it down. (I)

_______ C. helps me relax. (P)

_______ D. makes me dizzy. (S)

4 When I take my medication

_______ A. I stand in line. (I)

_______ B. I feel better. (P)

_______ C. I feel drowsy. (S)

_______ D. I feel worse. (N)

5 I feel that medication

_______ A. gives me a desire to get well. (P)

_______ B. is a part of hospital treatment. (I)

_______ C. does me no good. (N)

_______ D. makes me tired. (S)

6 With medication

_______ A. I drink water. (I)

_______ B. I feel worse. (N)

_______ C. I feel dizzy. (S)

_______ D. I feel better. (P)

7 Because of medication

_______ A. I do not feel well. (N)

_______ B. I feel better. (P)

_______ C. I come back to the ward. (I)

_______ D. I am drowsy. (S)

8 The fact I get medication

_______ A. helps me feel better. (P)

_______ B. means the nurse gives it to me. (I)

_______ C. makes my eyes blurry. (S)

_______ D. does not help me. (N)

9 The main thing about medication is that

_______ A. I take it three times a day. (I)

_______ B. it makes me feel worse. (N)

_______ C. it makes me thirsty. (S)

_______ D. it helps me get well. (P)

10 Right after taking my medication

_______ A. I feel groggy. (S)

_______ B. I leave the ward. (I)

_______ C. I feel sicker than before. (N)

_______ D. I feel better. (P)

11 Medication
_______ A. is necessary to a hospital. (I)
_______ B. is good for me. (P)
_______ C. makes me sleepy. (S)
_______ D. is of no value. (N)

12 Without the medication
_______ A. I am nervous and upset. (N)
_______ B. I feel fine. (P)
_______ C. there are no pills. (I)
_______ D. I am not so apt to get dizzy or sleepy. (S)

13 I take medication because
_______ A. it makes me sleepy. (S)
_______ B. I want to get better. (P)
_______ C. it is forced on me. (N)
_______ D. it is on the ward. (I)

14 My own feeling about taking medication is that I
_______ A. like to take it very much. (P)
_______ B. like to take it a little. (S)
_______ C. dislike to take it a little. (I)
_______ D. dislike to take it very much. (N)

ATTITUDES RELATED TO PRACTICES IN ECONOMICS

Social practices related to economic conditions are of greater interest during periods of economic depression when problems of earning a living are of paramount concern. It is no surprise, therefore, that few scales have been constructed in this category in recent years. Three scales are described that relate to economics: the Attitude toward Earning a Living Scale, the Attitude toward Work Relief as a Solution to the Financial Depression Scale, and the Attitude toward Farming Scale.

Attitude toward earning a living EXHIBIT 3-29

Description. This scale was constructed by Hinckley and Hinckley (1939) in connection with a study of the effects of a work relief program on attitudes. Approximately 800 statements were collected by reviewing work relief literature and by asking a number of persons to state their own opinions about earning a living. These were edited to 188 statements, which were scaled by the Thurstone method of equal-appearing intervals. Items were sorted by 250 judges working in groups of 12 to 15 persons. After discarding judges who appeared to be careless, 217 sortings were used to compute scale and Q values. After discarding items with large Q values, 27 items were selected to provide an even distribution from the lowest to the highest scale value. Q values of items in the final scale ranged from 0.19 to 1.26.

Subjects. The subjects used for the scaling procedure were 250 students in the summer session at the University of Florida.

Response Mode. Subjects respond to each item by placing a check mark to indicate agreement with the statement, a cross to indicate disagreement, and a question mark to indicate indecision.

Scoring. The attitude score is the median of the scale values of all items with which the subject indicates agreement. A high score indicates a favorable attitude toward personal responsibility for earning a living, whereas a low score indicates a favorable attitude toward dependence on others for a living.

Reliability. Split-half reliability was found to be .90 (E. D. Hinckley, private communication, 1964).

Validity. The method of selecting items suggests content validity of the scale, but no other evidence of validity is available.

Comments. This scale is a typical Thurstone-type scale, having adequate reliability and scanty evidence of validity. The referent of the attitude measured probably is not very salient for most of the present-day population of the United States, because of the healthy economic situation. Scale values should be recomputed before using this scale.

EXHIBIT 3-29

ATTITUDE TOWARD EARNING A LIVING

This is a study of attitudes toward earning a living. On this and the following page you will find twenty-seven statements expressing different attitudes toward the subjects.

Put a check mark (√) if you **agree** with the statement.
Put a cross (X) if you **disagree** with the statement.

If you cannot decide about a statement, you may mark it with a question mark.

This is not an examination. People differ in their opinions about what is right and wrong in this issue.

Please indicate your own attitude by a check mark when you agree and a cross when you disagree.

Scale Value

4.17 1 When I am trying to get a job, I think more about my rights as an individual than my duty to earn a living.

Scale Value		
10.24	2	The highest responsibility a man has is towards his job—his earning a living.
1.40	3	There is not enough work to go around; therefore I'll let the government feed me.
3.94	4	The responsibility of making a living should not weigh on a person's shoulders so much that he has no time for anything else.
6.58	5	I am trying to hold my job.
0.19	6	The world owes me a living.
8.99	7	The right thing to do is to work hard, earn your own living and not expect to have what you can't pay for.
4.56	8	My dream is for a job combining a minimum amount of labor with a maximum amount of wage.
9.70	9	A man should do all in his power to earn his own living.
0.62	10	It pays to do nothing and depend on the community for a living.
3.39	11	I'd never let earning a living greatly warp my life.
7.00	12	I want to work to keep the family out of debt.
4.99	13	I always have made my own living, but my responsibility in that matter is weakening.
1.80	14	My inability during the last few years to earn a living has made me firmly resolve that I will never waste any time trying to earn a living.
10.43	15	The first and most important duty of every man is to earn a living.
5.70	16	I have resigned myself to earning a living.
0.94	17	Work is something to be avoided if possible.
7.42	18	Since I have a family to support, I am never lazy.
5.44	19	Sometimes I think I want to earn my own living and sometimes I doubt it.
2.97	20	I have lost faith with the creed that makes me personally responsible for my own living.
8.55	21	You should earn your living by honest toil.
2.19	22	I never worry about material things such as food and clothing.
7.74	23	The man who helps himself need never worry.
9.30	24	We owe it to the very principles of democracy on which our country is founded to earn a living.
2.45	25	Being idle has made me want to keep on being idle.
6.07	26	I don't mind supporting myself.
8.20	27	I claim the right to work and share in the economic benefits of that work.

Attitude toward work relief as a solution to the financial depression EXHIBIT 3-30

Description. This is another scale developed by Hinckley and Hinckley (1939) in connection with the work relief program referred to in the preceding section. The method of construction was the method of equal-appearing intervals. A pool of 189 statements was collected and sorted by 250 judges. After excluding "careless" subjects, 214 sortings were retained and analyzed. Twenty-five items were selected for the final scale. Q values ranged from 0.19 to 0.79.

Subjects. Subjects were 250 students in the summer session at the University of Florida.

Response Mode. The respondent is asked to place a check mark beside each statement with which he agrees, a cross beside each statement with which he disagrees, and a question mark if he is unable to decide.

Scoring. The attitude score is the median of the scale values of all items agreed with by the respondent. A high score indicates a favorable attitude toward the work relief program.

Reliability. Split-half reliability was .91 (E. D. Hinckley, private communication, 1964).

Validity. The method of selecting the items suggests that the scale has content validity, but no other evidence is presented by the authors.

Comments. The work relief scale is even more outdated than the Attitude toward Earning a Living Scale; however, it may become more salient as the poverty program develops. Nevertheless, the prospective user should not only recompute the scale values, but also determine whether or not the respondents hold *any* attitude toward a work relief program. The scale might be useful in studies which attempt to develop attitudes experimentally.

EXHIBIT 3-30

ATTITUDE TOWARD WORK RELIEF AS A SOLUTION TO THE FINANCIAL DEPRESSION

This is a study of attitudes toward work relief as a solution to the financial depression. On this and the following page you will find twenty-five statements expressing different attitudes toward the subject.

Put a check mark (√) if you **agree** with the statement.
Put a cross (X) if you **disagree** with the statement.

If you cannot decide about a statement, you may mark it with a question mark.

This is not an examination. People differ in their opinions about what is right and wrong in this issue.

Please indicate *your own attitude* by a check mark when you agree and by a cross when you disagree.

Scale Value		
7.82	1	The work relief program has put industry in a position to plan more confidently for the future.

Scale Value		
6.91	2	The work relief program is being used as a temporary expedient to care for the worker until private business rallies.
3.57	3	The high wages of the work relief program have a tendency to harm legitimate business.
4.82	4	The work relief program is a last resort, but its success is doubtful.
0.46	5	The work relief program is no help; it should be abolished at once.
8.18	6	The work relief program is a valuable contribution to economic revival because it has increased purchasing power.
4.48	7	There is something wrong with the work relief program but I don't know what it is.
2.82	8	The work relief program favors the continued growth of the weaker element. This cannot help recovery.
0.00	9	Relief work is the greatest catastrophe that has hit the country.
2.40	10	The work relief program will retard, rather than expedite return of prosperity.
5.50	11	The result of the work relief program is uncertain. Recovery will be neither helped nor hindered by the work relief program.
3.22	12	Emergency methods, such as the work relief program, do not lay sure foundations for recovery.
1.27	13	It would be a good idea if all relief measures and procedures ceased immediately.
6.07	14	The usefulness of the work relief program is at best limited.
10.23	15	The work relief program is directly and positively ending the depression.
7.37	16	The work relief program will keep the country alive and give people time to prepare themselves for more effective action.
8.61	17	The work relief program is lifting prices out of their despairing ruts to normal levels.
1.63	18	Work relief is costing so much it is menacing our governmental and economic structure.
9.02	19	With the work relief program, the tide of recovery is rising unmistakably.
4.10	20	There is little indication that the work relief program will be successful in aiding business recovery.
9.85	21	We shall get for our money spent on the work relief program nothing less than national recovery.
2.00	22	The work relief program will destroy the kind of economic individualism and political democracy upon which this country was built.
6.53	23	The work relief program holds out the prospect for some incidental improvement in purchasing power and demand for goods.
9.38	24	The work relief program is bringing us swiftly toward normal conditions.
10.61	25	The work relief program is the greatest driving force toward recovery.

Attitude toward farming *EXHIBIT 3-31*

Description. The farming attitude scale (Myster, 1944) attempts to measure two aspects of the attitude toward farming: farming as a vocation and farming as a way of life. The scores on the two aspects correlated .672 (.839 when corrected for attenuation). Since this correlation approximates the reliability of the whole scale, it is doubtful that separation of the farming attitude into the two components is justified. The scale consists of 45 items cast in the Likert format, but no data concerning selection of items was presented by Myster.

Subjects. Three samples of subjects were used in Myster's study. These were 36 junior home economic students in the first course in rural sociology at Virginia State College; 56 Virginia State College students of agriculture; and 206 Iowa State College students of agriculture.

Response Mode. A five-alternative response mode is used. Subjects respond to each item by circling a letter or letters according to the following code: SA, strongly agree; A, agree; U, undecided; D, disagree; SD, strongly disagree.

Scoring. Each item response is scored on a 1 to 5 scale, with the higher score indicating the more favorable attitude toward farming. For the positive items, a score of 5 is assigned to the SA response, a 4 to the A response, a 3 to the U response, a 2 to the D response, and a 1 to the SD response. This scoring is reversed for the negative items. The attitude score is the sum of the item scores. The theoretical range is from 45 to 225.

Reliability. Split-half reliability was found to be .80 (corrected to .89), based upon the responses of 36 college students.

Validity. Validity was demonstrated by showing that students in two colleges of agriculture (Ns = 56 and 206) scored significantly higher ($p < .01$) than home economics students ($N = 36$). Mean scores on the farming scale were as follows: home economics students, 148.8; students at Virginia State Agricultural College, 171.6; and students at Iowa State Agricultural College, 180.8.

Comments. As a whole, the farming scale has acceptable reliability and some evidence of validity. More evidence of the method of selecting items would be very useful in evaluating the scale. As suggested earlier, use of the subscales cannot be recommended for most purposes, but they might be worthwhile for studies of attitude multiplexity.

EXHIBIT 3-31

ATTITUDE TOWARD FARMING

What are your opinions of the following statements? Your answer is correct if it expresses your true opinion. This is not a test and you are not to be graded. DO NOT OMIT ANY ITEM. In each case encircle the letter or letters which represent your own ideas about each statement.

SA—strongly agree; A—agree; U—undecided; D—disagree; SD—strongly disagree

1	Farming is a pleasant vocation.	SA	A	U	D	SD
*2	I can't say I'm wild about farming.	SA	A	U	D	SD
*3	Farm work is drudgery.	SA	A	U	D	SD
4	I would enjoy working with plants and animals.	SA	A	U	D	SD
*5	A farmer has more worries than do persons engaged in most other occupations.	SA	A	U	D	SD
*6	As a life's work, farming would be terrible.	SA	A	U	D	SD
7	Work on the farm is really enjoyable.	SA	A	U	D	SD
*8	The disadvantages of farming outweigh its advantages.	SA	A	U	D	SD
*9	Farming requires less intelligence than most other occupations.	SA	A	U	D	SD
10	The vocation of farming has its drawbacks, but I like it.	SA	A	U	D	SD
*11	Farming involves too many distasteful tasks.	SA	A	U	D	SD
*12	I have never wanted to be a farmer.	SA	A	U	D	SD
13	Farming is fascinating work.	SA	A	U	D	SD
*14	Farming requires less education than most other vocations.	SA	A	U	D	SD
15	I like farming well enough to make it my life's work.	SA	A	U	D	SD
*16	Farming is a monotonous vocation.	SA	A	U	D	SD
17	I have always wanted to be a farmer.	SA	A	U	D	SD
*18	Living on a farm is just too much hard work.	SA	A	U	D	SD
19	The advantages of farming far outweigh the disadvantages.	SA	A	U	D	SD
*20	Farming is uninteresting work.	SA	A	U	D	SD
*21	The average farmer enjoys farming more than I would.	SA	A	U	D	SD
22	Everything considered, I could be happier farming than engaging in any other occupation.	SA	A	U	D	SD
*23	Farming tends to isolate a person from the rest of the world.	SA	A	U	D	SD
*24	Farming yields less satisfaction than most other occupations.	SA	A	U	D	SD
25	The farm is the best place for young people.	SA	A	U	D	SD
*26	About all that can be said for farming is that it furnishes a means of existing	SA	A	U	D	SD
27	I could be satisfied to spend my life on the farm.	SA	A	U	D	SD
*28	Social well-being is impossible of attainment on the farm.	SA	A	U	D	SD
29	Farming would give me a great deal of pleasure.	SA	A	U	D	SD
*30	I feel that I would be doing my children an injustice by living on a farm.	SA	A	U	D	SD
*31	I dislike the farm with its many inconveniences.	SA	A	U	D	SD
32	Farming yields more satisfaction than most other vocations.	SA	A	U	D	SD
*33	Farming offers insufficient opportunity for contacts with people.	SA	A	U	D	SD
34	I feel that farm families as a whole are an interesting class of people.	SA	A	U	D	SD

* Items marked with an asterisk state a negative or unfavorable attitude toward farming.

*35	Farming has more social disadvantages than most other occupations.	SA	A	U	D	SD
*36	Farming deadens a person's ambitions.	SA	A	U	D	SD
37	I like farming as a way of life.	SA	A	U	D	SD
*38	On an average, the standard of living of farmers is below that of other persons in the United States.	SA	A	U	D	SD
39	The farm is a wonderful place to live.	SA	A	U	D	SD
*40	Farming tends to reduce one's social standing.	SA	A	U	D	SD
*41	For me life on a farm would be extremely dull.	SA	A	U	D	SD
42	The farmer enjoys many satisfactions which the average person never realizes.	SA	A	U	D	SD
*43	I think I would have less fun living on a farm than in town.	SA	A	U	D	SD
*44	Farming deprives one's children of an adequate education.	SA	A	U	D	SD
45	The independence of farm life appeals to me.	SA	A	U	D	SD

GENERALIZED SCALES TO MEASURE ATTITUDES TOWARD SOCIAL PRACTICES

In this section we will describe some generalized procedures for measuring attitudes toward social practices. These procedures include Remmers' master scales and the semantic differential. The semantic differential is described in Chapter 2. It is more general than Remmers' scales, since the same items may be used to measure any attitude, whereas Remmers' scales are designed to measure attitude toward classes of objects. The semantic differential has been used to measure attitude toward retirement (Kogan and Wallach, 1961), desegregation (Steiner and Field, 1960), dancing as a teaching aid and unusual music as a teaching aid (Asher and Evans, 1959), and similar social practices.

Generalized scales of the Remmers type have been constructed for measuring attitude toward any practice, toward any homemaking activity, and toward any vocation. Recently, Remmers (1960) edited these scales, reduced the number of items per scale to 17, and published them commercially. Since the data regarding construction of the scales were obtained using the longer forms, these are given in the following sections. Items selected by Remmers for the shorter forms are marked with an asterisk in Exhibits 3-32, 3-33, and 3-34.

Attitude toward any practice *EXHIBIT 3-32*

Description. The scale to measure attitude toward any practice was developed by Bues (1934) using the method of equal-appearing intervals. Items were selected from an original pool of 150 items. There are two 37-item forms, matched for scale and Q values as closely as possible. Q values ranged from 0.5 to 2.2 for items in Form A, and from 0.5 to 2.0 for items in Form B. Items and scale values are given in Exhibit 3-32, where the items making up the Remmers short form are marked with an asterisk.

Subjects. The nature of the sample used for scaling items was not given. Subjects for validation were four groups of 25 persons each, drawn from a fraternity, a sorority, a YWCA, and a Sunday school.

Response Mode. Subjects are asked to place a plus mark before each statement with which they agree with reference to the particular practice under consideration.

Scoring. The attitude score is the median of the scale values of the items marked to show agreement. A high score indicates a favorable attitude toward the practice.

Reliability. Bues did not report evidence on reliability, but Remmers (1960) reports reliability coefficients ranging from .71 to .92.

Validity. The scale was validated by the known-groups method, using drinking and petting as specific referents. It was expected that the fraternities should have the most favorable attitude toward these practices, sororities next most favorable, and YWCA and Sunday school groups the least favorable attitude toward these practices. For petting, the mean scores were 6.70 for the fraternity group, 5.26 for the sorority, 4.84 for the YWCA, and 4.06 for the Sunday school group. For drinking, the corresponding means were 6.00, 5.17, 4.22, and 3.42.

Comments. This scale appears to have adequate reliability, and the limited evidence concerning validity is encouraging. The criticisms directed toward generalized scales discussed in Chapter 2 are relevant to it and should be considered carefully by the potential user of the scale.

EXHIBIT 3-32

ATTITUDE TOWARD ANY PRACTICE

Directions: Following is a list of statements about practices. Place a plus sign (+) before each statement with which you agree with reference to the practice or practices listed. Your score will in no way affect your grade in any course.

Form A

Scale value		
11.0	1	Is better than anything else.
10.8	2	I like this practice better than anything I can think of.
10.8	3	Is profitable to everyone.
10.6	4	Is very worth while.
*10.0	5	Has an irresistible attraction for me.
9.8	6	I enjoy this practice.

* Items marked with an asterisk constitute the Remmers short form.

Reprinted with permission from Bues, H. W. The construction and validation of a scale to measure attitude toward any practice. *Purdue Univer. Studies in Higher Educ. XXVI,* 1934, 35, 64–67. Copies of the short form may be obtained from University Book Store, 360 State Street, West Lafayette, Indiana.

Scale value		
9.8	**7**	Is liked by almost everyone.
*9.7	**8**	I like this practice too well to give it up.
9.5	**9**	Makes for happier living.
*9.2	**10**	Serves a good purpose.
*8.9	**11**	Develops co-operation.
*8.6	**12**	Should be appreciated by more people.
8.4	**13**	Is being accepted more and more as time goes on.
*8.1	**14**	Has advantages.
7.9	**15**	If this practice were used more it would develop into a good one.
*7.5	**16**	There is no reason for stopping this practice.
7.2	**17**	Is all right as a pastime.
7.0	**18**	I like this practice a little.
6.9	**19**	Is all right in some cases.
*6.8	**20**	Is all right in a few cases.
*6.0	**21**	My likes and dislikes for this practice are balanced.
*5.6	**22**	I dislike this practice but I do not object to others liking it.
*4.9	**23**	Isn't so bad but it is very boring.
4.5	**24**	Has limitations and defects.
4.4	**25**	I like many practices better than this one.
4.0	**26**	Has several disadvantages.
*3.8	**27**	Has several undesirable features.
3.4	**28**	Is disliked by many people.
*3.2	**29**	Should not be tolerated when there are so many better ones.
3.0	**30**	Is not endorsed by logical-minded persons.
*2.6	**31**	Life would be happier without this practice.
2.5	**32**	Cannot benefit anyone who has common sense.
*2.2	**33**	Is a waste of time and money.
*1.8	**34**	Accomplishes nothing worth while either for the individual or society.
1.4	**35**	Is sinful.
1.2	**36**	I hate this practice.
*1.0	**37**	Is the worst thing I know.

Form B

11.0	**1**	Is the best of all.
10.9	**2**	I like this practice better than any other.
10.8	**3**	Is my favorite.
10.4	**4**	Develops high ideals.
*10.1	**5**	Should be practiced by all Americans.
9.9	**6**	Is a benefit to mankind.
9.7	**7**	Is beneficial to almost everyone.
*9.7	**8**	Aids in bringing civilization to a higher level.
9.5	**9**	Is fundamental for good social life.
*9.2	**10**	Is endorsed by sensible people.
*8.9	**11**	Many things about this practice are essential to normal living.
*8.6	**12**	Keeps us from being "one-sided."
8.4	**13**	Has value.
*8.1	**14**	As a rule, is good.
7.9	**15**	Should be liked.
*7.7	**16**	Has more merit than demerit.
7.2	**17**	Is not boring.
7.0	**18**	Is endorsed by sane people.
6.9	**19**	Is liked only fairly well.

Scale value		
*6.8	20	I would enjoy this practice if it were changed somewhat.
*6.0	21	I am not against this practice but neither am I for it.
*5.9	22	Isn't absolutely bad but isn't good either.
*4.8	23	Is a little foolish.
*4.5	24	Has drawbacks.
4.5	25	I am not interested in this practice.
4.0	26	Benefits too few people.
*3.9	27	Has more disadvantages than advantages.
3.4	28	Is frowned upon by the average person.
*3.1	29	Is annoying.
3.0	30	Is frowned upon by intellectual people.
*2.6	31	We would be better off without this practice.
2.4	32	Is approved by only stupid people.
*2.2	33	Is not endorsed by sane people.
*1.9	34	Serves no purpose.
1.4	35	Is of no use to anyone.
1.2	36	Is unfit for anyone.
*1.0	37	I hate this practice worse than I hate anything else.

Attitude toward any home-making activity EXHIBIT 3-33

Description. Kellar (1934) developed this scale, using the usual Thurstone procedure. The scale is intended for use in measuring attitude toward any activity that might be carried out in the home, but the content of the items suggests that it may be more appropriate for use with girls than with boys. The final scale consisted of two 45-item forms, roughly matched for scale and Q values. The Q values ranged from 0.5 to 2.3 for items of Form A, and from 0.6 to 2.3 for items of Form B. Exhibit 3-33 gives the items and scale values for both forms. Items marked with an asterisk constitute the Remmers short form.

Subjects. The sample consisted of 320 persons, including seventh grade girls, high school pupils, college students, and housewives.

Response Mode. The subject is asked to check each item with which he agrees by placing a plus mark beside the statement.

Scoring. The attitude score is the median of the scale values of the items checked.

Reliability. The scale was administered to the sample of subjects with caring for children and meal preparation as specific referents. The correlation between the scores on the two forms was .816 (corrected to .90) when caring for children was the referent and .790 (corrected to .88) when meal preparation was the referent.

Validity. The scale was shown to discriminate among students and housewives in the expected direction. The manner of selecting the items may also be taken as evidence of validity.

Comments. The same comments made in connection with the preceding scale apply to the scale for measuring attitude toward any home-making activity.

EXHIBIT 3-33

ATTITUDE TOWARD ANY HOME-MAKING ACTIVITY

Directions: Following is a list of statements about home-making activities. Place a plus sign (+) before each statement with which you agree with reference to the activity or activities listed. Your score will in no way affect your grade in any course.

Form A

Scale value		
10.9	1	I like to do this better than anything else I can think of.
10.8	2	! could go without my meals and go on doing this for a long time.
10.7	3	The most lasting satisfactions in life come to me in doing this.
10.6	4	This is my hobby.
*10.2	5	I really enjoy doing this.
10.1	6	It is a pleasure to do this.
9.8	7	This is very interesting.
*9.6	8	The more I do this the better I like to do it.
9.5	9	I like to do this because it is very interesting.
9.4	10	I like to spend my spare time in learning more about this.
*9.2	11	The feeling of mastery this gives me makes it worth while to me.
9.1	12	I like to do this even though I think it is terribly hard.
*8.9	13	This task is character building.
*8.6	14	I think it is a good thing for a girl to know how to do this.
*8.2	15	This seems to be a satisfactory thing to do.
*7.8	16	I don't mind doing this because I know it is my place to do it.
7.4	17	I like to do this when I can do it just the way I want to.
7.3	18	It is pleasant to do this some of the time.
7.1	19	I don't think doing this would harm anyone.
7.0	20	I don't mind doing this if I can take my own sweet time at doing it.
*6.8	21	I don't mind doing this if someone helps me.
6.1	22	It all depends on the mood I'm in whether or not I like to do this.
*6.0	23	I haven't any definite like or dislike for doing this.
5.9	24	I could be much more interested in this than I am.
*5.4	25	This would be all right if it weren't for a few disagreeable things connected with it.
5.1	26	I don't like to do this when I'm anxious to do something else.
4.9	27	Some people like to do this, but more of them dislike it.
*4.8	28	I don't care much about doing this.

* The items marked with an asterisk constitute the Remmers short form.

Reprinted with permission from Kellar, B. The construction and validation of a scale for measuring attitude toward any home-making activity. *Purdue Univer. Studies in Higher Educ. XXVI*, 1934, 35, 47–63. Copyright 1960 by the Purdue Research Foundation. Copies of the short form may be obtained from University Book Store, 360 State Street, West Lafayette, Indiana.

Scale value		
4.5	**29**	This takes more time than it is worth.
4.4	**30**	This is not hard, yet I have taken a dislike to it.
4.0	**31**	I get tired of doing this.
3.9	**32**	I think this takes up too much time.
3.8	**33**	This seems to make one's time drag.
*3.7	**34**	There are many more disadvantages than advantages in doing this.
3.4	**35**	This makes me too tired.
3.2	**36**	This seems very monotonous to me.
*3.1	**37**	Anyone who does this must be lacking in ambition.
*2.7	**38**	This has no place in the modern world.
2.5	**39**	This is a waste of time.
*2.2	**40**	It makes me tired to even think of doing this.
2.1	**41**	When I have a home of my own, I'll never do this myself.
*1.8	**42**	I get angry every time anyone mentions doing this.
1.3	**43**	I have a feeling of hatred for this.
1.2	**44**	This is hard to do and I hate it.
*1.1	**45**	I think there is no worse job in the world than this.

Form B

Scale value		
10.9	**1**	I love to do this.
10.8	**2**	I adore doing this.
10.6	**3**	I wouldn't mind doing this seven days a week.
10.5	**4**	This fascinates me.
*10.2	**5**	I get great pleasure out of doing this.
10.0	**6**	This gives me a great deal of pleasure.
9.8	**7**	I like to do this.
*9.6	**8**	I do this quite a lot and enjoy it.
9.5	**9**	The more I do this, the better I like it.
9.4	**10**	My enthusiasm remains great all the time I am doing this.
*9.2	**11**	I feel as though I were a benefit to mankind while I am doing this.
9.1	**12**	I like to do this by myself.
*8.9	**13**	I like to do this because it is appreciated by other people.
*8.8	**14**	I think everyone should know how to do this.
*8.1	**15**	I like to do this pretty well.
*7.8	**16**	I like to do this because it isn't so exerting as other tasks.
7.4	**17**	This has its merits.
7.3	**18**	I think I should learn to like to do this.
7.1	**19**	I like to do this when I'm in the mood.
7.0	**20**	I like this better when someone helps me.
*6.8	**21**	I like this only fairly well.
6.6	**22**	I enjoy only parts of this.
*6.0	**23**	My likes and dislikes for this about balance one another.
5.9	**24**	It is all right to do this when there is nothing else to do.
*5.8	**25**	Someday I might begin liking this.
5.0	**26**	I like to do many things better than this.
4.9	**27**	Many people do not like to do this.
*4.8	**28**	This is all right, but I wouldn't want to do it.
4.6	**29**	I dislike doing this if there is no one to help me.
4.1	**30**	This isn't what it is cracked up to be.
4.0	**31**	Why should one work on this when there are so many more pleasant things to do?

Scale value		
3.9	**32**	Quite a number of things about this annoy me.
3.8	**33**	This must be done, but why should I have to do it?
*3.7	**34**	To me this is more or less boring.
3.5	**35**	When I do this, it seems as though I'll never get done.
3.2	**36**	This is too hard to do.
*3.0	**37**	I get out of doing this whenever I can.
*2.7	**38**	This is a useless way to spend one's time.
2.5	**39**	This does one more harm than good.
*2.2	**40**	This benefits no one.
2.0	**41**	Only a very stupid person would enjoy doing this.
*1.8	**42**	I wish I had never heard of this.
1.7	**43**	There is nothing about this that I could ever like.
1.2	**44**	I certainly hate to do this.
*1.1	**45**	I absolutely refuse to do this.

Attitude toward any occupation *EXHIBIT 3-34*

Description. The scale to measure attitude toward any occupation was constructed by Miller (1934*a*). The Thurstone method of equal-appearing intervals was used. From the original list of 159 items, 90 items were selected and divided into two forms of 45 statements each. Q values ranged from 0.5 to 2.2 for items of Form A, and from 0.5 to 2.1 for items of Form B. Items and scale values are given in Exhibit 3-34.

Subjects. The subjects for this study were 160 instructors and students at Purdue University.

Response Mode. The respondent places a plus sign before each item with which he agrees, with respect to the occupation under consideration.

Scoring. The attitude score is the median of the scale values of the items with which the subject agrees. The higher the score, the more favorable the attitude toward the occupation in question.

Reliability. Reliability was given only in terms of P.E. of the median, the measure used by Thurstone. This was found to be .07. Note that this is an estimate of the reliability of the scale values rather than reliability of the whole scale. Remmers (1960) reports reliabilities ranging from .71 to .92.

Validity. No evidence of validity was given other than that implied by the method of item selection. In a later study (Miller, 1934*b*), scale scores with teaching as the referent were found to correlate .437 with scores on a scale designed specifically to measure attitudes toward teaching (see Exhibit 3-11).

Comments. The usual comments about generalized scales apply here also. This scale seems to be somewhat less valid than others considered in this section.

EXHIBIT 3-34

ATTITUDE TOWARD ANY OCCUPATION

Directions: Following is a list of statements about occupations. Place a plus sign (+) before each statement with which you agree with reference to the occupation or occupations listed. Your score will in no way affect your grade in any course.

Form A

Scale value		
10.4	1	I'd rather work at this occupation than eat.
*10.3	2	I love to do this work.
10.1	3	The most lasting satisfactions in life come to one in this work.
9.8	4	This work fascinates me.
*9.7	5	I wouldn't mind working seven days a week on this job.
9.5	6	This work is more enjoyable than most play.
9.4	7	I like this work too well to give it up.
9.3	8	This work is one of my favorite pastimes.
*9.2	9	This work gives me a great deal of pleasure.
9.1	10	I feel as though I am of benefit to mankind in this work.
9.0	11	This occupation offers one a chance to put his own ideas into operation.
*8.9	12	This occupation will mean a great deal to me when I am old.
8.6	13	This is a good job.
*8.4	14	This job will bring benefits to everyone who does it.
8.3	15	This job has several very decided advantages over most other jobs.
*8.1	16	This job is undoubtedly worth having.
7.9	17	Many things about this work are advantageous.
*7.6	18	This vocation is a good pastime.
7.5	19	This vocation has its merits.
6.8	20	This job is good enough for me.
6.7	21	This work seems to be satisfactory.
*6.5	22	This is a pleasant vocation some of the time.
*6.1	23	I don't think this work would harm anyone.
*5.5	24	The advantages and disadvantages of this work about balance each other.
*4.7	25	This job is all right when no others are available.
4.6	26	This work could be much more interesting.
4.2	27	This vocation is all right, but I wouldn't want it.
4.0	28	Some people like this work, but more of them dislike it.
3.9	29	Part of the time I enjoy this job; most of the time I don't.
3.7	30	To me this vocation is more or less boring.
*3.6	31	Many people do not like this work.
3.4	32	Why should one work on this job when so many other jobs are better?

* Items marked with an asterisk constitute the Remmers short form.

Reprinted with permission from Miller, H. E. The construction and evaluation of a scale of attitudes toward occupations. *Purdue Univer. Studies in Higher Educ. XXVI*, 1934, 35, 68–76. Copyright 1960 by the Purdue Research Foundation. Copies of the short form may be obtained from University Book Store, 360 State Street, West Lafayette, Indiana.

Scale value		
3.3	**33**	An intelligent person wouldn't be satisfied in this occupation very long.
*3.1	**34**	The advantages of this work will never outweigh the disadvantages.
2.8	**35**	There are many more disadvantages than advantages in this job.
*2.7	**36**	I have no desire to do this kind of work.
2.4	**37**	One cannot keep up a decent standard of living in this occupation.
*2.1	**38**	I would be better off without this job.
1.8	**39**	The less I see of this occupation, the better I like it.
*1.7	**40**	Only a very stupid person could be satisfied with this work.
1.3	**41**	This vocation can be buried for all I care.
1.1	**42**	The best one can hope for from this occupation is a long life which will end one in the poorhouse.
*1.0	**43**	I have a feeling of hatred for this vocation.
0.7	**44**	Under no conditions would I like this work.
0.6	**45**	This is the worst occupation in the country.

Form B

10.4	**1**	This is the ideal vocation for a life work.
*10.2	**2**	No matter what happens, this job always comes first.
10.0	**3**	I like this work better than any other I can think of.
9.8	**4**	Self-respect, social approval, reasonable pay and hours, and steady employment—these are the advantages in this occupation.
*9.7	**5**	This job is my hobby.
9.5	**6**	! really enjoy this work.
9.4	**7**	I always wanted this kind of a vocation.
9.3	**8**	I would enjoy this work even if I were independent.
*9.2	**9**	I can think of few jobs I would rather have than this one.
9.1	**10**	There are only a few vocations I would rather have than this one.
9.0	**11**	Anyone who dislikes this work is a fool.
*8.9	**12**	This work will bring one greater respect from both oneself and others than most other jobs.
8.6	**13**	This vocation develops a good character in one.
*8.4	**14**	Everyone should like this vocation.
8.3	**15**	This vocation is interesting.
*8.2	**16**	Most people like this kind of work.
7.9	**17**	This work develops a favorable attitude toward work in general.
*7.6	**18**	I can think of a lot more advantages than disadvantages in this work.
7.4	**19**	At least I'm not worn out when I come home from this work at night.
6.8	**20**	I like this occupation only fairly well.
6.7	**21**	This work could be made beneficial to one.
*6.5	**22**	The advantages of this vocation slightly outweigh the disadvantages.
*6.0	**23**	I enjoy only parts of this work.
*5.5	**24**	My likes and dislikes for this work about balance one another.
*4.7	**25**	There are a few unpleasant things connected with this work.
4.6	**26**	This work would be all right if it weren't for a few disagreeable things.
4.3	**27**	There are a few more disadvantages to this work than there are advantages.
4.0	**28**	I could get along without this job.
3.9	**29**	There are many occupations I like better than this one.
3.7	**30**	This used to be a good job, but not any more.

Scale value		
*3.5	**31**	Why should I do this when there are so many more pleasant vocations?
3.4	**32**	Quite a number of things about this job annoy me.
3.3	**33**	Anyone who does this work must be unambitious.
*3.2	**34**	I do not care about this job.
2.9	**35**	After the age of 45 one is useless in this occupation.
*2.7	**36**	There are too many undesirable qualities about this occupation.
2.4	**37**	This occupation does one more harm than good.
*2.1	**38**	I hate to think of Monday morning coming and having to come back to this job.
1.8	**39**	This occupation is a waste of time.
*1.7	**40**	This work has no place in the modern world.
1.3	**41**	More people hate this work than any other.
1.2	**42**	This occupation is all the bunk.
*1.0	**43**	This work is disliked by everyone.
0.7	**44**	I wouldn't take this job under any circumstances.
0.6	**45**	I would refuse this work even if I were starving.

SUMMARY

Our survey of scales to measure attitudes toward social practices revealed many scales that were so poorly developed that inclusion in this volume did not seem appropriate. We have included some scales for which there is little standardization data available, simply because they were the best ones found for measuring the attitude in question. The greatest deficiency was a lack of evidence concerning validity, perhaps because such evidence is very difficult to obtain.

The acceptability of the scales given in this chapter varies widely and in some cases, at least, will depend upon the outcome of further research.

CHAPTER 4

social issues and problems

All groups form norms regarding behaviors which are related to the goals of the group. An attitudinal or behavioral area becomes a problem for a group (1) when such norms are inconsistent, contradictory, or ambiguous, (2) when there are no available normative specifications to apply to a given behavioral area, or (3) when norm violation is sufficiently prevalent to threaten the integrity and continuity of the group. Social issues arise from similar conditions, but issues are further characterized by the fact that there are adherents to at least two different viewpoints regarding the area in question. As commentary, it seems worth noting that social issues may arise regarding practically anything from haircuts to beheading. Therefore, referents with which the reader is concerned and which are not found in this chapter should be sought in appropriate other chapters. For example, divorce has been treated in this book as a social practice rather than an issue, because of its prevalence and general acceptance in our society. This chapter largely contains scales which have as their referents events and situations which have been treated specifically as social issues or problems by the constructor or users of the scale.

ATTITUDES RELATED TO FAMILY ISSUES AND PROBLEMS

In this section are scales designed to measure attitudes toward such family-related issues and problems as birth control, effects of motion picture viewing, and the menstruation in girls. Birth control is contained in this section because it is pragmatically a family concern, although it might also be considered a religious or politico-legal problem.

Attitude toward birth control EXHIBIT 4-1

Description. This 20-item scale was developed by Wang and Thurstone (1930), who provided two equivalent forms. The items question the value of birth control on both moral and pragmatic bases. The range of Q values for these items is not available.

Subjects. The sample on which the scale was constructed is unknown.

Response Mode. The person is asked to respond to every item by placing a check mark beside those with which he agrees, a double check mark beside those with which he emphatically agrees, and a cross beside those with which he disagrees. This is somewhat different from the usual Thurstone procedure.

Scoring. The person's score is the median of the scale values of all items he double-checked. If he double-checked none of the items, it is the median of the scale values of the items he single-checked. A high score indicates an acceptant attitude.

Reliability. Likert et al. (1934) report reliability coefficients ranging from .62 to .93 for this scale. The range reported by Lorge (1939) is .68 to .84, and Ferguson (1944) reports a range from .72 to .84.

Validity. As with other Thurstone scales, this scale may be assumed to possess high content validity. Diggory (1953) reports a correlation of +.56 between this scale and the Thurstone scale of attitude toward the church ($N = 75$ males). Based on a sample of 103 females, he reports a correlation of +.28 between these two scales. As birth control is a religious issue, these correlations may be taken as evidence of some construct validity.

Comments. This scale possesses adequate validity and reliability. In fact, reliability coefficients for this scale are about average for Thurstone scales. Although devised some years ago, none of the items is dated. The somewhat different response mode on this scale introduces an intensity measure which might allow some investigation of the relation of position to intensity of attitude. It should not be expected, however, that the intensity measure on individual items will necessarily correlate with the score achieved by the computation of the median of items endorsed. Such correlations would reflect monotonic items, and the items in Thurstone scales are nonmonotonic. Readers interested in other studies using this scale may wish to consult Carlson (1933, 1934), Ferguson (1939), and Smith (1942, 1946).

EXHIBIT 4-1

ATTITUDE TOWARD BIRTH CONTROL

Put a check mark (√) if you agree with the statement. Put a double check (√√) if you agree emphatically. Put a cross (×) if you disagree with the statement.

Form A

Scale Value		
7.6	1	Birth control is a legitimate health measure.
7.4	2	Birth control is necessary for women who must help earn a living.
3.3	3	The practice of birth control may be injurious physically, mentally, or morally.
10.5	4	We simply must have birth control.
0.0	5	The practice of birth control is equivalent to murder.
5.4	6	Birth control has both advantages and disadvantages.
9.8	7	Only a fool can oppose birth control.
8.0	8	Birth control increases the happiness of married life.
2.3	9	Decency forbids the use of birth control.
0.9	10	Birth control should be absolutely prohibited.
9.6	11	Birth control is the only solution to many of our social problems.
1.7	12	Birth control reduces the marital relation to the level of vice.
6.6	13	Birth control has nothing to do with morality.
8.3	14	Birth control information should be available to everybody.
3.6	15	Birth control is morally wrong in spite of its possible benefits.
9.2	16	Uncontrolled reproduction leads to overpopulation, social unrest, and war.
1.1	17	Birth control is race suicide.
5.8	18	People should be free to do whatever they wish about birth control.
2.8	19	The practice of birth control evades man's duty to propagate the race.
4.5	20	The slight benefits of birth control hardly justify it.

Form B

Scale Value		
8.7	1	Uncontrolled reproduction is one fundamental cause of crime.
7.7	2	The distribution of birth control information should be legalized.
6.8	3	Scientific methods of birth control are not harmful.
10.8	4	The only salvation of the race is birth control.
9.3	5	Birth control information should be included in every person's education.
4.8	6	Birth control information should not be generally available.
1.3	7	The practice of birth control should be punishable by law.
4.1	8	Birth control is unnecessary from the standpoint of maternal health.

Scale Value		
2.1	9	The practice of birth control is immoral.
0.8	10	There is no justification for birth control under any conditions.
9.7	11	There should be no restriction whatever on the distribution of birth control information.
3.1	12	Birth control is an expression of individual selfishness.
1.5	13	Birth control is unjustifiable extermination of life.
10.3	14	We should not only allow but enforce limitation in the size of families.
6.2	15	Birth control is not a moral issue.
2.6	16	Birth control violates the purpose of the marital relation.
3.5	17	Contraceptive methods injure women's health.
5.5	18	The birth control question has little social significance.
8.2	19	I believe in children of choice and not of chance.
6.4	20	Birth control is justifiable only in cases of poverty or poor health.

Birth control (scale BC) scale *EXHIBIT 4-2*

Description. This is a 22-item, Likert-type scale developed by Wilke (1934). Item no. 6 is the only item which is dated. This item refers to the depression and to current unemployment and might be salvaged by dropping the reference to the depression. In such a case, it would be necessary to reanalyze the item to ensure that it still functioned in a monotonic fashion.

Subjects. The sample was composed of 1,174 unidentified persons.

Response Mode. Persons circle one of five alternative responses: strongly agree, agree, undecided, disagree, and strongly disagree.

Scoring. The responses for positive items are weighted from 5 (strongly agree) to 1 (strongly disagree). These weights must be reversed for negative items, which are indicated in Exhibit 4-2. The person's score is the sum of the weighted alternatives which he circles. High scores indicate acceptant attitudes.

Reliability. Wilke (1934) reported a split-half reliability coefficient of .91 (based on an *N* of 61) and test-retest reliabilities ranging from .88 to .83, using a retest interval of three weeks and based on a sample of 1,174 persons.

Validity. All items have content validity (with the exception of the dated item, no. 6) with regard to moral and pragmatic reactions to birth control. The only other evidence of validity lies in the fact that the author obtained small changes in test scores in the expected direction as a result of experimental treatment.

Comments. This is a scale with good reliability and relatively inadequate evidence of validity. Item no. 6 should be altered or dropped out because of its reference to the depression era in the United States.

EXHIBIT 4-2

BIRTH CONTROL (SCALE BC) SCALE

Will you please indicate your opinion on each of the accompanying statements. To indicate your opinion, draw a circle around the word which best describes your agreement as shown:

*1 We should be absolutely opposed to birth control.

Strongly Agree   Agree   Undecided   Disagree   Strongly Disagree

*2 Birth control reduces the marital relation to the level of vice.
3 We ought to approve of birth control because of the advantages to women's health resulting from the correct spacing of children.
4 Uncontrolled reproduction should be opposed on the grounds that it is a fundamental cause of crime.
*5 We should not approve of women taking the health risks involved in birth control.
6 The present depression and the attendant problem of unemployment makes more desirable than ever the general approval of birth control.
7 Wide-spread acceptance and approval of birth control is imperative.
*8 The practice of birth control is equivalent to murder.
9 Uncontrolled reproduction should be discouraged since it leads to many social evils.
*10 Birth control is race suicide.
11 Birth control is a legitimate health measure.
*12 Our laws should prohibit giving, even to adults, information concerning birth control.
13 We should not only allow but strongly urge birth control to limit the size of families of low income.
*14 Effective measures should be taken to prevent any sale of birth control devices.
15 Birth control would help to solve many of our social problems.
16 Birth control is highly desirable for women who must earn a living.
*17 The possible benefits of birth control do not alter the fact that it is morally wrong.
*18 Wide-spread knowledge of birth control methods should be opposed as likely to lead to the spread of social disease.
19 We should approve as socially desirable the program of those organizations supporting the movement for birth control.
*20 The practice of birth control evades man's duty to propagate the race.
21 Birth control increases the happiness of married life.
22 Every normal healthy couple should have as many children as is physiologically possible.

* These items are against birth control and weights for their response alternatives must be reversed for scoring. The same response categories are used for all items.

Reprinted with permission from Wilke, W. H. An experimental comparison of the speech, the radio, and the printed page as propaganda devices. *Arch. Psychol.*, 1934, No. 169.

Attitude toward menstruation EXHIBIT 4-3

Description. This 48-item scale was developed by McHugh and Wasser (1959), using the Thurstone scaling technique. Items were sorted on a continuum representing degree to which endorsement of the item would reflect a positive (good) or negative (bad) attitude toward menstruation from a mental hygiene point of view. They were sorted first by 58 female graduate students of mental hygiene and a second time by 11 female psychologists and mental hygienists. Exhibit 4-3 gives the scale values obtained by the two sortings.

Subjects. Fifty-eight female graduate students in mental hygiene and eleven professional females (psychologists and mental hygienists) served as the judges for the construction of the scale.

Response Mode. Persons endorse those items with which they agree.

Scoring. The individual's score is the median of the scale values for items which he endorses. A high score indicates a positive, or healthy, attitude.

Reliability. The authors report no reliability estimates for the scale. However, it is noteworthy that the scale values for the items changed very little from the first set of judges to the second set. This is not an estimate of reliability but seems sufficient basis on which to expect that reliability will be adequate.

Validity. Since this is a Thurstone-type scale, one may assume a good degree of content validity. Also, repeating the sorting process with a second sample of 11 professionals constitutes some cross validation of the scale values for the items.

Comments. While McHugh and Wasser used no specific instructions for administration to subjects, they suggest (McHugh, private communication, 1965) that their intention is reflected in their instructions to the judges. The instructions at the head of Exhibit 4-3 are a modification of the judges' instructions. For other means of measuring attitudes toward menstruation, see the section on generalized scales in this chapter.

EXHIBIT 4-3

ATTITUDE TOWARD MENSTRUATION

The following are 48 statements regarding menstruation. Please place a check (✓) beside those statements with which you agree. Place a cross

(×) beside those with which you disagree. If you simply cannot decide about a statement, you may mark it with a question mark.

Scale Values			
Students	Psychologists		
10.42	10.00	1	Menstruation is a normal biological function to me.
10.29	10.00	2	I feel that menstruation has an essential purpose.
10.22	9.50	3	I feel that menstruation is simply part of being a woman.
10.14	9.30	4	Menstruation to me is just another indication that I am part of life.
9.78	8.60	5	I am indifferent to menstruation; it doesn't bother me and I go ahead as usual.
9.69	7.00	6	I have no feeling of shame at all in connection with menstruation.
9.50	8.50	7	When I menstruate, I am happy that I am normal and healthy.
9.55	6.50	8	I am not ashamed to talk about menstruation.
8.00	9.00	9	Menstruation makes me feel a kinship with other women.
8.00	9.00	10	Menstruation means to me the ideal of having children.
8.43	7.50	11	I do not resent menstruation in the least.
8.00	7.00	12	Menstruation does not concern me enough to warrant much consideration.
8.00	6.00	13	I wish I knew more about menstruation.
7.11	7.90	14	Menstruation as a function makes me feel grown up.
5.66	7.30	15	Menstruation gives me a feeling of pride.
6.50	5.00	16	Menstruation makes me conscious of sex.
5.57	7.50	17	I feel older and more serious when I menstruate.
5.66	6.50	18	Pampering and special care during menstruation seem like a regression to me.
5.66	6.00	19	I don't mind mentioning menstruation to dates.
5.55	7.00	20	Menstruation makes me feel important.
5.53	5.30	21	I wonder about menstruation vaguely.
4.00	5.00	22	Menstruating gives me a kind of thrill.
4.75	5.00	23	I object to the interruption of my activities by menstruation.
4.00	5.00	24	Menstruation seems mysterious and wonderful.
4.66	3.00	25	I resent menstruation because of the pain.
4.25	4.00	26	I have always considered menstruation a terrible nuisance.
3.62	2.50	27	I am angry and annoyed at the material bother of menstruation.
3.14	3.25	28	I am annoyed because menstruation is something I cannot control.
2.75	4.00	29	When I menstruate, I feel that it is noticeable.
3.11	2.30	30	I am appalled to think of all the years menstruating will happen to me.
2.40	3.00	31	I want sympathy when I menstruate.
2.83	2.75	32	Menstruation frightens me a little.

Scale Values			
Students	Psychologists		
2.61	3.25	33	I am very self-conscious each time I menstruate.
2.73	2.00	34	I feel saddled with an unwarranted burden because of menstruation.
2.00	3.50	35	I get upset and nervous every time I menstruate.
2.60	2.30	36	I am resentful toward menstruation.
3.64	1.50	37	When I am menstruating, I am ashamed in front of boys.
2.37	2.75	38	I feel that menstruation is something to conceal.
2.31	3.00	39	I feel ashamed if someone discovers I am menstruating.
2.12	3.50	40	I am embarrassed about menstruation.
2.10	1.90	41	I am anxious about menstruation each time.
2.00	2.20	42	Menstruation makes me resent being a girl.
1.86	0.50	43	Menstruation represents to me the distasteful responsibility of adult sex life.
1.27	1.90	44	I am frightened by stories I have heard about menstruation.
1.38	1.50	45	I am afraid of all that menstruation means as a phase of development.
0.76	0.50	46	Menstruation revolts me.
0.82	1.00	47	I feel abnormal and peculiar when I menstruate.
0.74	1.60	48	I am very afraid of menstruating.

Attitude toward movies EXHIBIT 4-4

Description. This is a 40-item scale prepared by Thurstone (1930). It was developed on a 6-point sorting continuum, rather than the usual 11-point continuum; thus scale values range from 0.0 to 4.75. None of the items seem dated. The range of item Q values is unknown.

Subjects. The sample is unknown.

Response Mode. Subjects respond by checking those items with which they agree and placing a cross beside those with which they disagree. They place a question mark beside those about which they are uncertain.

Scoring. The subject's score is the median of the scale values of all items with which the person agrees. A high score indicates a positive attitude.

Reliability. Evidence of reliabilty is not available.

Validity. The scale possesses good content validity, but no other evidence of validity is available.

Comments. This is a scale on a timely issue, but it needs more work. Estimates of reliability and further demonstration of other forms of validity would increase its usefulness. Readers interested in this scale may also wish to see Thurstone (1932, 1959) and Williams (1933).

EXHIBIT 4-4

ATTITUDE TOWARD MOVIES

On the following pages you will find a number of statements expressing different attitudes toward the movies.

√ Put a check mark if you agree with the statement.
× Put a cross if you disagree with the statement.

If you simply cannot decide about a statement you may mark it with a question mark.

This is not an examination. There are no right or wrong answers to these statements. This is simply a study of people's attitudes toward the movies. Please indicate your own attitude by a check mark when you agree and by a cross when you disagree.

Scale Value		
1.5	**1**	The movies occupy time that should be spent in more wholesome recreation.
1.3	**2**	I am tired of the movies; I have seen too many poor ones.
4.5	**3**	The movies are the best civilizing device ever developed.
0.2	**4**	Movies are the most important cause of crime.
2.7	**5**	Movies are all right but a few of them give the rest a bad name.
2.6	**6**	I like to see movies once in a while but they do disappoint you sometimes.
2.9	**7**	I think the movies are fairly interesting.
2.7	**8**	Movies are just a harmless pastime.
1.7	**9**	The movies to me are just a way to kill time.
4.0	**10**	The influence of the movies is decidedly for good.
3.9	**11**	The movies are good, clean entertainment.
3.9	**12**	Movies increase one's appreciation of beauty.
1.7	**13**	I'd never miss the movies if we didn't have them.
2.4	**14**	Sometimes I feel that the movies are desirable and sometimes I doubt it.
0.0	**15**	It is a sin to go to the movies.
4.3	**16**	There would be very little progress without the movies.
4.3	**17**	The movies are the most vital form of art today.
3.6	**18**	A movie is the best entertainment that can be obtained cheaply.
3.4	**19**	A movie once in a while is a good thing for everybody.
3.4	**20**	The movies are one of the few things I can enjoy by myself.
1.3	**21**	Going to the movies is a foolish way to spend your money.
1.1	**22**	Moving pictures bore me.
0.6	**23**	As they now exist movies are wholly bad for children.
0.6	**24**	Such a pernicious influence as the movies is bound to weaken the moral fiber of those who attend.
0.3	**25**	As a protest against movies we should pledge ourselves never to attend them.

Reprinted with permission from Thurstone, L. L. A scale for measuring attitude toward the movies. *J. educ. Res.*, 1930, 22, 89–94. Copyright 1930 by Dembar Educational Research Services, Madison, Wis.

Scale Value		
0.1	26	The movies are the most important single influence for evil.
4.7	27	The movies are the most powerful influence for good in American life.
2.3	28	I would go to the movies more often if I were sure of finding something good.
4.1	29	If I had my choice of anything I wanted to do, I would go to the movies.
2.2	30	The pleasure people get from the movies just about balances the harm they do.
2.0	31	I don't find much that is educational in the current films.
1.9	32	The information that you obtain from the movies is of little value.
1.0	33	Movies are a bad habit.
3.3	34	I like the movies as they are because I go to be entertained, not educated.
3.1	35	On the whole the movies are pretty decent.
0.8	36	The movies are undermining respect for authority.
2.7	37	I like to see other people enjoy the movies whether I enjoy them myself or not.
0.3	38	The movies are to blame for the prevalence of sex offenses.
4.4	39	The movie is one of the great educational institutions for common people.
0.8	40	Young people are learning to smoke, drink, and pet from the movies.

ATTITUDES RELATED TO EDUCATIONAL ISSUES AND PROBLEMS

The only scales related to an educational issue are the Siebrecht (1941) scale concerning safe driving and the Academic Freedom Survey. The safe-driving scale is included in this chapter because of the current concern over highway safety, teen-age driving, and similar issues.

Attitudes toward safe driving *EXHIBIT 4-5*

Description. This scale, developed by Siebrecht (1941), includes 40 Likert-type items and two self-ratings using a graphic continuum. Siebrecht reports his group norms and has requested users of the scale to report any results to the Director, New York University, Center for Safety Education, New York.

Subjects. In construction of this scale, 100 driver-training students were used.

Response Mode. Persons indicate the extent to which they agree or disagree with the statement by checking one of five alternatives: strongly agree, agree, undecided, disagree, and strongly disagree.

Scoring. The alternatives are scored from 5 (strongly agree) to 1 (strongly disagree) for positively phrased items. Weights for negatively phrased items must be reversed. The subject's score is the sum of the weights for the alternatives endorsed by him. High scores indicate more positive attitudes. Scores from the last two items, using a graphic continuum, are not included in the subject's score. They are only informational questions.

Reliability. Siebrecht (1941) reports the split-half reliability to be .81, P.E. = ±.02.

Validity. The validity of the scale was assessed by Siebrecht (1941) on three bases: (1) the judgment of experts for content validity, (2) the selection of items which differentiate high and low scorers, (3) the prediction of known groups (driver-training and driving-experienced subjects). The critical ratio established was five times the desired minimum.

Comments. This seems to be a generally adequate scale, carefully constructed.

EXHIBIT 4-5

ATTITUDES TOWARD SAFE DRIVING: SIEBRECHT ATTITUDE SCALE

DIRECTIONS: Below is a series of statements about problems related to the driving of motor vehicles. There are no correct answers for these statements. They have therefore been set up in such a manner as to permit persons to indicate the extent to which they agree or disagree with the ideas expressed. Suppose the statement is

Only persons who have reached their nineteenth birthday should be permitted to drive a motor vehicle.

Strongly agree x Agree Undecided Disagree Strongly disagree

As you read the statement you will know whether you agree or disagree with the idea expressed. You must then indicate the extent to which you agree or disagree. If you agree fully, place an *x* before the words "Strongly agree"; if you agree but with reservation, that is you do not fully agree, place the *x* before the word "Agree," as in the sample above. If you disagree with the idea, indicate the extent to which you disagree by checking either "Disagree" or "Strongly disagree." But if you neither agree nor disagree, that is you are not certain, place the *x* before "Undecided." To indicate your attitude, read the statement carefully, then quickly check the position which best indicates your attitude. Do not spend much time with any statement. *But be sure to answer every statement*. You should complete the work in no more than *ten minutes*. Most persons will finish in less time. Work fast but carefully.

Statements

1 Drivers' examination should be more difficult to eliminate all but the best drivers.

Strongly agree Agree Undecided Disagree Strongly disagree

*2 The driver of an automobile should be the sole judge of the mechanical fitness of his car.
3 Drivers who pass on hills and curves should be considered incompetent.
4 Hit-and-run drivers should be classified as criminals.
*5 Drivers who have the right of way need not be concerned about sharing the road.
6 A person should be permitted to drive a car only as long as he does not abuse his privilege.
*7 The drinking of alcohol by drivers should be a matter for the consideration of the drivers alone.
8 Prospective drivers should take a course in the driving of the automobile.
9 Strict enforcement of traffic regulations is the only way to prevent accidents.
*10 Pedestrians should at all times be solely responsible for their own safety.
11 Every driver should be required to have his car inspected twice a year.
*12 Drivers who disregard traffic regulations should be punished only if they cause damage or injury.
13 Most drivers lack the ability to control automobiles at high speed.
*14 Because "things just happen" one should not be concerned with the prevention of accidents.
15 Drivers who handle cars carefully should not be denied the right to drive on public highways.
16 Drivers convicted of hit-and-run accidents should have their licenses revoked.
*17 The driver of a car should decide when it is safe to pass on curves.
18 A person should pass a physical examination before being issued a driver's license.
*19 A tired motorist should drive slowly until the drowsiness leaves him.
20 The rudeness of traffic officers discourages courtesy on the part of the motorist.
*21 The sturdy construction of automobiles assures safety at any speed.
22 Examinations for drivers' licenses should be required of all persons once a year.
*23 The present emphasis on the enforcement of traffic rules should be reduced.
24 Every motorist should be required to pass a driving-skill test once in five years.
*25 Motorists should be permitted to run signals and lights when there is no cross traffic approaching.
*26 Inexperienced drivers should not be arrested for running through traffic lights.
27 To accommodate the traffic, the cooperation of all drivers is necessary.
*28 The occurrence of accidents is a matter of chance and should be regarded as unavoidable.
29 Until a person passes a driving-skill test he should not be granted a license to drive.
*30 A driver really is the best judge of the speed he should be permitted to drive.
31 Drivers convicted of driving while under the influence of liquor should have their licenses revoked.
*32 People are as courteous "behind the wheel" as they are at any other time.
33 Every driver should be required to pass an examination on the rules of the road.
*34 No person should be denied the right to drive an automobile.

* Negative items must be reversed for scoring.

35 Examinations for drivers' licenses should be difficult enough to eliminate persons who are physically unfit and emotionally unstable.
*36 Pedestrians should yield the right of way to motorists.
37 Drivers of automobiles should be more concerned with the welfare of their passengers than of themselves.
*38 Improved construction of automobiles makes driving skill less necessary today than five years ago.
39 Driving is a cooperative affair in which the motorists share alike on the highways.
*40 Drivers with many years of experience should not be required to submit to reexamination in later years.

Answer only one—EITHER (A) OR (B)

(A) **If you now drive,** rate yourself as a driver by placing an x at that point along the line below from VERY POOR to EXPERT DRIVER which you believe will indicate the kind of driver you are:

VERY POOR ____ EXPERT DRIVER

(B) **If you do not now drive but hope to,** rate yourself as to the kind of driver you hope to become by placing an x at that point along the line below from VERY POOR to EXPERT DRIVER which you believe will best indicate the kind of driver you will be:

VERY POOR ____ EXPERT DRIVER

The academic freedom survey *EXHIBIT 4-6*

Description. This is a 23-item, modified Likert-type scale developed by the Academic Freedom Committee, Illinois Division of the American Civil Liberties Union, and published by Psychometric Affiliates (1954). It contains 12 items on rights of students, 7 on rights of teachers, and 4 items on general rights. It may be considered to measure attitude toward the institution in question on a basis of degree of freedom allowed by the institution. It could also be used to assess attitude toward the plight of the teacher and student in general in public educational institutions.

Subjects. Samples consisted of 50 administrative and 153 faculty representatives of 50 Illinois colleges, 34 college students at Northwestern University, and 30 students at the Illinois Institute of Technology (total $N = 144$).

Response Mode. Each item is answered by checking one of three alternatives reflecting the "extent to which right is effectively assured": complete, as a general rule, and very little or none.

Scoring. Answers are weighted from 3 (complete), to 1 (very little or none). Items which are left unanswered are given 2 points, as are all items answered by the alternative "as a general rule." The person's score is the sum of these weighted values. High scores indicate more positive attitudes.

Reliability. The split-half reliability (corrected), as reported in the manual provided by Psychometric Affiliates, is .92 for the full scale. The reliability estimate, based on the student sample only, is .90; based upon the staff sample, it is .86. Reliability coefficients for the separate sections of the scale are provided by the publishers.

Validity. These items possess content validity for attitude toward the institutional setting as being permissive and a place of freedom. The scale does *not* measure attitudes toward the merits of academic freedom or the propriety of such permissiveness, and it should not be used for such a purpose. It also does *not* measure the actual amount of freedom provided.

Comments. As each item states a freedom, all items may be considered positive. This lack of balance between positive and negative items allows for the operation of response set on the part of the respondent and may produce artificially high statistical results. The publishers provide norms for the scale as well as correlations of items with total scale score.

EXHIBIT 4-6

THE ACADEMIC FREEDOM SURVEY

IMPORTANT: Answer *every item:* If you omit an item, it will be scored "as a general rule."

	Extent to Which Right is Effectively Assured		
	COMPLETE	**AS A GENERAL RULE**	**VERY LITTLE OR NONE**
Rights of Students			
1 **Student Self-Government** by representatives freely elected.	_____	_____	_____
2 **Petition** to faculty and administration with respect to curriculum, tuition and other conditions of student life.	_____	_____	_____
3 **Due Process,** including fair notice, counsel and specification of charges in cases of suspension or expulsion.	_____	_____	_____

		COMPLETE	AS A GENERAL RULE	VERY LITTLE OR NONE
4	**Representation** on appropriate faculty-student or administration-student committees concerned with extracurricular activities.			
5	**Freedom to Hear** outside speakers on any subject without regard to unpopularity of speaker.			
6	**Freedom to Form Associations** for any lawful purposes and to affiliate these with national organizations, including political organizations, provided that these are not proscribed by law.			
7	**Freedom to Employ Facilities** of the institution such as rooms and bulletin boards.			
8	**Access to Counsel** by faculty advisers, freely chosen, so far as possible, by student groups.			
9	**Freedom of Press,** such as student newspapers and magazines, with free access to staffs of publications and with adequate provision in case of monopoly, for expression of minority views.			
10	**Freedom of Criticism,** by students, of faculty or administration.			
11	**Freedom of Off-Campus Activity,** subject to law or community standards of taste; in particular, freedom to engage in political activity with minority groups.			
12	**Equal Access to Admission,** scholarships or other aid, and to all recognized activities, without discrimination on account of race, creed or national origin.			
	Rights of Teachers			
13	**Faculty Self-Government,** by representatives freely elected, on organization and distribution of curriculum.			
14	**Freedom of Criticism** of curriculum and of conduct of administration.			
15	**Freedom of Association** in faculty societies and organizations provided these are legal.			
16	**Freedom from Special Requirements** such as special oaths of loyalty or any pledge other than a simple affirmation to support the Constitution and to follow and teach the truth.			

	COMPLETE	AS A GENERAL RULE	VERY LITTLE OR NONE
17 **Assurance of Tenure or Seniority** on established and declared principles relating solely to length and quality of service.	____	____	____
18 **Freedom of Research,** independent of restrictions emanating from political or religious considerations.	____	____	____
19 **Freedom to Maintain Citizenship Activities** and responsibilities without prejudice to academic status or advancement.	____	____	____
Other Rights			
20 **Freedom of Non-Academic Employees,** such as library and research staffs, to organize their own groups and represent themselves in dealings with faculty and administration.	____	____	____
21 Maintenance of free selection of books and magazines in library.	____	____	____
22 Freedom, in public institutions, from special influences to introduce sectarian religious education. In all other institutions, adherence to the respective institutional charter.	____	____	____
23 Any other rights. (You may well have in mind some infringements of academic freedom that are not well covered by the above list.)	____	____	____

ATTITUDES TOWARD HEALTH-RELATED ISSUES AND PROBLEMS

This section contains scales measuring attitudes related to issues in the area of health, including scales measuring attitudes toward mental health, medicare, and socialized medicine. Persons interested in attitudes toward mental illness may wish to see an information and opinion questionnaire by Nunnally (1961).

Opinions about mental illness EXHIBIT 4-7

Description. Developed by Cohen and Struening (1959) using factor analysis, this 51-item scale measures attitudes toward the causes and treatment of mental illness. The scale was designed for group administration under conditions of anonymity, but may be used otherwise. It contains five factors: A, authoritarianism; B, benevolence; C, mental hygiene; D, social restrictiveness; and E, interpersonal etiology.

Subjects. The sample consisted of 8,248 persons organized into 19 occupational groups; of these, 7,701 were members of 16 occupational groups employed in 12 VA mental hospitals in the United States (Cohen and Struening, 1963).

Response Mode. Persons respond to each item by checking one of six alternatives: strongly agree, agree, not sure but probably agree, not sure but probably disagree, disagree, strongly disagree.

Scoring. Each factor or dimension in the test is defined by a particular group of items. Responses to these items are weighted from 1 (strongly agree) to 6 (strongly disagree), regardless of the direction (positivity or negativity) of the item. In computing the factor scores, each item receives the appropriate number according to the respondent's position on the agree-disagree continuum. The formulas for these factors are as follows:

Factor	*Formula*
A	$= 67 - \Sigma(1, 6, 9, 11, 16, 19, 21, 39, 43, 46, 48)$
B	$= 31 + \Sigma(26, 32, 34, 36, 37, 40, 49) - \Sigma(2, 12, 17, 18, 22, 27, 47)$
C	$= 48 + (31) - \Sigma(3, 13, 23, 28, 33, 38, 44, 50)$
D	$= 47 + \Sigma(8, 41) - \Sigma(4, 7, 14, 24, 29, 42, 45, 51)$
E	$= 43 - \Sigma(5, 10, 15, 20, 25, 30, 35)$

Thus, if a person agrees strongly with all items defining Factor A, he receives a score of 67 — 11, or 56. If he disagrees with all items, he receives a score of 67 — 66, or 1. A high score indicates a positive attitude on that factor.

Reliability. Cohen and Struening (1962) report the results of a comparison of factor loadings on items for two geographically separate VA neuropsychiatric hospitals (using samples of 451 and 653 subjects). For each factor separately, the rotated factor loadings for the two hospitals were correlated over the items. The resulting correlations between hospitals ranged from .38 (Factor C) to .86 (Factor A). These results may be taken as an estimate of reliability (in the form of stability of internal consistency of the items) and further serve to increase the generality of usage of the scale. No other evidence of reliability is available.

Validity. Factor loadings for the five factors are as follows: A, 45 percent; B, 7 percent; C, 16 percent; D, 27 percent; and E, 5 percent. Correlations between these factors are reported by the authors (Cohen and Struening, 1959) as being "trivial or zero," indicating separate factors. Other evidence of validity is based upon the factorial validity coefficients for the five factors and upon the discrimination of occupational clusters (known groups) on the basis of these factors. With regard to concurrent validity, Costin and Kerr (1962) found that a course in abnormal psychology effectively changed the attitudes of students toward mental illness and mentally ill people in a desirable direction, as measured by this test.

Comments. Because it was developed through a factor-analytic procedure, much of the evidence of reliability and validity seems rather inferential. However, the scale is generally satisfactory in both of these regards. A test-retest reliability estimate and further demonstrations of validity would, of course, be valuable. The question of whether the scores obtained on the separate factors can be combined into a single total score must be answered empirically. Readers interested in this scale may also wish to see Cohen and Struening (1964).

EXHIBIT 4-7

OPINIONS ABOUT MENTAL ILLNESS

The statements that follow are opinions or ideas about mental illness and mental patients. By mental illness, we mean the kinds of illness which bring patients to mental hospitals, and by mental patients we mean mental hospital patients. There are many differences of opinion about this subject. In other words, many people agree with each of the following statements while many people disagree with each of these statements. We would like to know what *you* think about these statements. Each of them is followed by six choices:

strongly agree___ agree___ not sure but probably agree___ not sure but probably disagree___ disagree___ strongly disagree___

Please check (✓) in the space provided that choice which comes closest to saying how you feel about each statement. You can be sure that many people, including doctors, will agree with your choice. There are no right or wrong answers: we are interested only in *your opinion*. It is very important that you answer *every* item. Please do *NOT* sign your name.

*A 1 Nervous breakdowns usually result when people work too hard.

†strongly agree___ agree___ not sure but probably agree___ not sure but probably disagree___ disagree___ strongly disagree___

B 2 Mental illness is an illness like any other.

C 3 Most patients in mental hospitals are not dangerous.

D 4 Although patients discharged from mental hospitals may seem all right, they should not be allowed to marry.

* A, B, C, D, E: Items are marked with these letters to indicate that they are used in the computation of the score on that factor.

† The same response alternatives are used for all items.

Reference: J. Cohen and E. L. Struening. Opinions about mental illness in the personnel of two large mental hospitals. *J. abnorm. soc. Psychol.*, 1962, 64, 349–360. Items obtained from author and published with his permission. Copyright by Abacus Associates, Inc. Copies of the scale may be purchased from Abacus Associates, Inc., New York, N.Y.

E 5 If parents loved their children more, there would be less mental illness.
A 6 It is easy to recognize someone who once had a serious mental illness.
D 7 People who are mentally ill let their emotions control them: normal people think things out.
D 8 People who were once patients in mental hospitals are no more dangerous than the average citizen.
A 9 When a person has a problem or a worry, it is best not to think about it, but keep busy with more pleasant things.
E 10 Although they usually aren't aware of it, many people become mentally ill to avoid the difficult problems of everyday life.
A 11 There is something about mental patients that makes it easy to tell them from normal people.
B 12 Even though patients in mental hospitals behave in funny ways, it is wrong to laugh about them.
C 13 Most mental patients are willing to work.
D 14 The small children of patients in mental hospitals should not be allowed to visit them.
E 15 People who are successful in their work seldom become mentally ill.
A 16 People would not become mentally ill if they avoided bad thoughts.
B 17 Patients in mental hospitals are in many ways like children.
B 18 More tax money should be spent in the care and treatment of people with severe mental illness.
A 19 A heart patient has just one thing wrong with him, while a mentally ill person is completely different from other patients.
E 20 Mental patients come from homes where the parents took little interest in their children.
A 21 People with mental illness should never be treated in the same hospital as people with physical illness.
B 22 Anyone who tries hard to better himself deserves the respect of others.
C 23 If our hospitals had enough well trained doctors, nurses, and aides, many of the patients would get well enough to live outside the hospital.
D 24 A woman would be foolish to marry a man who has had a severe mental illness, even though he seems fully recovered.
E 25 If the children of mentally ill parents were raised by normal parents, they would probably not become mentally ill.
B 26 People who have been patients in a mental hospital will never be their old selves again.
B 27 Many mental patients are capable of skilled labor, even though in some ways they are very disturbed mentally.
C 28 Our mental hospitals seem more like prisons than like places where mentally ill people can be cared for.
D 29 Anyone who is in a hospital for a mental illness should not be allowed to vote.
E 30 The mental illness of many people is caused by the separation or divorce of their parents during childhood.
C 31 The best way to handle patients in mental hospitals is to keep them behind locked doors.
B 32 To become a patient in a mental hospital is to become a failure in life.
C 33 The patients of mental hospitals should be allowed more privacy.
B 34 If a patient in a mental hospital attacks someone, he should be punished so he doesn't do it again.
E 35 If the children of normal parents were raised by mentally ill parents, they would probably become mentally ill.
B 36 Every mental hospital should be surrounded by a high fence and guards.

B 37 The law should allow a woman to divorce her husband as soon as he has been confined in a mental hospital with a severe mental illness.

C 38 People (both veterans and non-veterans) who are unable to work because of mental illness should receive money for living expenses.

A 39 Mental illness is usually caused by some disease of the nervous system.

B 40 Regardless of how you look at it, patients with severe mental illness are no longer really human.

D 41 Most women who were once patients in a mental hospital could be trusted as baby sitters.

D 42 Most patients in mental hospitals don't care how they look.

A 43 College professors are more likely to become mentally ill than are business men.

C 44 Many people who have never been patients in a mental hospital are more mentally ill than many hospitalized mental patients.

D 45 Although some mental patients seem all right, it is dangerous to forget for a moment that they are mentally ill.

A 46 Sometimes mental illness is punishment for bad deeds.

B 47 Our mental hospitals should be organized in a way that makes the patient feel as much as possible like he is living at home.

A 48 One of the main causes of mental illness is a lack of moral strength or will power.

B 49 There is little that can be done for patients in a mental hospital except to see that they are comfortable and well fed.

C 50 Many mental patients would remain in the hospital until they were well, even if the doors were unlocked.

D 51 All patients in mental hospitals should be prevented from having children by a painless operation.

PLEASE CHECK BACK AND MAKE SURE THAT YOU HAVE NOT LEFT OUT ANY STATEMENTS OR *PAGES* OF STATEMENTS

The socialized medicine attitude scale EXHIBIT 4-8

Description. This is a 20-item scale developed by Mahler (1953). The form presented in Exhibit 4-8 is actually two equated 10-item forms used together. The author constructed this scale using the Edwards and Kilpatrick scale discrimination technique.

Subjects. In constructing the scale, 211 college students and 106 Stanford University students were used.

Response Mode. Persons respond on a five-point, modified Likert continuum: strongly agree, agree, undecided, disagree, and strongly disagree.

Scoring. Response alternatives for positive items are weighted from 4 (strongly agree) to 0 (strongly disagree). Weights must be reversed for negative items. The person's score is the sum of the weighted alternatives which he endorses. A high score indicates a positive attitude.

Reliability. Mahler (1953) reports the equivalent-forms reliability estimates to range from .81 to .84. The split-half reliability (corrected) was .96.

Validity. In addition to content validity, the scale has also been found to predict known groups (106 Stanford University students possessing pro- and anti-socialized medicine attitudes, as established by interview). With regard to concurrent validity, Libo (1957) found no correlation between F scale scores and scores on Mahler's scale for 97 senior medical students. This latter finding may be viewed as evidence of discriminant validity or may be considered to be the result of the fact that "correlations between personality traits and social attitudes are more easily found in populations where the social attitude is not a salient part of the group's ideology and hence can be allowed to vary in accordance with the individual's broader personal value system" (Libo, 1957, p. 136).

Comments. This seems to be a quite satisfactory scale with regard to both reliability and validity.

EXHIBIT 4-8

THE SOCIALIZED MEDICINE ATTITUDE SCALE

Please indicate your reaction to the following statements, using these alternatives:

Strongly Agree = SA
Agree = A
Undecided = U
Disagree = D
Strongly Disagree = SD

*1 The quality of medical care under the system of private practice is superior to that under a system of compulsory health insurance.

SA A U D SD

2 A compulsory health program will produce a healthier and more productive population.

*3 Under a compulsory health program there would be less incentive for young men to become doctors.

4 A compulsory health program is necessary because it brings the greatest good to the greatest number of people.

*5 Treatment under a compulsory health program would be mechanical and superficial.

6 A compulsory health program would be a realization of one of the true aims of a democracy.

*7 Compulsory medical care would upset the traditional relationship between the family doctor and the patient.

* These are negative items, and weights for their response alternatives must be reversed for scoring purposes. The same response alternatives are used with all items.

*8 I feel that I would get better care from a doctor whom I am paying than from a doctor who is being paid by the government.
9 Despite many practical objections, I feel that compulsory health insurance is a real need of the American people.
10 A compulsory health program could be administered quite efficiently if the doctors would cooperate.
11 There is no reason why the traditional relationship between doctors and patient cannot be continued under a compulsory health program.
*12 If a compulsory health program were enacted, politicians would have control over doctors.
*13 The present system of private medical practice is the one best adapted to the liberal philosophy of democracy.
14 There is no reason why doctors should not be able to work just as well under a compulsory health program as they do now.
15 More and better care will be obtained under a compulsory health program.
*16 The atmosphere of a compulsory health program would destroy the initiative and the ambition of young doctors.
*17 Politicians are trying to force a compulsory health program upon the people without giving them the true facts.
*18 Administrative costs under a compulsory health program would be exorbitant.
*19 Red tape and bureaucratic problems would make a compulsory health program grossly inefficient.
*20 Any system of compulsory health insurance would invade the privacy of the individual.

ATTITUDES RELATED TO POLITICAL AND LEGAL ISSUES

This section contains scales measuring attitudes toward issues and problems of a political and legal nature. Among these are attitudes toward censorship, the Constitution of the United States, capital punishment and treatment of criminals, racial integration, and school integration. One scale which was excluded from this section of the book was Thurstone's scale measuring attitudes toward prohibition. Not only were many of the items in the scale dated, but the issue itself is of low relevance to the present times. Readers interested in Thurstone's Attitude toward Prohibition Scale should consult Thurstone's book (1932, p. 15).

Attitude toward censorship scale *EXHIBIT 4-9*

Description. This is a 20-item scale developed by Rosander and Thurstone (1931), of which there are two equivalent forms, A and B. The items consider the moral, legal, and political implications of, and arguments surrounding, censorship. The Thurstone procedure was used in the construction of the scale. Information regarding the Q values for the items is not available.

Subjects. The sample on which this scale was constructed is unknown.

Response Mode. Persons place a check mark beside all items with which they agree and a cross beside those with which they disagree.

Scoring. The individual's score is the median of the scale values of the items with which he agrees. High scores indicate a positive attitude.

Reliability. Lorge (1939) reports the reliability estimates on this scale to range from .65 to .82, while Ferguson reports the range as being from .72 to .84. Goodstein (1953) tested the equivalent-forms reliability (with a two-week interval between administrations of the separate forms) and reports a correlation of .48 for a sample of 150 general psychology undergraduates. His design was counterbalanced.

Validity. The Thurstone scaling procedure tends to ensure greater content validity. Brim and Hoff (1957) tested the correlation between this scale and desire for certainty (as tested by projective means) and found no relation between scores on attitudes toward censorship and the desire for certainty. This result might be taken as indicative of discriminant validity, in the sense that the test is not measuring intellectual rigidity with its extreme items. Diggory (1953) reports correlations of +.16 to +.58 between this scale and Thurstone's scale measuring attitudes toward treatment of criminals. He also found this scale to correlate +.15 to +.46 with Thurstone's Attitude toward Capital Punishment scale. These correlations would seem to be a reflection of the construct validity of the scale.

Comments. This is a valid and reliable scale which has been used extensively. Readers interested in other studies using this scale may wish to see Ferguson (1939), Johnson (1940), and Fay (1939, 1940*a*,*b*).

EXHIBIT 4-9

ATTITUDE TOWARD CENSORSHIP SCALE

Place a check mark (✓) if you agree with the statement.
Place a cross (X) if you disagree with the statement.

Scale Value		Form A
6.9	1	Censorship is a good thing if there isn't too much of it.
3.6	2	The judgment of intelligent people is the only effective censorship.
0.3	3	Nobody has any right to dictate to me what I shall read.
8.0	4	Censorship is needed because most people are unable to judge for themselves.
5.5	5	There is much to be said on both sides of the censorship question.
4.1	6	Morality varies so much with different places and times that censorship is arbitrary.
2.2	7	Censorship is absurd because no two people agree about morality.
8.9	8	Our national morality is safeguarded by censorship.

Scale Value		
6.0	9	The censors are needed, but they go too far.
3.0	10	It is a shame that so many fine books and plays have been suppressed by the censors.
0.0	11	Censorship is a disgrace to our country.
7.2	12	Censorship when reasonably exercised is desirable for morality.
5.7	13	Whether censorship is good or not depends entirely on the censor.
2.8	14	People should be allowed to make their own distinctions between good and bad.
9.6	15	What we need is more and better censorship.
7.1	16	Our system of censorship isn't perfect but it is better than none.
3.8	17	The education of public opinion would be a great improvement over censorship.
1.4	18	Censorship can never be justified in a free country.
8.3	19	Some authorized power is certainly needed to keep obscene literature in check.
2.4	20	Censorship can never make people moral.
		Form B
4.2	1	I doubt if censorship is wise.
2.2	2	A truly free people must be allowed to choose their own reading and entertainment.
9.1	3	We must have censorship to protect the morals of young people.
6.7	4	The theory of censorship is sound, but censors make a mess of it.
3.1	5	Only narrow-minded Puritans want censorship.
0.0	6	The whole theory of censorship is utterly unreasonable.
7.5	7	Until public taste has been educated, we must continue to have censorship.
2.5	8	Many of our greatest literary classics would be suppressed if the censors thought they could get away with it.
9.9	9	Everything that is printed for publication should first be examined by government censors.
6.0	10	Plays and movies should be censored but the press should be free.
3.5	11	Censorship has practically no effect on people's morals.
0.5	12	Censorship is a gross violation of our constitutional rights.
8.2	13	Censorship protects those who lack judgment or experience to choose for themselves.
5.6	14	Censorship is a very difficult problem and I am not sure how far I think it should go.
7.1	15	Censorship is a good thing on the whole although it is often abused.
3.9	16	Education of the public taste is preferable to censorship.
1.7	17	Human progress demands free speech and a free press.
8.5	18	Censorship is effective in raising moral and aesthetic standards.
6.0	19	Censorship might be warranted if we could get reasonable censors.
2.8	20	Morality is produced by self-control, not by censorship.

Attitude toward the Constitution of the United States EXHIBIT 4-10

Description. Developed by Rosander and Thurstone (1931), this is a 21-item scale with equivalent forms. For the most part, the items question whether the Constitution should ever be criticized or changed. There are no questions regarding interpretation of the Constitution (a current issue), or the merit of having a Constitution, etc. Information regarding Q values for the items is missing.

Subjects. The population sample upon which the scale was originally constructed is unknown.

Response Mode. Subjects respond to items by placing a check mark beside them if they agree, a cross if they disagree, and a question mark if they cannot decide.

Scoring. The individual's score is the median of the scale values of the items with which he agrees. High scores indicate positive attitudes.

Reliability. Lorge (1939) reports the reliability estimates on this scale to range from .76 to .84, which is satisfactory.

Validity. The Thurstone procedure of construction tends to insure a degree of content validity. Other evidence of validity is lacking.

Comments. This seems to be a reliable scale which is valid for the question of whether the Constitution should be criticized or changed. It does not deal explicitly with the question of interpretation of the existing Constitution. The result is that two persons may agree that it should not be changed, but one person may mean that it should not be changed by formal amendment and the other person mean that it should not be changed in "interpretation" as it exists. Finally, it would be interesting to have a scale which measured attitudes toward interpretation of the constitution by the Supreme Court (as in the current civil rights issue). Readers interested in this scale may also consult Knode (1943) and Fay (1939, 1940*a*,*b*).

EXHIBIT 4-10

ATTITUDE TOWARD THE CONSTITUTION OF THE UNITED STATES

This is a study of attitudes toward the United States Constitution. On the following pages you will find twenty-one statements expressing different attitudes toward the Constitution.

Put a check mark (√) if you **agree** with the statement.
Put a cross (×) if you **disagree** with the statement.

If you cannot decide about a statement, you may mark it with a question mark.

This is not an examination. People differ in their opinions about what is right and wrong on this question.

Please indicate *your own attitude* by a check mark when you agree and by a cross when you disagree.

Form A

Scale Value		
4.8	1	The Constitution should be changed only after great deliberation and thought.
0.1	2	The Constitution should be overthrown.
8.8	3	Any foreigner who criticizes our Constitution should not be allowed to become a citizen.
10.0	4	I will oppose every attempt to revise the Constitution.
7.4	5	In schools we should present only the strong points of the Constitution.
2.7	6	The fundamental principles of our Constitution could be greatly improved.
1.1	7	The sooner we get a new Constitution, the better.
9.0	8	All right-thinking Americans believe heart and soul in the Constitution.
4.4	9	The Constitution is after all only a human document.
10.0	10	I'd give my life to preserve the Constitution.
7.8	11	We must protect our Constitution against the radicals.
3.3	12	The Constitution is not so perfect as most people think.
2.9	13	Destructive criticism of the Constitution should be allowed.
1.5	14	Our present Constitution is entirely inadequate.
5.7	15	Only the authorities should suggest changes in the Constitution.
9.2	16	Our Constitution is a model for all other governments to follow.
8.1	17	Public-school students should avoid all criticism of the Constitution.
6.4	18	Let us keep the Constitution even though it may be weak in places.
6.1	19	We should be cautious in suggesting changes in the Constitution.
1.9	20	Our industrial civilization requires a new Constitution.
4.3	21	I think there may be reasons for changing the Constitution.

Form B

Scale Value		
4.7	1	I suppose there may be some places where the Constitution is weak.
2.6	2	I believe that the Constitution is out of date.
7.9	3	We should show respect and reverence toward our Constitution.
4.0	4	Several parts of the Constitution might be improved.
9.0	5	Aliens who criticize our Constitution should be sent out of this country.
7.5	6	Our Constitution is a great document even though it is not perfect.
3.5	7	Complete freedom to criticize the Constitution should be allowed at all times.
5.3	8	I am undecided about changing the Constitution.
0.1	9	Our Constitution is in every way the worst governing document ever written.
8.4	10	Right-thinking Americans never criticize our Constitution.
10.1	11	Our Constitution is sacred.
9.8	12	The principles of government contained in our Constitution are as perfect as man can ever make them.
9.7	13	Our Constitution is the greatest document in all the world today.
1.0	14	We can never make any progress so long as we keep our present Constitution.
5.0	15	Any criticism of the Constitution should be constructive.

Scale Value		
6.6	16	Our Constitution should not be discarded because of a few evils connected with it.
2.2	17	The Constitution might have been great once but it isn't any more.
3.0	18	The Constitution has not been such a wonderful success as most people believe.
6.4	19	We should be careful about criticizing the Constitution.
7.0	20	Too much danger is involved in revising the Constitution.
1.3	21	We ought to have a new Constitution.

Attitude toward capital punishment *EXHIBIT 4-11*

Description. This 15-item scale was developed by Balogh and Mueller (1960), using a modified Thurstone procedure. This set of 15 items was selected from an original pool of 100 statements. Items were first selected on the basis of the degree to which they met Thurstone's criteria. The 20 items selected were then subjected to an item analysis and evaluated according to their ability to discriminate high and low scorers. Five items were dropped. As the items were originally sorted on a 7-point continuum, as opposed to the usual 11-point continuum, the possible scores range only from 1.1 to 6.8. No item in Exhibit 4-11 has a sigma larger than .84. There are two items (nos. 3 and 11) with confidence levels as low as .10. All others are at .05 or higher.

Subjects. The judges for sorting the items consisted of 15 criminology students. The item analysis was based upon a sample of an additional 24 unidentified persons.

Response Mode. Persons respond by checking those items with which they agree and placing a cross beside those with which they disagree.

Scoring. The individual's score is the mean of the scale values of the items with which he agrees. High scores indicate unfavorable attitudes toward capital punishment.

Reliability. There are no reliability estimates available for this scale.

Validity. The items have content validity for the question of whether murderers should face capital punishment, but they do not consider the question of capital punishment for any other forms of crime. The scale has relatively good content validity for this restricted content domain of capital punishment for murderers. It has been demonstrated to discriminate between mean scores of known groups (25 policemen and 25 subjects from the general population).

Comments. The scale seems to possess a satisfactory level of validity for attitude toward capital punishment for murderers. It is lacking in evidence for reliability. In view of the combination of Thurstone and Likert procedures for item selection (which results in violation of the assumptions underlying both models of scale construction), it may be expected that the reliability will be found to be only moderately good to poor. Overall, this scale seems less satisfactory than the scale by Thurstone, which follows, for measuring the same attitude.

EXHIBIT 4-11

ATTITUDE TOWARD CAPITAL PUNISHMENT

Put a check mark (✓) if you agree with the statement.
Put a cross (×) if you disagree with the statement.

If you simply cannot decide about a statement, you may mark it with a question mark.

Scale Value		
4.0	1	Capital punishment is not morally right or wrong; it is merely just one method of punishment.
1.1	2	A murderer deserves to die.
1.3	3	Murderers are social misfits and are useless to society; therefore it is best to execute them.
6.7	4	Society does not have the right to take a human life no matter what the circumstances.
2.6	5	The public would feel less secure if capital punishment were abolished.
6.7	6	When a murderer is sentenced to death, society is just as bad as the condemned.
5.1	7	Since capital punishment has not prevented murders, society should abolish it.
1.2	8	Murder is a sin and should be punished by death.
5.6	9	Statistics show that a person will only kill once; therefore, the murderer should be allowed to live and prove himself.
6.1	10	Since murderers can be rehabilitated, they deserve the chance to become useful citizens.
3.4	11	Capital punishment will do until something better is found.
5.5	12	Society should make murderers work for the state rather than execute them.
2.9	13	Capital punishment seems to have proven to be a fairly effective deterrent to murder.
6.8	14	When society sentences a murderer to death, we ourselves become murderers.
6.0	15	Rather than execute a murderer society should try to help him through treatment.

Reference: J. Balogh and M. A. Mueller. A scaling technique for measuring social attitudes toward capital punishment. *Sociol. soc. Res.*, 1960, 45, 24–26. Items obtained from authors and published with their permission.

Attitude toward capital punishment *EXHIBIT 4-12*

Description. This 24-item scale was developed by Thurstone (1932) and used by him on Illinois school children. It has the advantage of measuring attitude toward capital punishment in general, with items ranging from capital punishment for all criminals to those which reject capital punishment altogether. Information regarding Q values for the items was not available.

Subjects. The sample upon which the scale was originally constructed is unknown.

Response Mode. Subjects respond by placing a check mark beside those items with which they agree and a cross beside those with which they disagree. They are to place a question mark beside those about which they are uncertain.

Scoring. The individual's score is the median of the scale values of the items with which he agrees. A high score reflects a favorable attitude toward capital punishment.

Reliability. Lorge (1939) reports reliability estimates ranging from .59 to .88. The range of such estimates is reported by Ferguson (1944) as being from .79 to .88. This range is quite satisfactory. Thurstone (1932) established a test-retest reliability coefficient of .71 upon a sample of 501 Geneseo, Illinois, grade school children (grades 4 through 12 inclusive). The retest interval was fifteen days, during which time a treatment (exposure to a relevant motion picture) was administered. Thus, Thurstone's estimate may be taken as minimal.

Validity. The scale has good content validity. In addition, Diggory (1953) reports correlations of +.26 and +.42 between this scale and Thurstone's Attitude toward Punishment of Criminals Scale, which is indicative of construct validity. Finally, the reliability estimates allow for the possibility of adequate validity.

Comments. This is a valid and reliable scale for the measurement of attitude toward capital punishment in general. It is unfortunate that there is no equivalent form available for this scale. The interested reader may also wish to see Robinson (1941) and Smith (1939, 1940, 1945*b*).

EXHIBIT 4-12

ATTITUDE TOWARD CAPITAL PUNISHMENT

This is a study of attitude toward Capital Punishment. On the other side of this page you will find a number of statements expressing different attitudes toward Capital Punishment.

√ Put a check mark if you agree with the statement.
× Put a cross if you disagree with the statement.

Try to indicate either agreement or disagreement for each statement. If you simply cannot decide about a statement you may mark it with a question mark.

This is not an examination. There are no right or wrong answers to these statements. This is simply a study of people's attitudes toward Capital Punishment. Please indicate your own convictions by a check mark when you agree and by a cross when you disagree.

Scale Value		
7.2	1	Capital punishment may be wrong but it is the best preventative to crime.
0.0	2	Capital punishment is absolutely never justified.
6.2	3	I think capital punishment is necessary but I wish it were not.
10.4	4	Any person, man or woman, young or old, who commits murder, should pay with his own life.
2.4	5	Capital punishment cannot be regarded as a sane method of dealing with crime.
6.2	6	Capital punishment is wrong but is necessary in our imperfect civilization.
11.0	7	Every criminal should be executed.
2.7	8	Capital punishment has never been effective in preventing crime.
3.4	9	I don't believe in capital punishment but I'm not sure it isn't necessary.
8.5	10	We must have capital punishment for some crimes.
3.9	11	I think the return of the whipping post would be more effective than capital punishment.
0.1	12	I do not believe in capital punishment under any circumstances.
3.0	13	Capital punishment is not necessary in modern civilization.
1.5	14	We can't call ourselves civilized as long as we have capital punishment.
3.4	15	Life imprisonment is more effective than capital punishment.
0.9	16	Execution of criminals is a disgrace to civilized society.
9.6	17	Capital punishment is just and necessary.
5.8	18	I do not believe in capital punishment but it is not practically advisable to abolish it.
0.6	19	Capital punishment is the most hideous practice of our time.
9.4	20	Capital punishment gives the criminal what he deserves.
2.0	21	The state cannot teach the sacredness of human life by destroying it.
5.5	22	It doesn't make any difference to me whether we have capital punishment or not.
7.9	23	Capital punishment is justified only for premeditated murder.
9.1	24	Capital punishment should be used more often than it is.

Attitude toward punishment of criminals EXHIBIT 4-13

Description. This 34-item scale was originally developed by Wang and Thurstone (1931) for use with college students and later simplified for high school students. Both forms of the scale are given in Exhibit 4-13, but they should not be used as equivalent forms. The statements are concerned with the purpose of and appropriate use of punishment, as well as with the question of whether or not to punish criminals at all. Q values for the items could not be located.

Subjects. The exact sample upon which the test was constructed is uncertain but was probably University of Chicago students.

Response Mode. Persons respond by placing a check mark beside those items with which they agree and a cross beside those with which they disagree. A question mark is placed beside those about which they are uncertain.

Scoring. The individual's score is the median of the scale values of the items with which he agrees. High scores indicate favorable attitudes toward the punishment of criminals.

Reliability. Lorge (1939) reports reliability estimates for the original scale (the college form) to run from .69 to .76, while Ferguson (1944) reports the range as being from .57 to .73. It does not seem that the simplification of the items for use with high school students should appreciably affect the reliability of the second scale. Regarding this second scale, Thurstone (1932) found in his study of the effects of motion pictures upon attitudes that the children's form was relatively stable. He obtained a test-retest reliability coefficient of .66 in the face of exposure to a motion picture dealing with a relevant topic, using a retest interval of two weeks.

Validity. Both forms of the scale seem to have good content validity. Diggory (1953) reports that this scale (college form) correlates +.50 and +.30 with Thurstone's scale measuring attitude toward capital punishment. These correlations suggest that the college form of the scale possesses construct validity.

Comments. Although the characteristics of the children's form of the scale are less well known than those of the college form, both forms of the scale seem satisfactory with regard to both reliability and validity. The simplified children's form has the advantage of being useful for a larger range of educational levels. Readers interested in other studies using this scale should consult Telford (1934), Duffy (1941), and Smith (1940, 1943, 1945*a*,*b*).

EXHIBIT 4-13

ATTITUDE TOWARD PUNISHMENT OF CRIMINALS

This is a study of attitudes toward punishment of criminals. On the other side of this page you will find a number of statements expressing different attitudes toward punishment of criminals.

✓ Put a check mark if you agree with the statement.

× Put a cross if you disagree with the statement.

Try to indicate either agreement or disagreement for each statement. If you simply cannot decide about a statement you may mark it with a question mark.

This is not an examination. There are no right or wrong answers to these statements. This is simply a study of people's attitudes toward the punishment of criminals. Please indicate your own convictions by a check mark when you agree and by a cross when you disagree.

College Form

Scale Value		
5.8	**1**	A person should be imprisoned only for serious offenses.
1.1	**2**	It is wrong for society to make any of its members suffer.
9.0	**3**	Hard prison life will keep men from committing crime.
4.8	**4**	Some criminals do not benefit from punishment.
2.7	**5**	Most prisons are schools of crime.
8.2	**6**	We should not consider the comfort of a prisoner.
8.6	**7**	A criminal will go straight only when he finds that prison life is hard.
0.5	**8**	No punishment can reduce crime.
3.1	**9**	Prison influence is degenerating.
5.5	**10**	Only habitual criminals should be punished.
10.0	**11**	We should employ corporal punishment in dealing with all criminals.
5.3	**12**	I have no opinion about the treatment of crime.
0.8	**13**	Punishment of criminals is a disgrace to civilized society.
9.3	**14**	Solitary confinement will make the criminal penitent.
4.1	**15**	It is advantageous to society to spare certain criminals.
1.5	**16**	Only humane treatment can cure criminals.
3.1	**17**	Harsh imprisonment merely embitters a criminal.
9.8	**18**	No leniency should be shown to convicts.
3.4	**19**	Many petty offenders become dangerous criminals after a prison term.
8.1	**20**	Failure to punish the criminal encourages crime.
10.6	**21**	Only by extreme brutal punishment can we cure the criminal.
1.8	**22**	The more severely a man is punished, the greater criminal he becomes.
6.4	**23**	A criminal should be punished first and then reformed.
8.8	**24**	One way to deter men from crime is to make them suffer.
2.3	**25**	Punishment is wasteful of human life.
9.2	**26**	A bread and water diet in prison will cure the criminal.
3.2	**27**	Brutal treatment of a criminal makes him more dangerous.
7.6	**28**	A jail sentence will cure many criminals of further offenses.
10.3	**29**	Prison inmates should be put in irons.
4.6	**30**	We should consider the individual in treating crime.
0.0	**31**	Even the most vicious criminal should not be harmed.
7.4	**32**	It is fair for society to punish those who offend against it.
2.7	**33**	Humane treatment inspires the criminal to be good.
6.6	**34**	Some punishment is necessary in dealing with the criminal.

High School Form

5.8	**1**	A person should be put in prison only for very bad crimes.
1.1	**2**	It is wrong for the government to make any people suffer in prison.
9.0	**3**	Hard prison life will keep men from committing crime.
4.8	**4**	Punishment does not make some criminals any better.
2.7	**5**	In prison many men learn to be worse criminals.
8.2	**6**	We should not bother about the comfort of a prisoner.

Scale Value		
8.6	7	A criminal will go straight only when he finds that prison life is hard.
0.5	8	There isn't any punishment that will keep men from committing crime.
3.1	9	Prisons make men worse than they were.
5.5	10	Only men who have committed several crimes should be punished.
10.0	11	We should use physical punishment in dealing with all criminals.
5.3	12	I don't know anything about the treatment of crime.
0.8	13	We should be ashamed to punish criminals.
9.3	14	Putting a criminal in a cell by himself will make him sorry.
4.1	15	It is better for us to be easy on certain criminals.
1.5	16	Only kind treatment can cure criminals.
3.1	17	Cruel prison treatment makes criminals want to get even.
9.8	18	No kindness should be shown to prisoners.
3.4	19	Many men who aren't very bad become dangerous criminals after a prison term.
8.1	20	If we do not punish criminals, we will have more crime.
10.6	21	Only by very cruel punishment can we cure the criminal.
1.8	22	Severe punishment makes men worse criminals.
6.4	23	A criminal should be punished first and then reformed.
8.8	24	One way to keep men from crime is to make them suffer.
2.3	25	We cannot make a good citizen of a criminal if we punish him.
9.2	26	Having to live on bread and water in prison will cure the criminal.
3.2	27	Cruel treatment of a criminal makes him more dangerous.
7.6	28	A jail sentence will cure many criminals.
10.3	29	Prisoners should be chained.
4.6	30	In order to decide how to treat a criminal we should know what kind of person he is.
0.0	31	Even the very worst criminal should not be mistreated.
7.4	32	It is fair for the government to punish men who break the laws.
2.7	33	Kind treatment makes the criminal want to be good.
6.6	34	We have to use some punishment in dealing with criminals.

Attitudes toward school integration (IA) scale: form 1
EXHIBIT 4-14

Description. This is a 29-item scale developed by Greenberg, Chase, and Cannon (1957) to measure attitudes toward the issue of integration. An original pool of 60 items was developed based only on the logical validity of the items. The 29-items shown in Exhibit 4-14 were selected by testing each item for discriminatory power. This item analysis was performed using a sample of 50 college students. The items cover many different facets of the integration question from integration of public facilities to dating with a couple of another race. However, most of them refer to the context of an academic situation.

Subjects. The scale was originally constructed using a sample of 233 white high school students, 49 Negro high school students, and 860 white college students in western Texas.

Response Mode. Subjects respond to each question on a six-point continuum: strongly agree, agree, mildly agree, mildly disagree, disagree, and strongly disagree. Respondents must answer all questions; no neutral category is provided.

Scoring. The response alternatives are weighted from +3 (strongly agree) to −3 (strongly disagree) for negative items. These weights are reversed for the alternatives for positive items. A constant of 4 is added to all item scores to make all values positive. The person's score is the sum of the weighted alternatives endorsed by him. Should a question be left out, a score of 4 (the midpoint on the seven-point continuum) is assigned to it. If more than three questions are left out, the author (Greenberg, 1961) states that the subject should be excluded from the sample. High scores reflect negative attitudes toward integration.

Reliability. No evidence of reliability is reported.

Validity. The scale seems to have relatively good content validity, especially for testing the attitudes of students. Scores on this scale were found by Greenberg (1961) to correlate .71 with scores on the California E scale, which might be considered as evidence of construct validity.

Comments. The fact that reliability estimates and demonstrations of validity for this scale are lacking reduces the instrument's value. It does not seem to be as adequate as similar scales which follow (especially Exhibits 4-15 and 4-17). It has been included, nevertheless, because of the high relevance of many of its items to the school situation, a situation of focal concern in the process of integration of public facilities. Readers interested in the IA scale may also wish to see Greenberg and Hutto (1958).

EXHIBIT 4-14

ATTITUDES TOWARD SCHOOL INTEGRATION (IA) SCALE: FORM 1

This questionnaire has been devised to measure your attitudes. There are no "right" or "wrong" answers—the only right answer is the one which best reflects your true personal opinion toward the question considered.

To answer the questions, choose the answer below which corresponds most closely with your personal attitude toward the particular question, and place the corresponding number in the space provided at left.

+ (plus) 3 for strongly agree	— (minus) 3 for strongly disagree
+ (plus) 2 for agree	— (minus) 2 for disagree
+ (plus) 1 for mildly agree	— (minus) 1 for mildly disagree

*1 If another race were integrated into my school, I would do my best to accept them as classmates and equals.

2 I think the scholastic level of my school would fall if other races were integrated into the school program.

*3 I would be willing to accept, as an equal, a member of another race into a club to which I belonged.

4 I believe that members of the other race should have separate advisories and separate seats in assemblies.

*5 I believe that any student who has the ability should be eligible for the band and/or choir regardless of his race.

6 Racial groups should sit at separate tables in the cafeteria.

*7 It would make no difference to me if my teachers were of my own race or a different one.

8 I would hesitate to bring students of another race home with me because I do not think my parents would approve.

*9 Every student should have equal rights in regard to holding a class office, position as cheerleader, etc., regardless of his race.

10 I would not approve of a student of another race representing my school at statewide functions (Boy's State, Hi-Y conventions, etc.).

*11 I believe that every student, regardless of race, should be eligible for school athletic teams, if he has the ability to make the team.

12 Different racial groups mixing at school functions (dances, parties, etc.) will not be wise—it will only result in fights and ill feeling between races.

*13 Members of any race should be allowed to sit anywhere on busses, in movies, at ball games, etc.

14 Having members of other races on my school's athletic teams would result in more "dirty playing" and unsportsmanlike conduct.

*15 I believe that a member of the other race could become a very close friend of mine (possibly even my "best friend").

16 When integration is accomplished, separate shower facilities and locker rooms should be provided for the different races in Physical Education classes.

*17 I would not mind having a member of another race as a member of my church.

18 I do not think that my parents would want to work on school parent committees, such as the PTA, with parents of another race.

*19 If I liked a person of the other race well enough, I would accept him into my personal group of good friends ("My gang," etc.).

20 I believe that dating between races will be a serious problem soon after integration.

*21 I would not mind "double dating" with a couple both of whom were of the other race.

22 Regardless of what anyone else says, I believe that my race is superior and should be accepted as such.

*23 The Supreme Court's decision to integrate other races into white schools was just and timely.

†24 I do not think I would be willing to sit next to a member of another race in class.

*25 I would not mind dancing with a member of another race at a school or club function.

26 Separate rest room facilities and drinking fountains should be provided for each racial group.

* These are positive items and weights for their response alternatives must be reversed for scoring purposes.

† The author suggests that for college students, question 24 be replaced by the following item: "I would not accept a member of the other race as a roommate in the dormitory."

*27 There is no basic reason for feeling prejudiced against another race.
28 I would not vote for any candidate for student office unless he (she) was of my race.
*29 Restaurants, movies, etc., should serve anyone, regardless of race.

Attitude toward segregation scale EXHIBIT 4-15

Description. This is a 25-item, modified Likert-type scale developed by Rosenbaum and Zimmerman (1959). Items were selected upon the basis of item analysis, and all 25 items were found to discriminate the extreme quartiles of scorers at a high level of confidence.

Subjects. The scale was originally constructed upon a sample of 129 introductory psychology students at the University of North Carolina (Rosenbaum and Zimmerman, 1959). It was used further with a sample of 502 introductory psychology students (also presumably from the University of North Carolina) by the same authors.

Response Mode. Subjects respond on a modified Likert continuum: agree very much, agree pretty much, agree a little, disagree a little, disagree pretty much, and disagree very much. No neutral alternative is made available.

Scoring. Response alternatives to items are weighted from 6 (agree very much) to 1 (disagree very much) for prosegregation items. Scoring is reversed for antisegregation items. The subject's score is the sum of the alternatives he endorses. High scores indicate prosegregation attitudes. The range of possible scores is from 25 to 150. The authors report a mean of 85.4 and standard deviation of 26.2, based upon the 502 students at the University of North Carolina.

Reliability. The test-retest reliability coefficient is .89; the retest interval is not reported (Rosenbaum and Zimmerman, 1959).

Validity. The scale has reasonably good content validity. The high discriminatory power of the items is a testimony to its internal consistency.

Comments. This seems to be a quite adequate scale for measuring attitudes toward segregation.

EXHIBIT 4-15

ATTITUDE TOWARD SEGREGATION SCALE

This questionnaire represents an attempt to survey the opinions of students on the issue of segregation in our school systems. We feel that it is

Reference: M. E. Rosenbaum and I. A. Zimmerman. The effect of external commitment on response to an attempt to change opinions. *Publ. Opin. Quart.*, 1959, 23, 247–254. Items obtained from authors and reproduced with their permission.

a rather important issue that we are dealing with and so in order to permit you to present how you feel as frankly as possible, your name does not appear here. (The person is then asked to select one of six alternatives: Agree Very Much, Agree Pretty Much, Agree a Little, Disagree a Little, Disagree Pretty Much and Disagree Very Much).

1 Racial segregation is an effective and practical social arrangement which has no serious effect on the vitality of democratic ideals.

†Agree Very Much___ Agree Pretty Much___ Agree a Little___
Disagree a Little___ Disagree Pretty Much___ Disagree Very Much___

*2 The Negroes' main concern is with equal educational opportunities. They have no intention of interfering with the social patterns of the white community.

3 The best safeguard of a democracy is the solid stability of social tradition such as is involved in the maintenance of segregation.

4 Integration threatens one of the principles of democracy, the right of each citizen to choose his own associates.

5 The end of segregation would bring a continuing increase in social conflict and violence.

*6 Although the IQ of Negroes in the South is on the whole lower than the IQ of whites, this difference in intelligence is mainly due to lack of opportunity for the Negro and will eventually disappear under an integrated school system.

7 Since integration will require some painful adjustments to be made in changing from segregated schools, the best solution will be to leave the races segregated.

*8 Equal educational exposures in integrated schools will help both the Negro and white students to profit from the best of the two cultures.

*9 De-segregation can in most cases be accomplished without being followed by social conflict and violence.

*10 Improving Negro education via integration will lead to a higher standard of living in the South, accompanied by more and better jobs for everybody.

11 The Supreme Court's decision on segregation was a politically inspired invasion of states rights and represents a miscarriage of justice.

12 The Negro race is physically and mentally inferior to the white race and integration would not help to erase the innate differences between the two races.

*13 Integrated and therefore better education for the Negro via integration is certain to result in increased feelings of responsiblity and cooperation on his part.

*14 The successes of already completed integration attempts are clear evidence that the fears of extreme pro-segregationists are unfounded.

15 Negroes who are given the opportunity to go to integrated schools are apt to become demanding, officious, and overbearing.

16 Although certain radical Negro leaders try to make people think otherwise, the majority of Negroes do not want integration and would be satisfied with "equal but separate" school facilities.

17 De-segregation will develop a false sense of power among Negroes and will move us closer to having a "Negro party" in America.

*18 The South has failed to adequately draw upon the resources of the Negro race and integrated schools will enable the Negro race to make a greater

† The same response alternatives are used for all items.
* These items are antisegregation and weights for their alternatives are reversed for scoring purposes.

contribution to the South economically and socially than they have been able to make with segregated schools.

19 The de-segregation law is basically unfair to the Negroes who will now have to compete on equal terms with the whites.

20 Once you start letting Negroes attend the schools of whites, they will demand complete social equality in all respects including dating and club privileges.

*21 Negroes and whites will find it easier to get along together in the same school than most people think.

*22 In dealing with the problems of desegregation we should always act in terms of the Christian rule of brotherhood and justice for all and not in terms of social attitudes based on tradition.

*23 The practice of segregation cannot help but reduce our political influence in international affairs.

24 De-segregation will lead to a permanent lowering of standards in the public schools.

*25 De-segregation is economically wise since the South's poor economic state may in part be due to the double expense of segregation.

The segregation scale *EXHIBIT 4-16*

Description. This is a six-item scale developed by Peak, Morrison, Spivak, and Zinnes (1956), using Combs' unfolding technique. It measures attitudes toward the issue of allowing Negroes into white neighborhoods and was developed for a study of personality factors involved in attitude change.

Subjects. Peak (private communication, 1965) reports that the original population upon which the scale was constructed consisted of students in elementary psychology classes. Samples ranged in size from 86 to 208 persons.

Response Mode. The scale is composed of six items, rank ordered according to degree of favorability toward the segregation of Negroes in white neighborhoods. The respondent endorses three of the six alternatives, indicating the order of his preference by placing the number 1 before the statement which best agrees with his own position, 2 beside the statement which next best agrees with his own position, and 3 beside the statement which third best reflects his own position.

Scoring. The person's score is assigned on the basis of the pattern of responses given by him in assigning the three ranks to the responses. All 16 permutations of three endorsed items out of six alternatives are used. Labelling the items as a, b, c, d, e, and f, the permutations and their scores are as follows:

abc, 16; bac, 15; bca, 14; cba, 13; bcd, 12; cbd, 11; cdb, 10; dcb, 9; cde, 8; dce, 7; dec, 6; edc, 5; def, 4; edf, 3; efd, 2; fed, 1. (Peak, private communication, 1964.)

Thus, if the person assigned the numbers 1, 2, and 3 to the response alternatives a, b, and c respectively, he would receive a score of 16. If he assigned the numbers 1, 2, and 3 to the alternatives d, c, and e respectively, he would receive a score of 7. High scores indicate pro-segregation attitudes.

Reliability. The scale has a test-retest reliability of .68. The retest interval was seven weeks ($N = 86$).

Validity. The items of this ranking scale were administered with two other scales measuring attitude toward segregation. The intercorrelations between these three scales are reported by Peak and Morrison (1958) to range from .65 to .95, indicating good to excellent concurrent validity. The items sample a highly restricted content domain, as they are variations on a single question of opposition to allowing Negroes to move into white neighborhoods. Content validity would be considered seriously restricted for measuring attitudes toward segregation generally.

Comments. The scale is valid and reliable as a measurement of attitude toward segregation in neighborhoods.

EXHIBIT 4-16

THE SEGREGATION SCALE

In many parts of the country today there has arisen the question of whether Negroes should be allowed to move into neighborhoods that have previously been occcupied only by Whites.

****

Please read the statements below carefully.

Then *choose the three that come closest to representing your own Opinion on the issue stated above.*

Now *place number 1* before the statement which *best agrees* with your own position.

Now *place number 2* before the statement which *next best* reflects your own position.

Place number 3 before the statement which *third best* reflects your own position.

NOTE: USE EACH RANK (1, 2, and 3) ONLY ONCE—LEAVE BLANK THOSE STATEMENTS WITH WHICH YOU LEAST AGREE

_______ a. I am **completely opposed** to allowing Negroes into White neighborhoods.

_______ b. I am **much more opposed** to allowing Negroes into White neighborhoods than I am for it.

_______ c. I am **slightly more opposed** to allowing Negroes into White neighborhoods than I am for it.

Reference: H. Peak, H. W. Morrison, M. Spivak, and J. L. Zinnes. Some factors in resistance to attitude change. I. Personality factors. *Tech. Rep.* **No. 1, Office of Naval Research, August 15, 1956. Items obtained from authors and reproduced with their permission.**

_______ d. I am **slightly more in favor** of allowing Negroes into White neighborhoods than I am against it.

_______ e. I am **much more in favor** of allowing Negroes into White neighborhoods than I am against it.

_______ f. I am **completely in favor** of allowing Negroes into White neighborhoods.

****

In the space below, please indicate the degree of difficulty you had in making your first choice. Check the appropriate box.

Difficulty in making first choice: _______Great
_______Some
_______Little

The desegregation scale EXHIBIT 4-17

Description. This is a 26-item scale developed by Kelley, Ferson, and Holtzman (1958), using a combined Thurstone-Likert procedure. The final items selected for use in the scale were those demonstrating minimum variance and approximately equal interval distribution on an 11-point continuum. All items in Exhibit 4-17 have Q values smaller than 1.56. These items were originally interspersed in a larger survey covering many topics.

Subjects. The scale was developed using a sample of 547 male and female, native-born, undergraduate students at the University of Texas.

Response Mode. Although the scale values for the items are reported in Exhibit 4-17, Kelley's procedure required the subject to respond to each item on a five-point continuum from "strongly agree" to "strongly disagree."

Scoring. The alternative responses are weighted from 4 (strongly agree) to 0 (strongly disagree) for prosegregation items. These weights are reversed for response alternatives on antisegregation scores. The person's score is the sum of the weighted alternatives which he endorsed. High scores show intolerance of the Negro.

Reliability. The means of Kelley's sample were: males, 44.8; females, 45.1. These means should be compared with those from a second sample of 517 University of Texas students (Young, Benson, and Holtzman, 1960) taken three years later: males, 47.9; females, 42.3. The fact that there was little change in means and variances of the samples over a three-year period not only testifies to the well-known durability of attitudes and stereotypes, but also serves as a basis for inferring scale reliability.

Validity. Kelley et al. (1958) considered validity to be established on the basis of item selection: Items selected demonstrated minimum variance and approximately equal interval distribution on the 11-point scale. The scale seems to have at least average content validity.

Comments. Despite the fact that Kelley used a Likert-type response mode, it would seem feasible to also use this scale as a Thurstone scale and assign the median of the scale values of items endorsed as the subject's score (when the subject has been asked to check only those with which he agrees). This suggestion is advanced because items were selected for minimum variance, indicating that they are nonmonotonic. They may not be expected to correlate well with total score and may function best in a point-scale procedure such as Thurstone's. Used in this manner, they should discriminate the middle range better than if they were used as though they were monotonic; however, they may not, as there are no items with scale values between 4.30 and 7.34. Finally, further evidence of reliability and validity would be desirable.

EXHIBIT 4-17

THE DESEGREGATION SCALE

This is not an intelligence test nor an information test. There are no "right" or "wrong" answers. The best answer is your *honest, frank* opinion. You can be sure that whatever your opinion may be on a certain issue there are some people who agree, some who disagree. And this is what we want to find out: How is public opinion really divided on each of these socially important topics?

It must be emphasized that the sponsors of this survey do not necessarily agree or disagree with the statements in it. We have tried to cover a great many points of view. We agree with some of the statements and disagree with others. Similarly, you will probably find yourself agreeing strongly with some of the statements, disagreeing just as strongly with others, and being perhaps more neutral about still others.

We realize that people are very busy nowadays, and we don't want to take too much of your time. All we ask is that you:

a) Read each statement carefully and mark it according to your first reaction. It isn't necessary to take a lot of time for any one question.
b) *Answer every question.*
c) Give your personal point of view. Don't talk about the questions with anyone until you have finished.
d) Be as sincere, accurate, and complete as possible in the limited time and space.

For every item, please circle your personal reaction to the statement according to the following code:

SA—STRONGLY AGREE
A—AGREE
U—UNDECIDED OR UNCERTAIN
D—DISAGREE
SD—STRONGLY DISAGREE

Reference: J. G. Kelley, J. E. Ferson, and W. H. Holtzman. The measurement of attitudes toward the Negro in the South. *J. soc. Psychol.*, 1958, 48, 305–317. Items obtained from authors and published with their permission.

Scale Value		
10.59	3	The prospect of intermarriage is repulsive to me.
		†SA A U D SD
10.40	60	The Negro will remain ignorant and superstitious despite equal educational opportunities.
10.02	43	If one of my best friends married a Negro, I would stop inviting him to my home.
9.88	77	Negroes are often dishonest and would increase cheating if admitted to White schools.
9.50	73	If Negroes are allowed to share all public facilities and institutions with White people, they will soon become arrogant and overbearing.
9.25	55	The trouble with letting Negroes into White schools is that they would gradually give them a typical atmosphere.
8.94	33	Negroes living in White neighborhoods lower the standards of cleanliness.
8.43	61	Separate churches for White and colored people should be maintained, since church membership is a matter of individual choice.
8.24	37	One of the reasons for maintaining segregation is that the Negro will be able to find more equal opportunities with his own people.
7.96	30	A Negro Army officer could never do a good job leading White soldiers because they might lack confidence in him.
7.75	28	Admitting Negroes to White schools would not work because most Negroes do not have the necessary background to keep up with White students.
7.34	11	If a Negro were elected to public office, social pressures would prevent his doing a good job.
4.30	*17	The Negro race will eventually reach the cultural and intellectual level of White people.
3.76	*81	I would accept a traffic ticket as graciously from a Negro as from a White police officer.
3.71	*70	The fact that there is no racial segregation in certain European countries indicates that desegregation can be made to work here.
3.54	*62	The Army's desegregation policy is an advance toward interracial understanding.
3.42	*38	I would not object to participating in school athletics with Negroes.
3.33	*31	Negroes should be allowed to occupy any seats they can afford to pay for at a concert, sports event, or other public program.
3.00	*13	I would not mind sharing a table with Negroes in a crowded cafeteria.
2.71	*16	Negroes should be allowed to enter any university they choose.
2.40	*51	I would not mind having my children taught by a Negro school teacher.
2.32	*63	I would not object to sharing a public swimming pool with Negroes.
2.18	*89	I would not object to dancing with a good Negro dancer.
1.83	*71	I would not hesitate to join a fraternity or sorority which admitted Negroes.
1.34	*46	I would consider dating a Negro, providing he or she met all of my other standards.

† The same response alternatives are used with all items.
* These items are positive and must be reversed for scoring purposes, if a Likert response mode and scoring procedure are used (as is suggested by the authors).

Scale Value		
1.15	*42	The best way to solve the race problem is to encourage intermarriage so that there will eventually be only one race.

Attitude toward accepting Negro students in college
EXHIBIT 4-18

Description. This 20-item scale was developed by Grafton (1964) using the Thurstone procedure. It was constructed to poll student sentiment on the hypothetical question, "How would I feel if I learned that my college had accepted a Negro student?" A pool of 80 items was sorted by judges on a nine-point continuum from the most opposing to the most favoring statements. The items selected for the scale include both covert and overt reactions to the presence of a Negro student and to the general issue of segregation. The Q values for all items are between .71 and 2.84. Only two items have Q values as large as 2.0 (items no. 9 and 11), and the author points out that they are in the middle of the scale where greatest ambiguity would be expected to occur. In the form of the instrument used to obtain validation, the items in Exhibit 4-18 were arranged as follows: 8, 1, 5, 14, 11, 4, 13, 3, 20, 10, 17, 12, 18, 16, 2, 9, 7, 6, 15, 19.

Subjects. For sorting the items, 100 judges were used, most of whom were students from sociology classes in Mary Baldwin College. The scale was also administered to 280 students (103 freshmen, 101 sophomores, and 76 juniors and seniors) enrolled in classes in psychology, sociology, history, education, and religion.

Response Mode. Subjects respond by checking all items which they feel would represent their attitude; all other statements are left unchecked.

Scoring. The person's score is the arithmetic mean of the scale values of the items checked. High scores indicate positive attitudes. The theoretical range of scores is from 0.09 to 9.91.

Reliability. No evidence of reliability is available for this scale.

Validity. Grafton (1964) reports a significant difference in attitudes as related to regional differences, with students from the southern United States showing the greatest opposition. Further, he reports some difference between freshmen and older students, with freshmen being more opposed. It is a common finding that students become somewhat more liberal as a result of college experience. Thus, this latter result may be taken as evidence of construct validity.

Comments. This scale seems moderately satisfactory with regard to validity. Evidence of reliability would enhance its value. The author notes that item no. 1 was not checked by anyone and recommends that it be replaced by the following item: "I would participate in a public demonstration to show my disapproval." This item has a scale value of 0.17. Use of this scale is restricted to college student populations, of course.

EXHIBIT 4-18

ATTITUDE TOWARD ACCEPTING NEGRO STUDENTS IN COLLEGE

We ask you to make a serious effort to project yourself into a hypothetical situation and answer the question, "How would I feel if I learned that my college had accepted a Negro student?"

To answer this question you are asked to check every statement below which you believe would represent your attitude in such a situation, leaving all the other statements unchecked.

Scale Value		Item
.09	1	I would plan to make it so unpleasant that she would soon leave.
.55	2	I would transfer at the end of the year if I knew this would happen.
1.01	3	I would ask to be moved if seated at the same table with her.
1.40	4	It would be an unfriendly act, designed to humiliate Southern people.
1.91	5	I would oppose Negro students because their presence would make us more intolerant than we are now.
2.44	6	She should not expect to be included in the social life of the campus.
2.93	7	I do not believe a Negro student could keep up with our academic work.
3.63	8	I would not approve because I do not think she would be happy here.
4.29	9	I would favor her taking courses in summer school but not during the regular session.
4.84	10	I would wait and see how it worked, and then I could transfer if I didn't like it.
5.51	11	It would be the only thing to do although I would not like it personally.
6.10	12	I would approve only in the case of a very outstanding student.
6.59	13	I would not object to local Negro girls attending as day students.
7.05	14	I favor it because it would attract new donors to the College.
7.56	15	I think our students would quickly get used to it.
8.06	16	I think the presence of Negro students would help us all become more tolerant.
8.61	17	A Negro should have as much right to come as a foreign student.
9.06	18	I would try to enlist my parents in support of the idea.
9.51	19	I think all our colleges and universities should be desegregated.
9.91	20	I would be willing to be her roommate the first year.

ATTITUDES RELATED TO RELIGIOUS AND PHILOSOPHICAL ISSUES

Only two scales constitute this section—one by Webb and Kobler (1961) measuring attitude toward possible conflicts between religion and psychiatry and another by Molnar (1955) measuring attitudes toward vivisection.

Relation between religion and psychiatry scale *EXHIBIT 4-19*

Description. This 35-item scale was developed by Webb and Kobler (1961), using a combined Thurstone and Likert method. It measures only one side of the possible conflict between psychiatry and religion: Negative statements are all in terms of rejection of psychiatry because of religious conviction. There are no negative statements rejecting religion because of psychiatric convictions. All positive items emphasize the compatibility of these two approaches to man. In short, it measures the degree to which psychiatry is seen as compatible with religion, but not the degree to which religion is seen as compatible with psychiatry.

Subjects. The sample on which the scale was originally developed was made up of 268 Catholic seminarians.

Response Mode. The person responds to each item on a five-point continuum: strongly agree, agree, agree and disagree equally, disagree, and strongly disagree.

Scoring. Response alternatives for positive statements (indicating compatibility of religion and psychiatry) are weighted from 4 (strongly agree) to 0 (strongly disagree). Weights for the response alternatives must be reversed for negative items (rejecting psychiatry). The person's score is the sum of the weighted alternatives which he endorses. High scores indicate a positive attitude toward psychiatry, with regard to its compatibility with religion.

Reliability. The test-retest reliability coefficient for a two-week retest interval was .93. A split-half reliability estimate of .95 is also reported by the authors.

Validity. Validity was established through the prediction of known groups (two groups of seminary students, one of which received a course of a psychiatric nature taught by a priest-psychiatrist). The scale is probably restricted in its validity to use with samples possessing religious convictions. It may be expected to function less well with agnostic or atheistic samples.

Comments. This scale is probably a valid instrument for measuring an attitude involving rejection of psychiatry on religious grounds. It is best used on samples possessing religious convictions. There are no items to allow measurement of attitudes reflecting incompatibility between religion and psychiatry because of a rejection of religion.

EXHIBIT 4-19

RELATION BETWEEN RELIGION AND PSYCHIATRY SCALE

This questionnaire is an attempt to get your opinion on some vital issues. We are interested only in *your* agreement or disagreement with the following statements, and not in the truth or falsity of them. In some cases you may feel you do not have enough information to make a judgment; in such instances we would like you to make the best judgment possible.

Please read every statement and respond to it in terms of your personal agreement or disagreement according to the following plan:

Strongly agree	Agree	Agree and disagree equally	Disagree	Strongly disagree
A	B	C	D	E

Please circle the letter indicating your choice.

1 A psychiatrist can be effective regardless of his religion.

†A B C D E

2 There is a close relationship between religious and psychiatric ideals.
*3 Psychiatry ignores the supernatural side of man.
*4 A psychiatrist makes one feel uncomfortable because he is always analyzing his fellow man.
*5 Psychiatry denies free will in man's conduct by its emphasis on unconscious motivations.
6 Parishioners should be referred to a psychiatrist as readily as to another medical specialist.
7 There is no conflict between psychiatry and religion.
8 In our complex society it is essential for the priest to have a thorough knowledge of psychiatry.
*9 Current psychiatric practice allows people to express sexual impulses without moral inhibition.
*10 Common sense is a fitting substitute for psychiatric knowledge.
11 There is nothing in present day psychiatry that is contrary to Catholic teaching.
*12 A good Catholic should never undergo intensive psychiatric analysis.
13 Psychiatry is as important as philosophy in seminary training.
14 Religion and psychiatry are compatible.
*15 Psychiatrists are likely to misguide a Catholic when moral problems are involved.
*16 Psychiatrists often attempt to take the place of a priest.
*17 Psychiatry today is dominated by a materialistic philosophy of man.
*18 Psychiatric analysis usually requires too much time for treatment to be recommended to a parishioner.

† The same response alternatives are used with all items.
* These items are negative and must be reversed for scoring purposes.

Reference: N. J. Webb and F. J. Kobler. Clinical-empirical techniques for assessing the attitudes of religious toward psychiatry. *J. soc. Psychol.*, 1961, 55, 245–251. Items obtained from authors and published with their permission.

*19 Psychiatrists place an exaggerated emphasis on sex.
20 Psychiatric knowledge is essential in adjusting to life in the seminary.
*21 Psychiatry offers few facts and its teachings are mostly hypothetical and uncertain.
22 The findings of psychiatry should be taught to help the priest in his confessional work.
*23 In most cases a parishioner who thinks he needs psychiatric help would do better to improve his religious life.
24 Psychiatry is feared only because it is misunderstood.
*25 More consistent agreement among psychiatrists is necessary before their teaching can be brought into the seminary.
*26 Too much psychiatry is a bad thing.
27 More emphasis on teaching the findings of psychiatry is needed in the seminary curriculum.
*28 The present seminary curriculum is too crowded to include more teaching of psychiatric knowledge.
29 In dealing with mentally disturbed individuals psychiatry is essential.
*30 Psychiatry because of its exclusive concern with abnormal individuals is of little use to the priest.
*31 Psychiatry considers religion a mass delusion to be eliminated through analysis.
*32 The psychiatrist's use of electric shock therapy should be condemned.
33 The priest who utilizes psychiatric knowledge in his work is a more effective priest.
*34 Psychiatry is unacceptable because it deals too much with the unknown.
35 A priest should not hesitate to refer a parishioner to a psychiatrist.

The vivisection questionnaire EXHIBIT 4-20

Description. Molnar (1955) constructed this 10-item scale using a Likert procedure. It measures attitudes toward the use of animals in experimentation. The scale presented in Exhibit 4-20 is one obtained from Lana, as used by him in his 1959 study.

Subjects. The sample upon which the scale was constructed is unknown.

Response Mode. Subjects respond by checking in one of six columns labelled: disagree strongly, disagree moderately, disagree slightly, agree slightly, agree moderately, agree strongly. There is no neutral alternative. The columns have been eliminated from Exhibit 4-20.

Scoring. For provivisection items, the response alternatives should be weighted from 7 (strongly agree) to 1 (strongly disagree). These weights should be reversed for antivivisection items. The individual's score is the sum of the weighted alternatives which he has endorsed. Please note that this scoring procedure is not necessarily the one used by Molnar (1955) or Lana (1959). It is inferred to be the correct one on the basis of the modified Likert response mode used by Lana. If this procedure is used, items which are left blank should be scored as 4 (or neutral). If several items are left blank, the questionnaire for that subject should be discarded, since there are only 10 items.

Reliability. The corrected split-half reliability coefficient is reported by Lana (1959) to be .85, based on a sample of 132 University of Maryland students.

Validity. The scale is very abbreviated but seems to possess average content validity. The only other evidence of validity is the fact that scores changed in the expected direction as a result of experimental treatment: exposure to a taped provivisection argument (Lana, 1959).

Comments. This scale is satisfactory with regard to reliability, but evidence of validity is somewhat weak.

EXHIBIT 4-20

THE VIVISECTION QUESTIONNAIRE

This is a survey of what people think about a social question. The best answer to each statement below is *your own personal opinion.* We have tried to cover many different points of view. You may find yourself agreeing strongly with some of the statements, disagreeing just as strongly with others, and perhaps uncertain about others. Whether you agree or disagree with any statement, you can be sure many other people feel the same way that you do.

Please use the special answer sheet for making your answers. Each number of the answer sheet corresponds to a number on this sheet. Read each statement and then mark your response after the appropriate number on the answer sheet. Indicate your answer by placing a mark in the column which corresponds with your opinion.

1. I DISAGREE STRONGLY
2. I DISAGREE MODERATELY
3. I DISAGREE SLIGHTLY
4. I AGREE SLIGHTLY
5. I AGREE MODERATELY
6. I AGREE STRONGLY

*1 Most dogs destroyed in pounds would be of little value in medical research.

*2 Most surgical procedures are learned under the watchful eye of a surgeon while operating on humans—not on laboratory animals.

*3 Many times, the same vivisection experiment is performed again and again without conclusive results.

*4 Scientists should substitute new and better methods of carrying on their investigation for inconclusive operations on animals.

5 In animal experiments, animals do not suffer—anesthetics are always administered.

6 Animals in pounds would normally be destroyed, therefore, they should be used in animal experiments.

*7 Animals are man's friends and should not be treated cruelly.

8 Work done with animals in laboratories cannot be described as cruel.

* These items are negative and should be reversed for scoring purposes.

Reference: A. Molnar. The effects of styles, speakers, and arguments on the attitudes and perceptions of a listening audience. Unpublished M.A. thesis, Univer. of Maryland, 1955. Items obtained from R. E. Lana and published with the permission of A. Molnar and R. E. Lana.

9 All experiments on animals are serious efforts to find cures and better treatments for the ailments and diseases of men.
10 Animal experimentation is justified if the animals do not suffer.

ATTITUDES RELATED TO ECONOMIC ISSUES

The scales in this section are all designed to measure attitudes toward relatively specific economic issues or problems. They include as referents the employment of elderly persons, attitudes toward changes that are work related, and attitudes toward relief and receiving relief. Readers interested in more global economic attitudes should turn to Chapter 7. One scale on attitude toward relief which was excluded but which may be of interest is by Forsyth (1943).

Attitude toward employment of older people EXHIBIT 4-21

Description. This was originally a 27-item scale developed by Kirchner et al. (1952), using a Likert procedure. In a later study Kirchner (1957) used a 24-item version of the scale to measure attitudes of psychologists, supervisory trainees, personnel workers, and vocational guidance workers. It is the 24-item scale used in the later study which is given in Exhibit 4-21.

Subjects. The sample was composed of 62 supervisors and rank-and-file employees in a laundry.

Response Mode. Persons respond to each item on a Likert response continuum: strongly agree, agree, undecided, disagree, and strongly disagree.

Scoring. The scale should be scored by assigning weights for response alternatives to positive items (acceptance of hiring older persons) as follows: strongly agree, 5; agree, 4; undecided, 3; disagree, 2; strongly disagree, 1. These weights should be reversed for negative items indicating rejection of employment of older persons. The person's score would then be the sum of the weighted alternatives endorsed by him. High scores indicate positive attitudes toward employment of the elderly. This scoring procedure is inferred from the response mode used by Kirchner.

Reliability. Kirchner et al. (1952) report the split-half reliability coefficient (corrected) to be .90.

Validity. In addition to content validity, the scale differentiates between known groups (rank-and-file employees and supervisors) at a high level of significance; supervisors possess more negative attitudes (Kirchner et al. 1952). In a sample of 160 employees in a naval ordnance plant, Kirchner and Dunnette (1954) found the scale to differentiate older from younger rank-and-file employees, older employees being significantly more positive toward hiring older people. In the same study, it was also found that while supervisors had a significantly higher mean age, they possessed a significantly lower mean attitude score. Although the content domain seems relatively well sampled, it is contaminated by some seemingly irrelevant items (irrelevant to the topic issue) such as "I think Social Security payments are too small."

Comments. This scale is adequate with regard to both validity and reliability. Kirchner (1957) reports norms for responses from samples of psychologists and nonpsychologists for the response alternatives from each item. In these samples are included a number of personnel and vocational guidance specialists. Such norms may provide an interesting comparison base for other samples.

EXHIBIT 4-21

ATTITUDE TOWARD EMPLOYMENT OF OLDER PEOPLE

On this page and the following pages you will find a number of statements.

1. Read each statement carefully.
2. Choose the word that *best* tells how you feel about each statement.
3. Put an "X" in the space following the word.
4. Do this for all statements.

Here is an example:

There has been too much snow in Minnesota this winter.

Strongly agree___ Agree X___ Undecided___ Disagree___ Strongly disagree___

If you strongly agree with this statement, you would place an "X" in the space following the words "Strongly agree." If you agree with the statement you would place an "X" in the space following the word "Agree," as has been done in the example.

There are no "right" or "wrong" answers. Just tell how you feel about each statement.

Your answers are secret.

1 I think older employees have fewer accidents on the job.

†Strongly agree___ Agree___ Undecided___ Disagree___ Strongly disagree___

2 Most companies are unfair to older employees.

*3 Older employees are harder to train for jobs.

*4 Older employees are absent more often than younger employees (under age 30).

5 Younger people (under age 30) act too smart nowadays.

† The same response alternatives are used with all items.

* These are negative items and must be reversed for scoring purposes.

6 Younger employees (under 30) usually have more serious accidents than older employees.
7 In a case where two people can do a job about the same, I'd pick the older person for the job.
8 I think that Social Security payments are too small.
9 Occupational diseases are more likely to occur among younger employees (those under age 30).
10 The older employees usually turn out work of higher quality.
*11 I think that older employees are more grouchy on the job.
12 I believe that older people cooperate more on the job.
13 Older people seem to be happier on the job.
14 I feel that older people are more dependable.
*15 Most older people cannot keep up with the speed needed in modern industry.
*16 Supervisors find it hard to get older people to adopt new methods on the job.
17 Older people should get higher wages for their job.
18 You'll find that the employees who are most loyal to the company are the older employees.
*19 Older people are too set in their ways—they don't want to change.
20 I think older employees have as much ability to learn new methods as other employees.
21 I think companies should train middle aged employees (those aged 35–50) to handle many different jobs.
22 I think that older employees make better employees.
23 I think that most younger people are too radical in their ideas.
24 Pay should be based on length of service rather than on what a person does (how long a person has worked in a company should count more than the amount of work he turns out).

The (work related) change scale EXHIBIT 4-22

Description. This nine-item, Likert-type scale was developed by Trumbo (1961). It measures attitude toward changes that are work related. It includes items relevant to attitudes toward changes in ways of doing the job and transfers to new jobs. It has been included in the social issues chapter because of its relevance to the question of automation.

Subjects. The scale was constructed upon a sample of 46 supervisory and 232 nonsupervisory personnel of an insurance company involved in "office automation" changes. Of the nonsupervisory sample, 79 percent was female.

Response Mode. Persons respond to the first item on a five-point continuum from "is always the same" to "changes a great deal." The remaining eight items are responded to on a continuum from "strongly agree" to "strongly disagree" (Trumbo, 1961).

Scoring. For items reflecting a negative attitude toward change, the response alternatives to the items are weighted from 5 (strongly agree) to 1 (strongly disagree). For positive items (reflecting a preference for changes), weights for the response alternatives must be reversed. The individual's score is the sum of the weighted alternatives endorsed. High scores indicate an unfavorable attitude toward work-related changes.

Reliability. Trumbo (1961) reports the split-half reliability coefficient (corrected) to be .79.

Validity. The scale was found to predict attitudes toward specific change situations, particularly when the employee perceived or anticipated relatively extensive changes in his own job. The content domain sampled by the scale seems restricted. Item analysis demonstrated that all items discriminated between high and low scorers on the total score continuum.

Comments. While the scale seems average in validity and reliability for the sample on which it was used, this sample was also the one on which it was constructed. Further demonstrations of its reliability and validity would be valuable.

EXHIBIT 4-22

THE (WORK RELATED) CHANGE SCALE

There are no right or wrong answers to the following questions. All of the questions have to do with your attitudes and opinions.

Go through these questions quickly. Choose the one answer that comes closest to the way that you feel. Place a check mark (✓) in the space in front of your choice. Please try to answer every question.

1 The job that you would consider ideal for you would be one where the way you do your work:

_______ Is Always the Same
_______ Is Usually the Same
_______ Undecided
_______ Changes to Some Extent
_______ Changes a Great Deal

*2 If I could do as I pleased, I would change the kind of work I do every few months.

_______ I Strongly Agree
_______ I Agree
_______ Undecided
_______ I Disagree
_______ I Strongly Disagree

3 One can never feel at ease on a job where the ways of doing things are always being changed.

* This item is positive and should be reversed for purposes of scoring.

_______ I Strongly Agree
_______ I Agree
_______ Undecided
_______ I Disagree
_______ I Strongly Disagree

4 The trouble with most jobs is that you just get used to doing things in one way and then they want you to do them differently.

_______ I Strongly Agree
_______ I Agree
_______ Undecided
_______ I Disagree
_______ I Strongly Disagree

5 I would prefer to stay with a job that I know I can handle than to change to one where most things would be new to me.

_______ I Strongly Agree
_______ I Agree
_______ Undecided
_______ I Disagree
_______ I Strongly Disagree

6 The trouble with many people is that when they find a job they can do well, they don't stick with it.

_______ I Strongly Agree
_______ I Agree
_______ Undecided
_______ I Disagree
_______ I Strongly Disagree

7 I like a job where I know that I will be doing my work about the same way from one week to the next.

_______ I Strongly Agree
_______ I Agree
_______ Undecided
_______ I Disagree
_______ I Strongly Disagree

8 When I get used to doing things in one way it is disturbing to have to change to a new method.

_______ I Strongly Agree
_______ I Agree
_______ Undecided
_______ I Disagree
_______ I Strongly Disagree

9 It would take a sizeable raise in pay to get me to voluntarily transfer to another job.

_______ I Strongly Agree
_______ I Agree
_______ Undecided
_______ I Disagree
_______ I Strongly Disagree

Attitude toward receiving relief EXHIBIT 4-23

Description. Hinckley and Hinckley (1939) developed this 26-item, Thurstone-type scale. These items were drawn from an original pool of 132 items, sorted by 275 judges on an 11-point continuum. The question form is such as to make it appropriate only for persons who are receiving some sort of government relief. Item number 25 in this scale seems somewhat dated. Q values for the items range from 0.25 to 1.12. Two related scales by the same authors are given in Exhibits 3-29 and 3-30.

Subjects. Judges for item selection were 275 unidentified subjects.

Response Mode. The subject places a check mark beside those statements with which he agrees, a cross beside those with which he disagrees, and a question mark beside those about which he is uncertain.

Scoring. The subject's score is the median of the scale values of the items with which he agrees.

Reliability. The split-half reliability was found to be .90. (Hinckley, private communication, 1965).

Validity. The scale seems to have good content validity for attitudes of people who are on relief about receiving relief.

Comments. This appears to be a worthwhile scale and a timely one. However, the lack of information regarding its functional characteristics detracts from its value, and evidence of validity is seriously needed.

EXHIBIT 4-23

ATTITUDE TOWARD RECEIVING RELIEF

This is a study of attitudes toward receiving relief. On this and the following page you will find twenty-six statements expressing different attitudes toward the subject.

Put a check mark (√) if you agree with the statement.
Put a cross (×) if you disagree with the statement.

If you cannot decide about a statement, you may mark it with a question mark.

This is not an examination. People differ in their opinions about what is right and wrong in this issue.

Please indicate your own attitude by a check mark when you agree and by a cross when you disagree.

Scale Value		
4.37	**1**	Relief has enabled me to await with calm the chance of further employment.
2.19	**2**	I soon lost any feeling of reluctance toward living on public money.
9.33	**3**	Just leave me alone until I get work again—I don't want relief.
7.68	**4**	I'd hate to lose my independence by accepting relief.
4.93	**5**	I would accept relief if I needed it.
6.03	**6**	I am forced to receive relief, regardless of my ideals.
0.12	**7**	I would like to stay on the relief rolls forever.
1.63	**8**	I want relief so that I won't have to work so much.
6.63	**9**	I am not content on relief.
10.57	**10**	I would starve before I would accept relief.
8.14	**11**	I enjoy food bought with honest work rather than relief food.
5.31	**12**	Give me relief or give me a job.
2.82	**13**	I am beginning to prefer relief to work.
0.50	**14**	I will take all I can get.
8.63	**15**	Few men with respect for themselves and a sense of responsibility for society find it necessary to accept relief.
2.63	**16**	Since I cannot find work, I am perfectly willing, and even glad to accept relief.
10.28	**17**	No honest man would accept relief of any sort.
7.02	**18**	I am tired of living on the government.
1.33	**19**	I have every right to receive relief, and I accept it without shame.
5.74	**20**	Relief has been a help, but it is incidental. I still look to the future.
9.72	**21**	I need relief, but I won't take it.
3.40	**22**	I expect relief when I don't have a job.
8.99	**23**	By accepting relief I would consider myself a slave of the government.
0.88	**24**	As long as the government will feed me I'll let it.
3.73	**25**	It is practically impossible to pull out of this depression without some relief.
7.38	**26**	I would rather have a permanent job than be on relief.

Distribution of the wealth (DW) scale *EXHIBIT 4-24*

Description. This 20-item, Likert-type scale was developed by Wilke (1934). The items concern such issues as income and inheritance taxes and the sanctity of private property.

Subjects. The scale was constructed using 61 unidentified subjects. It was further used on a total sample of 1,174 subjects, in an experimental comparison of the impact of radio, the printed page, and speeches as propaganda devices.

Response Mode. Persons respond to each item by endorsing a Likert five-point continuum: strongly agree, agree, undecided, disagree, and strongly disagree.

Scoring. For positive items (favoring free enterprise), the response alternatives are weighted from 5 (strongly agree) to 1 (strongly disagree). Weights for response alternatives must be reversed for negative items (against capitalism and free enterprise). The person's score is the sum of the weighted alternatives endorsed by him.

Reliability. The author reports test-retest reliability coefficients of .87 and .90, based upon a sample of 1,174 persons and using a retest interval of three weeks. The split-half reliability coefficient (corrected) is reported as being .92, based on a sample of 61 persons.

Validity. Content validity for this scale is difficult to assess. The only other evidence of validity is the fact that the author reports small changes in scores in the expected direction as a result of experimental treatment.

Comments. This seems to be a reliable scale for measuring attitudes toward capitalism and mechanisms for redistribution of wealth. However, further evidence of its validity is required. Only two items are at all dated: Item 17 refers to the "present depression" and probably cannot be altered effectively; item 9 refers to the "colossal need" for relief and may or may not be considered dated at present.

EXHIBIT 4-24

DISTRIBUTION OF THE WEALTH (DW) SCALE

Will you please indicate your opinion on each of the accompanying statements. To indicate your opinion, draw a circle around the word which best describes your agreement as shown:

1 We should oppose the more even distribution of wealth since it is likely to stifle individual initiative.
†Strongly agree Agree Undecided Disagree Strongly disagree

*2 It would be far better for the country if great fortunes were not allowed to accumulate.

*3 Inheritance taxes should confiscate the bulk of all large private fortunes.

*4 Income taxes should be so high in the upper brackets that the greater portion of the larger incomes is confiscated.

*5 It is contrary to the interests of the people of the United States to permit the concentration of wealth into the hands of a few people.

6 Since only a few people are capable of handling the complex problems of large-scale industries, the wealth of this country is rightfully placed largely in their hands.

*7 It is socially undesirable that the children of the very rich should inherit the huge fortunes of their parents.

8 We should encourage the development of big fortunes as vitally necessary to supply large amounts of capital for our huge business and financial enterprises.

*9 The colossal need for relief in the face of an oversupply of food and other necessities shows that the ownership of wealth should be redistributed.

* These items are negative and must be reversed for scoring purposes.
† The same response alternatives are used with all items.

Reprinted with permission from Wilke, W. H. An experimental comparison of the speech, the radio, and the printed page as propaganda devices. *Arch. Psychol.*, 1934, No. 169.

*10 The enormous wealth of the extremely rich should be more uniformly distributed among all the people.
11 In gauging a nation's prosperity and wealth one should form his judgment on the basis of the greatest fortunes attained in that nation.
12 The wealth of this country is now distributed approximately as it should be.
*13 Most of our wealthy people do not deserve the huge fortunes which they have accumulated.
14 Individual thrift and initiative should not be dampened by any limitation or taxation of hereditary wealth.
15 The wealthiest people in the United States have amply justified the existence of great fortunes by the generous gifts to science and charity.
16 There should be no restriction except one's own ability upon the amount of money one may honestly acquire.
*17 Our government should get at the real basis of the present depression by taxing the wealthy sufficiently to give the masses of people enough to purchase what they need.
18 The wealthy are already doing more than their share in paying heavy taxes.
*19 The government ought to make it impossible for individuals to acquire such huge fortunes as are now in existence.
20 Money or property must be held inviolate and immune to seizure by governments, even in times of war, famine or national stress.

GENERALIZED SCALES TO MEASURE ATTITUDES TOWARD SOCIAL ISSUES AND PROBLEMS

The scales contained in this section are those which may be used to measure many different social issues with one instrument. Another generalized scale, the Osgood semantic differential is discussed in Chapter 2. It has been used in a number of studies to measure attitudes toward social issues. Steiner and Field (1960) have used it to measure attitudes toward desegregation. Asher and Evans (1959) measured attitudes toward the following referents with the Osgood semantic differential: public discussion of sex, public discussion of puberty in girls, and menstruation. Altrocchi and Eisdorfer (1961) used the semantic differential to measure attitudes toward the mentally ill. Nunnally (1957) has used it in a similar manner. The only other generalized scale to be discussed is the Attitudes toward Any Proposed Social Action scale.

Attitudes toward any proposed social action *EXHIBIT 4-25*

Description. This 17-item, Thurstone-type scale was developed by Remmers (1934, 1936, 1938) to measure attitudes toward any proposed social action. The consideration that such proposals would usually constitute bases for social issues led to its inclusion in this chapter. The scale has equivalent forms.

Subjects. The exact population upon which the scale was constructed is not known, but samples used in constructing Remmers' scales have included a wide range of subjects from grade 6 pupils to graduate students.

Response Mode. There are five blank columns beside the items. The person writes the names of the social issues in question at the head of these blank columns. He then places a plus (+) beside the item if he agrees with it with reference to the proposed social action or actions listed. These columns have been eliminated from Exhibit 4-25.

Scoring. The individual's score (for any one proposed social action) is the median of the scale values of the items endorsed by him for that referent.

Reliability. Remmers (1960) reports the following equivalent-forms reliability coefficients for this scale when applied to these proposed social actions: abolition of compulsory military training in college, $r = .92$; abolition of township trustees in Indiana, $r = .81$; compulsory sex education for adults, $r = .70$; divorce, $r = .81$; social insurance, $r = .75$; old age pensions, $r = .78$; outlawing communism, $r = .78$.

Validity. These items have at least some content validity, and the Thurstone procedure used to construct the scale normally ensures a degree of content validity. However, one cannot fully assess this characteristic without knowing the social action which is to serve as the referent for the scale. Thus, the scale may be valid for many social actions and invalid for others. One apparent basis for possible reduction in validity is that certain statements would not apply equally well to any action. For example, the first statement in this scale is "will bring lasting satisfaction"; this item is irrelevant to proposed stopgap social actions which are not expected to bring lasting satisfaction.

Comments. While the use of generalized scales would seem to have the advantage of eliminating variance due to differences in instruments, it may introduce variance due to differences in applicablity of items to the referents. Nonetheless, good reliability estimates are reported for the scale, and it seems a generally sound instrument. Test-retest reliability estimates would be valuable, of course, as would further demonstrations of validity.

EXHIBIT 4-25

ATTITUDES TOWARD ANY PROPOSED SOCIAL ACTION

Following is a list of statements about proposed social actions. Place a plus sign (+) before each statement with which you agree with reference to the proposed social action or actions listed at the left of the statements. The person in charge will tell you the proposed social action or actions to write in at the head of the columns to the left of the statements. Your score will in no way affect your grade in any course.

Form A

Scale Value		
10.3	1	Will bring lasting satisfaction.
9.6	2	Has unlimited possibilities.
9.2	3	Will solve some of humanity's greatest problems.
8.9	4	Will be an influence for right living.
8.5	5	Is sure to be effective.
8.1	6	Is a practical basis for future planning.
7.7	7	Places great emphasis upon fair-dealing.
6.5	8	Has its merits.
6.0	9	Can not do any serious harm.
5.5	10	Will be all right in some cases.
4.7	11	Can not meet the demands of a complex social order.
3.6	12	Will cause too much friction.
3.1	13	Will soon become an object of bitter distrust.
2.6	14	Will proceed to injurious limits.
2.2	15	Is a disgrace to society.
1.6	16	Will destroy our best American institutions.
1.0	17	Is perfectly absurd.

Form B

10.3	1	Is vitally necessary for the welfare of the country.
9.6	2	Will advance civilization to a higher level.
9.2	3	Will stand the test of time.
8.9	4	Shows great possibility of being a success.
8.5	5	Will be appreciated by the general public.
8.1	6	Shows common sense.
7.7	7	Probably will be accepted by the majority.
6.5	8	Will be liked only fairly well.
6.0	9	Will do just as much harm as it will good.
5.5	10	Is too much of a deviation from normal procedure.
4.7	11	Is too contradictory.
3.6	12	Will not fit into our modern world.
3.1	13	Is entirely a haphazard plan.
2.6	14	Is a foolish inconsistency.
2.2	15	Is an enemy of liberty.
1.6	16	Is a ridiculous plan.
1.0	17	Can mean only disaster.

SUMMARY

As with attitudes toward ethnic and national groups, many scales are available to measure attitudes toward such issues as segregation, civil rights, and integration. Many other contemporary issues are not represented, however. There are no scales for measuring attitudes toward such social issues as Bible reading in schools, authority of the Supreme Court, or birth control pills (and the possible accompanying increased sexual freedom of women). Similarly, many technological advances remain unrepresented: space travel and exploration, automation, the security impositions resulting in restriction of scientific and other information, nuclear power for home use, and the quality (or lack of it) and use of television.

CHAPTER **5**

international issues

A favorite concern of attitude investigators has been attitudes toward relations among nations. For example, Thurstone and his associates developed several scales to measure attitudes toward war and conducted many studies involving the measurement of these attitudes. More recently, greater interest has been directed toward nationalistic attitudes. Such attitudes are of great importance in determining the behavior of citizens in response to various governmental policies and actions in relation to other nations. A knowledge of these attitudes is essential to adequate understanding not only of the behavior of American citizens, but also of the reactions of other countries to our actions. Thus a comprehensive theory of international relations must include attitudes toward international issues.

Unfortunately, the number of issues for which scales are available is quite small. Eight scales given in this chapter deal with nationalistic attitudes, one with militarism-pacifism, five with war, and one with the tariff.

ATTITUDES RELATED TO POLITICAL RELATIONS

Although the scales in this section are variously labelled as measures of nationalism, internationalism, worldmindedness, and so on, their central concern is the measurement of attitudes along the nationalism internationalism continuum. This continuum ranges from extremely favorable attitudes toward other nations (high internationalism, low nationalism) to extremely unfavorable attitudes toward other nations (low internationalism, high nationalism). Seven scales are described under this general classification. Early attempts to measure this attitude that are not described in this volume include a scale by Manry (1927) and the Newman, Kulp, and Davidson International Attitudes Test (Kulp and Davidson, 1933).

Internationalism scale ***EXHIBIT 5-1***

Description. This 24-item scale was developed by Likert (1932). The various statements concern a wide variety of international relations, such as immigration laws, military training, international organizations, and wartime activities. Most of the items fall into the standard Likert format, but items 13, 14, and 15 are five-alternative multiple-choice items. Many of the items in Exhibit 5-1 are dated in the sense that they are not appropriate to the present world situation. For example, the question of whether the United States should enter the League of Nations is a meaningless question today. The scale is included here in view of the fact that a few wording changes could bring the item content up to date.

Subjects. The sample consisted of 650 college students drawn at random from a population of 2,000 students.

Response Mode. The response mode varied somewhat from item to item. The first 12 items require only a "yes," "?," or "no" response. Items 13, 14, and 15 require the subject to choose one of five alternatives which vary from item to item, and the remaining items require a choice among the following five alternatives: strongly approve, approve, undecided, disapprove, strongly disapprove.

Scoring. For items 1 through 12, a score of 4 is assigned for a "yes," 3 for a "?," and 2 for a "no" response when the statement expresses a favorable (positive) attitude toward internationalism; the order of scoring is reversed for negative statements. For items 13, 14, and 15, scores are assigned to each alternative as indicated in the right-hand column of Exhibit 5-1. For items 16 through 24, scores are assigned from 1 to 5, with the higher score being given to "strongly agree" for positive statements and to "strongly disagree" for negative statements. The attitude score is the sum of the item scores. The theoretical range is from 24 to 108, with the higher score indicating the more favorable attitude toward internationalism.

Reliability. Split-half reliability was found to be .81 (corrected to .90). Test-retest reliability after a thirty-day interval was .90.

Validity. In addition to content validity, scores on the Internationalism Scale were found to correlate .75 with the Droba war scale (see Exhibit 5-10).

Comments. The greatest problem with this scale is the inappropriateness of some of the items to current events. It was suggested above that these items might be updated by rewording. However, it should be evident that any rewording may alter the characteristics of the scale. Therefore, if such changes in item content are contemplated, the reliability and validity of the scale require reevaluation. We should also note that the evidence of validity of the scale in its present form is not strong.

EXHIBIT 5-1

INTERNATIONALISM SCALE

After each question underscore "Yes" or "No"; if you are undecided or not sure you understand the question, underscore the question mark.

*1 Do you favor the early entrance of the United States into the League of Nations?

YES ? NO

*2 Ought the United States to consult other nations in making her immigration laws?

3 Should the United States give naval demonstrations in the Pacific?

4 Is war at present a biological necessity?

*5 Should the United States recognize the Soviet government?

*6 Should the Treaty of Versailles be reconsidered, with greater leniency given to Germany?

*7 Should the United States cancel a large part of the Allied war debt in return for concessions as to disarmament and economic reconstruction abroad?

*8 Should there be a national referendum on every war?

9 Do you look with suspicion upon the idea of a Super-State as the future hope of international government?

10 Is it an idle dream to expect to abolish war?

*11 Are you in sympathy with the movement for the outlawing of war?

*12 Should the United States enter the World Court?

In each of the following you are given a preliminary statement which can be completed or answered in any one of five ways. Check whichever one of the five most closely approximates your own opinion.

13 How much military training should we have?

(a) We need universal compulsory military training. (1)

(b) We need Citizens Military Training Camps and Reserve Officers Training Corps, but not universal military training. (2)

(c) We need some facilities for training reserve officers but not as much as at present. (3)

(d) We need only such military training as is required to maintain our regular army. (4)

(e) All military training should be abolished. (5)

14 How large should our navy be?

(a) We should maintain the "two-power standard" formerly maintained by Great Britain (i.e., ours should be as strong as any two others). (1)

* Items expressing a favorable (positive) attitude toward internationalism are marked with an asterisk. The "Yes," "?," "No" response alternatives are used with items 1 through 12.

Reprinted with permission from Likert, R. A technique for the measurement of attitudes. *Arch. Psychol.*, 1932, No. 140.

(b) We should maintain a considerable margin over our nearest competitor. (2)
(c) We should share first place with another power as at present. (3)
(d) We should attempt only to maintain second place. (4)
(e) We should not be especially concerned with our rank as a naval power. (5)

15 Using the term "armaments" to mean equipment devised for war rather than for police purposes, our policy should be to favor:
(a) absolute and immediate disarmament of all nations. (5)
(b) rapid and drastic reduction of the armaments of all nations. (4)
(c) slow but steady reduction of all armaments. (3)
(d) maintenance for a long time approximately the present military and naval strength of all the powers. (2)
(e) our free military and naval expansion unembarrassed by agreements with other nations. (1)

After each statement please indicate your feelings by underscoring one of the five possible answers.

16 All men who have the opportunity should enlist in the Citizens Military Training Camps.

†Strongly Approve	Approve	Undecided	Disapprove	Strongly Disapprove

*17 The United States, whether a member or not, should co-operate fully in the humanitarian and economic programs of the League of Nations.
*18 In the interest of permanent peace, we should be willing to arbitrate absolutely all differences with other nations which we cannot readily settle by diplomacy.
*19 A person who loves his fellow men should refuse to engage in any war, no matter how serious the consequences to his country.
20 The United States should have the largest military and naval air fleets in the world.
21 We should be willing to fight for our country whether it is in the right or in the wrong.
22 We must strive for loyalty to our country before we can afford to consider world brotherhood.
*23 Our country should never declare war again under any circumstances.
24 Moving pictures showing military drill and naval maneuvers should be exhibited to encourage patriotism.

† The same response alternatives are used with items 16 through 24.

Nationalism scale: scale III EXHIBIT 5-2

Description. The Nationalism Scale was derived by Ferguson (1942, 1944*a*) from a factor analysis of Primary Social Attitudes. (See also Ferguson, 1940, 1952.) The Thurstone scales designed to measure attitudes toward war, patriotism, God, treatment of criminals, capital punishment, censorship, evolution, birth control, law, and communism were factor-analyzed. Three factors were extracted and labelled humanitarianism, religionism, and nationalism. Scales to measure the first two factors are described in Chapter 7.

The Nationalism Scale was constructed to measure Factor III, which subsumed attitudes toward patriotism, censorship, law, and communism as measured by the Thurstone scales. Sixty-four items were selected by item analysis and divided into two equivalent forms. The number of items in each form was later reduced to 25 (1944*a*). The shorter forms are given in Exhibit 5-2.

Subjects. The subjects used in Ferguson's studies were students at Stanford University and at the University of Connecticut. The number of subjects used varied from analysis to analysis.

Response Mode. Subjects are asked to check all statements with which they agree.

Scoring. For scoring purposes, weights were assigned to each item by a method described by Thomson (1939). The correlation of each item with the total score was rounded to the nearest one-digit number; the decimal was dropped; and the result was the scoring weight. Scoring weights are given in Exhibit 5-2. The attitude score is the algebraic sum of the weights of endorsed items. The higher the score, the more favorable the attitude toward nationalism.

Reliability. Equivalent-forms reliability was reported to be .79 (corrected to .88), based upon the responses of 178 college students.

Validity. Ferguson noted that the scale might be considered valid because it correlated .90 with scores on the nationalism factor which it was designed to measure ($N = 185$ college students). However, he suggested that this correlation begged the question, so a more direct attempt at validation was made. A group of 158 students was divided into a "nationalistic" and an "internationalistic" group, based upon their responses to a Survey of Opinion on Methods of Preventing War (Stagner, Brown, Gundlach, and White, 1942). As expected, the nationalistic group scored higher than did the internationalistic group.

Comments. The factor-analytic approach to the identification of "primary social attitudes" may be questioned on theoretical grounds, but the Nationalism Scale does appear to measure reliably the constellation of attitudes weighted on Ferguson's Factor III. See Lawson (1963) for an additional application of the scale.

EXHIBIT 5-2

NATIONALISM SCALE: SCALE III

Form A

Weights

−4	1	I believe that the United States is just as selfish as any other nation.
3	2	Censorship is a gross violation of our constitutional rights.
−3	3	We have too many laws.

Reprinted with permission from Ferguson, L. W. A revision of the Primary Social Attitude Scales. *J. Psychol.*, 1944, 17, 229–241.

3 4 Censorship is needed because people are unable to judge for themselves.

5 5 I'm for my country, right or wrong.

4 6 The law is more than the enactments of Congress; it is a sacred institution.

3 7 I have great respect for the American people.

4 8 Censorship might be warranted if we could get some reasonable censors.

−4 9 I prefer to be a citizen of the world rather than of any country.

−4 10 Workers can hardly be blamed for advocating communism.

5 11 The law is the true embodiment of eternal justice.

6 12 Our national morality is safeguarded by censorship.

−3 13 The American ideal of bigger, faster, and more doesn't appeal to me.

−6 14 The communists are on the right road.

−3 15 When I see so much corruption in the government of my country I can't support it wholeheartedly.

−4 16 We should have complete freedom of speech even for those who criticize the law.

−5 17 Nobody has any right to dictate to me what I shall read.

5 18 This is in every way the greatest nation in the world.

−4 19 Censorship can never be justified in a free country.

5 20 If Russia today is a sample of how communism works, we don't want it.

5 21 Censorship is effective in raising moral and aesthetic standards.

4 22 Plays and movies should be censored, but the press should be free.

−6 23 We should not reject communism until it has been given a longer trial.

−4 24 We had better keep our eyes on Russia for a while longer before making up our minds about communism.

4 25 The hatred of the United States by foreign countries is caused mostly by envy of our greatness.

Form B

5 1 I think the American people are the finest in the world.

4 2 In the long run law and justice are synonymous.

3 3 Foreign nations have done some very fine things but it takes America to do things in a big way.

−4 4 Censorship can never make people moral.

5 5 Some authorized power is certainly needed to keep obscene literature in check.

5 6 The whole communistic scheme is unsound.

5 7 Censorship protects those who lack judgment or experience to choose for themselves.

−4 8 Communism would not make much difference in the long run.

+5 9 There is hardly anything in the United States today that I would want different.

−3 10 Men are not all equal before the law.

−4 11 Commonsense keeps me from being too enthusiastic about the United States.

−6 12 The ideals of communism are worth working for.

4 13 I don't know much about other countries but I'm satisfied with the United States.

5 14 The law represents the wisdom of the ages.

4 15 Until public taste has been educated, we must continue to have censorship.

−3	16	Censorship has practically no effect on people's morals.
3	17	Censorship is a very difficult problem, and I am not sure how far I think it should go.
−6	18	More people would favor communism if they only knew something about it.
4	19	The individual who refuses to obey the law is a menace to civilization.
−4	20	It is too early to judge communism by its results in Russia.
3	21	Whether censorship is good or not depends entirely on the censor.
−4	22	Human progress demands free speech and a free press.
−4	23	People should be allowed to make their own distinctions between good and bad.
6	24	Our system of censorship isn't perfect but it is better than none.
−3	25	Americans are a mixture of all nationalities and are neither better nor worse than the nationalities that go into making them.

A survey of opinions and beliefs about international relations EXHIBIT 5-3

Description. This is a 16-item, Likert-type scale designed by Helfant (1952) to reflect an attitude of hostility in international relations. The attitude of hostility was defined as that of being able to criticize, reject, or coerce foreign countries or people, and that of feeling that we should take a more militant stand in international relations. In addition to the usual steps in scale construction by the Likert technique, Helfant subjected the final scale to an item analysis. The split-half method was used; all items discriminated between high and low scorers for each of three groups tested. The items in the final scale are given in Exhibit 5-3.

Subjects. The original sample of subjects consisted of 212 seniors at Teaneck High School, located in northeastern New Jersey. After eliminating those whose parents could not be reached and those who did not complete the tests, the final sample consisted of 84 senior boys and 82 senior girls, and their parents (165 mothers and 165 fathers).

Response Mode. The subject is asked to respond to each item by checking one of the following five alternatives: strongly agree, agree, don't know, disagree, strongly disagree.

Scoring. Each item response is scored from 1 to 5, with a favorable response being given the higher score. In Exhibit 5-3, the values assigned to each response are entered after each item under the response alternatives. The attitude score is the sum of the item scores. A high score indicates hostility toward other nations, whereas a low score indicates friendliness toward other nations. The theoretical range of scores is from 16 to 80.

Reliability. The corrected split-half reliability was .84 for the student sample, .71 for mothers, and .81 for fathers.

Validity. Validity was estimated by having students indicate their attitude toward international relations on a linear scale. The correlations between these self-ratings and scores on the attitude scale was .70.

Comments. This is a short, easily administered scale with reasonably good reliability and validity coefficients. However, the data concerning the selection of items is not as extensive as would be desirable.

EXHIBIT 5-3

A SURVEY OF OPINIONS AND BELIEFS ABOUT INTERNATIONAL RELATIONS

DIRECTIONS: Indicate your feeling about each statement by putting a check (✓) in the appropriate column. Be sure to put a check after every statement.

		Strongly Agree	Agree	Don't Know	Dis-agree	Strongly Disagree
1	In my opinion, the United States should give up trying to be on friendly terms with other countries.	1	2	3	4	5
*2	I think that if the United States is friendly toward other countries they are not as likely to be aggressive toward us.	5	4	3	2	1
3	In my opinion, only foolish dreamers believe that international friendliness can accomplish anything in the modern world.	1	2	3	4	5
*4	I feel that in international relations it is just plain common sense to "love thy neighbor as thyself."	5	4	3	2	1
*5	I believe that the U.S. should send food and materials to any country that needs them.	5	4	3	2	1
6	In my opinion, we shouldn't risk our happiness and well-being by getting involved with other countries.	1	2	3	4	5
7	I think that helping foreign countries is a waste of money.	1	2	3	4	5

* Items marked with an asterisk express a favorable attitude toward internationalism, whereas other items express a favorable attitude toward nationalism. Scoring weights are given after each item but of course are not present when the scale is administered.

		Strongly Agree	Agree	Don't Know	Dis-agree	Strongly Disagree
*8	In my opinion, international good will is essential to the welfare of the United States.	5	4	3	2	1
9	It is my belief that we should get even with any country that tries to take advantage of the United States.	1	2	3	4	5
10	I feel that we can't have "peace on earth, good will to men," because other nations are not of good will.	1	2	3	4	5
*11	I think that being friendly with other countries will do more good than harm.	5	4	3	2	1
*12	It is my feeling that we should try to help all nations, whether we get anything special out of it or not.	5	4	3	2	1
13	I think that other countries are always getting us into wars.	1	2	3	4	5
*14	I think that being friendly with other nations is a real help in solving international problems.	5	4	3	2	1
15	It is my belief that other nations are often plotting against us.	1	2	3	4	5
*16	In my opinion, all sensible people believe in trying to be friendly with other countries.	5	4	3	2	1

The internationalism-nationalism (IN) scale *EXHIBIT 5-4*

Description. The IN scale was developed by Levinson (1957). It is a 12-item, Likert-type scale, designed to measure nationalistic attitudes. The discriminatory power (DP) of an item was computed as the difference in scores between the upper and lower quarters of the total scale distribution. DPs ranged from 2.2 to 4.2 and all were significant beyond the 1 percent level of confidence. Four of the items express an internationalist position, and eight a nationalist position.

Subjects. The IN scale was administered to two classes in education and one in social relations at Harvard University during the 1951 summer session. The total sample of 84 subjects included undergraduates, graduates, and persons in teaching and related community work.

Response Mode. Subjects are allowed three degrees of agreement (+1, +2, +3) and three degrees of disagreement (—1, —2, —3) with each item. They respond by entering the appropriate number beside each item.

Scoring. Each item is given a score ranging from 1 to 7. For nationalistic items, a +3 response is given a score of 7; +2, a score of 6; +1, a score of 5; no response, a score of 4; —1, a score of 3; —2, a score of 2; and —3, a score of 1. For the internationalistic items (starred in Exhibit 5-4), the scoring is reversed. The total scale score is the mean of the item scores, multiplied by 10. The possible range of scores is therefore from 10 to 70, with the higher scores indicating a stronger nationalistic attitude.

Reliability. The split-half reliability was reported to be .86, and test-retest reliability, .90 after a six-week interval.

Validity. Some evidence of validity was provided by showing that scores on the IN scale correlated .52 with scores on a Religious Conventionalism Scale (developed by Lichtenberg and Levinson), .60 with a 12-item form of the F scale, .77 with the E scale, and .65 with the TFI scale (see Exhibit 3-10).

Comments. This is a short, easily administered and scored scale. Evidence concerning its characteristics, however, seems to be limited to that reported by Levinson and summarized above. Since this evidence is based upon the responses of only 84 subjects, further studies concerning the nature of the scale seem indicated.

EXHIBIT 5-4

THE INTERNATIONALISM-NATIONALISM (IN) SCALE

The following are statements with which some people agree and others disagree. Please mark each one on the left margin, according to the amount of your agreement or disagreement, by using the following scale:

+1: slight support, agreement	—1: slight opposition, disagreement
+2: moderate support, agreement	—2: moderate opposition, disagreement
+3: strong support, agreement	—3: strong opposition, disagreement

1 We need more leaders like MacArthur, who have the morals and the strength to put our national honor above appeasement.

2 If it weren't for Russia and her satellites, the world would be headed toward peace and prosperity by now.

*3 In the long run, it would be to our best interest as a nation to spend less money for military purposes and more money for education, housing, and other social improvements.

* Items marked with an asterisk take an "internationalist" position . . . ; the others represent a "nationalist" position.

Reprinted with permission from Levinson, D. J. Authoritarian personality and foreign policy. *Conflict Resolution*, 1957, 1, 37–47. Copyright 1957 The Journal of Conflict Resolution, Ann Arbor, Michigan.

4 The immigration of foreigners to this country should be kept down so that we can provide for Americans first.

5 The only way peace can be maintained is to keep America so powerful and well armed that no other nation will dare to attack us.

*6 Our best policy in China would be to forget about Chiang Kai-shek and to work for a coalition between the Communists and the "center" parties.

7 If the United Nations doesn't show more signs of getting rough with Russia soon, America must be prepared to carry on the fight by itself.

8 While we should give military aid to countries which are prepared to fight our enemies, we ought to cut down on foreign economic help, or else the other countries will just play us for a sucker.

9 In these troubled times, if we are to be strong and united against our common enemy, we must have more laws and safeguards against the spreading of dangerous ideas.

*10 One main trouble with American foreign policy today is that there is too much concern with military force and too little concern with political negotiation and economic reconstruction.

11 In view of America's moral and material superiority, it is only right that we should have the biggest say in deciding United Nations policy.

*12 The first principle of our foreign policy should be to join forces with any country, even if it is not very democratic, just as long as it is strongly anti-Communist.

The worldmindedness scale EXHIBIT 5-5

Description. The Worldmindedness Scale (Sampson and Smith, 1957) is a 32-item, Likert-type scale designed to measure nationalistic-internationalistic attitudes. Sampson and Smith called it a "social attitudes questionnaire" when discussing it with subjects. The items in the final scale were selected from a pool of 60 items on the basis of an item analysis and the requirements that there be 16 pro-worldminded and 16 anti-worldminded items and that each of eight dimensions of worldmindedness be represented by four items. All items retained discriminated between the upper and lower 10 percent by at least 2 scale points. In Exhibit 5-5 the items are arranged so that every eighth item pertains to the same dimension, in the following order: religion, immigration, government, economics, patriotism, race, education, and war. Thus items 1, 9, 17, and 25 pertain to religion, items 2, 10, 18, and 26 pertain to immigration, and so on throughout the scale.

Subjects. The subjects for development of this scale were 120 university students.

Response Mode. Subjects respond to each item by checking 1 of 6 degrees of agreement, as follows: strongly agree, agree, mildly agree, mildly disagree, disagree, strongly disagree.

Scoring. For pro-worldminded items, a score of 6 is given for strong agreement, 5 for agreement, 4 for mild agreement, 2 for mild disagreement, 1 for disagreement, and 0 for strong disagreement. For anti-worldminded items, this scoring is reversed. The attitude score is the sum of the item scores. The possible range of scores is from 0, for extreme nationalmindedness, to 192, for extreme worldmindedness.

Reliability. Based upon the responses of 56 college students, split-half reliability was found to be .87, corrected to .93. A test-retest reliability of .93 was obtained for 33 students after a twenty-eight-day interval.

Validity. Sampson and Smith suggested that the internal consistency of the scale argued for its validity, but they also provided some further empirical evidence. Scale scores correlated —.71 with an 11-item form of the E scale and —.53 with a 10-item form of the California Political-Economic Conservatism Scale. In addition, the Worldmindedness Scale discriminated between 192 students who went to Europe with student organizations as tourists and 25 persons who went to Europe with the Quaker International Volunteer Service—an organization known for a worldminded frame of reference.

Comments. The evidence provided by Sampson and Smith indicates that this scale has exceptionally high reliability and adequate validity. It has been used with some success by Garrison (1961), Allman (1961), and Smith (1955).

EXHIBIT 5-5

THE WORLDMINDEDNESS SCALE

Indicate your agreement or disagreement by underlining one of the following six degrees of agreement and disagreement: strongly agree, agree, mildly agree, mildly disagree, disagree, strongly disagree.

1 Our country should have the right to prohibit certain racial and religious groups from entering it to live.

*Strongly Agree	Agree	Mildly Agree	Mildly Disagree	Disagree	Strongly Disagree

2 Immigrants should not be permitted to come into our country if they compete with our own workers.

3 It would be a dangerous procedure if every person in the world had equal rights which were guaranteed by an international charter.

†4 All prices for exported food and manufactured goods should be set by an international trade committee.

†5 Our country is probably no better than many others.

* The same response alternatives used with each item.

† Pro-worldminded items are marked with a dagger.

6 Race prejudice may be a good thing for us because it keeps many undesirable foreigners from coming into this country.

7 It would be a mistake for us to encourage certain racial groups to become well educated because they might use their knowledge against us.

8 We should be willing to fight for our country without questioning whether it is right or wrong.

9 Foreigners are particularly obnoxious because of their religious beliefs.

†10 Immigration should be controlled by an international organization rather than by each country on its own.

†11 We ought to have a world government to guarantee the welfare of all nations irrespective of the rights of any one.

12 Our country should not cooperate in any international trade agreements which attempt to better world economic conditions at our expense.

†13 It would be better to be a citizen of the world than of any particular country.

†14 Our responsibility to people of other races ought to be as great as our responsibility to people of our own race.

†15 An international committee on education should have full control over what is taught in all countries about history and politics.

16 Our country should refuse to cooperate in a total disarmament program even if some other nations agreed to it.

17 It would be dangerous for our country to make international agreements with nations whose religious beliefs are antagonistic to ours.

†18 Any healthy individual, regardless of race or religion, should be allowed to live wherever he wants to in the world.

19 Our country should not participate in any international organization which requires that we give up any of our national rights or freedom of action.

†20 If necessary, we ought to be willing to lower our standard of living to cooperate with other countries in getting an equal standard for every person in the world.

21 We should strive for loyalty to our country before we can afford to consider world brotherhood.

22 Some races ought to be considered naturally less intelligent than others.

†23 Our schools should teach the history of the whole world rather than of our own country.

†24 An international police force ought to be the only group in the world allowed to have armaments.

25 It would be dangerous for us to guarantee by international agreement that every person in the world should have complete religious freedom.

†26 Our country should permit the immigration of foreign peoples even if it lowers our standard of living.

†27 All national governments ought to be abolished and replaced by one central world government.

28 It would not be wise for us to agree that working conditions in all countries should be subject to international control.

29 Patriotism should be a primary aim of education so our children will believe our country is the best in the world.

†30 It would be a good idea if all the races were to intermarry until there was only one race in the world.

†31 We should teach our children to uphold the welfare of all people everywhere even though it may be against the best interest of our own country.

†32 War should never be justifiable even if it is the only way to protect our national rights and honor.

The patriotism (NP) scale *EXHIBIT 5-6*

Description. Christiansen (1959) constructed the NP scale to reflect tendencies to see one's nation as superior to humanity. In formulating the statements used in the scale, it was assumed that a prominent aspect of patriotism would be a superordinate loyalty to one's own nation in relation to other reference and membership groups. Thus, Christiansen's concept of patriotism coincides closely with nationalistic attitudes measured by the scales described above.

The NP scale is essentially a Likert-type scale, although no systematic pretesting was undertaken. Item analysis revealed that item 1 discriminated between the highest and lowest quartiles at the 5 percent level of confidence, item 5 at the 1 percent level, and all other items at better than the 0.1 percent level of confidence.

Subjects. The subjects for evaluating this scale were 159 students at Oslo University, Norway.

Response Mode. The respondent is asked to indicate his agreement or disagreement with each item by circling one of the following alternatives: strong agreement, moderate agreement, slight agreement, moderate disagreement, strong disagreement. The usual "slight disagreement" alternative is not used with this scale.

Scoring. For items expressing a patriotic attitude, a "strong agreement" response is assigned a score of 5; "moderate agreement," a score of 4; "slight agreement," a score of 3; "moderate disagreement," a score of 2; and "strong disagreement," a score of 1. For items expressing a nonpatriotic attitude, this scoring is reversed. The attitude score is the sum of the item scores. The possible range of scores is from 9 to 45, with the higher score indicating a more patriotic attitude.

Reliability. Reliability was computed using Hoyt's formula and found to be .54 with a standard error of measurement of 3.13. The hypothetical reliability of the scale when lengthened to 40 items was reported to be .84.

Validity. Validity of the scale was evidenced by the finding that scale scores correlated in the expected direction with scores on a scale designed to measure preferred ways of reacting to international conflict situations (Christiansen, 1959). Correlations ranged from —.41 to .29 ($N = 154$). Some evidence of discriminant validity is indicated by the low correlation (.08) between the NP scale scores and number of conflict scores on the Blacky pictures test.

Comments. This is a short, easily administered scale, but its reliability and validity are lower than for the average scale. Also, the items are worded for use with residents of Norway. Presumably, this scale could be adapted for use in other countries by the substitution of that country's name, but there is no assurance that the characteristics of the scale would remain unchanged. Until further studies are completed, this scale can be recommended for use in only the most preliminary kind of exploratory study.

EXHIBIT 5-6

THE PATRIOTISM (NP) SCALE

Instructions: A series of statements is listed below. What is your opinion of each of the statements? Put a circle around the answer you think is most suitable.

*1 No duties are more important than duties toward one's country.

Strong agreement	Moderate agreement	Slight agreement	Moderate disagreement	Strong disagreement

2 Norway's frontiers should be open to all those who wish to settle in Norway.
3 When a national government is incompetent, the use of force to remove it can be justified.
4 Norway ought to be willing to give up its independence and submit to the authority of a United States of the World.
*5 One should always show greater loyalty to the King and the government than to a national political party.
6 All human beings are equally important. No Norwegian is of more value than any person from any other country.
7 Norway ought to support the establishment of a World Government that could solve international disputes by force.
8 The defence of Norway can never justify the taking of another human life.
9 One should show greater loyalty towards humanity than towards Norway as a nation.

* Strong agreement with starred items indicates extreme patriotism; for other items the relationship is reversed. The same response alternatives are used with each item.

Reprinted with permission from Christiansen, B. *Attitudes toward foreign affairs as a function of personality.* Oslo: Oslo University Press, 1959. Copyright 1959 by The Norwegian Research Council for Sciences and Humanities, Oslo, Norway.

Attitude toward patriotism scale EXHIBIT 5-7

Description. The Attitude toward Patriotism Scale (Thurstone, 1929–1934) was constructed using the familiar method of equal-appearing intervals. It is scale number 11 in the Thurstone series. It consists of two comparable 20-item forms. Q values were not reported, but Thurstone usually rejected items having Q values greater than 3.0.

Subjects. The subjects used in developing this scale were not described in the report, but the scale was developed at the University of Chicago. It is probably safe to infer that the subjects were students at that university.

Response Mode. The subject is asked to put a check mark beside each statement with which he agrees and a cross beside each statement with which he disagrees.

Scoring. The attitude score is the median of the scale values of the items endorsed. The higher the score, the more patriotic the attitude.

Reliability. Reliability estimates based upon the correlation between the two forms of the Patriotism Scale have been reported by Lorge (1939). These ranged from .69 to .83.

Validity. As with most Thurstone scales, validity is based largely upon content and the method of selecting the items.

Comments. This scale appears to have been much more carefully constructed than the NP scale described above. The items are appropriate for use in the United States but are inappropriate for use in other countries in their present form. Scale values were computed many years ago and should be recomputed before using the scale with modern-day subjects, although there is some evidence that scale values do not change over time as much as might be anticipated (Hinckley, 1963; Nickols, 1963). The scale has been used by Goodstein (1953) and by Brim and Hoff (1957).

EXHIBIT 5-7

ATTITUDE TOWARD PATRIOTISM SCALE

Put a check mark (√) if you agree with the statement.
Put a cross (×) if you disagree with the statement.

Form A

Scale values		
5.7	**1**	I am fond of this country because I was born here but I would be fond of any other country if I had been born there.
9.2	**2**	There is no room in the United States for people who find fault with this country.
1.0	**3**	The United States is one of the last places I would choose to live if I had my choice.
3.9	**4**	America surpasses other countries only in prosperity.
7.6	**5**	I wouldn't miss visiting foreign countries but I want to live in America.
10.9	**6**	I'm for my country, right or wrong.
2.2	**7**	The American is willing to sacrifice anything to profit.
8.5	**8**	The hatred of the United States by foreign countries is caused mostly by envy of our greatness.
0.3	**9**	I haven't an ounce of respect for the American people.
3.6	**10**	America by reason of the democratic ideal is committed to mediocrity.
7.0	**11**	In America there is rightly no room for Old-World sentimental idealism.
10.1	**12**	I think the American people are the finest in the world.
2.0	**13**	Americans are the most conceited people in the world.
5.2	**14**	Loyalty to one's country should not win over loyalty to one's moral convictions.
3.2	**15**	I can't feel patriotic because I see too many flaws in my country.

Scale values		
6.2	16	The fact that I love my country doesn't make me feel less kindly toward other countries.
9.8	17	The United States is closer to being an ideal country than any other nation has ever been.
1.5	18	I wouldn't care particularly if I never heard of the United States again.
4.8	19	I prefer to be a citizen of the world rather than of any country.
7.9	20	I don't know much about other countries but I'm satisfied with the United States.
		Form B
5.5	1	Americans are a mixture of all nationalities and are neither better nor worse than the nationalities that go into making them.
0.0	2	This is in every way the worst nation in the world.
3.3	3	When I see so much corruption in the government of my country I can't support it whole-heartedly.
6.6	4	The most I am willing to do for my country is to protect it in case of invasion.
10.0	5	I would like to see America expand to world-empire.
1.6	6	The hatred of the United States by foreign countries is justly deserved.
5.0	7	Commonsense keeps me from being too enthusiastic about the United States.
8.1	8	I have great respect for the American people.
8.8	9	Foreign nations have done some very fine things but it takes America to do things in a big way.
0.6	10	Americans combine the worst qualities of all nationalities.
3.7	11	The American ideal of bigger, faster, and more doesn't appeal to me.
7.4	12	Since I live in this country I want to be a part of it.
10.8	13	This is in every way the greatest nation in the world.
2.2	14	Americanism is nothing but a childish desire to "beat the world."
2.7	15	I don't feel any special pride in being identified with the United States.
6.1	16	I can accept the leadership of foreign countries in many fields.
9.3	17	There is hardly anything in the United States today that I would want different.
1.4	18	The American people are the most sordid, money-grubbing people in the world.
4.5	19	I believe that the United States is just as selfish as any other nation.
7.8	20	The equality of men in the United States is what holds my loyalty.

Attitude toward communism scale EXHIBIT 5-8

Description. The Attitude toward Communism Scale is another one of the Thurstone series (scale number 6) prepared by the method of equal-appearing intervals (Thurstone, 1929–1934). It consists of two matched forms of 20 items each, but little information is given concerning its construction.

Subjects. The subjects for developing this scale were students at the University of Chicago.

Response Mode. The respondent checks each statement with which he agrees and places a cross before each statement with which he disagrees.

Scoring. The attitude score is the median of the scale values of statements endorsed by the subject. Higher scores indicate a more favorable attitude toward communism.

Reliability. Reliability coefficients based upon a comparison of the two forms have been reported by several investigators. Likert, Roslow, and Murphy (1934) reported reliabilities ranging from .66 to .95; Lorge (1939) obtained reliabilities ranging from .81 to .95; and Ferguson (1944) reported reliabilities ranging from .78 to .88.

Validity. Little evidence of validity is available, other than item content and that indicated by the scaling procedure. Ferguson (1944) found scores on the communism scale correlated negatively with scores on the Thurstone scales to measure attitude toward patriotism (—.28 to —.37), toward God (—.22 to —.29), toward treatment of criminals (—.24 to —.27), toward capital punishment (—.19 to —.26), and toward law (—.23 to —.30). Scores correlated positively with attitude toward evolution (.20 to .25), whereas correlations with attitude toward war and toward birth control were essentially zero.

Comments. The communism scale appears to be comparable to other Thurstone scales. Again, recomputation of scale values is advisable before using the scale. The Attitude toward Communism Scale has been used, among others, by the following investigators: Carlson (1934), Newcomb and Svehla (1938), Ferguson (1940, 1942), Smith (1940), and Sappenfield (1942).

EXHIBIT 5-8

ATTITUDE TOWARD COMMUNISM SCALE

Put a check mark (✓) if you agree with the statement.
Put a cross (×) if you disagree with the statement.

Form A

Scale values		
5.4	1	Both the evils and the benefits of communism are greatly exaggerated.
2.2	2	It is only the ignorant and incompetent that want communism.
10.4	3	The whole world must be converted to communism.
7.0	4	Workers can hardly be blamed for advocating communism.
3.8	5	Communism is a much more radical change than we should undertake.
0.3	6	Police are justified in shooting down the communists.
8.4	7	Give Russia another twenty years or so and you'll see that communism can be made to work.

Scale values		
2.7	8	If Russia today is a sample of how communism works, we don't need it.
10.8	9	Communism should be established by force if necessary.
7.4	10	The communist may be rough but he has the right idea.
4.3	11	I am not worrying, for I don't think there's the slightest chance that communism will be adopted here.
0.9	12	The communists are the most destructive element in our civilization.
9.1	13	Communism is the solution to our present economic problems.
6.4	14	We should be open-minded about communism.
8.2	15	The ideals of communism are worth working for.
4.7	16	I am not sure that communism solves the problems of capital and labor.
1.9	17	The whole communistic scheme is unsound.
9.9	18	Communists should set up a dictatorship of the workers in the United States.
6.8	19	We should not reject communism until it has been given a longer trial.
3.3	20	If a man has the vision and the ability to acquire property, he ought to be allowed to enjoy it himself.
		Form B
6.8	1	Communists should have the same rights as other people.
3.4	2	The communist is too radical and extreme in his views.
5.5	3	Communism would not make much difference in the long run.
2.1	4	Let the Reds stay in Russia where they belong.
10.8	5	Communists should control the whole world.
7.2	6	Some parts of the commmunist program are entirely sensible and practicable.
3.8	7	Share-and-share-alike sounds well, but it won't work.
0.6	8	Every communist should be put in prison.
8.9	9	The only way for working people to get their rights against capitalists is through communism.
2.8	10	Most of the communistic doctrines are false.
11.3	11	Our government should be overthrown and a communistic one put in its place.
7.9	12	More people would favor communism if they only knew something about it.
4.5	13	Communists are too visionary for a practical world.
1.2	14	The communists are a menace to this nation and to the world in general.
9.2	15	The communists deserve our whole-hearted support.
5.8	16	It is too early to judge communism by its results in Russia.
8.0	17	The communists are on the right road.
5.1	18	We had better keep our eyes on Russia for a while longer before making up our minds about commmunism.
1.7	19	Communism would destroy the family and the home.
10.1	20	Communistic principles should be adopted everywhere.

ATTITUDES RELATED TO INTERNATIONAL CONFLICT

This category is represented most strongly by scales to measure attitude toward war, but it includes scales to measure militarism-pacifism.

It is not clear, however, that war and militarism-pacifism are different attitudes. One scale designed to measure attitude toward imperialism (Likert, 1932) was excluded because most of the items are meaningless in view of present-day world politics, and one set of items concerned with the prevention of war (Stagner et al., 1942) was not included because of insufficient data regarding its characteristics.

The Peterson war scale *EXHIBIT 5-9*

Description. The Attitude toward War Scale was prepared by Peterson under Thurstone's editorship, using the method of equal-appearing intervals. It is scale number 34 in the Thurstone series (Thurstone, 1929–1934). The final scale, given in Exhibit 5-9, consists of 32 items concerning war and the consequences of war.

Subjects. The subjects used in this study were 301 children in grades 7 through 12 in the public schools at Batavia, Illinois.

Response Mode. The subject is asked to place a check mark beside each statement with which he agrees and a cross beside each statement with which he disagrees.

Scoring. The attitude score is the median of the scale values of items endorsed. The higher the score, the more favorable the attitude toward war.

Reliability. The Peterson and Thurstone publication gives little information about the scale's reliability. However, they reported correlations of .63 for a sample of 301 children and .57 for a sample of 214 between successive administrations of the scale with a movie about war interposed. Lorge (1939) reported reliabilities ranging from .44 to .84; Ferguson (1944) reported reliabilities from .62 to .67; and Likert, Roslow, and Murphy (1934) obtained reliabilities ranging from .70 to .76.

Validity. Evidence of validity appears to be limited to content validity, the validity indicated by the scaling procedure, and the usefulness of the scale in research.

Comments. Despite the relatively low estimates of reliability, the Peterson War Scale has been widely used. Examples of studies using this scale are: Carlson (1934), Campbell and Stover (1933), Gardiner, (1935), Fehrer (1952), Sappenfield (1942), Miller (1934), Engle (1944), Ballin and Farnsworth (1941), Dudycha (1942*a*), Ferguson (1938, 1940), and Helson (1958).

Erickson (1942) questioned the validity of this scale, because it did not reflect specific changes in attitudes that he expected when the United States became involved in World War II. It should be noted, however, that the scale attempts to measure attitude toward war as an abstract concept, rather than as a specific event at a specific time.

EXHIBIT 5-9

THE PETERSON WAR SCALE

This is a study of attitude toward war. On the other side of this page you will find a number of statements expressing different attitudes toward war.

√ Put a check mark if you agree with the statement.
× Put a cross if you disagree with that statement.
Try to indicate either agreement or disagreement for each statement.

If you simply cannot decide about a statement you may mark it with a question mark.

Scale Values		
4.2	**1**	War is hardly necessary in the modern world.
1.4	**2**	War is a futile struggle resulting in self-destruction.
8.3	**3**	The desirable results of war have not received the attention they deserve.
3.3	**4**	A host of young men returned from the war disillusioned and cynical.
7.0	**5**	Another war would be terrible but it might be worth the price.
11.0	**6**	War is glorious.
7.8	**7**	War is sometimes necessary because right is more important than peace.
2.1	**8**	War destroys the finest of the nation's manhood.
4.6	**9**	We want no more war if it can be avoided without dishonor.
9.5	**10**	High idealism is born in war.
6.6	**11**	There are some arguments in favor of war.
3.0	**12**	There will be no more wars when people become really civilized.
0.0	**13**	Every last one of us should refuse to take part in any way in any war.
5.5	**14**	It is hard to decide whether wars do more harm than good.
2.4	**15**	War is an unnecessary waste of human life.
6.3	**16**	Peace and war are both essential to progress.
0.4	**17**	War should be avoided at any cost.
7.5	**18**	Under some conditions, war is necessary to maintain justice.
9.2	**19**	War develops the moral strength of men.
3.2	**20**	The benefits of war are not worth its misery and suffering.
10.8	**21**	The highest duty of man is to fight for the power and glory of his nation.
1.6	**22**	War in the modern world is as needless as it is terrible.
8.8	**23**	Every man should enlist as soon as war is declared.
0.2	**24**	There is no conceivable justification for war.
5.4	**25**	War brings out both good and bad qualities in men.
10.1	**26**	There can be no progress without war.
3.7	**27**	International disputes should be settled without war.
2.2	**28**	The soldier suffers terribly and gains nothing.
9.7	**29**	War is simply murder sanctioned by governments.
8.5	**30**	War is a satisfactory way to solve international difficulties.
6.0	**31**	War has some benefits; but it's a big price to pay for them.
9.8	**32**	War stimulates men to their noblest efforts.

A scale of militarism-pacifism EXHIBIT 5-10

Description. This scale was developed by Droba (1931*a*) by the method of equal-appearing intervals. Most of the statements concern war, and the scale is also referred to as the war scale (Droba, 1934). The final scale consisted of 44 items, selected so that differences between scale values were no greater than .6 and no smaller than .3. Q values ranged from 0.06 to 1.1.

Subjects. The subjects were 300 students at the University of Chicago. The sample included 8 freshmen, 136 sophomores, 96 juniors, 66 seniors, 83 graduate students, and 11 unclassified. Ages ranged from 17 to 44, with the mean age being 21.8. Subsequent validating studies involved the following samples: 129 Democrats, 447 Republicans, 21 Socialists, 385 Protestants, 78 Catholics, 158 Jews, and 111 persons with no religious preference.

Response Mode. The subject responds to each item by placing a plus sign beside the statement if he agrees with the statement and a minus sign if he disagrees with the statement.

Scoring. During development, the 44 items of the scale were divided into two matched forms of 22 items each. An "equivalent number" for each item was derived by assigning a 0 to the most extremely militaristic items and 21 to the most extremely pacifistic items in each form. Intermediate numbers were assigned according to degree of militaristic-pacifistic expression. The equivalent number for each item is given in the second column of Exhibit 5-10. The attitude score is the sum of the equivalent numbers of items marked with a plus sign. Scores may range from 0 to 462, with the higher score indicating the more pacifistic attitude.

The advantage of the equivalent number over the scale value is not immediately apparent, although perhaps the elimination of the decimal facilitates scoring.

Reliability. During the process of construction, the 44 items in Exhibit 5-10 were divided into two matched forms of 22 items each. The coefficient of equivalence was .83 (corrected to .99). A somewhat lower reliability (.71) was reported by Likert et al. (1934), although a simplified scoring procedure resulted in a reliability of .84.

Validity. In addition to content validity, Droba presented the results of several validating procedures. Attitude scores correlated .75 with self-ratings; men were found to be more militaristic than women; Republicans and Democrats were more militaristic than Socialists; and Catholics and Lutherans were more militaristic than Jews, Christian Scientists, and Protestants (Droba, 1931*a,b,c*). Some discriminant validity is indicated by the finding that attitude-toward-war scores correlated only .15 with scholarship (Droba, 1931*a*).

Comments. The Droba scale appears to have higher reliability and validity than the Peterson scale, and, according to Dudycha (1942) was more widely used than the Peterson scale at the time his review was completed. Examples of studies using the Droba war scale include: Cherrington and Miller (1933), Carlson (1934), Traxler (1935), Jones (1942*a*,*b*), Stump and Lewis (1935), Fehrer (1952), Diggory (1953), and Helson (1958).

EXHIBIT 5-10

A SCALE OF MILITARISM-PACIFISM

The purpose of this experiment is to measure differences in opinions relating to peace and war. Below you will find a number of statements expressing various degrees of opinion about militarism-pacifism.

If, on the whole, you agree with the sentiment of a statement, mark it with a *plus sign* in the parenthesis.

If, on the whole, you disagree with the sentiment of a statement, mark it with a *minus sign* in the parenthesis.

Please vote for each statement even if it seems ambiguous and you have to make some sort of guess.

Only mass results will be published which will not distinguish individual opinion.

Scale value	Equivalent number		
3.0	5	**1**	Multitudes are benefited by learning the lesson of wartime discipline.
9.5	18	**2**	War in the modern world is as needless as it is suicidal.
4.8	8	**3**	Those military units should be retained which afford training to the body and mind.
8.0	15	**4**	Army discipline injures self-respect and individuality.
9.0	17	**5**	The losses in human life and property, great as they are, are small evils compared to the undermining of morals and the lowering of standards of culture and civilization caused by war.
5.2	9	**6**	Wars are justifiable only when waged in defense of weaker nations.
1.0	1	**7**	War is ennobling and stimulative of the highest and best qualities of humankind.
10.7	21	**8**	It is the moral duty of the individual to refuse to participate in any way in any war, no matter what the cause.
0.5	0	**9**	Might is right.
5.6	10	**10**	The most that we can hope to accomplish is the partial elimination of war.
6.5	12	**11**	The evils of war are slightly greater than its benefits.
3.6	6	**12**	Until an equivalent discipline is organized war must have its own way.
4.2	7	**13**	Because right may be more important than peace, war may be the lesser of two evils.

Reprinted with permission from Droba, D. D. A scale to measure militarism-pacifism. *J. educ. Psychol.*, 1931, 22, 96–111.

Scale value	Equivalent number		
6.0	11	**14**	Along with patriotism world-citizenship should be taught in all secondary schools.
10.4	20	**15**	Persons should pledge themselves never to aid any future war.
7.0	13	**16**	It is almost impossible to have a large military force without being tempted to use it.
1.5	2	**17**	War is the tonic of races.
10.0	19	**18**	When the next war breaks out we should tell the diplomats who lead us to it that we will not follow them.
2.0	3	**19**	Militarism is necessary for the proper defense and protection of the individuals of a country.
2.5	4	**20**	So long as any people, white, black, brown or yellow, hold weapons in their hands, we must not commit the folly of disarming.
8.4	16	**21**	Under the scourge of war a nation has no opportunity for cultural development.
7.6	14	**22**	The soldier suffers tremendously and gains very little.
8.9	17	**23**	The evils that war brings in its train far outweigh any possible benefits.
4.4	8	**24**	We should have a moderate amount of military training in our schools.
7.4	13	**25**	No scheme of aggression or conquest can be pursued for any considerable length of time without enfeebling victor as well as vanquished.
10.5	20	**26**	When war threatens we should refuse the call to service and increase our anti-war activity.
2.5	4	**27**	It is foolish to talk of the abolition of war, since pugnacity is an ineradicable human instinct.
0.6	0	**28**	There is no progress without war.
8.4	16	**29**	Militarism should be abolished from the curriculum of the state schools.
2.1	3	**30**	It is not in war but in peace and prosperity that our worst vices develop and grow rank.
2.9	5	**31**	We cannot hope to do away with war, because it is part of the unending struggle for survival in a crowded world.
7.8	14	**32**	If armed conflict between individuals and cities can be outlawed, it is possible to outlaw armed conflict between nations.
9.5	18	**33**	Every war shows cowardice, murder, arson, graft, and leaves a trail of personal and national demoralization.
5.6	10	**34**	The most frequent cause of war is the rivalry of nations for possession of territory, markets, concessions, and spheres of influence.
10.7	21	**35**	There is no conceivable justification for war.
4.1	7	**36**	Military training is imperative, but it should be voluntary.
6.3	11	**37**	Nations should agree not to intervene with military force in purely commercial or financial disputes.
10.1	19	**38**	Concerning war we must be abolitionists.
1.6	2	**39**	The abolition of war would mean effeminacy, softness, debilitation, and degeneracy.
8.1	15	**40**	A host of young men entered the war in a spirit of idealism and unselfish devotion to a great cause, only to return disillusioned and cynical as to the value of ideals.

Scale value	Equivalent number		
3.4	6	41	For the liberty of oppressed nations wars should be fought.
1.0	1	42	Compulsory military training should be established in all countries.
6.8	12	43	Pugnacity, rivalry and self-interest are natural, but need not result in war any more than human desire for dominance need result in slavery.
5.4	9	44	Peace and war are both essential to progress.

Attitude toward defensive, cooperative, and aggressive war EXHIBIT 5-11

Description. This scale, developed by Day and Quackenbush (1942), consists of 13 items scaled by the method of equal-appearing intervals. In developing the scale, judges sorted 28 items into 9 piles, instead of the usual 11 used by Thurstone. The 13 items given in Exhibit 5-11 were selected from this pool of items. The scale values were not given in the article, nor could they be obtained from the authors. Therefore, items were rescaled by the present authors, and these values are given in Exhibit 5-11. Day and Quackenbush (1942) reported that their scale values ranged from 0.2 to 8.5. The new scale values range from 0.8 to 8.4 and thus compare favorably with the original range.

Although the items are about war in general, the scale was used to measure attitude toward three types of war by asking respondents to assume each of the referents: defensive war, cooperative war, and aggressive war. The same scale values are used regardless of the referent.

Subjects. The subjects used in scaling the items were 15 women and 35 men. Reliability scores were based upon the responses of 326 male students at the University of Mississippi.

Response Mode. Subjects are asked to respond to each item three times, once for each referent. A check mark indicates agreement with the statement, and a cross indicates disagreement with the statement.

Scoring. The attitude score for each referent is the median of the scale values of items endorsed by the subject for that referent. The higher the score, the more favorable the attitude toward war.

Reliability. Split-half reliabilities were reported as follows: defensive war, .77 (corrected to .87); cooperative war, .79 (corrected to .88); and aggressive war, .67 (corrected to .80).

Validity. Little evidence of validity is available beyond that indicated by content and the method of scaling items. Law students were found to have more favorable attitudes than other students, a finding which might have some bearing on validity.

Comments. This is a short scale and hence requires less time to administer and score than the Peterson and Droba scales. From the limited evidence available, it also appears to be as reliable and valid as these longer scales.

EXHIBIT 5-11

ATTITUDE TOWARD DEFENSIVE, COOPERATIVE, AND AGGRESSIVE WAR

This is a study of attitudes toward war. Below you will find a number of statements expressing various degrees of attitudes toward war or tendencies to act in case of war.

In expressing your agreement or disagreement with the statements, please put yourself in three possible situations. First, imagine that the United States had declared a *Defensive War* (war for the purpose of defending the United States in case of an attack). Please indicate in the first parenthesis, designated by the Roman numeral I, your agreement, disagreement, and doubt. Put a check mark (✓) if you agree with the statement, put a minus sign (—) if you disagree with the statement, and a question mark (?) if you are in doubt about the statement.

Second, imagine that the United States has declared a *Cooperative War* (war in cooperation with the democratic countries of Europe for the defense of democracy). Go over the statements again and indicate in the second parenthesis, designated by Roman II, your agreement, disagreement, and doubt in a similar way.

Third, imagine that the United States has declared an *Aggressive War* (war for the purpose of gaining more territory). Read the statements again and indicate in the third parenthesis, designated by Roman III, your agreement, disagreement, and doubt by a similar method.

*Scale value	I	II	III		
2.5	( )	( )	( )	1	I would support my country even against my convictions.
7.5	( )	( )	( )	2	I would immediately attempt to find some technicality on which to evade going to war.
0.8	( )	( )	( )	3	I would immediately go to war and would do everything in my power to influence others to do the same.
7.9	( )	( )	( )	4	I would rather be called a coward than go to war.
2.5	( )	( )	( )	5	I would offer my services in whatever capacity I can.
8.4	( )	( )	( )	6	I would not only refuse to participate in any way in war but also attempt to influence public opinion against war.
6.3	( )	( )	( )	7	I would take part in war only to avoid social ostracism.
5.9	( )	( )	( )	8	I would not go to war unless I were drafted.
4.6	( )	( )	( )	9	If possible, I would wait a month or two before I would enlist.

* Scale values were computed by the present authors.

Reprinted with permission from Day, D. D., and Quackenbush, O. F. Attitudes toward defensive, cooperative, and aggressive war. *J. soc. Psychol.*, **1942, 16, 11–20. Copyright 1942 by The Journal Press, Provincetown, Mass.**

*Scale value					
5.1	( )	( )	( )	10	I would go to war only if my friends went to war.
8.2	( )	( )	( )	11	I would refuse to participate in any way in war.
1.4	( )	( )	( )	12	I would disregard any possible exemptions and enlist immediately.
3.5	( )	( )	( )	13	I would not enlist but would give whatever financial aid I could.

Attitude toward war (scale W) *EXHIBIT 5-12*

Description. The scale was developed by Wilke (1934) following the Likert procedure. It was developed for the purpose of studying the influence of speech, radio messages, and written messages on attitude toward war. The final scale consists of 30 statements about war and preparations for war.

Subjects. The preliminary sample consisted of 243 students. The subjects for the main experiment consisted of 12 groups of students at Washington Square College, New York University. The total sample was 409 persons, but 68 gentiles were eliminated, leaving 341 Jewish students in the final sample. Most of these were sophomores and juniors, and most were natives of the metropolitan area.

Response Mode. The subject responds to each item by circling one of the following alternatives: strongly approve, approve, undecided, disapprove, strongly disapprove.

Scoring. Scores are assigned to response alternatives as follows: For pacifistic items (marked with an asterisk in Exhibit 5-12), a score of 5 is assigned to "strongly approve," a score of 4 to "approve," a score of 3 to "undecided," a score of 2 to "disapprove," and a score of 1 to "strongly disapprove." For militaristic items, this scoring is reversed. The attitude score is the sum of the item scores, with the higher scores indicating a less favorable attitude toward war.

Reliability. Split-half reliabilities were computed for several groups of varying size (total $N = 1{,}174$); coefficients ranged from .86 to .97. Test-retest reliability, with a three-week interval between testings, was reported to be .82 for a control group and .80 for an experimental group exposed to a propaganda appeal during the retest interval.

Validity. The scale appears to have content validity, but no other evidence of validity is available, unless the very small decrease in test-retest correlation as a result of the propaganda appeal is taken as evidence of validity.

Comments. This is a promising scale with good reliability indices, but evidence of validity is badly needed. Lack of equivalent forms decreases its usefulness in research.

EXHIBIT 5-12

ATTITUDE TOWARD WAR (SCALE W)

Will you please indicate your opinion on each of the accompanying statements. To indicate your opinion, draw a circle around the word which best describes your agreement as shown:

All final examinations should be abolished.

Strongly Approve	Approve	Undecided	Disapprove	Strongly Disapprove

*1 War should be avoided at any cost.
*2 The soldier suffers terribly and gains nothing.
3 It is an idle dream to abolish war.
*4 We should honor the heroes of peace as more worthy of recognition than those who die on the battlefield.
5 One who opposes war is probably a coward at heart.
6 The desirable results of war have not received the attention they deserve.
*7 A person who loves his fellow men should refuse to engage in any war, no matter how serious the consequences to his country.
8 War is justified when its purpose is defensive.
9 Under some conditions we should regard war as desirable to maintain justice.
*10 The costs of war far overshadow any possible benefits.
11 If a man's country enters a war which he does not consider justified, he should nevertheless serve at the front or wherever he is needed.
12 Adequate preparation for war is the best guarantee of international peace.
13 We should have compulsory military training.
*14 It is better to suffer indignities than to declare war.
15 In case of war, those who continue to oppose it should be imprisoned.
*16 Our country should never declare war again under any circumstances.
*17 Our policy should be to favor rapid and drastic reduction of the armaments of all nations.
18 We should have military training in our schools.
*19 We should make it a point to doubt the truth of all news reports likely to lead us into war.
20 Moving pictures showing military drill and naval maneuvers should be exhibited to encourage patriotism.
21 Our country should strive to have the largest military and naval air fleets in the world.
*22 War appeals to the basest of human motives and brings out all that is brutal in humanity.
*23 Armaments provoke war by creating suspicion, fear and hatred among nations.
*24 The selfish business interest of armament manufacturers should be given a prominent place among the causes of war.

* Items marked with an asterisk express a pacifistic attitude. The five response alternatives given in the instructions are provided for each item.

Reprinted with permission from Wilke, W. H. An experimental comparison of the speech, the radio, and the printed page as propaganda devices. *Arch. Psychol.*, 1934, No. 169.

*25 It is almost impossible to have a large military force without being tempted to use it.
*26 Military training (except as needed to maintain internal order) should be abolished.
27 The United States should have the world's largest navy.
28 We should reconcile ourselves to the fact that war is a necessary factor in the racial struggle for survival.
*29 Every last one of us should refuse to take part in any way in any war.
30 The highest duty of a man is to fight for the power and glory of his nation.

A scale for measuring attitude toward war *EXHIBIT 5-13*

Description. This is another scale designed to measure attitude toward war (Stagner, 1942). It was constructed by a variation of the Thurstone technique. A "method of absolute judgments" was used to determine scoring values for the items of the scale. Judges rated each item on a five-point scale, assigning a rating of 5 to statements judged to be favorable to war and a value of 1 to statements judged to be unfavorable to war. The median rating of each item was taken as its scale value. Two forms of the scale were prepared: a long form consisting of 27 items and a short form consisting of 15 items. Exhibit 5-13 gives the items of the longer form, with the items which were omitted from the short form marked with an asterisk.

Subjects. The subjects who rated the items consisted of five classes of graduates and undergraduates ($N = 125$). For evaluating the scale, four additional samples were used, consisting of 265 adult men, 191 adult women, 229 college men, and 181 college women. Except for 59 persons from Alabama, all were tested in Akron, Ohio.

Response Mode. Subjects are asked to place a check mark beside each item with which they agree.

Scoring. The attitude score is the mean of the scale values of items endorsed by the subject. The possible range of scores is from 1.24 to 4.76, with the higher scores indicating the more favorable attitude toward war.

Reliability. A reliability coefficient was reported only for the short form of the scale. This split-half coefficient was relatively low, being only .581 when corrected by the Spearman-Brown formula. In another article (Stagner, 1944*a*), a test-retest reliability of .83 ($N = 93$) after a one-month delay was reported. The second administration used a five-alternative response mode and an unweighted scoring procedure.

Validity. Validity was estimated by the known-groups method. Military training groups, veterans groups, and conservative political groups scored higher than labor groups and groups of professional men.

Comments. The relatively low reliability of this scale suggests that it is probably the least adequate of the war scales that we have considered thus far. This may be, in part, because of the narrow range of possible scores. However, the scale should be carefully reevaluated before it is used for any purpose other than exploratory research. For further studies using this scale, see Stagner (1944*b*,*c*).

EXHIBIT 5-13

A SCALE FOR MEASURING ATTITUDE TOWARD WAR

Instructions: Please read the following statements and check those which represent your own opinion. You may check as few or as many as you wish.

Scale value		Item
4.76	*1	War brings out the best qualities in men.
4.24	2	War is often the only means of preserving the national honor.
4.24	3	The desirable results of war have not received the attention they deserve.
4.67	4	There can be no progress without war.
4.72	5	War is the only way to right tremendous wrongs.
4.26	6	Patriotism demands that the citizens of a nation participate in any war.
4.10	*7	The United States has never fought an unjust war.
4.10	8	The United States should always be armed to the limit of its treaty rights.
4.62	*9	War is necessary to avoid overpopulation of nations.
4.19	*10	The Biblical command against killing does not apply to warfare.
4.05	*11	Nations should pay high honor to their military leaders.
3.90	12	College students should be trained in times of peace to assume military duties.
4.52	*13	Modern warfare provides a glorious adventure for men not afraid of danger.
3.76	14	Under some conditions, war is necessary to maintain justice.
3.81	15	Although war is terrible, it has some value.
3.48	16	Defensive war is justified but other wars are not.
2.97	*17	We should abolish armaments for offensive purposes.
3.29	*18	The average citizen can do nothing to oppose war.
2.33	19	Those who profit by war profit by the preparations for war.
1.72	*20	We expect war to endanger life and property rather than protect it.
1.72	21	The benefits of war rarely pay for its losses even for the victor.
1.24	22	There is no conceivable justification for war.
1.45	23	War is a futile struggle resulting in self-destruction.

* Starred items were omitted from the short form.

Reprinted with permission from Stagner, R. Some factors related to attitude toward war, 1938. *J. soc. Psychol.*, 1942, 16, 131–142. Copyright 1942 by The Journal Press, Provincetown, Mass.

Scale value		
1.32	24	The evils of war are greater than any possible benefits.
1.48	*25	International disputes should be settled without war.
1.36	*26	War breeds disrespect for human life.
1.43	*27	It is good judgment to sacrifice certain rights in order to prevent war.

The M-P opinion scale *EXHIBIT 5-14*

Description. The M-P Opinion Scale was first described by Zubin and Gristle (1937) and reported in detail by Gristle (1940). It was designed to measure militaristic-pacifistic attitudes. Ninety-five items were chosen to cover the causes of war, the results of war, the elimination of war, the purposes of war, preparedness, war and peace, and patriotism. Items were administered to a "militaristic" group and a "pacifistic" group, and items that discriminated between these two groups were selected for the final scale.

Subjects. The samples used in selection of items were 50 advanced ROTC students at City College of New York (the militaristic group) and 50 students in social sciences at City College (the pacifistic group). The reliability sample consisted of 260 college students.

Response Mode. Each item is provided with three response alternatives: yes, ?, no. The subject responds by circling one of these alternatives.

Scoring. Scoring is based upon the direction of item discrimination. Whenever the frequency of responses of the militaristic group was significantly greater than the frequency of the pacifistic group, the response was assigned a negative value; if the frequencies were reversed, the response was assigned a positive value; and if the frequencies were not significantly different for the two groups, the response was assigned a 0 value. The scoring values are indicated below the response alternatives to each item in Exhibit 5-14. The attitude score is the algebraic sum of the scoring values assigned to the subject's responses. The range of possible scores is from −65 to +65. A positive score indicates a pacifistic attitude, whereas a negative score indicates a militaristic attitude.

Reliability. Split-half reliability was found to be .89 (corrected to .95), based upon the responses of 260 college students.

Validity. The only evidence of validity is that provided by the content of the items and the fact that they discriminated between the militaristic and pacifistic groups.

Comments. The reliability of this scale is unusually high, but evidence of validity is average. Some cross validation would have been desirable but apparently was not undertaken by the scale constructors. There is also some question whether the attitude being measured is the same as that measured by the attitude-toward-war scales. Item content suggests that it is, but further studies would be useful.

EXHIBIT 5-14

THE M-P OPINION SCALE

DIRECTIONS:

Consider each statement separately. Draw a circle around either the word YES, or the word NO, or the question mark in order to indicate the way you feel toward that statement, as follows:

If you feel that the statement is **like** your own feelings, draw a circle around the word YES . . . . (YES) ? NO

If you feel that the statement is **opposed** to your own feelings, draw a circle around the word NO . . . . YES ? (NO)

If you feel that the statement is neither **like** or **opposed** to your own feelings or if you are in doubt about it, draw a circle around the question mark . . . . YES (?) NO

BE SURE TO MARK EVERY STATEMENT IN SOME WAY

	Statement	YES	?	NO
1	The benefits of war never make up for its losses, even to the victor.	*+	—	0
2	Every man in the country between the ages of 18 and 35 should be compelled to take military training.	—	0	+
3	The United States should give naval demonstrations in the large harbors of the country where the people may see them.	—	—	+
4	The greatest men in our history are those generals and admirals who have led our forces and country to victory in times of war.	0	—	+
5	The United States should have the largest army and navy in the world.	—	0	+
6	The Citizen Military Training Camps should be abolished.	+	—	0
7	All persons who love their fellow-men should refuse to engage in any war under any circumstances.	+	—	0
8	Moving pictures which show military drill should be exhibited to encourage patriotism.	—	—	+
9	It is unnecessary for us to spend hundreds of millions of dollars each year for military and naval preparations.	+	0	—
10	Unpreparedness lengthens war and greatly increases its suffering and losses.	—	0	+
11	Once the United States is drawn into a war it should fight to the finish.	—	0	+
12	War produces many evil qualities.	+	—	0
13	It is honorable to show other nations that we are courageous, even if it may lead to war.	—	—	+
14	Man is naturally a born fighter, and you cannot change his nature.	—	—	+
15	He who refuses to fight because he objects to war is a true hero.	+	0	—

* Scoring values are indicated below response alternatives for each item.

Reprinted with permission from Gristle, M. The construction of a scale for measuring attitude toward militarism-pacifism. *J. soc. Psychol.*, 1940, 11, 383–391. Copyright 1940 by The Journal Press, Provincetown, Mass.

No.	Statement	YES	?	NO
16	If a man's country enters a war which he does not consider justified he should, nevertheless, serve at the front, or wherever he is needed.	—	0	+
17	All nations should disarm immediately.	—	0	+
18	There should be in every public park a statue of a famous general or a captured gun.	0	—	+
19	War is horrible because in it men lose all traces of humaneness toward their fellow-men.	+	0	—
20	A country cannot amount to much without national honor, and war is the only means of preserving it.	0	—	+
21	War injures and kills the finest of a nation's manhood, leaving the physically unfit as the basis for coming generations.	+	0	—
22	The abolition of war might result, through the loss of fighting energy, in the fall of civilization.	0	—	+
23	So long as any people, white, black, brown or yellow, hold weapons in their hands, the United States must not disarm.	—	0	+
24	The fate of Belgium during the last war illustrates the need for preparedness.	—	0	+
25	Whether we like it or not, there must be war for ages to come.	—	0	+
26	Armaments are the only sure guarantee of peace.	—	—	+
27	People are greatly benefited by learning the lessons of war-time discipline.	—	—	+
28	Might is right.	—	0	+
29	Wars are justified only when waged in defense of weaker nations.	0	—	+
30	The discipline of the army injures self-respect and individualism.	+	+	—
31	The most we can ever hope to achieve, is the partial elimination of war.	—	0	+
32	War may be the lesser of two evils, because "right" is more important than peace.	0	—	+
33	It is impossible to have a large army without being tempted to use it.	+	0	—
34	War stimulates progress.	—	—	+
35	Soldiers suffer greatly and gain nothing.	+	—	—
36	Military training should be conducted in every high school and college in the country.	—	—	+
37	When war threatens we should increase our anti-war activity.	+	—	—
38	There is no justification for war.	+	—	—
39	Graft and corruption develop during periods of peace and prosperity and not during war-time.	—	0	+
40	Wars should be fought to free oppressed people.	0	—	+
41	America never has to fear an attack by any other nation at any time.	+	0	—
42	The Reserve Officers Training Corps furnishes excellent training in citizenship and patriotism.	—	0	+

		YES	?	NO
43	The government should always follow the advice offered by army and navy experts in all matters.	−	0	+
44	Armaments should be reduced in all countries, but not eliminated.	−	0	+
45	War should be abolished because it brings misery and suffering to innocent women and children.	+	−	0
46	It is our duty to serve in an offensive war.	−	−	+
47	A large army and navy are necessary for the proper defense of our country.	−	−	+
48	Once our country declares war, we should enlist without hesitation.	−	−	+
49	The assassination of an American official stationed in a foreign country is justification for war.	0	−	+
50	Mankind has the power to end war.	+	0	−
51	We should protect the weaker nations by threatening their oppressors with war.	0	−	+
52	All the conferences and leagues are useless, because war can never be eliminated.	−	−	+
53	The only real and effective way of solving international disputes is by war.	0	−	+
54	The "balance of power" must always be kept, and if one nation attempts to break it, war must result.	−	−	+
55	War is necessary for a nation to secure colonies for its surplus population.	−	0	+
56	God planned war just as He planned the force of gravity.	0	−	+
57	The people should have the right and power to vote on whether war should be declared.	+	−	0
58	A nation should always be ready to fight.	−	0	+
59	War is justified when one nation attempts to collect its debts from another nation which refuses to pay.	0	−	+
60	National honor is a small thing when it is compared to the seriousness of war.	+	−	−
61	War is a means of nature to reduce the population of the world.	−	−	+
62	We might as well try to do away with the force of gravity because of airplane accidents as to think of abolishing war because good women suffer and brave men die.	−	−	+
63	War in the modern world will lead to the destruction of all mankind.	+	0	−
64	If armed conflict between cities and individuals can be outlawed, it is possible to outlaw conflict between nations.	+	0	−
65	Adequate armaments tend to create security among nations.	−	−	+

ATTITUDES RELATED TO INTERNATIONAL ECONOMIC ISSUES

Only one scale falling into this category has been located: a scale designed to measure attitude toward the tariff.

Attitude toward the tariff EXHIBIT 5-15

Description. This is scale number 18 in the Thurstone series (Thurstone, 1929–1934). It was constructed by the usual method of equal-appearing intervals, and consists of 106 statements concerning the advantages and disadvantages of the tariff. The original scale values were not available; hence the scale values given in Exhibit 5-15 were computed by the authors. Q values range from 0.63 for item 8 to 8.90 for item 7, although most items have Q values less than 3.0. Other items having unusually large Q values are items 3 (5.10), 4 (5.15), 33 (7.90), 59 (4.89), 77 (4.80), and 79 (4.85).

Subjects. The subjects used in computing the scale and Q values given in Exhibit 5-15 were 89 students enrolled in an undergraduate course in social psychology at the University of Florida. The subjects used by Thurstone presumably were students at the University of Chicago.

Response Mode. The subject responds to each item by placing a check before the item if he agrees with it, a cross if he disagrees, and a question mark if he cannot decide whether he agrees or disagrees with the statement.

Scoring. The attitude score is the median of the scale values of those items agreed with. The possible scores range from 1.1 to 10.5, with the higher score indicating a positive (favorable) attitude toward the tariff.

Reliability. Test-retest reliability was estimated to be .84.

Validity. No evidence of the validity of this scale is available beyond that provided by content and the method of construction.

Comments. Relatively little information is available concerning this scale, but it seems to be reasonably reliable and probably valid. It is an old scale, and some of the items may not have meaning for modern subjects. However, there are enough items to permit the investigator to select those that appear to be most appropriate for use at the present time; however, further standardization will be required.

EXHIBIT 5-15

ATTITUDE TOWARD THE TARIFF

This is a study of attitudes toward the tariff. On the following pages you will find statements expressing different attitudes toward the tariff.

Put a check mark (√) if you **agree** with the statement.
Put a cross (X) if you **disagree** with the statement.

If you cannot decide about a statement, you may mark it with a question mark.

This is not an examination. People differ in their opinions about what is right and wrong in this issue.

Please check your own attitude by a check mark when you agree with a statement, by a cross when you disagree, and by a question mark when you cannot decide about a statement.

*Scale Value		
3.1	1	Conditions which once warranted a high tariff no longer exist.
8.9	2	Although a high tariff has some disadvantages, we must have it to protect our industries.
3.3	3	Commodities which cannot be produced in this country should be imported duty free.
6.7	4	The evils of free trade are somewhat greater than the benefits.
10.0	5	The advantages of the tariff far outweigh any possible disadvantages.
3.4	6	High tariffs assure high wages to only a comparatively small group of workers.
10.5	7	I am absolutely against free trade.
1.1	8	Everyone should oppose the tariff.
7.3	9	Free trade would not improve present conditions.
9.4	10	The success of the protective tariff has been demonstrated.
6.5	11	In spite of its advantages, there are certain objections to free trade.
4.0	12	The advantages of a high tariff are exaggerated because it creates a home market at the expense of foreign trade.
9.7	13	A protective tariff is necessary for maintaining our high standard of living.
9.5	14	Protective tariffs are an incentive to the pioneer in industry.
2.9	15	America should gradually be put on a free trade basis.
7.8	16	Free trade may be good in theory but it fails in practice.
7.7	17	We need a tariff but it does not have to be high.
2.0	18	We should have free trade between nations as between states.
8.3	19	The tariff helps the farmers by creating a greater demand for their products due to the establishment of manufactures.
5.0	20	The claims made by the advocates of high tariff are somewhat exaggerated.
1.5	21	Every intelligent person should support the doctrine of free trade.
8.8	22	The tariff is a legitimate business measure.
9.2	23	The protective tariff is desirable because it creates home markets.
7.9	24	Free trade is easier to talk about than to put into practice.
2.8	25	There would be fewer depressions under a free trade system.
9.6	26	Our high standard of living rests on the maintenance of a system of high duties.
1.5	27	The sooner this country adopts a system of free trade, the better for everybody.
1.4	28	Free trade is the solution to our economic problems.
5.3	29	The principles of free trade are sound but it is a more radical change than we should undertake at present.
5.0	30	Free trade is worthy of careful study.

* Scale values were computed by the authors of this book.

*Scale Value		
9.5	**31**	All our industrial progress has been due to our policy of a protective tariff.
3.4	**32**	More people would favor free trade if they knew something about it.
9.0	**33**	A system of free trade will never work anywhere.
6.9	**34**	The tariff would be more desirable if its disadvantages could be eliminated.
3.2	**35**	The tariff is economically unsound in spite of its possible benefits.
7.5	**36**	The benefits of free trade have been exaggerated.
2.3	**37**	Tariffs create hatreds among nations.
7.1	**38**	I do not believe in free trade even though it has some benefits.
4.6	**39**	Many tariff rates serve political rather than economic purposes.
8.2	**40**	A high tariff on certain articles may be desirable.
9.7	**41**	The tariff is necessary to enable American producers to meet foreign competition on terms of equality.
9.5	**42**	The tariff insures employment for our workers.
6.6	**43**	I believe in a tariff for revenue only.
8.5	**44**	The tariff is desirable because any system which decreases imports provides employment for our workers.
4.8	**45**	Necessities should be imported free of tariff.
4.0	**46**	The benefits of free trade are somewhat greater than the evils.
9.5	**47**	A high tariff is necessary for our industrial progress.
3.4	**48**	High tariffs are harmful to our export trade.
3.5	**49**	We are too prosperous to need a high tariff.
4.3	**50**	The benefits of the tariff have been exaggerated.
6.3	**51**	I'm not sure that free trade would be desirable.
9.2	**52**	The tariff protects both capital and labor.
4.6	**53**	The tariff question has little economic significance.
2.6	**54**	Protective tariff causes industry to turn to less advantageous fields, thus decreasing the efficiency of labor and lowering wages.
5.8	**55**	There is much to be said on both sides of the tariff question.
4.4	**56**	I doubt if a high tariff is wise.
4.0	**57**	There should be no tax on goods imported in exchange for domestic products.
8.7	**58**	On the whole, the tariff laws have been of benefit to the country.
9.3	**59**	Free trade would ruin our manufacturers.
6.4	**60**	Duties on imports should not exceed the amount necessary to equalize labor cost.
2.1	**61**	Free trade is necessary for industrial progress.
1.8	**62**	The tariff robs the consumer to protect the producer.
9.0	**63**	The tariff guarantees high wages for our workers.
7.2	**64**	The free trade theory does not take into account all existing facts.
3.3	**65**	Taxing imported goods helps only a few merchants.
4.1	**66**	Articles imported for private use should not be taxed.
9.9	**67**	The protective tariff has made us the richest nation in the world.
3.0	**68**	The tariff benefits only certain already powerful interests.
9.1	**69**	We need high tariffs to protect our infant industries.
6.2	**70**	We cannot be sure that abolishing the tariff would increase wealth.
2.8	**71**	Our industries no longer need tariff protection.
6.0	**72**	There is a little more to be said for a protective tariff than against it.

*Scale Value		
2.0	73	Robbing the consumer through high tariffs must be stopped.
2.4	74	High tariff is one cause of the uneven distribution of wealth.
8.8	75	The tariff helps to keep our money in our own country.
3.0	76	We no longer have infant industries that need tariff protection.
7.4	77	Free trade would decrease wages without decreasing living costs in proportion.
2.3	78	Tariffs ruin our foreign trade by provoking other nations to retaliate with similar tariffs.
9.7	79	The higher the tariff the more prosperous we will be.
9.7	80	A high protective tariff makes for prosperity.
4.7	81	There is a little more to be said for free trade than against it.
1.2	82	The protective tariff is a complete failure.
1.9	83	Tariffs are an unjustifiable burden on the consumer.
1.8	84	Tariffs destroy our foreign markets.
8.2	85	Lowering the tariff will cause hard times.
8.3	86	Tariffs should be high enough that foreign goods cannot compete with American goods.
2.6	87	The tariff has benefitted some individuals but has harmed the country as a whole.
9.2	88	The high tariff makes for a high standard of living.
3.4	89	High tariffs do not really help the people who need help.
9.0	90	Tariffs are necessary to prevent our markets from being flooded with foreign goods.
1.8	91	The tariff is unsound in principle.
5.5	92	The tariff helps a few basic industries.
7.6	93	The tariff rates on certain commodities should be higher.
1.5	94	I agree with the economists that free trade is the best policy.
9.8	95	Tariffs enable us to compete with cheap foreign labor and still maintain our high standard of living.
8.6	96	Our basic industries still need tariff protection.
3.2	97	The tariff increases the cost of living faster than it increases wages.
2.1	98	Free trade increases wealth and reduces the cost of commodities.
3.8	99	Efficiency of labor and advantageous conditions, not a protective tariff, keep wages high.
5.2	100	The tariff has been neither beneficial nor harmful to the country as a whole.
2.7	101	Free trade makes for general economic betterment.
2.5	102	The benefits of free trade greatly exceed the evils.
2.5	103	Living costs would be lower if we had free trade.
8.7	104	If the tariff were lowered, many factories would be forced to close.
5.2	105	The tariff question is of no practical consequence to most people.
5.7	106	Both the evils and the benefits of free trade have been exaggerated.

GENERALIZED SCALES FOR INTERNATIONAL ISSUES

No generalized scale for measuring attitudes toward international issues appears to have been developed, nor have we found references to any research using the semantic differential toward this end. The semantic differential, of course, is easily adaptable for this purpose.

SUMMARY

In this chapter we have described scales for measuring attitude toward internationalism or worldmindedness, war or militarism-pacifism, and the tariff. Except for the scale for measuring attitude toward the tariff, there is more supporting data for scales included in this chapter than for those in many other areas. However, the same lack of convincing data for scale validity is evident. Also, the international issues represented are very limited; scales for measuring attitudes toward foreign aid, cultural exchange, limited wars, and other current issues would be useful.

CHAPTER 6

abstract concepts

In addition to attitudes which are held toward persons, groups of persons, and other essentially social objects, individuals develop attitudes toward the events and situations produced by these objects and in which the objects occur or are involved. Thus many attitudes possess intangibles as their referents. The scales in this book which measure attitudes toward such abstract referents are contained, for the most part, in this chapter. However, scales measuring attitudes toward some abstracts are to be found in other chapters. The reader should look in the appropriate chapter (especially Chapter 7) for referents which are not located in this chapter.

The referents of the attitudes measured by scales in this chapter may be differentiated from those of other chapters on the following bases. First, all referents in this chapter are abstract. Secondly, the abstracts which serve as referents to the scales in this chapter are all relatively specific in nature (death, mathematics courses, problem solving, etc.). More global referents such as conservatism-radicalism are to be found in Chapter 7. Third, the concepts themselves are connotatively neutral and are very frequently dealt with in a nonevaluative manner. Thus, the concept of problem solving has no a priori evaluative connotation, but may be given one by the conceptualizer. Further, one often deals with problem solving in a nonevaluative manner.

The nonevaluative quality of the referents in this chapter is to be compared with referents occurring in the chapter on social practices (which possess the quality of preferability) and in the chapter on social issues (which are evaluative to the extent that they possess at least two connotations: the pros and the cons).

ATTITUDES TOWARD EDUCATION

Scales in this section measure attitudes toward the value of education or of being educated. Readers interested in scales regarding specific courses in educational curricula should see the following section of this chapter. For related scales, see Exhibits 3-14, 3-15, 3-16, 6-5, 6-6, and 10-1.

The education scale ***EXHIBIT 6-1***

Description. This 22-item, Likert-type scale was developed by Rundquist and Sletto (1936). The items are broad in content, ranging from effects of possessing an education upon one's leisure time and upon economic opportunity to conflict between education and work. Some of the items are mildly dated: "A good education is a great comfort to a man out of work." None are so seriously dated as to require alteration or elimination.

Subjects. College students, high school teachers, members of classes for the unemployed, and men on relief (2,882 subjects) were used in construction of this scale. For a further description of the sample, see Rundquist and Sletto (1936).

Response Mode. Persons respond to each item by selecting one of five Likert-type alternatives: strongly agree, agree, undecided, disagree, and strongly disagree.

Scoring. For items which are positive toward education, the alternative responses are weighted from 5 (strongly agree) to 1 (strongly disagree). Weights for negative items must be reversed. The person's score is the sum of the weighted alternatives endorsed by him. High scores indicate positive attitudes toward the value of education.

Reliability. Rundquist and Sletto (1936) report split-half reliabilities (corrected) of .82 and .83, based upon samples of 500 males and 500 females, respectively. They also report test-retest reliabilities of .84 for a sample of 70 males and .85 for a sample of 75 females.

Validity. The scale has good content validity for attitude toward high school education. The content domain is somewhat restricted by failure to include items dealing specifically with college education. Rundquist and Sletto (1936) also report some correlates with other measuring instruments which may be construed as evidence of some concurrent validity.

Comments. Although developed in 1936, none of the items in this scale is seriously dated. The items have content validity, and the size of the pool from which they were selected strengthens content validity. Lack of items regarding the value of college education (a more current interest than that of high school education) may restrict the content validity somewhat. Otherwise, this is a quite adequate scale for measuring attitude toward education and is probably preferable to the next scale (by Glassey) measuring the same attitude.

EXHIBIT 6-1

THE EDUCATION SCALE

READ EACH ITEM CAREFULLY AND UNDERLINE QUICKLY THE PHRASE WHICH BEST EXPRESSES YOUR FEELING ABOUT THE STATEMENT. Wherever possible, let your own personal experience determine your answer. Do not spend much time on any item. If in doubt, underline the phrase which seems most nearly to express your present feeling about the statement. WORK RAPIDLY. Be sure to answer every item.

*1 A man can learn more by working four years than by going to high school.
Strongly Agree Agree Undecided Disagree Strongly Disagree
2 The more education a person has the better he is able to enjoy life.
3 Education helps a person to use his leisure time to better advantage.
4 A good education is a great comfort to a man out of work.
*5 Only subjects like reading, writing, and arithmetic should be taught at public expense.
*6 Education is no help in getting a job today.
*7 Most young people are getting too much education.
8 A high school education is worth all the time and effort it requires.
9 Our schools encourage an individual to think for himself.
*10 There are too many fads and frills in modern education.
*11 Education only makes a person discontented.
*12 School training is of little help in meeting the problems of real life.
13 Education tends to make an individual less conceited.
14 Solution of the world's problems will come through education.
*15 High school courses are too impractical.
*16 A man is foolish to keep going to school if he can get a job.
17 Savings spent on education are wisely invested.
18 An educated man can advance more rapidly in business and industry.
*19 Parents should not be compelled to send their children to school.
20 Education is more valuable than most people think.
21 A high school education makes a man a better citizen.
*22 Public money spent on education during the past few years could have been used more wisely for other purposes.

* These are negative items, agreement wtih which is considered to reflect an unfavorable attitude. Their weights must be reversed for purposes of scoring. The same response alternatives are used with all items.
Reprinted with permission from Rundquist, E. A., and Sletto, R. F. *Personality in the depression.* Minneapolis: University of Minnesota Press, 1936.

Attitudes toward education *EXHIBIT 6-2*

Description. This is a 34-item, Thurstone-type scale developed by Glassey (1945) to measure attitudes toward the value of education and the effects of education upon people. Items and their scale values are given in Exhibit 6-2. There are enough items in the exhibit to create equivalent forms, if desired.

Subjects. In constructing the scale, British grammar school children (148 boys and 152 girls) between the ages of 11 and 18 years and 348 of their parents (173 fathers and 175 mothers) were used. Forty unidentified persons served as judges for sorting the items.

Response Mode. The person checks ("ticks") those items with which he fully agrees and places a cross in front of the items with which he does not fully agree. He may place a question mark in front of the item if he is totally unable to decide.

Scoring. The person's score is the median of the scale values of the items endorsed as "fully agree." Low scores indicate positive attitudes toward education.

Reliability. No reliability coefficients are reported for the scale.

Validity. The method of construction should ensure a degree of content validity. No other evidence of validity is available.

Comments. There is minimal evidence of validity for this scale and no evidence of reliability, which facts detract from its value. But it is a Thurstone-type scale, which gives it some merit in its own right, and the functional characteristics which are lacking can be readily assessed. Furthermore, despite the fact that it was developed on a sample of British subjects, the language of the items seems satisfactory for use with American samples as well. The items should be rescaled, however. The scale has the further advantage that it may be used with a wide range of ages and educational levels. In general, then, it is a promising scale which needs more work. If the user does not intend to assess its functional characteristics, he should use the scale by Rundquist and Sletto, presented earlier in this section, which is designed to measure the same attitude.

EXHIBIT 6-2

ATTITUDES TOWARD EDUCATION

Below are a number of statements about *education.* We want to know what you feel about this subject. Please read the statements carefully and then:

(i) Put a tick (✓) if you FULLY agree with a statement.
(ii) Put a cross (X) if you do not FULLY agree with a statement.

Reprinted with permission from Glassey, W. The attitude of grammar school pupils and their parents to education, religion, and sport. *Brit. J. educ. Psychol.*, **1945, 15, 101–104. Copyright 1945 by Methuen and Co., London, England.**

Scale Value		
1.0	1	I am intensely interested in education.
10.0	2	I go to school only because I am compelled to do so.
4.2	3	I am interested in education but think that one ought not to get too concerned about it.
6.4	4	I like reading thrillers and playing games better than studying.
0.5	5	Education is of first-rate importance in the life of man.
5.4	6	Sometimes I feel that education is necessary and sometimes I doubt it.
6.9	7	I should not do much work if I did not have to pass examinations.
8.4	8	Education tends to make people snobs.
10.1	9	I think time spent studying is wasted.
7.9	10	It is better for boys and girls to get jobs when they are fourteen than to continue at school.
5.7	11	It is doubtful whether education has improved the world or not.
10.9	12	I have no desire to have anything to do with education.
1.3	13	We cannot become good citizens unless we are educated.
2.2	14	More money should be spent on education.
3.7	15	I think my education will be of use to me after I leave school.
3.0	16	I always read newspaper articles on education.
9.3	17	Education does more harm than good.
11.4	18	I see no value in education.
3.3	19	Education enables us to live a less monotonous life.
7.4	20	I dislike education because it means that time has to be spent on homework.
4.5	21	I like the subjects taught in school but I do not like attending school.
10.5	22	Education is doing far more harm than good.
2.3	23	Lack of education is the source of all evil.
0.3	24	Education enables us to make the best possible use of our lives.
1.2	25	Only educated people can enjoy life to the full.
2.7	26	Education does far more good than harm.
7.1	27	I do not like school teachers so I somewhat dislike education.
4.9	28	Education is all right in moderation.
5.8	29	It is enough that we should be taught to read, write, and do sums.
8.9	30	I do not care about education so long as I can live comfortably.
9.9	31	Education makes people forget God and despise Christianity.
1.8	32	Education is an excellent character builder.
8.6	33	Too much money is spent on education.
6.7	34	If anything, I must admit a slight dislike for education.

ATTITUDES TOWARD SCHOOL COURSES

Scales contained in this section measure attitudes toward particular school courses, rather than toward education in general. Because most of the courses are those which would be encountered in college, and because the construction was almost always upon college populations regarding their encounter with their own courses, the validity of these scales for use in other educational contexts should be assessed carefully. The referents in this section include attitudes toward mathematics, physical education, and physical fitness. Readers interested in scales measuring attitudes toward physical education may also wish to see a scale by Drinkwater (1960) on attitudes toward physical education teaching as a career for women (see Exhibit 3-13). One scale for measuring attitude toward psychology courses was not included in this book because it uses an essentially projective technique; readers interested in that instrument will wish to see Knight and Hall (1957). Finally, there are two generalized scales for measuring attitudes toward any school subject (Silance and Remmers, 1934) and attitudes toward any college course (Hand, 1953), which are included in the last section of this chapter.

Attitudes toward mathematics EXHIBIT 6-3

Description. Gladstone, Deal, and Drevdahl (1960) developed this 12-item, modified Likert-type scale for use in the study of the effects of remedial mathematics courses. Most of the items ask for attitudes toward mathematics as compared with other academic subjects. The content of the items reflects fear of, or concern over, mathematics course grades. The items are given in Exhibit 6-3.

Subjects. The exact sample on which this scale was constructed is unknown, but it is presumed to have been a sample of undergraduate students in remedial mathematics courses.

Response Mode. Persons respond by endorsing one of a set of alternative responses. For all but two of the items, the person chooses one of six alternatives; for the other two, five alternatives per item are offered. The response alternatives vary in specific content, but all reflect degrees of favorability toward mathematics, usually in terms of fear and anxiety.

Scoring. The sixth alternative to these items always reflects a feeling that math courses are just like other courses. The other five items fall on a monotonic continuum. Thus, scoring the sixth alternative becomes a problem. It should probably be used separately as a control device or be substituted for the neutral alternative. If it is kept in and treated as a second neutral alternative, it poses the question of the effect of having two such alternatives upon the monotonicity of the item. If the sixth alternative is treated separately, or substituted for the other neutral alternative, the response alternatives should be weighted from 5 (most favorable toward mathematics) to 1 (least favorable toward mathematics). Weights for the alternatives for negative items should be reversed. The person's score would then be the sum of the weighted alternatives endorsed by him. High scores indicate positive attitudes.

Reliability. No reliability estimates are reported by these authors.

Validity. A cluster analysis of the 12 items of the scale indicated that the "question dealing with knowledge about the use of mathematics was independent of the other factors, that the question dealing with liking for mathematics was only moderately related to the remaining questions, and that the remaining questions could be treated as a cluster" (Gladstone et al., 1960). The authors also found the scores of an experimental group to change in the expected direction as a result of treatment more than did scores of the control group. However, the major item contributing to this change was found to be the question referring to liking for mathematics and not the cluster of other items which are related to one another. This indicates predictive validity of the scale for "liking mathematics," at least for that item.

Comments. Evidence of reliability is lacking for this scale, and further demonstrations of its validity are needed. It seems a potentially useful scale, but more work is required. The sixth alternative in these items creates, in effect, a parallel attitude continuum. This alternative should probably be used as a control device, or scored as 3, and substituted for the other neutral alternative; otherwise, it should be dropped altogether. In general, this scale seems less satisfactory than the Revised Math Attitude Scale by Aiken and Dreger (1961), which is described in the next section.

EXHIBIT 6-3

ATTITUDES TOWARD MATHEMATICS

Directions: Check the most *appropriate* response to the questions below. If you wish to change an answer, erase the wrong answer or cross it out heavily.

1 At the beginning of the fall semester, how well did you like mathematics as compared with other academic subjects such as English, Chemistry and History?

_____ a. I liked mathematics much better than other academic subjects.

_____ b. I liked mathematics about as well as or a little better than other academic subjects.

_____ c. I liked some academic subjects more, some less, than mathematics.

_____ d. I liked other academic subjects as well as or a little better than mathematics.

_____ e. I liked other academic subjects much better than mathematics.

_____ f. I liked all my academic subjects about equally well.

2 How well do you like mathematics now as compared with other academic subjects such as English, Chemistry and History?

_____ a. I like mathematics much better than other academic subjects.

_____ b. I like mathematics about as well as or a little better than other academic subjects.

_____ c. I like some academic subjects more, some less, than mathematics.

_____ d. I like other academic subjects as well as or a little better than mathematics.

Reference: R. Gladstone, R. Deal, and J. E. Drevdahl. An exploratory study of remedial Math. *Proc. Okla. Acad. Sci.*, 1960, 40, 81–85. Items obtained from authors and published with their permission.

_______ e. I like other academic subjects much better than mathematics.

_______ f. I like all my academic subjects about equally well.

3 At the beginning of the fall semester were you afraid of mathematics as compared with other academic subjects such as English, Chemistry and History?

_______ a. I was more afraid of mathematics than of any other academic subject.

_______ b. I was about as afraid or a little more afraid of mathematics than of my other academic subjects.

_______ c. In comparison with mathematics I was more afraid of some academic subjects, less afraid of others.

_______ d. I was about as afraid or a little more afraid of other academic subjects than of mathematics.

_______ e. I was more afraid of other academic subjects than of mathematics.

_______ f. I was not afraid of any of my academic subjects.

4 At the present time are you afraid of mathematics as compared with other academic subjects such as English, Chemistry and History; are you afraid of mathematics now?

_______ a. I am more afraid of mathematics than of any other academic subject.

_______ b. I am about as afraid or a little more afraid of mathematics than of my other academic subjects.

_______ c. In comparison with mathematics I am more afraid of some academic subjects, less afraid of others.

_______ d. I am about as afraid or a little more afraid of other academic subjects than of mathematics.

_______ e. I am more afraid of other academic subjects than of mathematics.

_______ f. I am not afraid of any of my academic subjects.

5 At the beginning of the fall semester, how willing were you to take a course in mathematics as compared with other academic courses such as English, Chemistry and History?

_______ a. I was much more willing to take a mathematics course.

_______ b. I was about as willing or a little more willing to take mathematics courses.

_______ c. I was more willing to take some, less willing to take others.

_______ d. I was about as willing or a little more willing to take other academic courses.

_______ e. I was much more willing to take other academic courses.

_______ f. I was equally willing to take all academic courses.

6 At the present time how willing are you to take another course in mathematics as compared with other academic courses?

_______ a. I am much more willing to take a mathematics course.

_______ b. I am about as willing or a little more willing to take mathematics courses.

_______ c. I am more willing to take some, less willing to take others.

_______ d. I am about as willing or a little more willing to take other academic courses.

_______ e. I am much more willing to take other academic courses.

_______ f. I am equally willing to take all academic courses.

7 At the beginning of the fall semester did concern about grades affect your attitude toward taking mathematics courses as compared with your concern about grades in other academic courses?

_______ a. I was much more concerned about the grade I might get in mathematics than I was about the grades I might get in other academic courses.

_______ b. I was somewhat more concerned about the grade I might get in mathematics than I was about the grades I might get in other academic courses.

_______ c. I was no more concerned about the grade I might get in mathematics than I was in most other academic courses.

_______ d. I was somewhat more concerned about the grades I might get in other academic courses than I was about the grade I might get in mathematics courses.

_______ e. I was much more concerned about the grades I might get in other academic courses than I was about the grade I might get in mathematics.

_______ f. I was not concerned about grades at all.

8 At the present time does concern about grades affect your attitude toward taking mathematics as compared with other academic courses?

_______ a. I am much more concerned about the grade I might get in mathematics than I am about the grades I might get in other academic courses.

_______ b. I am somewhat more concerned about the grade I might get in mathematics than I am about the grades I might get in other academic courses.

_______ c. I am no more concerned about the grade I might get in mathematics than I am in most other academic courses.

_______ d. I am somewhat more concerned about the grades I might get in other academic courses than I am about the grade I might get in mathematics courses.

_______ e. I am much more concerned about the grades I might get in other academic courses than I am about the grade I might get in mathematics.

_______ f. I am not concerned about grades at all.

9 At the beginning of the fall semester, how much confidence did you have in your ability to deal with mathematics in comparison with your ability to deal with other academic subjects?

_______ a. I had much less confidence in my ability to deal with mathematics than I had in my ability to deal with other academic subjects.

________ b. I had somewhat less confidence in my ability to deal with mathematics than I had in my ability to deal with most other academic subjects.

________ c. I had about average confidence in my ability to deal with mathematics as compared with other academic subjects.

________ d. I had somewhat more confidence in my ability to deal with mathematics than I had in my ability to deal with most other academic subjects.

________ e. I had a good deal more confidence in my ability to deal with mathematics than I had in my ability to deal with other academic subjects.

________ f. I was equally confident of my ability to deal with all academic subjects.

10 At the present time, how much confidence do you have in your ability to deal with mathematics in comparison with your ability to deal with other academic subjects?

________ a. I have much less confidence in my ability to deal with mathematics than I have in my ability to deal with other academic subjects.

________ b. I have somewhat less confidence in my ability to deal with mathematics than I have in my ability to deal with most other academic subjects.

________ c. I have about average confidence in my ability to deal with mathematics as compared with the academic subjects.

________ d. I have somewhat more confidence in my ability to deal with mathematics than I have in my ability to deal with most other academic subjects.

________ e. I have a good deal more confidence in my ability to deal with mathematics than I have in my ability to deal with other academic subjects.

________ f. I have equal confidence of my ability to deal with all academic subjects.

11 At the beginning of the fall semester, how well did you understand the way in which mathematics (exclusive of arithmetic) are used outside of the classroom?

________ a. I had no idea mathematics (exclusive of arithmetic) were good for anything except as a prerequisite for other courses or for graduation.

________ b. I knew mathematics were useful but had no idea how they were used.

________ c. I had some very vague notions about the uses of mathematics.

________ d. I had some knowledge about how mathematics were used but had little or no ideas about how the mathematics I had learned might be used.

________ e. I had some knowledge of the use of the mathematics I had been taught.

12 At the present time how well do you understand the way in which mathematics (exclusive of arithmetic) are used outside the classroom?

_______ a. I have no idea mathematics (exclusive of arithmetic) are good for anything except as a prerequisite for other courses or for graduation.

_______ b. I know mathematics are useful but have no idea how they are used.

_______ c. I have some very vague notions about the uses of mathematics.

_______ d. I have some knowledge about how mathematics are used but have little or no ideas about how the mathematics I have learned might be used.

_______ e. I have some knowledge of the use of the mathematics I have been taught.

Revised math attitude scale *EXHIBIT 6-4*

Description. This is a 20-item scale developed by Aiken and Dreger (1961) using the Likert scaling procedure. The scale was developed from paragraphs describing attitudes toward mathematics written by 310 college students. Ten of the items connote positive attitudes and ten connote negative attitudes toward mathematics.

Subjects. Items were developed on the basis of paragraphs written by 310 college students. Validity estimates were based upon a sample of 160 female college sophomores in a Southeastern women's college.

Response Mode. Persons respond to each item by choosing one of five Likert alternatives: strongly agree, agree, undecided, disagree, and strongly disagree.

Scoring. The response alternatives for positive items are weighted from 4 (strongly agree) to 0 (strongly disagree). These weights must be reversed for alternatives to negative items. The person's score is the sum of the weighted alternatives endorsed by him. High scores reflect positive attitudes toward mathematics.

Reliability. The authors (Aiken and Dreger, 1961) report a test-retest reliability coefficient of .94.

Validity. Scores on the attitude scale were found to be significantly related to final course grades of 67 females but not to the grades of 60 males. Scores on the attitude scale were positively correlated with numerical ability but unrelated to specified general personality variables. Scores on this scale also predicted gains in scores from initial to final administration of a mathematics achievement test when training intervened (Aiken and Dreger, 1961). In addition to content validity, the authors claim a degree of discriminant validity: "A test of independence between the scores on the attitude scale and scores on four items designed to measure attitudes toward academic subjects in general suggested that attitudes specific to mathematics were being measured" (Aiken and Dreger, 1961, p. 20).

Comments. This scale seems satisfactory with regard to both its reliability and validity. It is probably preferable to the scale by Gladstone et al., which also measures attitudes toward mathematics courses, presented in Exhibit 6-3. For interested readers, Aiken (1963) reports a matrix of intercorrelations among the Revised Math Attitude Scale and measures of personality variables to which it was significantly related.

EXHIBIT 6-4

REVISED MATH ATTITUDE SCALE

Directions: Please write your name in the upper right hand corner. Each of the statements on this opinionnaire expresses a feeling which a particular person has toward mathematics. You are to express, on a five-point scale, the extent of agreement between the feeling expressed in each statement and your own personal feeling. The five points are: Strongly Disagree (SD), Disagree (D), Undecided (U), Agree (A), Strongly Agree (SA). You are to encircle the letter(s) which best indicates how closely you agree or disagree with the feeling expressed in each statement AS IT CONCERNS YOU.

*1 I am always under a terrible strain in a math class.

SD D U A SA

*2 I do not like mathematics, and it scares me to have to take it.
3 Mathematics is very interesting to me, and I enjoy math courses.
4 Mathematics is fascinating and fun.
5 Mathematics makes me feel secure, and at the same time it is stimulating.
*6 My mind goes blank, and I am unable to think clearly when working math.
*7 I feel a sense of insecurity when attempting mathematics.
*8 Mathematics makes me feel uncomfortable, restless, irritable, and impatient.
9 The feeling that I have toward mathematics is a good feeling.
*10 Mathematics makes me feel as though I'm lost in a jungle of numbers and can't find my way out.
11 Mathematics is something which I enjoy a great deal.
*12 When I hear the word math, I have a feeling of dislike.
*13 I approach math with a feeling of hesitation, resulting from a fear of not being able to do math.
14 I really like mathematics.
15 Mathematics is a course in school which I have always enjoyed studying.
*16 It makes me nervous to even think about having to do a math problem.
*17 I have never liked math, and it is my most dreaded subject.
18 I am happier in a math class than in any other class.
19 I feel at ease in mathematics, and I like it very much.
20 I feel a definite positive reaction to mathematics; it's enjoyable.

* These are negative items, and must be reversed for purposes of scoring. The same response alternatives are used with all items.

Reprinted with permission from Aiken, L. R. Jr. Personality correlates of attitude toward mathematics. *J. educ. Res.*, 1963, 56, 576–580. Copyright 1963 by Dembar Educational Research Services, Inc., Madison, Wis.

Physical education attitude scale EXHIBIT 6-5

Description. This is a 30-item, Likert-type scale developed by Wear (1955). Equivalent forms are available. The items sample a broad content domain concerning the value of physical education for improvement of physical health, social skill, character, and understanding of others.

Subjects. The sample consisted of 100 male university freshmen.

Response Mode. Subjects respond to each statement on a separate answer sheet by checking below one of five alternatives: strongly agree, agree, undecided, disagree, and strongly disagree.

Scoring. For positive statements, response alternatives are weighted from 5 (strongly agree) to 1 (strongly disagree). Weights for alternatives must be reversed for negative items. The person's score is the sum of the weighted alternatives endorsed by him. High scores reflect positive attitudes toward physical education.

Reliability. The author reports split-half reliabilities (corrected) for Form A as .94 and for Form B as .96. The equivalent-forms reliability is reported as .96.

Validity. Scores on the two forms were found to correlate highly with other measures of attitude toward physical education, giving the scale a degree of concurrent validity. The content domain sampled by the scale is broad enough to allow for good content validity.

Comments. The scale is satisfactory with regard to reliability only. Test-retest reliability estimates would add to its value. Demonstration of validity is rather weak.

EXHIBIT 6-5

PHYSICAL EDUCATION ATTITUDE SCALE

DIRECTIONS—PLEASE READ CAREFULLY: Below you will find some statements about physical education. We would like to know how you feel about each statement. You are asked to consider physical education *only* from the standpoint of its place as an activity course taught during a regular class period. No reference is intended in any statement to interscholastic or intramural athletics. People differ widely in the way they feel about each statement. There are no right or wrong answers.

You have been provided with a separate answer sheet for recording your reaction to each statement. (a) Read each statement carefully, (b) go to the answer sheet and (c) opposite the number of the statement place an "x" in the square *which is under* the word (or words) which best expresses your feeling about the statement. After reading a statement you will know at once, in most cases, whether you *agree* or *disagree* with the statement. If you *agree,* then decide whether to place an "x" under "agree" or "strongly agree." If you *disagree,* then decide whether to place an "x" under "disagree" or "strongly disagree." In case you are undecided (or neutral) concerning your feeling about the statement, then place an "x" under "undecided." Try to avoid placing an "x" under "undecided" in very many instances.

Wherever possible, let your own personal experience determine your answer. Work rapidly, do not spend much time on any statement. This is not a test, but is simply a survey to determine how people feel about physical education. Your answers will in no way affect your grade in any course. In fact, we are not interested in connecting any person with any paper—so please answer each statement as you actually feel about it. *Be sure to answer every statement.*

Form A

*1 If for any reason a few subjects have to be dropped from the school program, physical education should be one of the subjects dropped.

*2 Physical education activities provide no opportunities for learning to control the emotions.

3 Physical education is one of the more important subjects in helping to establish and maintain desirable social standards.

4 Vigorous physical activity works off harmful emotional tensions.

*5 I would take physical education only if it were required.

*6 Participation in physical education makes no contribution to the development of poise.

7 Because physical skills loom large in importance in youth, it is essential that a person be helped to acquire and improve such skills.

8 Calisthenics taken regularly are good for one's general health.

*9 Skill in active games or sports is not necessary for leading the fullest kind of life.

*10 Physical education does more harm physically than it does good.

11 Associating with others in some physical education activity is fun.

12 Physical education classes provide situations for the formation of attitudes which will make one a better citizen.

*13 Physical education situations are among the poorest for making friends.

*14 There is not enough value coming from physical education to justify the time consumed.

15 Physical education skills make worthwhile contributions to the enrichment of living.

*16 People get all the physical exercise they need in just taking care of their daily work.

17 All who are physically able will profit from an hour of physical education each day.

18 Physical education makes a valuable contribution toward building up an adequate reserve of strength and endurance for everyday living.

*19 Physical education tears down sociability by encouraging people to attempt to surpass each other in many of the activities.

* These items are negative and their weights must be reversed for purposes of scoring.

20 Participation in physical education activities makes for a more wholesome outlook on life.
*21 Physical education adds nothing to the improvement of social behavior.
22 Physical education class activities will help to relieve and relax physical tensions.
23 Participation in physical education activities helps a person to maintain a healthful emotional life.
24 Physical education is one of the more important subjects in the school program.
*25 There is little value in physical education as far as physical well-being is concerned.
26 Physical education should be included in the program of every school.
*27 Skills learned in a physical education class do not benefit a person.
28 Physical education provides situations for developing desirable character qualities.
29 Physical education makes for more enjoyable living.
*30 Physical education has no place in modern education.

Form B

1 Associations in physical education activities give people a better understanding of each other.
2 Engaging in vigorous physical activity gets one interested in practicing good health habits.
*3 The time spent in getting ready for and engaging in a physical education class could be more profitably spent in other ways.
*4 A person's body usually has all the strength it needs without participation in physical education activities.
5 Participation in physical education activities tends to make one a more socially desirable person.
6 Physical education in schools does not receive the emphasis that it should.
*7 Physical education classes are poor in opportunities for worthwhile social experiences.
*8 A person would be better off emotionally if he did not participate in physical education.
9 It is possible to make physical education a valuable subject by proper selection of activities.
10 Developing a physical skill brings mental relaxation and relief.
*11 Physical education classes provide nothing which will be of value outside the class.
*12 There should not be over two one-hour periods per week devoted to physical education in schools.
13 Belonging to a group, for which opportunity is provided in team activities, is a desirable experience for a person.
14 Physical education is an important subject in helping a person gain and maintain all-round good health.
*15 No definite beneficial results come from participation in physical education activities.
16 Engaging in group physical education activities is desirable for proper personality development.
*17 Physical education activities tend to upset a person emotionally.
18 For its contributions to mental and emotional well-being physical education should be included in the program of every school.
19 I would advise anyone who is physically able to take physical education.

*20 As far as improving physical health is concerned a physical education class is a waste of time.
21 Participation in physical education class activities tends to develop a wholesome interest in the functioning of one's body.
22 Physical education classes give a person an opportunity to have a good time.
23 The final mastering of a certain movement or skill in a physical education class brings a pleasurable feeling that one seldom experiences elsewhere.
*24 Physical education contributes little toward the improvement of social behavior.
25 Physical education classes provide values which are useful in other parts of daily living.
27 Physical education should be required of all who are physically able to participate.
*28 The time devoted to physical education in schools could be more profitably used in study.
*29 The skills learned in a physical education class do not add anything of value to a person's life.
*30 Physical education does more harm socially than good.

Attitudes toward physical fitness and exercises EXHIBIT 6-6

Description. Although measuring attitudes toward physical fitness and exercise, Richardson (1960) developed this 19-item scale for use in measuring attitudes of college students toward physical education. He used a modified Thurstone procedure to produce the two equivalent forms shown in Exhibit 6-6. Using statements gathered from sentence-completion tests of college freshmen, expert judges (professors of health and physical education) sorted the items on a five-point continuum from "very unfavorable" to "very favorable." All items were selected so as to be evenly scaled with median values 0.2 points apart and to have small Q values. These items were arranged in order of their scale values for administration. Since they were scaled on a five-point continuum, the highest scale value obtained was 4.7.

Subjects. Items were obtained from eight college freshmen. Twenty professors of health and physical education in five universities served as judges. Reliability was assessed on a sample of 300 Southern Illinois University freshmen students.

Response Mode. Subjects respond by marking beside those items with which they agree. They make no mark beside those with which they disagree. No neutral or question mark alternative is provided.

Scoring. The person's score is the median of the scale values of items endorsed by him as "agree." High scores reflect positive attitudes.

Reliability. The author reports the equivalent-forms reliability of the scale to be .87, ± .03, based upon the sample of 300 freshmen. The test-retest reliability coefficient was .83, ± .06, using a test interval of three weeks and based upon a sample of 50 persons randomly selected from the original sample of 300.

Validity. The only evidence of validity of the scale lies in the fact that statistical treatment of the judges provided consensus. As with all Thurstone-type scales, the procedure used tends to assure a degree of content validity. Little other evidence of validity is available.

Comments. The reliability of the scale seems quite good, but bases for assuming validity are minimally satisfactory. Further evidence of validity would be helpful. The scale does have equivalent forms, which adds to its usefulness.

EXHIBIT 6-6

ATTITUDES TOWARD PHYSICAL FITNESS AND EXERCISE

The following items are not designed to test your knowledge. Instead, they are meant to explore some of your feelings and points of view toward certain health topics. There are no right or wrong answers. Further, your responses will not be made known to other students nor will they be used for grading purposes in this course. Please give a thoughtful and honest response to each item.

Read each item carefully and circle the number opposite each item with which you *agree.* Make no marks on the numbers opposite the items with which you *disagree.* Remember, circle the number only of the items with which you agree: your disagreement with the items is indicated by leaving the numbers of the items blank. There is no time limit but work rapidly.

Form A

Scale Value		
1.1	1	Physical fitness activity is the lowest type of activity indulged in by man.
1.3	2	Man has outgrown the need for physical fitness programs.
1.5	3	Physical fitness activity programs are necessary only in wartime.
1.7	4	Physical fitness activities are the least civilized of man's activities.
1.9	5	Physical activity should not be stressed so much in our present culture.
2.1	6	Planned physical activity programs have limited value.
2.3	7	Physical fitness activity is unnecessary.
2.5	8	The values of physical activity are debatable.
2.7	9	Physical fitness activity should be left to the individual.
2.9	10	Physical fitness programs are too soft.
3.1	11	Physical fitness activities appeal to man's highest nature.
3.3	12	Physical fitness is a most important aspect of life.
3.5	13	Physical fitness activities have not proved indispensable to society.
3.7	14	Physical fitness activities are retained in the world because of their value to mankind.

Scale Value		
3.9	15	Physical fitness programs are not sufficiently appreciated by college students.
4.1	16	Physical fitness activities are vital to life.
4.3	17	Physical activity benefits everybody.
4.5	18	Physical fitness activity programs should be stressed.
4.7	19	Physical fitness activity is a "must" in today's world.

Form B

1.1	1	Physical activity is a curse to modern men.
1.3	2	Physical fitness activities are "anti-intellectual" in effect.
1.5	3	Physical activity programs are an enemy to intellectual development.
1.7	4	Physical fitness is not worth the effort required.
1.9	5	Physical activity programs are more bad than good.
2.1	6	Physical fitness activities should be planned only on an individual basis.
2.3	7	Physical activity is not as important as intellectual activity.
2.5	8	Physical activity programs are decreasing in their value to mankind.
2.7	9	There are as many good as bad points in physical activity programs.
2.9	10	The world could exist without physical activity programs.
3.1	11	Planned physical activities develop good character.
3.3	12	Compulsory physical activity programs should be kept to a minimum.
3.5	13	Physical activity prorgams are in the process of change and will come out for the better.
3.7	14	Compulsory physical activity programs should be enforced in all schools.
3.9	15	Physical activities strengthen moral development.
4.1	16	Physical fitness activities are increasing in their value to mankind.
4.3	17	Physical fitness activities are valuable for maintaining health.
4.5	18	Physical fitness activities are not sufficiently practiced by college students.
4.7	19	Planning physical activity is fundamentally a sound practice.

ATTITUDES TOWARD THE LAW

The scales in this section measure attitudes toward the legal system, laws, legal ideology, and the functionaries of the legal system. Readers interested in legal issues should see Chapter 4, and a scale measuring attitude toward legal agencies for juvenile delinquency may be found in Chapter 10.

Attitude toward the law EXHIBIT 6-7

Description. This is a 20-item scale developed by Katz (Thurstone, 1931) using the Thurstone procedure. Equivalent forms of the scale are given in Exhibit 6-7. The items refer only to "law" and "the laws" and are more likely to be unidimensional than other scales in this section. Kimbrough (1955) submitted the items in this scale to a Guttman procedure and found 14 of the 20 items to survive this procedure. Interested readers should see Kimbrough and Cofer (1958).

Subjects. No information concerning the sample was given.

Response Mode. Persons respond by placing a check beside those items with which they agree and a cross beside those items with which they disagree.

Scoring. The person's score is the median of the scale values of the items endorsed. High scores reflect positive attitudes.

Reliability. Ferguson (1944) reports reliability estimates ranging from .47 to .64 for this scale. Goodstein (1953) reports the equivalent-forms reliability to be .33 ($N = 150$). While this correlation was statistically significant, it is very low for an equivalent-forms reliability estimate.

Validity. The scale seems to have good content validity. The analysis by Kimbrough (1955) would seem to indicate that the pool of items is relatively unidimensional. Regarding construct validity, Diggory (1953) reports correlations between this scale and the Thurstone scale measuring attitudes toward treatment of criminals of .30 and .50, based on samples of 75 men and 103 women, respectively. The test has also been found to correlate highly with the two forms of Thurstone's Attitude toward Patriotism Scale (Goodstein, 1953.)

Comments. This Thurstone scale has been shown to be useful in the past. However, its reliability estimates are quite low, overall. Kimbrough and Cofer (1958) have developed a Guttman modification of this scale, which was found to have predictive validity when attitude scale scores were compared with the content of free associations to verbal stimuli. Interested readers may consult Kimbrough (1955) and Kimbrough and Cofer (1958). Other studies using this scale include Fay and Middleton (1939, 1940), Ferguson (1939), Barkley (1942), Ferguson and Lawrence (1942), Gregory (1939), Middleton and Wright (1941), and Smith (1940, 1944, 1945).

EXHIBIT 6-7

ATTITUDE TOWARD THE LAW

Put a check mark (✓) if you agree with the statement.
Put a cross (×) if you disagree with the statement.

Form A

Scale Value		
4.1	1	We have too many laws.
10.1	2	Law is the greatest of our institutions.
0.8	3	The law is just another name for tyranny.
7.4	4	Individual laws are frequently harmful but the law as a whole is sound.
8.8	5	In the long run law and justice are synonymous.
0.2	6	I believe in the use of force to overthrow the law.

Scale Value		
4.6	**7**	We should have complete freedom of speech even for those who criticize the law.
5.7	**8**	Between a society completely bound by law and a state of anarchy there is a happy medium.
10.5	**9**	The law is more than the enactments of Congress, it is a sacred institution.
9.7	**10**	The law represents the wisdom of the ages.
3.4	**11**	Men are not all equal before the law.
6.7	**12**	We should obey the law even though we criticize it.
5.2	**13**	After all, the law is merely what people do.
9.1	**14**	The sanctity of the law should be taught in all schools.
2.9	**15**	The law is made in response to the pressure of lobbies in Washington.
6.1	**16**	Some laws command our respect while others are mere regulations.
2.2	**17**	The law is often the refuge of the scoundrel.
7.9	**18**	It is not judges who punish criminals, it is the law.
1.5	**19**	Law is the enemy of freedom.
8.3	**20**	The law prevents wholesale crime and murder.

Form B

3.7	**1**	Individual laws are frequently unjust.
9.0	**2**	The law should take its course no matter how individuals may suffer.
4.4	**3**	Some parts of the law are bad.
8.1	**4**	The law is fundamentally sound in spite of mistakes by Congress and courts.
6.3	**5**	Though it is our duty to obey all laws, we can try to have them changed.
9.3	**6**	The individual who refuses to obey the law is a menace to civilization.
2.4	**7**	The law is for the poor to obey, and for the rich to ignore.
8.5	**8**	Disobedience of the law leads to anarchy.
0.0	**9**	All law should be overthrown.
1.9	**10**	The law is a means of enslaving the mass of humanity for the benefit of a small minority.
5.5	**11**	Since law is made by man, it may be either good or bad.
5.9	**12**	Individual liberty and legal restrictions are equally important factors in society.
7.8	**13**	The law is superior to individual codes of conduct.
9.9	**14**	No man can violate the law and be my friend.
3.3	**15**	The law does not benefit the common man.
4.9	**16**	Though we obey the law, we can still criticize it.
1.1	**17**	We would be better off without any laws at all.
10.4	**18**	The law is the true embodiment of eternal justice.
0.3	**19**	The law is rotten to the core.
7.0	**20**	The less one tampers with the law, the better.

The law scale *EXHIBIT 6-8*

Description. This 22-item scale was developed by Rundquist and Sletto (1936). It is a Likert-type scale measuring attitudes toward laws, judges, juries, court decisions, lawyers, etc. This and other scales by Rundquist and Sletto (1936) in this book were developed in a study of the relative merits of Thurstone and Likert procedures. A set of 162 items was given to graduate students in psychology and advanced students in sociology, who commented on the items (especially on their ambiguity). They also indicated which items were responded to on the basis of their personal experience. Items were selected which were unambiguous and based on personal feelings without focusing upon personal problems. A third selection criterion for items was reliability. Items that were unreliable over a one-week interval were rejected. New items were added to those passing all three of these criteria, increasing the total to 212. This set of items was then administered to 184 juniors in sociology classes. An item analysis was completed on these, and items were chosen on the basis of their ability to discriminate the upper and lower quartiles of the total score distribution.

Subjects. The subjects were 2,882 college and high school students, high school teachers, students in classes for the unemployed, and men on relief.

Response Mode. Subjects respond to each item by choosing one of five aternatives: strongly agree, agree, undecided, disagree, and strongly disagree.

Scoring. Response alternatives for positive items are weighted from 5 (strongly agree) to 1 (strongly disagree). Weights for negative items must be reversed. The person's score is the sum of the weighted alternatives endorsed by him. High scores indicate positive attitudes toward the law.

Reliability. The authors report split-half reliabilities (corrected) of .84 and .82 for 500 males and 500 females, respectively. The test-retest reliability coefficient was .78 for a sample of 70 males and 75 females.

Validity. The scale has above-average content validity. The authors also offer some evidence of concurrent validity (Rundquist and Sletto, 1936).

Comments. This seems to be a satisfactorily valid and reliable scale for measuring attitudes toward the law. Further evidence of validity would be valuable, however. It is to be noted that this scale was originally a part of the Minnesota Scale for the Survey of Opinions, and its items were embedded in a set of other items measuring other attitudes. It would, therefore, be valuable to reassess the functional characteristics of these items when they are used out of the context of the items of the Minnesota scale.

EXHIBIT 6-8

THE LAW SCALE

READ EACH ITEM CAREFULLY AND UNDERLINE QUICKLY THE PHRASE WHICH BEST EXPRESSES YOUR FEELING

ABOUT THE STATEMENT. Wherever possible, let your own personal experience determine your answer. Do not spend much time on any item. If in doubt, underline the phrase which seems most nearly to express your present feeling about the statement. WORK RAPIDLY. Be sure to answer every item.

*1 The law protects property rights at the expense of human rights.
Strongly Agree Agree Undecided Disagree Strongly Disagree
*2 A person should obey only those laws that seem reasonable.
*3 It is all right to evade the law if you do not actually violate it.
*4 The sentences of judges in court are determined by their prejudices.
5 On the whole, judges are honest.
*6 Juries seldom understand a case well enough to make a really just decision.
7 On the whole, policemen are honest.
8 A man should obey the laws no matter how much they interfere with his personal ambitions.
9 Court decisions are almost always just.
10 In the courts a poor man will receive as fair treatment as a millionaire.
11 Personal circumstances should never be considered as an excuse for law-breaking.
12 A man should tell the truth in court, regardless of consequences.
*13 A person who reports minor law violations is only a trouble-maker.
*14 A person is justified in giving false testimony to protect a friend on trial.
*15 A hungry man has a right to steal.
16 All laws should be strictly obeyed because they **are** laws.
*17 Laws are so often made for the benefit of small selfish groups that a man cannot respect the law.
*18 Almost anything can be fixed up in the courts if you have enough money.
19 It is difficult to break the law and keep one's self-respect.
20 On the whole, lawyers are honest.
21 Violators of the law are nearly always detected and punished.
*22 It is all right for a person to break the law if he doesn't get caught.

* These are negative items and their weights must be reversed for purposes of scoring. The same response alternatives are used with all items.

The ideological and law-abidingness scales
EXHIBIT 6-9

Description. Both of these Thurstone-type scales are by Gregory (1939). The Ideological Scale measures six continua: (1) reification (the degree of definiteness with which the statement seems to suggest or imply that law is a thing or process which exists apart from human beings), (2) vivification (the degree of definiteness with which the statement seems to suggest or imply that law is a living thing), (3) super-individual control (the degree of definiteness with which the statement seems to suggest or imply that law in itself exerts control over individuals, or otherwise influences their behavior), (4) individual control (the degree of definiteness with which the statement seems to suggest or imply that control by law is really merely control by a superhuman agency or institution), (5) degree of control (the degree of control or influence exerted by or through law over individuals), (6) individual realistic (the degree of definiteness with which the statement seems to suggest or imply that law is nothing outside of or apart from human beings, but usually consists of the behavior of the majortiy of citizens). Actually, these six continua constitute six scales which have some items in common. Each scale consists of four or more items. To construct a scale for administration, the items which are repeated in the several continua should be used only once and then scored for each continuum in which they occur. This will result in a scale of 39 items.

To construct the Ideological Scale the author obtained definitions of law from a variety of persons, texts, dictionaries, and other reference books. The resulting 75 statements were scaled and selected to have low Q values (less than 3.7) and for approximately equal unit distribution on the scale value continuum. All 75 items were scaled on all six continua.

The Law-abidingness Scale consists of 14 items asking the respondent to indicate the frequency and extent to which he conforms to laws. Each stem has a set of five or more alternative responses. These items and the items for the Ideological Scale are given in Exhibit 6-9. The purpose of the Law-abidingness Scale was to measure conformity to law. The author defined conformity to law as the extent to which the person complies with the behavior expectancy stated in the law. A number of criteria were used in item development. First, laws which were selected to be included had to have daily or frequent relevance to the person and be laws on which the subject would report his behavior accurately. Second, laws were selected to represent a range of motives for conformity and to include local, state, and national laws. Items on this scale measure both extent and frequency of conformity. Frequency items include items 7, 8, 9, 10, 11, 12, 13, and 14. Extent-of-conformity items are items 1, 2, 3, 4, 5, and 6. To sort the items, the judges first pinned them in rank order to a sheet of paper (from greatest to least conformity). The judges were allowed to leave equal or unequal distances between items. The paper was then divided into 11 equal units. Scale values and Q values were then computed on the basis of this physical dimension, the use of which is rather unique in scaling. All items in the Law-abidingness Scale have Q values less than 2.4.

Subjects. For scaling the ideological statements, 48 persons were used: 20 social science faculty members and graduate students, 20 undergraduates in psychology at Syracuse University, and 8 adult residents of Syracuse. Judges for the law-abidingness items were 40 undergraduate students in psychology at Syracuse University.

Response Mode. Persons place a check mark in front of each statement with which they agree completely. They do not check those with which they disagree in any way. They may check as many or as few statements as they like. For the Law-abidingness Scale, the person is asked to underscore that alternative in each set of alternatives which best describes his behavior in that setting.

Scoring. For the Ideological Scale, the person receives a score for each continuum to which an item he checks is relevant. His score is determined by the median of the scale values for the items he checks on that continuum. For the Law-abidingness Scale, three scores are computed: a frequency score, an extent-of-violation score, and a total score. The frequency score is the median of the scale values of statements endorsed by the person on items 7, 8, 9, 10, 11, 12, 13, and 14. The extent-of-violation score is the median of the scale values of items 1, 2, 3, 4, 5, and 6. This lowest scale value would represent the greatest extent of nonconformity ever demonstrated by the person in the situation described. To secure a general law-abidingness score, the mean between the total frequency score and the total extent score is computed. High scores on the ideological continua reflect a tendency to adopt that perspective. High scores on the degree-of-control continuum indicate that the person sees law as strongly controlling. High scores on the Law-abidingness Scale indicate a report of infrequent violations of small extent.

Reliability. In order to establish reliability, the author presented the following argument: Because Scales I, III, IV, and VI could be classed as being either institutionalistic or individualistic, and because these two categories were logically opposites, it was possible to reverse the scale values of the statements on the individualistic scales (IV and VI) (by subtracting the scale value of each statement on these two scales from 10.5, deriving a figure that theoretically would be the scale value of that statement if it were scaled on the institutionalistic continua). In this fashion, these two scales were transposed into institutionalistic scales. The mean of the scale values of all statements that each of the subjects checked on Continua I, III, IV, and VI (the latter two with scale values reversed) was computed and taken as the score that represented the individual's location on a general institutionalistic continuum. Correlation of this combined score with scores on the separate scales resembled a reversed split-half technique. "The r between the original scores on Continuum VI (Individual-realistic) and this combined scale was $-.78, \pm .03$, and that between Continuum I (Reification) and the combined scores was $+.88, \pm .02$, indicating a rather high reliability for these two scales" (Gregory, 1939, p. 270). This is a rather ingenious way of assessing reliability, but it is of questionable merit. For the Law-abidingness Scale, a modified split-half technique was also used. The scores for each subject on five of the scales were averaged (scales number 1, 3, 8, 12, 14). Then the averages of these five scores were correlated with the total law-abidingness scores of the same subjects, yielding a correlation of $.81, \pm.03$.

Validity. Because Continua I, II, and III of the Ideological Scale were considered by the author to be institutionalistic, and Continua IV and VI individualistic, Gregory (1939) hypothesized that correlations between individualistic and institutionalistic scales would be negative if the scales were valid. Also, correlations between individualistic scales would be positive, as would correlations between institutionalistic scales. His hypotheses were borne out, and the author takes this as evidence of validity for the Ideological Scale. To establish the validity of the Law-abidingness Scale, the author correlated scores on this scale with scores on two other scales which he had also created (the Civic Participation

Scale and the Social Regard Scale). He considers that the low correlations obtained between the Law-abidingness Scale and each of the other two scales indicate that the subjects were not merely rating themselves highly on the law-abidingness scale for the sake of good appearance. However, it is to be pointed out that the distribution of scores could account for the low correlations, if all subjects did rate themselves high on *all* scales. Both scales seem to have good content validity, which is in part a result of the care with which dimensions of the referent were specified in advance.

Comments. These scales have the merit of providing a number of separate scales which could possibly be used separately if one were, for example, interested only in tendency to reify the law, etc. The disadvantage of the scales is the ingenious, but roundabout, manner in which the author attempted to establish their validity and reliability. Nonetheless, the scales possess construct validity, content validity, and (apparently) some degree of reliability. Further work on these characteristics (and especially upon the characteristic of reliability) would be necessary to make effective use of the scales. The referents of the scales are themselves theoretically interesting in terms of tendency to concrete thinking, reification of abstract concepts, etc., in conjunction with perception of degree of control exercised over one externally.

EXHIBIT 6-9

THE IDEOLOGICAL AND LAW-ABIDINGNESS SCALES

*THE IDEOLOGICAL SCALE

Following is a list of thirty-nine statements about law.

Please place a check mark (✓) in front of each statement with which you *completely* agree.

If you disagree with a statement *in any way*, do not put any mark in front of it.

Please check as many or as few statements as you wish, but be sure that you place a check mark in front of every statement with which you fully agree.

Continuum I (Reification)

Scale Values

0.4 1 Law is nothing more than certain acts, beliefs, and attitudes of the majority of individuals in their daily relations with others.

* The items of this scale are presented as the author presented them in his article. Although they are arranged under the continuum to which they refer, some items are common to more than one continuum. To create the actual scale, they should be included only once, giving rise to a 39-item scale as indicated in the instructions.

Reprinted with permission from Gregory, W. S. Ideology and affect regarding "law" and their relation to law-abidingness. Part I, *Char. and Pers.* 1939, 7, 265–284. Copyright 1939 by Duke University Press, Durham, N.C.

Scale Values		
0.9	**2**	Law is nothing and does nothing of itself; it is a written statement which is enforced by police and court officials.
1.9	**3**	The functioning of law results only in the satisfaction of the purposes of those who make and enforce the law.
2.8	**4**	Law is passed by a group of officials who represent a group of citizens.
4.0	**5**	Law contains the accepted code of civil conduct.
5.1	**6**	The purpose of law is to protect each citizen from the possible misdeed of others.
6.0	**7**	Law is essential to the enjoyment by each citizen of his inalienable rights.
6.8	**8**	The functioning of law results in the prevention of behavior harmful to others.
7.7	**9**	Law is the rules which govern the people.
8.7	**10**	Law sets itself up as the standard of civil conduct.
9.6	**11**	Law controls the conduct of the citizens.
10.3	**12**	Law is something over and above human beings.

Continuum II (Vivification)

0.0	**1**	Law is nothing more than certain acts, beliefs, and attitudes of the majority of individuals in their daily relations with each other.
0.8	**2**	The purposes ascribed to law are only the purposes of the officials and citizens.
1.4	**3**	Law is a formula of civil conduct which it is the duty of everyone to obey.
2.5	**4**	Law is designed so that the greatest number will derive the most good when it is universally obeyed.
3.5	**5**	Law is the curbing of one's action by authorized power outside and superior to oneself.
4.3	**6**	Law is essential to the enjoyment by each citizen of his inalienable rights.
5.4	**7**	Law is the embodiment of justice and equality.
6.7	**8**	Law keeps the action of individuals from interfering with the rights of others.
7.9	**9**	The purpose of law is to guarantee the liberty of the individual.
8.7	**10**	Law rightly claims the allegiance of every citizen at all times.
9.7	**11**	Law punishes the bad and protects the good.

Continuum III (Super-individual control)

0.0	**1**	Law is nothing more than certain acts, beliefs, and attitudes of the majority of individuals in their daily relations with others.
1.2	**2**	Law is formulated and passed by persons with status as officials to protect and promote the interests of the majority.
2.2	**3**	Law is the principles according to which we consent to be governed.
3.3	**4**	Law is designed so that the greatest number will derive the most good when it is universally obeyed.
4.0	**5**	Law serves as a means by which society compels or restrains its members.
4.7	**6**	Law is a formula of civil conduct which it is the duty of everyone to obey.
6.0	**7**	Law is to secure justice and order among the people.
7.3	**8**	The purpose of law is to guarantee the well-being of the individual.

Scale Values		
8.0	9	The functioning of law results in the prevention of behavior harmful to others.
9.0	10	Law keeps the action of individuals from interfering with the rights of others.
10.0	11	Law punishes the bad and protects the good.

Continuum IV (Individual control)

0.3	1	Law is something over and above human beings.
0.8	2	Law controls the conduct of the citizens.
1.9	3	Law is the rules which govern the people.
2.6	4	Law keeps the actions of individuals from interfering with the rights of others.
3.4	5	Law is the formula of civil conduct which it is the duty of everyone to obey.
4.0	6	Law contains the accepted code of civil conduct.
5.2	7	Law is the statement of regulations which in general promote the welfare of those who obey them.
5.8	8	Law serves as a means by which society compels or restrains its members.
7.0	9	Law represents the rule or procedure of the people in situations where the satisfaction of one person's needs is likely to come in conflict with the satisfaction of the needs of others.
8.2	10	The functioning of law results only in the satisfaction of the purposes of those who make and enforce the law.
8.8	11	Law embodies the principles by which civil authorities regulate the behavior of citizens.
9.7	12	Law is the statements written by officials which contain the official rules of conduct.

Continuum V (Degree of control)

0.6	1	Law is nothing more than certain acts, beliefs, and attitudes of the majority of individuals.
1.4	2	Law's purpose is only a generalization of the common purposes or desires of the majority of citizens.
2.0	3	Law originates in the common needs and desires of the people.
2.8	4	Law is designed so that the greatest number will derive the most good when it is universally obeyed.
4.4	5	Law is the principles according to which we consent to be governed.
5.3	6	Law is a statement of the circumstances under which public force will be brought to bear on men through the courts.
6.1	7	Law is the guardian of social welfare.
7.4	8	Law attempts to regulate human behavior.
8.3	9	Law is the curbing of one's actions by authorized powers outside and superior to oneself.
9.3	10	Law has to be obeyed regardless of the personal interests at stake.

Continuum VI (Individual realistic)

0.3	1	Law punishes the bad and protects the good.
1.3	2	Law attempts to regulate human behavior.
2.4	3	The purpose of law is to protect each citizen from the possible misdeed of others.

Scale Values		
3.2	4	Law is to be obeyed regardless of the personal interest at stake.
4.8	5	Law is the statements written by officials which contain the official rules of conduct.
5.7	6	Law contains the accepted code of civil conduct.
6.5	7	Law is passed by officials who represent a group of citizens.
7.5	8	Law states regulations of behavior with which individuals comply in preference to sanctions applied by force by officials.
8.4	9	The purposes ascribed to law are only the purposes of the officials and citizens.
9.2	10	Law is nothing or does nothing of itself; it is a written statement which is enforced by police and court officials.
10.3	11	Law is nothing more than certain acts, beliefs, and attitudes of the majority of individuals in their daily relations with others.

THE LAW-ABIDINGNESS SCALE

On the following pages are listed various activities that people do in different degrees, such as speed of driving, frequency of voting, making out applications, listening to radio talks, and other things. It is recognized that there are differences of opinion and many different practices in regard to the behaviors listed.

This study is being conducted to find out which of these behaviors are being performed by the largest number of people. You are asked to help in finding the prevalence of these behaviors by *underscoring* the answer that most accurately describes your behavior in each of the situations named.

You may not be able to remember exactly what you do in some of the situations named, but please give the most accurate approximation possible.

If on any question you feel you cannot give an opinion that is even approximately correct or for any other reason do not wish to answer, please omit that question. All questions answered should represent your best judgment or the most accurate estimate possible.

Do *not* sign your name. All returns are anonymous.

Scale Value		
	1	(Underscore as many of the following as are correct for you.) I have at some time in my life:
0.8		(a) Sent a long written document in a parcel post package.
1.7		(b) Sent a letter in a parcel post package.
5.2		(c) Sent a short note in a parcel post package.
8.1		(d) Sent a sentence or two in a parcel post package.
10.5		(e) I have never sent any writing in a parcel post package.
	2	(Underscore as many of the following as apply to you in connection with the filing of your income tax returns.)
0.5		(a) I have omitted or reported items incorrectly so that I did not have to pay any tax at all.

Scale Value	
2.7	(b) I have omitted or reported items incorrectly so that my taxes were very much lower than they should have been.
4.5	(c) I have omitted or reported items incorrectly so that my taxes were considerably lower than they should have been.
6.5	(d) I have omitted or reported items incorrectly so that my taxes were slightly lower than they should have been.
8.3	(e) I have omitted or reported items incorrectly so that my taxes were very slightly lower than they should have been.
10.5	(f) I neither omitted nor reported incorrectly any items.
	3 (Underscore as many as are correct for you.) Before driving your car into or across a "throughtraffic" street from a side street on which a stop sign is posted have you ever:
0.5	(a) increased speed?
2.4	(b) retained your customary speed?
5.2	(c) slowed down a little?
8.2	(d) slowed down to a very slow speed without actually stopping?
10.5	(e) brought your car to a complete stop?
	4 What is the fastest you have ever driven a car in Syracuse?
10.5	(a) Twenty-five miles per hour.
8.4	(b) Thirty-five miles per hour.
6.1	(c) Forty-five miles per hour.
4.1	(d) Fifty-five miles per hour.
2.2	(e) Sixty-five miles per hour.
0.5	(f) Seventy-five miles per hour.
	5 What is the longest time you have left your car parked at a place where parking was prohibited.
0.5	(a) Not more than four hours.
1.3	(b) Not more than three hours.
2.2	(c) Not more than two hours.
3.3	(d) Not more than one hour.
4.4	(e) Not more than thirty minutes.
5.2	(f) Not more than twenty-five minutes.
6.2	(g) Not more than twenty minutes.
7.1	(h) Not more than fifteen minutes.
8.2	(i) Not more than ten minutes.
9.2	(j) Not more than five minutes.
10.5	(k) Not parked there at all.
	6 What is the longest time that you have ever left your car parked in a place where parking was limited to forty-five minutes?
10.5	(a) Not more than forty-five minutes.
9.3	(b) Not more than fifty minutes.
8.4	(c) Not more than fifty-five minutes.
7.2	(d) Not more than sixty minutes.
5.6	(e) Not more than one hour and fifteen minutes.
4.6	(f) Not more than one hour and thirty minutes.
3.5	(g) Not more than two hours.
2.6	(h) Not more than three hours.

Scale Value		
1.6		(i) Not more than four hours.
0.5		(j) Not more than a half day.
	7	Before driving your car into or across a "throughtraffic" street from a side street on which a "stop" sign is posted, about how often do you bring your car to a complete stop before entering the "through" street?
0.5		(a) Never.
2.3		(b) Rarely.
5.2		(c) Sometimes.
8.1		(d) Frequently.
10.5		(e) Always.
	8	When driving your car in Syracuse, about how regularly do you drive at a speed of more than twenty-five miles per hour?
10.5		(a) Never.
8.3		(b) Rarely.
5.3		(c) Sometimes.
2.5		(d) Frequently.
0.5		(e) Very frequently.
	9	About how often have you parked at a place where parking is prohibited?
10.5		(a) Never.
8.4		(b) Rarely.
5.7		(c) Sometimes.
2.7		(d) Frequently.
0.5		(e) Very frequently.
	10	About how often have you parked at a place where parking was limited to a certain length of time, and exceeded the parking time limit?
10.5		(a) Never.
8.1		(b) Rarely.
5.2		(c) Sometimes.
2.5		(d) Frequently.
0.5		(e) Very frequently.
	11	About how often do you send written material in a parcel post package?
10.5		(a) Never.
8.4		(b) Rarely.
5.6		(c) Sometimes.
2.3		(d) Frequently.
0.5		(e) Very frequently.
	12	How often have you taken hotel or restaurant towels, silverware, ash trays, etc., to keep for yourself?
10.5		(a) Never.
8.8		(b) Once or twice.
8.1		(c) Rarely.

Scale Value		
5.4		(d) Sometimes.
2.7		(e) Frequently.
1.5		(f) Make a hobby of collecting them.
0.5		(g) Every time you patronize a hotel, restaurant, etc.
	13	In filling out forms or stating information verbally when applying for work, any kind of license, bonus, relief, etc., about how often have you omitted or reported facts incorrectly?
10.5		(a) Never.
8.1		(b) Rarely.
5.3		(c) Sometimes.
2.5		(d) Frequently.
0.5		(e) Always.
	14	About how often have you visited in their sick rooms persons ill with the measles?
10.5		(a) Never.
8.3		(b) Rarely.
5.3		(c) Sometimes.
2.3		(d) Frequently.
0.5		(e) Very frequently.

Attitudes toward law and justice EXHIBIT 6-10

Description. This is a set of eight Likert-type items developed by Watt and Maher (1958) to measure attitudes toward law and justice. It was originally used with an 11-item, incomplete-sentence blank measuring the same attitude and an 8-item questionnaire measuring attitudes toward home and parents. Persons interested in the latter scale should see Chapter 9.

Subjects. The sample consisted of 79 prisoners at Indiana State Prison who had been confined for the following crimes: murder, 20; violent crimes (armed robbery, burglary, and larceny), 18; "intellectual crimes" (fraud, forgery, and embezzlement), 16; and sexual offenses, 10.

Response Mode. Persons respond to each item by checking one of three alternatives: agree, disagree, or no opinion.

Scoring. The scale is scored by a ratio in which the percentage of positive answers is divided by the sum of the percentages of positive and negative answers. The maximum value of this ratio is 1.0. Since half of the items are worded negatively, care must be taken to score disagreement with negative items as reflecting positive answers. High scores indicate positive attitudes toward law and justice.

Reliability. No evidence of reliability is available.

Validity. The scale was validated by the multitrait-multimethod procedure, providing an estimate of convergent and discriminant validity

(Maher, Watt, and Campbell, 1960). The structured and projective forms of the attitudes toward law and justice forms correlated .50 with one another in a matrix including noncritical correlations of .13 and .12. Such a result testifies to the validity of the scales. When the sample was broken down into the five subgroups of crimes for which they had been incarcerated, the authors found positive, significant correlations between the two forms of the test for the prisoners as a whole and for all groups except intellectual and sex offenders (Watt and Maher, 1958). However, the scales did not discriminate type of crime. Ten point-biserial correlations between type of crime and scores on the tests provided only one significant correlation (a highly significant correlation between intellectual crime and attitudes toward law and justice as measured by the structured attitude scale presented in Exhibit 6-10).

Comments. This seems a valid estimate of attitude toward law and justice. The lack of reliability estimates seriously detracts from the value of the scale. Also, equivalent forms are quite valuable for short scales such as this one. Items in the scale have content validity. Readers interested in the incomplete-sentence blank accompanying this scale should see Watt and Maher (1958).

EXHIBIT 6-10

ATTITUDES TOWARD LAW AND JUSTICE

Mark the statements which you agree with in the first column, those you disagree with in the second column and those you have no opinion about in the third column.

Agree	Disagree	No Opinion		
______	______	______	*1	Cops often carry a grudge against men who get in trouble with the law and treat them cruelly.
______	______	______	2	For the most part, justice gets done by the police and the courts.
______	______	______	*3	Many of the people in prisons are actually innocent of the crimes they were convicted for.
______	______	______	4	Most policemen are honest.
______	______	______	*5	Any jury can be fixed and most of them are fixed.
______	______	______	6	We would have less crime if our laws were more strict.

* These items are negative and disagreement with them should be counted as a positive response; agreement is counted as a negative response.

______	______	______	*7	The big-time crooks never get arrested in this country. It's just the little guy that gets caught.
______	______	______	8	Most judges are honest and kind-hearted.

ATTITUDES TOWARD FORMAL ABSTRACT CONCEPTS

The referents for scales included in this section are all concepts for which formal definitions are available and whose definitions have some generality of acceptance. Included among these are evolution, problem solving, God, and death. Concepts for which no standard, formal definition exists are contained in the following section of this chapter. Persons interested in measuring attitudes toward evolution will find another item pool available in Dudycha (1930, 1934). There are several questionnaires available for measuring reactions to death which were not included in this book because they were not sufficiently well known with regard to their functional characteristics, or their method of construction. Among these are a set of items by Diggory and Rothman (1961) and an adjective checklist by Swenson (1958, 1961*a*,*b*).

Attitudes toward evolution *EXHIBIT 6-11*

Description. This is a 20-item, Thurstone-type scale developed by Thelma Thurstone (Thurstone, 1931). Apparently there were originally two forms of this scale, but only Form A could be located. The scale items bear directly upon the theory of evolution without specification of which theory. They tend to contrast the evolutionary doctrine with religious doctrines.

Subjects. The population sample was not specified, but it is assumed that the subjects were University of Chicago undergraduates.

Response Mode. Persons respond by placing a check mark beside those items with which they agree and a cross beside those with which they disagree.

Scoring. The person's score is the median of the scale values of items endorsed by him. High scores indicate positive attitudes toward evolution.

Reliability. Reliability estimates are reported by Likert et al. (1934) as ranging from .67 to .86. Lorge (1939) reports these reliabilities as being from .71 to .92, and Ferguson (1944) reports the range as being from .82 to .90.

Validity. The method of construction would tend to ensure a degree of content validity. Other demonstrations of validity are lacking.

Comments. The scale has moderately good reliability but is below average in demonstrations of validity for measurement of attitudes toward evolutionary doctrine, especially as that doctrine may conflict with religious doctrine. Readers interested in this scale may also wish to see Woodruff and Di Vesta (1948), Carey (1940), Ferguson (1939, 1942, 1945), and Barkley (1942).

EXHIBIT 6-11

ATTITUDES TOWARD EVOLUTION

Put a check mark (✓) if you agree with the statement.
Put a cross (×) if you disagree with the statement.

Scale Values		
0.4	1	I am beginning to think that the theory of evolution may be right.
5.2	2	The idea of evolution is no more convincing than the account of creation given in the Bible.
1.7	3	The theory of evolution is a lot of unsupported guesses.
4.2	4	I am not quite ready to accept the doctrine of evolution.
9.7	5	Only the ignorant and the superstitious oppose evolution.
1.4	6	The Bible gives the true explanation of the world's creation and the origin of man.
3.1	7	Evolution may apply to plants and animals, but never to man.
9.1	8	If the biblical accounts conflict with the findings of science, then the Bible must give way.
8.4	9	The evolutionary theory is the most satisfactory explanation of life we yet have.
4.0	10	We must be cautious in accepting such a radical doctrine as evolution.
10.8	11	The theory of evolution is complete to the last detail.
6.8	12	The evolutionary theory may contain errors but it is a step in the right direction.
1.0	13	The theory of evolution is absurd and harmful to society.
4.7	14	I do not entirely understand the evolutionary theory, so I am doubtful of its truth.
8.7	15	Anti-evolution legislation is ridiculous in a civilized nation.
5.5	16	There is much to be said on both sides of the evolution controversy.
0.4	17	Books supporting the evolutionary theory should be destroyed.
2.2	18	We should oppose the theory of evolution because it undermines our faith in God.
9.8	19	The biological demonstrations of evolution are beyond dispute.
7.4	20	Evidence points to an evolutionary explanation of life.

Death attitudes scales EXHIBIT 6-12

Description. This is a 16-item, Likert-type scale developed by Kalish (1963). It measures attitudes toward eight issues regarding death: birth control, abortion, euthanasia, wartime killing, capital punishment, fear of death, belief in afterlife, belief in God. For each issue there are two items, one worded positively and one negatively. Seventy-five items were originally obtained from 200 essays on "How I Feel about Death." Factor analysis indicated one constellation of attitudes referred to by Kalish (private communication, 1963) as prosecular and another constellation referred to by him as prosacred. The prosecular constellation espoused basically humanistic values; the prosacred variables were those espousing traditional Judeo-Christian values. The author also reports a third set of factors involving fear and anxiety directly related to death and dying. Factors in this third set were intercorrelated with one another.

Subjects. Persons contributing the 200 essays were primarily nonstudents. The 75-item form was developed upon a sample including 280 college students (primarily in evening classes attended by fully employed adults and housewives) and 427 residents of metropolitan Los Angeles. The author (Kalish, 1963) reports developing the scale presented in Exhibit 6-12 upon a sample of 210 students in advanced psychology classes at Los Angeles State College. These latter students were mostly part-time students with ages ranging from 18 to 64. The median age was 28. They included 93 Protestants, 38 Catholics, 25 Jews, 35 atheist-agnostics, and 19 of unknown religious affiliation. Of the sample, 24 were Negroes; 6 were Asian; 163 were Caucasian; and 17 were unknown regarding race. The sample included 130 men and 67 women; 13 persons failed to indicate their sex.

Response Mode. Persons respond to each item by choosing one of five alternatives: strongly agree, agree, question mark, disagree, and strongly disagree.

Scoring. Kalish (1963) scored the eight variables individually by summing the weighted alternatives chosen for the two items relevant to the variable. The range of possible scores for a variable ranged from 2 to 10. For positive items, weights were assigned the alternative responses from 5 (strongly agree) to 1 (strongly disagree). Weights for negative items were reversed. There does not seem to be any reason, however, to prevent summing across all items for a total score (after reversing negative items). Low scores would indicate negative attitudes toward death.

Reliability. No reliability estimates are available for this scale.

Validity. This scale should possess very good content validity. On the larger, 75-item scale Kalish (private communication, 1963) has reported significant relationships between the scale and such biographical variables as sex, racial origin, religious affiliation, etc.

Comments. This scale should have very good content validity. However, there is a problem in this regard because of the fact that the scale seems to possess at least two dimensions: secular–sacred and fear–no fear. It is unfortunate that there are no reliability estimates available, since these would enhance its value. These are easily obtainable, however, and, if found to be reliable, the scale should be very useful. For another death attitudes scale, see the Metaphor Scales by Knapp (1960).

EXHIBIT 6-12

DEATH ATTITUDES SCALE

DIRECTIONS: This form measures your attitudes on a number of important issues. Each item is a statement of belief or attitude. At the right of each statement is a place for you to indicate your feeling. Please circle the symbols that best express your point of view. Please respond in terms of how *you* feel, not how you think others feel or what society wants you to feel.
WORK QUICKLY AND PLEASE RESPOND TO EVERY ITEM.

SA—Strongly Agree
A—Agree
?—Neutral, don't know
D—Disagree
SD—Strongly Disagree

4 In many instances, married couples should be encouraged to use birth control devices.

†SA A ? D SD

7 Mercy-killing, assuming proper precautions are taken, will benefit people on the whole.
*9 Preventing conception by mechanical birth control devices is as wrong or almost as wrong as taking a human life after birth.
*10 Laws which provide the death penalty for crimes are morally wrong.
*11 Although my definition of God may differ from that of others, I believe there is a God.
*14 Physical or mental illness, no matter how severe or hopeless, should never be the basis for taking the life of the involved person.
*16 Killing during war is just as indefensible as any other sort of killing.
18 As unfortunate as it is, killing during wartime may be justifiable.
19 The possibility that God exists today seems very unlikely.
23 If a mother's life is seriously endangered, forced abortion of the fetus may be necessary.
26 Life after death seems an improbable occurrence.
*27 I find the prospect of my eventual death disturbing.
29 There is some sort of existence after our present life ends.
*30 Forced abortion of the fetus is wrong, regardless of the health of the mother or the social conditions involved.

* The items are negative and their weights must be reversed for purposes of scoring.
† The same response alternatives are used with all items.

31 In the long run, appropriate use of the death penalty for crimes will benefit society.
32 I don't think I am really afraid of death.

Problem-solving attitude scale EXHIBIT 6-13

Description. This 18-item, Likert-type scale was developed by Carey (1958). The alternate forms of the scale are given in Exhibit 6-13. From an original pool of 63 items, 36 items were selected on the basis of their ability to differentiate between high and low scorers. These 36 items were divided into the two 18-item alternate forms.

Subjects. The original 63 items were developed upon a sample of 32 male and 100 female Stanford University elementary psychology students. The functional characteristics of the scale were assessed upon a second sample of 59 women and 50 men and a third sample of 48 women and 48 men, all of whom were Stanford University students in elementary psychology.

Response Mode. Subjects respond to each item by choosing one of five alternatives, as shown below each item in Exhibit 6-13.

Scoring. Response alternatives for positive statements should be weighted from 5 (strongly agree or almost always) to 1 (strongly disagree or almost never). Weights for negative items should be reversed. The person's score is the sum of the weighted alternatives endorsed by him. High scores indicate a positive attitude toward problem-solving situations and demands.

Reliability. The author (Carey, 1958) reports an equivalent-forms reliability of .94, based upon a sample of 32 males and 100 females. The equivalent-forms reliability based upon a sample of 59 women and 50 men was .83.

Validity. Most of the items in the test have content validity, although the content validity of some items is reduced by the use of general terms (e.g. "philosophy".) The scale also has predictive validity, for the scores were found to have a positive relationship to performance in experimental problem-solving situations. Also, as hypothesized by the author, men were found to have significantly higher scores on the scale than women: Means for males on Forms A and B are 62.12 and 58.19, respectively; means for females on Forms A and B are 57.61 and 53.17, respectively. Finally, women showed a change to a more favorable attitude toward problem solving (the expected change) as a result of experimental treatment.

Comments. This seems to be a relatively reliable instrument for measuring attitudes toward problem solving. It is average or above in demonstrations of validity. The referent chosen for the scale is unique and should provide interesting information in further research. Test-retest reliability estimates are all that are lacking for the scale.

EXHIBIT 6-13

PROBLEM-SOLVING ATTITUDE SCALE

DIRECTIONS: (Given Orally) Place a check mark beside the answer which best expresses your opinion.

Form A

1 I would prefer a job involving technical responsibility to a job involving supervisory responsibility.
Strongly agree; Agree; Uncertain; Disagree; Strongly disagree

2 Chess is a game that appeals to me.
Strongly agree; Agree; Uncertain; Disagree; Strongly disagree

3 I like to solve equations.
Strongly agree; Agree; Uncertain; Disagree; Strongly disagree

4 When a question is left unanswered in class I continue to think about it afterwards.
Almost always; Frequently; Occasionally; Rarely: Almost never

5 I would rather have been Thomas Edison than John Rockefeller.
Strongly agree; Agree; Uncertain; Disagree; Strongly disagree

6 As a child I liked arithmetic better than spelling.
Strongly agree; Agree; Uncertain; Disagree; Strongly disagree

7 I would rather be an engineer than a doctor.
Strongly agree; Agree; Uncertain; Disagree; Strongly disagree

8 I enjoy being the score keeper when playing bridge or canasta.
Almost always; Frequently; Occasionally; Rarely: Almost never

*9 I would rather listen to a comedy than to a "Facts Forum" type of radio program.
Almost always; Frequently; Occasionally; Rarely: Almost never

10 I wish I had taken more math courses than I have.
Strongly agree; Agree; Uncertain; Disagree; Strongly disagree

11 Once I pick up a puzzle book I find it hard to put it down.
Almost always; Frequently; Occasionally; Rarely: Almost never

12 In high school I preferred algebra to English.
Strongly agree; Agree; Uncertain; Disagree; Strongly disagree

13 For me the most important thing about a job is the opportunity for independent thinking.
Strongly agree; Agree; Uncertain; Disagree; Strongly disagree

*14 I would rather have someone tell me the solution to a difficult problem than to have to work it out for myself.
Strongly agree; Agree; Uncertain; Disagree; Strongly disagree

*15 It is hard for me to concentrate on what I'm doing.
Almost always; Frequently; Occasionally; Rarely: Almost never

16 I like games which involve intellectual problems.
Strongly agree; Agree; Uncertain; Disagree; Strongly disagree

17 I would like to major in philosophy.
Strongly agree; Agree; Uncertain; Disagree; Strongly disagree

* These items are negative and their weights must be reversed for scoring purposes.

Reference: G. L. Carey, Sex differences in problem-solving performance as a function of attitude differences. *J. abnorm. soc. Psychol.*, 1958, 56, 256–260. Items obtained from author and published with her permission.

*18 I would rather participate in a spelling contest than in a multiplication contest.
Strongly agree; Agree; Uncertain; Disagree; Strongly disagree

Form B

1 I am more interested in the theoretical than the applied aspects of my major field.
Strongly agree; Agree; Uncertain; Disagree; Strongly disagree

2 I like to play anagrams.
Strongly agree; Agree; Uncertain; Disagree; Strongly disagree

3 Mathematics is one of my favorite subjects.
Strongly agree; Agree; Uncertain; Disagree; Strongly disagree

4 When a problem arises that I can't immediately solve I stick with it until I have the solution.
Almost always; Frequently; Occasionally; Rarely; Almost never

5 I would rather be Einstein than the president of General Motors.
Strongly agree; Agree; Uncertain; Disagree; Strongly disagree

6 I like to try new games.
Almost always; Frequently; Occasionally; Rarely; Almost never

7 I am more interested in the physical sciences than the humanities.
Strongly agree; Agree; Uncertain; Disagree; Strongly disagree

*8 I find it helpful to count on my fingers when doing arithmetic.
Almost always; Frequently; Occasionally; Rarely; Almost never

*9 I prefer fiction to non-fiction.
Almost always; Frequently; Occasionally; Rarely; Almost never

10 Every college student should take at least one math course.
Strongly agree; Agree; Uncertain; Disagree; Strongly disagree

11 I like puzzles.
Strongly agree; Agree; Uncertain; Disagree; Strongly disagree

*12 English is one of my favorite subjects.
Strongly agree; Agree; Uncertain; Disagree; Strongly disagree

13 I would like to do scientific research.
Strongly agree; Agree; Uncertain; Disagree; Strongly disagree

14 I am challenged by situations I can't immediately understand.
Almost always; Frequently; Occasionally; Rarely; Almost never

15 I enjoy problem solving of many kinds.
Strongly agree; Agree; Uncertain; Disagree; Strongly disagree

*16 I avoid games which involve intellectual problems.
Almost always; Frequently; Occasionally; Rarely; Almost never

17 I would rather be a philosopher than an artist.
Strongly agree; Agree; Uncertain; Disagree; Strongly disagree

18 I am as good at solving puzzles as most of my friends are.
Strongly agree; Agree; Uncertain; Disagree; Strongly disagree

The existence of God scale (scale G) EXHIBIT 6-14

Description. This is a 20-item, Likert-type scale developed by Wilke (1934). The items concern the reality of God, the value of atheism as an alternative to religion, and the value of believing in God in order to preserve the morals of society, etc. It was used by Wilke (1934) in a comparative study of the merits of speech, radio, and printed page as propaganda vehicles.

Subjects. Several groups of subjects were used, composing a total sample of 1,174 persons.

Response Mode. Persons respond to each statement by choosing one of five alternatives: strongly agree, agree, undecided, disagree, and strongly disagree.

Scoring. For positive statements, the response alternatives are weighted from 5 (strongly agree) to 1 (strongly disagree). Weights for negative items must be reversed. The person's score is the sum of the weighted alternatives endorsed by him. High scores indicate positive attitudes toward the existence of God.

Reliability. Wilke (1934) reports a split-half reliability of .96, based upon a sample of 61 persons. He reports a test-retest reliability of .95, using a retest interval of three weeks. Split-half reliability estimates for the total sample of 1,174 persons ranged from .72 to .98.

Validity. The scale seems to have at least minimum content validity. As further evidence of validity, the author obtained small changes in scores in the expected direction as a function of treatment.

Comments. This scale seems adequate with regard to validity and reliability. It may be noted that some of the items are the same as those used on the Thurstone scale which follows; this is puzzling since a Likert-type scale requires monotonic items, while a Thurstone-type scale uses nonmonotonic items.

EXHIBIT 6-14

THE EXISTENCE OF GOD SCALE (SCALE G)

Will you please indicate your opinion on each of the accompanying statements. To indicate your opinion, draw a circle around the word which best describes your agreement as shown:

*1 The idea of God is mere superstition.

Strongly agree Agree Undecided Disagree Strongly Disagree

*2 It would be desirable to point out to all school children that science has made it unnecessary to assume the existence of God.

3 An atheist should be regarded as an enemy of the community.

*4 It would be an encouraging sign of progress if the people of this country would free themselves from the influence of belief in God.

5 Those who advocate atheism should be prevented by law from having such views published and circulated as printed matter.

6 I am opposed to atheism.

*7 The idea of God is a hindrance to clear thinking.

* These are negative items and their weights must be reversed for purposes of scoring. The same response alternatives are used with all items.

Reprinted with permission from Wilke, W. H. An experimental comparison of the speech, the radio, and the printed page as propaganda devices. *Arch. Psychol.*, 1934, No. 169.

*8 I am an atheist and am delightfully free from what some regard as duty toward God.
9 The American Association for the Advancement of Atheism should be suppressed.
10 It would be a fine thing if the schools of this country made a determined and organized effort to counteract any atheistic leanings among the students.
*11 A belief in atheism is the beginning of wisdom.
12 We may well fear the spread of atheism as likely to encourage crime.
*13 To teach children desirable habits and ideals without any mention of God would be more sensible than teaching them about God.
*14 College authorities should encourage the formation of clubs wishing to promote atheism.
15 No decent, law-abiding citizen should endorse atheism.
16 We should actively oppose any spread of disbelief in God as ruinous to morals.
17 My faith in God is complete for "though he slay me, yet will I trust Him."
*18 In view of the demonstrated failure of religion to solve our social problems, we ought to build up a scientific approach on an atheistic basis.
19 Students preparing essays or speeches as part of school work should be prohibited from expressing atheistic sentiments.
*20 Belief in God is of no value in ridding the world of such social evils as war.

Attitude toward God: the reality of God EXHIBIT 6-15

Description. This is a 20-item scale developed by Chave and Thurstone (Thurstone, 1931). Equivalent forms are available. The items concern the existence of God and the effects upon the individual of believing in God. These items are to be contrasted to those of the Chave and Thurstone scale given in the next exhibit which question the influence of believing or disbelieving in God upon one's conduct. The two scales are quite similar, and the four forms composing them were numbered by Chave and Thurstone as Forms A, B, C, and D, of one scale (scale number 22). A fifth form (Form E, concerning definitions of God) was not included in the book since it lacks the formal characteristics of a scale. The two forms given in Exhibit 6-15 are Forms A and B of scale number 22. Ayad and Farnsworth (1953) rescaled these items and found the scale values of the items to have shifted after 20 years. Therefore, both sets of scale values for the items are given in the exhibit.

Subjects. The population sample was not specified, but it is assumed to have been a sample of University of Chicago undergraduates.

Response Mode. Persons respond by placing a check beside those items with which they agree, a double check beside those with which they agree emphatically, and a cross beside those with which they disagree.

Scoring. The person's score is the median of the scale values of all items he has double-checked. If he has not double-checked any items, his score is the median of the scale values of the items he has checked. This is somewhat different from the usual Thurstone procedure and seems to be an attempt to measure intensity as well as direction of the attitude. High scores reflect acceptance of the reality of God.

Reliability. Likert et al. (1934) report estimates of reliability on this scale ranging from .79 to .93, while Lorge (1939) reports a range from .81 to .91. Ferguson (1944) reports estimates ranging from .85 to .92. All these estimates are quite good. They are as good as Likert-type scale reliabilities and better than many Thurstone scales.

Validity. The scale construction procedure should ensure a degree of content validity. Diggory (1953) reports correlations between this scale and Thurstone's scale measuring attitude toward the church of .78 and .90 for samples of 75 males and 103 females, respectively. For the male sample, Diggory reports correlations between this scale and the Attitude toward Communism scale and the Attitude toward Birth Control scale of .31 and .46, respectively. For the female sample, he reports correlations between this scale and the Attitude toward Communism scale and the Attitude toward the Law scale of .65 and —.43, respectively. These correlations provide strong evidence for construct validity.

Comments. This is a highly valid and reliable scale which has been widely used. The provision of new scale values by Ayad and Farnsworth should enhance still further its value. The scale is very similar to the Attitude toward God: Influence upon Conduct scale which follows. Taken together, they provide four equivalent forms and a very large item pool for research purposes. Readers interested in this scale may also wish to see Ferguson (1942, 1939, 1944), Carlson (1934, 1933), Carey (1940), Allen (1947), Middleton and Wright (1941), Hirschberg (1942), Nelson (1939, 1940), Gragg (1942), Nelson and Nelson (1940), and Barkley (1942).

EXHIBIT 6-15

ATTITUDE TOWARD GOD: THE REALITY OF GOD

Put a check (✓) if you agree with the statement.
Put a double check (✓✓) if you agree emphatically.
Put a cross (×) if you disagree with the statement.

*Chave and Thurstone Scale Values	Ayad and Farnsworth Scale Values		Form A
3.4	2.0	1	I do not believe in God and would be a coward if I pretended to do so.

* Since the original manuscripts were faded, many of the Thurstone scale values were obtained from a list provided by Ayad (private communication). All the Ayad and Farnsworth scale values were obtained from Ayad, and are reproduced with his permission.

*Chave and Thurstone Scale Values	Ayad and Farnsworth Scale Values		
1.2	1.8	2	It is absurd for any thinking man to use such a concept as God.
8.0	10.0	3	I trust in God to support the right and condemn the wrong.
6.4	6.9	4	I think I believe in God, but really I haven't thought much about it.
9.6	11.0	5	I am thrilled in contemplation of the divine Creator.
4.5	5.4	6	I am tolerant toward those who still believe in God.
2.2	2.6	7	The idea of God is a hindrance to clear thinking.
1.5	1.8	8	It is stupid to insist that there is a God.
6.7	7.9	9	I believe in God but my idea of God is vague.
10.4	11.4	10	My faith in God is complete for "though he slay me yet will I trust Him."
7.6	8.8	11	My idea of God develops with experience.
4.4	5.3	12	Although I do not believe in God, I am open-minded about the mysteries of life.
5.5	6.5	13	I haven't yet reached any definite opinion about the idea of God.
0.5	1.5	14	I hate the word God and everything associated with it.
7.1	8.8	15	I have a strong desire to believe in God.
8.8	10.2	16	I am quite convinced of the reality of God.
5.5	6.4	17	I do not know whether I ought to believe in God.
3.1	3.2	18	The idea of God seems quite unnecessary.
9.5	10.8	19	God is the underlying reality of life.
2.4	2.7	20	God has no place in my thinking.

Form B

2.9	3.1	1	There is a far better way of explaining the working of the world than to assume any God.
5.5	6.3	2	The ideas of God are so confusing that I do not know what to believe.
8.3	10.0	3	The idea of God means much to me.
4.5	5.5	4	I don't believe in God but the idea has value for many people.
1.9	2.2	5	The idea of God is useless.
4.4	5.5	6	I wish I could believe in God but I don't.
3.4	3.1	7	I try to rule out all ideas of God, irrespective of tradition and sentiment.
7.2	8.9	8	Though at times I am perplexed, I still trust in the underlying reality of God.
9.8	9.6	9	Anyone who questions the reality and goodness of God cannot be honest in anything.
7.6	9.8	10	The idea of God gives me a sense of security.
3.6	3.6	11	I would openly reject the idea of God except for the feelings of parents and friends.

*Chave and Thurstone Scale Values	Ayad and Farnsworth Scale Values		
5.5	6.5	12	I fluctuate between believing and denying the reality of God.
8.8	10.3	13	The idea of God is the best explanation for our wonderful world.
6.9	7.9	14	I still hold on to my belief in God without any clear reason.
1.4	2.4	15	It is simple-minded to picture any God in control of the universe.
6.5	7.1	16	I still believe in God because it is hard to give up an old habit.
10.5	11.4	17	I would rather die than give up my faith in God.
1.1	1.6	18	I have no patience with those who still cling to the stupid idea that there is a God.
9.5	11.1	19	The belief in God is fundamental in my life.
2.3	2.3	20	The idea of God is mere superstition.

Attitude toward God: influence on conduct EXHIBIT 6-16

Description. This is a 22-item scale developed by Chave and Thurstone (Thurstone, 1931). Equivalent forms are available. The items deal with the influence upon one's conduct of believing or disbelieving in God. These items are to be compared with the Chave and Thurstone scale given in the previous exhibit which deal with the existence of God and the effects upon the individual of believing in God. The two scales are very similar, and the four forms composing them were numbered by Chave and Thurstone as Forms A, B, C, and D, of one scale (scale number 22). A fifth form (Form E, Definition of God) was excluded from this book because it lacks the formal characteristics of a scale. The two forms given in Exhibit 6-16 are Forms C and D of scale number 22. Ayad and Farnsworth (1953) rescaled these items and found the scale values of the items to have shifted during the two decades since the original scaling. Both the Thurstone and the Ayad and Farnsworth scale values for the items have been included in the exhibit.

Subjects. The population sample was not specified, but it is assumed to have been a sample of University of Chicago undergraduates.

Response Mode. The subjects respond by placing a check beside those items with which they agree and a double check beside those with which they agree emphatically. They place a cross beside those with which they disagree.

Scoring. The person's score is the median of the scale values of all items he has double-checked. If he has not double-checked any items, his score is the median of the scale values of the items he has checked. This is somewhat different from the usual Thurstone procedure and seems to be an attempt to measure intensity as well as direction of the attitude. On this scale Thurstone reversed the weighting, thus high scores on this set of forms reflect strong atheistic attitudes toward God. Note that high scores on the Attitude toward God: Reality of God Scale reflect acceptance of the reality of God.

Reliability. Likert et al. (1934) report a range of reliability estimates from .84 to .92 for this scale.

Validity. The construction method used for the scale should ensure a degree of content validity. The high degree of similarity between this scale and the Attitude toward God: Reality of God Scale, together with the excellent demonstrations of validity of the reality of God scale, argue for a high degree of validity.

Comments. This seems to be as valid and reliable a scale as the Attitude toward God: Reality of God Scale described above. It has been used extensively, although somewhat less than the other scale. Interested readers should see Nelson (1939, 1940), Nelson and Nelson (1940), Gragg (1942), and Ferguson (1939, 1944, 1946).

EXHIBIT 6-16

ATTITUDE TOWARD GOD: INFLUENCE ON CONDUCT

Put a check (✓) if you agree with the statement.
Put a double check (✓✓) if you agree emphatically.
Put a cross (×) if you disagree with the statement.

*Chave and Thurstone Scale Values	Ayad and Farnsworth Scale Values		Form C
0.1	0.6	1	I pattern my life after Jesus Christ and yield my whole life to God.
5.6	5.4	2	I am uncertain whether the idea of God influences my conduct or not.
8.3	7.9	3	I get all kinds of good thrills out of life without assuming God.
1.6	1.4	4	I never attempt any major activity without praying for guidance.
9.5	8.8	5	I am much happier since I gave up all pretense of believing in God.
1.0	1.0	6	To me God is the constant inspiration and support of the best we try to achieve.
10.8	10.3	7	I am doing all I can to eradicate such religious rubbish as the idea of God.

* Since the original manuscripts were faded, many of the Thurstone scale values were obtained from a list provided by Ayad (private communication). All the Ayad and Farnsworth scale values were obtained from Ayad, and are reproduced with his permission.

*Chave and Thurstone Scale Values	Ayad and Farnsworth Scale Values		
7.1	6.7	8	I don't think the idea of God influences my daily living.
0.5	0.6	9	I would not hesitate to die rather than deny my faith in God.
8.8	8.0	10	I guide my conduct by the findings of good scientific men and not by the idea of God's will.
5.8	5.7	11	I neither approve the idea of God by worship nor show disapproval of the idea by any careless word or act.
2.0	1.9	12	I feel a growing power to achieve my ideals as I reflect upon the way of God.
4.4	4.1	13	I am afraid of losing my faith in God.
10.3	10.0	14	I am an atheist and am delightfully free from what some regard as duty toward God.
2.4	1.9	15	I need God as I struggle to realize my ideals.
9.1	7.8	16	My rules of conduct are based upon experience and are quite unrelated to any ideas of God.
4.2	4.1	17	I think it is necessary to believe in God but I do not devote a lot of time to religion.
3.1	2.9	18	I believe in God but I find that God helps me when I help myself.
6.0	6.2	19	I'm not opposed to the idea of God but personally do not find any values in it.
7.9	7.2	20	The idea of God is not necessary to me as I attempt to achieve the good life.
3.7	4.7	21	My loyalty to God is very dependent upon being with good religious persons.
6.6	6.8	22	Whatever may be the truth about God I do not let the question prevent me from having a good time.
			Form D
0.1	0.6	1	I have completely surrendered my life to God.
5.6	5.7	2	I make all my statements about God as noncommittal as I can.
8.3	8.1	3	I have greater happiness in living a day at a time without worry about God.
1.4	1.6	4	God is a hidden force directing my life as I strive for the best.
9.4	9.3	5	I don't steer my life by any foolish ideas about what is God's way.
1.1	1.0	6	I feel the call of God in every human need.
10.6	10.2	7	Only fools and hypocrites talk about God influencing them.
7.2	7.8	8	I am gaining freedom from old fears and superstitions about God influencing my conduct.
0.5	1.1	9	God is a tremendous reality and I adjust all my life to this fact.
8.8	8.3	10	My satisfaction is in life itself and I'll enjoy it as fully as I can without any God.

*Chave and Thurstone Scale Values	Ayad and Farnsworth Scale Values		
5.8	5.6	11	The idea of God neither helps nor hinders my endeavor to live a decent life.
2.0	1.7	12	My faith in God makes me struggle for a new world order.
4.4	4.5	13	If I could get any satisfactory idea of God I believe it would make a difference in the way I live.
10.6	9.6	14	I have no faith in God; I live as I please and defy the fates to do their worst.
2.6	2.9	15	I never trust anyone who denies that he believes in God.
9.1	9.0	16	I feel that none of the ideas of God have any value for ordinary living.
4.2	4.1	17	I am far more careless about my duty toward God than I ought to be.
3.2	2.8	18	I believe that one has to be faithful to God in order to prosper in life and I act accordingly.
6.2	7.1	19	I have given up the idea of God but the old customs still have a pull on me.
7.7	7.2	20	I find every day full of opportunities for doing good and for enjoying life without assuming God.
3.7	3.8	21	I love God but I am too selfish to love my neighbor as myself.
6.4	6.4	22	I have reluctantly given up my idea of God but I continue to act as squarely as I ever did.

ATTITUDES TOWARD INFORMAL CONCEPTS

The referents for the scales in this section are abstract concepts for which no formal definition exists that would gain wide acceptance. These include attitudes toward feminism, freedom of information, dependability, and the aesthetic value. For scales measuring attitudes toward concepts having formal definitions with wide acceptance, see the preceding section of this chapter, which includes attitudes toward evolution, problem solving, God, and death. A number of scales or questionnaires were excluded from this section, e.g., Dudycha's (1933*a*) Moral Beliefs Scale, and (1933*b*) Superstitious Beliefs Scale, a battery of metaphor scales by Knapp (1960) measuring attitudes toward love, death, conscience, and success, and a Misanthropy Scale by Rosenberg (1960).

Attitudes toward feminism belief patterns scale *EXHIBIT 6-17*

Description. This 80-item scale was developed by Kirkpatrick (1936) using his own method. Three alternate forms (Forms A, B, and C) were developed and are given in the exhibit. The items concern the adequacy, rights, and prerogatives of women, especially married women. For belief pattern scales by Kirkpatrick regarding humanitarianism and religion, see Chapter 7.

Subjects. The items were judged as feminist or antifeminist by 13 judges. The scale was constructed upon a sample of 545 students, feminists, and ministers.

Response Mode. Subjects place a check mark beside those items they accept as expressing their own personal way of thinking and feeling. They place a double check mark beside those statements about which they feel strongly.

Scoring. The person's score is the algebraic sum of the feminist and anti-feminist propositions accepted. Thus, the person would receive 1 point for items single-checked as "agree" and 2 points for items double-checked as "agree." If the items are feminist items, the person receives positive points; if the items are antifeminist, the person receives negative points. High positive scores reflect profeminist attitudes.

Reliability. The equivalent-forms reliability for this scale is reported as being .85 (Kirkpatrick, 1936*a*). Kirkpatrick (1936*b*) also reported an equivalent-forms reliability of .89.

Validity. The scale has content validity for a domain of female dominance, and female equality in social, political, and business affairs. A further demonstration of validity was made by the author using known groups (National Women's Party members and Lutheran pastors).

Comments. The scale needs more work in the form of estimates of reliability and demonstrations of validity. It is quite usable as it stands, however. The value of the intensity ratings remains a question, as does the form of the scale. It is possible that a Likert response continuum ("strongly agree" through "strongly disagree") would serve as well as the response mode suggested by the author. In this case, the scale might be shortened and improved by application of a Likert-type item analysis.

EXHIBIT 6-17

ATTITUDES TOWARD FEMINISM BELIEF PATTERNS SCALE

(1) You are requested to check (✓) from the following list those statements which you accept as expressing your own personal way of thinking and feeling. Opinions differ and your own view is as good as that of anybody else. If you feel in a certain way check (✓) the statements which express that feeling and leave other spaces blank.

Reprinted with permission from Kirkpatrick, C. The construction of a belief pattern scale for measuring attitudes toward feminism. *J. soc. Psychol.*, **1936, 7, 421–437. Copyright 1936 by the Journal Press, Provincetown, Mass. Forms B and C obtained from author.**

(2) If there are statements which you accept and feel strongly about then check them twice (✓✓).

Form A

1 Women have the right to compete with men in every sphere of economic activity.

*2 As head of the household the father should have final authority over his children.

3 Disposal of real property or of common earnings by the husband without the consent of the wife should be forbidden by law.

*4 The unmarried mother is morally a greater failure than the unmarried father.

5 Women have as much right to sow wild oats as do men.

*6 A husband should have the right to dispose of family property as he may please.

7 Parental authority and responsibility for discipline of the children should be equally divided between husband and wife.

*8 The influx of women into the business world in direct competition with men should be discouraged.

9 The relative amounts of time and energy to be devoted to household duties on the one hand and to a career on the other should be determined by personal desires and interests rather than by sex.

*10 A woman who refuses to bear children has failed in her duty to her husband.

11 There should be a strict merit system of public appointment and promotion without regard to sex.

*12 Women should be guided by men's view of decency in dress.

13 Women have the right to decide for themselves what is proper in feminine dress.

*14 Women should not be permitted to hold political offices that involve great responsibility.

15 The wife's desires concerning the number of children she is to bear should be respected by the husband.

*16 A woman who continues to work outside the home after marriage is shirking her fundamental duty to home and children.

17 Women should be their own judges of fitness to enter a particular occupation.

*18 Retention by a wife of her maiden name is selfish and fanatical.

19 It is medieval to permit a man to bring a damage suit for "loss of services" of his wife due to an accident.

*20 Only the very exceptional woman is justified in attempting participation in civic affairs.

21 Contemporary social problems are crying out for increased social participation by women.

*22 The husband should be regarded as the legal representative of the family group in all matters of law.

23 It is servile for a woman to give up her own name at marriage.

*24 Women should not be allowed entire freedom in their choice of occupation.

25 Women should be given equal opportunities with men for vocational and professional training.

*26 No woman is too cultured to take responsibility for housework.

27 If a husband is permitted to divorce his wife on account of insanity the same right should be accorded to the wife.

* These are anti-feminist items and are scored as −1 when endorsed with a single check; they are scored as −2 if endorsed with a double check. All other items are scored positively; they are scored as 1 if endorsed with a single check, and 2 if endorsed with a double check.

*28 There should be a sharp distinction drawn between men's and women's sports.
29 Any form of athletics should be open to women who care to indulge.
*30 Fewer grounds for divorce should be permitted the wife as compared with the husband.
31 Married women should struggle against enslavement by domestic obligations.
*32 Far too much money is wasted on vocational and professional training for women.
33 Regardless of sex, there should be equal pay for equal work.
*34 A husband has the right to expect that his wife be obliging and dutiful at all times.
35 A father has no more right to the earnings of offspring than does the mother.
*36 A woman to be truly womanly should gracefully accept chivalrous attentions from men.
37 There is no particular reason why a girl standing in a crowded street car should expect a man to offer her his seat.
*38 The father should have a better claim to the earnings of a minor offspring than the mother.
39 It is absurd to regard obedience as a wifely virtue.
*40 It is only fair that male workers should receive more pay than women even for identical work.
41 There should be no legal restriction upon night work by women.
*42 The "clinging vine" wife is justified providing she clings sweetly enough to please her husband.
43 To deny mothers the right of equal guardianship of their children is to perpetuate a ridiculous inequality.
*44 There are many words and phrases which are unfit for a woman's lips.
45 The use of profane or obscene language by a woman is no more objectionable than the same usage by a man.
*46 A father should have preference as the legal guardian of a child.
47 It is degrading for a woman to hold a husband by sheer physical charm.
*48 As newcomers into industry women should accept the arrangements of men in regard to hours and conditions of work.
49 Acceptance by women of an inferior economic status is disgraceful.
*50 A man has the right to insist that his wife accept his view as to what can or can not be afforded.
51 There is no valid reason why women should take the nationality of their husbands upon marriage.
*52 One should never trust a woman's account of another woman.
53 It is unjust to say that women think in more personal terms than do men.
*54 The law which requires that women take the nationality of their husbands is a most logical one.
55 Women should demand money for household and personal expenses as a right rather than as a gift.
*56 On the average women should be regarded as less capable of contributing to economic production than are men.
57 The general belief that women are by nature too high-strung to hold certain jobs is no more true than many of our superstitions.
*58 Women who insist upon removing the word "obey" from the marriage service succeed in making complete fools of themselves.
59 It is desirable that women be appointed to police forces and empowered to protect the rights of women offenders.

*60 A woman should not expect to go to the same places or to have quite the same freedom of action as a man.

61 The morals of women should not be given any protection not given to the morals of men.

*62 It is absurd to appoint women as police.

63 It is insulting to women to have the "obey" clause remain in the marriage service.

*64 Women are too nervous and high-strung to make good surgeons.

65 It is foolish to regard scrubbing floors as more proper for women than mowing the lawn.

*66 An aversion on the part of a wife to sex intimacy with her husband should be repressed for the good of the family.

67 The working wife who claims economic equality has no more right to alimony from her husband than he has right to alimony from her.

*68 Women should accept the intellectual limitations of their sex.

69 It is foolish to question the intellectual equality of woman with man.

*70 Alimony is an appropriate protection for women as members of the weaker sex.

71 Married women should have full control of their persons and give or withhold sex intimacy as they choose.

*72 Woman's work and man's work should be fundamentally different in nature.

73 Society should seek to further the economic status of mothers through family allowances paid directly to the mother.

*74 It is naturally proper for parents to keep a daughter on the average under closer control than a son.

75 The married woman should have the same right to make a will that is accorded to her husband.

*76 Women should always take the passive role in courtship.

77 It is mere prejudice which prevents women from freely taking the initiative in courtship.

*78 It is a mistake to permit women to make legal wills.

79 A daughter in a family should have the same privileges and opportunity as the sons.

*80 It is obviously more logical that a state family allowance be paid to the father than to the mother.

Form B

1 Women should assume their rightful place in business and the professions along with men.

*2 In general the father should have greater authority than the mother in the bringing up of children.

3 A vigorous effort should be made to prevent joint control of family property from meaning masculine control of property.

*4 It is more important for a woman to maintain her virtue prior to marriage than it is for a man.

5 Adultery is no greater sin for a woman than it is for a man.

*6 The husband should be favored by law in the disposal of family property or income.

7 A mother's authority as regards the children should be equivalent to that of the father's.

*8 It is a disgrace to have one's wife working outside the home in competition with men.

9 Women should not be expected to subordinate their careers to home duties to any greater extent than men.

*10 A husband has the right to expect his wife to bear him children.
11 Women should have equal opportunity with men for jury service.
*12 Women in their dress should place feminine modesty before utility.
13 Women should have the same right as men to appear on a bathing beach clad only in trunks if they care to do so.
*14 The privilege and obligation of jury service should be restricted to men.
15 The ultimate decision as regards the desirability of having children should rest with the wife.
*16 Women should be concerned with their duties of child-rearing and house-tending, rather than with foolish desires for professional and business careers.
17 As free human beings, women's right of choice concerning vocation should not be restricted.
*18 A woman should be proud to take her husband's name at marriage.
19 A married woman rather than her husband should receive any damages which may be forthcoming as the result of an accident which she has suffered.
*20 The intellectual leadership of a community should be largely in the hands of men.
21 Women should express their views more frequently from the platform and through the press and radio.
*22 A husband should represent his wife in court in all save criminal trials.
23 To take the husband's name after marriage implies unwarranted loss of individuality.
*24 A woman's choice of occupation should by all means be restricted.
25 It is unfair for schools which offer vocational or professional training to limit the enrollment of women students in favor of males.
*26 Attention to little details of household management are worthy of the attention of any good wife.
27 Both husband and wife should be allowed the same grounds for divorce.
*28 Women should not go in for unwomanly forms of recreation.
29 Intoxication among women is no more repulsive than intoxication among men.
*30 A woman who has been divorced for adultery should be prohibited by law from a second marriage.
31 Women should protest against their burden of domestic drudgery.
*32 Expensive vocational and professional training should be given only to men.
33 The principles of economic justice make it apparent that workers doing equivalent work should receive equal remuneration, regardless of sex.
*34 A wife should make every effort to minimize irritation and inconvenience to the male head of the family.
35 The law is manifestly unfair to women wherever it allows the father sole right to the earnings of offspring.
*36 A woman walking with a man should wait to be helped over a stone wall.
37 The modern woman should put on her own overshoes without expecting aid from her male friends.
*38 An inheritance from a deceased offspring should go to the father rather than to the mother.
39 Conventional wifely submissiveness is a disgraceful role for the modern wife.
*40 Women certainly do not deserve equal pay for equal work with men.
41 Women workers should have an equal voice with men in determining their particular conditions of work.
*42 A woman should keep herself an attractive love object and not worry about her rights.
43 Women should have equal privileges in regard to guardianship of children.

*44 It is infinitely more disgusting to hear profanity from the lips of a woman than from a man.
45 Women have as much right to swear as men.
*46 It is entirely reasonable that legal guardianship of a child should be vested exclusively in the father.
47 Stress on the wifely duty of maintaining physical charm should be regarded as a vestige of sex parasitism.
*48 If women need special hours and conditions of work in industry it proves that their true place is in the home.
49 Society should regard the services rendered by the women workers of the world as valuable as those of men.
*50 The husband as head of the family has in general no obligation to inform his wife of his financial plans.
51 A woman is being treated like a mere child when she is forced by law to take the nationality of her husband.
*52 Women as a sex are unreliable in their personal relations.
53 It is absurd to say that women are more petty than men.
*54 A wife should take the nationality of her husband.
55 It is humiliating for a woman to wheedle money from her husband.
*56 Women should recognize that it is foolish to attempt to equal men in business and the professions.
57 The time-worn argument that women are too unstable emotionally to be successful in certain vocations such as surgery or law is false.
*58 The "obey" clause in the marriage service should be retained as indicating the spirit of a true marriage.
59 There should be policewomen appointed in every city to insure fairness and consideration in law enforcement for women as well as for men.
*60 An unmarried woman should not visit a man's apartment without a chaperon.
61 The modern girl is entitled to the same freedom from regulation and control that is given to the modern boy.
*62 Police duty is a man-sized job that should be restricted to men.
63 The "obey" clause in the marriage service is hostile to the highest ideals of modern woman.
*64 Women's general lack of emotional stability makes them obviously unfit for many occupations involving nervous strain.
65 Economic freedom is worth far more to women than acceptance of the ideal of femininity which has been set up by men.
*66 The satisfaction of her husband's sexual desires is a fundamental obligation of every wife.
67 Women should claim alimony not as persons incapable of self-support but only when there are children to provide for or when the burden of starting life anew after the divorce is obviously heavier for the wife.
*68 Women should recognize their intellectual limitations as compared with men.
69 It is unjust to deny the intellectual equality of women with men.
*70 Women should be concerned with being good wives rather than with demanding support and alimony laws.
71 It is degrading for a married woman to submit to sex intimacy with her husband when she is not emotionally responsive.
*72 It would be improper for women to enter certain occupations that detract from feminine charm.
*73 Family allowances should be granted to mothers in recognition of the value of children to the community.
*74 A father is under obligation to see to it that his daughter makes a wise choice of a husband.

75 Every person of normal mentality should have the right to make a will, regardless of sex.
*76 A woman should never be forward in her relations with men.
77 Women should have equal rights with men to take the initiative in courtship.
*78 A married woman should prove herself legally competent before being allowed to make business contracts.
79 Girl children should be made to feel that they are fully equal to the boys in the family.
*80 In any system of family allowance it is only fair that the money should be paid directly to the father rather than to the mother.

Form C

1 A married woman has an equal right with her husband to work outside the home.
*2 The father should be the final source of authority over children.
3 Inequality in the property rights of men and women is grossly unfair.
*4 Unmarried mothers are fully deserving of the scorn and contempt that society heaps upon them for their transgressions.
5 There should be a single standard in sex matters for both men and women.
*6 The joint earnings of husband and wife should legally be under control of the former.
7 In deciding whether a serious operation should be performed on a child the mother should have equal authority with the father.
*8 Married women should not be allowed to teach school if their husbands are able to support them.
9 Women should not permit home duties to interfere with economic activity outside of the home.
*10 Bearing children for her husband is the duty of the wife.
11 Every political office in the United States should be open to women.
*12 Women have an obligation to uphold modesty and decorum in dress.
13 Women have the same right as men to wear shorts in public.
*14 Women do not belong in politics.
15 No wife should be urged by a husband to bear a child against her will.
*16 Women who seek a career are selfishly ignoring a nobler career of devotion to husband and children.
17 It is both unjust and illogical that men should determine whether or not women are fit for certain kinds of work.
*18 It is childish for a woman to assert herself by retaining her maiden name after marriage.
19 A husband has no more right to sue for the loss of a wife's services than has a woman to sue for the loss of her husband's services.
*20 Training for educational and cultural leadership should be largely restricted to men.
21 Women should take increasing responsibility for leadership in solving the intellectual and social problems of the day.
*22 Greater leniency should be adopted towards women convicted of crime than towards male offenders.
23 A woman has the same right as a man to retain the same name after marriage.
*24 The physical handicaps of women should be recognized as sufficient reason for men to disbar them from certain occupations.
25 Women should be given equal opportunity with men for apprenticeship in the various trades.
*26 A good wife is a good housekeeper.

27 It is unjust to make pre-marital sex experience grounds for divorce in the case of women but not in the case of men.
*28 It is disgusting to see women play basket-ball with men.
29 There is no form of athletics which is not equally proper for both men and women.
*30 A man should have the right to divorce a wife who is found to have been sexually intimate with another man prior to marriage.
31 Under modern economic conditions involving activity of women outside the home men should share in household tasks such as washing dishes.
*32 If women must have a college education, they should be limited to a general cultural course and stay out of the professional schools entirely.
33 It is absurd that salesgirls employed in department stores should receive less pay than the salesmen, in spite of the fact that the nature and amount of the work done is equivalent for both.
*34 A wife should consider it her duty to stand by her husband, even though he is disrespectful and insulting to her.
35 Women should have an equal right with men to inherit property from a deceased child who has died without making a will.
*36 A woman on the average needs male protection and guidance.
37 The modern woman should resent being patted on the head by a man or helped over fences.
*38 A son's property at death should be assigned by law to his father rather than to his mother.
39 Wifely submission is an outworn virtue.
*40 Women should not receive equal remuneration with men in industry.
41 Legal restrictions concerning minimum hours in industry should be the same for both sexes.
*42 It is the wife's own fault if she loses her husband through failure to maintain an attractive appearance.
43 Equity with the husband in the guardianship of children should be made the inalienable right of every mother.
*44 The habit of swearing is much more repulsive in a woman than it is in a man.
45 There should be no difference in effect on a mixed group when a woman as compared with a man tells a "suggestive" story.
*46 The father rather than the mother should be regarded in law and custom as the natural guardian of offspring.
47 The modern wife has no more obligation to keep her figure than her husband to keep down his waist line.
*48 It is perfectly fair that men should determine the hours and conditions of work for women who enter industry.
49 It is unjust to hold that women workers in general are inferior to men because of lack of ability.
*50 A husband in general has a right to invest money as seems best without consulting his wife.
51 Married women should have the right to citizenship independent to that of their husbands.
*52 Women are more likely than men to be underhanded in obtaining their ends.
53 No one should say that women are selfish as compared with men.
*54 It is proper to exclude foreign women from citizenship in the United States if their husbands are ineligible for citizenship.
55 It is humiliating for a woman to have to ask her husband for all the money which she receives.
*56 Men are much better fitted to run business enterprises or direct the building of bridges than are women.

57 There is no occupation which should be closed to women because of alleged emotional instability.
*58 A woman should "love, honor, and obey" her husband in the full sense of the phrase.
59 Every police department should contain policewomen having status and authority equal to that of the men on the force.
*60 No woman who stays out all night alone with a man should expect to keep her reputation.
61 A woman should have the same freedom from rules and regulations as a man.
*62 The demand that women be appointed on police forces is preposterous.
63 The phrase "obey" should not be permitted to remain in the marriage service.
*64 Women are too emotional and impractical to be good judges or attorneys.
65 Women doctors are just as desirable as men doctors in the case of a serious illness.
*66 The married woman should not permit personal feeling to interfere with the performance of her "conjugal duty."
67 Legal pressure should be brought to bear to insure responsibility and support from the fathers of illegitimate children.
*68 Women should give up their false ideal of intellectual equality with men.
69 It is foolish to question that the intelligence of women entitles them to equal social status with men.
*70 The law very properly deals more severely with the illegitimate mother than with the illegitimate father.
71 Women should not submit to sex slavery in marriage.
*72 It is ridiculous for a woman to run a locomotive and for a man to darn socks.
73 In any system of family endowment, the money should be given to the mother rather than to the father.
*74 Sons in a family should in general be given training for careers in preference to the daughters.
75 There should be equality between the sexes in regard to the right to make a will.
*76 The initiative in courtship should come from the man.
77 Women earning as much as their escorts should bear equally the expense of common recreation.
*78 A married woman should not be permitted to will any of her property away from her husband.
79 A father has no more right to interfere in his daughter's choice of a marriage partner than he has in the case of a son.
*80 Any family allowances which are paid to aid in the rearing of children should be paid to the father.

Attitude toward freedom of information *EXHIBIT 6-18*

Description. This is an eight-item, Guttman-type scale, developed by Rogers (1955) along with a scale for attitude toward the newspapers. The latter scale may be found in Chapter 10. The present scale for attitude toward freedom of information has as its content questions about legal restrictions upon the freedom of newspapers to publish, freedom of reporters to gather news, etc. The scale was originally composed of 39 questions, which were subjected to a scalogram analysis. It was then revised and its functional characteristics assessed upon a new sample.

Subjects. The sample upon which the 39 questions were evaluated was 92 undergraduate and graduate students and 109 secondary education students in seven state-supported teacher-training institutions for white students in Texas. It was upon this latter sample that the functional characteristics of the present scale were assessed.

Response Mode. Subjects check one of five alternatives for each item: strongly approve, approve, undecided, disapprove, and strongly disapprove.

Scoring. The person is given +1 point for every item with which he disagrees, except item 4. He is given +1 point for agreeing with item 4. His score is the sum of the points given for his endorsements. High scores indicate positive attitudes toward freedom of the newspapers.

Reliability. No information regarding reliabilty was reported by the author.

Validity. The scale is reported by the author (Rogers, 1955) to have a reproducibility coefficient of .861 (quasi-scale), based upon a sample of 109 secondary education students. The scale is very restricted in content validity for the general question of freedom of information. The author reports that the mean score of the sample of 686 undergraduates was 4.53 (with a possible score of 8) and the standard deviation, 1.64. Intensity analysis gave a U-shaped curve with a very broad, flat base and a zero-point approximation at the 50.25 percentile. These results would indicate an even division of attitudes in the sample and would suggest that a large portion of the sample did not hold intense attitudes toward the topic in question.

Comments. The scale seems restricted in its use to the question of freedom of information to newspapers. The generality of responses to this question—to the question of freedom of information—is an empirical question. The scale is a quasi-scale by Guttman standards but seems to be valid for the restricted referent. Estimates of its reliability would increase the value of the scale.

EXHIBIT 6-18

ATTITUDE TOWARD FREEDOM OF INFORMATION

(These) statements present hypothetical situations related to the news which may be printed. Mark an "X" in the space in front of the answer that best expresses your approval or disapproval of the situation. Answer every item.

†1 A state legislature passes a law which prohibits police from giving reporters the names of persons arrested for major crimes. Do you approve of this law?

________strongly approve
________approve
________undecided
________disapprove
________strongly disapprove

2 A wealthy young man is brought to trial on charges of operating a prostitution ring. The judge rules that the press may not attend the trial and print the testimony. Do you approve of the judge's ruling?

3 A state legislature establishes a board to examine magazines and censor all items dealing with crime or sex. Each issue of a magazine must receive approval before it can be sold in the state. Do you approve of this action?

*4 A business man makes an income tax settlement with the Federal Government for less than the amount he owes. At a newspaper's insistence, the Department of Justice allows this information to be published over the businessman's protest. Do you approve of publication of this information?

5 An Air Force training plane crashes in a private farm field. A newspaper photographer, with the consent of the owner of the farm, takes a picture of the crashed plane. But an Air Force officer at the scene forces the photographer to surrender the exposed film. Do you approve of the officer's action?

6 A state legislature establishes a state board of examiners to issue and revoke licenses to newspaper reporters. Requirements include education, moral character, and passage of a written examination. Do you approve of such a license?

7 A law is passed by Congress prohibiting the Socialist Party from publishing newspapers in this country. Do you approve of this law?

8 A state legislature authorizes its appropriations committee to meet and debate money bills without newsmen present. Do you approve of this action?

† The same response alternatives are used with all items.
* The subject receives 1 point if he agrees with this statement. He receives 1 point if he disagrees with any other statement.

Attitudes toward dependability: the attitude scale for clerical workers EXHIBIT 6-19

Description. This is a 27-item scale developed by Dudycha (1941), using a modified Thurstone procedure. The scale possesses the following number of items in each of the various categories of dependability used by the author: accuracy, 3; persistence, 3; punctuality, 4; regularity, 3; consistency, 3; honesty, 3; fidelity, 4; responsibility, 3; and dependability, 1. These items were selected to have small Q values and to represent 0.4 of a scale unit along the scale continuum. All Q values range between 1.1 and 3.6. Dudycha referred to this as the Attitude Scale for Clerical Workers in order to disguise its content.

Subjects. Dudycha (1941) used a total sample of 123 judges to scale the items; 56 were men, and 67 were women. Of the subjects, 85 were of college age, and 38 were mature women and men ranging in age from the middle twenties to the late sixties.

Response Mode. Subjects respond by checking those items with which they agree and placing a cross beside those with which they disagree. If they cannot decide, they place a question mark beside the item.

Scoring. The individual's score is the median of the scale values of the items endorsed by him. High scores indicate negative attitudes toward dependability.

Reliability. No evidence of reliability is offered by the author.

Validity. The use of an original pool of 200 statements would seem to ensure good content validity. Also, the scores differentiated known groups (students who were observed to be either markedly early or late to classes).

Comments. The value of this scale is detracted from by the lack of reliability estimates. However, it seems a valid scale and should produce satisfactory reliability coefficients when tested. The scale seems satisfactory otherwise. For persons interested in a large pool of items regarding this topic, Dudycha (1941) reports his entire list of 200 items with scale and Q values.

EXHIBIT 6-19

ATTITUDES TOWARD DEPENDABILITY: ATTITUDE SCALE FOR CLERICAL WORKERS

Below you will find twenty-seven statements expressing different attitudes held by clerical workers.

Put a check (✓) if you agree with the statement.
Put a cross (×) if you disagree with the statement.
If you cannot decide about a statement you may mark it with a question mark.

Scale Values		
2.1	1	Punctuality makes for success.
6.8	2	It is fun to be inconsistent at times.
.5	3	One should always work to the best of his ability.
9.2	4	Punctuality is of minor importance.
10.0	5	To assume responsibility is too much trouble.
2.4	6	A daily routine makes work easier.
5.1	7	There are times when it is permissible to break a promise.
.8	8	If one does not succeed at first one should try again and again.
6.5	9	Exaggeration is often necessary to prove a point.

Scale Values		
10.4	**10**	Promises are made to be broken.
7.6	**11**	A persistent person is usually annoying.
9.6	**12**	One gets no satisfaction out of being accurate.
1.6	**13**	Only a weak-kneed individual gives up when faced with difficulty.
1.2	**14**	Honesty is the best policy.
4.0	**15**	Routine work is usually easy.
4.7	**16**	Inaccurate people are liable to be dishonest.
8.4	**17**	A faithful employee is seldom rewarded.
3.0	**18**	One should usually be consistent.
10.7	**19**	Only a fool is faithful in his work.
7.3	**20**	A person coming late may make a very effective entrance.
3.2	**21**	Every man is responsible for his own actions.
6.1	**22**	When in Rome, do as the Romans do.
8.0	**23**	One should be honest but not in all things.
5.6	**24**	Varied speed of work is a sign of instability.
3.6	**25**	Although it is wrong to be late it is sometimes necessary.
8.8	**26**	Accurate people are usually socially undesirable.
4.8	**27**	A person should work regularly at some tasks, but not at others.

Attitude toward the aesthetic value *EXHIBIT 6-20*

Description. This is a 20-item, Thurstone-type scale developed by Cohen (1941). The equivalent forms of the scale are given in Exhibit 6-20. The items measure attitudes toward aesthetic education, interests, occupations, and so forth. Aesthetic is defined for the respondent as the "beautiful" or "appreciation of the beautiful." All Q values are between 0.5 and 2.3.

Subjects. The sample consisted of 201 students from the University of Maine.

Response Mode. Persons respond by checking those items with which they agree and placing a cross beside those items with which they disagree.

Scoring. The person's score is the median of the scale values of items endorsed by him as "agree." High scores reflect negative attitudes toward aesthetic value.

Reliability. The author (Cohen, 1941) reports the equivalent-forms reliability to be .85. The test-retest reliability is reported as .92.

Validity. The construction procedure used should ensure a degree of content validity. Additional evidence of validity comes from a correlation of .38 between attitudes expressed on this scale and aesthetic scores on the Allport-Vernon study of values.

Comments. This scale seems satisfactory in most regards. Further demonstrations of validity would be valuable, however. The scale values of the items are not so well spaced as they might be, but this is not critical.

EXHIBIT 6-20

ATTITUDE TOWARD THE AESTHETIC VALUE

The word *Aesthetic* has reference to the beautiful or to the appreciation of the beautiful.

Put a check mark (√) if you agree with the statement.
Put a cross (×) if you disagree with the statement.

Form A

Scale Value		
3.0	1	I believe that aesthetic interests promote desirable relationships between nations.
7.0	2	I believe that individuals engaged in purely aesthetic occupations are parasites on society.
8.0	3	I do not care for highly aesthetic people because their interests seem to me to be more emotional than rational.
1.6	4	I have a great interest in aesthetic matters.
4.3	5	I believe that everyone should have a little training in aesthetic matters.
6.1	6	I would be willing to give money to support aesthetic enterprises if it were not for the "highbrow" atmosphere surrounding them.
1.8	7	I am interested in anything in which I can see an aesthetic quality.
9.9	8	I have no desire to join or have anything to do with any organization devoted to aesthetic activities.
.8	9	It is in the aesthetic experiences of life that I find my greatest satisfaction.
9.3	10	I see very little worth while in aesthetic interests.
2.1	11	Attendance at an aesthetic entertainment (such as a concert or an art exhibition) gives me inspiration.
5.0	12	I am in favor of aesthetic entertainments (such as concerts and art exhibitions) for they do no harm to anyone.
5.5	13	Aesthetic matters do not interest me now, but I expect that sometime I shall find time to pursue them actively.
6.7	14	Practical considerations should come first, beauty second.
2.2	15	I believe that the pursuit of aesthetic interests increases one's satisfaction in living.
3.4	16	I am attracted to individuals who pursue aesthetic interests.
10.4	17	Aesthetic education is nonsense.
5.2	18	I believe that the teaching of aesthetic appreciation is all right, but the type of person now teaching it fails to "get it across."
7.7	19	I do not believe that I would receive any benefit from lectures concerning aesthetic subjects.
8.9	20	I see no reason for the government to spend money on aesthetic objects and activities.

Form B

6.0	1	Aesthetic appreciation does not play an especially large part in my life.

Reprinted with permission from Cohen, J. B. A scale for the measurement of attitude toward the aesthetic value. *J. Psychol.*, **1941, 12, 75–79.**

Scale Value		
5.5	**2**	Sometimes I feel that aesthetic interests are necessary and sometimes I doubt it.
10.5	**3**	The pursuit of aesthetic interests is a sheer waste of time.
8.8	**4**	I believe that aesthetic interests are rarely genuine and sincere.
2.1	**5**	Appreciation of beautiful things aids in making my life happier.
2.3	**6**	I believe that aesthetically sensitive people are fine people.
6.6	**7**	I can enjoy the beauty of such things as paintings, music, and sculpture only occasionally for I feel that they are impractical.
7.6	**8**	I find the life of people pursuing aesthetic interests too slow and uninteresting.
9.7	**9**	Education in artistic things is a waste of public funds.
9.5	**10**	It is hard for me to understand how anybody can be stupid enough to concentrate all his energies on aesthetic activities.
3.8	**11**	Aesthetic interests are not essential but make for happy existence.
8.4	**12**	The "highbrow" attitude of individuals having a great deal of aesthetic interest is quite distasteful.
4.8	**13**	I believe in the value of aesthetic interests but I do not like the stilted way in which the ideas on this subject are presented to me.
5.0	**14**	I believe that aesthetic interests have value, but I seldom take time to pursue them.
2.9	**15**	I believe that aesthetic pursuits are satisfying.
5.3	**16**	I go to such things as symphony orchestras, art exhibitions, etc., occasionally, but I have no strong liking for them.
1.8	**17**	I believe that the great leaders of the world come from the ranks of those individuals who are aesthetically inclined.
7.2	**18**	I have no interest in aesthetic objects (such as fine paintings and pottery) because I do not understand their technical aspects.
1.6	**19**	I like beautiful things because they give me genuine pleasure.
.7	**20**	I find more satisfaction in aesthetic pursuits than in anything else.

GENERALIZED ATTITUDE SCALES TO MEASURE ATTITUDES TOWARD ABSTRACT CONCEPTS

There are two scales in this section, one to measure attitude toward any school subject (Silance and Remmers, 1934) and one to measure attitude toward any college course (Hand, 1953). The Osgood semantic differential technique is also applicable to any of the referents included in the present chapter. For a discussion of this technique, see Chapter 2.

Attitude toward any school subject *EXHIBIT 6-21*

Description. This 45-item, Thurstone-type scale was developed by Silance and Remmers (1934). Two equivalent forms were developed. The scale was the basis for the later, shorter scale developed by Remmers (1960) to measure attitudes toward the same referent. Those items used by Remmers in his scale have been marked with an asterisk in the exhibit.

Subjects. The exact population upon which the scale was constructed is uncertain, but it was apparently developed upon a large sample (several thousand) of high school students and college undergraduates.

Response Mode. Persons respond by checking those items with which they agree.

Scoring. The individual's score is the median of the scale values of the items endorsed by the person.

Reliability. The authors report equivalent-forms reliabilities ranging from .81 to .90, using both high school and college students and using different school subjects as attitudinal referents. Ferguson (1952) cites the reliabilities for the following courses as being: biology, .81 (N = 269); chemistry, .70 (N = 771); English, .68 (N = 705); mathematics, .74 (N = 579).

Validity. The scale should have adequate content validity. Bolton (1938) has validated this scale using criterion groups measured for interests and values. The object of the attitude in Bolton's study was mathematics. Strunk (1957) has advanced some evidence of concurrent validity, obtaining a correlation of .39 between this scale and scores of 130 subjects on a graphic rating scale of expression of interest in a psychology course. Strunk did not obtain an expected correlation between attitude toward psychology, as measured by this scale, and judgments of reading ease of psychology course textbooks, as measured by a graphic rating continuum. This latter result may be considered to detract somewhat from the validity of the scale or may be explained on the basis of a general reading ability on the part of his subjects.

Comments. This scale seems reasonably valid and reliable and is long enough to provide additional equivalent forms, should they be desired for research purposes. While Remmers' shorter form would take less time to administer, the longer form may be expected to be more reliable.

EXHIBIT 6-21

ATTITUDE TOWARD ANY SCHOOL SUBJECT

NOTE: The following instructions are not necessarily those used by the original authors. They are suggested by the construction procedure and response mode used.

Please read each of the following statements carefully.
Put a check mark (✓) if you agree with the statement.
Put a cross (×) if you disagree with the statement.
If you simply cannot decide about a statement, you may place a question mark beside it.

There are no right or wrong answers to these questions. People differ in their opinions on them. Just indicate your own opinion by checking those statements with which you agree and placing a cross beside those with which you disagree.

Form A

Scale Values		
*10.3	**1**	No matter what happens, this subject always comes first.
10.2	**2**	I would rather study this subject than eat.
9.8	**3**	I love to study this subject.
9.7	**4**	This subject is of great value.
*9.6	**5**	This subject has an irresistible attraction for me.
9.4	**6**	I really enjoy this subject.
*9.2	**7**	This subject is profitable to everybody who takes it.
9.1	**8**	This subject develops good reasoning ability.
9.0	**9**	This subject is very practical.
*8.9	**10**	Any student who takes this subject is bound to be benefited.
8.8	**11**	This subject teaches me to be accurate.
8.7	**12**	This subject is a universal subject.
*8.5	**13**	This subject is a good subject.
8.4	**14**	All of our great men studied this subject.
8.3	**15**	This subject is a cultural subject.
*8.1	**16**	All lessons and all methods used in this subject are clear and definite.
7.9	**17**	This subject is O.K.
*7.7	**18**	I am willing to spend my time studying this subject.
7.6	**19**	This subject is not receiving its due in public high schools.
7.3	**20**	This subject saves time.
6.8	**21**	This subject is not a bore.
*6.5	**22**	This subject is a good pastime.
*6.1	**23**	I don't believe this subject will do anybody any harm.
5.8	**24**	I am careless in my attitude toward this subject, but I would not like to see this attitude become general.
*5.5	**25**	I haven't any definite like or dislike for this subject.
*4.7	**26**	This subject will benefit only the brighter students.
*3.6	**27**	My parents never had this subject; so I see no merit in it.
3.5	**28**	I could do very well without this subject.
3.4	**29**	Mediocre students never take this subject; so it should be eliminated from schools.
3.3	**30**	The minds of students are not kept active in this subject.
*3.1	**31**	I am not interested in this subject.
2.9	**32**	This subject does not teach you to think.
2.8	**33**	This subject is very dry.
*2.6	**34**	This subject reminds me of Shakespeare's play—"Much Ado About Nothing."
2.5	**35**	I have no desire for this subject.
2.4	**36**	I have seen no value in this subject.
*2.2	**37**	I would not advise any one to take this subject.
2.1	**38**	This subject is based on "fogy" ideas.
*1.6	**39**	This subject is a waste of time.

* Items marked with an asterisk constitute the Remmers short form.

Scale Values		
1.5	**40**	It is a punishment for anybody to take this subject.
1.3	**41**	This subject is disliked by all students.
*1.0	**42**	I look forward to this subject with horror.
0.8	**43**	I detest this subject.
0.7	**44**	This subject is the most undesirable subject taught.
0.6	**45**	I hate this subject.

Form B

*10.3	**1**	I am "crazy" about this subject.
10.3	**2**	The very existence of humanity depends upon this subject.
9.8	**3**	If I had my way, I would compel everybody to study this subject.
9.7	**4**	This subject is one of the most useful subjects I know.
*9.6	**5**	I believe this subject is the basic one for all high school courses.
9.4	**6**	This is one subject that all young Americans should know.
*9.2	**7**	This subject fascinates me.
9.1	**8**	The merits of this subject far outweigh the defects.
9.0	**9**	This subject gives pupils the ability to interpret situations they will meet in life.
*8.9	**10**	This subject will help pupils socially as well as intellectually.
8.8	**11**	This subject makes me efficient in school work.
8.7	**12**	There are more chances for development of high ideals in this subject.
*8.5	**13**	This subject is interesting.
8.4	**14**	This subject teaches methodical reasoning.
8.3	**15**	This subject serves the needs of a large number of boys and girls.
*8.1	**16**	All methods used in this subject have been thoroughly tested in the classroom by experienced teachers.
7.9	**17**	This subject has its merits and fills its purpose quite well.
*7.7	**18**	Every year more students are taking this subject.
7.6	**19**	This subject aims mainly at power of execution or application.
7.3	**20**	This subject is not based on untried theories.
6.7	**21**	I think this subject is amusing.
*6.5	**22**	This subject has its drawbacks, but I like it.
*6.0	**23**	This subject might be worth while if it were taught right.
5.9	**24**	This subject doesn't worry me in the least.
*5.5	**25**	My likes and dislikes for this subject balance one another.
*4.7	**26**	This subject is all right, but I would not take any more of it.
*3.6	**27**	No student should be concerned with the way this subject is taught.
3.5	**28**	To me this subject is more or less boring.
3.4	**29**	No definite results are evident in this subject.
3.3	**30**	This subject does not motivate the pupil to do better work.
*3.1	**31**	This subject has numerous limitations and defects.
2.9	**32**	This subject interferes with developing.
2.8	**33**	This subject is dull.
*2.6	**34**	This subject seems to be a necessary evil.
2.5	**35**	This subject does not hold my interest at all.
2.4	**36**	The average student gets nothing worth having out of this subject.
*2.2	**37**	All of the material in this subject is very uninteresting.
2.1	**38**	This subject can't benefit me.
*1.6	**39**	This subject has no place in the modern world.
1.5	**40**	Nobody likes this subject.
1.3	**41**	This subject is more like a plague than a study.

Scale Values		
*1.0	42	This subject is all bunk.
0.8	43	No sane person would take this subject.
0.7	44	Words can't express my antagonism toward this subject.
0.6	45	This is the worst subject taught in school.

A scale to study attitudes toward college courses *EXHIBIT 6-22*

Description. This 45-item scale was developed by Hand (1953) largely to demonstrate a method of weighting scale items which would minimize the number of judges needed and which would take less time in construction than standard scale construction techniques. All items were selected to meet Wang's criteria for attitude statements. After administration to subjects, items were weighted in the following manner: The most frequently checked favorable item received 528 endorsements, and the most frequently checked unfavorable item received 317 endorsements. These two items were considered as neutral because 259 of the 586 subjects would have had to have endorsed both of these statements. An attitude continuum was postulated which extended through 20 equal units from —10 (unfavorable) to +10 (favorable). Favorable items were located on the favorable end of the continuum by dividing the number of endorsements for any statement by 528 (the number of endorsements for the most frequently checked favorable statement), multiplying the fraction by 10, and measuring this distance from the favorable end of the continuum. Thus, the most frequently checked positive statements would be assessed as located $528/528 \times 10$, or 10 units from the favorable end of the continuum, giving it a weight of 0, or neutral. In assigning scale values to the unfavorable items, the denominator would be 317 (the number of endorsements of the most frequently checked unfavorable item). The items and their weights are given in Exhibit 6-22.

Subjects. The subjects used for construction of the scale were 586 college students.

Response Mode. Persons respond to each item by checking whether they feel that it is a false statement or a true statement.

Scoring. The subject's score is obtained by computing the mean of the weights of the positive items endorsed and the mean of the weights of the negative items endorsed and summing these means algebraically (Hand, private communication, 1965). Positive scores indicate positive attitudes.

Reliability. The author (Hand, 1953) reports a split-half reliability estimate of .92, based upon a sample of 100 subjects.

Validity. Clark's validity index, which gives an index of the power of a statement to discriminate between favorable and unfavorable subjects, was used to estimate the validity of the scale. The median index for all statements was .86, where 1.0 would indicate perfect discrimination. Validity of the scale was also indicated by: (1) the positive relation between attitude scores and effort in a course, (2) close agreement between attitude scores and self-ratings of attitude, and (3) the demonstrated ability of the scale to differentiate between group attitudes in a direction expected from logical considerations (Hand, 1953).

Comments. The advantages and disadvantages of this method of scale construction are still relatively unknown, but the procedure involved is not without precedent. It is apparently based on the assumption that the least that a scale (item) can do is to indicate the most popular item (response alternative). Of course, such popularity highly conditions the reproducibility of the scale. The author's construction procedure seems to rest upon the following premises and argument. It may be assumed that attitudes are distributed normally in the population in such a way that most persons have attitudes falling in, or near, the neutral range (on an attitude continuum running from positive, through neutral, to negative). Items which are more frequently endorsed should be closer to the neutral point of such a continuum than less frequently endorsed items. Frequency of endorsement could, then, be used as an index of the point occupied on the attitude continuum by the item. However, this whole argument rests upon the further assumption that more frequently endorsed items are not simply irrelevant to the attitude in question, or ambiguous in nature. Thurstone has provided formal procedures for assessing ambiguity and relevance of an item. The relevance of the item may be further assessed by determining its content validity. As content validity increases, the probability that the item is irrelevant decreases. Whether the premise that attitudes are normally distributed in the population is valid is an empirical question. Some attitudes (in particular populations) would not be expected to be so distributed; for example, it is doubtful that attitudes toward God are normally distributed in a population of nuns.

EXHIBIT 6-22

A SCALE TO STUDY ATTITUDES TOWARD COLLEGE COURSES

Below is a list of statements to enable you to evaluate the course in which you receive this questionnaire. For example, if you receive this questionnaire in an English-11 classroom, then respond to each question in terms of how you feel about English-11. If you receive this questionnaire in an Orientation classroom, then respond to each question in terms of how you feel about Orientation.

Reference: J. Hand. A method of weighing attitude scale items from subject responses. *J. clin. Psychol.*, 1953, 9, 37–39. Items obtained from author and published with his permission.

If you agree with a statement (feel that it is a TRUE statement) **mark answer No. 1 on the answer sheet.** If you disagree (feel that it is a FALSE statement) **mark answer No. 2 on the answer sheet.**

If you change your mind, be careful to erase your first answer completely. Make marks glossy-black and firmly up and down between the dotted lines.

THIS IS NOT AN INTELLIGENCE TEST. THE CHOICES YOU MAKE WILL IN NO WAY AFFECT YOUR GRADE IN ANY COURSE.

Weight		
+4.3	**1**	This course should be considered one of the most valuable courses offered here.
+4.0	**2**	This course encourages the development of ideals.
+2.2	**3**	My likes for this course outweigh my dislikes.
−5.6	**4**	The material covered by this course is uninteresting.
−7.1	**5**	The time that I spend studying for this course is completely wasted.
−1.2	**6**	Only about 10% of the students enjoy this course.
+3.7	**7**	This course increases my qualifications to associate with educated people.
+2.6	**8**	This course helps the student to feel that he belongs in college.
+1.0	**9**	This course is of some value in promoting university life.
−4.0	**10**	The value of this course is overestimated by most people.
+2.6	**11**	This course is an important part of the educational system at this university.
−8.9	**12**	No university should offer a course of this type.
−1.2	**13**	A passing grade on the final examination should be the only requirement for this course.
+4.3	**14**	Usually I enjoy studying the lesson assignments of this course.
+1.9	**15**	There is a definite need for this course on the campus.
−7.4	**16**	This course limits individualistic thinking to an unwholesome degree.
+0.5	**17**	This course has its defects but is still worthwhile.
−5.9	**18**	The students do not remember the information they obtain from this course.
+7.0	**19**	I estimate that 90% of the students enjoy this course.
+6.3	**20**	This course helps prepare the students to face the problems of everyday life.
0.0	**21**	I shall be able to use the information obtained from this course at various times during my college career.
+2.8	**22**	This course is based upon sound educational principles.
−3.4	**23**	The number of unexcused absences should be increased in this course.
−6.9	**24**	Sometimes this course makes me doubt the value of a college education.
−6.5	**25**	This course is not worth the time and effort it requires.
+4.8	**26**	This course is essential to adequate cultural development.
+4.1	**27**	Through this course I am better acquainted with the problems of acquiring an education.
0.0	**28**	The students who do not enjoy this course slightly outnumber the ones who do enjoy it.
+2.4	**29**	I believe that a course of this type is needed by all college students.
−1.7	**30**	Sometimes the class is interesting but more often it is uninteresting.
+3.9	**31**	This course helps in promoting proper conduct among college students.

Weight		
+2.2	**32**	I feel that all new students should be required to take this course.
+1.4	**33**	A person who teaches this course should feel that he is performing a valuable service.
+1.6	**34**	Even though I fail to appreciate it, this course may be an important part of my education.
−2.5	**35**	This course has no integrating influence upon the values and ideals of the students.
+4.1	**36**	After graduation from college the information obtained from this course will be valuable.
+6.4	**37**	After studying this course I shall be able to enjoy life more fully.
+4.0	**38**	This course gives ample opportunity for self-expression.
+1.0	**39**	I have no antagonistic feeling toward this course.
−5.9	**40**	The basic principles of this course are outmoded.
+3.0	**41**	The amount of valuable information derived from this course is very large.
−5.4	**42**	No time should be devoted to this subject outside of class.
−2.8	**43**	This course requires time which I could use more beneficially.
+5.3	**44**	The material covered by this course is extremely interesting.
+5.1	**45**	I am inspired by this course to make full use of my capabilities.

SUMMARY

Many of the scales in this chapter are unsatisfactory with regard to their functional characteristics. Also, there were very many scales that had to be excluded because of inadequate definition of the referent or casual use of untested procedures for construction. Many of these latter scales were pointed out in the text in the hope that use could be made of the item pools.

Regarding the lack of scales, it is interesting that psychologists have never constructed a formal scale to assess attitudes toward psychology and psychology courses. The only scales available for these purposes are a projective technique by Knight and Hall (1957) and some scales in other chapters on attitudes toward psychologists, counseling centers, and mental hospitals. Really adequate scales are also missing for the measurement of attitudes toward such referents as time, sexuality, leisure, and social responsibility, all of which should be theoretically and diagnostically interesting.

CHAPTER 7

political and religious attitudes

The scales contained in this chapter have as their referents various political, religious, and economic ideologies and issues. As used here, *ideology* refers to the kinds of thinking characteristic of an individual or a group, especially as it influences and shapes their political and economic procedure or social structure. These ideologies are, in brief, the various "isms" with which human beings are afflicted. Among the scales included herein are those measuring attitudes toward conservatism, religionism, fascism, and liberalism. Those scales measuring attitudes related to issues involving nations have been placed in the chapter on international issues (e.g., communism, nationalism, and patriotism).

In selecting scales for this chapter, we included only those scales measuring attitude toward a particular ideology; scales or tests measuring tendency to follow or accept ideologies in general as a personality trait (e.g., authoritarianism) have not been included in this book.

The scales in this chapter have been grouped into two major sections. In the first section are scales measuring attitudes toward political and economic ideologies. The second section includes scales measuring attitudes toward religion, articles of religious faith, and similar referents.

ATTITUDES TOWARD POLITICAL, ECONOMIC, AND SOCIAL SYSTEMS

In the modern world, the political and economic domains have become so closely related that they are extremely difficult to separate in scale construction or in categorizing scales. There is apparently a multitude of dimensions along which one may order political and economic attitudes. This section includes scales for such dimensions as liberalism-conservatism, conservatism-radicalism, fascism-individualism, and progressivism-nonprogressivism.

Conservatism-radicalism (C-R) opinionnaire EXHIBIT 7-1

Description. This is one of the earliest ideological scales to be developed (Lentz, 1930). The test includes two forms (J and K), each with 60 controversial items toward which a person might take a conservative or liberal view. These statements were drawn from various fields of interest: ethics, education, feminism, freedom of speech, international affairs, sex and marriage, politics, race relations, religion, sport, transportation, mechanics, etc. (Lentz, 1930). Using "opposition to change" as a working definition of conservatism, and "belief in, or expectation of change" as a definition of radicalism, Lentz found that "several judges showed very little disagreement among themselves as to which statements were radical and which were conservative" (1930, p. 538). The test was called the Social Science Opinionnaire in its original form, which consisted of two forms (H and I) composed of 100 items each. Readers interested in obtaining this item pool should see Lentz (1934). Allport (1937, p. 431) has referred to this test as "one of the most satisfactory" tests for measuring conservatism-radicalism.

Subjects. The original sample consisted of 324 undergraduate students in psychology, engineering, and education. In his manual, the author also provides norms based upon 580 college students.

Response Mode. The person places a plus sign beside the item if he agrees with it more than he disagrees; he places a minus sign beside it if he disagrees with the item more than he agrees with it. Omissions are permissible but undesirable.

Scoring. The subject receives 1 point for conservatism for each conservative statement with which he agrees and 1 for each radical statement with which he disagrees, plus one half of the number of items omitted. High scores indicate conservatism.

Reliability. Lentz (1935) reports the equivalent-forms reliability between these forms of the scale to be .835 ($N = 580$). The reliability of the 100-item forms (H and I) was .94. The predicted reliability (see Handy and Lentz, 1934) of the two forms J and K was: Form J, .910; Form K, .834; forms J and K combined, .935. Using a sample of 901 students from 16 universities and colleges in the United States, Nelson (1938, 1954) measured attitude persistence on this scale over a fifteen-year interval (1936–1950) and obtained a test-retest correlation of .57. Nelson also reports finding a trend toward more liberal attitudes during postcollege years and discusses some differences related to the sex and geographical location of his sample.

Validity. Lentz (1935) offered the following evidence of the validity of the scale. Experienced judges agreed with regard to direction of scoring of the items. It was also found to distinguish between known groups: Conservative or middle-of-the-road persons who had not changed their church, who had not voted for Hoover or Smith, or Roosevelt, or who were enrolled in the small denominational colleges made higher conservatism scores on the test than those who rated themselves as radical, who had changed their church, who had voted for Norman Thomas, or who were enrolled in large universities. Based upon a sample of 93 persons, Alpert and Sargent (1941) have reported a correlation of .71, $\pm.035$ ($N = 93$), between Form J of the scale and a test of "immediate emotional reactions." This latter test involved reactions to 24 terms such as "investment capital, private enterprise," and so forth. Alpert and Sargent's study lends support to the scale in the form of construct validity. In a similar study, Havron, Nordlie, and Cofer (1957) reported a correlation of .42 between this scale and a controlled word-association test of conservatism-radicalism. Regarding the earlier 100-item forms, Lentz (1930) reports that "as negative evidence on validity, conservatism scores were correlated" negatively or not at all with the Otis Intelligence Test. "These figures imply that, whatever the test measures, it does not measure intelligence" (p. 539).

Comments. This is a moderately well validated and highly reliable scale which has been used extensively. Fortunately, equivalent forms of the scale are available. While few of the items are dated, phrasing of many of the items is somewhat dated. The vocabulary level in these scales is quite high, thus restricting the educational range of samples for which it is feasible.

EXHIBIT 7-1

THE CONSERVATISM - RADICALISM (C - R) OPINIONNAIRE

Here are some statements listed to see what people think about many questions. These are opinions and each person will agree with some and disagree with others.

If you *agree* more than you disagree with a statement, mark a plus (+). If you disagree more than you agree with a statement, mark a minus (—). Be sure to place either a plus or a minus mark to the left of each number.

Reprinted with permission from Lentz, T. F., Jr., and Colleagues, *Manual for C-R Opinionnaire (Conservatism-Radicalism). Forms J and K.* St. Louis, Mo.: Character Research Association, Department of Education, Washington University, 1935.

Form J

1 Three meals a day will always be the best general rule.
*2 The metric system of weights and measures should be adopted instead of our present system.
3 Cleanliness is a more valuable human trait than curiosity.
*4 We should celebrate Pasteur's birthday rather than Washington's as he has done the world a greater service.
5 The proposal to change the present calendar to one having 13 months of 28 days is unsound.
6 Even in an ideal world there should be protective tariffs.
*7 Our courts should be in the hands of sociologists rather than lawyers.
*8 Not the young men, but the old men, should fight our wars.
9 In the Sunday School chiefly the Bible should be taught.
*10 Socially-minded experts, rather than voters, should decide the policies of government.
11 Cat meat is out of the question for the human diet.
12 Conscience is an infallible guide.
13 The English and the Americans have the highest standards of morality.
*14 Our universities should have as many research workers as teachers.
15 Ministers should preach more about immortality than about social justice.
16 A commission form of government would not be desirable for the nation.
*17 Negroes should be permitted to attend educational institutions with whites.
18 People who are religious will be happier in the future life than will others.
19 Married women should not be allowed to teach in public schools.
20 Any science which conflicts with religious beliefs should be taught cautiously, if at all, in our schools.
21 It is more important to believe in God than to be unselfish.
*22 Since the theory of evolution has been accepted by most scientists, it should be taught in our schools.
23 Skirts which do not come to the knee should not be worn by grown women.
*24 Criminals should be treated like sick persons.
*25 It is to be hoped that men will improve the comfort of their dress by abandoning or replacing the present necktie and collar.
*26 Cremation is the best method of burial.
27 Conservative people are usually more intelligent than radical people.
28 Trial by jury has been, and always will be, the most effective way of securing justice.
*29 Our spelling should be revised and simplified.
*30 Capital punishment will some day be done away with.
31 The average person needs greater caution more than greater daring.
32 One is never justified in taking another's life, even when it would be a merciful act.
33 The Star-Spangled Banner is the most stirring in theme and noble in sentiment of national anthems.
*34 At the age of 21, people should have the privilege of changing their given names.
*35 The Bible is valuable primarily because it contains some of the world's best literature, and not because it is the word of God.
36 Race prejudice is, on the whole, beneficial as it keeps many undesirable foreigners from the country.

* These are radical items. The person receives one point if he rejects them. He also receives one point for acceptance of the unmarked, conservative items.

37 Democracy as practiced in the United States is the best of all modern governments because it is most suited to the needs of modern times.
*38 Freedom of teaching, that is, allowing teachers to teach what they think is the truth, is necessary for real education.
*39 American civilization may some day be wiped out as was Roman civilization.
40 It is not probable that wood ever will be converted into humanly edible food.
41 The Japanese race is, on the whole, crafty and treacherous.
42 Children should be brought up to have higher respect for our ancestors (generally).
*43 Radical agitators and propagandists should be allowed to speak publicly in parks and streets.
*44 Telling a lie is worse than taking the name of God in vain.
*45 National boundaries may some day become as truly obliterated as state lines have become in America during the past 150 years.
*46 In college, students should be allowed to attend class as much or as little as they like.
*47 Our present system of athletics in America is at fault in that it does not provide for mass participation.
48 The A.B. degree should continue to require four and only four years of work above the high school.
*49 We should Europeanize our native Americans, as well as Americanize Europeans among ourselves.
*50 We cannot say whether Christianity is sound or not because we have never practiced it systematically.
51 Preaching is one of the most effective ways of teaching people to lead better lives.
*52 Our present system of law, based upon outgrown conditions, should be replaced by a progressive system based upon the conditions of our present order.
*53 We owe our progress to radically minded people rather than to the "middle of the road" folk.
54 Generally speaking, Americans are more intelligent and enterprising than people of most any other country.
*55 The naval custom for a captain to stay with his ship until she sinks is outmoded, sentimental, and unnecessary.
56 It would not be possible to invent an ice cream which could be made merely by opening a tin can and exposing the contents to the air.
*57 Deformed babes of whose permanent helplessness we can be sure, should be put to death at the outset.
*58 Something more effective than our present brooms and mops and vacuum cleaners should be devised for cleaning our homes.
59 All children should have some sectarian religious training either on Sunday or week days.
*60 Most members of the D.A.R. would repudiate as dangerous characters modern personalities equivalent to the progenitors through whom they claim membership in the organization.

Form K

1 The age of six is the logical time to start school.
2 Free Trade is economically unsound.
3 Any science which conflicts with religious beliefs should not be taught in our schools.
4 School boards are right in barring married women from teaching positions.

5 College or university professors should not put forth their own radical views in the class room.
6 A man should be a booster for his city to help it grow.
*7 The present tendency among women to wear less clothing should be encouraged, especially in warm weather or climates.
*8 The world needs a new religion.
*9 Our responsibility to people of other races should be as great as our responsibility to our own race.
10 Science will never be able to create life.
*11 Workers in industry should receive a part of the profits of their company in addition to their salary.
*12 Woman should have as much right to propose dates to men as men to women.
13 The ministry is a more noble calling than the law.
14 The ceremony of baptism is more than a symbolic rite of the church, and is essential for the spiritual welfare of the individual.
*15 Church hymns should be revised to fit modern discovery.
16 Radical foreigners who wish to visit the United States should not be admitted.
17 Capital punishment will never be done away with.
18 Turkish people should not be admitted to our country as citizens.
19 The mind and spirit of man have kept pace with the rapid change in his material environment.
*20 In case of war, men's wealth, as well as their lives, should be drafted so that no war debts exist after the war is over.
*21 Censorship of speech, press and entertainment should be completely abolished.
*22 In presidential campaigns, the nominee receiving the second greatest number of votes should become the Vice-President, and the Vice-President given a more important role.
23 No individual, even though he feels that life is not worth living, is justified in committing suicide.
*24 We should change our minds and policies progressively and constantly.
*25 Facilities should be increased for open forum discussions among the people where grievances against the existing social or political order could be voiced.
26 Advertising is worthwhile because it increases purchasing power.
27 Race prejudice is useful in that it prevents inter-marrying.
*28 Historic heroes should be 'debunked.'
*29 We should make our immigration restrictions with regard to the desirability of an individual, regardless of his nationality, and abolish the practice of a fixed quota for each nationality.
30 As long as our captains of industry are as humane to their employees, and as long as wealthy people are as philanthropic as at present, there will be no need for socialism.
*31 All legislative bodies should be so constituted as to give representation to all groups in proportion to their voting strength (Republicans, Democrats, Socialists, Communists, Anarchists, etc.).
*32 All oil beneath the earth's surface should be common property of all men, and he who pumps it out should pay royalty to society as a whole, and not to any one man or group of men.
*33 Divorce by mutual consent would be a much better system than our present one.
*34 Aristocracies of worth should replace those of wealth or birth.

*35 Cremation should be made compulsory.
*36 Taxation should be used to mitigate the inequalities and to secure a greater socialization of wealth.
*37 The chivalry of women to men and of men to weaker (less intelligent, less informed) men is about as essential as the chivalry of men to women.
38 World patriotism should be second to national patriotism.
*39 Faith healing is not miraculous, but always psychologically explainable.
40 Most all men should wear neckties.
41 There should be a definite and appreciable amount of compulsory military training.
*42 The Continental attitude towards mistresses is saner than ours.
43 Much more energy should be expended in conserving what mankind does know, than in discovering what it does not know.
*44 If Russia demonstrates very clearly that communism is better than capitalism, then we should accept the former.
45 It is bad for a married man to take another man's wife to the movies.
46 "My country, may she always be right, but my country, right or wrong," is a good slogan.
47 The best way to remedy the modern divorce situation would be to make the conditions of divorce more stringent, so that marriage would be considered in a more serious light.
48 It would not be desirable to have a Chinese family move in next door.
49 The presidential term of office of four years is as it should be.
*50 Well-trained elementary teachers should receive the same salary as well-trained high school teachers, if not more.
51 It is not fitting that a statue of Einstein should occupy a niche in Dr. Fosdick's Riverside Drive Church.
52 Modern fiction should be required to pass a board of censors before publication.
*53 The Government should own the water power sites and distribute the power.
*54 Children should be encouraged to choose, independently of parents and relatives, their own religion.
55 Criminals retard our moral progress more than all other people combined.
*56 A marriage code should be in force in the United States, whereby the wife is not only given a right in the common property, but is made jointly responsible for the support of the family.
*57 Our national government should appropriate for the next twenty years at least 20 billion dollars for research work (chiefly in the social sciences of psychology, education, sociology, politics, and government).
*58 Science should endeavor to discover and develop a harmless liquor, retaining almost all the good features, but lacking the harmful ones, of alcoholic beverages.
59 Football helps put a college on the map, and should be heartily supported by all the alumni.
*60 The United States should enter a world federation of nations.

The Florida scale of civic beliefs *EXHIBIT 7-2*

Description. This scale was developed by Kimbrough and Hines (1963) and is composed of 60 Likert-type items. Referents of these items include the following: foreign affairs (4 items), economics (15 items), function of government (16), public finance (10), nature of man and society (15). Constructed by factor analysis, the scale is considered by the authors to measure conservatism versus two forms of liberalism (classical and new liberalism). Items for the scale were obtained from newspaper editorials, books, and university faculty members. These were sent to 15 University of Florida and University of Tennessee professors of education, psychology, economics, political science, and sociology. The professors acted as judges, evaluating the items as being liberal or conservative and adding new items. For these purposes, no definition of the terms liberal or conservative were supplied to the judges. Items were then categorized if 12 or more respondents agreed upon their nature. Then 121 such items were sent to 370 subjects who answered them on a three-point scale (agree, disagree, undecided). These subjects also reported whether they viewed themselves as conservative or liberal. An item analysis was performed, resulting in 80 surviving items. The procedure was then repeated with 185 subjects, and this analysis (together with a factor analysis) resulted in the scale of 60 items in Exhibit 7-2. All items in the scale show a first factor loading of .46 or above. None is loaded above .50 on any of the remaining 14 factors (Hines, undated mimeograph).

Subjects. The sample consisted of 370 subjects, most of whom had completed high school, and four-fifths of whom were attending college; 185 unidentified subjects; and 100 subjects who included leaders in the formal and informal power structure of one Florida county, middle-class householders, and University of Florida staff members.

Response Mode. Subjects respond to the test by circling one of five alternatives: strongly agree, agree, neither agree nor disagree, disagree, strongly disagree.

Scoring. Responses are weighted from 1 (strongly disagree) to 5 (strongly agree) for conservative statements. Weights are reversed for liberal statements. The score is the sum of the weighted responses to the 60 items. Liberal items are indicated by an asterisk in Exhibit 7-2. High scores indicate conservatism.

Reliability. The authors report a split-half correlation (corrected) of .934, based upon 75 graduate student subjects. (Hines, undated mimeograph).

Validity. The content validity of the items was checked by 15 judges from the faculties of the Universities of Tennessee and Florida. The content domain of the scale is somewhat restricted and emphasizes the issue of the Federal government versus free enterprise. Also, the factor loadings discussed above and used in the selection of the items may be taken as evidence of validity to the extent that the first factor reflects liberalism-conservatism.

Comments. Other forms of validity estimates (concurrent and predictive) would be welcome for this scale. Estimates of the test-retest reliability would also be useful. The fact that there is no alternative form to the test may detract somewhat from its usefulness.

EXHIBIT 7-2

THE FLORIDA SCALE OF CIVIC BELIEFS

Following are some statements with which you may agree or disagree. Circle the symbol which best represents your position on each statement as follows:

SA. . . . Strongly Agree
A. . . . Agree
N. . . . Neither agree nor disagree
D. . . . Disagree
SD. . . . Strongly Disagree

1 Socialized medicine would ruin medical standards and fill our nation with people having imaginary ailments.

†SA A N D SD

*2 The idea of equality should not be restricted to political equality.

3 Centralization of government tends to destroy the rights of the individual.

*4 History shows that economic and social planning by governments does not necessarily lead to dictatorship.

*5 Federal participation in local affairs can exist without undesirable federal control.

6 Moderates, who preach appeasement by urging us to give up our fight against centralized government and liberal constitutional interpretation, do so mostly for their personal political gain.

*7 What a state does with its schools should be its business, not the Supreme Court's.

8 The most serious political issue of our day is the encroachment of the federal government upon states' rights.

9 Local government is grass-roots democracy at work and represents the voice of the people better than centralized government.

10 The federal government taxes the states and then sends this money back, minus what is wasted in Washington.

*11 The federal government is often more representative of the people than some state governments.

12 Free enterprise, with an absolute minimum of governmental control, is the best way to assure full productivity in our country.

13 Private enterprise is the only really workable system in the modern world for satisfying our economic wants.

14 When individual producers and consumers are left free to follow their own self-interest, natural economic laws operate to produce the greatest public good.

*15 The growth of our economy depends upon an increase in the activities of government to satisfy human wants as well as an increase in our private economy.

† The same response alternatives are used with all items.
* These are liberal items whose weights must be reversed for purposes of scoring.

Reprinted with permission from Kimbrough, R. B., and Hines, V. A. The Florida Scale of Civic Beliefs. Gainesville, Fla. College of Education, University of Florida, 1963. Copyright 1963 by the College of Education, University of Florida, Gainesville, Fla.

16 The principle of free competition is a natural law which should govern our business system without governmental interference.

*17 The growth of large corporations makes government regulation of business necessary.

18 Government regulation of the market should occur only in cases of monopolies such as public utilities.

19 Money taken in by taxes is lost to the economy, since government is nonproductive.

20 We should get back to hard work to cure our country's ills.

*21 A growing national debt is nothing to worry about if the national income is growing at the same rate.

22 The price of aid to education, from a larger unit of government to a smaller one, is that the smaller one must do what it is told.

*23 Income taxes are more equitable than sales taxes.

24 To keep taxes from rising is commendable but in reality taxes should be cut.

25 The government is doing things which we simply cannot afford at public expense.

26 Deficit spending is a bad public policy except possibly in time of war.

27 All government spending should be on a pay-as-you-go basis.

28 In ordinary times public buildings, roads, and other permanent construction are the only things for which the government should borrow money.

*29 The government should meet the needs of the people, if necessary, through borrowing money or increasing taxes.

*30 If the country and the state are to make progress we are going to need additional taxes.

31 Good financial principles for private enterprise are equally good principles for government.

32 Government spending is naturally wasteful.

33 We are spending more than the people can really afford to spend for government services.

34 The collecting and spending of tax money is most wasteful at the federal level, not so wasteful at the state level, and least wasteful at the local level of government.

*35 We could still increase spending for important government services without harming the nation's economy.

36 Congress should accept the sensible virtue other businesses and individuals have learned—that of living within one's means.

*37 Our government can and should do more to promote the general welfare.

38 Private enterprise could do better many of the things that government is now doing.

39 The best governed is the least governed.

40 It is more important to teach Americanism than to teach democracy in our public schools.

41 Charitable services for those in need should be left to voluntary groups.

*42 Government in the United States is not the enemy of business.

*43 Increased government services in the social welfare programs may increase an individual's freedom.

44 Legislative reapportionment is undesirable because city residents do not understand rural and small town problems.

45 The Supreme Court has assumed powers not given to it by law or by custom.

46 Federal aid to schools, aid to the aged through social security, more stringent civil rights laws, and laws of like nature, are dangerously parallel to methods used in socialistic countries.

*47 The government should increase its activity in matters of health, retirement, wages, and old-age benefits.
48 Some races are by nature inferior mentally, emotionally, and physically.
49 If one has enough ambition and is willing to work hard, nothing but extremely bad luck can stop him.
*50 Unless we change social conditions, many children of minority groups will be unable to realize their full potentialities.
51 The Monroe Doctrine should be revitalized and maintained by the Armed Forces of the United States.
52 The United Nations has become an international debating society paid for by the United States.
53 Our foreign policy has been motivated too long by a spirit of do-goodism.
54 People of most underdeveloped countries are by nature incapable of self-government.
*55 We could recognize nations such as Red China without implying that we approve of their forms of government.
56 Production is greatest in an economic system based upon competition and some pressure.
57 If everyone would "take care of number one" there would be little need for such things as social security, health services, and other social welfare measures.
*58 Government has a responsibility for protecting not only property rights but human rights as well.
59 Providence is the proper source for social change.
60 This country was made great by persons who were willing to pull themselves up by their own bootstraps.

The economic conservatism scale *EXHIBIT 7-3*

Description. This is a 22-item scale developed by Rundquist and Sletto (1936), using a Likert procedure. Principally, it measures attitudes toward control of the economic institution by government, labor, and management. The developers of the scale gave 162 items to graduate students in psychology and advanced students in sociology, who commented on the items (especially on their ambiguity). They also indicated which items were responded to on the basis of their personal experience. Items were selected which were unambiguous and based on personal feelings without focusing upon personal problems. A third selection criterion for items was reliability. Items that were unreliable over a one-week interval were rejected. New items were added to those passing all three of these criteria, increasing the total to 212. This set of items was then administered to 184 juniors in sociology classes. An item analysis was completed on these responses, and 22 items were chosen on the basis of their ability to discriminate the upper and lower quartiles of the total score distribution. This scale was part of the Minnesota scale for the survey of opinions.

Subjects. The sample was composed of 2,882 subjects, including the following groups: college and high school students, high school teachers, men on relief, and persons enrolled in classes for the unemployed.

Response Mode. Persons respond by checking one of five alternatives: strongly agree, agree, undecided, disagree, and strongly disagree.

Scoring. Responses are weighted from 1 (strongly disagree) to 5 (strongly agree) for conservative statements. Weights for liberal statements are reversed. The score is the sum of the weighted response alternatives endorsed by the person. High scores indicate conservatism.

Reliability. The authors report split-half reliabilities (corrected) of .85 and .82 (based upon samples of 500 males and 500 females respectively). They reported test-retest reliability coefficients (for samples of 70 males and 75 females, using a sixty-day test interval) of .86 and .82 respectively (Rundquist and Sletto, 1936).

Validity. When taken as a measure of attitudes toward *who* should *control* the economic institution, the scale has good content validity. The scale is reported by the authors to correlate positively with several measures of personal adjustment, which may confer upon it a degree of construct validity. However, it correlated not at all with educational level. This detracts from its construct validity only if one is willing to generalize from results obtained on tests of authoritarianism, which indicate a negative correlation between education and authoritarianism. If one does not assume conservatism to be associated with authoritarianism, the construct validity of the scale is undamaged by its failure to correlate with educational level.

Comments. Despite the fact that this scale was constructed in the 1930s, the items are not dated and may still be used with success. It is a reliable scale but could benefit from further validation studies. However, as its title indicates, it emphasizes economic conservatism. In view of findings by Kerr (1946) and Voor (1953), one would not expect that scores on this scale would reflect conservatism in other domains such as politics or religion, nor should one expect to assess a general factor of conservatism using this scale. Other studies using it include Darley (1938), Ferguson (1941), and Sewell and Amend (1943).

EXHIBIT 7-3

THE ECONOMIC CONSERVATISM SCALE

READ EACH ITEM CAREFULLY AND UNDERLINE QUICKLY THE PHRASE WHICH BEST EXPRESSES YOUR FEELING ABOUT THE STATEMENT. Wherever possible, let your own personal experience determine your answer. Do not spend much time on any item. If in doubt, underline the phrase which seems most nearly to express your present feeling about the statement. WORK RAPIDLY. Be sure to answer every item.

*1 The government should take over all industries.

Strongly Agree Agree Undecided Disagree Strongly Disagree

2 Labor should have much more voice in deciding government policies.
3 Legislatures are too ready to pass laws to curb business freedom.
4 For men to do their best, there must be the possibility of unlimited profit.
*5 Poverty is chiefly a result of injustice in the distribution of wealth.
6 The government should not attempt to limit profits.
7 The more a man learns about our economic system, the less willing he is to see changes made.
*8 The government ought to guarantee a living to those who can't find work.
*9 Large incomes should be taxed more than they are now.
10 Men would not do their best if government owned all industry.
11 Most great fortunes are made honestly.
12 Private ownership of property is necessary for economic progress.
*13 Without sweeping changes in our economic system, little progress can be made in the solution of social problems.
14 On the whole, our economic system is just and wise.
*15 Labor does not get its fair share of what it produces.
*16 When a rich man dies, most of his property should go to the state.
*17 If our economic system were just, there would be much less crime.
18 The incomes of most people are a fair measure of their contribution to human welfare.
*19 A man should strike in order to secure greater returns to labor.
20 A man should be allowed to keep as large an income as he can get.
*21 Money should be taken from the rich and given to the poor during hard times.
22 Our economic system is criticized too much.

* These items must be reversed for scoring purposes. Agreement is regarded as a liberal attitude. The same response alternatives are used with all items.

Questionnaire on politico-economic attitudes EXHIBIT 7-4

Description. This was originally a 20-item modified Likert scale developed by Sanai (1950*a*). The original form of the scale contained items measuring attitude toward a diversity of political and economic referents. In a later 16-item version of essentially the same scale (Sanai, 1950*b*), the domain of content being sampled was extended to include items dealing with religious issues and differences between the sexes. The author apparently considers this latter version of his scale to measure an attitude of alterationism (which may be taken as akin to radicalism, and reflects a desire for or expectation of change). This concept is similar to the underlying Lentz's C-R Opinionnaire, discussed at the beginning of this section. The original 20 items of the scale were included in Exhibit 7-4 because of the more adequate sampling of the content domain.

Subjects. The sample on which the scale was constructed was 250 British subjects, including 119 London University students, 61 working-class people, and 70 college girls.

Response Mode. Persons respond by marking one of seven alternatives: when you are in complete agreement; when, on the whole, you agree; when you are in doubt, but if forced to choose, will agree; when you are totally unable to decide; when you are in doubt, if forced to choose, will disagree; when, on the whole, you disagree; when you are in complete disagreement.

Scoring. The seven alternatives are weighted from +3 (when you are in complete agreement) to −3 (when you are in complete disagreement), for statements reflecting an attitude of alterationism. Weights for the response alternatives for conservative statements should be reversed. The person's score is the sum of the weighted alternatives endorsed by him. High scores reflect radicalism and an attitude of alterationism.

Reliability. The author reported a split-half (odd-even) reliability coefficient (corrected) of .86. The shorter, 16-item test (containing many of the same items) is reported by him as possessing a split-half reliability estimate of .88. Both of these estimates are based upon the sample of 250 subjects.

Validity. The content validity of the 20-item scale seems only fair in that a very broad domain is being sampled with very few items. That of the 16-item scale was reduced still further by decreasing the number of items in the scale while increasing the number of different referents to which items allude. The scale seems further lacking in content validity in that some of the items do not appear to measure anything one could call "alterationism" or "radicalism." Nevertheless, the author (Sanai, 1952) reports a correlation of .90 between scores on the scale and membership in the Socialist party. Also, in a factor analysis of the items, he found a general factor loading interpreted by him as socialism versus *laissez faire* which contributed to 41 percent of the variance. A second, bipolar factor was determined, interpreted by him as Marxism versus Fabianism, or revolutionary versus evolutionary change. It contributed to 8 percent of the variance. Also, the factor reflecting Marxian communism is orthogonal to the general factor of socialistic-mindedness (radicalism). These latter findings would indicate that the scale is a moderately valid measure of socialistic attitudes.

Comments. The scale seems reliable, as assessed using a British sample. It may not be as reliable for an American population. Also, at least some of the items would have to be changed or discarded for use in the United States. For example, item number 6 refers to the Labor party; other items refer to the British and American governments from a British viewpoint. Before it is used in the United States, the scale items should be altered and the functional characteristics of the scale reassessed. Further studies of the validity of the scale would be valuable.

EXHIBIT 7-4

QUESTIONNAIRE ON POLITICO - ECONOMIC ATTITUDES

Below are 20 questions which represent widely held opinions on various political questions. They are chosen in such a way that most people are likely to agree with some and disagree with others.

You are requested to observe the following Rule of Markings:

In the left hand margin before the statement put:

+3 When you are in complete agreement with the statement.
+2 When, on the whole, you agree with the statement.
+1 When you are in doubt, but if forced to choose, will agree with the statement.
0 When you are totally unable to decide.
−1 When you are in doubt, if forced to choose, will disagree with the statement.
−2 When, on the whole, you disagree with the statement.
−3 When you are in complete disagreement with the statement.

Your answers will be kept secret. Please answer *carefully* and *frankly.*

1 Industries such as electricity, mines and railways should be owned and operated by the State—not for private profit.
*2 If 10 percent of the population owns 90 percent of the country's wealth it is because the most able rise to the top.
3 In practice the rich and the poor are not equal before the law.
4 Slumps and unemployment are inevitable consequences of capitalism.
5 It is clearly unfair that some people should acquire large incomes, not through any work of their own, but by inheritance.
6 But for the controls which the Labor Government maintained there would have been economic chaos in this country.
*7 Socialism leads to too much bureaucracy.
*8 Capitalism is a misleading term in Britain now that the majority of the population have invested savings or buy their own homes.
9 Many of the errors in our foreign policy are due to the diplomatic service being drawn so exclusively from the "Upper Class."
10 Before any satisfactory measure of social progress can be achieved the working class must exercise a temporary dictatorship.
*11 British Governments have so far aligned themselves in foreign countries with reactionary elements.
*12 It is not possible to put democratic principles into practice owing to wide differences in innate intelligence between individuals.
13 Stable peace will only be possible in a Socialist world.
14 Capitalism is immoral because it exploits the worker by failing to give him the full value of his productive labor.
15 In the present state of capitalist societies genuine social progress is impossible without the aid of revolution.

* These are conservative statements and must be reversed for purposes of scoring.

16 In capitalist countries the economic system impels the capitalists and the workers into irreconcilable conflict with one another.
17 All large scale means of production and distribution must be owned and operated by the State.
18 In the interest of peace we must give up a large part of our national sovereignty.
19 Unrestricted freedom of discussion on every topic is desirable in the press, in literature, on the stage, etc.
20 In a capitalist country, like the United States for example, it is really big business that controls the State, not the people at large.

Conservatism-radicalism (C-R) battery *EXHIBIT 7-5*

Description. This scale was developed by Centers (1949) and is composed of six items intended to measure a dimension of conservatism-radicalism on attitudes toward political and economic issues. Centers originally selected the items (through repeated piloting) to be understandable to the general public. Case (1953) applied a Guttman scaling procedure to the items to assess their unidimensionality and obtained a quasi-scale, presented in Exhibit 7-5.

Subjects. The original sample (Centers, 1949) consisted of 1,100 male Caucasians twenty-one years of age and over, selected by stratified random sampling to represent the following criteria: geographical area, urban-rural residence, socio-economic status, occupation. He reports some bias in the sample by overrepresentation of managerial and professional types. His data were obtained by interview two weeks before the end of World War II. Case (1953) used a sample consisting of 441 respondents drawn by the Washington Public Opinion Laboratory and polled at the time of the 1950 United States presidential election.

Response Mode. The items in Exhibit 7-5 appear as they did on Poll No. 23, October, 1950 (Case, 1953). They vary in the type of response continuum used, offering from two to five alternative responses to an item and offering a variety of types of responses including "agree-disagree," nouns such as "workers" or "employees," and long verbal statements. Subjects respond by checking that alternative which best describes their attitude.

Scoring. Centers divided persons into conservative and radical groups on the basis of the consistency of their adherence to a single position throughout the six questions. Persons endorsing five or six items conservatively are "ultra-conservative"; three or four such endorsements indicate a "conservative"; persons endorsing five or six in a radical manner are "ultra-radical"; three or four such endorsements indicate a "radical"; any other pattern of endorsement is referred to as "indeterminate." Conservative and radical endorsements are indicated in Exhibit 7-5.

Reliability. No evidence of reliability is available.

Validity. Case obtained a coefficient of reproducibility of .813, treating the items as six trichotomies. When treated as two trichotomies and four dichotomies, the coefficient was .884 (a quasi-scale). Content validity seems weak. It is to be noted that item number 3 is dated; alteration of the item to read "As you know, during the *past* war, . . . *were* taken over . . ." would improve its applicability. The content domain is otherwise restricted by the small number of somewhat similar questions being asked. Centers (1949, p. 42) reports an item analysis which demonstrates that persons tend to respond consistently from one item to the next, which seems to justify his scoring procedure. He also reports the intercorrelations (tetrachoric) between items. The degree of association measured by tetrachoric correlation varied from .12 between belief that "America is truly a land of opportunity" and siding with employers in strikes and disputes with workers, to .68 between belief in "individualism" and endorsement of "private ownership" of industry.

Comments. The scale seems to have minimally satisfactory validity. Some form of reliability estimate is necessary to further assess the scale. Also, equivalent forms are especially desirable for very short scales such as this. The scale concentrates on conservatism with regard to economic issues as they are influenced by political factors. It should not be expected to necessarily reflect political conservatism otherwise, nor should it be used to measure religious, aesthetic, or general conservatism.

EXHIBIT 7-5

CONSERVATISM - RADICALISM (C - R) BATTERY

NOTE: No instructions were provided for the scale since the author obtained his data through an interview procedure. Any instructions which require the subject to choose one of the alternatives provided and to answer every question will probably suffice.

1 Do you agree or disagree that America is truly a land of opportunity and that people get pretty much what is coming to them here?

1. ( ) agree 2. ( ) disagree 3. ( ) don't know

*2 Would you agree that everybody would be happier, more secure and more prosperous if the working people were given more power and influence in government, or would you say we would all be better off if the working people had no more power than they have now?

1. ( ) agree 2. ( ) no more power 3. ( ) don't know

*3 As you know, during this war, many private businesses and industries have been taken over by government. Do you think wages and salaries would be fairer, jobs more steady, and that we would have fewer people out of work

* If subjects endorse the first response alternative on these items, they are responding radically; endorsement of response alternative No. 2 is conservative. For the unmarked items, the reverse is true.

if the government took over and ran our mines, factories, and industries in the future, or do you think things would be better under private ownership?

1. ( ) better under government
2. ( ) better under private ownership
3. ( ) other
4. ( ) don't know

4 Which of these statements do you most agree with?

1. ( ) The most important job for government is to make it certain that there are good opportunities for each person to get ahead on his own.
2. ( ) The most important job for government is to guarantee every person a decent and steady job and standard of living.

*5 In strikes and disputes between working people and employers do you usually side with the workers or with the employers?

1. ( ) Workers 2. ( ) Employers 3. ( ) Neither 4. ( ) Won't say 5. ( ) Don't know

*6 Do you think working people are fairly and squarely treated by their employers, or that employers sometimes take advantage of them?

1. ( ) Fair treatment 2. ( ) Employers take advantage 3 ( ) Don't know

Tulane factors of liberalism-conservatism attitude values profile *EXHIBIT 7-6*

Description. This 76-item scale was developed by Kerr (1946). It is the author's contention that there is no generalized liberalism-conservatism factor which would obtain across all areas of the individual's life. Therefore, his scale is constructed to measure attitudes on a liberal-conservative continuum in five separate areas: political, economic, religious, aesthetic, and social. It is copyrighted by Psychometric Affiliates, Inc., and is available through them.

Subjects. The subjects were 291 males enrolled in Protestant and nondenominational colleges (New Orleans, 242; New York, 32; Chicago, 17).

Response Mode. The first 51 items are answered by checking one of five columns labelled as follows: yes, probably yes, undecided, probably no, and no. Five columns labelled "like very much" through "dislike very much" are used for the aesthetic items. These columns have been eliminated from Exhibit 7-6.

Scoring. Subscale scores are obtained by summation of the weighted response alternatives endorsed by the person. Responses are weighted from 1 (most conservative or reactionary reply) to 5 (most liberal or radical reply). Omissions are weighted as 3 (undecided). There are no items to be reversed. In his manual, the author reports norms for his samples. He also provides an arbitrary set of standards for interpretation of scores using "conventional emotional stereotype labels." Unless one is willing to accept the premise of a generalized attitude of conservatism-liberalism, it would not be valuable to sum the scores obtained from the subscales to obtain one score for the entire test.

Reliability. The author (Kerr, 1946) reports the following split-half correlations (corrected) for the subscales based on an N of 246 males: political, .55; economic, .82; religious, .77; social, .95; aesthetic, .88. As may be seen, the political subscale is least satisfactory with regard to reliability.

Validity. The author reports the economic subscale to yield a significantly higher liberalism for Democrats than for Republicans. The religious subscale is reported by him to differentiate significantly among Catholics, Protestants, Jews, and "no religion" groups. Kerr also presents a table of tetrachoric intercorrelations among the five subscales as evidence of their relative independence. These correlations range from —.02 (political and economic) to +.40 (social and political). Using a sample of 251 seminarians studying for Roman Catholic priesthood, Voor (1953) reports a set of Pearsonian intercorrelations (corrected) in a cross validation of the independence of the five subscales. These range from —.20 (religious and political) to +.29 (social and aesthetic). Thus it would appear that, as measured by these scales, liberalism and conservatism are specific to the content domain being sampled.

Comments. This seems to be a reliable scale (excepting the low correlation on the political subscale). There are several items on the political subscale that are suspicious: Item 3 quite possibly does not function monotonically, as the Likert procedure would require, and item 5 may also be questioned. Rewriting or discarding these items may improve this subscale. Regarding validity, there are several problems. First, there are no negative items in the scale, allowing the operation of response sets. Second, the definition of liberalism changes from scale to scale. These definitions should be examined carefully by the user. In this latter regard, the validity of the aesthetic subscale may be questioned, as it may measure indiscriminant acceptance of music, art, etc. In general, the approach taken by the author of the scale in measuring conservatism-liberalism in specific content areas adds value to the potential use of the scales. There is some support for his assumption that there is no general trait of conservatism across all areas of a person's values. Interested readers may also wish to see Kerr (1952).

EXHIBIT 7-6

TULANE FACTORS OF LIBERALISM - CONSERVATISM ATTITUDE VALUES PROFILE

The questions which follow attempt to measure what you *believe* in various fields of human opinion. The "correct" answer to each item is merely your honest opinion. Answer every question. When you agree strongly with an item, place a check (✓) mark in the "yes" column at the right; place a mark in the "Probably Yes" column when you agree weakly; check "Undecided" when you have no opinion; "Probably No" and "No" are checked to show disagreement.

Example: Do you favor repeal of the laws against homicide?

Yes Probably Yes Undecided Probably No No

Political Items:

1 Do congressmen try to do a good job in representing the People?
2 Are most elected politicians honest?
3 Should all able adults be permitted to vote?
4 Is a country harmed by having only one recognized political party?
5 Should all races and creeds have the right to vote?
6 Should the international world government have the right to overrule decisions of member nations?
7 Would the country be harmed by being governed permanently by a strong person chosen because of his good standing in some prominent organization?
8 Should rural and city areas be represented in the government in proportion to their population?
9 Should you send your opinion on an important issue to your congressman?
10 Should any special group of citizens have the right to organize and support or oppose candidates for public office?
11 Would you feel honored at being elected to a public office?
12 Should local citizens have a voice in solving local problems?

Economic Items:

13 Should every family be guaranteed a minimum standard of living?
14 In hard times should the government invent jobs for the unemployed?
15 Should farmers be guaranteed a minimum annual income?
16 Is old age insurance paid by the government a good idea?
17 Should employees have the right to organize and bargain for wages?
18 Should employees have the right to go on strike for higher wages?
19 Should the government provide medical care for all citizens?
20 Should the government closely regulate companies which employ thousands of workers?
21 Should dental service be provided to all citizens at public expense?
22 Should every capable young person be entitled to vocational training at government expense?
23 Should all adults be entitled to a month's vacation with pay each year?
24 Should the government take over the ownership and operation of any national industry?
25 Do you favor a heavy tax on large incomes?

Religious Items:

26 Can you be psychologically complete without believing in God?
27 Do you think "God listens to prayers" is a false statement?
28 Do you think your chances of life after death are equally good by belonging to any one of several similar religious denominations?
29 Do you think form of worship (music, communion, ritual, etc.) is unimportant?
30 Is it proper for a church to maintain social and recreational organizations?
31 Do you believe that the holy scriptures are not divine?

32 Is it improper for the church to decide what you can read in your own home?
33 Do you think any one of the other religions in the world is as good as Christianity?
34 Do you think it unnecessary to fast on certain days each year?
35 Do you think it unnecessary to abstain from eating any certain food on any designated day?
36 Do you believe that church property not used for worship should be taxed?
37 Do you think stories about miracles happening within the last few hundred years are false?
38 Do you think any nation's government should oppose establishment of any one church as the favored church of a country?
39 Is one's marriage likely to be just as successful if one regards the family as something that is not sacred?

Social Items:

40 Do you enjoy talking with citizens of small towns?
41 Do you enjoy talking with citizens of large cities?
42 Do you enjoy talking with rural citizens?
43 Do you enjoy talking with members of **all** other races?
44 Do you believe that all races are equally good?
45 Do you think that people of all nations are equally good?
46 Should whites and Negroes be permitted to intermarry?
47 Have immigrants from southern Europe become good citizens?
48 Have immigrants from northern Europe become good citizens?
49 Have oriental immigrants become good citizens?
50 Have Negroes become good citizens?
51 Have Jews become good citizens?

Aesthetic Items:

How Much Do You Like the Following?
Like It Much, Like It Some, Don't Care, Dislike It Some, Dislike It Much.

52 Patriotic music.
53 Fast dance music.
54 Hawaiian music.
55 Popular "hit parade" music.
56 Humorous and novelty music.
57 Semi-classical and standard music.
58 Waltzes.
59 Polkas and square dances.
60 Negro spirituals and blues.
61 Marches.
62 Classical music.
63 Hillbilly and western music.
64 Sacred and religious music.
65 Greek sculpture.
66 Paintings by the old masters.
67 Realistic paintings of present-day scenes.
68 Surrealistic imaginative painting.
69 Primitive pottery.
70 "Modernistic" architecture.
71 Colored comic cartoons (Newspaper).
72 Flowers.
73 Planting flowers and shrubs yourself.

74 Doing woodwork, carving, or sewing.
75 Seeing and hearing birds.
76 Seeing woods, fields, and streams.

The social attitudes scale EXHIBIT 7-7

Description. This is an as yet unpublished scale developed by Kerlinger (private communication, 1963) to measure attitudes on a dimension of liberalism-conservatism. It is composed of 26 modified Likert-type items which were selected by factor analysis. The two title factors (liberalism and conservatism) are actually a combination of four complementary factors. The author selected items from earlier social attitude instruments by Eysenck, Vetter, Lentz, Sanai, and others and also wrote an additional 80 items. From this pool, he finally selected 40 items (20 to reflect liberalism and 20 to reflect conservatism). A factor analysis of these 40 items produced four factors: complementary Factors A and C on the one hand, all with liberal items, and Factors B and D on the other hand with all conservative items. This 40-item pool was then further reduced to the best 13 liberal and 13 conservative items to produce the scale given in Exhibit 7-7 (Kerlinger, private communication, 1965).

Subjects. Samples included 210 graduate students in education, 251 undergraduates, and 205 individuals outside the university setting. The main analysis was performed on a sample of 415 subjects composed of the graduates and persons outside the university.

Response Mode. Persons respond to each item by checking one of six alternatives: agree very strongly, agree strongly, agree, disagree, disagree strongly, and disagree very strongly.

Scoring. For liberal items, response alternatives are weighted from +3 (agree very strongly) to −3 (disagree very strongly). Weights for the response alternatives for conservative items are reversed. The subject's score is the sum of the weighted alternatives endorsed by him. Higher scores are indicative of liberalism.

Reliability. The author (1965) reported the split-half reliability estimates (corrected) to be .78 (liberalism) and .79 (conservatism), based on a sample of 168 unidentified subjects.

Validity. Kerlinger administered this scale along with a number of other instruments to 161 of the 168 subjects used to assess reliability. Among the other instruments administered were Kerlinger's education scales (measuring progressivism-traditionalism), the F scale, Rokeach's Opinionation Scales, Edwards's Social Desirability Scale, Bass's Social Acquiescence Scale, Keniston and Couch's Agreement Response Scale, the Gough Rigidity Scale, and the Wonderlic Intelligence Scale. All these were intercorrelated and factor-analyzed. Among other results, the conservative items of the Social Attitudes Scale fell together with the F scale. The only other response set measure that also fell on this factor (.66) was the Bass Social Acquiescence Scale. Most important, the liberalism and conservatism items fell on different factors as the author predicted, indicating construct validity. The conservatism items loaded .86 on one factor (A) and hardly at all on any other factor. The liberalism items loaded .57 on a different factor (C) and .29 on a second factor (B). The scale has adequate content validity.

Comments. This scale has not had an opportunity to be widely used as yet. It seems satisfactory thus far with regard to reliability and validity. Test-retest reliability coefficients and further demonstrations of validity would be valuable. Equivalent forms would also enhance the usefulness of the scale.

EXHIBIT 7-7

THE SOCIAL ATTITUDES SCALE

Given below are statements on various social problems about which we all have beliefs, opinions, and attitudes. We all think differently about such matters, and this scale is an attempt to let you express your beliefs and opinions. There are no right and wrong answers. Please respond to each of the items as follows:

Agree very strongly	+3	Disagree very strongly	−3
Agree strongly	+2	Disagree strongly	−2
Agree	+1	Disagree	−1

For example, if you agree very strongly with a statement, you would write +3 in the left margin beside the statement, but if you should happen to disagree with it, you would put −1 in front of it. Respond to each statement as best you can. Go rapidly but carefully. Do not spend too much time on any one statement; try to respond and then go on. Don't go back once you have marked a statement.

*1 Individuals who are against churches and religions should not be allowed to teach in colleges.
2 Large fortunes should be taxed fairly heavily over and above income taxes.
3 Both public and private universities and colleges should get generous aid from both state and federal governments.
*4 Science and society would both be better off if scientists took no part in politics.
5 Society should be quicker to throw out old ideas and traditions and to adopt new thinking and customs.
6 To ensure adequate care of the sick, we need to change radically the present system of privately controlled medical care.
*7 If civilization is to survive, there must be a turning back to religion.
*8 A first consideration in any society is the protection of property rights.
*9 Government ownership and management of utilities leads to bureaucracy and inefficiency.

* These are conservative items whose weights should be reversed for scoring purposes. All unmarked items are liberal.

Items obtained from F. N. Kerlinger and published with his permission. No reference is available.

*10 If the United States takes part in any sort of world organization, we should be sure that we lose none of our power and influence.
11 Funds for school construction should come from state and federal government loans at no interest or very low interest.
*12 Inherited racial characteristics play more of a part in the achievement of individuals and groups than is generally known.
13 Federal Government aid for the construction of schools is long overdue, and should be instituted as a permanent policy.
14 Our present economic system should be reformed so that profits are replaced by reimbursements for useful work.
15 Public enterprises like railroads should not make profits; they are entitled to fares sufficient to enable them to pay only a fair interest on the actual cash capital they have invested.
*16 Government laws and regulations should be such as first to ensure the prosperity of business since the prosperity of all depends on the prosperity of business.
17 All individuals who are intellectually capable of benefiting from it should get college education, at public expense if necessary.
*18 The well-being of a nation depends mainly on its industry and business.
19 True democracy is limited in the United States because of the special privileges enjoyed by business and industry.
20 The gradual social ownership of industry needs to be encouraged if we are ever to cure some of the ills of our society.
*21 There are too many professors in our colleges and universities who are radical in their social and political beliefs.
*22 There should be no government interference with business and trade.
*23 Some sort of religious education should be given in public schools.
24 Unemployment insurance is an inalienable right of the working man.
*25 Individuals with the ability and foresight to earn and accumulate wealth should have the right to enjoy that wealth without government interference and regulations.
26 The United Nations should be whole-heartedly supported by all of us.

Political and economic progressivism (PEP) scale *EXHIBIT 7-8*

Description. This is a 26-item, Likert-type scale developed by Newcomb (1943). It is adapted from and remains essentially the Stagner Fascism Scale in content, although some changes were made in order to make it applicable to a Likert procedure. The present 26 items were selected from an original 30 items on the basis of their correlation with the total score.

Subjects. Subjects included 322 Williams College students and 252 Skidmore College students. The samples were drawn in 1939.

Response Mode. A standard Likert response continuum is used: strongly agree, agree, uncertain, disagree, strongly disagree. The respondent circles that alternative which best represents the degree of his agreement or disagreement.

Scoring. Response alternatives for conservative statements are weighted from +3 (strongly agree) to −3 (strongly disagree). The weights must be reversed for response alternatives for liberal statements. The liberal statements are indicated by an asterisk in Exhibit 7-8. The score is the sum of the weighted alternatives endorsed by the respondent. High scores indicate conservatism.

Reliability. The author (Newcomb, 1943) reported split-half reliabilities (corrected) of .94 ($N = 322$) and .82 ($N = 252$). Reliabilities were higher for junior and senior college students than for freshmen and sophomores, indicating that the attitudes were more clearly formulated for them. In a retest, a correlation of .90 was obtained between the number of favorable responses from subjects when they were freshmen and when they were seniors. Only a few individuals showed a significant rank order difference between the two scores over the four-year period.

Validity. Newcomb reported differences in PEP scores among freshmen entering different major divisions of the college, and these differences increased after three or four years in college. To the extent that freshmen select majors on the basis of finding compatible attitudes among persons in that major division, it would be expected that their already existing attitudes would be supported and solidified during their education. If this interpretation is valid, the finding of increased differences in attitudes over time in different major divisions would lend supportive evidence to the validity of the scale. Also the fact that the attitude measurement of juniors and seniors is more reliable probably indicates increased validity of the measurement due to increased certainty of the respondents.

Comments. This is a cleanly constructed scale which has provided good reliability estimates in the past. It is presently somewhat dated and needs to be overhauled. If it is to be used with younger persons who do not remember the depression or who were largely uninfluenced by it, there is some question of whether overhauling the scale would be worth the work involved. Items 2, 7, 18, and 19 in Exhibit 7-8 are especially dated and should be altered or discarded before using the scale. Some of the other items regarding the depression and the rights of labor organizations may not function as well today as they did in 1939 because of decreased saliency of their referents.

EXHIBIT 7-8

POLITICAL AND ECONOMIC PROGRESSIVISM (PEP) SCALE

Directions

On the following pages appear statements about certain contemporary public issues. You will agree with some of the statements, disagree with some, and be uncertain of others. There are no "right" or "wrong" answers. Whatever you happen to think about it is the right answer for you.

Please indicate your replies as follows:

Encircle A if you **agree** with the statement, thus	SA	(A)	?	D	SD
Encircle SA if you **strongly agree** with it, thus	(SA)	A	?	D	SD
Encircle D if you **disagree** with the statement, thus	SA	A	?	(D)	SD
Encircle SD if you **strongly disagree** with it, thus	SA	A	?	D	(SD)
Encircle ? if you are **uncertain**, thus	SA	A	(?)	D	SD

*1 The only true prosperity of the nation as a whole must be based upon the prosperity of the working class.

SA A ? D SD

2 Recovery has been delayed by the large number of strikes.

*3 Some form of collective society, in which profits are replaced by reimbursements for useful mental or manual work, is preferable to our present system.

*4 The depression occurred chiefly because the working classes did not receive enough in wages to purchase goods and services produced at a profit.

*5 A "planned economy" is not enough unless it is planned for the welfare of workers rather than of business men.

6 Most labor trouble happens only because of radical agitators.

7 The people who complain most about the depression wouldn't take a job if you gave it to them.

*8 The standard of living of the working class can be kept above the poverty line only as workers force it up by the use of strikes.

*9 Labor organizations have as much right to bring in outside agitators as do business men to import outside technical experts.

10 Any able-bodied man could get a job right now if he tried hard enough.

11 Most people on relief are living in reasonable comfort.

12 The budget should be balanced before the government spends any money on social security.

*13 Our government has always been run primarily in the interests of big business, and so it is those interests which are chiefly responsible for the depression.

14 Labor unions are justifiable only if they refrain from the use of strikes.

*15 Since it is impossible for working people to make any substantial savings, they have fully earned their right to old-age pensions.

16 It is all right to try to raise the standard of living of the lower classes, provided that existing property rights are continually safeguarded.

*17 Most employers think only of profits and care little about their employees' welfare.

18 Unemployment insurance would saddle us with a nation of idlers.

19 Organizations of the unemployed are just a group of chronic complainers.

*20 We have no true democracy in this country, because only business and industrial concerns have economic opportunity.

21 If the government didn't meddle so much in business everything would be all right.

22 You can't expect democracy to work very well as long as so many uneducated and unintelligent people have the vote.

* These items are liberal and their weights must be reversed for scoring purposes. All items use the same response alternatives.

23 The vast majority of those in the lower economic classes are there because they are stupid or shiftless, or both.

24 Those who have the ability and the foresight to accumulate wealth ought to be permitted to enjoy it themselves.

*25 The middle classes will never enjoy security or prosperity until they understand that their welfare is identified with that of the working class, and not with that of business and industrial groups.

*26 The real threat to prosperity in this country is the repressive activities of those who wish to keep wealth and economic power in the hands of those who now possess them.

Public opinion questionnaire *EXHIBIT 7-9*

Description. This was originally a 26-item, Likert-type scale designed by Edwards (1941) to measure fascist attitudes. The items were collected from a variety of sources including studies by Stagner and Gundlach and the writings of Childs, Mann, and Kolnai. These statements were then rated by five judges concerning whether they expressed pro- or antifascist attitudes. The 26 items upon which the judges agreed were retained. Four more items were later dropped after item analysis. The remaining 22 items were given in Exhibit 7-9.

Subjects. The sample consisted of 91 students in general psychology classes at the University of Akron (Ohio).

Response Mode. The scale uses a standard Likert response continuum: strongly agree, agree, uncertain, disagree, and strongly disagree. The person chooses that alternative which best describes his attitude.

Scoring. Responses are weighted from 5 (strongly agree) to 1 (strongly disagree) for all items but one. The third item (original number 5) is negative, and its weights must be reversed. The subject's score is the sum of the weighted alternatives endorsed by him. High scores are profascist.

Reliability. The author reports a split-half reliability (corrected) of .84, based upon a sample of 146 students at Ohio State University.

Validity. The items were subjected to an item analysis and the 22 items in Exhibit 7-9 retained because they discriminated significantly between the median scores of the 16 highest and 16 lowest scorers. Retention only of items on which five judges agreed provides some assurance of the content validity of the scale, which is probably satisfactory in view of the number of sources from which statements were taken. The major question with regard to validity arises because all but one of the items have the same direction. This allows response set to operate. It is possible that the high and low scorers that are being discriminated by the items are "yea-sayers" and "nay-sayers."

Comments. Although developed some years ago, these items are not dated. Reliability is adequate, but some further demonstrations of validity seem required. The scale would be better if additional negative or antifascist items were included.

EXHIBIT 7-9

PUBLIC OPINION QUESTIONNAIRE

This is an attempt to find out the extent to which people are agreed in their opinions about various problems which confront society today. What we are interested in finding out is: What is public opinion on these statements. *There are of course no "right" or "wrong"* answers to these statements; they are merely expressions of opinion. Will you please help us to get a cross section of public opinion by indicating *your* opinion on these statements. Just place an X on the line which most nearly expresses your opinion. *Do not sign your name on this blank.*

†1 Children should be taught to be more obedient and to have more respect for authority by the public schools.

_______ I strongly agree with this statement
_______ I agree with this statement
_______ I am uncertain about this statement
_______ I disagree with this statement
_______ I strongly disagree with this statement

2 Whatever best serves the interests of government is generally right.

*5 The masses of people are capable of determining what is and what is not good for them.

6 America has reached a higher state of civilization than any other country in the world and as a consequence has a culture which is superior to any other.

8 Over 10% of the population is incapable of democratic participation in government by reason of their lack of inherited abilities.

9 Generally speaking, women are less intelligent and efficient than men.

10 The superior people in any culture are justified in dominating national affairs by force if necessary, because of the very fact that they are superior.

12 Because many of the minor political parties merely confuse national issues, all political parties except the two major ones should be abolished.

13 The right to vote should be restricted to those individuals who have a specified amount of private property and therefore have a direct concern in the welfare of the country.

14 A large percent of the taxes which citizens pay is wasted in an effort to educate individuals who are not capable or worthy of being educated.

15 The right of the working classes to call a general strike should be abolished because it is a potential threat to democracy and is not in the general interest of society.

† The same response alternatives are used with all items.
* These items are negative and should be reversed for purposes of scoring.

Reprinted with permission from Edwards, A. L. Unlabelled fascist attitudes. *J. abnorm. soc. Psychol.*, 1941, 36 575–582.

16 Patriotism and loyalty to one's country are more important than one's intellectual convictions and should have precedence over them.
17 A standing army of 2,000,000 men or over is necessary for our national defense at all times.
18 Government should attempt to persuade people to have more children and if necessary restrict birth control information for the benefit of our national defense.
19 In the national interest, private schools should either be abolished or restricted in their teachings so that the control of education is largely in the hands of the federal government.
20 Regardless of who our next president is, he must be a strong intelligent man and be given full power to run things in the interest of the people.
21 Certain religious sects whose beliefs do not permit them to salute the flag, should either be forced to conform or else be abolished.
22 There will always be superior and inferior races in the world and in the interests of all concerned it is best that the superior continue to dominate the inferior.
23 Our foreign markets are a vital necessity to our prosperity and must be protected at all costs.
24 Women have more ability and are more efficient at tasks around the home and as a result their rightful place is in the home and not in the business world.
25 Minor forms of military training such as drill, marching, and simple commands should be made a part of the elementary school educational program.
26 Academic freedom is all right in principle, but instructors in high schools and colleges should not be allowed to express their convictions concerning their subject matter.

ATTITUDES TOWARD RELIGIOUS AND PHILOSOPHICAL SYSTEMS

The scales contained in this section include as their referents Christianity, religionism (and its opposite, humanitarianism), religious liberalism, religious ideologies, and religion as a sociological institution. Persons interested in attitudes toward such other religious referents as God and the church should see Chapter 6 and Chapter 10. There is also a scale on Sunday observance in Chapter 3, and a scale on religion and psychiatry in Chapter 4.

Religionism scale: scale I EXHIBIT 7-10

Description. This scale is one of a set of three developed by Ferguson (1939, 1940*b*, 1944*a*) and called by him the Revised Primary Social Attitudes Scale. Readers interested in the Humanitarianism Scale should see Exhibit 7-17. The Nationalism Scale is available in Chapter 5. The Religionism Scale possesses two equivalent forms each containing 25 items. To develop this scale, the author used a factor-analytic procedure, applied to the Thurstone scales measuring attitude toward the following: God, patriotism, treatment of criminals, censorship, evolution, capital punishment, birth control, law, and communism. Generally, items were selected on the basis of four criteria: (1) All items were eliminated with dichotomies between the yes-no answers (in a Thurstone response mode) more extreme than 10–90 percent; (2) items were chosen to represent equally all intervals along the attitudinal continuum from 1 to 11; (3) items possessing the highest correlations with the total score of the particular scale involved were chosen in preference to items with lower correlations; (4) all items retained significantly differentiated between the upper and lower quartiles of extreme scores.

Subjects. The total sample included 1,255 students, sampled at different times for varying purposes in groups of 185, 144, 136, and 790.

Response Mode. Subjects answer by checking one of three alternatives: agree, uncertain, disagree.

Scoring. The score is the algebraic sum of the weights, or index values, for each item endorsed as "agree." These weights were derived by reducing the item correlations with the attitude continuum to the nearest one-digit figures and then dropping the decimal point. Weights are indicated in Exhibit 7-10. Positive scores indicate acceptant attitudes toward religion and religious precepts.

Reliability. The author (1944*a*) reports equivalent-forms reliabilities of .86 and .87 for the total battery of three scales. The equivalent-forms reliability for the Religionism Scale is .90. The combined reliability estimate for the two forms is .96.

Validity. To establish the validity of the scale, responses to the scale were compared with responses to the original Thurstone scales. The estimates for the Religionism Scale are: Form A, .89; Form B, .91; combined A and B, .92. Dreger (1958) reports correlations from .75 to .84 between scores on the Religionism Scale and responses to certain religious items on a personal data sheet, providing further evidence of concurrent validity.

Comments. Although a great deal of work went into the construction of this scale, the author seems to have submitted Thurstone's essentially nonmonotonic items to procedures used to select monotonic items. The score on the scale is weighted with the correlation of the item with the attitude continuum, items with higher correlations being retained. As a result, these items should be the ones which are least clearly nonmonotonic. As a result of the selection of items possessing small Q values, Thurstone and his associates had previously selected those items which were presumably least monotonic. The final result should be that the items in this battery would be those that are least clearly monotonic or nonmonotonic. More importantly, they should not be expected to function as well as would items which were either monotonic or nonmonotonic. No studies exist to assess the empirical value of such a procedure, but it is clear that the procedure violates the assumptions underlying the selection of monotonic and nonmonotonic items.

EXHIBIT 7-10

RELIGIONISM SCALE: SCALE I

Put a check mark in front of each statement with which you *agree.*

Form A

Weights		
3	1	My idea of God develops with experience.
7	2	I am quite convinced of the reality of God.
−4	3	Opposition to evolution is due simply to ignorance.
6	4	The idea of God gives me a sense of security.
−5	5	The evidences of evolution are unquestionable.
6	6	I trust in God to support the right and condemn the wrong.
−4	7	Birth control increases the happiness of married life.
6	8	There is much to be said on both sides of the evolution controversy.
6	9	The idea of God means much to me.
−6	10	There is a far better way of explaining the working of the world than to assume any God.
−3	11	We simply must have birth control.
−5	12	I am beginning to think that the theory of evolution may be right.
−4	13	I haven't yet reached any definite opinion about the idea of God.
4	14	The evolutionary theory sounds logical but I don't know if it's true.
4	15	Birth control is justifiable only in cases of poverty or poor health.
7	16	I am not quite ready to accept the doctrine of evolution.
7	17	My faith in God is complete for "though he slay me, yet will I trust Him."
−3	18	Anti-evolution legislation is ridiculous in a civilized nation.
5	19	We must be cautious in accepting such a radical doctrine as evolution.
4	20	The practice of birth control evades man's duty to propagate the race.
−3	21	The ideas of God are so confusing that I do not know what to believe.
−4	22	I fluctuate between believing and denying the reality of God.
−5	23	The biological demonstrations of evolution are beyond dispute.
−4	24	There should be no restriction whatever on the distribution of birth control information.
−6	25	If the biblical accounts conflict with the findings of science, then the Bible must give way.

Form B

7	1	I have a strong desire to believe in God.
−4	2	I believe in children of choice and not of chance.
4	3	The idea of evolution is no more convincing than the account of creation given in the Bible.
7	4	It is better to believe in God than in evolution.
−3	5	Only a fool can oppose birth control.
6	6	I am thrilled in contemplation of the divine creator.

Weights		
6	7	I do not entirely understand the evolutionary theory, so I am doubtful of its truth.
−4	8	All books on biology should stress the evolutionary viewpoint.
−5	9	Although I do not believe in God, I am open minded about the mysteries of life.
4	10	Contraceptive methods injure women's health.
6	11	God is the underlying reality of life.
−6	12	No intelligent person can believe the Bible in preference to the theory of evolution.
−3	13	I do not know whether I ought to believe in God.
−4	14	Birth control has nothing to do with morality.
−6	15	The evolutionary theory is the most satisfactory explanation of life we yet have.
−6	16	I don't believe in God, but the idea has value for many people.
−6	17	The evolutionary theory is the only reasonable viewpoint of life.
7	18	The belief in God is fundamental in my life.
−5	19	Only the ignorant and the superstitious oppose evolution.
5	20	Though at times I am perplexed, I still trust in the underlying reality of God.
−4	21	It is simple minded to picture any God in control of the universe.
3	22	Birth control is necessary for women who must help earn a living.
6	23	The idea of God is the best explanation for our wonderful world.
3	24	The practice of birth control may be injurious physically, mentally or morally.
7	25	I am still somewhat hesitant about accepting the theory of evolution.

Belief pattern scale; attitude of religiosity *EXHIBIT 7-11*

Description. This is one of two scales developed by Kirkpatrick (1935, 1949) to measure religiosity and humanitarianism. The humanitarianism scale (Scale II) is in Exhibit 7-18. They are reminiscent of Ferguson's Revised Primary Social Attitudes Scale. The religiosity belief pattern scale by Kirkpatrick (1935) is composed of 69 items emphasizing the acceptance of doctrinaire statements and values. A total of 134 propositions were submitted to 11 judges for classification in one of eight categories (social, personal, etc.). They also classified the statements as being favorable or unfavorable toward religion. The items were selected from the original 134 statements on three bases: (1) Judges were in complete agreement regarding the favorableness of the item; (2) 75 percent of the judges agreed upon the category to which the item belonged; (3) 75 percent of the judges gave the same rating as to the word strength of the item.

Subjects. The sample included 468 Minneapolis residents and 11 unidentified judges.

Response Mode. In responding to the religiosity scale, persons check those propositions with which they agree.

Scoring. Endorsement of proreligion items is scored +1, and endorsement of antireligious items is scored —1. The person's score is the algebraic sum of the item scores. High scores reflect positive attitudes toward religion.

Reliability. Kirkpatrick (1949) reported a test-retest reliability coefficient of .94 for the religiosity scale.

Validity. Ratings were made by experts concerning the religiosity of various groups of religious and intellectual leaders. Schedules were filled out by such leaders to yield a known-groups form of validation. In the case of students, there was an association between their scores and their overt behavior (as reported by them). Denominational differences in scores were also interpreted by the author as suggesting validity: Mean score of 77 psychologists, —6.8; mean score of 42 conservative Catholics and Lutherans, 24.44; mean score of 52 liberal Congregational-Unitarians, 12.3 (Kirkpatrick, 1935).

As further possible evidence of concurrent validity, it is interesting that Kirkpatrick (1949) obtained negative correlations between the religiosity and humanitarianism scales on 13 out of 14 groups tested.

Comments. The religiosity scale seems satisfactory with regard to both its reliability and its validity. However, Ferguson's scale (Exhibit 7-10) measuring the same attitude may be preferred to this scale because equivalent forms are available.

EXHIBIT 7-11

BELIEF PATTERN SCALE; ATTITUDE OF RELIGIOSITY

Please check in the parenthesis those propositions with which you *agree.* Indicate your acceptance of a proposition only when you agree with it in its *entirety.*

( ) 1 The church has done as much as any existing social institution to combat modern evils.

( ) *2 Those people to whom "God has revealed Himself" have been subject to delusions.

( ) *3 The so-called spiritual experience of men cannot be distinquished from the mental and emotional, and thus there can be no transference from this world to a so-called spiritual one.

( ) 4 Immortality is certain because of Christ's sacrifice for all mankind.

( ) 5 The gift of immortality has been revealed by prophets and religious teachers.

( ) *6 As our body of scientific knowledge has increased, organized religion has steadily lost ground.

* These items are negative and are scored —1 when endorsed. All other items are scored +1 when endorsed.

( ) *7 Modern astronomy has revealed a world in which human wishes and aspirations can have little significance.

( ) *8 The belief in a God is merely another way of "explaining" phenomena in terms of the unknown.

( ) *9 The church has always had the tendency to establish antagonism toward those outside the fold.

( ) *10 No critically-minded person of the twentieth century could accept the ancient and medieval superstitions with which the modern church is largely concerned.

( ) 11 Acceptance of the God-concept furnishes us with an adequate explanation of the origin of life.

( ) 12 No scientific law has yet given a satisfactory explanation of the origin of life.

( ) 13 Since there are laws of nature, there must be a Law Giver.

( ) *14 The soul is mere supposition, having no better standing than a myth.

( ) *15 The church can do little for the individual person, since it is too much concerned with conflicting doctrine.

( ) 16 The solace one finds in the belief in some after-life aids one in obtaining an emotional adjustment in this earthly life.

( ) 17 At all times and at all places men have believed in God; such universal belief could not be based on illusion.

( ) *18 The church has claimed for itself the position of moral authority without knowledge of modern conditions.

( ) *19 The belief that "since there are laws of nature, there must be a Law Giver" is due to confused thinking.

( ) *20 The fact that as knowledge becomes greater the figure of God becomes smaller, is an indication that the God concept is due to ignorance.

( ) *21 The religious leaders of the past who spoke of retribution in a future life were subject to all the fallacious notions concerning life and death which prevailed at their time.

( ) 22 Belief in God makes life on earth worthwhile.

( ) *23 The findings of modern science leave many mysteries unsolved, but they are still incompatible with a personal God concept.

( ) *24 The orderliness of the universe is due to the working out of natural laws.

( ) *25 The notion of retribution in a future life is due to wishful thinking.

( ) 26 The church is the means by which moral leadership is still assured in the modern world.

( ) 27 It is inconceivable that what is most valuable in human life should perish at death.

( ) 28 There are many events which cannot be explained except on the basis of divine or supernatural intervention.

( ) 29 The existence of God is proven because He revealed Himself directly to the prophets described in the Old Testament.

( ) 30 All human beings need an adjustment of self to a supreme value outside of self, and faith in God provides such an adjustment.

( ) *31 The believer in a personal God is in danger of the shock of disillusionment.

( ) 32 Since science has left much unexplained concerning the origin of life, one must accept the existence of an Almighty God.

( ) 33 Organized religion has acted as a powerful agency in the development of social justice.

( ) 34 It is by means of the church that peace and good-will may replace hatred and strife throughout the world.

( ) 35 It is inconceivable that misery and suffering should exist in this world if ultimate compensation were not part of the divine plan.

( ) *36 In this world of scientific fact-finding, one who believes in a personal God must eventually suffer much emotional conflict.

( ) 37 The church is a powerful support of good citizenship and political stability.

( ) *38 The great majority of men of science do not believe in God.

( ) 39 The church, in spreading the doctrine of the brotherhood of man, has been a powerful agency in making for world peace.

( ) *40 It is inconceivable for a rational mind to believe that all the people who have lived since the beginning of time are still existing somewhere.

( ) 41 There must be life after death because the spirits of dead persons have appeared to those still alive.

( ) 42 Since Christ brought the dead to life, He can give eternal life to all who have faith.

( ) 43 There is reason to think that there is less mental disorder among people who have faith in a God who aids them in meeting the crises of life.

( ) *44 The church cannot be considered a progressive social institution since it has not renounced modern warfare.

( ) *45 Since neurology, psychology, and comparative anatomy have demonstrated the inter-dependence of the "mind" and the nervous system, therefore one cannot believe that the soul of mental self survives the disintegration of its physical basis.

( ) 46 Since the findings of modern science have left many things unexplained one must accept the concept of a God.

( ) *47 The doctrine of immortality is a fiction of the human mind.

( ) 48 The existence of God is proven by the fact that He has repeatedly revealed Himself to men on earth.

( ) 49 The church is an effective agency for organizing the social life of a community.

( ) 50 In the long run, one who believes in God leads a more satisfying life than does the skeptic.

( ) *51 The fact that a man is a church member can tell us absolutely nothing about his moral character.

( ) 52 The orderliness of the universe is the result of a divine plan.

( ) 53 The existence of God is shown by the fortunate results through approaching Him in prayer.

( ) 54 Without the church there would be a collapse of morality.

( ) *55 The fact that the church is extending its functions to include the social as well as the spiritual is an indication of its weakening control over the spiritual life of the people.

( ) *56 The church is too bound up with dogma and medieval superstition to enable it to cope with present day problems.

( ) 57 Man is a creature of faith and to live without faith in some Supreme Power is to suffer a homesickness of the soul.

( ) *58 There is no evidence in modern science that the natural universe of human destiny is affected by faith or prayer.

( ) *59 The church has acted as an obstruction to the development of social justice.

( ) 60 The belief in immortality follows from the fact that the human soul partakes of the divine.
( ) 61 Specialists in religion tend to accept the doctrine of immortality and we should rely upon their authority.
( ) 62 Human values cannot perish with the death of our physical existence.
( ) *63 Religious beliefs may furnish solace to some people vexed by troubles, but these beliefs do not furnish truthful answers to individual problems.
( ) 64 There must be life after death since otherwise man would be no more than an animal.
( ) 65 Religion with its fear-inspiring supernaturalism is responsible for a large amount of mental suffering.
( ) *66 The modern rejection of the God concept is an intellectual one.
( ) *67 The notion of immortality is unintelligible and creates more mysteries than it solves.
( ) *68 The affirmation of the belief in an after life is no proof of its existence.
( ) *69 The idea of creation out of nothing is incomprehensible.

Religious ideology scale *EXHIBIT 7-12*

Description. This scale is actually composed of three subscales: the Orthodoxy Subscale, the Fanaticism Subscale, and the Importance Subscale. The subscales possess six Likert-type items each, the total scale being 18 items. It was developed by Putney and Middleton (1961) to investigate the dimensions of religious ideologies. A fourth dimension investigated by them was that of ambivalence. It was measured by a single question asking for a Likert-type rating of the statement: "Although one is stronger than the other, there is part of me which believes in religion and part of me which does not." Items were selected through item analysis, those with low discriminatory power being discarded.

Subjects. Subjects included 1,126 students in social science courses at 13 colleges and universities located in New York, New Jersey, Pennsylvania, Florida, Georgia, and Alabama. About half of the students were in institutions in the Northeastern states and half in the Southeastern states. All were Christians.

Response Mode. Subjects respond on a modified seven-point Likert continuum of alternatives: strong disagreement, moderate disagreement, slight disagreement, no response or don't know, slight agreement, moderate agreement, and strong agreement.

Scoring. Scores for the subscales are derived as follows: For positive items, response alternatives are weighted from 7 (strong agreement) to 1 (strong disagreement). Weights for negative items (indicated in Exhibit 7-12) must be reversed. The person's score on any subscale is the sum of the weighted alternatives endorsed by him. In view of the high interrelationships between the three subscales, it would seem appropriate to derive a total scale score by summing scores on the subscale.

Reliability. The author does not report any estimate of reliability.

Validity. Subjects were classified into the categories of "skeptics" (do not believe in a personal God), "modernists" (who believe in a personal God but do not interpret the Bible literally), and "conservatives" (who believe that every word of the Bible is literally true). Contingency coefficients were obtained for these three categories for each of the subscales of fanaticism, orthodoxy, and importance and for the dimension of ambivalence as well. All values were significant at the .001 level. However, the fanaticism, orthodoxy, and importance dimensions were found to be highly positively intercorrelated (using Yule's Q as a measure of association), leading to a question of whether they are measuring separate dimensions of the attitude. The dimension of ambivalence was found to be significantly and negatively related to the other three dimensions. Regarding construct validity, the following other information is relevant: Highly orthodox persons tended to be authoritarian, to be conservative in political and economic questions, and not to acknowledge any ambivalence in their faith.

Comments. This scale, like the foregoing ones, seems to measure the degree to which individuals accept doctrinaire values and ideologies. It seems doubtful that the separate subscales are actually measuring different things. Further work is required to assess the merit of considering the subscale scores separately. Although the scale seems valid for measurement of conservative attitude toward religion, the lack of reliability estimates detracts from its value.

EXHIBIT 7-12

RELIGIOUS IDEOLOGY SCALE

The authors state that they used no special instructions. The following instructions are suggested by the form of the response mode:

Please read the following statements carefully, and then indicate your agreement according to the following conventions:

Strong Agreement	7
Moderate Agreement	6
Slight Agreement	5
No Response	4
Slight Disagreement	3
Moderate Disagreement	2
Strong Disagreement	1

Orthodoxy Subscale:

1 I believe that there is a physical Hell where men are punished after death for the sins of their lives.

2 I believe there is a supernatural being, the Devil, who continually tries to lead men into sin.

3 To me the most important work of the church is the saving of souls.
4 I believe that there is a life after death.
5 I believe that there is a Divine plan and purpose for every living person and thing.
*6 The only benefit one receives from prayer is psychological.

Fanaticism Subscale:

1 I have a duty to help those who are confused about religion.
2 Even though it may create some unpleasant situations, it is important to help people become enlightened about religion.
*3 There is no point in arguing about religion because there is little chance of changing other people's minds.
*4 It doesn't really matter what an individual believes about religion as long as he is happy with it.
5 I believe the world would really be a better place if more people held the views about religion which I hold.
6 I believe the world's problems are seriously aggravated by the fact that so many people are misguided about religion.

Importance Subscale:

1 My ideas about religion are one of the more important parts of my philosophy of life.
2 I find that my ideas on religion have a considerable influence on my views in other areas.
3 Believing as I do about religion is very important to being the kind of person I want to be.
4 If my ideas about religion were different, I believe that my way of life would be very different.
*5 Religion is a subject in which I am not particularly interested.
6 I very often think about matters relating to religion.

* These items are negative and must be reversed for purposes of scoring.

The religious attitude inventory EXHIBIT 7-13

Description. This is a 50-item, Likert-type scale developed by Ausubel and Schpoont (1957). It measures attitudes toward the following religious referents: religious doctrine, immortality, God, and the church. It was developed to study accuracy of perception of persons holding extreme versus neutral views on a relevant topic. In the composition of the scale, 159 statements were collected and administered to subjects, and the mean item rating was determined. The final scale was constructed by choosing the 25 items at each extreme of the distribution of item values.

Subjects. The sample included 38 graduate students in education, at the University of Illinois; 95 freshmen and sophomores (82 of whom were women) in the College of Education and in the Liberal Arts College at the University of Illinois. The mean age of the latter group of subjects was 20.5 years.

Response Mode. Subjects respond to a modified set of Likert alternatives, on a five-point scale: strongly agree, tend to agree more than disagree, neither agree nor disagree, tend to disagree more than agree, and strongly disagree.

Scoring. The response alternatives for positive (proreligious) items are weighted from 5 (strongly agree) to 1 (strongly disagree). Weights for alternatives of the negative (antireligious) items must be reversed. The person's score is the sum of the weighted alternatives endorsed by him. High scores indicate acceptance of religion and religious doctrine.

Reliability. The authors report a split-half reliability coefficient (corrected) of .97, based on an N of 95.

Validity. Items were chosen for their ability to discriminate extreme scorers. Further, on the responses of the 95 undergraduates, the authors tested the significance of the difference between mean scores of the high, middle, and low groups of subjects and found them significant at the .01 level. The scale apparently possesses content validity.

Comments. This seems to be a reliable scale for measurement of attitude toward religion and its teachings, but evidence of validity is limited. Test-retest reliability estimates would be a valuable addition to the supportive information on the scale.

EXHIBIT 7-13

THE RELIGIOUS ATTITUDE INVENTORY

Respond to each of these items on a 1 to 5 scale:

1 Means that you **strongly agree** with a given statement.
2 Means that you **tend to agree more than disagree** with a given statement.
3 Means that you **neither agree nor disagree** with a given statement.
4 Means that you **tend to disagree more than agree** with a given statement.
5 Means that you **strongly disagree** with a given statement.

1 God made everything, the stars, the animals, and the flowers.
2 The gift of immortality has been revealed by prophets and religious teachers.
*3 The church has acted as an obstruction to the development of social justice.
4 There are many events which cannot be explained except on the basis of divine or supernatural intervention.
*5 The church is a monument to human ignorance.
*6 The idea of God is useless.
7 God hears and answers one's prayers.
*8 The soul is mere supposition, having no better standing than a myth.

* These items are negative, and the weights for their alternatives must be reversed for purposes of scoring.

Reference: D. P. Ausubel and S. H. Schpoont. Prediction of group opinion as a function of extremeness of predictor attitudes. *J. soc. Psychol.*, 1957, 46, 19–29. Items obtained from authors and published with their permission.

*9 The universe is merely a machine. Man and nature are creatures of cause and effect. All notions of a Diety as intelligent Being or as a "spiritual force" are fictions, and prayer is a useless superstition.
10 It is by means of the church that peace and good-will may replace hatred and strife throughout the world.
11 God created man separate and distinct from the animals.
*12 The church is a harmful institution, breeding narrow-mindedness, fanaticism, and intolerance.
13 Christ, as the Gospels state, should be regarded as divine, as the human incarnation of God.
*14 There is no evidence in modern science that the natural universe of human destiny is affected by faith or prayer.
*15 The notion of retribution in a future life is due to wishful thinking.
*16 The good done by the church is not worth the money and energy spent on it.
17 The orderliness of the universe is the result of a divine plan.
*18 The church is a stronghold of much that is unwholesome and dangerous to human welfare. It fosters intolerance, bigotry, and ignorance.
19 The existence of God is proven because He revealed Himself directly to the prophets described in the Old Testament.
20 The church is the greatest influence for good government and right living.
*21 God is only a figment of one's imagination.
22 Man is a creature of faith and to live without faith in some Supreme Power is to suffer a homesickness of the soul.
23 God will, depending on how we behave on earth, reward or punish us in the world to come.
*24 People who advocate Sunday observance are religious fanatics.
*25 It is simple-minded to picture any God in control of the universe.
26 The church is the greatest agency for the uplift of the world.
*27 The idea of God is mere superstition.
28 The world was created in six solar days.
*29 The idea of God is unnecessary in our enlightened age.
30 God has good reason for everything that happens to us, even though we cannot understand it sometimes.
31 The soul lives on after the body dies.
32 The existence of God is shown by the fortunate results through approaching Him in prayer.
*33 The country would be better off if the churches were closed and the ministers were set to some useful work.
*34 The so-called spiritual experience of men cannot be distinguished from the mental and emotional, and thus there can be no transference from this world to a so-called spiritual one.
35 The first writing of the Bible was done under the guidance of God.
*36 The church is hundreds of years behind the times and can not make a dent on modern life.
37 Belief in God makes life on earth worthwhile.
38 God cares whether we repent or not.
*39 Man cannot be honest in his thinking and endorse what the church teaches.
*40 There is no life after death.
41 Since Christ brought the dead to life, He can give eternal life to all who have faith.
*42 The church represents shallowness, hypocrisy and prejudice.
43 There is an infinitely wise, omnipotent creator of the universe, whose protection and favor may be supplicated through worship and prayer.

*44 The paternal and benevolent attitude of the church is quite distasteful to a mature person.
*45 The church deals in platitudes and is afraid to follow the logic of truth.
46 God protects from harm all those who really trust him.
47 Immortality is certain because of Christ's sacrifice for all mankind.
*48 There is a far better way of explaining the working of the world than to assume any God.
*49 It seems absurd for a thinking man to be interested in the church.
50 The idea of God is the best explanation for our wonderful world.

The religion scale EXHIBIT 7-14

Description. This is a 25-item, Likert-type scale developed by Bardis (1961). It measures positivity of attitude toward religious faith and other religious referents. The author secured 200 brief statements dealing with various religious beliefs and practices. Most of these were taken from publications on the subject of religion; the rest were supplied by male and female adolescents and adults representing different faiths. In a pretest using 500 Midwestern Jews and Christians, only 46 of the items seemed to discriminate. These 46 items were given to a similar group of 100 Midwesterners. The 25 items discriminating the extremes of the score distribution in this sample were selected for the final scale.

Subjects. Subjects included 324 members of various religious faiths, ministerial students, agnostics, and college students.

Response Mode. Subjects respond on a Likert continuum: strongly disagree, disagree, undecided, agree, and strongly agree.

Scoring. Response alternatives to all items are weighted from 5 (strongly agree) to 1 (strongly disagree). There are no negative items to be reversed. The person's score is the sum of the weighted alternatives endorsed by him. High scores indicate positive attitudes toward religion.

Reliability. Bardis (1961) reports a split-half reliability of .90, based upon an N of 130. He also reports test-retest reliabilities of .94 and .84 based upon a sample of 52 subjects (time interval unspecified).

Validity. The scale is reported by the author to differentiate between agnostics and religious persons and between ministerial and nonministerial students. The items were selected to discriminate between high and low scorers. The items sample the content domain of acceptance of religious teachings and positively valuing religion. The large number of items collected originally and the variety of sources should provide a degree of content validity.

Comments. A major difficulty with the scale is the fact that all items are in the same direction. Since the scale contains no negatively phrased items, it allows for the operation of response sets, thereby reducing the validity of measurement. Otherwise, the scale seems to be a relatively valid and reliable way of measuring attitude toward the value of and acceptance of a religious way of life.

EXHIBIT 7-14

THE RELIGION SCALE

Below is a list of issues concerning religion. Please read *all* statements very *carefully* and respond to *all* of them on the basis of *your own true* beliefs *without* consulting any other persons. Do this by reading each statement and then writing, in the space provided at its left, *only one* of the following numbers: 0, 1, 2, 3, 4. The meaning of these figures is:

0: Strongly Disagree
1: Disagree
2: Undecided
3: Agree
4: Strongly Agree

_____ 1 A sound religious faith is the best thing in life.
_____ 2 Every school should encourage its students to attend church.
_____ 3 People should defend their religion above all other things.
_____ 4 People should attend church once a week if possible.
_____ 5 Belief in God makes life more meaningful.
_____ 6 Every person should give 10 percent of his income to his church.
_____ 7 All people are God's children.
_____ 8 People attending church regularly develop a sound philosophy of life.
_____ 9 We should always love our enemies.
_____ 10 God rewards those who live religiously.
_____ 11 Prayer can solve many problems.
_____ 12 Every school should have chapel services for its students.
_____ 13 There is life after death.
_____ 14 People should read the Scriptures at least once a day.
_____ 15 Teachers should stress religious ideals in class.
_____ 16 Young people should attend Sunday School regularly.
_____ 17 People should pray at least once a day.
_____ 18 A religious wedding ceremony is better than a civil one.
_____ 19 Religious people should try to spread the teachings of the Scriptures.
_____ 20 People should say grace at all meals.
_____ 21 When a person is planning to be married, he should consult his minister, priest, or rabbi.
_____ 22 Delinquency is less common among young people attending church regularly.
_____ 23 What is moral today will always be moral.
_____ 24 Children should be brought up religiously.
_____ 25 Every person should participate in at least one church activity.

Reference: P. D. Bardis. A Religion Scale. *Soc. Sci.*, **1961, 36, 120–123. Items obtained from the author and published with his permission.**

Religious belief scale EXHIBIT 7-15

Description. This 41-item scale was developed by Martin and Nichols (1962) to test certain personality and demographic correlates of religiosity. Content of the items centers around belief in the Bible, in the efficacy of prayer, in an afterlife, in a personal God, and in the necessity of church and religion for a good life. In short, it measures acceptance of religious teachings and valuing religion positively. The 41 items for the scale were selected from 50 such items by item analysis. The original 50 items were taken for the most part from religious belief scales used by other authors.

Subjects. The sample consisted of 59 male and 104 female undergraduate students.

Response Mode. Subjects respond "true" or "false" to each item on a separate answer sheet.

Scoring. Nichols (private communication, 1965) states that subjects receive 1 point for each positive item that they mark as "true," and 1 point for each negative item that they mark as "false." The person's score is the sum of the points received. Negative items are indicated by an asterisk in Exhibit 7-15. High scores reflect acceptance of religion and religious teachings.

Reliability. The authors (Martin and Nichols, 1962) reported a Kuder-Richardson reliability estimate of .95, based on a sample of 83 persons.

Validity. Predicted personality and demographic characteristics did not demonstrate significant correlations with the scale scores, detracting from its construct validity. Significant correlations were obtained, but do not present an interpretable picture. Content validity of this scale seems somewhat restricted in comparison with other scales in this section.

Comments. Although the authors performed an item analysis which would be appropriate for selection of monotonic items, many of these items read nonmonotonically. Also, the use of the true-false alternatives would seem to be more appropriate for point scale items. Nevertheless, the reliability estimate provided by the authors is strikingly high. Evidence for the validity of this scale is very limited.

EXHIBIT 7-15

RELIGIOUS BELIEF SCALE

This booklet contains a series of statements. Read each one, decide how you feel about it, and then mark your answer on the special answer sheet. MAKE NO MARKS ON THE TEST BOOKLET. If you *agree* with a statement or feel that it is true about you or true to the best of

Reference: C. Martin and R. C. Nichols. Personality and religious belief. *J. soc. Psychol.*, 1962, 56, 3–8. Items obtained from authors and published with their permission.

your knowledge, answer TRUE. If you *disagree* with a statement, or feel that it is not true about you, or not true to the best of your knowledge, answer FALSE. In marking your answers on the answer sheet, make sure that the number of the statement is the same as the number on the answer sheet. Be sure to answer either TRUE or FALSE for every statement, even if you have to guess at some.

1 Religious faith is better than logic for solving life's important problems.
*2 I don't think it makes any difference if one is a Christian so long as he has good will for others.
3 I often think that I couldn't do without my religion.
4 I believe the Bible is the inspired Word of God.
*5 I think there were many men in history as great as Jesus.
6 God is constantly with us.
*7 Christ's simple message of concern for your fellow man has been twisted by superstitious mysticism.
8 I attend church to worship God with devotion and to gain guidance for everyday life.
*9 A person can be happy and enjoy life without believing in God.
10 I believe that eternal life is a gift of God to those who believe in Jesus Christ as Savior and Lord.
*11 Man can solve all his important problems without help from a Supreme Being.
12 It is through the righteousness of Jesus Christ and not because of our own works that we are made righteous before God.
*13 I don't think prayers go above the ceiling of the room in which they are uttered.
14 I am sometimes very conscious of the presence of God.
*15 "God" is an abstract concept roughly equivalent to the concept "Nature."
*16 I think that the Bible is full of errors, misconceptions, and contradictions.
17 If I were without my religion and my understanding of God, I would have little left in life.
18 I think God is revealed in every person who feels and acts unselfishly.
19 I believe that man working and thinking together can build a just society without superhuman help.
20 I believe that God exists as Father, Son, and Holy Spirit.
*21 The Bible in many ways has held back and retarded human progress.
22 I think of God as present wherever there is genuine beauty.
*23 I am not a religious person.
*24 Science makes me doubt that man has a soul.
25 When in doubt, it is best to stop and ask God what to do.
*26 Christ was not divine but his teachings and the example set by his life are important.
27 I believe that following the gospel of Christ is the only way for mankind to be saved.
28 God exists in all of us.
29 I think that God's purposes are best shown by Christ.
30 God created man separate and distinct from animals.
*31 I can take religion or leave it.
32 I think that Jesus was born of a Virgin.

* These items are negative and must be reversed for purposes of scoring.

*33 I think that God may **possibly** have created the world, but he does not show Himself or interfere in it today.
*34 I think there is no life after death.
*35 As science advances, religion will fade out in importance and eventually no religion will be needed.
36 God is very real to me.
*37 A person should follow his own conscience—not prayer—in deciding right and wrong.
38 I believe there is a Heaven and a Hell.
39 Because of His presence we can know that God exists.
40 Religion gives meaning to my life.
*41 I don't believe that history reveals the working out of God's plan.

A survey of attitudes toward religion and philosophy of life EXHIBIT 7-16

Description. This is a battery of seven scales developed by Funk (1958) to study the relation of anxiety to religious attitudes. Funk developed six of the scales and used as the seventh an adapted version of the Myers Orthodoxy Scale. The total battery is composed of 113 items. Items for all scales, except the Religious Attitude Change Scale, were chosen on the basis of their ability to discriminate high and low scorers. All seven scales will be described together and are presented in Exhibit 7-16 as Funk (1958) presented them. The battery is composed of scales measuring the following: religious conflict, orthodoxy, philosophy of life, religious tranquility, religious solace, hostility to the church, and religious attitude change.

The Religious Conflict Scale is a 22-item scale designed to measure "simultaneous tendencies to react in opposing and incompatible ways to the same religious attitude object" (Funk, 1958, p. 240).

The Religious Orthodoxy Scale is composed of nine items. *Orthodoxy* was defined by the author as the tendency to accept the teachings of religious authorities and to conform to prescribed religious practices.

The Philosophy of Life Scale is a five-item scale. Regarding the scale, Funk states: "A philosophy of life is an integrated system of meanings and purposes which relates the individual's goals to the goals of humanity and the wider structure of the universe. Although religion may form the basis of a philosophy of life, a religious value system has a different meaning than does a nonreligious code of ethics. The purpose of this scale was to isolate a group of subjects for whom a philosophy of life is a substitute for religion. Consequently, the five items contain a philosophical viewpoint with a rejection of religious beliefs" (Funk, 1958, p. 241).

The Religious Tranquility Scale is a six-item scale. The author states, "Religious tranquility is an arbitrary term, characterizing the attitude of those who see religion, not as a compensation, but as an aid to happiness and favorable socio-psychological adjustment" (Funk, 1958, p. 242).

In brief, this scale is considered by her to measure a psychologically healthy acceptance of religion.

The Religious Solace Scale is composed of seven items. The author defines religious solace as the use of religion as a means of compensating for the unhappiness and disappointments of life. As such, it constitutes a defense mechanism which, when used to excess, reflects maladjustment. The author seems to consider that the attitude is maladjustive, or at least less adjustive than the attitude measured by her scale of religious tranquility.

The Hostility to the Church Scale is composed of seven items. The author states that hostility to religion is an affectively toned predisposition to react with aggression or withdrawal toward religious attitude objects. The hostility scale contains items expressing negative and indifferent attitudes toward religion and the church.

The Religious Attitude Change Scale contains 10 multiple-choice items designed to measure stability or instability of religious beliefs since college entrance and to measure the change in subjects' attitudes toward 10 traditional religious concepts.

Subjects. The subjects were 255 students in an introductory psychology course at a Midwestern university.

Response Mode. Subjects respond to each item of the Religious Attitude Change Scale by endorsing one of three alternatives: the same (S), partly different (P), and very different (D). On all other scales, the subject responds "true" or "false" or, for multiple-choice items, chooses among alternatives.

Scoring. Except for the Religious Attitude Change Scale, all items are weighted either 1 or 2. These weights are indicated in Exhibit 7-16. The person's score is the sum of the weighted alternatives endorsed by him as "true" on any one scale. For the Religious Attitude Change Scale, the alternatives are weighted from 2 (very different) to 0 (the same). High scores on the Religious Conflict Scale indicate an ambivalent attitude toward religion. A low score on the Religious Attitude Change Scale indicates a stable attitude toward religion. Acceptance of religious teaching, substitution of a philosophy of life for religion, and hostility to the church are reflected by high scores on the Religious Orthodoxy Scale, the Philosophy of Life Scale, and the Hostility to the Church Scale, respectively. A high score on the Religious Tranquility Scale is taken as reflecting a healthy attitude toward religion, and a high score on the Religious Solace Scale is considered indicative of an unhealthy attitude toward religion.

Reliability. Based on a sample of 31 persons and a three-week test interval Funk (private communication, 1958) reported the following test-retest reliability estimates for these scales: the Religious Conflict Scale, .72 (rank order R) and .84 (product moment r); the Philosophy of Life Scale, .69 (R) and .81 (r); the Hostility to the Church Scale, .84 (R) and .88 (r); the Religious Tranquility Scale, .78 (R) and .84 (r); the Orthodoxy Scale, .95 (R) and .95 (r); the Religious Solace Scale, .87

(*R*) and .87 (*r*); the Religious Attitude Change Scale, .92 (*R*) and .90 (*r*).

Validity. The author (Funk, undated mimeograph) reported a highly significant positive correlation between scores on the Taylor Manifest Anxiety Scale and the Religious Conflict Scale, giving it a degree of construct validity. The scale seems to have fair content validity.

Regarding the Religious Orthodoxy Scale, the content domain is sufficiently restricted to produce fairly good content validity even with so few items. One problem with its content is that items number 98 and 100, which question frequency of church attendance and belief that prayer is answered, do not allow for a response of "never" or "seldom." The fact that scores on the Religious Orthodoxy Scale are negatively correlated with scores on the Religious Conflict Scale gives this scale a degree of construct validity.

Regarding the Philosophy of Life Scale, the content domain is defined so as to make it difficult to assess content validity. Little other evidence of validity is available for this scale.

As defined by the author, the items in the Religious Tranquility Scale seem to have good content validity. No other evidence of validity is available. It is difficult to discriminate the items of the Religious Solace Scale from those of the Religious Tranquility Scale, and the constructs underlying these two scales are not necessarily discrete; that is, compensation may be a healthy mechanism under certain circumstances. No evidence is available to indicate the degree to which this pair of scales is measuring different dimensions of attitude toward religion.

Most of the items in the Hostility to the Church Scale refer to religion generally. Thus, the scale seems to lack content validity as it is presently labelled. It might better be titled Hostility toward Religion.

There are two problems with regard to the validity of the Religious Attitude Change Scale, as compared with other scales in this battery. First, there is no indication of the direction of change in the score. Although subjects indicate whether their beliefs are the same or different than they were upon entrance into college, there is no indication of their nature upon entry. Second, the concept of content validity (difficult as it is to apply to statements) is extremely difficult to apply to a list of concepts (frequently single nouns), as in this scale. One suspects that these single words and phrases mean different things to different subjects, increasing the variance in the meaning of any response and reducing the validity of the instrument.

Comments. First, it should be pointed out that these scales were parts of a total battery by Funk and were administered together. Although presented separately in Exhibit 7-16, probably no one of them could be used with great success by itself. If they are used outside the context of the battery, their functional characteristics should be reassessed.

The rationale upon which the Religious Conflict Scale was constructed is somewhat different from the usual attitude scale rationale. The fact that conflict as measured by this scale correlates with anxiety as measured by the Taylor Manifest Anxiety Scale brings up the question of whether this conflict is specific to religion. It is conceivable that persons scoring high on this scale would have a general tendency to give conflicting and contradictory answers to any referent. Is it measuring religious conflict or the diffuse effects of anxiety?

The Religious Orthodoxy Scale seems to be at least minimally valid and reliable for measuring attitudes toward orthodoxy (in the form of acceptance of religious teachings). The merit of the scale is increased by the specificity with which the author identifies the content domain being sampled.

The Philosophy of Life Scale and the Religious Solace Scale are the weaker scales in this battery with regard to validity. Increasing the number of items in the Philosophy of Life Scale would probably improve its reliability. To add items to the scale, however, better definition of the content domain would be necessary.

The Religious Tranquility Scale seems satisfactorily reliable, but more evidence of its validity would be required to enhance its value as a tool. Knowledge of the intercorrelations between these scales would be of great value in assessing the degree to which different attitudes are being measured.

The Religious Solace Scale is satisfactory with regard to reliability. Further information is required for adequate use of both this scale and the Religious Tranquility Scale.

With regard to the Hostility toward the Church Scale, unless it is demonstrated that the scale measures hostility toward the church, it might be better to consider it a measure of negative attitude toward religion generally. Of course, it is to be expected that there would be a positive correlation between hostility toward the church and negative attitude toward religion.

The Religious Attitude Change Scale is the weakest of the battery in terms of its conceptualization. Unless the direction of change is established and the commonality of meaning of terms can be demonstrated, the use of the scale becomes an exercise in semantics. There is the further problem of relying upon the self-report of the subject regarding the nature of his attitudes upon admission to school. The score is better interpreted as a reflection of the degree to which the individual *feels* that he has changed his attitudes.

EXHIBIT 7-16

A SURVEY OF ATTITUDES TOWARD RELIGION AND PHILOSOPHY OF LIFE

This inventory consists of numbered statements. Read each statement and decide whether it is *true as applied to you* or *false as applied to you.*

If the question is multiple choice, blacken in the space corresponding to your choice.

You are to mark your answers on the answer sheet you have. If a statement is TRUE OR MOSTLY TRUE, as applied to you, blacken between the lines in the column headed T. If a statement is FALSE OR NOT USUALLY TRUE, as applied to you, blacken between the lines in the column headed F.

Religious Conflict Scale

Original Item Number	
1	I cannot decide what to believe about religion.
10	I sometimes wonder just what life is all about and why we are here.
12	I am actively trying to decide by reading or other means, what the truth is about religion.
14	At times I have felt guilty because of my religious upbringing.
20	I sometimes feel disloyal to my parents because I cannot entirely accept their religious beliefs.
24	I wish I was perfectly sure of my belief in God.
26	I am not as strict in my religious practices as I feel I should be.
28	My church is too strict.
38	There are too many things about religion I don't understand.
42	I am in danger of losing my faith.
44	Sometimes I feel guilty because of my lack of faith.
46	Education has led me to question some teachings of my church.
50	Sometimes I believe in Hell and sometimes I don't.
56	I wish I could be sure my religious beliefs are correct.
60	Contradictory religious ideas make one wonder which ones to accept.
64	I feel that I shouldn't question my religion, but I sometimes do, anyway.
66	I feel that I should be more religious than I am.
68	I might be happier if I did not believe in my religion.
72	I wish I did not believe in Hell, but I do.
76	I sometimes wonder why God lets terrible things happen to people.
84	It is hard to reconcile science with religion.
86	Although basically I believe in my religion, my faith often wavers.

The Orthodoxy Scale

1	(a) I believe in the basic teachings of my church and attend regularly.
4	I believe firmly in the teachings of my church.
6	I never doubted the teachings of the church.
90	I believe that religious faith is better than logic for solving life's important problems.
92	I believe that our fate in the hereafter depends on how we behave on earth.
94	I believe God knows our every thought and movement.
96	I believe God controls everything that happens everywhere.
98	I think my prayers are answered *(a) Always (b) Sometimes
100	I attend church *(a) Once a week or more (b) Once a month or more

* These items are assigned a weight of 2 if endorsed. All other items are assigned a weight of 1 when endorsed, except on the Religious Attitude Change Scale. On this scale, the alternatives are weighted as follows: S, 0; P, 1; D, 2.

Philosophy of Life Scale

Number

1 (d) I do not believe in any particular religion; instead, I have a philosophy of life.
8 Although at one time I believed in a religion, I now believe in a code of ethics.
62 If you are a strong person, you do not need religion.
82 Promoting a better world is more important to me than religion is.
88 We make our own heaven or hell here on earth.

The Religious Tranquility Scale

30 Religion has brought me peace of mind.
32 Religion's chief purpose is to make people happy.
40 Religion makes me feel safe and secure.
70 Religion helps me to be a better person.
74 I feel secure in the knowledge that God is always with me.
80 I believe in a merciful God, not a punishing one.

Religious Solace Scale

16 Religion helps me when I feel blue.
18 Some unhappy experiences have made me turn to God for help.
22 Sometimes religion is the only thing we can rely on.
34 If I were to lose my belief in God, there would be little comfort left.
36 I feel a strong need to believe in God.
52 You can always turn to God when you are in trouble.
78 At times only my belief in God has prevented me from feeling hopeless.

Hostility to the Church Scale

*1 I believe that religion is of little use in present-day society.
2 I am indifferent to the subject of religion.
48 I have little use for religion.
54 Religion has not kept pace with the times.
58 Religion has too often been used to promote prejudice.
†62 If you are a strong person, you do not need religion.
‡82 Promoting a better world is more important to me than religion is.

Religious Attitude Change Scale

(Here are a number of beliefs. Please indicate, by checking the appropriate column, whether your attitude toward each is the same (S), partly different (P) or very different (D) than it was when you entered college.)

Item No.	Item	*S	P	D
104	The Church.	______	______	______
105	A personal God.	______	______	______
106	The immortality of the soul.	______	______	______
107	Hell.	______	______	______
108	Heaven.	______	______	______

† Dropped from the Hostility to the Church Scale after item analysis.
‡ This item also contributed to the Philosophy of Life Scale score.

Item No.	Item	*S	P	D
109	Adam and Eve.	____	____	____
110	Angels.	____	____	____
111	The divine inspiration of the Bible.	____	____	____
112	The power of prayer.	____	____	____
113	The divine authority of the Church.	____	____	____

Humanitarianism scale: scale II EXHIBIT 7-17

Description. This scale is one of a set of three developed by Ferguson (1939, 1940*b*, 1944*a*) and called by him the Revised Primary Social Attitudes Scale. Readers interested in the Religionism Scale should see Exhibit 7-10. The third scale, the Nationalism Scale, is available in Chapter 5. The Humanitarianism Scale possesses two equivalent forms, each containing 25 items. To develop this scale, the author used a factor-analytic procedure, applied to the Thurstone scales measuring attitudes toward the following: God, patriotism, treatment of criminals, censorship, evolution, capital punishment, birth control, law, and communism. Generally, items were selected on the basis of four criteria: (1) All items were eliminated with dichotomies between the yes-no answers (in a Thrustone response mode) more extreme than 10–90 percent; (2) items were chosen to represent equally all intervals along the attitudinal continuum from 1 to 11; (3) items possessing the highest correlations with the total score of the particular scale involved were chosen in preference to items with lower correlations; (4) all items retained differentiated significantly between the upper and lower quartiles of scale scores.

Subjects. The total sample included 1,255 students, sampled at different times for varying purposes in groups ranging in size from 185 to 790.

Response Mode. Subjects answer by checking one of three alternatives: agree, uncertain, disagree.

Scoring. The subject's score is the algebraic sum of the weights for all items endorsed as "agree." These weights were derived by reducing the item correlations with the attitude continuum to the nearest one-digit figures and then dropping the decimal point. Weights are indicated in Exhibit 7-17. Positive scores indicate acceptant attitudes toward a philosophy of humanitarianism.

Reliability. The author (Ferguson 1944*a*) reported equivalent-forms reliabilities of .86 and .87 for the total battery of three scales. For the Humanitarianism Scale, the author reports an equivalent-forms reliability estimate of .85. The combined reliability estimate for the two forms is .92.

Validity. To establish the validity of the scale, responses to the scale were compared with responses to the original Thurstone scales. The validity estimates for the Humanitarianism Scale are Form A, .94; Form B, .88; combined Forms A and B, .92.

Comments. This scale seems reasonably reliable for measurement of acceptant attitudes toward a philosophy of humanitarianism. Further studies of its validity would be helpful. It is to be expected that positive attitudes as measured by this scale would be negatively correlated with attitudes toward religion as measured by Scale I. For further comments on the use of an item analysis with nonmonotonic items, see the comments section under the Religionism Scale (Exhibit 7-10).

EXHIBIT 7-17

HUMANITARIANISM SCALE: SCALE II

Check each statement with which you agree.

Form A

Weights		
−3	1	War is a futile struggle in self-destruction.
−5	2	All criminals are victims of circumstances and deserve to be helped.
4	3	Capital punishment is a very definite deterrent to major crimes.
4	4	One way to deter men from crime is to make them suffer.
−2	5	War is hardly necessary in the modern world.
−7	6	Society can deal with crime effectively without resorting to capital punishment.
−4	7	Only humane treatment can cure criminals.
−4	8	I don't believe in capital punishment but I'm not sure it isn't necessary.
−2	9	There is no conceivable justification for war.
−4	10	Correction is civilized; punishment is brutal.
4	11	Justice demands the punishment of criminals.
6	12	Capital punishment may be wrong but it is the best preventive to crime.
−4	13	Correction is more effective than punishment in preventing crime.
2	14	Under some conditions, war is necessary to maintain justice.
5	15	Capital punishment should apply to other than murder cases.
4	16	I think capital punishment is necessary but I wish it were not.
2	17	There are some arguments in favor of war.
6	18	Capital punishment is the only adequate punishment for murder.
7	19	Capital punishment gives the criminal what he deserves.
−5	20	No thinking individual can believe in capital punishment as a method of preventing crime.
2	21	On the whole, wars do the world some good.
5	22	Until we find a more civilized way to prevent crime we must have capital punishment.
2	23	It is hard to decide whether wars do more harm than good.
−3	24	Capital punishment is the most hideous practice of our time.
−5	25	Capital punishment has never been effective in preventing crime.

Form B

Weights		
−3	**1**	Harsh imprisonment merely embitters a criminal.
−2	**2**	War is an international catastrophe.
5	**3**	Any person, man or woman, young or old, who commits murder, should pay with his own life.
−5	**4**	Capital punishment is not an effective deterrent to crime.
−3	**5**	War should be avoided at any cost.
7	**6**	We must have capital punishment for some crimes.
2	**7**	Peace and war are both essential to progress.
5	**8**	The death penalty should be given for major crimes.
4	**9**	Criminals must be punished.
5	**10**	Capital punishment is very undesirable but it is essential for the safety of the group.
3	**11**	Another war would be terrible but it might be worth the price.
−4	**12**	I don't believe in capital punishment but I'm not sure it isn't necessary.
2	**13**	War has some benefits; but it's a big price to pay for them.
−3	**14**	Petty offenders can be reformed without punishment.
−7	**15**	Criminals are pathological people who should be corrected, not executed.
−7	**16**	Capital punishment cannot be regarded as a sane method of dealing with crime.
2	**17**	Although war is terrible it has some value.
6	**18**	Capital punishment is justified because it does act as a deterrent to crime.
−6	**19**	The state cannot teach the sacredness of human life by destroying it.
2	**20**	War is sometimes necessary because right is more important than peace.
6	**21**	Capital punishment is good because it deters others from crime.
3	**22**	Failure to punish the criminal encourages crime.
−2	**23**	Every last one of us should refuse to take part in any way in any war.
−4	**24**	Life imprisonment is more effective than capital punishment.
−3	**25**	The death of a comrade in prison embitters all the inmates against the state.

Belief pattern scale; attitude of humanitarianism *EXHIBIT 7-18*

Description. This is one of two scales developed by Kirkpatrick (1935, 1949) to measure religiosity and humanitarianism. Readers interested in the religiosity scale should see Exhibit 7-11. The items for the humanitarianism scale (Kirkpatrick, 1949) were developed as follows: A large number of humanitarian and nonhumanitarian items were gathered and subjected to an item analysis, items being selected which differentiated between the high and low quartiles on the total score continuum. Then, 107 students classified these items as being positive, negative, or undecided with regard to humanitarianism. Items obtaining less than 70 percent agreement among these judges were dropped out. The resulting 44 items are given in Exhibit 7-18.

Subjects. The sample included 297 students, who served as judges of the items.

Response Mode. The person responds on a standard Likert-type response continuum: strongly agree, agree, undecided, disagree, and strongly disagree.

Scoring. Weights are assigned to the response alternatives for the humanitarian items from 5 (strongly agree) to 1 (strongly disagree). Weights for the nonhumanitarian items are reversed. The person's score is the sum of the weighted alternatives endorsed by him. High scores indicate positive attitudes toward a philosophy of humanitarianism.

Reliability. The test-retest reliability estimate for the humanitarianism scale is reported as being .94. The split-half reliability (corrected) is .62.

Validity. The author validated the humanitarianism scale by the known-groups method, reporting the scale to differentiate between the sexes and between religious and social action groups. As further evidence of validity, Kirkpatrick (1949) obtained negative correlations between this scale and the religiosity scale (Exhibit 7-11) on 13 out of 14 groups tested.

Comments. The humanitarianism scale is less than satisfactory with regard to its reliability and validity on two bases. First, the split-half reliability estimate is not particularly good, indicating some lack of internal consistency. Second, 18 of the 44 items in this scale are rather dated. Some are less seriously dated than are others and could be easily salvaged. Others would probably have to be dropped from the scale altogether. Those items which appear dated include at least the following: items number 2, 3, 4, 5, 7, 9, 14, 16, 18, 27, 29, 30, 31, 36, 38, 40, 41, and 42. Of course, this still leaves 26 items, which would provide a scale of greater length than many Likert-type scales. If these items are dropped, however, it would be necessary to reevaluate the characteristics of the scale. In general, the scale by Ferguson (Exhibit 7-17) measuring the same attitude is probably preferable to this one.

EXHIBIT 7-18

BELIEF PATTERN SCALE; ATTITUDE OF HUMANITARIANISM

Read each item carefully and underline the phrase that most nearly represents your own personal belief.

1 Criminals should be regarded as victims of circumstances in the same sense as sick persons are so regarded.

† Strongly Agree Agree Undecided Disagree Strongly Disagree

*2 Enemy atrocities against American war prisoners should be revenged by corresponding treatment of enemy prisoners.

3 We should be willing to accept strict food rationing in this country after the war in order to provide for victims of starvation which may develop in Germany.

*4 Unrestricted bombing of the enemy is justified as it gives them a taste of their own medicine.

5 American citizens of Japanese descent should be guaranteed civil rights in spite of risk to the war effort.

*6 There are many criminals in United States prisons who could be best controlled by physical punishment.

7 Defeated leaders in enemy countries should be merely restrained from doing further harm to the peace and happiness of the world.

*8 An American soldier who risks the lives of his comrades by failing to do his duty under fire should be shot as a cowardly deserter.

9 The economic resources of the world should be shared evenly with the people of defeated enemy countries.

*10 Victims of disaster in distant foreign countries are to a considerable extent responsible for their own plight.

11 Negroes in the United States should be given especially kindly consideration as members of an underprivileged group.

*12 Charity begins at home in the sense of upholding local, national, and religious loyalties.

13 Conscientious objectors should be regarded as sincere idealists.

*14 Captured German spies should be electrocuted as an example to other enemies of our country.

15 European refugees should be welcomed to this land of liberty even at the risk of economic competition.

*16 Nazi children taught by Hitler to worship force can be dealt with only by force.

17 Unmarried mothers should be treated as misguided and unfortunate persons in need of help.

*18 The children in enemy countries should suffer as other children have been made to suffer for the sins of their parents.

19 Prostitutes should be treated as socially maladjusted persons.

*20 No punishment is too severe for a Negro guilty of the sex killing of a white child.

21 Alcoholics and drug addicts should be regarded like the tubercular as victims of a disease.

*22 A child who steals money from his parents should be shown by punishment the sinful nature of his act.

23 A child who steals money from his parents should be given understanding help and forgiveness.

*24 Alcoholics and drug addicts should be condemned for their moral weakness.

25 A Negro guilty of sex killing of a white child should be dealt with under existing laws as a mentally abnormal person.

*26 Prostitutes deserve contempt and punishment as enemies of decent living.

27 After the war the children in enemy countries should be treated in exactly the same way as war victims in other countries.

*28 Unmarried mothers should be treated as violators of the established moral code and be made to suffer the consequences of their actions.

† The same response alternatives are used with all items.
* These items are negative and their weights must be reversed for scoring purposes.

*29 European refugees should not be permitted to menace the economic well being of our own citizens.

30 Captured German spies as servants of their country should be made harmless, but in a way that reveals the humanitarianism of the United States.

31 After the war Nazi youth should be regarded as a problem in re-education.

*32 Conscientious objectors should be made to pay a heavy price for refusal to accept the responsibility of citizenship.

33 The old custom of giving a tenth of one's income to charity, if applied, should disregard the religious beliefs of the beneficiaries.

*34 Negroes in the United States should be regarded as responsible for their difficulties in adjusting to American life.

35 Financial sacrifices should be made by American citizens to aid Hindu victims of famine in India.

*36 Punitive economic sanctions should be applied against axis powers for a long period of time after the war.

37 An American soldier who risks the lives of his comrades by going to pieces under fire should be treated as a victim of nervous instability.

*38 Responsible officials in defeated enemy countries should be made to suffer for their crimes as their innocent victims have suffered.

39 Bodily punishment should not be applied to prison inmates regardless of their behavior.

*40 American citizens of Japanese descent should be treated with all the severity necessary to further our national interests.

41 Bombing should be restricted to protect innocent persons even at the cost of some American lives.

*42 Sooner or later the German people should receive a heavy dose of the suffering they have inflicted on the helpless people of Europe.

43 Regardless of provocation we should indulge in no brutality against enemy prisoners.

*44 Criminals should be punished for their sins.

SUMMARY

This chapter is somewhat unique in that the scales possess much broader referents than is typical of attitude scales in other chapters. As a result, it is difficult to assess their content validity, and it may be expected that their reliabilities would be lowered also. Many of the scales in the chapter measure attitudes on some dimension of liberalism-conservatism (political, economic, religious, etc.). However, there does not seem to be a general factor of liberalism-conservatism which may be expected to permeate the whole of an individual's attitudinal system. Rather, as Kirkpatrick (1946) has suggested, liberalism and conservatism seem specific to the various content domains being sampled. It begins to appear that a scale measuring attitude toward *changes* of various sorts would have as much success as these more general scales. Perhaps what is being dealt with is the question of the merit and proper pace of social change.

The number of scales in the chapter has been reduced in part because of the tendency of "isms" to constitute social and international issues. Among the gaps in this area, it would seem worthwhile to have a scale measuring an attitude of sciencism (or sciolism). This seems an especially appropriate instrument for psychology, in view of the modern tendency to displace religion with science and to expect science to answer essentially philosophical questions.

CHAPTER 8

ethnic and national groups

The concept of group is a major one in the social sciences today. One of the principal classifications of groups divides them into primary groups (small groups which are characterized by face-to-face interaction) and secondary groups (larger groups which are not possessed of face-to-face interaction). In the formation of these groups, and the accompanying development of ingroup "feelings," norms and attitudes are formed toward outgroup members that are usually negative or hostile in content. This process seems to occur in the development of new nations and political parties (secondary groups), as well as in the formation of boys' gangs (primary groups). Like all attitudes, these hostile attitudes toward outgroup members are very durable and difficult to change. While their development in the newly forming group may not be inevitable, Sherif and Sherif (1956) have demonstrated that it is a difficult process to suppress or to overcome.

The earliest attitude scales (Bogardus, 1925) were developed to measure attitudes toward such secondary groups as races and nationalities. Interest in the measurement of attitudes toward such groups, especially toward minority groups, continues today. The study of such attitudes is most relevant for the investigation of prejudice and intergroup relations and seems essential both to such theoretically important areas as understanding group formation and to applied areas such as the development of understanding and peace at the international level.

Scales contained in this chapter have as their referents ethnic and national groups. A fine, and sometimes rather arbitrary, delineation has been made between scales measuring attitudes toward these groups and scales which measure issues and problems surrounding the groups. Thus, we have included scales measuring attitude toward the Negro in this chapter but have placed scales measuring attitude toward segregation and integration in Chapter 4. The scales in this chapter have been grouped under five rubrics. Because of the great interest in measuring attitudes toward Negroes and Jews, scales to measure attitudes toward these ethnic groups have been given separate sections (the first and second sections, respectively). A third section includes scales measuring attitudes toward ethnic and national groups other than Negroes or Jews. The fourth section includes mixed scales measuring attitudes toward several ethnic groups simultaneously, and the last section includes generalized scales which may be used to measure attitudes toward any group (except, perhaps, the subjects' own ingroups).

ATTITUDES TOWARD NEGROES

In this section are scales measuring attitudes toward Negroes as a group, toward the behavior of Negroes, and toward contacts with Negroes. Scales measuring attitudes toward segregation are to be found in Chapter 4. There are also a number of mixed scales in the fourth section which have Negroes (among others) as referents. A number of scales for measuring attitude toward Negroes which might be of interest were excluded for various reasons. These include scales by Garrison and Burch (1933), Baumgartner (1935), Horowitz (1939), and Ash (1954).

Attitude toward the Negro *EXHIBIT 8-1*

Description. This is perhaps the best known and one of the earlier scales to be developed on this topic. It was constructed by Hinckley (1932), using the Thurstone procedure. The scale has two forms (A and B), composed of 16 items each. The questions refer to the equality, the rights, and the prerogatives of the Negro. All Q values were between 4.0 and 1.8.

Subjects. The sample on which the scale was constructed consisted of between 800 and 1,000 college students, including both Negro and white subjects.

Response Mode. Subjects place a check mark beside those items with which they agree and a cross beside those with which they disagree. They may place a question mark beside those about which they are unable to decide.

Scoring. The person's score is the median of the scale values of the items endorsed by him as "agree." A high score reflects a favorable attitude toward the Negro.

Reliability. The equivalent-forms reliability is reported by Stephenson (1955) to be .76 ± .02, established on 200 Miami (Ohio) University education majors. Bolton (1935) reports an equivalent forms of .62, based on a sample of 162 Southern female college students. Sims and Patrick (1936) give the equivalent-forms reliability as being .70 to .78.

Validity. In addition to the content validity of the scale, Sims and Patrick (1936) found the scale to differentiate known groups (Northern and Southern college students), while Bolton (1935) validated the scale against objective rankings of prejudiced and nonprejudiced subjects. Rosander (1937) obtained correlations of .68 to .89 between this scale and his scale measuring attitudes toward Negro behavior. Ritt (1964) obtained a correlation of .89 between this scale and a scale developed by a procedure for short-forming structured psychological tests.

Comments. This scale is superior to most in evidence for its validity. However, its reliability estimates are somewhat low. It has been used widely to validate other instruments and in other research projects. For revisions of this scale, see Katz (1947) and Smith (1939*a*). Interested readers may also wish to consult Upshaw (1962), Chase (1939, 1940), Droba (1932), Bolton (1933), Barkley (1942), and Hinckley (1963).

EXHIBIT 8-1

ATTITUDE TOWARD THE NEGRO

This is a study of attitudes toward the Negro. On the following page you will find sixteen statements expressing different attitudes toward the Negro.

Put a check mark (✓) if you **agree** with the statement.
Put a cross (×) if you **disagree** with the statement.
If you cannot decide about a statement, you may mark it with a question mark.

This is not an examination. People differ in their opinions about what is right and wrong in this issue.

Please indicate *your own attitude* by a check mark when you agree and by a cross when you disagree.

Form A

Scale Value		
4.9	1	The difference between the black and white races is not one of mere degree, but of kind.
8.9	2	The educated Negro is less of a burden on the courts and is less likely to become a dependent or a defective than the educated white man.
2.3	3	No Negro should hold an office of trust, honor, or profit.

Scale Value		
7.2	**4**	The Negro should not be simply the doormat of American civilization.
0.0	**5**	I place the Negro on the same social basis as I would a mule.
9.6	**6**	The Negro should be given the same educational advantages as the white man.
5.7	**7**	I am not at all interested in how the Negro rates socially.
10.3	**8**	Inherently, the Negro and the white man are equal.
3.5	**9**	The inability of the Negroes to develop outstanding leaders dooms them to a low level in society.
1.1	**10**	No Negro has the slightest right to resent, or even question the illegal killing of one of his race.
4.2	**11**	After you have educated the Negro to the level of the white man, there will still be an impassable gulf between them.
8.3	**12**	The Negro is fully capable of social equality with the white man, but he should not be so recognized until he is better trained.
1.8	**13**	The Negro is by no means fit for social equality with the commonest white people.
2.9	**14**	I would not patronize a hotel that accommodates Negroes.
6.6	**15**	It is possible for the white and Negro races to be brothers in Christ without becoming brothers-in-law.
7.7	**16**	The Negro should have the advantage of all social benefits of the white man but be limited to his own race in the practice thereof.

Form B

Scale Value		
4.6	**1**	Negroes must undergo many years of civilization before they may be said to reach the social level of the whites.
2.0	**2**	Negroes should not be allowed to mingle with whites in any way.
8.7	**3**	Although the Negro is rather inferior mentally, he has a fuller and deeper religious life than the white man, and thus has an emphatic claim upon our social approval.
5.3	**4**	In our efforts to help the Negro, we must not blind ourselves to the definite and marked differences which actually exist between the two races.
3.1	**5**	The white man has clearly shown the dominance of his race and should continue to exercise his power of leadership over the Negro.
0.5	**6**	The great majority of Negroes should be treated as well-trained apes.
9.3	**7**	Social recognition should be based on culture, without regard for color.
10.6	**8**	I believe that the Negro is entitled to the same social privileges as the white man.
6.0	**9**	So great is the social range between the highly educated Negro and the "nigger" that the race as a whole cannot be assigned to any one notch in the social scale.
1.4	**10**	The feeble-mindedness of the Negro limits him to a social level just a little above that of the higher animals.
8.1	**11**	The Negro is perfectly capable of taking care of himself, if the white man would only let him alone.
9.9	**12**	Give the Negro a high position in society and he will show himself equal to it.
2.6	**13**	The Negro is a necessary evil and is to be endured.
7.4	**14**	There are some Negroes with whom I would esteem it a privilege to travel, but I would not spend an hour with a miscellaneous multitude of the Negro race.

Scale Value		
6.9	15	The Negro should not be condemned forever to a lower place than the white man, but to a different place.
3.7	16	The instinctive aversion which the white man has for the Negro will forever keep the latter far beneath the notice of the former.

Attitude toward Negroes EXHIBIT 8-2

Description. This scale was developed by Thurstone (1931) and used by him (1932) in research on the effects of movies upon children. The scale contains 24 items considering the status and the capabilities of the Negro and solutions to the racial problem. The Q values for these items could not be located but may be expected to be satisfactory.

Subjects. The sample is unknown, but it is assumed to have consisted of University of Chicago undergraduate students.

Response Mode. Subjects respond by checking those statements with which they agree, placing a cross beside those with which they disagree, and placing a question mark beside those about which they are uncertain.

Scoring. The person's score is the median of the scale values of the items endorsed by him as "agree." High scores indicate favorable attitudes toward the Negro.

Reliability. Thurstone (1932) administered this scale twice to 434 Illinois school children (grades 6 to 12 inclusive) with a one-week interval between administrations. He reports a correlation of .55 between these two administrations, which may be taken as a very conservative estimate of reliability, since there was an experimental treatment (exposure to a relevant motion picture) which may have affected attitudes of the sample. Ferguson (1944) indicates that the reliabilities on this scale range from .44 to .77; Likert et al. (1934) report estimates from .57 to .73. Generally, estimates of reliability on this scale are lower than usual for Thurstone scales; they appear adequate for group research.

Validity. In addition to the content validity of this scale, Diggory (1953) found scores on the scale to correlate —.68 and —.48 with Thurstone's treatment of criminals scale, based upon a sample of 103 females and 75 males, respectively. It is also to be noted that this scale was one of those used by Grice (1934) to successfully validate his generalized scale to measure attitudes toward any defined group; the correlation between the two scales was .67. Finally Osgood et al. (1957) have also obtained significant correlations between this scale and their semantic differential when measuring attitude toward the Negro. These findings confer upon the scale a degree of construct and concurrent validity.

Comments. Although superior in evidence for its validity, this scale seems to be somewhat below average on reliability. In these regards, it is comparable to the Hinckley scale presented in the previous section. The somewhat low reliability estimates on these two scales is typical of

Thurstone scales, but reliability seems satisfactory for group work. The Hinckley scale has the advantage of possessing equivalent forms.

EXHIBIT 8-2

ATTITUDE TOWARD NEGROES

* This is a study of attitudes toward the Negro. On the following page you will find 24 statements expressing different attitudes toward the Negro.

Put a check mark (✓) if you **agree** with the statement.
Put a cross (×) if you **disagree** with the statement.

If you cannot decide about a statement, you may mark it with a question mark.

This is not an examination. People differ in their opinions about what is right and wrong in this issue. Please indicate *your own* attitude by a check mark when you agree and by a cross when you disagree.

Scale Values		
5.4	**1**	I am not at all interested in how the Negro rates socially.
7.3	**2**	You cannot condemn the entire black race because of the actions of some of its members.
2.7	**3**	Under no circumstances should Negro children be allowed to attend the same schools as white children.
0.8	**4**	The white race must be kept pure at all costs, even if the Negroes have to be killed off.
8.9	**5**	Give the Negro time. Within the next fifty years he will astonish you.
4.3	**6**	The Negro should have freedom but should never be treated as the equal of the white man.
1.8	**7**	No person with the slightest trace of Negro blood should associate with white people or be classed as a white man.
10.3	**8**	I believe that the Negro deserves the same social privileges as the white man.
9.6	**9**	Give the Negro a high position in society and he will show himself equal to it.
6.8	**10**	In a thousand years the Negro might become the white man's equal; then his social position should be equal to the white man's.
4.7	**11**	I think the colored race should hold a somewhat lower social position than the white race.
2.1	**12**	I can stand a "nigger" in his place but I cannot stand him as th equal of the white man.
0.9	**13**	The Negro will always remain as he is—a little higher than t animals.
10.3	**14**	The Negro should be considered as equal to the white man and given the white man's advantages.

* These instructions are not necessarily those used by Thurstone. They are, however, standard Thu instructions and should be satisfactory for use with this scale.

Scale Values		
7.9	15	Our refusal to accept the Negro is not based on any fact in nature but on a prejudice which should be overcome.
6.5	16	The courts are far more unfair to the Negro than the real differences between the races justify.
3.2	17	The Negro and the white man must be kept apart in all social affairs where they might be taken as equal.
1.7	18	Negroes should not be allowed to associate with white people in any way.
9.6	19	The white and colored races should enjoy the same privileges and protection.
5.5	20	The Negro problem will settle itself without our worrying about it.
3.6	21	The Negro should be treated and thought of as a servant for the white man.
0.9	22	The Negro should be considered in the lowest class among human beings.
10.0	23	By nature the Negro and the white man are equal.
7.7	24	The Negro is perfectly capable of taking care of himself, if the white man would only let him alone.

Attitude toward the Negro scale EXHIBIT 8-3

Description. This 15-item scale was developed by Likert (1932) using his own procedure. In addition to the usual questions regarding the traits and characteristics of the Negro, many of the items question the proper behavior on the part of whites in interaction with, or reaction to, Negroes. Likert (private communication, 1965) states that items 6, 8, and 15 should be omitted because of social changes. He also points out hat item number 11 is a double-barreled item.

Subjects. The sample consisted of 650 college students.

esponse Mode. Most of the questions possess the standard Likert nuum of five alternatives: strongly agree, agree, undecided, dis- and strongly disagree. The alternatives for some items are '?," and "no," and a few items have clauses or phrases that are ves.

For positive statements, the response alternatives should be the following manner: For the three-point items, "yes" is ht of 4; "?," a weight of 3; and "no," a weight of 2. For the e items, responses are weighted from 5 (most favorable 1 (most unfavorable alternative). Weights for response egative items must be reversed. The person's score is the ted alternatives endorsed by him. High scores indicate oward the Negro.

(1932) reports the split-half reliability (corrected) etest reliability coefficient as .85, using a thirty-day

Validity. Likert obtained a significant difference in the mean scores of groups of Northern and Southern students, thus validating the scale by the known-groups method. McKeachie (1954) obtained a highly significant correlation between changes in scores on this scale and changes in perceptions of group norms as a result of experimental treatment.

Comments. This seems a relatively valid and highly reliable scale for measuring attitude toward the Negro. It does not have equivalent forms, but is superior in its reliability estimates to the Hinckley scale presented in the first paragraph of this section. Likert feels that recent social changes have made some of the more extreme negative items less useful, but this would depend greatly upon the nature of the population upon which the scale is used. For another study using this scale, see Seeleman (1940).

EXHIBIT 8-3

ATTITUDE TOWARD THE NEGRO SCALE

PART I: After each question *underscore* "yes" or "no"; or if you are undecided or not sure you understand the question, underscore the question mark.

*1 Would most negroes, if not held in their place, become officious, overbearing, and disagreeable?

YES	?	NO
(2)	(3)	(4)

2 If you went into a cafeteria in a northern city, sat down, and then realized you were at the table with a negro, would you leave the table?

YES	?	NO
(2)	(3)	(4)

3 Would you shake hands with a negro?

YES	?	NO
(4)	(3)	(2)

4 Do you disapprove of the use of the term "nigger"?

YES	?	NO
(4)	(3)	(2)

5 If you heard of a negro who had bought a home or a farm would you be glad?

* Numbers in parentheses indicate the proper weight to be assigned to that alternative.

Reprinted with permission from Likert, R. A technique for the measurement of attitudes. *Arch. Psychol.*, 1932, 22, 5–55.

YES	?	NO
(4)	(3)	(2)

PART II: In each of the following you are given a preliminary statement which can be completed or answered in any one of five ways. Check whichever one of the five most closely approximates your own opinion.

6 In a community in which the negroes outnumber the whites, under what circumstances is the lynching of a negro justifiable?
(a) Never (5)
(b) In very exceptional cases where a specially brutal crime against a white person calls for swift punishment. (4)
(c) As punishment for any brutal crime against a white person. (3)
(d) As punishment for any gross offense (felony or extreme insolence) committed against a white person. (2)
(e) As punishment for any act of insolence against a white person. (1)

7 How far in our educational system (aside from trade education) should the most intelligent negroes be allowed to go?
(a) Grade school (1)
(b) Junior high school (2)
(c) High school (3)
(d) College (4)
(e) Graduate and professional school (5)

8 In a community where the negroes outnumber the whites, a negro who is insolent to a white man should be:
(a) excused or ignored (5)
(b) reprimanded (4)
(c) fined and jailed (3)
(d) not only fined and jailed but also given corporal punishment (whipping, etc.) (2)
(e) lynched (1)

PART III: The following list of sentences is in the form of statements of what should or should not be done. If you strongly approve of the statement as it stands, *underscore* the words "strongly approve," and so on, with regard to the other attitudes (approve, undecided, disapprove, strongly disapprove) which follow each statement.

9 All negroes belong in one class and should be treated in about the same way.

Strongly Approve	Approve	Undecided	Disapprove	Strongly Disapprove
(1)	(2)	(3)	(4)	(5)

10 Negro homes should be segregated from those of white people.

Strongly Approve	Approve	Undecided	Disapprove	Strongly Disapprove
(1)	(2)	(3)	(4)	(5)

11 Where there is segregation, the negro section should have the same equipment in paving, water, and electric light facilities as are found in the white districts.

Strongly Approve	Approve	Undecided	Disapprove	Strongly Disapprove
(5)	(4)	(3)	(2)	(1)

12 If the same preparation is required, the negro teacher should receive the same salary as the white.

Strongly Approve	Approve	Undecided	Disapprove	Strongly Disapprove
(5)	(4)	(3)	(2)	(1)

13 Practically all American hotels should refuse to admit negroes.

Strongly Approve	Approve	Undecided	Disapprove	Strongly Disapprove
(1)	(2)	(3)	(4)	(5)

14 No negro should be deprived of the franchise except for reasons which would also disfranchise a white man.

Strongly Approve	Approve	Undecided	Disapprove	Strongly Disapprove
(5)	(4)	(3)	(2)	(1)

15 In a community of 1,000 whites and 50 negroes, a drunken negro shoots and kills an officer who is trying to arrest him. THE WHITE POPULATION IMMEDIATELY DRIVES ALL NEGROES OUT OF TOWN.

Strongly Approve	Approve	Undecided	Disapprove	Strongly Disapprove
(1)	(2)	(3)	(4)	(5)

The anti-Negro scale EXHIBIT 8-4

Description. This is a 16-item, Likert-type scale developed by Steckler (1957) for use with Negro samples. Only one item, number 14 in the exhibit, restricts its use to such a sample, however. Alteration of this item would allow more general use of the scale. The scale is interesting as it stands, being one of the few scales designed for measuring attitudes toward the reference group of the subject. The items sample heavily the cultural stereotype of the Negro.

Subjects. The sample was composed of 299 college students and members of church groups, all of whom were Negro. The sample represented both Northern and Southern Negroes.

Response Mode. Persons respond to each item on a Likert-type continuum: strongly agree, agree, undecided, disagree, and strongly disagree.

Scoring. For negative items, weights are assigned the response alternatives from 5 (strongly agree) to 1 (strongly disagree). Weights for positive items must be reversed. The person's score is the sum of the weighted alternatives endorsed by him. Higher scores reflect anti-Negro attitudes.

Reliability. Steckler (1957) reports a split-half reliability of .84 for the scale.

Validity. This scale was found by its author to correlate .24 with an antiwhite scale (see the third section of this chapter). It also correlated .40 and .57 with the California E and F scales, respectively. These correlations may be taken as evidence of construct validity. The scale possesses content validity for Negro samples.

Comments. This is a quite interesting scale which is average in validity and reliability. Its value is enhanced still further by the fact that the author provided an antiwhite scale to accompany it. The two scales together should produce valuable research regarding generality of hostility in attitudes, strength of attitude and group membership, and so forth.

EXHIBIT 8-4

THE ANTI - NEGRO SCALE

This is a study of what people think about a number of social questions. The best answer to each statement below is *your personal opinion.* We have tried to cover many different points of view. You may agree strongly with some statements, disagree just as strongly with others, and perhaps be uncertain about others. Whether you agree or disagree with any statements, you can be sure that many other people feel the same way that you do.

Please mark each statement in the left margin according to how much you agree or disagree with it. *Please Mark Every One.* Write +1, +2, +3 or —1, —2, —3, depending on how you feel in each case.

+1: I Agree a Little	—1: I Disagree a Little
+2: I Agree Pretty Much	—2: I Disagree Pretty Much
+3: I Agree Very Much	—3: I Disagree Very Much

1 A large part of the problems facing Negroes today are caused by Negroes themselves.

2 I would rather not marry a person who has very kinky hair, wide nostrils, and thick lips.

3 The lower-class Negro is to blame for a lot of anti-Negro prejudice.

4 Whites and Negroes can get along on jobs until too many Negroes try to push themselves in.

5 One big reason why racial prejudice is still so strong is that Negroes offend people by being so sensitive about racial matters.

6 One important reason why Negroes are discriminated against in housing is that they don't keep up the property.

7 One reason why racial prejudice still exists today is the fact that many Negroes are dirty, loud, and generally offensive in their ways.
8 One trouble with Negroes is that they are even more jealous of each other's success than are whites.
9 Too many Negroes have abused the privilege of attending baseball games by being rowdy, noisy, and cheering only for the colored ballplayers.
10 Segregation and jimcrow will never end unless the average colored person becomes better educated and better mannered.
11 Colored people can hardly be expected to gain social equality until many more of them exert some effort to better themselves and live more decently.
12 With all of the drinking, cutting, and other immoral acts of some Negroes, white people are almost justified for being prejudiced.
13 Too many Negroes, when they get a little money, spend it all on whiskey, flashy cars, or expensive clothes.
14 One is almost ashamed to be a Negro when he sees so many of them who look and act like cotton pickers fresh from the fields.
15 A great many Negroes become officious, overbearing, and disagreeable when given positions of responsibility and authority.
16 Negroes would solve many of their social problems if so many of them were not irresponsible, lazy, and ignorant.

Negro behavior attitude scale EXHIBIT 8-5

Description. This is a 22-item scale developed by Rosander (1937). The author has provided equivalent forms (A and B). Although constructed using the Thurstone method, it is somewhat different from the usual Thurstone-type scale in that each item is coupled with a proposition of action to be taken. The subject then indicates whether or not he would have acted as stated. This is apparently an attempt to measure a component similar to Guttman's closure. Although this item form makes the item somewhat more complex, Rosander found that reliable scale values could be obtained.

Subjects. The sample consisted of 372 college students from the Northern and Southern United States.

Response Mode. Subjects respond by checking the statement if they would act as stated. They place a cross in front of the statement if they would not act as stated.

Scoring. The person's score is the median of the scale values of the items endorsed by him (i.e., when he indicates that he would act as stated). A high score indicates a favorable attitude toward Negroes.

Reliability. The author (Rosander, 1937) reports split-half reliability estimates of .71 and .89 for Forms A and B, respectively.

Validity. The validity of the scale is based upon correlations of .68 to .89 with the Hinckley Attitude toward the Negro Scale (described in the first paragraph of this section). It was also found to differentiate between Northern and Southern college students. Finally, the method of construction should ensure a degree of content validity.

Comments. This is a satisfactorily valid and reliable scale for measuring attitudes toward Negroes, but it should not be taken as a measure of what persons would actually do in these situations; it is a measure only of their report of what they would do. No doubt there is some correlation between the two, but not one which is strong enough to allow close prediction from report to actual behavior.

EXHIBIT 8-5

NEGRO BEHAVIOR ATTITUDE SCALE

Put a check mark (✓) in front of statement if you would *act* as stated. Put a cross (×) in front of statement if you would *not act* as stated.

Form A

Scale Value		
6.2	1	In the community where you live a Negro marries a white girl. You do nothing about it.
1.2	2	You are bathing at a beach. Some Negroes approach and enter the water near you. You start a fight with them.
11.5	3	A Negro family moves into the residential district where you live. You invite them to your home.
10.8	4	A Negro with a college education is a qualified candidate for Congress from your district. You vote for him on the basis of race alone.
10.3	5	Your sister takes a friendly interest in an educated and unmarried Negro boy to whom she has been introduced. You commend her for her broad-mindedness.
9.2	6	A Negro family moves into the apartment building in which you live. You act friendly toward them.
7.0	7	You stop at a hotel which you discover caters to Negroes as well as to whites. You remain in the hotel.
2.6	8	You are reading in a public library. A Negro enters and sits down beside you. You leave the library at once.
10.2	9	A well-educated Negro applies for membership in a high school or college society of which you are a member. You move that the constitution of the club be amended to allow Negro members.
5.8	10	You attend a conference at a hotel which will not allow the Negro delegates to register. You propose that the Negroes attend the meetings but live in another hotel.
1.0	11	In a community where you live a Negro attacks a white girl. You demand that all the Negroes be driven out of town.
3.4	12	You are bathing at a beach. Some Negroes approach and enter the water near you. You go to some other beach.
2.0	13	In the community where you live a Negro marries a white girl. You fight for the maintenance of the color line.

Scale Value		
6.3	14	The congregation of the church you attend has always been white. One Sunday morning a Negro attends the services. You do nothing about it.
4.0	15	A Negro is put to work in the same department with you so that you have to associate with him every day. You try to have as little to do with him as possible.
9.7	16	In a community where you live a Negro attacks a white girl. You try to break up the mob which forms.
4.9	17	A Negro family moves into the apartment building in which you live. You treat them coolly.
9.4	18	A Negro is put to work in the same department with you so that you have to associate with him every day. You act friendly toward him.
3.6	19	You attend a conference at a hotel which will not allow the Negro delegates to register. You advise the Negroes to withdraw.
1.6	20	You see a white girl whom you know walk down the street with a Negro boy. You never speak to her after that.
8.1	21	A well-educated Negro applies for membership in a high school or college society of which you are a member. You consider his application the same as you would that of any other student.
3.8	22	Your sister takes a friendly interest in an educated and unmarried Negro boy to whom she has been introduced. You warn her of the possible consequences of her behavior.

Experiences with Negroes *EXHIBIT 8-6*

Description. This scale, constructed by Ford (1941), may not be considered an attitude scale per se, but it may be used for this as well as for other purposes. It is a 26-item scale which was developed using a combined Likert-Thurstone method. The scale has questions which inquire about two types of contacts with Negroes: community contacts and personal contacts. The item pool was derived from books, articles, and notes kept by the author on situations involving Negroes and whites. Persons were interviewed informally about their actual contacts with Negroes and how they felt toward the Negro as a result of such contacts. About 800 statements of contact situations were developed for the pool. Items were selected according to Wang's (1932) informal criteria for selection. Also, no word appears in the items which falls outside the 10,000 most frequently used words in the English language. Most of the words are within the first 5,000. Although developed using a Likert procedure, the author had seven college graduates sort the response alternatives to each item on a five-point scale from friendliness to unfriendliness. Items were selected whose response alternatives were considered unambiguous on the basis of this scaling procedure. The items themselves were then scaled on a five-point response continuum.

Subjects. The subjects used in scale construction were 554 college students at the University of Pittsburgh, the University of Mississippi, and Tulane University.

Response Mode. Persons respond to each item by checking that alternative which most nearly corresponds with their personal experience.

Scoring. Response alternatives for positive items are weighted from 5 (most favorable response) to 1 (most unfavorable response). For negative items, these weights are reversed, as shown in Exhibit 8-6. The person's score is the sum of the weighted alternatives endorsed by him. High scores reflect positive attitudes.

Reliability. The author (Ford, 1941) reports the split-half reliability (corrected) to be .82 and .92 for the two parts of the scale (community and personal contacts), respectively.

Validity. The scale was validated by the known-groups method and was found to differentiate significantly between the scores of the University of Mississippi and University of Pittsburgh students.

Comments. This seems to be a satisfactory scale for measuring attitudes by tapping reports of personal experiences with Negroes. Its use as an attitude scale requires the assumption that persons will distort their experiences as a function of the direction and intensity of the attitude held. This is a frequent and reasonable assumption which is well borne out by research on attitudes. The scale has the advantage of having a wide range of usage because of the control exercised over vocabulary level in its construction. It is a somewhat different, but interesting, approach to attitude measurement.

EXHIBIT 8-6

EXPERIENCES WITH NEGROES

This is a study of the experiences which you, your friends, and your relatives have had with Negroes. Below, you will find 26 situations indicating possible experiences you may have had.

Each situation has five possible responses. Pick the one which most nearly corresponds with your personal experiences and place a check mark (✓) on the dotted line in front of it. Try to answer every item.

There is no need to sign your name. This is not an examination. However, your experiences are of great interest to social scientists. Therefore, it is important that you select the items carefully and thoughtfully.

Community Contacts

Please begin here, placing a check (✓) in front of one response:

1 Are there separate arrangements for Negroes who travel in the area where you were reared?

*1. ________ Always; a fixed custom.

2. ________ Usually separate arrangements.

3. ________ Never noticed.

* These numbers are weights to be assigned the alternatives when endorsed.

4. ________ Negroes not required to sit apart, but they usually do so voluntarily.
5. ________ Same privileges as whites; sit where they like.

2 When do whites address a Negro as Mr. or Mrs. in the community where you were reared?
1. ________ Never; a fixed custom.
2. ________ Rarely, as in addressing a famous Negro.
3. ________ Never noticed.
4. ________ When the occasion demands it.
5. ________ Same as in addressing whites.

3 Were Negroes allowed to use public buildings, such as libraries and museums, in the area where you were reared?
5. ________ Yes, whites and Negroes used buildings at same time.
4. ________ Same privileges as whites, but Negroes generally stayed away.
3. ________ No chance to observe.
2. ________ Limited privileges.
1. ________ Not allowed.

4 How are the Negro children educated in the community where you were reared?
5. ________ Never noticed any difference in treatment of white and Negro children.
4. ________ Same schools and teachers as white children had.
3. ________ Can't say; Negroes lived in another part of area.
2. ________ Separate schools, but same amount of education provided.
1. ________ Separate schools which were not as good as the white schools.

5 How do whites in the area where you were reared look upon other whites who treat Negroes as equals?
1. ________ Severely criticized for such conduct.
2. ________ Disliked.
3. ________ No set community attitude on the matter.
4. ________ Seldom anything said.
5. ________ Such conduct is never questioned.

6 May a Negro enter the front door of a white man's house in the area where you were reared?
1. ________ Under no circumstances.
2. ________ Only if invited.
3. ________ No set custom in the community.
4. ________ Yes, but they seldom use the privilege.
5. ________ Same as for whites in similar circumstances.

7 Do whites call Negroes "niggers" to their faces in the community where you were reared?
1. ________ Yes, that is a common term of address.
2. ________ Quite often, but usually in anger or disgust.

3. ________ Too few opportunities for me to observe.
4. ________ Rarely used.
5. ________ No, the term is carefully avoided when Negroes are near.

8 How is the Negro who wants to vote treated at the polls in the community where you were reared?
5. ________ Same privileges as whites, which they exercise freely.
4. ________ Same privileges as whites.
3. ________ Don't know.
2. ________ Permitted to vote but not wanted.
1. ________ Not allowed to vote.

9 Do whites in the area where you were reared favor educating Negroes?
1. ________ No; spoils the Negro.
2. ________ Not beyond learning to read and write.
3. ________ Never heard the subject discussed enough to know.
4. ________ Yes, with emphasis on manual training.
5. ________ Yes, same privileges as whites.

10 Were your parents in favor of treating whites and Negroes alike?
5. ________ Strongly in favor.
4. ________ In favor.
3. ________ Never said.
2. ________ Opposed.
1. ________ Strongly opposed.

11 Do mobs ever seize Negroes in the area where you were reared?
1. ________ Many times.
2. ________ Occasionally.
3. ________ Never had reason to, so far as I know.
4. ________ No, our community depends on the courts.
5. ________ Never.

12 May a Negro run for election to public office in your home area?
5. ________ Yes; some hold or have held public office.
4. ________ Yes, they may try.
3. ________ Don't know of any such an attempt.
2. ________ Legally yes, but they never do.
1. ________ Whites simply would not allow it.

Personal Contacts

1 Have you ever walked with a Negro for other than business reasons?
5. ________ Yes, just as I do with whites.
4. ________ When I thought it suitable.
3. ________ Situation calling for a decision never arose.
2. ________ Yes, but I was uncomfortable while doing it.
1. ________ Never under any circumstances.

2 Under what conditions have you shaken hands with a Negro?

5. ________ Follow same rules that I follow for whites.
4. ________ When I meet a Negro friend who would expect me to.
3. ________ Situation calling for a decision never arose.
2. ________ To show friendship for a Negro, provided he knew his place.
1. ________ Under no circumstances.

3 Have you ever been annoyed by white people who were acting too friendly toward Negroes?

1. ________ Yes, on many occasions.
2. ________ Yes, a few times.
3. ________ Haven't had much chance to observe.
4. ________ No.
5. ________ Never; my observation has been that whites are too unfriendly.

4 Have you warned whites to be more strict in handling Negroes?

1. ________ Several times.
2. ________ No, but there have been times when I should have.
3. ________ Never had reason to.
4. ________ My experience has been that whites are generally too strict.
5. ________ No, I have advised them to be less strict.

5 Have you ever noticed that Negroes have a disagreeable body odor?

1. ________ Many times.
2. ________ A few times.
3. ________ Never noticed.
4. ________ Yes, but under circumstances where whites smell just as disagreeable.
5. ________ The Negroes whom I have met are as clean or cleaner than whites.

6 Have you ever approved of quick justice, as sometimes dealt by white men outside of court, to a Negro who has been accused of a crime against a white person?

5. ________ Never under any circumstances.
4. ________ Yes, but I no longer would approve.
3. ________ Don't know of such a case at first hand.
2. ________ Yes, but only when the offense was a very serious one.
1. ________ Yes.

7 Can you recall actual cases where Negroes in public places seemed to be looking for trouble?

1. ________ Many of them.
2. ________ A few.
3. ________ Few chances to observe such situations.
4. ________ Yes, but under circumstances where whites would have done the same.
5. ________ None.

8 Under what circumstances have you gone to the home of a Negro?

5. ______ For a friendly visit.
4. ______ Usually on business, but sometimes for other reasons.
3. ______ Never had reason to.
2. ______ On business or to show friendship, provided the Negro knew his place.
1. ______ Under no circumstances.

9 Think of the Negro who has the finest qualities of character of all the Negroes whom you know. Where would you rate him in comparison with the whites whom you know.

5. ______ Above any whites I know, outside of my family.
4. ______ Equal to my white acquaintances.
3. ______ Cannot answer: don't know any Negroes well enough.
2. ______ Below whites in general.
1. ______ Below the meanest of white people.

10 What has been your policy in the past when a Negro came into a public place, such as theatre, railroad waiting room or restaurant?

1. ______ Let the Negro know he wasn't wanted.
2. ______ Let him alone so long as he knew his place.
3. ______ Situation never arose.
4. ______ Tried to pay no attention to the situation.
5. ______ Treated him as I did whites in similar circumstances.

11 Have you ever had trouble with Negroes because you thought that they were getting out of their place?

5. ______ On the contrary, I have defended Negroes who were being put in their place.
4. ______ No trouble.
3. ______ Have seldom been in position where this might have happened.
2. ______ On a few occasions.
1. ______ Many times.

12 Have you ever permitted Negroes to come into your home for friendly visits?

1. ______ Positively never.
2. ______ Yes, if they knew their place.
3. ______ Situation calling for a decision never arose.
4. ______ On a few occasions.
5. ______ Yes frequently.

13 Have you ever called Negroes "niggers" when talking to them?

5. ______ Never.
4. ______ Yes, but I have since regretted it.
3. ______ Never had reason to.
2. ______ Yes, when sufficiently aroused.
1. ______ Many times.

14 Which of the following descriptions most accurately represents Negro workers whom you have seen?
1. ________ Very poor workers; did the least possible amount of work.
2. ________ Poor workers even when directed.
3. ________ Not enough opportunity to make such a judgment.
4. ________ Good workers when directed.
5. ________ Very good workers; even showed initiative.

The social situations questionnaire EXHIBIT 8-7

Description. This is an eight-item, Guttman-type scale, developed by Kogan and Downey (1956) to measure discriminatory attitudes toward Negroes. Three clusters of five items each were developed and classified as to the person, or persons, manifesting the discriminatory behavior described in the item. The three types of stimulus persons upon which the items were classified were peers, authorities, and strangers. Guttman scales were obtained for these three clusters, and another scale was developed taking all items from the three scales together. Each item presents a number of social situations, and the alternative responses are various ways of resolving the situation of conflict.

Subjects. The sample consisted of 50 boys and 50 girls (ages twelve to twenty) who were members of a New England city youth organization.

Response Mode. For each item, subjects choose one of four alternatives for resolving an anti-Negro conflict situation. The alternatives vary in form and content, but all are arranged on a continuum of positivity toward the Negro and negativity toward discrimination.

Scoring. The items were treated by Kogan and Downey as dichotomies and scored as 1 (a positive response) or 0 (a negative response). The subject's score was the sum of the weighted alternatives endorsed by him. High scores were taken to reflect a militantly positive attitude toward the Negro. Kogan (private communication, 1965) indicated that the sample employed was quite unprejudiced and suggested that it would be valuable to rescale these items to determine their cutoff points when used with other samples.

Reliability. No reliability coefficients were provided.

Validity. The three scales in Exhibit 8-7 possess the following reproducibility coefficients: peers, .93; authorities, .96; strangers, .95. All three may be considered true scales. The reproducibility coefficient for the three scales taken together is .91, which is still a true scale in the Guttman sense. These coefficients reflect the unidimensionality of the scale. Scale scores were also validated against prediction of actual participation in youth club activities, yielding a highly significant correlation between militant antiprejudice and youth club participation. The scale possesses content validity for attitudes toward modes of resolution of social conflicts involving discrimination against the Negro. The content domain is too restricted, however, to provide content validity for the larger question of attitude toward the Negro.

Comments. This scale seems above average in validity for the measurement of attitudes toward the Negro as reflected in the resolution of conflictive social situations involving discrimination. As usual with Guttman scales, the content domain being sampled seems restricted. However, the scale possesses content validity for the referent as defined. It is a true scale, and the approach is an interesting one. Reliability estimates for the scale would be a valuable addition to knowledge of its functional characteristics.

EXHIBIT 8-7

THE SOCIAL SITUATIONS QUESTIONNAIRE

This test is a study of what different people will do in different situations. A situation is given followed by four possible actions that you might take. After reading the situation, pick out that response which you think you would make. Even though it might not be exactly what you would do, check that action which is *closest* to that which you would probably take. Remember that there is no right or wrong answer, for different people will naturally answer differently.

S 1 Imagine yourself as a private who has just been drafted into the Army. After a few days you discover that most of the men in your barracks are quite prejudiced against Negroes. One day, the commander of your outfit comes around looking for volunteers for a mixed Negro-white battalion. You know that anybody who joined would be looked down on and called a "Nigger-lover" by many of the boys in your barracks. Under these conditions,

______ I would definitely volunteer.

______ I would probably volunteer.

______ I probably would not volunteer.

______ I definitely would not volunteer and would disapprove of anyone who did.

P 2 Imagine that you are walking around town one Halloween Night with a large group of your friends (boys and girls). As you come to one street corner you see four or five Negro girls across the street. Someone in your crowd yells to them, "Hey, girls, what are you all wearing the dark masks for?" Everyone in your crowd laughs and passes it off as a joke, not meaning any harm to the girls. You know that if you criticize

S, P, A: The letters beside the items indicate whether they are items involving peers (P), authorities (A), or strangers (S).

Reference: N. Kogan and J. F. Downey. Scaling norm conflicts in the area of prejudice and discrimination. *J. abnorm. soc. Psychol.*, 1956, 53, 292–295. Items obtained from authors and published with their permission.

the fellow who yelled, your friends will probably scoff at you and say you shouldn't be so sensitive over a harmless little joke like that. Under these conditions,

_______ I would definitely bawl him out for what he said.

_______ I would probably say that it wasn't a good joke.

_______ I probably wouldn't say anything, but would feel a little uneasy about it.

_______ I definitely would say nothing and would think that it was a harmless joke.

A 3 Imagine that you are in a class that has four or five colored boys and girls in it. You notice that one of your teachers always seems to be picking on them and criticizing their work—more so than she does the white boys and girls. For example, if two boys are unprepared or are fooling around, she will usually punish the colored boy more. A few of the other kids in the class have also noticed this. Under these conditions,

_______ I would feel that the colored kids should just be more careful about how they act in class.

_______ I would keep quiet and feel that how the teacher runs the class is her own business.

_______ I would try to persuade the kids that we should do something about this.

_______ I would go directly to the principal and tell him what was going on.

A 4 Imagine that as you are sitting at home one day, a neighbor comes in to ask your parents to sign a petition which would prevent Negroes from buying or renting land on your block. He explains that it would not hurt the Negroes because there are plenty of other good places in town to live. This move would not only save your section just for white people, but would also make your land worth more money. Your folks are just about to sign the petition. Under these conditions,

_______ I would insist that they were wrong and try to persuade them not to sign the petition.

_______ I would probably tell my parents that I didn't think that they were doing the right thing.

_______ I would probably keep quiet because it wouldn't make much difference to me one way or the other.

_______ I would definitely approve.

P 5 Imagine that you are trying to form a new social club (e.g. fraternity or sorority) among your friends at school. After five or six of you have gotten the club started, one of them proposes that B, a fairly well-liked Negro you know, be asked to join. Most of the others seem to be very much against this proposal, not because they don't like B, but because they don't want to have any Negroes in the club at all. Under these conditions,

_______ I would side with those who were against admitting any Negroes at all to the club.

_______ I would probably wait and see what the majority thought about it and then go along with them.

_______ I would probably say that future members should be judged by their own personal merits, and not by whether they are Negroes or not; but I would go along with any decision the majority made.

_______ I would say that if they were going to automatically rule out all Negroes that I wouldn't want to be in the club.

S 6 Imagine that you are at a drug store waiting to make a phone call. As you are standing there, you notice a Negro woman coming up to the counter, followed in a few seconds by a white woman. As the clerk starts to wait on the colored woman, the white woman says in a snobbish voice, "would you mind waiting on me first—I'm in a hurry. This colored woman can wait." The clerk doesn't know quite what to do. Under these conditions,

_______ If the clerk hesitated, I would say that since the white woman was in a hurry, he should wait on her first.

_______ I would feel that I shouldn't interfere.

_______ I would remind the clerk that the other woman was first.

_______ I would definitely speak up and criticize the white woman for what she said.

P 7 Imagine that you are walking down the street with a fellow you know pretty well. On the way down the street he accidentally bumps into a colored boy coming the other way. Immediately he becomes angry and says, "Listen, Darky, who do you think you're bumping? I'm not going to let any Nigger push me around—" and is just about to start a fight with him, but the colored boy runs away. Under these conditions,

_______ I wouldn't criticize him for what he did.

_______ I would probably say that he was making a mountain out of a molehill and let it go.

_______ I would probably say something about the colored boy having just as much right to walk down the street as he did.

_______ I would definitely criticize him for becoming angry over the accident, just because the fellow was a Negro.

A 8 Imagine that your mother has just been asked to give a tea for the P.T.A. In it all the mothers of the children in your class would be invited to spend the afternoon at your house. Your mother at first seemed to be pretty happy about being able to do this, but when she found out that there were three or four Negro mothers who would have to be invited, she decided to call up and say that she couldn't give the party after all. Under these conditions,

_______ I would insist that she was wrong, and that the Negro mothers were no different from the white mothers.

_______ I probably would tell her that I couldn't see why she wouldn't want to give the party just because there would be some Negro women present.

_____ I would probably keep quiet, not wanting to make an issue of the matter.

_____ I would agree with her and say that she should call up and say that she couldn't give the party.

P 9 Imagine that you are planning to go out to a show with three other fellows and your dates. The day before you go out, one of the fellows calls you and asks you if it would be all right if Sam Johnson (a Negro whom you do not know) could come along with his date. You're pretty sure that the other kids in the party would not like this. Under these conditions,

_____ I would definitely say "no" or else get out of the party.

_____ I would probably say I would rather not, because of how the other kids would feel about it.

_____ I would probably say that it would be O.K. with me.

_____ I would definitely say that it would be O.K. and would try to convince the others that this was a good idea.

S 10 Imagine that, coming back from a trip, you have a large suitcase to carry, so you decide to take a cab home. Waiting on the corner for a cab, you glance across the street and see a well-dressed colored man also waiting for a cab. After a few minutes, a cab comes by and both of you whistle for it. The cab goes right by the Negro, turns around, and comes back to pick you up. When the driver opens the door, he remarks, "I really saw that colored fellow first, but I always go by the rule that whites come first." Under these conditions,

_____ I would definitely tell the cabbie that he had done the wrong thing.

_____ Although I didn't like what he said, I would probably get into the cab without saying anything.

_____ I would think that the cabbie was a pretty good guy and that he had done the right thing.

_____ I would probably get into the cab and mind my own business.

S 11 Imagine that you are visiting a friend of yours out of town. You decide to go swimming at a local swimming pool. Getting into line to pay your admission, you notice a young colored boy in line just in front of you. As he gets up to the booth to get his ticket, the woman in the booth tells him that they don't allow Negroes in the pool. Under these conditions,

_____ I would complain to the woman about this policy.

_____ I would voice a complaint to my friend making sure that the woman would hear.

_____ I wouldn't say anything about it then, but might make a criticism to my friend later.

_____ I would say nothing, feeling it is the right of the pool owners to reject Negroes if they want.

A 12 Imagine that you are graduating from high school, and your aunt who lives here in town, is giving a (stag/hen) party for you and your friends.

A week before the party, you call her up and ask her if it would be all right if a colored friend of yours comes to the party. Your aunt says that she would rather not give the party if a Negro is going to come. You know that you can't change her mind. Under these conditions,

_______ I can't answer this question, because I never would have invited a Negro to my party in the first place.

_______ I would apologize and say that we would leave my friend out of the party.

_______ I would probably try to get out of this party and go to some other party where my friend could come.

_______ I would tell my aunt she was taking a poor attitude, and that if my friend couldn't come, I would rather not have the party at all.

A 13 Imagine that you have a 19 year old brother who has been going pretty steadily with an attractive colored girl for the past month or so. Although your parents admit that she is a very nice girl, they have been trying to force your brother to stop taking her out, because they are afraid that they might get serious about each other. They don't mind him having her as a friend, but they don't want him to date her or call her "his girl." One night, during an argument, when your brother is present, your parents ask you what you think. Under these conditions,

_______ I would disagree with my parents and say that, as long as she was a nice girl, it was O.K.

_______ I would probably try to keep out of it, saying that my brother should make up his own mind.

_______ I would probably tend to side with my parents.

_______ I would definitely side with my parents, saying that this could only lead to a disgrace to the family.

S 14 Imagine that as you are walking down town one day, you see five or six boys, who are about five years younger than you, teasing a little colored boy, calling him "Black boy," etc., and threatening to hurt him. The little fellow starts to cry, breaks away from the white boys and runs up to you asking you to make them leave him alone. Under these conditions,

_______ I would stop them from teasing him, and try to show them why they shouldn't pick on a boy just because of his race.

_______ I would stop them from teasing him, and make sure that the Negro got away safely, but wouldn't say anything much.

_______ I would try to keep out of it if I could, unless I was sure they were going to hurt him.

_______ I would definitely stay out of it and let the colored boy take care of himself.

P 15 Imagine that as you are coming home from school one day, you saw one of your friends in a serious argument with a colored boy. You don't know what has caused the argument but as you draw nearer, you hear him insulting the colored boy by calling him various names ("dirty Nigger," etc.). You know that if you interfere and criticize him for his name calling, he will think you are taking the colored boy's side. On the other hand, unless you do say something it appears that he might hurt the colored boy, who is a little smaller. Under these conditions,

_______ I would definitely say nothing.
_______ I would probably say nothing or else just try to break up the fight.
_______ I would probably butt in and tell my friend he was wrong for his name calling.
_______ I would definitely butt in and tell my friend that no matter what the other boy had done, he had no right to call him names like that.

ATTITUDES TOWARD JEWS

Scales contained in this section measure anti-Semitic attitudes. There are several scales in the fourth section of this chapter which include Jews among their other referents and should be considered as possible alternatives to the following scales.

The anti-Semitism (A-S) scale EXHIBIT 8-8

Description. This scale was developed by Levinson and Sanford (1944) upon a sample of 128 college students. It is a 52-item scale containing questions which deal with the ethics, morality, and personality traits of Jews, as well as with their patriotism and religion.

Subjects. The sample consisted of 128 college students.

Response Mode. Subjects respond to each item on a six-point, modified Likert-type continuum: firm, strong agreement (undoubtedly true in general); moderate agreement (true in many cases; often true); slight agreement (true in some cases; occasionally); slight disagreement (more false than true); moderate disagreement (usually not the case; probably wrong); strong disagreement (an absolute misconception; false). No neutral alternative is provided.

Scoring. Weights are assigned to the response alternatives from +3 (strong agreement) to —3 (strong disagreement). No neutral alternative is provided, and a constant of 4 is added to make all values positive. The person's score is the sum of the weighted alternatives endorsed by him. High scores reflect anti-Semitism.

Reliability. Levinson and Sanford (1944) report split-half reliabilities from .96 to .98. The split-half reliability is reported by O'Reilly and O'Reilly (1954) as being .96 (corrected).

Validity. The authors based the validity of the scale upon the discrimination between known groups with liberal and conservative leanings (as measured by their approval or disapproval of such groups and movements as labor unions, socialism, racial equality, and the United States

Communist party). With regard to predictive validity, Weatherley (1961) found that high A-S scorers have a greater specific tendency than low scorers to displace experimentally aroused aggression selectively onto Jews, and very low scorers have a specific tendency to avoid expression of aroused aggression toward Jews. Weatherly (1963) also reported that child-rearing practices likely to lead to the development of a strong readiness to displace hostility were related to subsequent anti-Semitism in children, as measured by the A-S scale and by the Osgood semantic differential. In the same vein, Pulos and Spilka (1961) report that high A-S scorers were more accurate in identifying Jewish photographs and remembered accurately significantly more Jewish than non-Jewish photographs. Low A-S scorers remembered significantly more non-Jewish photographs than Jewish, and were also more accurate in their identifications of the non-Jewish photographs than were the high A-S scorers. These studies by Weatherley, and by Pulos and Spilka, may be taken as very strong evidence of the construct validity of the scale.

Comments. This is an extremely well validated, highly reliable scale which has been widely used in research. It has contributed to the development of a number of other instruments and will no doubt continue to do so. The scale is somewhat long, however, and it might be possible through item analysis to shorten the scale while retaining quite satisfactory reliability and validity estimates. Such shortening would seem valuable in terms of reduced cost.

EXHIBIT 8-8

THE ANTI - SEMITISM (A - S) SCALE

This is an investigation of general public opinion concerning Jewish people. The following are statements with which some people agree and others disagree. Please mark each one in the left margin, according to the amount of your agreement or disagreement, by using the following scale:

+3 firm, strong agreement; undoubtedly true in general.
+2 moderate agreement; true in many cases; often true.
+1 slight agreement; true in some cases; occasionally.
—1 slight disagreement; more false than true.
—2 moderate disagreement; usually not the case; probably wrong.
—3 strong disagreement; an absolute misconception; false.

1 It would hurt the business of a large concern if it had too many Jewish employees.

2 The Jews should make sincere efforts to rid themselves of their conspicuous and irritating faults, if they really want to stop being persecuted.

3 In order to maintain a nice residential neighborhood it is best to prevent Jews from living in it.

4 War shows up the fact that the Jews are not patriotic nor willing to make sacrifices for their country.
5 The best way to eliminate the Communist menace in this country is to control the Jewish element which guides it.
6 Jews seem to prefer the most luxurious, extravagant and sensual way of living.
7 Much resentment against Jews stems from their tendency to keep apart and to exclude Gentiles from Jewish social life.
8 Colleges should adopt a quota system by which they limit the number of Jews in fields which have too many Jews now.
9 The Jews must be considered a bad influence on Christian culture and civilization.
10 In order to handle the Jewish problem, Gentiles must meet fire with fire and use the same ruthless tactics with the Jews that the Jews use with Gentiles.
11 The Jewish districts in most cities are results of the clannishness and stick-togetherness of Jews.
12 Jews may have moral standards that they apply in their dealing with each other, but with Christians they are unscrupulous, ruthless and undependable.
13 On the whole, the Jews have probably contributed less to American life than any other group.
14 One thing that has hindered the Jews from establishing their own nation is the fact that they really have no culture of their own; instead, they tend to copy the things that are important to the native citizens of whatever country they are in.
15 A step toward solving the Jewish problem would be to prevent Jews from getting into superior, profitable positions in society, for a while at least.
16 The true Christian can never forgive the Jews for their crucifixion of Christ.
17 Jews go too far in hiding their Jewishness, especially such extremes as changing names, straightening noses, and imitating Christian manners and customs.
18 It is not wise for a Christian to be seen too much with Jews, as he might be taken for a Jew, or be looked down upon by his Christian friends.
19 When Jews create large funds for educational or scientific research (Rosenwald, Heller, etc.) it is mainly a desire for fame and public notice rather than a really sincere scientific interest.
20 There is something different and strange about Jews; one never knows what they are thinking or planning, nor what makes them tick.
21 The Jewish problem is so general and deep that one often doubts that democratic methods can ever solve it.
22 A major fault of the Jews is their conceit, overbearing pride, and their idea that they are a chosen race.
23 One of the first steps to be taken in cleaning up the movies and generally improving the situation in Hollywood is to put an end to Jewish domination there.
24 There is little hope of correcting the racial defects of the Jews, since these defects are simply in their blood.
25 One big trouble with Jews is that they are never contented, but always try for the best jobs and the most money.
26 The trouble with letting Jews into a nice neighborhood is that they gradually give it a typical Jewish atmosphere.
27 It is wrong for Jews and Gentiles to intermarry.
28 One trouble with Jewish business men is that they stick together and connive, so that a Gentile doesn't have a fair chance in competition.
29 No matter how Americanized a Jew may seem to be, there is always something basically Jewish underneath, a loyalty to Jewry and a manner that is never totally changed.

30 Jewish millionaires may do a certain amount to help their own people, but little of their money goes into worthwhile American causes.
31 Most hotels should deny admittance to Jews, as a general rule.
32 The Jew's first loyalty is to Jewry rather than to his country.
33 It is best that Jews should have their own fraternities and sororities, since they have their own particular interests and activities which they can best engage in together, just as Christians get along best in all-Christian fraternities.
34 Jewish power and control in money matters is far out of proportion to the number of Jews in the total population.
35 Jewish leaders should encourage Jews to be more inconspicuous, to keep out of professions and activities already over-crowded with Jews, and to keep out of the public notice.
36 I can hardly imagine myself marrying a Jew.
37 The Jews should give up their un-Christian religion with all its strange customs (kosher diet, special holidays, etc.) and participate actively and sincerely in the Christian religion.
38 There is little doubt that Jewish pressure is largely responsible for the U.S. getting into the war with Germany.
39 The Jews keep too much to themselves, instead of taking the proper interest in community problems and good government.
40 Jews seem to have an aversion to plain hard work; they tend to be a parasitic element in society by finding easy, non-productive jobs.
41 It is sometimes all right to ban Jews from certain apartment houses.
42 Jews tend to remain a foreign element in American society, to preserve their old social standards and to resist the American way of life.
43 Districts containing many Jews always seem to be smelly, dirty, shabby and unattractive.
44 It would be to the best interest of all if the Jews would form their own nation and keep more to themselves.
45 There are too many Jews in the various Federal agencies and bureaus in Washington, and they have too much control over our national policies.
46 Anyone who employs many people should be careful not to hire a large percentage of Jews.
47 One general fault of Jews is their over-aggressiveness, a strong tendency always to display their Jewish looks, manners, and breeding.
48 There are a few exceptions, but in general Jews are pretty much alike.
49 Jews should be more concerned with their personal appearance, and not be so dirty and smelly and unkempt.
50 There seems to be some revolutionary streak in the Jewish make-up as shown by the fact that there are so many Jewish Communists and agitators.
51 The Jews should not pry so much into Christian activities and organizations, nor seek so much recognition and prestige from Christians.
52 Jews tend to lower the general standard of living by their willingness to do the most menial work and to live under standards that are far below average.

Attitude toward Jews scale EXHIBIT 8-9

Description. This 12-item, Likert-type scale was developed by Harlan (1942) to measure attitudes toward Jews in the college situation. The items are paragraphs which tell "stories" in which some action is taken or some attitude is expressed by non-Jews toward Jewish students or teachers. Each story is followed by a single question to be answered by the respondent.

Subjects. The sample consisted of 534 male and female college students from Northern and Southern colleges.

Response Mode. Subjects respond to each item on a five-point Likert continuum: strongly approve, approve, undecided, disapprove, and strongly disapprove. On the original form, there was also a calibrated linear continuum on which the subject marked how favorable or unfavorable his attitude toward Jews was.

Scoring. For positive items, the response alternatives are weighted from 5 (strongly approve), to 1 (strongly disapprove). Weights for the response alternatives for negative items must be reversed. The person's score is the sum of the weighted alternatives endorsed by him. High scores reflect positive attitudes toward Jews.

Reliability. Harlan (1942) reports split-half reliability coefficients (corrected) ranging from .81 to .88.

Validity. Validity is based upon the fact that the difference between the means of answers of 32 Jews and 502 non-Jews is 10.79 times its standard error, with the mean for Jewish subjects being higher than non-Jews. To further establish validity, each subject was asked to mark on a nine-point scale, ranging from most friendly to most unfriendly, his own estimate of his attitude toward Jews. These estimates correlated .66 with the test scores of the 502 non-Jewish subjects, giving the scale a degree of concurrent validity.

Comments. The use of stories rather than single sentence items can become very complex and difficult. In this case, however, each story has a single theme and, following it, a clear-cut question to which the subject is to reply. As a result, the scale seems average or above in its validity and reliability. For the interested reader, Harlan (1942) presents normative information regarding the scores of his various samples, which may be useful for longitudinal or cross-cultural comparisons.

EXHIBIT 8-9

ATTITUDE TOWARD JEWS SCALE

Here are twelve stories in which some action toward Jews is described. After you have read each story, indicate the extent of your agreement with or approval of the action described by checking one of the five responses listed under each story: strongly agree, agree, don't know, disagree, strongly disagree.

*I Although he was strongly recommended by his college teachers, Irving Pindar was rejected by the medical schools to which he applied for admittance. Since other students with poorer college records and less strongly recommended than he were accepted by the same schools to which he applied, it was plain that the reason for Irving's rejection was the fact that he was Jewish.

Question: Do you approve or disapprove of the action of the medical schools with regard to Irving's application for admittance?

Strongly Agree Agree Don't Know Disagree Strongly Disagree

II When Dr. Harry Katz was appointed as teacher of chemistry in a small midwestern college, four members of the board of trustees protested. They asserted that the relations between teacher and student in a small college are close and intimate, and they did not want the students associating in such ways with a Jew. The president of the college, however, fought against their objection on the ground that Dr. Katz was an able teacher and well qualified for the position, and he was successful in having the appointment confirmed.

Question: Do you approve or disapprove of the action of the president?

III Sylvia Morton hadn't been at the University a month before Bob Jenks asked her for a date. Bob knew that Sylvia was Jewish; he also knew that she was one of the prettiest and most attractive girls in her class. All during their freshman year Bob took Sylvia to movies, dances, games, parties, etc.

Question: Do you approve or disapprove of Bob having dates with Sylvia?

*IV Fraternity Row at one of the eastern Universities is lined with large and expensive houses. When the local chapter of a Jewish national social fraternity attempted to buy a lot in order to build a house on the Row, the members of the fraternities already there petitioned the authorities of the University not to sell the land to the Jewish fraternity.

Question: Do you approve or disapprove of the action of the fraternities?

V For years ______________ College, a privately endowed college in New England, had followed the policy of admitting Jewish students in numbers no greater than 8 percent of the freshman class. When a new president took office he dropped this policy and proposed to admit Jews on the same basis as other students.

Question: Do you approve or disapprove of the action of the new president?

VI When Jack Henderson proposed Leon Teller for membership in the national social fraternity of which Jack was a member, his proposal met with opposition by other members. Their objection to Leon was based on the fact that he was Jewish. Jack pleaded with his fraternity brothers to realize that Leon was a bright, charming and popular boy. He argued that the fact that Leon was a Jew should not influence their decision.

Question: Do you approve or disapprove of Jack's action?

*VII Jim Todd was the last member of the squad to vote in the election of captain for next year's football team. It so happened that when it came his turn to vote there was a deadlock between White and Levine, the two outstanding guards on the team. Jim voted for White. He later explained that he did so because "it just wouldn't do to have a Jew for football captain."

Question: Do you approve or disapprove of Jim's attitude?

*VIII The Cosmos Club at ______________ University is composed of some twenty or so of the graduate students in the social sciences. Once a month they have an informal meeting at which a paper on some subject of general

* These items are negative and weights for their response alternatives must be reversed for purposes of scoring. The same response alternatives are used with each question.

interest is read and discussed. When Henry Berstein, a brilliant student in economics, was proposed for membership, one of the members objected, saying, "Henry is all right, but once we start letting Jews in we'll be overrun with them."

Question: Do you approve or disapprove of the attitude expressed by this member?

IX Harry Myers and Mary Babcock have been going together for six years—ever since they were in college together. Harry is Jewish, Mary is not. Although her friends urge her to break off the relationship, Mary has decided that she loves Harry and intends to marry him.

Question: Do you approve or disapprove of Mary's decision?

*X One of the large state universities had a vacancy in its English department. After a careful consideration of the qualifications of all the applicants for the position, the head of the English department and the dean of the college agreed that Dr. Harold Bowman was by far the best qualified for the job. An interview with Dr. Bowman confirmed them in their judgment. He was pleasant, attractive in manner, and obviously competent in his field. However when they learned that Dr. Bowman was Jewish they decided not to appoint him to the position.

Question: Do you approve or disapprove of the decision made in this case?

XI Tom Jackson, in his freshman year at a southern state university, found himself assigned to a room in the dormitory with Philip Klein, a Jewish boy. Tom's friend urged him to get the university authorities to give him another room. Tom, however, said that he found Philip a very pleasant and cooperative roommate and refused to ask for any change.

Question: Do you approve or disapprove of Tom's action?

*XII In his senior year Bill Smith had to take a course in economic history. There were two sections of the course offered: one taught by Prof. Jones, the other by Prof. Lovenstein. Bill chose Prof. Jones' section and justified his choice to his advisor by saying, "I don't think you ought to study economics under a Jew. They're all communists or something, and you're liable to get the wrong ideas."

Question: Do you approve or disapprove of Bill's attitude in this case?

Opinions on the Jews EXHIBIT 8-10

Description. This 24-item scale was developed by Eysenck and Crown (1949) using a combined Thurstone and Likert procedure. The content of the items deals with the question of inferiority of Jews in terms of morality, intellect, loyalty, and power seeking. The original item pool, 150 statements regarding Jews, was submitted to a Thurstone sorting procedure. Of these, 24 items were retained and tested for reliability. The items were then tested for reliability using a Likert response continuum on a second sample of 200 university students. The same data on the 24 items were then scored using the authors' scale product method (in which the Thurstone scale value is multiplied by the weight assigned the response alternative endorsed to produce the score for the item), in order to compare reliability coefficients. Finally, the same 24 items were subjected to a factor analysis and a scalogram analysis. No further item selection was performed on the basis of these analyses.

Subjects. The sample for the Thurstone sorting procedure was 80 (mostly nonacademic) judges, whose views on the attitudinal referent were assessed by the Primary Social Attitudes Questionnaire (Eysenck, 1947). The sample for the assessment of the split-half reliability of the Thurstone form of this scale was 200 university students. A second sample of 200 university students was used to assess the reliability of the Likert form of the scale; data from this sample were also used in the assessment of the reliability of the scale product method. To assess validity, the scale (in Likert form) was administered to 250 nonacademic, middle- and working-class subjects (urban, both sexes, all ages) who were contacted through students.

Response Mode. If the scale product scoring procedure is followed, the subjects respond to each item by endorsing one of five Likert-type alternatives: strongly agree, agree, uncertain, disagree, and strongly disagree.

Scoring. Each item is scored by multiplying the Thurstone scale value of the item (indicated in Exhibit 8-10) by the weight assigned the Likert-type alternative endorsed by the subject. The weights to be assigned the alternative are shown beside it in the exhibit. Weights for alternatives to negative items have been reversed. The subject's score is the sum of the weighted alternatives multiplied by the scale values of the items. High scores indicate anti-Semitic attitudes.

Reliability. The split-half reliability (corrected) for the Thurstone form of the scale was found by the author to be .83 ($N = 200$). For the Likert form of the scale, the split-half reliability (corrected) was .90, $N = 200$ (which is significantly higher than that for the Thurstone form). The split-half reliability (corrected) for the scale product method of scoring was .94 ($N = 200$). Again, the reliability estimate for the scale product method is significantly higher than that for the Likert form.

Validity. This use of the Thurstone construction procedure should provide a degree of content validity. To further assess the validity of the scale, students were asked to give the scale to five persons. These students then wrote essays describing the characteristics of these persons (temperament, social background, any personal knowledge of the respondent's social attitudes, comments of the respondents to the questionnaire, and a summary by the student of the relation between known attitudes and answers on the questionnaire). The students were sophisticated in regard to scale construction and factors influencing questionnaire answers; the respondents presumably were not. The author reports a very close degree of agreement between the answers given by the respondent and the ratings given the respondents by the student administrators. The impression of the students that the sample was largely anti-Semitic was confirmed by the distribution of scores on the scale, which fact is taken as further evidence of validity by the authors. The theoretical neutral point in this scale would be 96, or the mean score for the range of possible scores. The neutral point, when assessed using Guttman's procedures, was found to fall in the score class interval of 62 to 66, or one standard deviation below the mean of possible scores. In a factor analysis, the first factor accounted for 48 percent of the variance and was interpreted as being pro-Semitism. The second factor accounted only for 5 percent of the variance and is attributed to error or to response set. The first factor reflecting anti-Semitism was correlated with radicalism ($r = -.48$) and with tendermindedness ($r = -.11$), using the Primary Social Attitudes Questionnaire to assess radicalism and tendermindedness. Further evidence for validity is the reproducibility coefficient of .85, indicating a quasi-scale by Guttman's standards.

Comments. This scale may be used in any one of three procedures: the scale product method devised by its authors, the Thurstone procedure, or the Likert procedure. However, evidence of comparability of these methods with regard to changes in subjects' scores is not available. It should be noted that Eysenck and Crown have been criticized by Green (1954) for their combination of the Thurstone and Likert procedures for scale construction because the two procedures require different item forms. However, the scale authors obtained high reliability estimates using their procedure. The effects on validity of combining the two procedures is an empirical question which has not been answered as yet. This scale is average or above in reliability, but further studies of its validity would be valuable. The authors (Eysenck and Crown, 1949) report their factor analysis, the scalogram analysis, and the score distributions, which should be useful for further research on the problems involved in the scale product method.

EXHIBIT 8-10

OPINIONS ON THE JEWS

In this questionnaire you will find 24 different opinions on the Jews. We want to know in each case whether you agree or disagree with the view expressed. Underneath the statement of each opinion you will find five alternative reactions:

strongly agree; agree; uncertain; disagree; strongly disagree.

Underline whichever alternative gives the most correct picture of your own view. *Please do not leave out any statements* even when you find it difficult to make up your mind. Your views will remain quite anonymous; you are asked not to sign your name.

Scale Value | **Item**

4.7 1 Dislike of the Jews comes mainly from misunderstanding.
strongly agree; 3 agree; 3 uncertain; 4 disagree; 5 strongly disagree; 5.

Reprinted with permission from Eysenck, H. J., and Crown, S. National stereotypes: An experiment and methodological study. *Internat. J. Opin. Attitude Res.*, 1948, 2, 26–39.

Scale Value		
8.8	*2	Jews monopolize everything to the detriment of the English. strongly agree; 7 agree; 5 uncertain; 4 disagree; 3 strongly disagree; 1.
5.9	3	The Jews are an isolated group in society because of their religion. strongly agree; 3 agree; 4 uncertain; 4 disagree; 4 strongly disagree; 5.
9.5	*4	Jews will stoop to any kind of deceit in order to gain their own ends. strongly agree; 7 agree; 6 uncertain; 4 disagree; 2 strongly disagree; 1.
2.3	5	Jews are as valuable, honest, and public-spirited citizens as any other group. strongly agree; 1 agree; 2 uncertain; 4 disagree; 6 strongly disagree; 7.
3.0	6	There are both "good" and "bad" Jews, as there are both kinds of Englishmen, and there is not much to choose between them on the whole. strongly agree; 1 agree; 3 uncertain; 4 disagree; 5 strongly disagree; 7.
5.6	7	The Jews as a whole cannot be held responsible for misdeeds of a minority who run foul of the laws and customs of this country. strongly agree; 8 agree; 6 uncertain; 4 disagree; 4 strongly disagree; 5.
10.2	*8	Jews corrupt everything with which they come into contact. strongly agree; 3 agree; 4 uncertain; 4 disagree; 2 strongly disagree; 0.
3.9	9	There is no reason to believe that innately the Jews are less honest and good than anyone else. strongly agree; 2 agree; 3 uncertain; 4 disagree; 5 strongly disagree; 6.
7.2	*10	The dislike of many people for the Jews is based on prejudice, but is nevertheless not without a certain justification. strongly agree; 5 agree; 5 uncertain; 4 disagree; 3 strongly disagree; 3.
1.5	11	The Jews are mentally and morally superior to most other people. strongly agree; 0 agree; 2 uncertain; 4 disagree; 6 strongly disagree; 8.
7.9	*12	The Jews have too much power and influence in this country. strongly agree; 6 agree; 5 uncertain; 4 disagree; 3 strongly disagree; 2.

* These items are negative and their weights have been reversed for purposes of scoring.

Scale Value		
8.3	*13	The Jews have a stranglehold on this country. strongly agree; 6 agree; 5 uncertain; 4 disagree; 3 strongly disagree; 2.
2.0	14	The Jews have survived persecution because of the many admirable qualities they show. strongly agree; 0 agree; 2 uncertain; 4 disagree; 6 strongly disagree; 8.
9.1	*15	Jews in their dealings with others are an absolute menace, money-grabbing and unscrupulous. strongly agree; 7 agree; 5 uncertain; 4 disagree; 3 strongly disagree; 1.
2.7	16	Jews are just as loyal to the country in which they live as any other citizens. strongly agree; 1 agree; 2 uncertain; 4 disagree; 6 strongly disagree; 7.
7.5	*17	Jews lack physical courage. strongly agree; 5 agree; 5 uncertain; 4 disagree; 3 strongly disagree; 3.
9.9	*18	The Jews are a menace to any nation and to any country in which they happen to live. strongly agree; 7 agree; 6 uncertain; 4 disagree; 2 strongly disagree; 1.
3.5	19	The Jews are a decent set of people on the whole. strongly agree; 1 agree; 3 uncertain; 4 disagree; 5 strongly disagree; 7.
6.3	*20	The Jews should give up their separate customs and become average citizens of this country. strongly agree; 5 agree; 4 uncertain; 4 disagree; 4 strongly disagree; 3.
6.7	*21	There are too many Jews in the highly paid professions. strongly agree; 5 agree; 4 uncertain; 4 disagree; 4 strongly disagree; 3.
4.4	22	Jews can't be expected to behave any better toward the rest of the world than the rest of the world behaves toward them. strongly agree; 2 agree; 3 uncertain; 4 disagree; 5 strongly disagree; 6.
10.7	*23	The Jews are the most despicable form of mankind which crawls on this earth. strongly agree; 8 agree; 6 uncertain; 4 disagree; 2 strongly disagree; 0.
5.1	24	The Jewish menace has been much exaggerated. strongly agree; 3 agree; 3 uncertain; 4 disagree; 5 strongly disagree; 5.

ATTITUDES TOWARD OTHER ETHNIC AND NATIONAL GROUPS

In this section are those scales which measure attitudes toward ethnic and national groups other than Negroes and Jews. In some instances, it is difficult to determine whether the scale measures attitudes toward the national group as a political entity or toward the people as a social group (e.g., the Thurstone scale measuring attitudes toward the German people). Scales in this section include measures of attitudes toward Caucasians (an antiwhite scale), Germans, Chinese, and Russians. A number of instruments were excluded from this section because they were not scales, or because of difficulties in their construction and in assessment of their characteristics. Readers interested in a projective measure of attitudes toward Americans should see Graham (1954). For an incomplete-sentence approach to measurement of attitudes toward Russia, see Frymier (1961). There is also a scale measuring attitudes toward communism in Chapter 5. Johnson (1950) has developed a projective device for measurement of ethnic attitudes, and a similar instrument is reported upon by Vaughan and Thompson (1961). The first scale in this section is an antiwhite scale by Steckler, who also developed an anti-Negro scale to accompany it (see the first section of this chapter).

The anti-white scale *EXHIBIT 8-11*

Description. This 18-item scale was developed by Steckler (1957) and used concurrently with his anti-Negro scale to measure the attitudes of Negroes in a study of authoritarianism in Negroes. The items are such that they lend themselves more to the testing of nonwhite than of white samples, and would be best used with Negro samples. Steckler (1957) reports the means and standard deviations of the scale scores on his sample for readers interested in making comparisons.

Subjects. The sample consisted of 299 college students and members of church groups, all of whom were Negro; the sample represented both Northern and Southern Negroes.

Response Mode. Persons respond to each item on a Likert-type continuum: strongly agree, agree, undecided, disagree, and strongly disagree.

Scoring. For negative items, weights are assigned the response alternatives from 5 (strongly agree) to 1 (strongly disagree). Weights for positive items must be reversed. The person's score is the sum of the weighted alternatives endorsed by him. Higher scores reflect antiwhite attitudes.

Reliability. Steckler (1957) reports the split-half reliability of this scale as .88.

Validity. The scale seems to have very good content validity. In addition, Steckler reports correlations of .60 and .55 between the Anti-White

Scale and the California E and F scales, respectively. This scale correlates .24 with the Anti-Negro Scale. These correlations may be taken as evidence of construct validity for the scale.

Comments. This seems to be a reasonably valid and reliable scale for measuring antiwhite attitudes among Negroes or other "colored" samples. It is not very applicable to white samples. This scale, together with its counterpart (the Anti-Negro Scale) should produce interesting data on self-hate in minority groups, the generality of hostility in attitudes, and so forth.

EXHIBIT 8-11

THE ANTI - WHITE SCALE

This is a study of what people think about a number of social questions. The best answer to each statement below is *your personal opinion.* We have tried to cover many different points of view. You may agree strongly with some statements, disagree just as strongly with others, and perhaps be uncertain about others. Whether you agree or disagree with any statement, you can be sure that many other people feel the same way that you do.

Please mark each statement in the left margin according to how much you agree or disagree with it. *Please Mark Every One.* Write +1, +2, +3, or −1, −2, −3, depending on how you feel in each case.

+1: I Agree A Little	−1: I Disagree A Little
+2: I Agree Pretty Much	−2: I Disagree Pretty Much
+3: I Agree Very Much	−3: I Disagree Very Much

1 There is nothing lower than white trash.
2 White people may be all right, but they carry it too far when they try to butt into the Negro's affairs and go around with Negro women.
3 The whites have shown by their actions that they are naturally immoral, vicious, and untrustworthy.
4 No matter how nicely they treat a colored person, white people don't really mean it.
5 It is usually a mistake to trust a white person.
6 Any Negro who marries a white is a traitor to his people.
7 There may be a few exceptions, but white musicians and athletes are definitely inferior to Negro musicians and athletes.
8 White people are only friendly to Negroes when they want something out of them.
9 Negroes can expect no real help from white people in the fight against racial discrimination.

10 Most white people are always looking for ways to cheat and steal from the colored people.

11 The colored race has been pushed around long enough; it's about time that the whites were made to get out of the Negro communities.

12 If there is a Heaven, it is hard to imagine that there are many white people up there.

13 Although the white man now rules the world, it will be a happy day when the tables are turned and the colored people become the rulers.

14 The world might be a better place if there were fewer white people.

15 When the Bible says, "The bottom shall rise to the top," it gives hope that the Negro people will someday give the orders in this country instead of whites.

16 It may be wrong to damn all whites, but it's plain that whites have all the money and power, and that they look down on anyone who is colored.

*17 There are many white people who are not prejudiced and who sincerely believe that Negroes are equals.

18 When it comes to such things as sports, dancing, music, and making love, the white man is not as talented as the Negro.

* This item is positive and must be reversed for scoring purposes.

Attitude toward the German people EXHIBIT 8-12

Description. Although developed by Peterson (Thurstone, 1931) prior to World War II, this 27-item scale is not at all dated in content. The items tend to emphasize the militancy (or lack of it) of the German people. Some items refer to the people of Germany, while others seem to imply as their referent the German immigrant to America.

Subjects. The sample on which this scale was constructed is unknown but is presumed to have been University of Chicago undergraduate students.

Response Mode. Subjects respond by checking those statements with which they agree and placing a cross beside those statements with which they disagree.

Scoring. The subject's score is the median of the scale values of the items endorsed by him as "agree."

Reliability. Lorge (1939) reports the reliability coefficients on this scale to range from .51 to .58. Likert et al. (1934) give the range as being from .42 to .59. While these reliabilities are lower than are desirable, they may reflect the conflictive nature of the historical era in which they were obtained; i.e., they were estimated in the 1930s. The estimates are minimal even for purposes of group testing, nonetheless.

Validity. The content validity of this scale would be improved by altering the scale (or its items) to make it refer either to the nation of Germany or the Germans (especially if it were made clear whether it referred to German immigrants or to nationals). Dudycha (1942) reports a continual decline in the mean test scores of college students measured before World War II, before the European invasion, and just after that invasion. This decline would seem to indicate the predictive validity of the scale.

Comments. One of the primary difficulties with this scale is the fact that subjects may have in mind any combination of four possible referents: Americans of German descent, German immigrants to America, the people of East Germany, or the people of West Germany. Failure to effectively distinguish between these possible referents reduces the content validity of the scale and probably accounts in part for its very low reliability estimates. These estimates are much lower than the average Thurstone scale. Improvement of the scale would involve primarily an improvement in delineation of its content domain. Also, in view of continual changes in the international situation, it would seem wise to reassess the scale values of the items in this scale. This is one of the few Thurstone scales that strongly requires further attention to functional characteristics, but for successful use of this scale such attention does seem essential.

EXHIBIT 8-12

ATTITUDE TOWARD THE GERMAN PEOPLE

This is a study of attitudes toward the Germans. On the following page you will find 27 statements expressing different attitudes toward the Germans.

Put a check mark (✓) if you **agree** with the statement.
Put a cross (×) if you **disagree** with the statement.
If you cannot decide about a statement, you may mark it with a question mark.

This is not an examination. People differ in their opinions about what is right and wrong in this issue.

Please indicate *your own attitude* by a check mark when you agree and by a cross when you disagree.

Scale Value		
4.6	1	The Germans as a race are very pleasant people.
9.1	2	I'm prejudiced against people of German descent.
6.4	3	German people are no better and no worse than any other people.
1.8	4	I admire the German people unreservedly.
12.3	5	The German people are the most despicable people in the world.
4.1	6	Some of our best American citizens are of German descent.
.7	7	The German people are the finest in the world.
10.6	8	The German soldiers were, almost without exception, cruel and brutal.

Scale Value		
8.4	9	Germans are slow and unimaginative.
3.7	10	The more I know about the German people the better I like them.
11.5	11	If Germany had been wiped out by the war the world would be better off.
7.4	12	I don't object to German people but I don't like the German Government.
4.8	13	The German people were not responsible for and did not want war.
9.7	14	I don't trust the Germans.
9.1	15	The German military officer is typical of the German people.
9.0	16	German parents are harsh to their children.
11.9	17	I hate all the Germans.
4.0	18	The rank and file of the German army were kindly admirable young men.
2.7	19	The Germans are the most desirable class of immigrants.
2.4	20	I'd rather have my sister marry a German than any other foreigner.
5.7	21	The arrogance of the German officer is not typical of the German People.
7.0	22	I have no particular love nor hate for the Germans.
10.9	23	There is nothing about the Germans that I could ever like.
7.8	24	I suppose Germans are all right but I've never liked them.
3.0	25	German home life is ideal.
10.4	26	The people of Germany are gluttonous, militaristic and overbearing.
.5	27	Germans are superior to any other nationality.

Attitude toward the Chinese *EXHIBIT 8-13*

Description. Thurstone (1931) developed this 26-item scale using his own procedure. Regarding content, it is still applicable to non-Communist Chinese, but a number of the items are stated in such a manner as to make it inapplicable to Red China today. When it is used, the instructions should make clear that the items refer only to Nationalist China. Even then, the scale values probably need to be reassessed, and the content domain may not be adequately sampled. Q values for these items could not be located.

Subjects. The sample upon which the scale was constructed is unknown but presumably consisted of University of Chicago undergraduate students.

Response Mode. Subjects respond by checking those items with which they agree and by placing a cross beside those with which they disagree.

Scoring. The person's score is the median of the scale values of the items endorsed as "agree." High scores indicate negative attitudes toward the Chinese.

Reliability. Like the attitude toward Germans scale presented above, this scale is of doubtful reliability. Likert et al. (1934) report reliability estimates ranging from .57 to .86 for this scale, while Lorge (1939) gives the range as being from .39 to .67. Using 182 Illinois school children (grades 9 through 12), Thurstone (1932) reports a test-retest reliability coefficient of .57 with an intervening test interval of one week. This coefficient is not actually a reliability coefficient but may be treated as one. It is to be noted that the subjects were subjected to a relevant motion picture during the test interval, which may have conditioned their attitudes and makes the figure reported by Thurstone a conservative one.

Validity. This scale possesses reduced content validity because of the dated items and because of historical and political events which would allow for the development of many new, meaningful items. It was used by Grice (1934) to validate his scale measuring attitudes toward any defined group, the correlation between the two scales being .57. The scale is presently in the position of being an instrument which was once quite valid but is now questionable.

Comments. The use of instructions which clarify to what group of Chinese (immigrant American Chinese, American-born Chinese, Red Chinese, or Nationalist Chinese) the items refer would probably improve the reliability and validity of this scale. However, there are many items which could be added to the item pool to improve its contemporary content validity. If it is used, it would seem necessary to reassess the characteristics of the scale and the Q values of the items.

EXHIBIT 8-13

ATTITUDE TOWARD THE CHINESE

This is a study of attitudes toward the Chinese. On the following page you will find 26 statements expressing different attitudes toward the Chinese.

Put a check mark (✓) if you **agree** with the statement.
Put a cross (×) if you **disagree** with the statement.
If you cannot decide about a statement, you may mark it with a question mark.

This is not an examination. People differ in their opinions about what is right and wrong in this issue.

Please indicate *your own attitude* by a check mark when you agree and by a cross when you disagree.

Scale Value		
6.5	1	I have no particular love nor hate for the Chinese.
10.1	2	I dislike the Chinese more every time I see one.
4.7	3	The Chinese are pretty decent.

Scale Value		
7.2	4	Some Chinese traits are admirable but on the whole I don't like them.
.5	5	The Chinese are superior to all other races.
8.7	6	The Chinese as part of the yellow race are inferior to the white race.
3.5	7	I like the Chinese.
2.8	8	The more I know about the Chinese the better I like them.
11.0	9	The Chinese are aptly described by the term "yellow devils."
1.8	10	The high class Chinese are superior to us.
5.2	11	The Chinese are different but not inferior.
11.5	12	I hate the Chinese.
4.1	13	Chinese parents are unusually devoted to their children.
7.7	14	Although I respect some of their qualities, I could never consider a Chinese as my friend.
1.2	15	I would rather live in China than any other place in the world.
9.7	16	There are no refined nor cultured Chinese.
6.0	17	The Chinese are no better and no worse than any other people.
8.4	18	I think Chinese should be kept out of the United States.
2.2	19	I consider it a privilege to associate with Chinese people.
10.6	20	The Chinese are inferior in every way.
9.4	21	I don't see how anyone could ever like the Chinese.
3.0	22	Chinese have a very high sense of honor.
8.6	23	I have no desire to know any Chinese.
1.4	24	Chinese people have a refinement and depth of feeling that you don't find anywhere else.
9.8	25	There is nothing about the Chinese that I like or admire.
3.9	26	I'd like to know more Chinese people.

A survey of opinions and beliefs about Russia: the Soviet Union EXHIBIT 8-14

Description. This 12-item, Likert-type scale was developed by Smith (1946). The items involve questions of acceptance of and trust in Russia, its leaders, and its form of government. It is more a measure of attitudes toward Soviets than of attitudes toward Russians in general. How much differentiation between the two would be made by respondents is an empirical question.

Subjects. The sample consisted of 560 college students and 150 adults.

Response Mode. Subjects respond to each item on a modified Likert-type continuum: strongly agree, moderately agree, undecided, moderately disagree, and strongly disagree.

Scoring. The response alternatives for positive items are weighted from 5 (strongly agree) to 1 (strongly disagree). Weights for response alternatives to negative items must be reversed. The person's score is the sum of the weighted alternatives endorsed by him. High scores reflect positive attitudes toward Russia.

Reliability. Smith (1946) reported odd-even reliability coefficients (corrected) of .86 to .92. Test-retest reliabilities of .95 and .79 were reported, using a ten-day test interval. Helfant (1952) used 166 high school seniors and their mothers (165) and fathers (165) as his sample and reported split-half reliabilities (corrected) of .86, .89, and .92 for the mothers, fathers, and students, respectively.

Validity. Smith (1946) based the validity of the scale upon three rather loose criteria. First, the scale scores were consistent with subjects' verbalizations during a one-hour nondirective interview; second, six subjects earning maximum scores were members of organizations with pro-Soviet policy; third, the political beliefs and readings of high and low scorers on the scale were consistent with expectation. Helfant (1952) has established concurrent validity for the scale on the basis of a .78 correlation between scale scores and self-ratings by subjects of their attitudes toward Russia.

Comments. This seems a satisfactory scale in most regards. If there were equivalent forms, its value would be enhanced somewhat.

EXHIBIT 8-14

A SURVEY OF OPINIONS AND BELIEFS ABOUT RUSSIA: THE SOVIET UNION

On this page you will find 12 statements. READ EACH STATEMENT CAREFULLY AND UNDERLINE QUICKLY THE WORD WHICH BEST EXPRESSES YOUR FEELING ABOUT THE ITEM. You should guide yourself by this key.

AGREE or DISAGREE (in large letters) = **strongly** agree or disagree with the statement.

agree or disagree (in small letters) = **moderately** agree or disagree with the statement.

Undecided = undecided, indifferent, or do not understand the statement.

There is no "right or "wrong" about any of these answers; the statements do not form a test, but simply a survey of opinions. BE SURE TO ANSWER EVERY ITEM. If in doubt, underline the word which seems most nearly to express your present feeling about the statement. Put down what you actually feel, rather than what you think you ought to feel; and do not be especially concerned about whether your opinions are "consistent" or not.

1 In my opinion, the Russian leaders will honestly support a United Nations plan to keep the peace.

Reprinted with permission from Smith, G. H. Attitude toward Soviet Russia: I. The standardization of a scale and some distributions of scores. *J. soc. Psychol.*, 1946, 23, 3–16.

*2 I have an unfavorable attitude toward Russia.
*3 Even in peacetime, the Soviet leaders use force to hold the mass of Russian people in place—make them do things against their will.
4 I like more things about Stalin than I dislike.
*5 I would not like to see any other European country set up a Russian type of government.
6 I approve the methods the Soviet Union has used to strengthen the country and "get things done."
7 I feel friendly toward Russia.
*8 It is my feeling that the Soviet Union is likely to start another European war, sooner or later.
9 I think Russia's treatment of the church is all right.
10 I believe Russia sincerely wants to see the people in the small countries of Europe decide their own form of government.
*11 I feel a sense of distrust and suspicion toward Russia.
*12 I am disturbed by what has happened to the home and the family under the Russian system.

* These items are negative and must be reversed for purposes of scoring.

MIXED SCALES TO MEASURE ATTITUDES TOWARD ETHNIC GROUPS

In this section are contained scales which measure attitudes toward more than one ethnic or national group. These scales do not always provide separate scores for each of the referent groups and are often an attempt to measure some more global attitude. If the scales are broken down into separate scores for the different referents contained in them, it would be valuable to reassess the functional characteristics of the subscales thus used. The two mixed scales included here are the California E scale and the Intolerant-Tolerant (IT) Scale. For an interesting mixed scale using logical syllogisms as the item form, see Thistlethwaite (1950).

Ethnocentrism scale EXHIBIT 8-15

Description. This scale was initially developed by Levinson (1949) and used by Adorno et al. (1950) to study ethnocentricism and authoritarianism. It has enjoyed a great deal of usage in the past decade and a half. The scale was constructed using a Likert procedure. The items given in Exhibit 8-15 are those from the final, suggested form (Levinson, 1949). It is a 20-item scale containing three subscales which measure attitudes toward (1) Jews, (2) Negroes, (3) other minorities and patriotism. This form represents a compromise between the longer forms and the short (10-item) Form 45. Although the E scale seems to measure a highly general response predisposition, rather than a specific attitude, it may be used to measure the specific attitudes represented by its subscales.

Subjects. A very large sample was used, including such groups as penitentiary inmates, female extension-class students, psychiatric clinic women, psychiatric clinic men, and working-class men and women.

Response Mode. Subjects respond to each item on a six-point continuum: strong support, agreement; moderate support, agreement; slight support, agreement; slight opposition, disagreement; moderate opposition, disagreement; and strong opposition, disagreement.

Scoring. All items in the scale are negatively phrased. Thus, weights are assigned to response alternatives for all items from +3 (strong agreement) to −3 (strong disagreement). A constant of 4 is added to make all values positive. The person's score is the sum of the weighted alternatives endorsed by him. High scores reflect negative (ethnocentric) attitudes.

Reliability. Adorno et al. (1950) estimate the reliability of the total E scale to be .85 on the average. The equivalent-forms reliability of the Forms 45 and 40 (10- and 5-item scales respectively) is about .79. The split-half reliability for the Form 45 is .87. It is expected that the scale contained in the exhibit would have a reliability coefficient above .80. Levinson (1949) reported reliabilities in the neighborhood of .90.

Validity. The validity of the E scale has been generally called into question on two bases: First, the scale attempts to measure such a global concept as ethnocentrism or authoritarianism; second, the items are all negatively phrased, thus rendering it vulnerable to response set on the part of the subject. The fact that the items all have one direction, coupled with the extremity of these statements, indicates that the scale score will be affected by any tendency to acquiescence as well. If the scale presented here is used to measure specific attitudes toward the referents involved (Jew, Negro, or other minorities), the question of validity is more readily resolved. First, some of the items are dated. Second, the items measuring attitudes toward Jews are known to correlate well (.80) with Levinson's A-S scale (Levinson, 1949). Siegel and Siegel (1957) have demonstrated predictive validity for the scale as a whole. McGinnies and Altman (1959) found the high, middle, and low scorers on the E scale could be differentiated on the basis of variables measured by the Chapple interaction chronograph. Finally, the authors of the scale (Adorno et al., 1950) found that the E scale would differentiate known groups such as penitentiary inmates, female extension-class students, psychiatric clinic women, psychiatric clinic men, and working-class men and women.

Comments. Although developed as a measure of a global construct, this scale (or its subscales) may be used to measure attitudes toward specific referents. Before the scale is used in this manner, however, further estimates of validity and reliability are necessary. For any use, some of the items (all of which read negatively) should be altered to read positively to avoid the effects of acquiescence and other response sets on the part of subjects. Some of the items in the scale are dated (i.e., items referring to "Zootsuiters" and the "new" world organization) and are of doubtful value.

EXHIBIT 8-15

ETHNOCENTRISM SCALE

The following statements refer to opinions regarding a number of social groups and issues, about which some people agree and others disagree. Please mark each statement in the left-hand margin according to your agreement or disagreement as follows:

+1: slight support, agreement	−1: slight opposition, disagreement
+2: moderate support, agreement	−2: moderate opposition, disagreement
+3: strong support, agreement	−3: strong opposition, disagreement

A. Jews

1 One trouble with Jewish businessmen is that they stick together and prevent other people from having a fair chance in competition.

2 I can hardly imagine myself marrying a Jew.

3 There may be a few exceptions, but in general Jews are pretty much alike.

4 The trouble with letting Jews into a nice neighborhood is that they gradually give it a typical Jewish atmosphere.

5 To end prejudice against Jews, the first step is for the Jews to try sincerely to get rid of their harmful and irritating faults.

6 There is something different and strange about Jews; it's hard to tell what they are thinking and planning, and what makes them tick.

B. Negroes

1 Negroes have their rights, but it is best to keep them in their own districts and schools and to prevent too much contact with whites.

2 It would be a mistake ever to have Negroes for foremen and leaders over whites.

3 Negro musicians may sometimes be as good as white musicians, but it is a mistake to have mixed Negro-white bands.

4 Manual labor and unskilled jobs seem to fit the Negro mentality and ability better than more skilled or responsible work.

5 The people who raise all the talk about putting Negroes on the same level as whites are mostly radical agitators trying to stir up conflicts.

6 Most Negroes would become overbearing and disagreeable if not kept in their place.

C. Other Minorities and Patriotism

1 Zootsuiters prove that when people of their type have too much money and freedom, they just take advantage and cause trouble.

2 The worst danger to real Americanism during the last 50 years has come from foreign ideas and agitators.

3 Now that a new world organization is set up, America must be sure that she loses none of her independence and complete power as a sovereign nation.
4 Certain religious sects who refuse to salute the flag should be forced to conform to such a patriotic action, or else be abolished.
5 Filipinos are all right in their place, but they carry it too far when they dress lavishly and go around with white girls.
6 America may not be perfect, but the American Way has brought us about as close as human beings can get to a perfect society.
7 It is only natural and right for each person to think that his family is better than any other.
8 The best guarantee of our national security is for America to have the biggest army and navy in the world and the secret of the atom bomb.

Intolerant-tolerant (IT) scale EXHIBIT 8-16

Description. Prentice (1956) developed this 32-item scale to measure attitudes toward Negroes and Jews. Of the items, 16 are positive (stating a tolerant or supportive position of the ethnic group), and 16 are negative (stating an intolerant position). The items are similar in content to the California E scale. This scale consists of the conclusions to individual syllogisms from a test of syllogistic reasoning (the Woodbridge Reasoning Test) also developed by Prentice (1957).

Subjects. The sample consisted of 66 freshmen at Boston University, all of whom were native, white, Christian males.

Response Mode. Subjects respond to each item on a six-point, modified Likert-type continuum: I agree a little, I agree pretty much, I agree very much, I disagree a little, I disagree pretty much, I disagree very much.

Scoring. For negative items, the response alternatives are weighted from +3 (I agree very much) to —3 (I disagree very much). Weights for the response alternatives of positive items must be reversed. A constant of 4 is added to make all values positive. The person's score is the sum of the weighted alternatives endorsed by him. High scores reflect intolerant attitudes when scored in the manner described.

Reliability. The split-half reliabilities for the whole scale, and for the positive and negative halves of the scale, are reported to be .90, .78, and .85, respectively.

Validity. An estimate of validity is given by the correlation of the IT scale with an 18-item form of the California E scale. The E scale correlates .86 with the negative half of the IT scale, and .64 with the positive half. The length of the scale allows for good content validity.

Comments. This seems to be a satisfactory mixed type of scale with regard to both reliability and validity. If the items are separated into two subscales of Negro and Jew, it would be well to reassess the functional characteristics of these subscales. It may be that one set of these items is functioning better than is the other.

EXHIBIT 8-16

INTOLERANT - TOLERANT (IT) SCALE

Here are a number of statements about which most people have strong opinions. You are to indicate how you feel about them. Try to rate each statement the way you really feel about it.

Rate each statement on the line drawn to its left according to how much you agree with it. Please mark each one. Do not spend too long on any one as your first reaction is what is wanted. Write in +1, +2, +3, or —1, —2, —3, depending on how you feel in each case.

+1: I AGREE A LITTLE	—1: I DISAGREE A LITTLE
+2: I AGREE PRETTY MUCH	—2: I DISAGREE PRETTY MUCH
+3: I AGREE VERY MUCH	—3: I DISAGREE VERY MUCH

1 No exclusive hotels should generally be open to any Negro.
*2 The Negroes are a biologically identical group with the whites.
3 Jews are shady, clannish businessmen who are likely to use cut-throat practices.
*4 The Negro is an honest, stable worker.
*5 No Jews are powerful persons controlling the best of everything.
6 The Jew is eager to escape plain hard work because he really likes a soft life.
*7 No Negroes are pretty much content with things as they are.
*8 Jews are smart capable workers who are likely to contribute much to America.
9 No Jews are living modestly and without much showiness.
*10 No Jews are especially loud, noisy and overbearing.
*11 No nice neighborhoods should usually be closed to any Negro.
12 No Jews are well-bred, cultured people whom others like.
13 Many Jews are distinguished by foreign customs and irritating ways.
14 Many Jews should not mingle with people who don't think money is their god.
15 No Negroes should really be allowed to intermingle freely with whites at dances and schools.
16 Many Negroes are to be shunned for freely expressing sexual and aggressive urges.
*17 The Jew is contributing to the richness, wisdom, and vitality of the American Way of Life.
18 No Negroes are really interested in changing their place in life.
*19 Many Negroes should not be restricted from supervising or directing whites.
20 The Negroes are a mentally inferior group compared with whites.
21 No Jews mix very well with other people.
22 Many Jews do not give their first loyalty to America but instead to their own kind.
*23 No Negroes should be in favor of submitting to social convention without thinking for themselves.
*24 Many Jews are eager to help out any less fortunate Gentile.

* These are positive items and their weights must be reversed for purposes of scoring.

Reference: N. M. Prentice. The comparability of positive and negative items in scales of ethnic prejudice. *J. abnorm. soc. Psychol.*, **1956, 3, 420–421. Items obtained from author and published with his permission.**

*25 No Jews are ruining a nice neighborhood around them.
*26 Many ambitious Negroes are not to be discouraged from making their position equal to whites.
27 The Negro is a sharp flashy dresser.
*28 Many Jews do not neglect their duty towards community problems but instead work hard on them.
*29 Many Negroes are to be encouraged in dating white girls who like them.
*30 Many Jews should not be denied admission to the best schools, neighborhoods, or social clubs.
31 Many Negroes should not be given education they will not use.

GENERALIZED SCALES TO MEASURE ATTITUDES TOWARD ANY GROUP

Two scales to measure attitude toward any group are included in this section. In addition to these scales, it should be pointed out that the semantic differential has been used frequently to measure attitudes toward various ethnic and national groups. Asher and Evans (1959) measured attitudes toward Negroes, Negro professors, and intelligent Negroes with it, and Weatherly (1963) used the semantic differential to measure attitudes toward Jews. The scale has been found to correlate with the Levinson and Sanford A-S scale and with the Thurstone attitude toward Negroes scale, when applied to these referents. For a discussion of the characteristics of the semantic differential, see the third section of Chapter 2.

The social distance scale EXHIBIT 8-17

Description. This scale was originally developed by Bogardus (1925) to measure social distance, or the degree of intimacy an individual would allow to members of outgroups. The items in the scale are arranged in descending order of intimacy. *Social distance* is defined for the responding subjects as "the different degrees of sympathetic understanding that exist between persons." The items presented in Exhibit 8-17 are from an equal-appearing intervals modification of the scale by Bogardus (1933). This scale and its modification have been used to measure social distance with regard to racial groups, political and economic groups, occupational groups, and religious groups. In the development of the equal-appearing intervals modification, 100 judges sorted 60 items on a seven-point continuum of the degree to which the item reflected sympathetic understanding between two persons or between a person and a group. These seven items were selected to fall one scale interval apart (from 1.0 to 6.98) to represent the entire continuum. The wording of items Nos. 6 and 7 originally read "would debar from" and was changed to read "would have live outside" in order to be more uniform with the wording of the other statements (Bogardus, 1933). Bogardus did not report any dispersion measures for these items.

Subjects. The total sample on which the scale was originally constructed and validated included 1,725 Americans descended from many ethnic groups, but chiefly from Northern Europeans. Bogardus (1928, p. 24) gives the frequencies for the racial descent of his subjects. The 100 judges used in developing the equal-appearing intervals modification included 66 faculty members and graduate students and 34 undergraduates. Included among them were 62 women and 38 men.

Response Mode. The subject is asked to check those alternatives (among the seven alternatives) which reflect his feeling reactions to the ethnic group in question as a group, and not to react to the best or worst members of the group that he has known. Subjects may mark as many of the seven alternatives as they care to mark.

Scoring. The subject's score for a particular group is the rank of the lowest (most intimate) relationship among all the relationships he checks as ones he would allow the group in question. If a number of groups are used, several quotients may be computed for the individual: a racial distance quotient (Ra. D.Q.), an occupational distance quotient (O.D.Q.), a religious distance quotient (Re. D.Q), and a political and economic distance quotient (P. and E.D.Q). Thus, if a number of racial groups are used as the referents, the Ra. D.Q. is computed by addition of the ranks of the lowest items checked for each of the groups and division by the number of groups used. A social distance quotient is computed by summing the person's racial distance, occupational distance, religious distance, and political and economic distance quotients and dividing by 4. Larger scores reflect greater distance (and thereby greater prejudice).

Reliability. Newcomb (1950) states that the split-half reliability of the Bogardus scale is as high as .90 (or higher on the average). Over time (twenty years), it has shown highly consistent results in its measurement of attitudes which prevail in the United States toward various minority and dominant groups. This fact reflects not only the durability of stereotypes, but the reliability of this scale as well.

Validity. Although the items in the scale have content validity, Nunnally (1959) has criticized such devices as this scale for failing to measure the extreme negative attitudes. In an equal-interval version of this scale developed for use in the Far East, Dodd (1935) included a statement, "I wish someone would kill all of them." Such an item might be included in this scale but would, of course, necessitate rescaling the items. Regarding the Bogardus scale, "for measuring an individual's general social distance, and measuring his order of preference among ethnic groups . . . both its reliability and validity seem satisfactory" (Newcomb, 1950, p. 167).

Comments. This scale seems quite valid and reliable for measuring attitudes of subjects toward outgroups, but it should not be used to measure their attitudes toward their own reference or membership groups. Miller and Biggs (1958) have developed a modified Bogardus scale for use with children. Readers interested in this type of scale may also wish to see Dudycha (1953), Dodd (1935), and Zeligs (1937, 1947, 1948, 1953).

EXHIBIT 8-17

THE SOCIAL DISTANCE SCALE

You are urged to give yourself as complete freedom as possible. In fact, the greater the freedom you give yourself, the more valuable will be the results. Use only checkmarks or crosses.

Seven Kinds of social contacts are given.

You are asked to give in every instance your first feeling reactions. Proceed through the tests without delaying. The more you "stop to think," the less valuable will be the results. Give your reactions to every race, occupation, or religion in the following lists which you have ever heard of.

Social distance means the different degrees of sympathetic understanding that exist between persons. This test relates to a special form of social distance known as personal-group distance, or the distance that exists between a person and groups, such as races, occupations, and religions.

By taking this test at intervals of six months or a year, a person can discover what some of the changes in attitudes are that he is undergoing. If given to a group at intervals, changes in group attitudes may likewise be gauged.

Remember to give your first feeling reactions in every case. Give your reactions to each race as a group. Do not give your reactions to the best or the worst members that you have known.

Put a cross after each race in as many of the seven columns as your feeling reactions dictate.

	1 Would marry into group	2 Would have as close friends	3 Would have as next door neighbors	4 Would work in same office	5 Have as speaking acquaint-ances only	6 Have as visitors only to my nation	7 Would debar from my nation
Armenians							
Americans (U.S. white)							
Canadians							
Chinese							
Czechs							
English							
Filipinos							
Finns							
French							

	1	2	3	4	5	6	7
	Would marry into group	Would have as close friends	Would have as next door neighbors	Would work in same office	Have as speaking acquaintances only	Have as visitors only to my nation	Would debar from my nation
Germans							
Greeks							
Hollanders							
Indians (American)							
Indians (of India)							
Irish							

1. Please remember to give your **first feeling reactions** for every group.
2. Remember to give feeling reactions to your **chief picture** of each group as a whole.
3. Also, to check as many columns for each group as you can, and to work rapidly.

Italians							
Japanese							
Japanese Americans							
Jews							
Koreans							
Mexicans							
Mexican Americans							
Negroes							
Norwegians							
Poles							
Russians							
Scots							
Spanish							
Swedish							
Turks							

Scale to measure attitudes toward defined groups EXHIBIT *8-18*

Description. This scale was developed by Grice (1934) and is the scale from which Remmers (1960) developed his shorter 17-item form for measuring the same attitude. The items used by Remmers in developing his scale are indicated with an asterisk beside the items in the exhibit. This scale was constructed using a Thurstone scaling procedure, and has 46 items in each of two equivalent forms (A and B). All Q values for these items are between 0.5 and 3.5.

Subjects. Subjects were 120 high school and college students, 63 of whom were Negroes.

Response Mode. The person responds by checking those items with which he agrees.

Scoring. The person's score is the median of the scale values of the items endorsed by him as "agree." A high score indicates a favorable attitude toward the group in question.

Reliability. Equivalent-forms reliability of this scale is .84, the P.E. being .013, when used to test attitudes toward Negroes.

Validity. Validity was based upon a correlation of .67 and .57 with the Thurstone scales of attitude toward Negroes and attitude toward Chinese, respectively (when applied to those referents).

Comments. This scale is satisfactory in most regards. For longitudinal data resulting from its application, see Albright et al. (1956) and Remmers (1943, 1946, 1947). See also Kasheiva and Smith (1943).

EXHIBIT 8-18

SCALE TO MEASURE ATTITUDES TOWARD DEFINED GROUPS

Following is a list of statements about any group. Place a plus (+) before each statement with which you agree with reference to the group listed at the left of the statements. The person in charge will tell you the group to write in at the head of the columns to the left of the statements. Your score will in no way affect your grade in any course.

Form A

Scale Values		
10.9	1	Show a high rate of efficiency in anything they attempt.
*10.2	2	Can be depended upon as being honest.
10.0	3	Are mentally strong.
9.9	4	Are fine people.
9.8	5	Are very patriotic.
*9.5	6	Are far above my own group.
9.3	7	Are noted for their industry.
*9.2	8	Some of our best citizens are descendants from this group.
9.0	9	Are a tactful group of people.
*8.9	10	Deserve much consideration from the rest of the world.
8.8	11	I would be willing to trust these people.
8.7	12	Should be permitted to intermarry with any other group.
*8.5	13	Command the respect of any group.
8.4	14	Are generous to others.

* Items marked with an asterisk are those used by Remmers (1960) to develop his 17 item version of the same scale.

Reprinted with permission from Grice, H. H. The construction and validation of a generalized scale to measure attitudes toward defined groups. *Purdue Univ. Stud. high Educ.*, 1934, 35, 37–46. Copyright by Purdue University Research Foundation, Lafayette, Ind. Copies of the short form of this scale may be purchased from Purdue University Bookstore, Lafayette, Ind.

Scale Values		
8.2	15	Are of a self-sacrificing nature.
*8.1	16	Are quick to apprehend.
8.0	17	Should be permitted to enter this country as immigrants.
7.9	18	Are good mixers.
*7.7	19	Are a God-fearing group.
*6.8	20	Have an air of dignity about them.
*6.0	21	Are highly emotional.
*5.8	22	Take an exceptional pride in themselves.
*4.6	23	Are superstitious.
4.4	24	Are fond of display.
4.2	25	Are unimaginative.
*3.6	26	Are self-indulgent.
3.2	27	So far as I am concerned this group can stay in their native country.
*3.1	28	Do not impress me favorably.
3.0	29	Are frivolous.
2.8	30	Are extravagant with their means.
*2.5	31	I am not in sympathy with these people.
2.4	32	Tend to lower the standards of living of their neighbors.
2.3	33	Are tactless.
*2.2	34	Would likely prove disloyal to our government.
1.9	35	Are despised by the better groups.
1.8	36	Have many undesirable traits.
*1.6	37	Belong to a low social level.
1.5	38	Have nothing about them that I admire.
1.4	39	Should not be permitted to associate with other groups.
1.3	40	Should not be permitted to enter this country.
1.2	41	All members of this group should be deported from this country.
*1.0	42	Are mentally defective.
0.9	43	Respect only brute force.
0.8	44	I hate anyone belonging to this group.
0.7	45	Are our worst citizens.
0.4	46	Are inferior in every way to the rest of the world.

Form B

10.5	1	Are the finest in the world.
*10.2	2	Are honest.
10.0	3	Are the most desirable class of immigrants.
9.9	4	Have an ideal home life.
9.8	5	Have a high standard of living.
*9.5	6	Tend to improve any group with which they come in contact.
9.3	7	Are superior in every way to the rest of the world.
*9.2	8	I consider it a privilege to associate with this group.
9.0	9	Have an unusual ability for leadership.
*8.9	10	Are on a level with my own group.
8.8	11	The world is better off by having these people in it.
8.7	12	Are sincere in their actions.
*8.5	13	Are religiously inclined.
8.4	14	Are sociable.
8.2	15	The higher class of this group are superior to us.
*8.1	16	Are considerate of others.
8.0	17	Are courageous in wars.

Scale Values		
7.9	**18**	Are sympathetic to others.
*7.7	**19**	Can be resourceful when necessary.
*6.8	**20**	Should be regarded as any other group.
*6.1	**21**	Are equal in intelligence to the average person.
*5.4	**22**	I have no particular love or hatred for this group.
*4.5	**23**	Are of a gregarious nature.
4.4	**24**	Have a great love of power.
4.2	**25**	Are stingy.
*3.6	**26**	I suppose these people are all right, but I've never liked them.
3.3	**27**	Must imitate others to succeed.
*3.1	**28**	Have a tendency toward insubordination.
3.0	**29**	Will not bear acquaintance.
2.7	**30**	Are always suspicious of others.
*2.5	**31**	Are envious of others.
2.4	**32**	Have a tendency to fight.
2.3	**33**	Must undergo many years of civilization before they may be said to have reached our own level.
*2.2	**34**	Are discourteous.
1.9	**35**	Are sluggish in action.
1.8	**36**	Are unreasonable in their attitude toward other groups.
*1.6	**37**	Are slow and unimaginative.
1.5	**38**	Are disorderly in conduct.
1.4	**39**	I do not see how anyone can be fond of this group.
1.3	**40**	Are a necessary evil to be endured.
1.2	**41**	Are generally sly and deceitful.
*1.0	**42**	Are the most despicable people in the world.
0.9	**43**	We should cultivate a national hatred for these people.
0.8	**44**	Cannot be trusted.
0.7	**45**	Are the least respected people in the world.
0.4	**46**	Are inferior in every way to the rest of the world.

SUMMARY

Many of the scales contained in this chapter were developed before World War II. At least some of these have dated content and are in need of updating; otherwise, their use is restricted. It is noteworthy that there are many scales measuring attitudes toward Negroes or Jews, or both, but very few measuring attitudes toward other specific ethnic and national groups. Thus, there are no scales measuring attitudes toward the French, Mexicans, or Americans. Such scales as these latter could have a great deal of applicability in research on international relations, although translation and cross-cultural differences create a hazard. It is also notable that some of the more recent scaling methods (e.g., the unfolding technique) are not represented in these scales. The application of these methods would provide an expanded instrumentation for assessing validity.

It should be pointed out that it is particularly important for authors of scales which measure attitudes toward ethnic and national groups to report as fully as possible such characteristics of their subjects as ethnic origin, regional location, etc. These most relevant characteristics are major determinants of how and whether items will scale.

Finally, a number of suggestions for future development of scales to measure attitudes toward groups of persons are to be found in the present examples. Thus, using the behavior of individuals or kinds of contacts with individuals as the attitudinal referent might be expected to improve the predictive validity of such scales (1) by increasing the specificity of the content and (2) by relating the content of the scale more directly to the situations to be predicted.

CHAPTER 9

significant others

Every person everywhere comes into contact with and interacts with a great many other persons. Some of these other persons are relatively unimportant to the individual, and he develops no attitude toward them. Many of these other persons, however, are important to him, and consequently he develops varying attitudes toward them. These *significant others* are often individuals such as "father," "mother," "my supervisor," etc. They may also be classes or categories of persons such as old people, mentally ill persons, psychiatrists, and similar groups of persons. Classes of significant others frequently are based upon role relations but sometimes are based upon physical or biological characteristics. This chapter includes scales to measure attitudes toward both types of significant others.

ATTITUDES TOWARD MEMBERS OF THE FAMILY

Family-related attitudes have already been discussed in Chapter 3 where scales were described for measuring attitudes toward child-rearing practices and intrafamily relations. In this section we shall be concerned with attitudes toward the family as a unit and toward generalized members of the family such as father, mother, and children. Four scales in this category are described below.

Familism scale EXHIBIT 9-1

Description. This scale was developed by Bardis (1959*a*). It is a Likert-type scale designed to measure attitudes toward the family as a social entity. Conceived in this way, family includes not only the members of the home, but also relatives such as uncles, parents-in-law, etc. The author failed to indicate the number of items originally formulated, nor did he give precise information regarding the outcome of item-analysis procedures. There are 16 items in the final scale.

Subjects. The sample consisted of 68 white, native American students and their 136 parents who were also white, native Americans and who were still married. The student sample consisted of 18 males and 50 females, ranging in age from 18 to 24 years. Of this sample, 1 was Catholic, 66 were Protestant, and 1 had no religious affiliation; 1 was married, and 65 were single; 3 were seniors, 23 were juniors, and 42 were sophomores. Of the fathers, who ranged in age from 41 to 69 years, 2 were Catholic, and 66 were Protestant; 5 had only a grade school education, 22 were high school graduates, 26 had at least some college, and 15 had done graduate work. Occupations and socioeconomic level varied greatly. Of the mothers, who ranged from 38 to 59 years of age, 2 were Catholic, and 66 were Protestant; 6 had a grade school education, 23 had finished high school, 34 had some college, and 5 had some graduate work.

Response Mode. Subjects respond to each item by entering a number from 0 to 4 in the space provided to the left of each statement. A zero means "strongly disagree"; a 1, "disagree"; a 2, "undecided"; a 3, "agree"; and a 4, "strongly agree."

Scoring. The attitude score is obtained by summing the individual item scores. The theoretical range of scores is therefore from 0 to 64. Since all items are stated in the positive direction, a high score indicates a favorable attitude toward the family. This also means that the score may be contaminated by response bias.

Reliability. Split-half reliability was reported to be .79, corrected to .88, based upon the responses of 30 college students.

Validity. No evidence of validity was given. The mean attitude-toward-family score did not differ for students, mothers, and fathers. These means were 28.50, 28.22, and 30.16, respectively.

Comments. The lack of evidence of validity is a serious shortcoming of this scale, and validation studies are advisable before it is used in research.

EXHIBIT 9-1

FAMILISM SCALE

Below is a list of issues concerning the family *in general,* not your own. Please read *all* statements very carefully and respond to *all* of them on the basis of *your own true* beliefs *without* consulting any other persons. Do this by reading each statement and then writing, in the space provided at its left, *only one* of the following numbers: 0, 1, 2, 3, 4. The meaning of each of these figures is:

0: Strongly disagree
1: Disagree
2: Undecided
3: Agree
4: Strongly agree

(For research purposes, you must consider all statements as they are, without modifying any of them in any way.)

________ 1 A person should always support his uncles and aunts if they are in need.

________ 2 Children below 18 should give almost all their earnings to their parents.

________ 3 The family should consult close relatives (uncles, aunts, first cousins) concerning its important decisions.

________ 4 Children below 18 should almost always obey their older brothers and sisters.

________ 5 A person should always consider the needs of his family as a whole more important than his own.

________ 6 At least one married child should be expected to live in the parental home.

________ 7 A person should always be expected to defend his family against outsiders even at the expense of his own personal safety.

________ 8 The family should have the right to control the behavior of each of its members completely.

________ 9 A person should always support his parents-in-law if they are in need.

________ 10 A person should always avoid every action of which his family disapproves.

________ 11 A person should always share his home with his uncles, aunts or first cousins if they are in need.

________ 12 A person should always be completely loyal to his family.

________ 13 The members of a family should be expected to hold the same political, ethical, and religious beliefs.

________ 14 Children below 18 should always obey their parents.

________ 15 A person should always help his parents with the support of his younger brothers and sisters if necessary.

________ 16 A person should always share his home with his parents-in-law if they are in need.

The family scale EXHIBIT 9-2

Description. Like the Familism Scale, this scale was designed to measure attitude toward the family, but it appears to limit the definition of family to members of the home. It was developed by Rundquist and Sletto (1936) by the Likert method of scale construction. It is one of six scales included in a Survey of Opinions. In the studies reported by Rundquist and Sletto, the items of the Family Scale were interspersed among the items of the other scales, which included measures of attitude toward school, law, and economics, and sections on morale and inferiority feeling. The discriminative values of the items in each scale were computed as the difference between the first and the fourth quartiles. The mean discriminative value of the items of the Family Scale was 1.251. The items of the Family Scale are given in Exhibit 9-2 and are numbered as they appeared in the original questionnaire. The potential user of this scale should recognize that the data concerning the scale presented below are based upon responses to the items embedded in the larger questionnaire.

Subjects. The samples were drawn from a variety of populations. These samples included 560 University of Minnesota students (200 from an elementary sociology class, 200 from a General College class, 100 from the freshman class in law, and 60 from a group of students receiving Federal aid); 1,024 persons drawn from night school classes in the adult education department of the Minneapolis Public Schools; 412 drawn from special classes for the unemployed, supervised by the same department; 813 high school students; 21 high school teachers; and 52 men on relief. There were 1,316 men and 1,566 women in the total sample. Approximately 94 percent of the men and 90 percent of the women fell within the 17 to 29 age range. Occupation, education, and socioeconomic status varied widely.

Response Mode. The standard Likert response alternatives are used: strongly agree, agree, undecided, disagree, strongly disagree. However, Rundquist and Sletto included the numbers assigned as scores in the printing of their scales, whereas the usual Likert response mode does not include these numbers. Subjects respond by underlining one of the five alternatives.

Scoring. Weights ranging from 1 to 5 are assigned to each response alternative, with a weight of 1 given to "strongly agree" for items expressing a favorable attitude toward the family. The scoring is reversed for negative items. The attitude score is obtained by summing the item scores. Possible scores range from 22 to 110. A high score on the Family Scale indicates an unfavorable attitude toward the family.

Reliability. Split-half reliabilities were computed for samples of 500 men and 500 women. Corrected by the Spearman-Brown formula, these were found to be .84 for men and .82 for women. Test-retest reliabilities after a sixty-day interval were found to be .83, based upon the responses of 70 men, and .78, based upon the responses of 75 women.

Validity. The Family Scale was designed to reflect parent-child relations and family tensions, and the items appear to reflect this intent. Other evidence of validity is limited, although the attitude scores of men were related in the expected direction to the following variables: occupational security, overageness, separation of parents, retired father, and mother deceased. Similarly, the attitude scores of women were related to separation of parents, mother deceased, mother employed, divorce, and unemployed who are married.

Comments. Although this scale was constructed many years ago, the items are still useful. The scale has been used only to a limited degree. A follow-up study by Ramsey and Nelson (1956) found only one change in attitude toward the family from 1939 to 1952: Girls in the 1952 sample had somewhat less favorable attitudes toward the family than did girls in the earlier study.

EXHIBIT 9-2

THE FAMILY SCALE

READ EACH ITEM CAREFULLY AND UNDERLINE QUICKLY THE PHRASE WHICH BEST EXPRESSES YOUR FEELING ABOUT THE STATEMENT. Whenever possible, let your own personal experience determine your answer. Do not spend much time on any item. If in doubt, underline the phrase which seems most nearly to express your present feeling about the statement. WORK RAPIDLY. Be sure to answer every item.

3 Home is the most pleasant place in the world.

Strongly agree   Agree   Undecided   Disagree   Strongly Disagree

*9 Parents expect too much from their children.
15 One ought to discuss important plans with the members of his family.
21 In making plans for the future, parents should be given first consideration.
27 A man should be willing to sacrifice anything for his family.
*33 Parents too often expect their grown-up children to obey them.
*39 One cannot find as much understanding at home as elsewhere.

* Items marked with an asterisk express an unfavorable attitude toward the family.

45 One owes his greatest obligation to his family.
*51 It is hard to keep a pleasant disposition at home.
57 People in the family can be trusted completely.
*63 One becomes nervous at home.
*69 The joys of family life are much over-rated.
75 One's parents usually treat him fairly and sensibly.
81 One should confide more fully in members of his family.
87 One feels most contented at home.
93 Family ties are strengthened when times are hard.
*99 Parents are inclined to be too old-fashioned in their ideas.
*105 Members of the family are too curious about one's personal affairs.
111 Parents keep faith in their children even though they cannot find work.
*117 Parents are too particular about the kind of company one keeps.
*123 Obligations to one's family are a great handicap to a young man today.
*129 So far as ideas are concerned, parents and children live in different worlds.

Attitudes toward parents (Form F) *EXHIBIT 9-3*

Description. The Attitudes toward Parents Scale was developed by Itkin (1952) as a part of a battery of scales to measure attitudes related to the family. Related scales dealing with child-rearing practices and discipline are given in Chapter 3. This scale was prepared in two forms, one for measuring attitude toward father (Form F) and one for measuring attitude toward mother (Form M). Since these two forms are identical except that in Form M the word "mother" is substituted for the word "father" in Form F, the two are discussed together, and only the items for Form F are given in Exhibit 9-3.

The form of the scale does not fit any standard model. It consists of 35 items, including 11 items answered "true" or "false," 8 multiple-choice items, and 16 personality traits that are rated on a five-point scale from "possesses to a very great degree" to "possesses only to a very slight degree or not at all." The number of items originally formulated was not given, but the discriminability of the items was estimated by phi coefficients using Guilford's (1941) graphic method. All items retained in the final form discriminated between high and low scoring subjects at the 5 percent level or better.

Subjects. The samples used for scale development were drawn from the student body at the Chicago junior colleges in November and December, 1947. The size of the samples ranged from 57 to 323.

Response Mode. The response mode varied for different items as indicated above and in Exhibit 9-3. Items 1 through 11 are answered by circling either "true," "?," or "false"; items 12 through 19 are answered by checking one of the five alternatives provided; and items 20 through 35 are answered by circling A, B, C, D, or E.

Scoring. In Exhibit 9-3 the numerical value assigned to each response is below or beside each alternative. The attitude score is the sum of the values for each item endorsed. The theoretical scores thus range from 46 to 164. A high score indicates a favorable attitude toward parents.

Reliability. Split-half reliabilities were reported to be .917 (corrected to .956) for Form F, based upon the responses of 311 students, and .851 (corrected to .920) for Form M, based upon the responses of 323 students.

Validity. A validation study was conducted to determine whether attitude scores correlated with self-ratings, using students at Herzl and Wright Junior Colleges. Attitude scores on Form F correlated —.700 with self-ratings ($N = 57$), and attitude scores on Form M correlated —.798 with self-ratings ($N = 61$), where low self-ratings and high attitude scores indicated favorable attitudes toward parents.

Comments. Although this scale was not developed by a standard scaling technique, the evidence indicates that it is reliable and reasonably valid. It can certainly be recommended for research and perhaps for studies of individual attitudes as well. The scale does not appear to have been widely used, but some additional data may be found in Itkin (1955).

EXHIBIT 9-3

ATTITUDES TOWARD PARENTS (FORM F)

Following is a list of statements which might be answered as true, false, or uncertain. If you believe the statement true of your father or your feelings toward your father, *encircle* the "True" in front of the statement; if false, *encircle* the "False," and if your answer might be "Yes and No" or "Not Certain," *encircle* the "?."

True	?	False		
*4	3	2	1	I consider myself very close to my father.
4	3	2	2	My father generally has good reasons for any requests he might make.
4	3	2	3	I would like to be the same kind of a parent that my father has been.
2	3	4	4	I believe that my father underestimates my ability.
2	3	4	5	I believe my father finds fault with me more often than I deserve and seems never to be satisfied with anything I do.
2	3	4	6	I believe that my father has insufficient respect for my opinions.

* The numbers by each response alternative are scoring weights. These numbers are omitted when the scale is administered.

Reference: W. Itkin. Some relationships between intra-family attitudes and preparental attitudes toward children. *J. genet. Psychol.*, 1952, 80, 221–252. Items obtained from author and published with his permission.

True	?	False		
2	3	4	7	In my estimation, my father is insufficiently interested in whether or not I have friends.
True	?	False		
2	3	4	8	In my judgment, my father did not treat me fairly when I was young.
True	?	False		
4	3	2	9	I believe that my father is one of the most admirable persons I know.
True	?	False		
4	3	2	10	My father has been one of the best friends I have ever had.
True	?	False		
4	3	2	11	My father considers the rearing of his children his most important job in life.

In each of the following you are given a preliminary statement which can be completed in any one of five ways or a question which can be answered in any one of five ways. Check whichever one of the alternative choices most closely approximates your own opinion or feeling.

12 My father . . .

___5___ (a) takes a very great interest in everything that concerns his children

___4___ (b) takes a moderate amount of interest in things which concern his children

___3___ (c) does not take very much interest in things which concern his children

___2___ (d) takes little interest in things which concern his children

___1___ (e) takes no interest in things which concern his children

13 I get along with my father . . .

___5___ (a) Very well

___4___ (b) Well

___3___ (c) Fairly well

___2___ (d) Not very well

___1___ (e) Poorly

14 In regard to taking my father into my confidence, I . . .

___5___ (a) feel free to ask him intimate questions

___4___ (b) often ask him intimate questions

___3___ (c) sometimes ask him intimate questions

___2___ (d) rarely if ever ask him intimate questions

___1___ (e) wouldn't think of asking him any intimate questions

15 Check whichever of the following terms best describes your feelings toward your father.

___5___ (a) I idealize my father

___4___ (b) I admire my father

___3___ (c) I respect my father

___2___ (d) I do not particularly respect my father

___1___ (e) I do not respect my father at all

16 Check whichever of the following descriptions most nearly fits your father.

___1___ (a) Is always critical of his children, and nothing his children do ever seems to please him

___2___ (b) Is rather critical of his children, and is not often pleased by what his children do

___3___ (c) Is not very critical of his children, but on the other hand, does not show particular pleasure at what his children do

___4___ (d) Often shows pleasure at what his children do, and often praises them for their accomplishments

___5___ (e) Very seldom complains about his children, and is liberal in his praise of them

17 I consider my father . . .

___5___ (a) always willing to think only the best of his children

___4___ (b) generally inclined to think well of his children

___3___ (c) neither inclined to think only well or only poorly of his children

___2___ (d) sometimes inclined to be critical of his children

___1___ (e) always ready to think only the worst of his children

18 My father . . .

___1___ (a) never does little things for his children to show affection or consideration

___2___ (b) seldom does little things for his children to show affection or consideration

___3___ (c) sometimes does little things for his children to show affection or consideration

___4___ (d) often does little things for his children to show affection or consideration

___5___ (e) is always doing little things for his children to show affection or consideration

19 In my opinion, my father . . .

___5___ (a) is so attached to his children that he wants to have them around all of the time

___4___ (b) enjoys spending some of his time with his children

___3___ (c) likes to spend a little of his time with his children

___2___ (d) does not like to spend time with his children

___1___ (e) dislikes very much spending any of his time with his children

Following is a list of traits of personality. If in your opinion your father possesses a trait in a very great degree, *encircle* the "A" in front of the trait. If he possesses the trait to a greater than average degree, *encircle* the "B"; if he possesses the trait to about an average extent, *encircle* the "C"; if he possesses the trait to a less than average extent, *encircle* the "D"; and if he possesses the trait only to a very slight degree or not at all, *encircle* the "E" in front of the trait.

A	B	C	D	E			A	B	C	D	E		
5	4	3	2	1	20	Fair	1	2	3	4	5	28	Envious
A	B	C	D	E			A	B	C	D	E		
1	2	3	4	5	21	Selfish	5	4	3	2	1	29	Affectionate

A	B	C	D	E	22	Helpful	A	B	C	D	E	30	Understanding
5	4	3	2	1			5	4	3	2	1		
A	B	C	D	E	23	Sarcastic	A	B	C	D	E	31	Cold
1	2	3	4	5			1	2	3	4	5		
A	B	C	D	E	24	Considerate	A	B	C	D	E	32	Suspicious
5	4	3	2	1			1	2	3	4	5		
A	B	C	D	E	25	Bossy	A	B	C	D	E	33	Sympathetic
1	2	3	4	5			5	4	3	2	1		
A	B	C	D	E	26	Agreeable	A	B	C	D	E	34	Courteous
5	4	3	2	1			5	4	3	2	1		
A	B	C	D	E	27	Kind	A	B	C	D	E	35	Trustful
5	4	3	2	1			5	4	3	2	1		

Parents' judgment regarding a particular child *EXHIBIT 9-4*

Description. This scale was also developed by Itkin (1952) as a part of the intrafamily survey (see above and Chapter 3). Like the scales described in the preceding section, the items are mixed in form. Of the items, 18 are typical Likert items, 5 are multiple-choice items, and 12 are ratings of the degree to which specified traits are possessed by the child.

Item discriminability was estimated by the graphic method suggested by Guilford (1941). This method showed that 33 of the 35 items discriminated between high and low scorers for male subjects and that 34 of the 35 items discriminated between high and low scorers for female subjects ($p < .05$ or better).

Subjects. Subjects for scale development were parents of students at Chicago junior colleges during November and December, 1947. The number varied from study to study.

Response Mode. The response mode varies from item to item. Subjects respond to items 1 through 18 by underlining one of the following alternatives: strongly agree, agree, uncertain, disagree, or strongly disagree. Items 19 through 23 call for checking one of five choices, and items 24 through 35 require the subject to draw a line through the description which most nearly describes the child.

Scoring. For items 1 through 18, a weight of 5 is assigned to "strongly agree" for positive (favorable) statements and to "strongly disagree" for negative statements. The weight assigned to each response for the remaining items is indicated below or beside each alternative in Exhibit 9-4. The attitude score is computed by summing item scores. The possible range of scores is therefore from 35 to 175. A high score indicates a favorable attitude toward the child.

Reliability. Split-half reliability was found to be .903 (corrected to .949), based upon the responses of 412 parents drawn from the population described above.

Validity. Attitude scores of parents ($N = 68$) were found to correlate —.623 with self-ratings. Again, the favorability of the scores was reversed for the two measures.

Comments. This scale was developed by the same procedure as the Attitude toward Parents Scale, but the validating evidence is not as strong. For further data, see Itkin (1955).

EXHIBIT 9-4

PARENTS' JUDGMENT REGARDING A PARTICULAR CHILD

By this scale it is hoped to discover the qualities in children which satisfy or dissatisfy their parents. Because we desire to measure both qualities in children which satisfy and which dissatisfy their parents, it would not be desirable that either mostly favorite or mostly least favored children be reported upon. Therefore, in order to assure that some subjects in this study will be the favorites of their parents, others the least favored, and others in between, it is requested that parents fill out this scale according to the way they feel about *the particular child who brought these scales home.*

We realize that some parents may dislike answering some of these questions, and if we did not believe that the study was an important one, we would not ask them. However, this information is being used for a scientific study only, and will be held strictly confidential. In fact, we want this to be so confidential that even one parent would not know how the other parent answered these questions, and it is for this reason that we ask each parent to fill these forms out independently.

Following is a list of statements to which you might have any one of five reactions. You might strongly agree, agree, be uncertain, disagree, or strongly disagree. Please draw a line under whichever of these choices best describes the way you feel about the particular child who brought these scales home.

*1 I consider myself very close to this child.

Strongly Agree   Agree   Uncertain   Disagree   Strongly Disagree

2 I feel that this child does not have enough respect for his (or her) parents.
3 I feel that this child does not love me enough.
4 I find myself being nice to this child at one moment and being very angry at it the next.
*5 I love this child so much that I cannot bear to be away from him (or her) for even a short time.
6 This child has been a difficult child to bring up.
7 I feel that this child does not appreciate the sacrifices his (or her) parents make for him (or her).
*8 I am extremely proud of this child.
9 I feel that this child complains too much.
10 I am somewhat disappointed in this child.
11 This child has always been difficult to control.

* The same set of response alternatives is used with each item numbered 1 through 18; items expressing a favorable attitude toward the child are marked with an asterisk.

Reference: W. Itkin. Some relationships between intra-family attitudes and preparental attitudes toward children. *J. genet. Psychol.*, 1952, 80, 221–252. Items obtained from author and published with his permission.

12 In my judgment this child does not sufficiently appreciate his (or her) parents.
13 I am often annoyed by this child.
14 When this child is out of my sight, I always worry for fear that something will happen to him (or her).
15 In my opinion, this child expects to be waited on too much.
16 This child is too great an expense to the family.
*17 This child is everything that I could hope a child of mine to be.
*18 I like to spend as much of my spare time as I can with this child.

In each of the following you are given a statement which can be completed in any one of several ways. Place a check in front of whichever of the alternative choices most nearly resembles your own feeling.

†19 When this child was in elementary school, it was necessary for his (or her) parents to punish him (or her) . . .

__1__ (a) Very frequently
__2__ (b) Quite often
__3__ (c) Sometimes
__4__ (d) Seldom
__5__ (e) Never

20 I find myself becoming angry at this child . . .

__1__ (a) Very frequently
__2__ (b) Quite often
__3__ (c) Sometimes
__4__ (d) Seldom
__5__ (e) Never

21 I feel that I get along with this child . . .

__5__ (a) Very well
__4__ (b) Well
__3__ (c) Fairly well
__2__ (d) Not very well
__1__ (e) Poorly

22 This child gets on my nerves . . .

__1__ (a) Frequently
__2__ (b) Quite often
__3__ (c) Sometimes
__4__ (d) Seldom
__5__ (e) Never

23 I get . . .

__5__ (a) Very much satisfaction from this child
__4__ (b) Considerable satisfaction from this child
__3__ (c) Some satisfaction from this child
__2__ (d) Very little satisfaction from this child
__1__ (e) No satisfaction from this child

† Numbers by each response alternative for items 19 through 35 are scoring weights. These numbers are omitted when the scale is administered.

Following is a list of traits of personality. Below each trait are five expressions which describe five different degrees of the trait. The first of these descriptions would indicate that the child being described possesses the trait considerably more than the average, the second would indicate that the child possesses the trait noticeably more than the average, the third average, the fourth noticeably below average, and the fifth considerably less than the average.

Please draw a line below whichever of the descriptions most nearly describes your child.

24 SELFISHNESS

Very Selfish	More Selfish than the average	Average	Less Selfish than the average	Very Unselfish
1	2	3	4	5

25 HELPFULNESS

Very Helpful	More Helpful than the average	Average	Less Helpful than the average	Not Helpful at all
5	4	3	2	1

26 AFFECTIONATENESS

Very Affectionate	More Affectionate than average	Average	Less Affectionate than average	Very Unaffectionate
5	4	3	2	1

27 CONSIDERATENESS

Very Considerate	More Considerate than the average	Average	Less Considerate than the average	Very Inconsiderate
5	4	3	2	1

28 COURTEOUSNESS

Very Courteous	More Courteous than the average	Average	Less Courteous than the average	Very Discourteous
5	4	3	2	1

29 RESPECTFULNESS

Very Respectful	More Respectful than the average	Average	Less Respectful than the average	Very Disrespectful
5	4	3	2	1

30 OBEDIENCE

Very Obedient	More Obedient than the average	Average	Less Obedient than the average	Very Disobedient
5	4	3	2	1

31 AGREEABILITY

Very Agreeable	More Agreeable than the average	Average	Less Agreeable than the average	Very Disagreeable
5	4	3	2	1

32 LAZINESS

Very Lazy	More Lazy than the average	Average	Less Lazy than the average	Not Lazy at all
1	2	3	4	5

33 CARELESSNESS

Very Careless	More Careless than the average	Average	Less Careless than the average	Not Careless at all
1	2	3	4	5

34 DEPENDABILITY

Very Dependable	More dependable than the average	Average	Less Dependable than the average	Very Un-dependable
5	4	3	2	1

35 REASONABLENESS

Very Reasonable	More Reasonable than the average	Average	Less Reasonable than the average	Very Un-reasonable
5	4	3	2	1

ATTITUDES TOWARD SELF AND OTHERS

Individuals form conceptions of themselves as a person or "object" and through their experiences develop attitudes toward this object. In the literature, this attitude is most commonly referred to as degree of self-acceptance. Since the individual may evaluate himself favorably or unfavorably, self-acceptance measures are essentially measures of attitude toward self. Similarly, attitudes toward generalized others (or sometimes specific others, such as "my boss") are referred to as acceptance of others, and the same procedures are used to measure this attitude as attitude toward self.

Perhaps the most common technique of measuring acceptance of self or acceptance of others is by the Q sort. A number of descriptive adjectives or phrases are rated according to the degree to which they apply to the rater and then rated again according to the degree to which they apply to the rater as he would like to be ideally. The self–ideal self discrepancy is taken as an inverse measure of self-acceptance. (See for example Bills, Vance, and McLean, 1951; Brownfain, 1952; Crowne and Stephens, 1961; Crowne, Stephens, and Kelly, 1961; Ewing, 1954; Jourard, 1957; Wylie, 1961.) These checklists do not form scales as we have defined them; hence we have not included them in this volume. A few investigators, however, have prepared scales for measuring attitude toward self and others, and these are described below.

The self-others questionnaire *EXHIBIT 9-5*

Description. According to the author (Phillips, 1951), this scale was developed for use in hypothesis testing only. It is essentially a Likert-type scale, except that it uses a modified response mode, and the author reported no evidence concerning item analysis or other means of item selection. It consists of 50 items, 25 to measure attitude toward self and 25 to measure attitude toward others.

Subjects. The samples used in evaluating the scale were drawn from college and high school populations. One sample consisted of 48 students in general psychology courses in the 1949 summer session at George Washington University. These were mostly older, part-time students. Another sample consisted of 77 students, most of whom were freshmen. Two samples were drawn from a high school in a middle-class, suburban area in Washington, D.C. One consisted of 45 sophomores, and the other of 41 seniors.

Response Mode. A five-alternatives response mode is used. Subjects respond to each item by entering the letter A for "rarely or almost never true for me," the letter B for "sometimes but infrequently true for me," C for "occasionally true for me," D for "very often true for me," and E for "true for me all or most of the time."

Scoring. Each item response is given a weight, ranging from 1 for an A response to 5 for an E response. The attitude-toward-self score is obtained by summing the weighted score for each item on the self scale. Similarly, the attitude-toward-others score is the sum of the item scores for the others scale. Since there are 25 items on each scale, each score has a theoretical range from 25 to 125. A high score indicates an unfavorable attitude toward self or others.

Reliability. Test-retest reliability, after a five-day interval, was .84 for the self scale and .82 for the others scale ($N = 45$ college students).

Validity. No direct evidence of validity was reported. However, substantial correlations were reported between self scores and others scores (.74 for 48 college students in the George Washington University summer session, .54 for 77 regular college students, .67 for the 45 high school sophomores, and .51 for the 41 high school seniors).

Comments. Supporting data for this scale are quite limited, and further studies are indicated. The author is especially emphatic in stating that the scale should be used for research purposes only.

EXHIBIT 9-5

THE SELF - OTHERS QUESTIONNAIRE

Answer each item by writing one letter (A, B, C, D, or E) in the space provided. The meaning of these letters is:

A Rarely or almost never true for me
B Sometimes but infrequently true for me
C Occasionally true for me
D Very often true for me
E True for me all or most of the time

Reference: E. L. Phillips. Attitudes toward self and others: A brief questionnaire report. *J. consult. Psychol,.* 1951, 15, 79–81. Items obtained from author and published with his permission.

Scale			
*S	______	1	My own decisions regarding problems I face do not turn out to be good ones.
*O	______	2	I find it easy to exert considerable influence over some of my friends.
O	______	3	When others make an error in my presence I am almost certain to point it out to them.
O	______	4	When others fail to agree with me on some topic I know well, I am somewhat "taken back" by this.
S	______	5	I find that I feel the need to make excuses or apologize for my behavior.
S	______	6	If someone criticizes me to my face it makes me feel very low and worthless.
S	______	7	I change my opinion (or the way I do things) in order to please someone else.
O	______	8	I find it hard to take a genuine interest in the activities of some of my friends.
S	______	9	I regret my own past action I have taken when I find that my behavior has hurt someone else.
O	______	10	I am critical of the dress, manner, or ideas of some of my friends.
O	______	11	Some of my friends consistently do things of which I disapprove.
S	______	12	It worries me to think that some of my friends or acquaintances may dislike me.
O	______	13	I find it hard to accept some minority group members as equals.
S	______	14	I feel inferior as a person to some of my friends.
S	______	15	I have to be careful at parties and social gatherings for fear I will do or say things that others won't like.
S	______	16	It bothers me because I cannot make up my mind soon enough or fast enough.
O	______	17	I think that a large share of the world's ills are due to certain groups of people who are basically stubborn, dishonest, or inferior.
S	______	18	I feel that I have very little to contribute to the welfare of others.
O	______	19	When I am first getting to know a person, I try to size him (or her) up to see wherein I am better (or not as good) as this person.
O	______	20	Students who get elected to honor societies are mostly grinds or people with the right sort of pull.
O	______	21	One cannot be too careful in his efforts not to hurt others because some people are just naturally hard to deal with.
O	______	22	Becoming a close friend to another person always involves a risk and may turn out to the detriment of one of the persons.
S	______	23	I feel that I might be a failure if I don't make certain changes in my behavior (or my life).
S	______	24	It takes me several days or longer to get over a failure that I have experienced.
O	______	25	On the whole, college students are not very mature socially or emotionally.

* S indicates items of the self scale, and O indicates items of the others scale.

Scale		No.	Item
O	______	26	Some people whom I know become conceited or "hard to live with" when they experience some success or receive some honor.
S	______	27	When meeting a person for the first time, I have trouble telling whether he (or she) likes (or dislikes) me.
O	______	28	At least one of my friends depends upon me for advice and help with decisions he has to make.
O	______	29	One cannot afford to give attention to the opinions of others when he is certain he is correct.
S	______	30	I become panicky when I think of something I have done wrong (or might do wrong in the future).
S	______	31	Although people sometimes compliment me, I feel that I do not really deserve the compliments.
S	______	32	I regard myself as different from my friends and acquaintances.
O	______	33	One soon learns to expect very little of other people.
S	______	34	I keep still, or tell "little white lies" in the company of my friends so as not to reveal to them that I am different (or think differently) from them.
O	______	35	The "success" of most people whom I know stems primarily from the breaks they got.
O	______	36	The success and social standing of others means little to me unless they can prove themselves to be loyal, personal friends.
S	______	37	My feelings are easily hurt.
S	______	38	As I think about my past there are some points about which I feel shame.
S	______	39	I think I would be happier if I didn't have certain limitations.
O	______	40	I am not concerned with the opinions of others as long as I am fairly certain I am headed toward my goals.
S	______	41	I doubt if my plans will turn out the way I want them to.
S	______	42	I think that I am too shy.
S	______	43	In class, or in a group, I am unlikely to express my opinion because I fear that others may not think well of it (or of me).
O	______	44	I find it hard to sympathize with people whose misfortunes I believe are due mainly to their own shortcomings.
O	______	45	People who fail to work hard toward the attainment of respectable goals can depend upon no help from me when they are in trouble.
S	______	46	I criticize myself afterwards for acting silly or inappropriately in some situations.
O	______	47	Strikers, extreme conservatives, or extreme radicals have only a nuisance value as far as I am concerned.
O	______	48	Some people are always trying to get more than their share of the good things in life.
O	______	49	A small group of obnoxious people stir up most of the troubles which we read about in the papers.
S	______	50	If I hear that someone expresses a poor opinion of me, I do my best the next time I see this person to impress him (or her) as favorably as I can.

Acceptance of self and others EXHIBIT 9-6

Description. This instrument is really two scales, one to measure attitude toward self and one to measure attitude toward others, but it is administered as a single test. It was developed by Berger (1952) using the Likert procedure. The self-acceptance scale is made up of 36 items and the acceptances of others scale of 28 items. These items were selected from an initial pool of 47 statements on self-acceptance and 40 statements on acceptance of others on the basis of an item analysis. The top and bottom 25 percent of a sample of 200 were selected, and the difference between the mean scores of these criterion groups was used as an index of the discriminating power of the item. The standard error of the difference between means did not exceed .30 for any item, and all items in the final scales had critical ratios of 3.0 or more, except three which had critical ratios close to 2.0.

Subjects. The subjects used in selecting items for these scales were 200 students who were in first-year sociology or psychology courses. They differed widely in socioeconomic backgrounds and vocational interests. Ages ranged from 17 to 45, but about 90 percent of the subjects were in the 17-to-30 age group. For reliability and validation studies, samples were drawn from day and evening session college students, prisoners, stutterers, speech-problem cases, adult classes at YMCA, and counselees.

Response Mode. The response mode is a modified Likert type. The subject responds to each item by entering a 1 for "not at all true of myself," a 2 for "slightly true of myself," a 3 for "about half-way true of myself," a 4 for "mostly true of myself," and a 5 for "true of myself."

Scoring. The score for any item ranges from 1 to 5. For items expressing a favorable attitude toward self or others, a score of 5 is assigned to a response of "true of myself," a score of 4 for "mostly true of myself," a score of 3 for "about half-way true of myself," a score of 2 for "slightly true of myself," and a score of 1 for "not at all true of myself." The direction of the scoring is reversed for negatively worded items. After this adjustment has been made, the acceptance-of-self score is computed by summing the item scores for all items on that scale. Similarly, the acceptance-of-others score is obtained by summing item scores for that scale. A high score indicates a favorable attitude toward self or others.

Reliability. Split-half reliabilities were obtained for five groups ranging in size from 18 to 183. These were reported to be .894 or better for the self-acceptance scale for all but one group, which was .746. Similar reliabilities for the acceptance-of-others scale ranged from .776 to .884. All estimates were corrected by the Spearman-Brown formula.

Validity. Several estimates of validity were obtained for these scales, in marked contrast to most of the scales described in this volume. First, one group ($N = 20$) was asked to write freely about their attitudes toward themselves, and another group ($N = 20$) was asked to write about their attitudes toward others. These "essays" were then rated by four judges and the mean ratings correlated with the corresponding scale scores. The correlation was .897 for self-acceptance and .727 for acceptance of others.

Second, a group of stutterers ($N = 38$) were compared with a group of nonstutterers, matched for age and sex. The stutterers had lower mean scores than nonstutterers ($p < .06$) on the self-acceptance scale. For the acceptance-of-others scale, a group of prisoners was compared with a group of college students, matched for age, sex, and race. As expected, prisoners scored lower on the acceptance-of-others scale than the students (p about .02). The prisoners also scored lower on the self-acceptance scale ($p < .01$).

Finally, members of a speech rehabilitation group ($N = 7$) were rated for self-acceptance by clinical assistants. This score correlated .59 with the self-acceptance score, which was not significantly higher than chance. This is not consistent with other results, but the small number of cases and the probable unreliability of the ratings by the clinical assistants raise some question about this estimate of validity.

In general, these scales appear to have been carefully developed, and the author has provided more than the usual amount of evidence of validity.

Comments. This is the most carefully developed scale to measure attitude toward self that we found in the literature. Evidence of validity is more extensive than for most scales in this book.

EXHIBIT 9-6

ACCEPTANCE OF SELF AND OTHERS

This is a study of some of your attitudes. Of course, there is no right answer for any statement. The best answer is what you feel is true of yourself.

You are to respond to each question on the answer sheet according to the following scheme:

1	2	3	4	5
Not at all true of myself	Slightly true of myself	About halfway true of myself	Mostly true of myself	True of myself

Remember, the best answer is the one which applies to you.

Reference: E. Berger. The relation between expressed acceptance of self and expressed acceptance of others. *J. abnorm. soc. Psychol.*, **1952, 47, 778–782. Items obtained from author and published with his permission.**

*Scale		
†S	1	I'd like it if I could find someone who would tell me how to solve my personal problems.
S	2	I don't question my worth as a person, even if I think others do.
O	3	I can be comfortable with all varieties of people—from the highest to the lowest.
O	4	I can become so absorbed in the work I'm doing that it doesn't bother me not to have any intimate friends.
†O	5	I don't approve of spending time and energy in doing things for other people. I believe in looking to my family and myself more and letting others shift for themselves.
†S	6	When people say nice things about me, I find it difficult to believe they really mean it. I think maybe they're kidding me or just aren't being sincere.
†S	7	If there is any criticism or anyone says anything about me, I just can't take it.
†S	8	I don't say much at social affairs because I'm afraid that people will criticize me or laugh if I say the wrong thing.
†S	9	I realize that I'm not living very effectively but I just don't believe that I've got it in me to use my energies in better ways.
†O	10	I don't approve of doing favors for people. If you're too agreeable they'll take advantage of you.
S	11	I look on most of the feelings and impulses I have toward people as being quite natural and acceptable.
†S	12	Something inside me just won't let me be satisfied with any job I've done—if it turns out well, I get a very smug feeling that this is beneath me, I shouldn't be satisfied with this, this isn't a fair test.
†S	13	I feel different from other people. I'd like to have the feeling of security that comes from knowing I'm not too different from others.
†S	14	I'm afraid for people that I like to find out what I'm really like, for fear they'd be disappointed in me.
†S	15	I am frequently bothered by feelings of inferiority.
†S	16	Because of other people, I haven't been able to achieve as much as I should have.
†S	17	I am quite shy and self-conscious in social situations.
†S	18	In order to get along and be liked, I tend to be what people expect me to be rather than anything else.
†O	19	I usually ignore the feelings of others when I'm accomplishing some important end.
S	20	I seem to have a real inner strength in handling things. I'm on a pretty solid foundation and it makes me pretty sure of myself.
†O	21	There's no sense in compromising. When people have values I don't like, I just don't care to have much to do with them.
†O	22	The person you marry may not be perfect, but I believe in trying to get him (or her) to change along desirable lines.
†O	23	I see no objection to stepping on other people's toes a little if it'll help get me what I want in life.
†S	24	I feel self-conscious when I'm with people who have a superior position to mine in business or at school.
†O	25	I try to get people to do what I want them to do, in one way or another.
†O	26	I often tell people what they should do when they're having trouble in making a decision.

* Items of the self scale are labelled S, and those of the others scale are labelled O.

† Items marked with a dagger are worded negatively; item scores are reversed before the scale is scored.

*Scale		
†O	27	I enjoy myself most when I'm alone, away from other people.
†S	28	I think I'm neurotic or something.
O	29	I feel neither above nor below the people I meet.
O	30	Sometimes people misunderstand me when I try to keep them from making mistakes that could have an important effect on their lives.
†S	31	Very often I don't try to be friendly with people because I think they won't like me.
†O	32	There are very few times when I compliment people for their talents or jobs they've done.
O	33	I enjoy doing little favors for people even if I don't know them well.
S	34	I feel that I'm a person of worth, on an equal plane with others.
†S	35	I can't avoid feeling guilty about the way I feel toward certain people in my life.
†O	36	I prefer to be alone rather than have close friendships with any of the people around me.
S	37	I'm not afraid of meeting new people. I feel that I'm a worthwhile person and there's no reason why they should dislike me.
†S	38	I sort of only half-believe in myself.
O	39	I seldom worry about other people. I'm really pretty self-centered.
†S	40	I'm very sensitive. People say things and I have a tendency to think they're criticizing me or insulting me in some way and later when I think of it, they may not have meant anything like that at all.
†S	41	I think I have certain abilities and other people say so too, but I wonder if I'm not giving them an importance way beyond what they deserve.
S	42	I feel confident that I can do something about the problems that may arise in the future.
†O	43	I believe that people should get credit for their accomplishments, but I very seldom come across work that deserves praise.
O	44	When someone asks for advice about some personal problem, I'm most likely to say, "It's up to you to decide," rather than tell him what he should do.
†S	45	I guess I put on a show to impress people. I know I'm not the person I pretend to be.
†O	46	I feel that for the most part one has to fight his way through life. That means that people who stand in the way will be hurt.
†O	47	I can't help feeling superior (or inferior) to most of the people I know.
S	48	I do not worry or condemn myself if other people pass judgment against me.
†O	49	I don't hesitate to urge people to live by the same high set of values which I have for myself.
O	50	I can be friendly with people who do things which I consider wrong.
†S	51	I don't feel very normal, but I want to feel normal.
†S	52	When I'm in a group I usually don't say much for fear of saying the wrong thing.
†S	53	I have a tendency to sidestep my problems.
†O	54	If people are weak and inefficient I'm inclined to take advantage of them. I believe you must be strong to achieve your goals.
†O	55	I'm easily irritated by people who argue with me.
†O	56	When I'm dealing with younger persons, I expect them to do what I tell them.

*Scale		
†O	57	I don't see much point to doing things for others unless they can do you some good later on.
†S	58	Even when people do think well of me, I feel sort of guilty because I know I must be fooling them—that if I were really to be myself, they wouldn't think well of me.
S	59	I feel that I'm on the same level as other people and that helps to establish good relations with them.
†O	60	If someone I know is having difficulty in working things out for himself, I like to tell him what to do.
†S	61	I feel that people are apt to react differently to me than they would normally react to other people.
†S	62	I live too much by other people's standards.
†S	63	When I have to address a group, I get self-conscious and have difficulty saying things well.
†S	64	If I didn't always have such hard luck, I'd accomplish much more than I have.

People in general EXHIBIT 9-7

Description. This scale was developed by Banta (1961) using the UPRO technique. Items were selected from a pool of 72 items originally formulated by Christie in an attempt to measure the extent to which people are disposed to act in an exploitative or manipulative manner toward other people. Twenty of the original items make up the final scale. As described in Chapter 3, the unique aspect of the UPRO technique is that attitude scores and scale values can be obtained from a single administration. Since the scale values are computed with the subjects' own responses as the starting point, they are determined for each population as the scale is used.

In Banta's (1961) study the same items were analyzed by Likert and Thurstone procedures as well as by UPRO. Exhibit 9-7 lists both UPRO and Thurstone scale values, although the two sets of values are highly correlated ($r = .96$).

Subjects. Subjects were drawn from introductory psychology classes of Columbia University, School of General Studies, during the 1958 summer session. Twenty-eight subjects responded to the People in General Scale on three different occasions, once using the Likert format, once the Thurstone format, and once the UPRO format.

Response Mode. For the UPRO-type scale, the subject is given six alternatives ranging from "much too favorable for me," through "expresses my own opinion," to "much too unfavorable for me," plus an undecided category (see Exhibit 9-7).

Scoring. Banta suggested three possible scores: UPRO mean agree score, UPRO summated rating score, and UPRO summated psychometric score. The mean agree score is simply the mean of the scale values of the items checked as expressing "my own opinion." The summated rating score is the mean of the responses to all items, whereas the summated psychometric score is the percent of items the subject considers to be either too unfavorable or with which he agrees. Since the mean agree score correlated higher with Likert and Thurstone scores, it is the one recommended for use with this scale.

Reliability. No reliability estimates were reported, although Banta suggests that the relatively high correlations among Thurstone, Likert, and UPRO scores "reflect very desirable test-retest reliabilities."

Validity. The People in General Scale appears to have content validity, and attitude scores correlated .71 with Likert scores and .72 with Thurstone scores. It is unclear whether these correlations should be treated as estimates of reliability or validity, since the same items were given with different response formats.

Comments. The People in General Scale is one of the few scales developed by the unfolding technique. It appears to be minimally reliable, and items have content validity; however, other evidences of validity are lacking. It might be noted that the UPRO procedure adds little to the Thurstone technique insofar as scale values are concerned. However, the advantage seems to lie in the greater ease with which scale values can be obtained.

EXHIBIT 9-7

PEOPLE IN GENERAL

Instructions

Read carefully

Some of the following statements may reflect your own views, while others may not. Of these statements that do not reflect your own views, there are likely to be some that are too favorable toward the issue; on the other hand, there are also likely to be some that are too unfavorable toward the issue to represent your own views.

Please read each statement carefully and indicate your reaction to it in accordance with the following rules:

Circle

—— – (O) + ++ ?	If the statement expresses your own feelings regarding the issue.
—— – O (+) ++ ?	If the statement is somewhat too favorable toward the issue in question to represent your own views.
—— – O + (++) ?	If the statement is much too favorable to represent your own views.
—— (–) O + ++ ?	If the statement is too unfavorable to represent your own views.

Reference: T. J. Banta. Social attitudes and response styles. *Educ. psychol. Measmt,* 1961, 21, 543–557. Items obtained from author and published with his permission.

Circle

(−−) − O + ++ ? If the statement is very definitely too unfavorable to represent your own views.

−− − O + ++ (?) If the statement is not one that expresses your own feelings but you can't determine whether it is too favorable or too unfavorable toward the issue in question.

Scale Values			
UPRO	Thurstone		
3.22	3.35	1	Most men will fight back when insulted.
2.75	2.74	2	Generally speaking, most people do not truly believe in anything new until they have experienced it.
2.20	2.18	3	Anyone who completely trusts anyone else is asking for trouble.
1.83	1.88	4	Generally speaking, men won't work hard unless they're forced to do so.
3.27	3.74	5	Even the most hardened and vicious criminal has a spark of decency somewhere within him.
4.00	4.00	6	Any normal person will stand up for what he thinks is right even if it costs him his job.
2.69	2.35	7	Most people really don't know what is best for them.
2.74	2.40	8	Some of the best people have some of the worst vices.
2.06	1.79	9	Most men forget more easily the death of their father than the loss of their property.
3.42	3.40	10	Men are quicker to praise than they are to blame.
3.76	3.90	11	Most men like to tackle new and difficult problems.
3.83	3.84	12	Most men are brave.
2.37	2.23	13	Nature has so created men that they desire everything but are unable to attain it.
1.95	1.80	14	The biggest difference between most criminals and other people is that criminals are stupid enough to get caught.
2.81	2.83	15	The best way to handle people is to tell them what they want to hear.
2.06	2.00	16	It is safest to assume that all people have a vicious streak and it will come out when they are given the chance.
3.49	4.05	17	Most people are basically good and kind.
2.62	2.98	18	Barnum was very wrong when he said that there's a sucker born every minute.
2.33	2.23	19	When you come right down to it, it's human nature never to do anything without an eye to one's own advantage.
2.85	2.63	20	The great majority of men are more satisfied with what seems true than with the truth.

ATTITUDES RELATED TO STATUS

Attitudes toward groups of persons based upon status and role relations play an important part in any organized society. In this category, scales are available to measure attitude toward superiors, policemen, and probation officers. A scale to measure attitude toward employers (Hall, 1934) was not included because the items appear inappropriate to the current industrial situation.

Attitude toward the supervisor (AS) scale *EXHIBIT 9-8*

Description. This scale was constructed by Schmid, Morsh, and Detter (1956) as part of a larger program designed to measure job satisfaction. It was developed by a combination of the homogeneous keying procedure (Loevinger, Gleser, and DuBois, 1953) and bifactor analysis. Initially, 60 items were written concerning various aspects of the job situation and were administered to 238 airmen. The homogeneous keying procedure consisted of taking the three most highly correlated items as a nucleus of the proto-scale and successively adding items which increased the internal consistency of the composite set of items, as measured by Kuder-Richardson formula 20 (K-R 20). When additional items failed to increase consistency, the scale was considered complete. The AS scale was the second of three scales derived from the original 60 items. It consisted of 17 items and achieved a K-R 20 of .90. A multiple-group factor analysis was then performed using items from the three homogeneous scales. Only 7 of the 17 items of the AS scale were unique, and these were used to locate a factor axis. The multiple-group factor analysis was then converted to a bifactor solution. The final outcome of these procedures was three scales: the 14-item AS scale shown in Exhibit 9-8, plus scales interpreted as measuring "sense of personal achievement" and "stress." Bifactor loadings on the AS scale ranged from .31 to .57.

Subjects. Subjects were 238 airmen stationed at one Air Force base. The career ladders included: organizational supply specialist, petroleum supply specialist, clerical specialist, and personnel specialist. All were receiving on-the-job training.

Response Mode. Subjects respond to each item by selecting one of five alternatives: strongly agree, agree, undecided, disagree, or strongly disagree.

Scoring. The items are scored by giving a 1 for agreement with a positive (favorable) statement or for disagreement with a negative (unfavorable) statement. The authors did not specify the method of computing the total score, but it seems apparent that the scale score should be the sum of the item scores. The range of possible scores is therefore from 0 to 14. The higher the score, the more favorable the attitude toward supervisors.

Reliability. The only evidence of reliability reported was the measure of internal consistency (K-R 20 = .90) of the original set of 17 items derived by the homogeneous keying procedure; however, it is probable that the final scale is also internally consistent, since all of the 14 items were contained in the original 17.

Validity. Evidence of validity is not great. The content of the items suggests that the scale does indeed measure attitude toward supervisors, since each statement begins with "My supervisor. . . ." It is not clear, however, that the total range is represented by the items. The scale appears to be factorially pure, but additional evidence of validity would be desirable.

Comments. The procedure followed in developing this scale is unusual, but appears to have resulted in a unidimensional scale of relatively high reliability. It is unfortunate that more evidence concerning validity is not available. Further validation studies are recommended before the scale is used for any purpose other than preliminary (pilot) research.

EXHIBIT 9-8

ATTITUDE TOWARD THE SUPERVISOR (AS) SCALE

Answer each item by entering the appropriate letter in the space provided according to the following scale:

A. Strongly agree
B. Agree
C. Undecided
D. Disagree
E. Strongly Disagree

_____ 60 My supervisor is admired and respected by all of his men.
_____ 6 My supervisor praises his men for a job well done.
_____ *27 My supervisor ignores opinions of those who disagree with him.
_____ 30 My supervisor confidently handles emergency situations.
_____ *9 My supervisor takes all the credit when others do good work.
_____ *3 My supervisor ignores the feelings of his men.
_____ 12 My supervisor always backs up his men.
_____ 24 My supervisor treats his men unusually well.
_____ 15 My supervisor considers the safety of his men above all else.
_____ *45 My supervisor gives instructions that are hard to understand.
_____ *33 My supervisor has the wrong opinion of some of his men.
_____ 39 My supervisor has genuine interest in his work.
_____ 57 My supervisor works hard and welcomes additional responsibilities.
_____ *51 My supervisor is not always fair in judging our work.

* Items marked with an asterisk indicate negative attitudes.

Reprinted with permission from Schmid, J. Jr., Morsh, J. E., and Detter, H. M. *Analysis of job satisfaction.* Research Report AFPTRC-TN-57-30, March 1957, ASTIA Document No. 098935.

The superior-subordinate (SS) scale EXHIBIT 9-9

Description. The SS scale was designed to measure the direction of identification in situations involving conflict between a superior and a subordinate (Chapman and Campbell, 1957). From a pool of 130 items, the 37 items of the SS scale were selected by item analysis. Item scale correlations ranged from .19 to .44. In the final form of the scale, there were 20 Likert-type items and 17 forced-choice items.

Subjects. During the item-selection phase, the subjects were 195 officers and instructors and 439 flight cadets tested during the spring of 1954. In a later application of the scale, the subjects were 142 male students at Northwestern University.

Response Mode. The 20 Likert items have the usual five alternatives: A, strongly agree; a, agree; ?, undecided; d, disagree, and D, strongly disagree. Most other items have two alternatives, the nature of which varies from item to item. The authors used an IBM response sheet, but the responses may be entered on the test form if desired.

Scoring. The scoring is dichotomized for all items. The responses scored in the positive direction are shown in parentheses after each Likert item and underlined for each multiple-choice item in Exhibit 9-9. The attitude score is the total number of positive responses. Therefore, the theoretical range is from 0 to 37, with the higher score representing the more favorable attitude toward the superior (and/or the less favorable attitude toward subordinates).

Reliability. Based upon the responses of the 142 students at Northwestern, the Kuder-Richardson reliability was reported to be .69.

Validity. The pattern of correlations of the SS scale with other scales provides some limited evidence of construct validity. The SS scale correlated nonsignificantly with the F scale (.21), with a scale to measure alienation (.08), and with a scale to measure attitude toward cooperation (—.20). It correlated positively (.25, $p < .01$) with a scale to measure identification with discipline.

Comments. The SS scale has been developed carefully and has at least minimum reliability and validity. It has been used with some success by Burwen, Campbell, and Kidd (1956) and by Campbell and Damarin (1961).

EXHIBIT 9-9

THE SUPERIOR - SUBORDINATE (SS) SCALE

PURPOSE: This test is a survey of people's opinions on problems of leadership, administration, supervision, and other aspects of life in general. The object is to better understand how students feel about such matters. There are no right or wrong answers; we are interested only in your frank opinions.

Reference: L. J. Chapman and D. T. Campbell. An attempt to predict the performance of three-man teams from attitude measures. *J. soc. Psychol.,* **1957, 46, 277–286. Items obtained from authors and published with their permission.**

Part I. Mark the answer sheet as follows:

A. Strongly agree
a. Agree
? Undecided
d. Disagree
D. Strongly disagree

*1 The advantage of any extra privileges that go with higher job status is more than outweighed by the burden of increased responsibilities. **(A a ?)**

2 Most workers would do a better job if they weren't always being checked on by a boss. **(d D)**

3 In the long run, the boss does best who looks out for the interests of his men above all else. **(d D)**

4 Students will not work well for a teacher whom they are afraid of. **(d D)**

5 A tough teacher who cracks the whip can, in the long run, get more work out of the men than the kind who is easier and better liked by the men. **(A a ?)**

6 Too often the person in charge of a job takes credit that should rightfully go to the men under him who actually did the job. **(? d D)**

7 Most workers would "goof off" the job if a boss did not supervise their work closely. **(A a ?)**

8 Getting workers to make their own individual work decisions is the best way of getting things done. **(? d D)**

9 Life is probably tougher in the armed forces for the man in the lower ranks than for the man higher up. **(d D)**

10 Despite what some people say about handling men, in practice being nice to them gets better results than being tough. **(? d D)**

11 Although the students may not like a strict teacher as well, they usually have more confidence in him than the type who is a good Joe. **(A a)**

12 Great business firms today could use a little more kindness in dealing with workers. **(d D)**

13 Most businesses and military units would be run a lot more efficiently if the managers listened more to what the underlings had to say. **(? d D)**

14 On most jobs it doesn't hurt for a boss to give in to the men on an unreasonable request once in a while. **(d D)**

15 The average student likes it better in the long run if his superiors are strict and tell him exactly what to do. **(A a)**

16 The life of an enlisted man is in general more carefree than the life of an officer. **(A a)**

17 In general, the tougher a boss is with himself and his men, the higher the morale. **(A a ?)**

18 Confidence in one's workers is good, but it should be tempered with keeping a close eye on things to see that they get done. **(A a)**

19 Praising your men too much makes them try and get by with less work. **(A a ?)**

20 If a boss does not keep close check on the men under him, he would not know the good ones from the bad ones. **(A a)**

PART II. Mark the answer sheet according to your choice.

21 When a supervisor is inclined to be excessively tough on the men, should the foreman under him

A. make things easier for the men when it is possible.
<u>B.</u> conduct things exactly as the supervisor would do.

* The responses that are scored as favorable toward superiors are indicated in parentheses after each Likert item and by underlining of A or B for the multiple-choice items.

22 A high school teacher can be a "good Joe":
A. but discipline usually starts to get slack.
B. and still maintain strict discipline.

23 On the job, whose approval gives you the greater pleasure?
A. The approval of your bosses.
B. The approval of the men you supervise.

24 A man is less likely to make a mistake a second time if:
A. he is severely reprimanded by the person in charge.
B. the person in charge encourages him to do his best and takes the attitude that an occasional mistake is only human.

25 A foreman has been driving his men to the limit to get an emergency job done. His supervisor said it had to be done faster. Should he:
A. explain that the men were doing their best.
B. try driving the men even harder.

26 If workers were given less work to do, it would most likely lead to the men:
A. pitching in with more energy on the next job.
B. getting spoiled.

27 A worker who is usually efficient and conscientious has slipped up on something rather minor that the "big boss" is particular about. Should the man's foreman:
A. stick his own neck out and try to cover up for the man.
B. let the man take his punishment.

28 Giving lots of praise is likely to result in the students doing:
A. more work.
B. less work.

29 The schools today are in danger of being too:
A. soft with the students.
B. strict with the students.

30 In general, the tougher a boss is with himself and the men:
A. the lower the morale.
B. the higher the morale.

31 A commanding officer is a stickler for discipline and going by the regulations, even in trivial matters that other commanding officers are not enforcing. The men have protested to their immediate officer. Should he:
A. explain to the men in as sympathetic a way as possible that these are the regulations.
B. present the situation to the commanding officer and see if he will let up somewhat.

32 For an officer preparing for wartime conditions, the most important consideration is:
A. winning the loyalty of his men.
B. teaching his men to carry out an order without question.

33 What do you do when the men you supervise ask some favor which goes against company policy?
A. grant the favor and take the rap if it comes to that.
B. explain the company policy to the men, and turn down their request.
C. ask your boss for permission to grant the men's request.
D. postpone action and hope the men will forget it.
E. grant the favor but explain the company policy to the men and tell them not to expect it again.

34 On the job, whose disapproval do you usually fear more?
A. The disapproval of my bosses.
B. The disapproval of the men I supervise.

35 It's more important for a military officer to be:
A. well liked by his men.
B. feared and respected by his men.

36 A man who is very conscientious and efficient is due for a promotion. The foreman feels he deserves it, but is also aware that his own supervisor dislikes this man. Should he:
A. put through the man's promotion anyway.
B. let the matter ride.

37 The workers are asking to do something that the foreman feels is all right but that his supervisor disapproves of. Should the foreman:
A. risk his supervisor's displeasure by requesting this permission for the men.
B. turn down the men on the basis that the supervisor would disapprove it.

Attitude toward the supervisor EXHIBIT 9-10

Description. This is a questionnaire designed to measure attitude toward the supervisor (Nagle, 1953). It consists of 22 items about the respondent's immediate supervisor. In constructing the scale, 56 items were administered to 223 employees in 14 departments of an industrial plant. Of these, 93 percent (208) responded. The 22 items in the final scale were selected from the original pool by item analysis.

Subjects. The subjects on which the scale was constructed were 208 employees in 14 departments in the Louisville works of the International Harvester Company. All subjects were part of the office staff.

Response Mode. Each item in the scale consists of a question, followed by from two to four response alternatives. The subject responds by checking the alternative which best represents his feeling about his own immediate supervisor.

Scoring. Responses reflecting a favorable attitude toward the supervisor are marked by an asterisk in Exhibit 9-10. Each favorable response is given a score of 1, and all others a score of 0. The attitude score is the sum of the item scores. The theoretical range is therefore from 0 to 22, with the higher score indicating the more favorable attitude.

Reliability. Split-half reliability was found to be .865 (corrected to .92).

Validity. The sampling of the content domain appears to be adequate. In addition, it was found to correlate as expected with scores on several other scales designed to measure various aspects of the company: —.71 with a company sensitivity scale, —.90 with a measure of the supervisor's sensitivity, and .67 with a cooperation scale. The attitude toward supervisor score also correlated negatively with department size (—.40).

Comments. Further data on this scale may be found in reports by Lawshe and Nagle (1953) and by Guion and Robins (1964). It appears to have relatively good reliability and acceptable evidence of validity.

This scale is copyrighted by Purdue University. Permission to reproduce it must be obtained from the president of the university or from the chairman of the psychology department acting on behalf of the president.

EXHIBIT 9-10

ATTITUDE TOWARD THE SUPERVISOR

Answer each question by checking the alternative which best represents your feeling about your immediate supervisor.

1 Does your immediate supervisor give you an opportunity to prove your ability?
- *a. ______ Frequently
- b. ______ Yes, but not as often as he could
- c. ______ Rarely

2 In your opinion, does your immediate supervisor spend sufficient time planning the work of your department?
- *a. ______ Yes
- b. ______ No

3 Does your immediate supervisor criticize you in front of others?
- a. ______ Criticizes in front of others
- *b. ______ Saves criticism for private occasions

4 Does your immediate supervisor 'follow through' on his promises?
- a. ______ No
- *b. ______ Yes

* Starred responses are scored 1; nonstarred responses are scored 0.

5 Do you feel that you have proper opportunity to present a problem, complaint, or suggestion?
*a. ______ Yes
b. ______ No

6 Does your immediate supervisor avoid you when he knows you want to see him about a problem?
a. ______ Usually avoids me
b. ______ Occasionally avoids me
*c. ______ Never avoids me

7 Does your immediate supervisor take an interest in you as a person as well as in how well you do your job?
a. ______ Yes
*b. ______ No

8 In your opinion, does your immediate supervisor spend sufficient time directing the work of your department?
*a. ______ Yes
b. ______ No

9 Are you criticized by your immediate supervisor for happenings over which you have no control?
a. ______ Often
b. ______ Occasionally
*c. ______ Never

10 Does your immediate supervisor explain to you the 'why' of an error to prevent recurrence of the error?
*a. ______ Usually
b. ______ Occasionally
c. ______ Never

11 When a change is ordered in your work procedure, are you usually given sufficient explanation of why the change is necessary?
*a. ______ Yes
b. ______ No

12 Does your immediate supervisor give you 'straight answers' when you ask him something?
*a. ______ Usually
b. ______ Occasionally
c. ______ Never

13 On the job does your immediate supervisor take a reasonably democratic attitude toward you?
*a. ______ Yes
b. ______ No

14 Does your immediate supervisor delay in taking care of your complaints?
- a. ________ Usually delays
- b. ________ Occasionally delays
- *c. ________ Never delays

15 Do you feel that your immediate supervisor is interested in getting your ideas and suggestions?
- a. ________ No
- *b. ________ Yes

16 Does your immediate supervisor give you recognition for work well done?
- *a. ________ Usually
- b. ________ Occasionally
- c. ________ Never

17 Do you know how you stand with your immediate supervisor?
- a. ________ No
- *b. ________ Yes

18 If something happens which puts your immediate supervisor 'on the spot,' what is he most likely to do?
- *a. ________ Almost always takes the responsibility himself
- *b. ________ Usually takes the responsibility himself
- c. ________ Usually puts the responsibility on the employee
- d. ________ Almost always puts the responsibility on the employee

19 Is your immediate supervisor courteous and friendly to you?
- *a. ________ Always
- b. ________ Usually
- c. ________ Seldom

20 Do you feel promotions in your department are usually based more on ability than on 'personality'?
- *a. ________ Yes
- b. ________ No

21 How well does your immediate supervisor keep you informed about what is going on around the plant?
- *a. ________ He usually keeps me well informed
- b. ________ He rarely keeps me well informed

22 Do you feel at ease around your immediate supervisor?
- *a. ________ Yes
- b. ________ No

Attitude toward the police EXHIBIT 9-11

Description. This scale was developed by Chapman (1960) as a part of a battery of tests to measure delinquents' attitudes toward legal agencies and authorities (police, probation officers, juvenile court, detention home, and boys' industrial school). The scale for measuring attitudes toward probation officers is discussed in the next section, and those relative to the juvenile court, the boys' industrial school, and the detention home are described in Chapter 10. The items in the boys' industrial school scale are specific to the institution familiar to the sample studied, however.

Likert's method was used in constructing the scale. Items were selected by the internal consistency method; each item retained in the final scale yielded a critical ratio of 2.0 or better. The 26 items of the police scale in Exhibit 9-11 are numbered as they were in the larger test battery.

Subjects. The sample used for scale construction consisted of 160 boys in Springfield, Ohio, ranging in age from 13 to 17 years with a mean age of 14.7. Forty of the boys had been in juvenile court. Educational level ranged from seventh to eleventh grade.

Validation data were obtained from a second sample, consisting of 133 delinquents and 133 nondelinquents, matched for age, intelligence, educational level, father's occupation, and residence. They ranged in ages from 13 to 18, with the larger number falling into the 15-year group. Educational level ranged from seventh to eleventh grade.

Response Mode. The response alternatives for each item are the usual Likert type: strongly agree, agree, undecided, disagree, strongly disagree. Subjects respond to each item by checking one of the five alternatives.

Scoring. Following Likert, arbitrary weights are assigned to each response. For favorable (positive) items, a weight of 5 is assigned to "strongly agree," a weight of 4 to "agree," a weight of 3 to "undecided," a weight of 2 to "disagree," and weight of 1 to "agree." The scoring is reversed for negative items. The attitude score is the sum of item scores. A high score indicates a favorable attitude toward the police.

Reliability. Reliability coefficients were computed by both the test-retest and the split-half method, but the exact values were not reported. However, test-retest coefficients for the five scales in the larger battery were reported to range from .85 to .98, and split-half reliabilities, from .92 to .98. Therefore, it may be inferred that the reliabilities of the police scale fall within these ranges.

Validity. In addition to content validity, the scale scores discriminated significantly (CR = 4.95) between delinquents and nondelinquents, with the nondelinquents having the more favorable attitude toward the police.

Comments. The Attitude toward the Police Scale has adequate reliability and appears to be valid. The prospective user should note that the scale items were administered by Chapman (1960) in a larger battery which to some extent disguised the intent of the investigator. Consideration should be given to this factor when using the scale.

EXHIBIT 9-11

ATTITUDE TOWARD THE POLICE

The following pages contain a number of statements about which all boys don't feel the same way. Boys differ a great deal in the way they feel about each statement. There is no such thing as right or wrong answers. We would like to have your honest opinion about each of the statements. They will help many boys in the United States.

Read each statement carefully and then place an *X* in the space which expresses the way you feel about the statement. Wherever possible, let the things which have happened to you help you make a choice. Be sure to answer each statement.

*1 Boys believe that the police could do more to help people.

___Strongly Agree ___Agree ___Undecided ___Disagree ___Strongly Disagree

2 Policemen try to protect things which belong to you.
11 Policemen do more for boys than preachers.
16 The city would be better off if there were more policemen.
*21 The police have it in for boys.
*26 Most policemen will let you buy your way off.
*31 Boys must always be on the lookout for policemen who want to do them dirt.
*36 Policemen try to trick boys.
41 Policemen are pretty nice guys.
46 Boys like most policemen.
51 Boys believe that they can talk about anything with a policeman.
56 Boys believe that they can get as much from a policeman as anyone else.
61 I would like to be a policeman when I grow up.
66 Boys don't believe policemen want to kill people.
*71 Policemen are dumb.
76 Policemen don't do the bad things people say they do.
81 Policemen should get a lot of money for their work.
86 Policemen are always around when they are needed.
*87 Things would be better off if there were fewer policemen.
*89 Policemen don't care what happens to you after they pick you up.
*91 Policemen enjoy kicking boys around.
*93 Policemen don't arrest boys who have rich parents.
*95 Policemen don't know how to be friendly to boys.
96 Policemen are a great help to boys.
*97 Policemen are just as crooked as the people they arrest.
98 On the whole, policemen are honest.

* Negative items are marked with an asterisk. The same set of response alternatives is used with each item.

Reference: A. W. Chapman. Attitudes toward legal agencies of authority for juveniles: A comparative study of one hundred thirty-three delinquent and one hundred thirty-three non-delinquent boys in Dayton, Ohio. *Dissert. Abstr.*, **1960, 20, No. 7. Items obtained from author and published with his permission.**

Attitude toward probation officers *EXHIBIT 9-12*

Description. This is one of the scales in the battery described above (Chapman, 1960). It is a Likert-type scale consisting of 22 items. These items are given in Exhibit 9-12, numbered in the order in which they appeared in the larger battery. The method of construction and item selection were the same as described above.

Subjects. The samples used in construction and validation are described in the preceding section.

Response Mode. The five-alternative Likert response mode is used: strongly agree, agree, undecided, disagree, strongly disagree. The subject checks one alternative for each item.

Scoring. Scoring is again by the arbitrary assignment of weights, with a weight of 5 for responses most favorable to probation officers and weight of 1 for least favorable responses. Weights of 4, 3, and 2 are assigned to intermediate responses. Item scores are summed to obtain the attitude score; thus a high score indicates a favorable attitude toward probation officers.

Reliability. Corrected split-half reliability was reported to be .92. As reported above, test-retest reliability was reported to range from .85 to .98 for the five scales in the battery; therefore, the test-retest reliability of the probation officers scale falls within this range.

Validity. The scale seems to have content validity, but it failed to discriminate between delinquents and nondelinquents (CR = 1.0).

Comments. The evidence for reliability is satisfactory, but there is some question concerning the validity of the scale. Further standardization is indicated. Again, the prospective user is cautioned that the items were interspersed among items from other scales.

EXHIBIT 9-12

ATTITUDE TOWARD PROBATION OFFICERS

The following pages contain a number of statements about which all boys don't feel the same way. Boys differ a great deal in the way they feel about each statement. There is no such thing as right or wrong answers. We would like to have your honest opinion about each of the statements. They will help many boys in the United States.

Reference: A. W. Chapman. Attitudes toward legal agencies of authority for juveniles. A comparative study of one hundred thirty-three delinquent and one hundred thirty-three non-delinquent boys in Dayton, Ohio. ***Dissert. Abstr.*, 1960, 20, No. 7. Items obtained from author and published with his permission.**

Read each statement carefully and then place an *X* in the space which expresses the way you feel about the statement. Whenever possible, let the things which have happened to you help you make a choice. Be sure to answer each statement.

*3 Probation officers expect too much from boys.

___Strongly Agree ___Agree ___Undecided ___Disagree ___Strongly Disagree

*8 Probation officers visit boys in their homes too much.
*13 Probation officers are just like policemen.
*18 Boys would rather take a whipping than to talk to a probation officer.
23 Probation officers seem to know how boys feel when they are in trouble.
*28 Probation officers talk to too many people about boys.
*33 Probation officers are too strict about the kind of friends a boy keeps.
*38 Probation officers try to trick boys into telling the truth.
*43 Probation officers keep many boys from making money by watching them.
48 Probation officers are just like big brothers to boys.
*53 Probation officers think that they are smarter than most people.
58 Probation officers like to help boys.
63 Boys don't mind turning to probation officers when they are in trouble.
*68 Probation officers are of more help to the city than to boys.
73 Boys can always trust probation officers.
*78 Probation officers make it tough for boys.
83 Boys don't mind telling probation officers the truth.
86 Boys will do anything for probation officers.
88 I would like to be a probation officer when I grow up.
*90 Things would be better off if there were no probation officers.
*92 Boys get little satisfaction from probation officers.
94 Probation officers treat boys better than their teachers.

* Negative items are marked with an asterisk. The same set of response alternatives is used with each item.

The juvenile delinquency attitude (JDA) scale *EXHIBIT 9-13*

Description. The JDA scale (Alberts, 1962, 1963) appears to measure a complex attitude toward juvenile delinquency. We have chosen to list it under the significant others rubric since a major aspect of the attitude measured seems to be attitude toward the delinquent as a person. The scale was designed to measure ministers' attitudes toward juvenile delinquency on an authoritarian-supportive continuum, where authoritarian-supportive refers to contrasting orientations toward the juvenile delinquent. The authoritarian orientation is characterized by punitive, moralistic attitudes, whereas the supportive orientation is characterized by acceptant, youth-centered, educative, understanding attitudes toward the juvenile delinquent. The 23 items in the final scale were selected from a pool of 38 items by item analysis. All items discriminated between high and low scorers at the 5 percent level or better.

Subjects. The subjects were 74 Protestant ministers who were serving churches in which juvenile offenders associated with the church had been brought into juvenile court during the period from 1957 to 1959. All were Protestant, representing 14 denominations. All were located in or near Boston. Item selection was based upon the responses of 50 ministers from the same population. The scale was also administered to 22 staff members of the Division of Legal Medicine of the Commonwealth of Massachusetts, consisting of 16 psychiatric social workers and six psychologists.

Response Mode. A six-category response mode is used: +1, I slightly agree; +2, I moderately agree; +3, I strongly agree; —1, I slightly disagree; —2, I moderately disagree; —3, I strongly disagree. The subject responds to each item by entering the appropriate number in the space provided.

Scoring. Responses to items are converted into scores as follows: —3, 1 point; —2, 2 points; —1, 3 points; +1, 5 points; +2, 6 points; +3, 7 points. The attitude score is the total of the item scores. An individual's total score could range from 23 to 161 points. A high score indicates an unfavorable attitude toward juvenile delinquency.

Reliability. A test-retest reliability coefficient of .95 was reported for 33 ministers from the experimental sample. The average item-test correlation was .93.

Validity. The author reports that most of the high scorers agreed with the majority of the items on the scale, whereas most of the low scorers disagreed with 19 of the 23 items. Validity was also seen in an analysis of interview data. High scorers (the upper 27 percent) avoided, condemned, rejected youth, demanded obedience, and resorted to fear and force in handling delinquents; low scorers (the lower 27 percent) tended to accept and understand delinquents, to hold up ethical values to them, to provide them with wholesome activities, and to help them readjust to the community.

The fact that the group of 16 psychiatric social workers and 6 psychologists had mean scores on the JDA scale (55) similar to the mean score of the lower 27 percent of the experimental group (57) is also considered as evidence of validity by Alberts (1962).

Finally, the JDA scale was found to correlate .81 with the TFI scale (see Chapter 3) and .83 with the F scale (see Chapter 7).

Comments. The JDA scale has adequate reliability, but the complex nature of the items and the nature of the validation data raise questions about the referent. The content of many of the items, as well as the high correlation between the JDA scale and the F scale, also raises questions about the referent. The prospective user should consider this question in more detail before adoption of the scale for any purpose other than exploratory research.

Finally, the items are all stated in the same direction, which means that response bias is likely to be a contaminating factor.

EXHIBIT 9-13

THE JUVENILE DELINQUENCY ATTITUDE (JDA) SCALE

This is a survey of the opinion of clergymen concerning the rearing of children with specific application to the problem of juvenile delinquency. The following are statements with which some people agree and others disagree. Similarly, you will probably find yourself agreeing strongly with some statements, disagreeing just as strongly with others, and being perhaps more neutral about still others. There are no right or wrong answers. The best answer is your personal opinion. Please mark each one in the left margin according to the amount of your agreement or disagreement by using the following scale:

+1: I slightly agree	**—1:** I slightly disagree
+2: I moderately agree	**—2:** I moderately disagree
+3: I strongly agree	**—3:** I strongly disagree

1 Each member of a gang that becomes involved in a gang war, commits robbery, sets fires, etc., is equally guilty and all should receive the same punishment.

2 While psychology can contribute to our understanding of why children steal, become truant, run away from home, and are stubborn, there are some kinds of violent and wanton behavior that cannot be understood by the human mind.

3 Youngsters who get into trouble have to suffer the consequences in order to learn that wrong living does not pay and can only lead to punishment and suffering.

4 Young people who commit sex crimes, such as raping or molesting girls or forcing other young people into homosexual acts, deserve more than mere imprisonment; they ought to be dealt with severely.

5 Living is too soft for kids today; less of them would get into trouble if they had a job to occupy their time and minds.

6 While looks can be deceiving, physical appearance, such as tidiness or sloppiness, tells a lot about a young person; it would seem that even the delinquent child who is tidy and neat would be easier to help than the delinquent whose appearance is rough and untidy.

7 If delinquents expect adults to like them, they have to show respect and obedience.

8 Character, honesty, and obedience will tell in the long run; most boys and girls get what they deserve.

9 The boy who commits a destructive or assaultive act should be locked up where he can do no more harm.

10 A major cause of delinquency stems from magazines and movies that play up the sordid and seamy side of life, exposing the minds of young people to all sorts of immoral ideas and criminal schemes.

11 On the whole, juvenile delinquents are not as much the unfortunate and helpless victims of circumstances as some people think; they know right from wrong and can do better if they try.

12 It would be difficult, if not impossible, to help the juvenile offender who refused to repent and confess his guilt.

13 With regard to juvenile delinquency, we are putting too much faith in the psychological approach, when what we really need are stiffer laws and more vigilant law enforcement.

14 We are coddling juvenile delinquents and their parents by shielding them from the newspapers; if the names of the delinquents and their parents were published, the disgrace might have the effect of keeping such youths out of further trouble.

15 Young people should not be allowed to hang out on street corners for it is often there that delinquent gangs are formed and malicious acts planned.

16 It would be easier to help a younger and smaller boy who became involved in delinquency than an older and bigger boy.

17 Help to delinquents is better carried on in the church and synagogue than in the demoralizing setting of the home.

18 It is almost too late for the church or synagogue to help the persistent delinquent after he has finally been sentenced to a correctional institution.

19 Church- or synagogue-sponsored activities, such as scouting, arts and crafts, and basketball, while of value to delinquent youngsters in the forming of wholesome relationships with peers and adult leaders, do not offer as much corrective influence as religious instruction classes.

20 Most juvenile delinquents are vicious and destructive and present a growing threat to life and property.

21 Behavior is either right or wrong, good or bad, and young people should be rewarded or punished accordingly as the case may be.

22 Psychologists who deal with delinquents in guidance centers and reformatories should be less concerned with the subconscious life of these youths and more concerned with their moral life.

23 In the final analysis, the only way to stop some kids from getting into further trouble is to instill fear in them whether it be the fear of God, or the fear of the police, or the fear of punishment.

ATTITUDES RELATED TO BIOLOGICAL CHARACTERISTICS

This category contains scales to measure attitudes toward subcultural groups based upon biologically determined characteristics of persons in these groups. Here we are concerned only with those subgroups that are based directly upon such characteristics. Biologically determined characteristics also play a role in the development of prejudices toward ethnic and national groups, which are considered in Chapter 8.

Theoretically, there might be a large number of subgroups based directly upon biological characteristics; in fact, we found only scales for measuring attitudes based upon age and sex. A scale to measure attitude toward the employment of older workers (Kirchner, Lindbom, and Paterson, 1952) is given in Chapter 4.

The "value inventory" EXHIBIT 9-14

Description. Jarrett and Sherriffs (1953) designed this scale to measure attitude toward the relative "value" of men and women in our culture. Thus the attitude which the scale attempts to measure is a complex one. None of the formal attitude scaling techniques was used in developing the scale; instead, each item was selected on the basis of judgments by the investigators and "several colleagues" as to whether it was positively or negatively valued by the general population and whether it was generally included within the stereotypes of males and females. For the final scale, 58 items were chosen. Of these, 17 were judged as appropriate to stereotypes for men, 17 for women, and 24 as unrelated to male-female stereotypes.

Subjects. The subjects were drawn from classes in personal and social adjustment at the University of California in 1950 and 1951. These classes were not open to psychology majors; about 42 major fields were represented. The earlier sample consisted of 179 men and 212 women, and the later sample consisted of 159 men and 266 women.

Response Mode. The subject is required to indicate whether the behavior referred to in each item applies more appropriately to men or women. (Jarrett and Sherriffs attempted to disguise the intent of the scale by asking subjects to also indicate whether the behavior best characterized other classes of people, such as Catholics, Jews, or Protestants.)

Scoring. An attitude score is obtained by assigning a +1 to any positively valued statement ascribed to men and any negatively valued statement ascribed to women, and a —1 to any negatively valued behavior ascribed to men or positively valued behavior ascribed to women. The attitude score is the algebraic sum of item scores. Thus the possible score ranges from +58 for a person who ascribes only good things to men and bad things to women to —58 for one who ascribes only good things to women and bad things to men.

Reliability. Only indirect evidence of reliability is available. A total of 815 college students responded to this scale on two successive occasions, either in control groups or in experimental groups with an interposed treatment. For one sample, the mean change in attitude score from pre- to posttest was 1.77 for men ($N = 35$) and —1.42 for women ($N = 38$). Similarly, in the other sample the mean change was 2.86 for men ($N = 44$) and —0.33 for women ($N = 48$). These small changes in mean scores may be taken as at least minimal evidence of reliability, but the interpretation is complicated by the fact that the change was positive for men and negative for women.

Validity. Limited evidence of validity comes from the changes in attitude scores as a result of promale or profemale arguments. Promale arguments produced mean changes in the positive direction (4.86 to 10.75), whereas profemale arguments produced mean changes in the negative direction (—6.57 to —9.17).

Comments. A major question with regard to this scale is whether the items represent the entire range. There is no way of knowing, from the procedure followed in construction of the scale, whether the scale can discriminate equally well between persons at different points on the attitude continuum. This is in part a problem of validity, suggesting the need for further evidence that the scale actually measures the value attributed to men and women. The lack of more definitive reliability data is also a weakness of this scale.

EXHIBIT 9-14

THE "VALUE INVENTORY"

Indicate whether each of the following statements best characterizes men or women. Write a W after the statement if it best characterizes women, and an M after the statement if it best characterizes men. Please respond to every statement.

1 Proportional to their numbers, most responsible for auto accidents in 1939 were:
2 Having the most understanding of the real needs of children are:
3 Most likely to be careless in matters of personal cleanliness are:
4 Most subject to violent outbursts of temper are:
5 Predisposition to insanity is more frequent among:
6 More likely to hold a grudge are:
7 Showing most consideration for persons older than themselves are:
8 Best losers at card games are:
9 Most conscientious in preparing for going to the polls on election day are:
10 Least likely to get upset over small details are:
11 Best equipped for the medical profession, other things being equal, are:
12 Life is **endured** more than enjoyed more often by:
13 More marital difficulties arise from the jealousy of persons who are:
14 Showing greatest warmth toward those less fortunate than themselves are:
15 More courageous in the face of social disapproval are:
16 Most insightful are:
17 Most faithful in marriage are:
18 Reasoning ability is poorest in:
19 Showing greatest emotional balance in crises are:
20 "Carriers" of disease are more often found among:
21 Least likely to have an opinion of themselves which is higher than the opinion of them by their peers are:
22 Most likely to give up a principle in order to obtain social status are:
23 Least willing to accept responsibility for actions which will affect the happiness of others are:
24 Prone to defend stubbornly their own point of view against overwhelming evidence that it is incorrect are:
25 More people report their greatest happiness was given them by:

26 The members of social service organizations who make the greatest individual contributions of time, effort and results are:
27 Most often likely to resort to unfair tactics in competitive situations are:
28 If in charge of finances, most likely to go dangerously in debt are:
29 Most likely to make pretenses socially rather than to reveal their real attitudes are:
30 Prone to take advantage of any situation to further their own selfish ends are:
31 Individuals who are so dependent upon others that they have difficulty adjusting to life situations are more often:
32 Possessing the keenest sense of humor are:
33 More often tending to be competitive even in the most cooperative situations are:
34 Most able to base actions on objective facts rather than on irrational personal feeling are:
35 Most imaginative are:
36 Fundamentally more prone to impose one's will on others are:
37 More courageous in the face of physical danger are:
38 Most prone to punctuality out of consideration for others are:
39 Personal conscience fails to inhibit reprehensible behavior most frequently in:
40 Most creative are:
41 More courageous in the face of pain are:
42 The best leaders of small groups—5 to 10 individuals—more often are:
43 General intelligence is highest in:
44 The persons who remain most loyal to friends and causes under fire are:
45 Most often swayed against their best interests by newspaper editorials are:
46 Physical defects are more common among:
47 Basic moral character is found to represent the highest values generally in:
48 Least likely to exaggerate their personal difficulties are:
49 Poorest losers at sports are:
50 Trustworthiness has been found to be highest in:
51 More likely to find satisfaction in daydreams than in actual life situations are:
52 More inclined to exhibitionism are:
53 Having least poise in awkward situations are:
54 The sexual codes of their own groups are more often violated by:
55 Impetus for future social progress will come to the greatest degree from:
56 Most likely to be sensitive to the feelings of others are:
57 "Vanity" is a term applicable to more members of:
58 "Keeping up with the Joneses" is more often a preoccupation of:

The open subordination of women (OSW) scale EXHIBIT 9-15

Description. This is a 20-item, Likert-type scale, developed by Nadler and Morrow (1959). It was designed to tap several aspects of attitude toward women: restrictive policies, alleged inferiority, alleged narrowness, and alleged offensiveness. The number of items before selection was not given, but item discriminatory powers were computed by subtracting low quartile means from high quartile means. These values ranged from 1.50 to 3.65. The items were intermingled with three other scales; Exhibit 9-15 gives the items of the OSW scale, numbered as they were in the composite instrument.

Subjects. Subjects were taken from three undergraduate classes in psychology at a large university and from one psychology class in a smaller college. Both institutions were located in a large Midwestern city. Two classes were given in the daytime, and students were mostly on a full-time basis. The other two were evening classes and were attended by part-time students. All were men, and their average age was 25. Most were single, and the majority reported at least one sister. Total number was 83.

Response Mode. A six-point Likert response mode is used. These are: agree very much, agree pretty much, agree, disagree, disagree pretty much, and disagree very much.

Scoring. Items are scored on a seven-point scale, with the midpoint treated as a hypothetical zero which was scored if the item was not answered. That is, "agree very much" was given a value of 1; "agree pretty much," a value of 2; "agree," a value of 3; no response, a value of 4; "disagree," a value of 5; "disagree pretty much," a value of 6; and "disagree very much," a value of 7. The attitude score is the sum of the item scores. A high score indicates a favorable attitude toward women.

Reliability. Split-half reliability was .83, corrected by the Spearman-Brown prophecy formula.

Validity. Evidence of validity is limited, but some discriminant validity is indicated by the finding that OSW scores correlated .66 with the F scale and .45 with the E scale. The OSW scale also correlated .73 with the C scale described below.

Comments. This scale seems to have adequate reliability and some evidence of validity, but further standardization studies are indicated.

EXHIBIT 9-15

THE OPEN SUBORDINATION OF WOMEN (OSW) SCALE

This is a study of what people think regarding a number of social questions, especially regarding women. The best answer to each statement is *your own personal opinion.* We have tried to cover many different points of view. You may find yourself agreeing strongly with some of the statements, disagreeing just as strongly with others, and perhaps uncertain about others. Whether you agree or disagree with any statement, you can be sure that many other people feel the same way that you do.

Mark each statement in the left margin according to how much you agree or disagree with it. *Please mark every one.* Write in a +1, +2, +3, or −1, −2, −3, depending upon how you feel in each case.

+1: I agree a little	−1: I disagree a little
+2: I agree pretty much	−2: I disagree pretty much
+3: I agree very much	−3: I disagree very much

1 Because of their inborn limitations, women have contributed but little to the discoveries and inventions of civilization.

4 It goes against nature to have a woman as foreman or boss over men.

7 The man should "wear the pants" in the family.

11 Constant petting and cuddling have the same cheapening effect on a woman as that produced on merchandise which through repeated handling has become faded and rumpled.

14 A major fault that women have is their personal vanity as shown by the exaggerated importance they attach to minute details of dress and grooming.

17 Women naturally tend to be self-centered, so that for them to be loved is a greater need than to love someone else.

21 Women seem to be inherently less capable than men of logical and scientific thinking.

24 Because men are strong and women are weak, it is only right that this be a man's world.

27 No matter how they are treated, the majority of women seem to be bossy and nagging.

31 Women are much more prone to engage in jabbering, chattering talk than are men.

34 There is hardly anything more revolting than seeing a woman dress, act and cuss like a man.

37 Women have far less control over their emotions than do men.

41 Although women play a part in many important jobs today, woman's proper place is still in the home.

44 Despite the American ideal of equality of the sexes, there are certain jobs, like that of President of the United States, which are just too important to be held by a woman.

47 Although there are exceptions, nagging and domineering traits, however subtle, seem to be pretty typical among women.

51 Men are naturally more capable than women in financial matters.

54 Even with the right to vote and hold office, few women participate actively in politics; thus it is clear that the average woman's political interests are inherently narrower than those of men.

57 It must be admitted that the average woman has a rather narrow sense of justice.

61 The majority of women are gold-diggers when they get the chance.

64 It seems to be a law of nature that men are dominant and women are submissive.

The chivalry (C) scale EXHIBIT 9-16

Description. The C scale was developed by Nadler and Morrow (1959) in connection with the OSW scale described above. The items were selected to reflect several aspects of men's attitudes toward women:

superficial "protection and assistance," special "deference" in conduct toward women, and special pseudorespectful "deference" toward women as a value. Items were evaluated by item discriminative power as described above. DP values ranged from 1.31 to 3.48. Exhibit 9-16 lists the 18 items of the C scale, numbered as they were in the composite scale.

Subjects. Subjects used in the construction of the C scale were the same as those used in the construction of the OSW scale.

Response Mode. The six-point Likert response mode is used, as outlined in the description of the OSW scale.

Scoring. Like the OSW scale, items are scored on a seven-point scale, with the midpoint being treated as a hypothetical zero point. Items are again scored so that a high score indicates a favorable attitude toward women. Item 29 is the only item that is stated in the opposite direction, and scoring is reversed for this item. The attitude score is the sum of the item scores.

Reliability. Split-half reliability (corrected) was found to be .86, but no other estimates of reliability were reported.

Validity. Again, evidence of validity is limited. However, scores on the C scale correlated .60 with the F scale and .73 with the E scale.

Comments. Like the OSW scale, the C scale shows some promise as a useful research tool, but additional studies of reliability and validity are needed.

EXHIBIT 9-16

THE CHIVALRY (C) SCALE

This is a study of what people think regarding a number of social questions, especially regarding women. The best answer to each statement is *your own personal opinion.* We have tried to cover many different points of view. You may find yourself agreeing strongly with some of the statements, disagreeing just as strongly with others, and perhaps uncertain about others. Whether you agree or disagree with any statement, you can be sure that many other people feel the same way that you do.

Mark each statement in the left margin acccording to how much you agree or disagree with it. *Please mark every one.* Write in a +1, +2, +3, or —1, —2, —3, depending upon how you feel in each case.

+1: I agree a little	—1: I disagree a little
+2: I agree pretty much	—2: I disagree pretty much
+3: I agree very much	—3: I disagree very much

3 No gentleman should allow a lady to soil her hands with messy work if he can possibly convince her that it is easier for him to do it.

6 A gentleman should remove his hat and hold it in his hand when a lady enters the elevator in which he is a passenger.

9 In alighting from an automobile, the most desirable procedure when possible is for the man to walk around in front of the car and hold the door open for the lady.

13 Although fighting a duel for the honor of a lady is a custom which is not practiced in the modern world, the idea behind this custom should certainly be maintained.

16 In the light of their interests in domestic affairs, their fondness for babies and devotion to their children's success, women are deserving of a special respect and admiration by men.

19 Every boy should be taught from an early age to feel a special honor and respect for womanhood.

22 It is inexcusable when a man escorting a lady fails to help her on with her coat.

26 A true gentleman should not invite a young lady to come alone to his house, especially at night.

29 The custom that a man should rise from his seat while being introduced to a lady, while the lady being introduced to the man is supposed to remain seated, is really rather silly and should be dropped.

33 In accompanying a lady anywhere at night, a gentleman should never fail to offer his arm.

36 It is disrespectful for a man to swear in the presence of a lady.

39 No real man can help but admire the essential tenderness and purity of women.

43 No right-thinking person would question the sanctity of motherhood.

46 In being introduced a gentleman should never shake hands with a lady unless she offers her hand first.

49 When sitting down at the table, proper respect demands that the gentleman hold the lady's chair.

53 When entering a room, it is inexcusably boorish for a man to precede a lady.

56 When walking with a lady, genuine respect demands that the gentleman should always walk on the curb side of the pavement or with the lady on his right.

59 Except perhaps in very special circumstances, a gentleman should never allow a lady to pay the taxi, buy the tickets, or pay the check.

Attitudes toward old people *EXHIBIT 9-17*

Description. This scale was developed by Tuckman and Lorge (1953*a*). It consists of 137 items, classified into 13 categories: physical, financial, conservatism, family, attitudes toward the future, insecurity, mental deterioration, activities and interests, personality traits, best time of life, sex, cleanliness, and interference. Items of the scale given in Exhibit 9-17 are not identified by class but this information may be obtained from the original report by Tuckman and Lorge (1952*a*).

No standard procedure was followed in constructing the scale, although judgments of a sizable number of "experts" were obtained for purposes of item selection.

Subjects. The subjects used in the original study consisted of 95 men and 55 women at Teachers College, Columbia University. Their ages ranged from 20 to 51, with a mean of 29.5 for men and 33.3 for women. Other samples were used in later studies, from which much of the evidence concerning reliability and validity is obtained. These samples are described in connection with the appropriate data.

Response Mode. Respondents are required only to indicate, by circling either "yes" or "no," whether each statement applies to old people.

Scoring. The attitude score is the number of "yes" responses. A high score indicates an unfavorable attitude toward old people.

Reliability. Data relevant to reliability comes largely from reports of research using the scale. In one study (Tuckman and Lorge, 1954) 30 items from the old people scale and 10 items from the older workers scale (Tuckman and Lorge, 1952*b*; see below) were given under two response directions: the usual "yes-no" response and an estimation of the percentage of old people to which the statement applies. The sample consisted of 29 men, aged from 21 to 48 years, and 18 women, aged from 21 to 51 years. The correlation between the two sets of scores was .94 before instruction in a psychology course and .90 after instruction. Test-retest reliabilities were .96 for the "yes-no" response mode and .83 for the percentage estimate. As the authors indicated, selection of the items for the shorter scale probably resulted in the more reliable items being included.

Validity. Aside from item content, the best evidence of validity also comes from the use of the scale in research. In one study (Tuckman and Lorge, 1952*a*) it was shown that institutionalized persons (29 men and 19 women, aged from 61 to 88 years) scored significantly higher (mean score, 81.8) than did noninstitutionalized persons (a community group composed of 11 men and 10 women, aged from 60 to 80 years, had a mean score of 61.7; and an apartment-house group composed of 5 men and 15 women, aged from 65 to 84 years, had a mean score of 66.9). This finding is consistent with the hypothesis that as individuals become less able to cope with the problems of everyday life, they will subscribe more to the stereotypes about old people; hence, it provides some evidence of construct validity. In another study (Tuckman, Lorge, and Spooner, 1953) sizable correlations were reported between scores of fathers, mothers, and children on the old people scale and the older workers scale (.86 for fathers, .75 for mothers, and .79 for children; $N = 50$ in each case).

The best study of validity, however, is that undertaken by Axelrod and Eisendorfer (1961). They utilized an approach called stimulus-group validity. The Tuckman-Lorge scale was administered to 280 students at Duke University. Random fifths of each group of subjects were instructed to apply the statements to either 35-year-olds, 45-year-olds, 55-year-olds, 65-year-olds, or 75-year-olds. Mean number of "yes" responses increased monotonically with age of the stimulus group. An item analysis using the stimulus-group criterion indicated that 96 of the 137 are valid.

Comments. Additional data relevant to the old people scale are cited in other reports by the authors of the scale (Tuckman and Lorge, 1952*d*; 1953*b*; 1958*a,b*), and in a study by Drake (1957). The scale appears to be valid as a whole, but caution should be exercised in interpreting scores derived from subcategories.

EXHIBIT 9-17

ATTITUDES TOWARD OLD PEOPLE

DIRECTIONS: Below are statements about old people. If you are in general agreement with these statements, put a circle around the Yes. If you are in general disagreement with the statement, put a circle around the No. Answer all questions. If you are not sure, guess.

Yes	No	1	Old people need glasses to read.
Yes	No	2	They are absent-minded.
Yes	No	3	They need less food than younger people.
Yes	No	4	They are in the happiest period of their lives.
Yes	No	5	They spoil their grandchildren.
Yes	No	6	They are kind.
Yes	No	7	They repeat themselves in conversation.
Yes	No	8	They cannot learn new things.
Yes	No	9	They are poor eaters.
Yes	No	10	They get upset easily.
Yes	No	11	They prefer to live alone.
Yes	No	12	They prefer to be alone.
Yes	No	13	They have to be careful of their diet.
Yes	No	14	They are proud of their children.
Yes	No	15	They are set in their ways.
Yes	No	16	They need less sleep than younger people.
Yes	No	17	They are not important in the family affairs.
Yes	No	18	They vote for the political candidate who promises the largest old age pensions.
Yes	No	19	They are grouchy.
Yes	No	20	They worry about unimportant things.
Yes	No	21	They are better off in old age homes.
Yes	No	22	They have to go to bed early.
Yes	No	23	They expect their children to support them.
Yes	No	24	They are forgetful.
Yes	No	25	They are easily moved to tears.
Yes	No	26	They are more interested in religion.
Yes	No	27	They have many accidents in the home.
Yes	No	28	They are old-fashioned.
Yes	No	29	They are a burden to their children.
Yes	No	30	They feel sorry for themselves.
Yes	No	31	They need a nap every day.
Yes	No	32	They like just to sit and dream.

Yes No 33 They are calm.
Yes No 34 They are hard to get along with.
Yes No 35 They feel cold even in warm weather.
Yes No 36 They are unproductive.
Yes No 37 They think the world is headed for destruction.
Yes No 38 They become insane.
Yes No 39 They never take a bath.
Yes No 40 They never fully recover if they break any bone.
Yes No 41 They usually live with their children.
Yes No 42 They are conservative.
Yes No 43 They are very talkative.
Yes No 44 They are hard of hearing.
Yes No 45 They are out of step with the times.
Yes No 46 They like old songs on the radio.
Yes No 47 They are stubborn.
Yes No 48 They die soon after retirement.
Yes No 49 They cannot taste differences in food.
Yes No 50 They believe in a life after death.
Yes No 51 They have too much power in business and politics.
Yes No 52 They like to be helped across the street.
Yes No 53 They like to give advice.
Yes No 54 They make friends easily.
Yes No 55 They are suspicious of others.
Yes No 56 They think the future is hopeless.
Yes No 57 They worry about their health.
Yes No 58 They cannot manage their own affairs.
Yes No 59 They would like to be young again.
Yes No 60 They are touchy.
Yes No 61 They have a few friends.
Yes No 62 They never had it better.
Yes No 63 They are good to children.
Yes No 64 They have lost most of their teeth.
Yes No 65 They like religious programs on the radio.
Yes No 66 They respect tradition.
Yes No 67 They walk slowly.
Yes No 68 They feel that their children have failed them.
Yes No 69 They are selfish.
Yes No 70 They frequently quarrel with their children and relatives.
Yes No 71 They should not marry.
Yes No 72 They suffer from constipation.
Yes No 73 They hold on to their opinions.
Yes No 74 They are afraid of the dark.
Yes No 75 They like to be waited on.
Yes No 76 They spend much time in bed because of illness.
Yes No 77 They cannot remember names.
Yes No 78 They are lonely.
Yes No 79 They collect many useless things like string, paper and old shoes.
Yes No 80 They have poor coordination.
Yes No 81 They get no sympathy from their relatives.
Yes No 82 They like to play checkers or dominoes.
Yes No 83 They object to women smoking in public.
Yes No 84 They hide their money.
Yes No 85 They like to doze in a rocking chair.
Yes No 86 They like to think about the good old days.

Yes No 87 They feel tired most of the time.
Yes No 88 They are bad patients when ill.
Yes No 89 They are in their second childhood.
Yes No 90 They feel that their children neglect them.
Yes No 91 They are afraid of death.
Yes No 92 They are fussy about food.
Yes No 93 Their voices break.
Yes No 94 They prefer old friends rather than make new ones.
Yes No 95 They love life.
Yes No 96 They spend most of their time reading or listening to the radio.
Yes No 97 They would like to live their lives over again.
Yes No 98 They die of cancer or heart disease.
Yes No 99 They avoid going out in bad weather.
Yes No 100 They are untidy and careless about their appearance.
Yes No 101 They take a keen interest in politics.
Yes No 102 They frequently are at loose ends.
Yes No 103 They develop infection easily.
Yes No 104 They should not become parents.
Yes No 105 They worry about financial security.
Yes No 106 They are critical of the younger generation.
Yes No 107 They are tight in money matters.
Yes No 108 They dislike any changes or interference with established ways of doing things.
Yes No 109 They are usually supported by their children or old-age pensions.
Yes No 110 They are very sensitive to noise.
Yes No 111 They are in the way.
Yes No 112 They marry persons much younger than themselves.
Yes No 113 They are anxious about the future.
Yes No 114 They are cranky.
Yes No 115 They suffer much discomfort.
Yes No 116 They expect obedience and respect from their children and grandchildren.
Yes No 117 They meddle in other people's affairs.
Yes No 118 They are bossy.
Yes No 119 They prefer to read newspapers rather than books.
Yes No 120 They have no interest in the opposite sex.
Yes No 121 They cannot concentrate, even on simple tasks.
Yes No 122 They have a high automobile accident rate.
Yes No 123 They get love and affection from their children.
Yes No 124 They like to gossip.
Yes No 125 They feel miserable most of the time.
Yes No 126 They are careless about their table manners.
Yes No 127 They become less intelligent.
Yes No 128 They frequently talk to themselves.
Yes No 129 They do not take part in sports.
Yes No 130 They feel that young parents do not know how to bring up children properly.
Yes No 131 They die after a major operation.
Yes No 132 They are a nuisance to others.
Yes No 133 They are helpless.
Yes No 134 They are insecure.
Yes No 135 They have a high suicide rate.
Yes No 136 They are not useful to themselves or to others.
Yes No 137 They have a chance to do all the things they wanted to do.

Older workers questionnaire EXHIBIT 9-18

Description. The Older Workers Questionnaire (Tuckman and Lorge, 1952*d*) is similar to the old people scale described above except that the items have to do with stereotypes of the older worker rather than old people. Again, no standard scaling technique was used, reliance being placed on the judgment of experts in the field of gerontology. The 51 items of the scale were selected to represent nine categories: physical, mental, resistance to new, reaction to criticism, keeping youth down, employer attitudes-costs, waiting for retirement, interpersonal, and jobs.

Subjects. The subjects to whom this questionnaire was given were 147 graduate students enrolled in a psychology course at Teachers College, Columbia University. Of the students, 92 were men, and 55 were women. The men ranged in age from 20 to 48 years (mean age, 29.5), and the women ranged from 20 to 51 years (mean age, 38.3).

Response Mode. Each item is preceded by "yes-no" response alternatives. Subjects respond to each item by circling either "yes" or "no."

Scoring. The attitude score is simply the number of "yes" responses.

Reliability. Reliability data are all but lacking for this scale. The research reported above in connection with the old people scale (Tuckman and Lorge, 1954) using 10 items from this scale is relevant but provides only slight evidence of reliability.

Validity. Some evidence of validity is provided by a study of differences between institutionalized and noninstitutionalized groups (Tuckman and Lorge, 1952*d*). The mean scores of the institutionalized group ($N = 48$) was 28.3 as compared with a community ($N = 21$) mean of 18.9 and an apartment-house group ($N = 19$) mean of 15.9. The difference between the institutionalized group and each of the other groups was statistically reliable ($p < .01$).

The high correlations between the Attitudes toward Old People Scale and the Older Workers Questionnaire (.75 to .86) reported by Tuckman et al. (1953) are evidence of validity, but also suggest that the two scales are measuring the same attitude.

Comments. This questionnaire appears to be a reasonably adequate instrument, as indicated by its heuristic value in research (cf. Tuckman and Lorge, 1952*c*; 1952*e*; 1953*b*). However, standardization studies are badly needed, especially with reference to reliability.

EXHIBIT 9-18

OLDER WORKERS QUESTIONNAIRE

DIRECTIONS: Below are statements about older workers. If you are in general agreement with the statement, put a circle around the Yes. If you are in general disagreement with the statement, put a circle around the No. Answer all questions. If you are not sure, guess.

Yes No 1 Older workers fail in emergencies.
Yes No 2 They are slow.
Yes No 3 They cannot win the confidence and loyalty of fellow workers.
Yes No 4 They take jobs away from younger workers.
Yes No 5 They fail to keep up with changing methods of work.
Yes No 6 They are unsure of themselves.
Yes No 7 They have a high rate of absenteeism.
Yes No 8 They are in a rut.
Yes No 9 They make many errors.
Yes No 10 They get rattled when rushed.
Yes No 11 They lose jobs often.
Yes No 12 They increase production costs.
Yes No 13 They get all the breaks.
Yes No 14 They show poor judgment.
Yes No 15 They take credit for the work done by younger men.
Yes No 16 They are interested only in putting in their hours.
Yes No 17 They have no ambition.
Yes No 18 They are unable to smooth out disagreements between other workers.
Yes No 19 They have difficulty in planning their work.
Yes No 20 They cannot supervise others well.
Yes No 21 They are paid too much for the amount of work they do.
Yes No 22 They will not take on additional responsibilities.
Yes No 23 They just wait for retirement.
Yes No 24 They need longer rest periods more often.
Yes No 25 They increase costs of pensions for employers.
Yes No 26 They have accidents often.
Yes No 27 They get occupational diseases more often.
Yes No 28 They cannot concentrate.
Yes No 29 They are interested more in security than job advancement.
Yes No 30 They will not carry out plans assigned by supervisor.
Yes No 31 They spoil much of their work.
Yes No 32 They are critical of younger workers.
Yes No 33 They cannot take criticism without getting angry.
Yes No 34 They do not produce as much as younger workers.
Yes No 35 They need more time to learn new operations.
Yes No 36 They are not physically able to keep up with the work.
Yes No 37 They dislike to work under younger supervisors.
Yes No 38 They resist new ways of doing things.
Yes No 39 They take longer in getting over illness.
Yes No 40 They are critical of their fellow workers.
Yes No 41 They are slow to catch new ideas.
Yes No 42 They are suspicious of labor saving machines.
Yes No 43 They look to the past.
Yes No 44 They are suspicious of other workers.
Yes No 45 They are mentally unable to keep up with the job.
Yes No 46 They take longer in getting over injuries.
Yes No 47 They keep younger men from getting ahead.
Yes No 48 They are difficult to work with.
Yes No 49 They cannot listen to other people's complaints without getting irritated.
Yes No 50 They quit jobs frequently.
Yes No 51 They have limited skill.

Old people (OP) scales EXHIBIT 9-19

Description. The OP scale was designed to measure attitudes toward old people with respect to norms and individual differences (Kogan, 1961*a*). Items are concerned with such things as the residential aspect of old people's lives, vague feelings of discomfort and tension in the presence of old people, qualities of old people, and interpersonal relations across age generations. The scale consists of 17 positive and 17 negative statements about old people, designated OP+ and OP— scales, respectively. The set of items expressing negative sentiments about old people was constructed, and then the set of positive items was formulated in such a way that the content was the reverse of the negative ones. Items 7P, 9P, and 10P were reworded after administration to two samples; the revised items are given in Exhibit 9-19. Correlation of item scores with total scores ranged from .19 to .70 for the OP— scale and from .09 to .67 for the OP+ scale.

Subjects. Subjects were drawn from introductory psychology courses at Northeastern University (two male samples, *N*s = 128 and 186) and at Boston University (87 males and 81 females).

Response Mode. Each item is provided with six response categories: strongly disagree, disagree, slightly disagree, slightly agree, agree, and strongly agree. Subjects check one alternative for each item.

Scoring. Response categories are scored 1, 2, 3, 5, 6, and 7, respectively. A score of 4 is assigned if the subject fails to respond to an item. The attitude score is obtained by adding the individual item scores for each scale taken separately. Thus a high score on the OP+ scale indicates a favorable attitude toward old people, whereas a high score on the OP— scale indicates an unfavorable attitude toward old people. (In actual practice, Kogan used means rather than sums and subtracted the positive means from 8.0 to make the two scales comparable. When this is done, a high score reflects more unfavorable attitudes for both scales.)

Reliability. Odd-even reliabilities were computed for each scale separately and for each of the three samples. Corrected reliabilities for the OP— scale were reported as follows: .73 and .83 for the Northeastern University samples and .76 for the Boston University sample. Corresponding values for the OP+ scale were .66, .73, and .77, respectively.

Validity. Like many of the scales in this volume, the OP scales have reasonably good content validity. In addition, Kogan (1961*a*) reported significant correlations between scores on these scales and attitudes toward ethnic minorities and physically disabled groups. Scores on the OP scales correlated .08 to .46 with scores on the CMI scale (Gilbert and Levinson, 1956; see Chapter 3), .21 to .50 with attitude toward deafness, and .21 to .53 with attitude toward cripples, where a correlation of .14 is significant at the .05 level of confidence. [Attitudes toward deafness and cripples were measured by five-item scales prepared by Kogan by converting items taken from the Cowen, Underberg, and Verrillo

(1958) Attitude to Blindness Scale, shown in Exhibit 9-22. Corrected split-half reliabilities of these five-item scales ranged from .51 to .60. Items are given in Kogan's article.]

In addition, Kogan derived a nuturant factor from a brief personality inventory given to his subjects, which was significantly correlated with OP scale scores. Since the more nuturant subjects were more positively disposed toward old people, this may be taken as some evidence of validity.

Comments. The OP scales have been rather carefully developed and have been used with some success in a subsequent study (Kogan, 1961*b*). However, the fact that the two scales correlate only from .46 to .52 indicates that some effects of response bias are involved. The matched positive and negative items should compensate for this, at least to some extent.

The potential user of the OP scales should note that Kogan disguised his items somewhat by interspersing them among other attitude and personality items. The effects of this upon the attitude score is not known, but it probably is advisable to use filler items when using these scales.

EXHIBIT 9-19

OLD PEOPLE (OP) SCALES

On the following pages, you will find a number of statements expressing opinions with which you may or may not agree. Following each statement are six boxes labelled as follows:

Strongly Disagree	Disagree	Slightly Disagree	Slightly Agree	Agree	Strongly Agree
☐	☐	☐	☐	☐	☐

You are to indicate the degree to which you agree or disagree with each statement by checking the appropriate box.

Please consider each statement carefully, but do not spend too much time on any one statement. *Do not skip any items.*

There are no "right" or "wrong" answers—the only correct responses are those that are true *for you.* THIS INVENTORY IS BEING USED FOR RESEARCH PURPOSES ONLY AND IS COMPLETELY ANONYMOUS.

		Strongly Disagree	Disagree	Slightly Disagree	Slightly Agree	Agree	Strongly Agree
*1N	It would probably be better if most old people lived in residential units with people their own age.	☐	☐	☐	☐	☐	☐

* Items are listed in pairs, N representing the negatively worded form and P the positively worded form.

Reprinted with permission from Kogan, N. Attitudes toward old people: The development of a scale and an examination of correlates. *J. abnorm. soc. Psychol.*, 1961, 62, 44–54.

		Strongly Disagree	Disagree	Slightly Disagree	Slightly Agree	Agree	Strongly Agree
*1P	It would probably be better if most old people lived in residential units that also housed younger people.	☐	☐	☐	☐	☐	☐
2N	There is something different about most old people: it's hard to figure out what makes them tick.	☐	☐	☐	☐	☐	☐
2P	Most old people are really no different from anybody else: they're as easy to understand as younger people.	☐	☐	☐	☐	☐	☐
3N	Most old people get set in their ways and are unable to change.	☐	☐	☐	☐	☐	☐
3P	Most old people are capable of new adjustments when the situation demands it.	☐	☐	☐	☐	☐	☐
4N	Most old people would prefer to quit work as soon as pensions or their children can support them.	☐	☐	☐	☐	☐	☐
4P	Most old people would prefer to continue working just as long as they possibly can rather than be dependent on anybody.	☐	☐	☐	☐	☐	☐
5N	Most old people tend to let their homes become shabby and unattractive.	☐	☐	☐	☐	☐	☐
5P	Most old people can generally be counted on to maintain a clean, attractive home.	☐	☐	☐	☐	☐	☐
6N	It is foolish to claim that wisdom comes with old age.	☐	☐	☐	☐	☐	☐
6P	People grow wiser with the coming of old age.	☐	☐	☐	☐	☐	☐
7N	Old people have too much power in business and politics.	☐	☐	☐	☐	☐	☐
7P	Old people have too little power in business and politics.	☐	☐	☐	☐	☐	☐
8N	Most old people make one feel ill at ease.	☐	☐	☐	☐	☐	☐
8P	Most old people are very relaxing to be with.	☐	☐	☐	☐	☐	☐
9N	Most old people bore others by their insistence on talking about the "good old days."	☐	☐	☐	☐	☐	☐
9P	One of the most interesting qualities of old people is their accounts of their past experiences.	☐	☐	☐	☐	☐	☐
10N	Most old people spend too much time prying into the affairs of others and in giving unsought advice.	☐	☐	☐	☐	☐	☐

		Strongly Disagree	Disagree	Slightly Disagree	Slightly Agree	Agree	Strongly Agree
10P	Most old people respect others' privacy and give advice only when asked.	☐	☐	☐	☐	☐	☐
11N	If old people expect to be liked, their first step is to try to get rid of their irritating faults.	☐	☐	☐	☐	☐	☐
11P	When you think about it, old people have the same faults as anybody else.	☐	☐	☐	☐	☐	☐
12N	In order to maintain a nice residential neighborhood, it would be best if too many old people did not live in it.	☐	☐	☐	☐	☐	☐
12P	You can count on finding a nice residential neighborhood when there is a sizeable number of old people living in it.	☐	☐	☐	☐	☐	☐
13N	There are a few exceptions, but in general most old people are pretty much alike.	☐	☐	☐	☐	☐	☐
13P	It is evident that most old people are very different from one another.	☐	☐	☐	☐	☐	☐
14N	Most old people should be more concerned with their personal appearance; they're too untidy.	☐	☐	☐	☐	☐	☐
14P	Most old people seem to be quite clean and neat in their personal appearance.	☐	☐	☐	☐	☐	☐
15N	Most old people are irritable, grouchy, and unpleasant.	☐	☐	☐	☐	☐	☐
15P	Most old people are cheerful, agreeable, and good humored.	☐	☐	☐	☐	☐	☐
16N	Most old people are constantly complaining about the behavior of the younger generation.	☐	☐	☐	☐	☐	☐
16P	One seldom hears old people complaining about the behavior of the younger generation.	☐	☐	☐	☐	☐	☐
17N	Most old people make excessive demands for love and reassurance.	☐	☐	☐	☐	☐	☐
17P	Most old people need no more love and reassurance than anyone else.	☐	☐	☐	☐	☐	☐

ATTITUDES TOWARD HEALTH–RELATED REFERENTS

The attitudes considered in this section are directed toward groups of individuals who are in some way involved with disabilities. In some cases, the group is composed of persons who are themselves disabled (e.g., mentally retarded persons); in other cases, the group consists of individuals who are attempting to help disabled persons (e.g., psychiatrists). Scales are described to measure attitude toward mentally ill persons, mentally retarded persons, disabled persons, the blind, psychiatrists, and psychologists.

The "CI" attitude scale *EXHIBIT 9-20*

Description. The "CI" Attitude Scale was constructed to assess attitudes toward "criminally insane" patients (Khanna, Pratt, and Gardiner, 1962). Criminally insane patients were defined as mental patients having criminal charges against them. The CI scale is a Likert-type scale consisting of 75 items distributed among several categories, as follows: 26 items regarding CI patients (including 3 items differentiating CI patients from non-CI patients, 10 items about CI patients in general, and 13 items about types of CI patients); 9 items regarding mental illness; 12 items concerning the treatment of CI patients; 5 items regarding aides; and 15 items from the L scale of the Minnesota Multiphasic Personality Inventory (Hathaway and McKinley, 1951). The five items regarding aides are filler items, and the L scale is used as an indicator of the honesty of the subjects.

The items were formulated by eight clinical psychologists. Direction (favorable versus unfavorable) was determined on the basis of the pooled judgments of these eight psychologists. Unanimity was achieved on all but six items, and on these seven of the eight judges were in agreement.

Subjects. The sample came from employees at a mental hospital. It consisted of 7 attendants, 20 Psychiatric Aide I's, and 4 Psychiatric Aide II's. They ranged in age from 22 to 74 years, with a mean age of 45, and in education from eighth grade to three years college work. They had been employed by the hospital from 1 to 14 years.

Response Mode. The response mode was a four-point forced choice: strongly agree, A; mildly agree, a; mildly disagree, d; and strongly disagree, D. The subject is required to respond to every item.

Scoring. Weights of 3, 2, 1, 0 are assigned to response alternatives, with the higher numbers indicating more favorable attitudes. An attitude score is obtained by summing the weights for individual item responses. A high score represents a psychiatrically favorable attitude, and a low score an unfavorable attitude.

Reliability. Reliability computed by Hoyt's technique was found to be .87, based upon the responses of the 31 subjects that were described above.

Validity. In addition to consensual validity, a factor analysis yielded favorable results. The analysis was carried out using the CI scores, age, education, length of employment, aide status, performance ratings, intelligence, social service orientation, and selected personality attributes. Six factors were extracted. The "CI" Attitude Scale had a high factor loading (.841) on Factor I and low factor loadings on other factors. The authors suggested that this indicates the scale is measuring a relatively unitary trait, which lends support to the factorial validity of the scale. However, intelligence (measured by the Otis) also had a high loading (.766) on Factor I; and the CI attitude correlated .64 with intelligence. Significant positive correlations were also reported between CI attitude scores and social service orientation (.40), age (.44), and performance ratings (.41).

Comments. The "CI" Attitude Scale has been rather carefully constructed, and the reliability and validity evidence is at least average. It seems to be measuring a rather complex attitude, however, and knowledge of its relationship to other attitudinal measures would be enlightening.

EXHIBIT 9-20

THE "CI" ATTITUDE SCALE

Read each of the statements below and then rate them as follows:

A	a	d	D
strongly agree	mildly agree	mildly disagree	strongly disagree

Indicate your opinion by drawing a circle around the "A" if you strongly agree, around the "a" if you mildly agree, around the "d" if you mildly disagree, and around the "D" if you strongly disagree.

Be sure to answer each question according to your own opinion. It is very important to the study that *all* questions be answered. Many of the statements will seem alike but all are necessary to show differences of opinion.

		Agree		Disagree	
*1	For the public protection all murderers should be hung.	A	a	d	D
2	At times I feel like swearing.	A	a	d	D
3	Only a few mental patients are dangerous.	A	a	d	D
*4	Mental disease appears suddenly without any warning.	A	a	d	D
5	I do not read every editorial in the newspaper every day.	A	a	d	D

* Disagreement with starred items indicates a favorable attitude.

Reference: J. L. Khanna, S. Pratt, and G. Gardine. Attitudes of psychiatric aides toward "criminally insane" patients. *J. crim. Law, crim. and police Sci.*, 1962, 53, 55–60. Items obtained from authors and published with their permission.

		Agree			Dis-agree
*6	It doesn't pay to give privileges because CI's only take advantage of them.	A	a	d	D
7	I do not like everyone I know.	A	a	d	D
8	Thorazine will not cure most mental illnesses.	A	a	d	D
*9	Just talking to the patient, as in psychotherapy, is of little or no value.	A	a	d	D
*10	If you give a CI an inch he will want to take a mile.	A	a	d	D
11	Some CI patients should be treated differently than other CI patients depending on their crimes.	A	a	d	D
12	I would rather win than lose in a game.	A	a	d	D
13	I like to know some important people because it makes me feel important.	A	a	d	D
*14	You can always pick out a "queer" (homosexual) from the rest of the patients.	A	a	d	D
15	CI patients are no harder to handle than any other patients.	A	a	d	D
16	Masturbation ("playing with oneself") can never cause insanity.	A	a	d	D
17	Most criminals are mentally sick people and should be in a mental hospital rather than in prison.	A	a	d	D
*18	Anyone who has ever raped a child should die in the "electric chair."	A	a	d	D
*19	For the good of the public all sex offenders should be castrated or sterilized.	A	a	d	D
*20	Most CI's are dangerous.	A	a	d	D
21	Sometimes at elections I vote for men about whom I know very little.	A	a	d	D
22	Through ward government by CI patients they can become more responsible for themselves.	A	a	d	D
23	I gossip a little at times.	A	a	d	D
*24	CI patients are generally stupid.	A	a	d	D
25	Many patients who have killed someone long ago are now completely harmless.	A	a	d	D
*26	Mental illness is a disgrace.	A	a	d	D
27	My table manners are not quite as good at home as when I am out in company.	A	a	d	D
28	Some people can't keep from stealing even though they know its bad.	A	a	d	D
*29	Murderers and sex offenders should always be separated on the ward.	A	a	d	D
30	I would rather work on Dillon Building than anywhere else in the hospital.	A	a	d	D
*31	Mental illness is caused by bad blood.	A	a	d	D
*32	Most CI patients are sex crazed.	A	a	d	D
*33	Ward government by CI patients is dangerous.	A	a	d	D
34	Other people at the hospital don't appreciate the job we aides do.	A	a	d	D
*35	For CI's, preventing escape is more important than the treatment for their mental illness.	A	a	d	D
*36	If mental patients had used will power they wouldn't be here in the first place.	A	a	d	D

		Agree		Dis-agree	
*37	Given a chance most CI's will try to escape.	A	a	d	D
38	If I could get into a movie without paying and be sure I was not seen I would probably do it.	A	a	d	D
39	Once in a while I put off until tomorrow what I ought to do today.	A	a	d	D
*40	Physical punishment of CI's is occasionally necessary.	A	a	d	D
41	Wet packs are not the best form of treatment.	A	a	d	D
*42	Most mental illness is really physical.	A	a	d	D
43	Most aides are under paid for the job they do.	A	a	d	D
*44	All CI patients who have committed a murder are still extremely dangerous.	A	a	d	D
*45	Most CI's should be in prison instead of the hospital.	A	a	d	D
*46	If a patient makes a lot of trouble he should be given shock treatment to quiet him down.	A	a	d	D
*47	Patients who are here on bad check charges are not really mentally ill.	A	a	d	D
48	Once in a while I think of things too bad to talk about.	A	a	d	D
*49	Most of the CI's sent from the pen are here for a soft touch.	A	a	d	D
*50	If you put a CI on an open ward you'll probably have trouble.	A	a	d	D
*51	All homosexuals ("queers") were born that way and can never change.	A	a	d	D
52	CI patients are generally no different from other patients.	A	a	d	D
53	Most aides would rather work anywhere in the hospital than on Dillon Building.	A	a	d	D
*54	Electric shock is a good punishment for CI patients.	A	a	d	D
*55	If you show that you are weak CI patients will step all over you.	A	a	d	D
*56	CI's guilty of robbery should be in prison instead of the hospital.	A	a	d	D
*57	You can always tell a "queer" by the way he looks.	A	a	d	D
*58	CI patients should first of all be treated as criminals.	A	a	d	D
*59	If a "queer" makes a pass at somebody they should beat him up.	A	a	d	D
60	Sometimes when I am not feeling well I am cross.	A	a	d	D
61	Since the aides know more about the patients they should have more to say about them.	A	a	d	D
62	CI patients are generally as friendly as other patients.	A	a	d	D
*63	Electric shock treatment usually improves any patient's personality.	A	a	d	D
64	Most mental disease starts in childhood.	A	a	d	D
*65	Most "CI's" need religion more than anything else.	A	a	d	D
66	Electric shock treatment is bad for the patient's brains.	A	a	d	D
*67	If more discipline were handed out in childhood there would be less patients in mental hospitals.	A	a	d	D
*68	Insanity runs in the family.	A	a	d	D
69	I get angry sometimes.	A	a	d	D
70	I do not always tell the truth.	A	a	d	D
71	Once in a while I laugh at a dirty joke.	A	a	d	D

		Agree		Dis- agree	
*72	Most "Cl's" guilty of stealing did it because they needed the money.	A	a	d	D
*73	Most "Cl's" are basically bad people.	A	a	d	D
*74	Sometimes for the patient's own good he has to be beaten up.	A	a	d	D
*75	"Cl" patients are people who just had bad luck.	A	a	d	D

Attitudes toward mentally retarded people EXHIBIT 9-21

Description. This is a 24-item Likert scale developed to measure the attitudes of attendants at an institution for the mentally retarded (Bartlett, Quay, and Wrightsman, 1960). Initially, 175 statements were written which were believed to reflect the attendants' attitudes. These statements were then analyzed by factor analysis, revealing a general factor and several specific factors. The general factor was interpreted as reflecting the most important attitude. The items in the final scale given in Exhibit 9-21 all had loading on the general factor of .30 or above.

Subjects. The subjects were drawn from attendants at an institution for the mentally retarded. The sample used in the initial selection of items consisted of 99 attendants. A second sample of 97 attendants drawn from another institution for the mentally retarded was used in estimating reliability and validity.

Response Mode. Each item was provided with a three-point response scale: T, ?, and F. Subjects respond to each item by circling the T if the statement is believed to be true, the F if false, and the ? if undecided.

Scoring. A weight of 0 is assigned for an unfavorable response, a weight of 1 for an undecided (?) response, and weight of 2 for a favorable response. The attitude score is the sum of the item scores. Thus, the theoretical range is from 0 to 48, with the higher score indicating the more favorable attitude. In Exhibit 9-21 an asterisk indicates items to which a T response is unfavorable; for all other items, an F response is unfavorable.

Reliability. Split-half reliability was reported to be .80 after correction by the Spearman-Brown prophecy formula, based upon the responses of 68 attendants. Test-retest reliability with a two-week intertest interval was found to be .71, based upon the responses of 17 attendants.

Validity. Little evidence of validity is available. The scale correlated only .22 (corrected for attenuation to .39) with a forced-choice scale designed to measure the same attitude. However, this scale was prepared by pairing an item with a high loading on the general factor (see above) with an item having a low factor loading. It is not clear exactly what such a scale is measuring. The Attitude toward Mentally Retarded People Scale was used in an attitude change study (Quay, Bartlett,

Wrightsman, and Catron, 1961) with only partial success. They attempted to change attitude toward the mentally retarded by three methods: lecture, a booklet, and discussion. Only the lecture resulted in a significant change.

Comments. The Attitude toward Mentally Retarded People Scale shows some promise, although the evidence of validity is not as convincing as one might desire. It might also be noted that many of the items seem to be positive-negative counterparts, i.e., a negative statement often is identical with a positive statement except that negation is indicated, such as changing the verb from "are" to "are not." Only the very naive would be expected to agree with both pairs of statements. One might suspect that this would have the same effect as reducing the length of the scale. It could also lead to a spuriously high reliability estimate.

EXHIBIT 9-21

ATTITUDES TOWARD MENTALLY RETARDED PEOPLE

Directions

Read each of the following sentences and decide whether the sentence is true or false. If you think the sentence is true, make a circle around the *T*. If you think it is false, make a circle around the *F*. If you cannot decide whether it is true or false, make a circle around the *?*. There is no right or wrong answer to any of the sentences. Just give your personal opinion about each sentence.

*1 T ? F I don't get paid enough for this job.
*2 T ? F I don't trust retarded people.
*3 T ? F I don't want to work with the mentally retarded all my life.
4 T ? F I want to work with the mentally retarded all my life.
5 T ? F I would like this job even if I didn't get paid.
*6 T ? F Mentally retarded people are dangerous.
*7 T ? F Mentally retarded people are mean.
8 T ? F Mentally retarded people are not crazy.
9 T ? F Mentally retarded people are not dangerous.
10 T ? F Mentally retarded people are not mean.
11 T ? F Mentally retarded people are not stubborn.
*12 T ? F Mentally retarded people are not very easy to take care of.
*13 T ? F Mentally retarded people should not be allowed to vote.
*14 T ? F Mentaly retarded people try to outsmart you.
15 T ? F Mentally retarded people will listen to reason.
*16 T ? F Mentally retarded people won't listen to reason.

* A "true" response to items marked with an asterisk is unfavorable and is scored 0; to all other items a "false" response is unfavorable and is scored 0.

Reference: C. J. Bartlett, L. C. Quay, and L. S. Wrightsman, Jr. A comparison of two methods of attitude measurement: Likert-type and forced choice. *Educ. psychol. Measmt*, 1960, 20, 699–704. Items obtained from authors and published with their permission.

17 T ? F Most retarded people wouldn't steal.
*18 T ? F Most retarded people would steal if they had the chance.
19 T ? F Retarded people can be trusted.
*20 T ? F Retarded people like to be dirty.
*21 T ? F The church should not provide religious training for the retarded.
*22 T ? F The mentally retarded are born stubborn.
*23 T ? F The retarded can't learn right from wrong.
24 T ? F The retarded have something to live for.

Attitude to blindness scale EXHIBIT 9-22

Description. The Attitude to Blindness Scale was constructed by Cowen, Underberg, and Verrillo (1958). The items in the final scale were selected from a pool of 97 items taken from questionnaires by Steingisser (1954) and Fitting (1954). The selection procedure deviated from the standard Likert procedure in that items were first given to five workers with the blind, who judged whether agreement with a given statement indicated a positive or a negative attitude by a sighted person toward the blind. Judges agreed perfectly on 56 items. The items in the final scale were then selected from these 56 items by Flanagan's tetrachoric *r* method of item analysis. The range of item-test correlations for the three-item scale was from .44 to .75. Ten items had been judged to indicate a positive attitude and twenty, a negative attitude.

Subjects. The subjects were 101 students drawn from several adult education courses in psychology.

Response Mode. Four response alternatives are provided for each item: strongly agree, mildly agree, mildly disagree, strongly disagree. Subjects are asked to respond to each item by selecting one of these alternatives.

Scoring. The above response alternatives are weighted 1, 2, 3, and 4, respectively, when the statement is positive, and exactly opposite when the statement is negative. The attitude score is the sum of item scores; hence the higher the score, the more unfavorable the attitude toward blindness.

Reliability. Split-half reliability was .83 before correction and .91 after correction.

Validity. Validity estimates, in addition to that provided by the original judges and item analysis, were obtained by correlating scores on the Attitudes to Blindness Scale with the California scales. Correlations were .36 with the Anti-Minority Scale, .45 with the Anti-Negro Scale, and .33 with the F scale.

Comments. Once again, we find a scale that has adequate reliability but insufficient evidence of validity. The agreement of judges seems to be the best indication of validity.

EXHIBIT 9-22

ATTITUDE TO BLINDNESS SCALE

Read each of the statements below and then rate them as follows:

A	a	d	D
Strongly Agree	Mildly Agree	Mildly Disagree	Strongly Disagree

Indicate your opinion by drawing a circle around the "A" if you strongly agree, around the "a" if you mildly agree, around the "d" if you mildly disagree, and around the "D" if you strongly disagree.

There are no right or wrong answers, so answer according to your own opinion. It is very important to the study that all questions be answered. Many of the statements will seem alike but all are necessary to show slight differences of opinion.

*1 A blind person might as well accept the fact that blindness makes people pretty helpless. (A a d D)

*2 On the whole, blind children seem to be less intelligent than sighted children. (A a d D)

*3 Blinded people are used to failing in most of the things they do. (A a d D)

*4 A blind person should not have to meet the same standards as others. (A a d D)

*5 Blind people are constantly worried about the future. (A a d D)

6 Blindness has little or no effect upon intelligence. (A a d D)

7 A blind person is not afraid to express his feelings. (A a d D)

*8 A blind person can never really be happy. (A a d D)

*9 Most blind people are dissatisfied with themselves. (A a d D)

*10 A blind person can't afford to talk back to people. (A a d D)

11 One can live in a competitive society and still compete successfully without sight. (A a d D)

*12 It makes me feel a little guilty to know that I can see and others cannot. (A a d D)

*13 You should not expect too much from a blind person. (A a d D)

*14 Most blind people feel that they are worthless. (A a d D)

15 It is possible to know the beauty of the world without sight. (A a d D)

16 My attitude towards a blind person would be based more upon his personality than upon the fact that he is blind. (A a d D)

*17 Blind people do not have as much initiative as sighted people. (A a d D)

*18 It is very difficult to make a blind person change his mind once he has decided on something. (A a d D)

*19 It must be bitterly degrading for a blind person to depend so much upon others. (A a d D)

20 Many blind people are economically independent. (A a d D)

*21 Blind people are more easily upset than sighted people. (A a d D)

*22 Most blind people think and act alike. (A a d D)

* Agreement with items marked with an asterisk indicates a negative attitude toward blind persons, whereas agreement with all other items indicates a positive attitude.

*23 It's difficult to understand the blind because they keep so much to themselves. **(A a d D)**
24 There are things worse than being blind. **(A a d D)**
25 Acceptance of blindness is the same thing as acceptance of anything else in life. **(A a d D)**
*26 The blind adult is not quite as mature or "grown-up" as the sighted adult. **(A a d D)**
27 Blindness does not change the person any more than any other physical handicap. **(A a d D)**
28 The blind have as many interests as the sighted have. **(A a d D)**
*29 I feel that blindness is as hard to bear as complete paralysis. **(A a d D)**
*30 A blind person is constantly worried about what might happen to him. **(A a d D)**

Attitude toward disabled people (ATDP) scale *EXHIBIT 9-23*

Description. The ATDP scale (Yuker, Block, and Campbell, 1960), unlike the scales described above, attempts to measure attitudes toward disabled persons in general. The original form of the scale consisted of 20 items, but later work resulted in two equivalent 30-item forms. Each statement suggests that disabled persons are either the same as or different from physically normal people. Approximately half of the items refer to similarities or differences in personality characteristics, whereas the other half deal with the question of special treatment for the disabled. Items were selected on the basis of item analysis.

Subjects. The ATDP scale had been administered by its authors to a large number of subjects. Estimates of reliability were obtained from samples of physically normal college students at Hofstra College. For purposes of validation, a sample of disabled persons was drawn from employees of Abilities, Inc. ($N = 248$).

Response Mode. Subjects are given a six-point response scale: I agree very much, I agree pretty much, I agree a little, I disagree a little, I disagree pretty much, and I disagree very much. These alternatives are weighted +3, +2, +1, −1, −2, and −3, respectively. The subject responds to each item by either entering the appropriate weight in a space provided to the left of each item or by circling the appropriate weight on an answer sheet. (When an answer sheet is used, the response values are entered on the answer sheet after the number corresponding to each item.)

Scoring. Forms A and B of the ADTP scale are scored as follows: (1) Change the signs of the weights of positive items (Form A items 5, 9, 12, 14, 17, 19, 21, 22, 23, 24, 25, and 29; Form B items 1, 3, 4, 6, 7, 10, 12, 13, 22, 26, and 28); (2) add all the responses algebraically; (3) change the sign of the algebraic resultant; and (4) add 90. With disabled subjects, high scores are interpreted as self-acceptance; for nondisabled subjects, high scores are interpreted to represent acceptance of disabled persons, i.e., a favorable attitude toward disabled persons.

Reliability. Several estimates of reliability are reported. Split-half reliabilities range from .78 ($N = 72$) to .84 ($N = 110$). Coefficients of equivalence (Form A versus Form B) ranged from .41 ($N = 58$) to .83 ($N = 57$).

Validity. The ATDP scale has reasonably good content validity, and additional evidence is provided by correlation of ATDP scores with other scales. Significant correlations were found between ATDP and semantic differential scores (—.266), scores on a job satisfaction scale (+.463), and the Edwards Personal Preference Schedule (+.252). Nonsignificant correlations were found between ATDP and the following: Attitude toward Intellectualism (Block and Yuker, unpublished), the F scale, the Machiavellianism Scale (Christie, 1956), the IPAT Self Analysis Forms (Cattell, 1957), and the Attitudes toward Old People Scale (Block and Yuker, unpublished).

Comments. The authors of this scale have done a considerable amount of work on it, and the supporting data are better than for most scales. There is still some question concerning its validity, but it seems adequate for research purposes.

EXHIBIT 9-23

ATTITUDE TOWARD DISABLED PEOPLE (ATDP) SCALE

Mark each statement in the left margin according to how much you agree or disagree with it. Please mark every one. Write +1, +2, +3; or —1, —2, —3; depending on how you feel in each case.

+3: I agree very much
+2: I agree pretty much
+1: I agree a little
—1: I disagree a little
—2: I disagree pretty much
—3: I disagree very much

Form A

1 Disabled people are often unfriendly.
2 Disabled people should not have to compete for jobs with physically normal persons.
3 Disabled people are more emotional than other people.
4 Most disabled persons are more self-conscious than other people.
*5 We should expect just as much from disabled as from non-disabled persons.
6 Disabled workers cannot be as successful as other workers.
7 Disabled people usually do not make much of a contribution to society.
8 Most non-disabled people would not want to marry anyone who is physically disabled.
*9 Disabled people show as much enthusiasm as other people.

* Agreement with items marked with an asterisk indicates a favorable attitude; agreement with other items indicates an unfavorable attitude.

10 Disabled persons are usually more sensitive than other people.
11 Severely disabled persons are usually untidy.
*12 Most disabled people feel that they are as good as other people.
13 The driving test given to a disabled person should be more severe than the one given to the non-disabled.
*14 Disabled people are usually sociable.
15 Disabled persons usually are not as conscientious as physically normal persons.
16 Severely disabled persons probably worry more about their health than those who have minor disabilities.
*17 Most disabled persons are not dissatisfied with themselves.
18 There are more misfits among disabled persons than among non-disabled persons.
*19 Most disabled persons do not get discouraged easily.
20 Most disabled persons resent physically normal people.
*21 Disabled children should compete with physically normal children.
*22 Most disabled persons can take care of themselves.
*23 It would be best if disabled persons would live and work with non-disabled persons.
*24 Most severely disabled people are just as ambitious as physically normal persons.
*25 Disabled people are just as self-confident as other people.
26 Most disabled persons want more affection and praise than other people.
27 Physically disabled persons are often less intelligent than non-disabled ones.
28 Most disabled people are different from non-disabled people.
*29 Disabled persons don't want any more sympathy than other people.
30 The way disabled people act is irritating.

Form B

*1 Disabled persons are usually friendly.
2 People who are disabled should not have to pay income taxes.
*3 Disabled people are no more emotional than other people.
*4 Disabled people can have a normal social life.
5 Most physically disabled persons have a chip on their shoulder.
*6 Disabled workers can be as successful as other workers.
*7 Very few disabled persons are ashamed of their disabilities.
8 Most people feel uncomfortable when they associate with disabled people.
9 Disabled people show less enthusiasm than non-disabled people.
*10 Disabled people do not become upset any more easily than non-disabled people.
11 Disabled people are often less aggressive than normal people.
*12 Most disabled persons get married and have children.
*13 Most disabled persons do not worry any more than anyone else.
14 Employers should not be allowed to fire disabled employees.
15 Disabled people are not as happy as non-disabled ones.
16 Severely disabled people are harder to get along with than are those with minor disabilities.
17 Most disabled people expect special treatment.
18 Disabled persons should not expect to lead normal lives.
19 Most disabled people tend to get discouraged easily.
20 The worst thing that could happen to a person would be for him to be very severely injured.
21 Disabled children should not have to compete with non-disabled children.
*22 Most disabled people do not feel sorry for themselves.

23 Most disabled people prefer to work with other disabled people.
24 Most severely disabled persons are not as ambitious as other people.
25 Disabled persons are not as self-confident as physically normal persons.
*26 Most disabled persons don't want more affection and praise than other people.
27 It would be best if a disabled person would marry another disabled person.
*28 Most disabled people do not need special attention.
29 Disabled persons want sympathy more than other people.
30 Most physically disabled persons have different personalities than normal persons.

Medical information test *EXHIBIT 9-24*

Description. The Medical Information Test was developed by Perricone (1964) to measure attitude toward physicians. The scale is an error-choice type of scale, consisting of 24 factual items and 12 nonfactual items. The critical items are the nonfactual ones. The nonfactual items were selected by item analysis and cross validation from an initial pool of 21 items. The 12 items in the final scale discriminated between the upper and lower 27 percent at the .01 level of confidence or better. Exhibit 9-24 gives the items of the Medical Information Test and indicates the critical (nonfactual) items.

Subjects. Several samples were used. In the original selection of items, the subjects were 108 students enrolled in sociology courses at the University of Florida in the summer of 1964. In addition, three other samples were used for validation: another group of 108 sociology students, 47 medical students, and 80 students in nursing.

Response Mode. As in the typical error-choice scale, the subject is asked to choose between two alternatives for each item. Each choice is indicated by placing a check mark in the space provided.

Scoring. Only the nonfactual items are scored. A weight of 1 is assigned to each favorable alternative checked, and the attitude score is the total of these weights. Thus the theoretical range of scores is from 0 to 12, with the higher score indicating a more favorable attitude toward physicians.

Reliability. Split-half reliability was .72 before correction and .84 after correction.

Validity. Perricone attempted to establish validity by the known-groups method. The rationale was that persons who were committed to the medical profession would have more favorable attitudes toward physicians and that the degree of commitment would likewise be related to attitude favorability. The mean scores of various subgroups were: junior medical students, 8.1; senior medical students, 8.8; student nurses, 7.2; premedical student related to a physician, 9.2; premedical student unrelated to a physician, 8.1; students related to a physician, 6.4; students who were friends of physicians, 6.0; students with no commitment, 6.2. With some variation, these means are generally in the expected order.

Comments. This is a promising scale, although some further standardization is desirable. It probably would be improved if additional critical items could be added. The disguised aspect of the scale should make it useful in many situations in which the more obvious type of scale could yield invalid results.

EXHIBIT 9-24

MEDICAL INFORMATION TEST

DIRECTIONS: A purpose of this study is to ascertain the level of knowledge of the general public concerning medical practice. We are not interested in individual scores, as such, so no names are required or desired.

A number of factual statements or questions with two alternatives are given below. Indicate the answer you think makes the statement correct by writing in the blank before each question the letter found in parenthesis before the chosen answer. No one is expected to know all the answers. On those questions which you do not know the correct answer, you should select the one you have a "hunch" is correct. There is no time limit, but you should work as quickly as possible. Do not linger on any one statement. PLEASE DO NOT LEAVE ANY BLANKS EVEN IF YOU HAVE TO GUESS.

______ 1 The physician who specializes in the treatment of disorders of the eye is called an . . . .
(a) ophthalmologist (b) obstetrician

______ 2 The part of medical training which puts emphasis on a specialty is . . . .
(a) residency (b) internship

______ 3 Last year, physicians ordered patients who **did have** hospital insurance to remain in hospitals . . . .
(a) 8.7 days (b) 5.9 days

______ 4 Physicians, in general . . . the King-Anderson Bill.
(a) favor (b) oppose

______ 5 The non-specialist must spend a total of . . . in medical education and internship before he may set up a private practice.
(a) 5 years (b) 4 years

______ 6 Physicians in solo practice (as opposed to group or partnership) make up . . . percent of all physicians.
(a) 52 percent (b) 64 percent

Reference: P. J. Perricone. Doctor-patient interaction: Formulation of a hypothesis and development of a test for measuring attitudes toward physicians. Unpublished master's thesis, Univ. of Florida, December, 1964. Items obtained from author and published with his permission.

* A 7 A survey revealed that the average waiting time in the office of physicians who see patients by appointment only is . . . .
(a) less than 15 minutes (b) more than 30 minutes

8 Since 1930, the number of hospital beds has increased by . . . .
(a) 70 percent (b) 90 percent

* A 9 The average yearly wage of a medical intern is . . . .
(a) $3,019 (b) $3,059

10 During the first six months of 1960, the American Medical Association spent approximately . . . in congressional lobbying activities.
(a) $28,000 (b) $46,000

11 Recently, doctors protesting a new national insurance law staged a strike. The country where this occurred is . . . .
(a) England (b) Belgium

12 Approximately . . . of all practicing physicians belong to the American Medical Association.
(a) 80 percent (b) 90 percent

13 There are . . . doctors for every 100,000 persons in the population.
(a) 108.6 (b) 132.4

14 The greatest need for doctors is in . . . .
(a) rural areas (b) urban areas

15 Women comprise . . . of all U.S. doctors.
(a) 4 percent (b) 6 percent

16 Numerically, the largest specialty within medicine is . . . .
(a) surgery (b) internal medicine

* A 17 Of every 100 persons who **have** surgical insurance, doctors ordered . . . to undergo surgery last year.
(a) 6 (b) 8

* A 18 Doctors' fees have risen by . . . in the last 20 years.
(a) 85 percent (b) 95 percent

19 Physicians . . . a higher incidence of peptic ulcers than members of the other professions.
(a) have (b) do not have

20 Surgeons win . . . of all malpractice suits filed against them.
(a) slightly more than half (b) slightly less than half

21 Interns . . . receive a salary.
(a) do (b) do not

22 The function of Good Samaritan laws is . . . .
(a) to make it obligatory that doctors render aid in emergencies.
(b) to exempt doctors from liability for harm resulting from emergency care.

* B 23 Physicians . . . well protected by the law.
(a) are (b) are not

24 The majority of medical schools are . . . institutions.
(a) public (b) private

25 Today, of every 40 patients the doctor sees, . . . are in the patient's home.
(a) 3 (b) 5

* Critical items are marked with an asterisk, and the favorable alternative is indicated by the letter in the space to the left of each critical item.

Key	No.	Item
	26	The average hospital stay of slightly more than a week costs . . . . (a) $270 (b) $290
	27	A specialist in the treatment of children's diseases is a . . . . (a) pediatrician (b) obstetrician
* A	28	The average person spends . . . out of every dollar for medical care. (a) 4 cents (b) 8 cents
	29	In 1963, . . . of the U.S. population never saw a doctor. (a) 11 percent (b) 21 percent
* B	30	More than half of all physicians in private practice work approximately . . . . (a) 57 hours a week (b) 63 hours a week
* A	31	There . . . a shortage of physicians in the United States today. (a) is (b) is not
	32	The average physician subscribes to . . . professional journals. (a) two (b) six
* B	33	According to various studies, fee-splitting is . . . . (a) fairly common (b) not very common
* B	34	Most physicians oppose "socialized medicine" because . . . . (a) they feel it would result in restriction of medical practice and income. (b) they feel it would lower the quality of medicine.
	35	A group which is rapidly receiving recognition from physicians is . . . . (a) osteopaths (b) chiropractors
	36	Doctors are known for their . . . office manners. (a) poor (b) excellent
	37	A comparison of college grades and I.Q.'s shows that today's medical students compare . . . with medical students of 30 years ago. (a) favorably (b) unfavorably
	38	Specialists make up . . . of all practicing physicians. (a) 38.4 percent (b) 47.6 percent
* A	39	A recent survey revealed that most physicians entered the profession . . . . (a) because of a need to serve mankind (b) because of the financial security it offered.
	40	The undergraduate major of most pre-medical students is . . . . (a) biology (b) chemistry
	41	There is a definite trend today for more physicians to go into . . . . (a) solo practice (b) group practice
* B	42	The average physician has an income of . . . than $25,000 per year. (a) more (b) less

ATTITUDES TOWARD EDUCATIONAL WORKERS

This section deals with scales measuring attitudes toward classes of persons involved in the educational process. Only one scale was found that was judged to be appropriate to this category and sufficiently standardized to merit inclusion. This is a scale to measure attitude toward psychologists (Costin, 1963). A scale by Weaver (1959) contains items concerning teachers, but is described in Chapter 10 since the majority of the items refer to the classroom, study hall, study, high school, and school rules. A set of items concerning attitudes toward athletes and scholars was formulated by Dudycha (1932), but no supporting data were given. The interested reader can obtain the items from Dudycha's report. Nickols (1963) scaled items from a generalized scale to measure attitudes toward any defined group (Grice, 1934) with college professors as the referent, but since this is a generalized scale, it is described elsewhere (see Chapter 8).

Knowledge about psychology (KAP) test *EXHIBIT 9-25*

Description. The KAP test (Costin, 1963) consists of two 30-item scales. Scale P is designed to measure attitudes toward psychologists, whereas Scale S attempts to measure understanding of the scientific nature of psychology. Scale S is not an attitude scale, but it might be useful in relation to attitudes toward psychologists and serves the secondary purpose of disguising Scale P. The items in the two forms were selected by item analysis from an original pool of 100 items. Also, no item was retained unless all members of a panel of 10 psychologists agreed with the author's keyed answer. Scale P is composed of the even-numbered items and Scale S of the odd-numbered items. The "correct" response to each item is underlined.

Subjects. Three samples were used: 51 students who had not taken courses in psychology, 77 students who had taken at least one course in psychology, and 280 students representing a variety of class levels and who had not taken a course in psychology.

Response Mode. The items in these scales are multiple choice, with each item having three alternatives. Subjects respond to each item by blackening the letter (A, B, or C) on an answer sheet which corresponds to the alternative chosen. (Note: The answer may also be indicated directly on the test form.)

Scoring. The attitude score is merely the number of choices which agree with the keyed response on each scale. (The keyed response to each item is underlined in Exhibit 9-25.) Each scale is of course scored separately, so the range of possible scores is from 0 to 30. A high score on Scale P indicates a favorable attitude toward psychologists, whereas a high score on Scale S indicates greater knowledge about psychology.

Reliability. Measures of test-retest reliability after a six-week interval were obtained from responses of 51 students who had not taken psychology, yielding *r*s of .70 for Scale S and .78 for Scale P. For a sample of 77 students who had taken a psychology course, the values were .75

for Scale S and .81 for Scale P. Internal consistency was estimated (by K-R 20) to be .45 for Scale S and .76 for Scale P, based upon the responses of 280 students in the heterogeneous sample.

Validity. In addition to content validity, an appraisal of construct validity was made by comparing samples of students who had taken varying numbers of psychology courses. Those who had taken more courses scored higher on the KAP test, especially on Scale P. (Note: Assuming that students who take many psychology courses have a favorable attitude toward psychologists, this procedure reduces to the known-groups method.) Scale P was also found to be less closely related to academic aptitude as measured by the verbal scale of the School and College Ability Test ($r = .19$) than Scale S ($r = .34$).

Comments. Evidence of reliability is satisfactory, but the validation data once again is less than desirable. Scale P is better in this respect, and of course is the one of interest in this volume.

EXHIBIT 9-25

KNOWLEDGE ABOUT PSYCHOLOGY (KAP) TEST

Directions: This is a test of your general knowledge about psychology and psychologists. Each of the items in this test has three suggested answers. For each item choose the ONE alternative which best answers the question or completes the statement. Then *blacken* the letter on your answer sheet which corresponds to your correct choice.

Answer every item, even if you are not sure of your answer.

***Scale**

S 1 Which of the following usually contribute most to scientific research?
- <u>A.</u> psychologists
- B. psychiatrists
- C. psychoanalysts

P 2 In his leisure time a psychologist would be most likely to:
- A. go on bird-watching expeditions
- B. go to the horse races
- <u>C.</u> play chess, bridge, or poker

S 3 Which of the following problems is least suitable for a psychological study?
- <u>A.</u> Who is the better musician, Mozart or Beethoven?
- B. Can dreams forecast the future?
- C. Is it possible to read another person's mind?

* S indicates items of scale S, and P items of scale P. The keyed response is underlined.

Reference: F. Costin. The knowledge about psychology test. *J. exp. Educ.*, 1963, 31, 395–400. Items obtained from author and published with his permission.

P **4** Compared to the general population, psychologists are:
A. below average physically but above average intellectually
B. above average physically and intellectually
C. average physically and average intellectually

S **5** In the field of science, the psychologist:
A. has respect for the opinions of others
B. refuses to accept opinions of others
C. has respect for facts but not for opinions

P **6** The main difference between psychologists and other people of equal intelligence is that psychologists:
A. have received special training
B. are less interested in enjoying life
C. believe that knowledge is power

S **7** One way in which psychology is like other sciences is that it employs the "scientific method." Which of the following is the best statement of what is meant by the scientific method?
A. Scientific method is one which uses special instruments or mathematical equations.
B. Scientific method means to do research according to a theory.
C. Scientific method is a way of examining and evaluating evidence.

P **8** As a group, psychologists are probably:
A. about as persistent and charming as businessmen
B. more persistent than businessmen
C. less charming than businessmen

S **9** Psychological experiments should be carried out:
A. in the laboratory
B. at colleges and universities
C. wherever the materials are available

P **10** Three men visit the public library at the same time.
Man No. 1 selects a detective story.
Man No. 2 selects a detective story and a popular novel.
Man No. 3 selects a detective story, a popular novel, and a biography.
These men are a psychologist, a newspaper writer, and a lawyer. In identifying them, which of the following statements is most likely to be true?
A. No. 1 is the lawyer, but it is difficult to distinguish between the other two.
B. No. 3 could very well be any one of the three men.
C. No. 1 is the lawyer, No. 2 is the psychologist, and No. 3 is the writer.

S **11** Which of the following statements describes the most important way that psychologists serve our society?
A. They provide advice to other people.
B. They provide people with knowledge about themselves.
C. They show people what they should strive for.

P 12 Helen is very serious and highly intelligent. Betty is friendly, cheerful, and also highly intelligent. Which could become a successful psychologist?
A. Helen
B. Betty
C. Both Helen and Betty

S 13 Of the following, which is the most important characteristic of how the psychologist works?
A. He acquires and classifies as many facts as possible.
B. He does not make statements unless they are true.
C. He tries to discover his own mistakes and correct them.

P 14 The early childhood of most psychologists is probably:
A. less exciting then that of most children
B. much like that of most children
C. less happy than that of most children

S 15 The psychologist is a scientist because he:
A. makes systematic measurements of human behavior
B. uses his discoveries to help people with their everyday problems
C. speculates about the human mind

P 16 As compared with businessmen in general, psychologists are on the average:
A. less poised
B. more precise
C. about as poised and precise

S 17 When well-trained psychologists develop explanations of human behavior, their explanations:
A. are almost always correct
B. will probably be right more often than they are wrong
C. will probably be wrong more often than they are right

P 18 Which of the following statements best describes the mental health of psychologists?
A. A few successful psychologists are "queer ducks."
B. People with neurotic tendencies never become good psychologists.
C. Too much study often causes our best psychologists to lose their minds.

S 19 To be scientific, a psychological experiment must:
A. discover important facts
B. control factors other than those being investigated
C. take place in a laboratory

P 20 Children of psychologists are most likely to be proud of their fathers because:
A. psychologists do useful work

B. psychologists can tell their children about the exciting things they do in their work
C. most children are apt to be proud of their fathers

S 21 Which of these is the most highly controlled method the psychologist has of observing behavior?
A. clinical
B. experimental
C. survey

P 22 Below are the descriptions of three men:
Man No. 1—Low forehead, steady, penetrating eyes, wears glasses
Man No. 2—Low forehead, blinks eyes frequently, no glasses
Man No. 3—High forehead, steady gaze, wears glasses
These men are a businessman, a psychologist, and a lawyer. In identifying them, which of the following statements would you consider most likely to be true?
A. Any of the descriptions could fit all three persons equally as well.
B. No. 1 is the businessman, No. 2 is the lawyer, and No. 3 is the psychologist.
C. No. 3 is the psychologist, but it is difficult to distinguish between the businessman and the lawyer.

S 23 Psychologists sometimes use animals for experiments because:
A. animal behavior is less complex than human behavior
B. facts obtained from observing animals are usually true of human behavior
C. studying animal behavior is more scientific than studying human behavior

P 24 Most psychologists when they have a day off would probably prefer to:
A. visit a museum
B. plan their next study
C. spend their time with their families

S 25 Which of these are most likely to do psychotherapy in their everyday work?
A. clinical psychologists
B. educational psychologists
C. social psychologists

P 26 If a person hopes to be an outstanding psychologist, he probably will need to be:
A. average in intelligence
B. above average in intelligence
C. a genius

S 27 Most psychologists work for:
A. colleges and universities
B. private business and industry
C. government agencies

P 28 George always makes good grades in school but is a practical joker. Fred also makes good grades but has no sense of humor. Which of the boys probably could become a psychologist?
A. George
B. Fred
C. Both George and Fred

S 29 Most advances in psychological theory are the result of:
A. the work of some one great psychologist
B. pooling the ideas of many psychologists
C. discoveries of a genius who may not even be a professional psychologist

P 30 The major contributions of psychologists have resulted from:
A. brilliant flashes of imagination
B. hard work
C. accidental discoveries

S 31 Sometimes a psychological theory has to be discarded. Why?
A. Newer discoveries prove it to be false.
B. It is dangerous to man's welfare.
C. It is found to have no practical use.

P 32 Three men all work for the same company. The first is a research psychologist, the second is a plant foreman, and the third is a salesman. The answer to which of the following questions would help you select the research psychologist?
A. Which man has had the most college training?
B. Which man is the hardest worker?
C. Which man is the most serious-minded?

S 33 The most important objectives of a psychologist is to discover:
A. how to cure mental illness
B. why people behave as they do
C. how to prevent mental illness

P 34 Which one of the following characteristics would be most likely to interfere with a psychologist's everyday work?
A. "absent-mindedness"
B. lack of understanding of statistics
C. radical political opinions

S 35 Which of these is most likely to have a medical degree?
A. clinical psychologist
B. psychoanalyst
C. psychiatrist

P 36 One of the satisfactions that a person can get from his work as a psychologist is that most other people:
A. follow the advice of a psychologist
B. have respect for persons who are psychologists
C. enjoy talking to psychologists

S **37** Which one of the following is the best way to help advance psychology as a science?
A. Provide well-equipped laboratories and classrooms
B. Develop systems for classifying new facts
C. Choose very competent people to do the work

P **38** Which of the following characteristics is most important for a person to develop if he plans to become a psychologist?
A. aggressiveness
B. curiosity
C. thriftiness

S **39** A good psychologist:
A. recognizes problems that need to be solved
B. waits until a problem presents itself before he works on it
C. accepts only those problems which are of practical value to people

P **40** In order for a psychologist to be successful he must be willing to:
A. stick to his work
B. have faith in other people
C. believe that his results will be right

S **41** Two prominent psychologists announce a discovery at about the same time. It is most likely that:
A. one psychologist is not honest and copied the work of the other
B. both just happened to conclude their work at the same time
C. each knew of the other's work and attempted to finish first

P **42** Below are the descriptions of three women:
Woman No. 1—Pretty, well-dressed, outgoing in behavior
Woman No. 2—Not very pretty, rather plainly dressed, outgoing in behavior
Woman No. 3—Pretty, well-dressed, reserved in behavior
These 3 women are a business executive, a stenographer, and a psychologist. In identifying them, which of the following statements would you consider most likely to be true?
A. No. 1 is the stenographer, No. 2 is the psychologist, and No. 3 is the business executive.
B. No. 1 could very well be any one of the three.
C. No. 2 is the psychologist, but it is difficult to distinguish between the stenographer and the business executive.

S **43** Most of the greatest psychological discoveries have been made by:
A. carefully planned studies
B. trying everything the psychologists could think of
C. a lucky chance

P **44** Among psychologists as a group you would expect to find:
A. an unusually large proportion of high-strung persons
B. about the same proportion of high-strung persons that you would find in most groups
C. an unusually small number of high-strung persons

S 45 Most psychological research today is the result of:
A. teamwork
B. individual work
C. competitive work

P 46 On his vacation, a psychologist is most likely to:
A. visit a scientific exhibit
B. take a trip around the country
C. study a different branch of science

S 47 It is the duty of all psychologists to:
A. tell how people can use their discoveries
B. report their discoveries in such a way that other psychologists may repeat their studies
C. be as economical in their work as possible, since psychological studies are often very expensive

P 48 Children of psychologists generally enjoy spending time with their fathers because:
A. most children enjoy spending time with their fathers
B. psychologists are able to tell their children interesting stories
C. psychologists are able to help their children understand themselves

S 49 As a scientist, the main function of a psychologist is to:
A. invent new techniques which further human happiness
B. discover new ways of doing things important for humanity
C. explore new ideas in a systematic way

P 50 Below are the descriptions of three men:
Man No. 1—short, thin, slightly stooped, wears glasses
Man No. 2—medium height, average weight, wears glasses
Man No. 3—tall, broad-shouldered, well-built
These are a psychologist, a physician, and a plumber. In identifying them, which of the following statements would you consider most likely to be true?
A. No. 3 is the plumber, but it is difficult to distinguish between the physician and the psychologist.
B. No. 1 is the psychologist; No. 2 is the physician; and No. 3 is the plumber.
C. Any of the descriptions could fit very well either the psychologist, the physician or the plumber.

S 51 The most important goal of the educational psychologist is to:
A. show students new techniques for learning school subjects
B. discover how students learn
C. prevent students from failing in school

P 52 As compared with lawyers as a group, psychologists are on the average:
A. less humorous
B. less friendly
C. about as humorous and friendly

S 53 Which of these are most closely related in their work to what psychiatrists do?
A. clinical psychologists
B. industrial psychologists
C. social psychologists

P 54 Good character in a psychologist is shown best by the fact that other people:
A. like him
B. ask him for advice
C. can depend upon him

S 55 Which of the following problems is the best example of "applied psychology?"
A. predicting success in law school students
B. relationships between anxiety and changes in skin temperature of college students
C. relationships between blood sugar content and hunger in the white rat

P 56 In their relations with their children, psychologists tend to:
A. have more problems than most other people
B. have about as many problems as most other people
C. have less problems than most other people

S 57 In which of these fields of specialization is the largest number of psychologists?
A. clinical psychology
B. educational psychology
C. social psychology

P 58 Three men are dining together at a restaurant.
Man No. 1 is very interested in the food.
Man No. 2 spends a great deal of time admiring the furnishings.
Man No. 3 pays most attention to the other people in the restaurant.
The three men are a psychologist, a corporation executive, and an architect. In identifying them, which of the following statements is most likely to be true?
A. No. 1 is the corporation executive, No. 2 is the architect, and No. 3 is the psychologist.
B. No. 3 is the psychologist, but it is difficult to distinguish between the corporation executive and the architect.
C. No. 3 could very well be any one of the three men.

S 59 Which of these best defines "psychology"?
A. psychoanalysis of personal problems
B. reading people's minds
C. explanation and prediction of human behavior

P 60 As a group, psychologists are:
A. less self-confident than businessmen

B. about as self-confident as businessmen and lawyers
C. less self-confident than lawyers

GENERALIZED SCALES TO MEASURE ATTITUDES TOWARD SIGNIFICANT OTHERS

A number of more or less generalized scales have been found to measure attitudes toward significant others. Remmers and his associates developed at least two scales that might be used for this purpose: a scale to measure attitudes toward any defined group (Grice, 1934; Remmers, 1934) and a scale to measure attitude toward any teacher (Hoshaw, 1936). The first of these scales is described in Chapter 8, and the second one is presented below.

The semantic differential has also been used to measure attitude toward various persons and classes of persons that fit our definition of significant others. Osgood et al. (1957) used this device to measure attitudes toward labor leaders and Senator Robert Taft, reporting test-retest coefficients after a five-week interval ranging from .87 to .93. Also using the semantic differential, Asher and Evans (1959) measured attitude toward the Negro professor and intelligent Negroes; Eisendorfer and Altrocchi (1961) measured attitude toward self, ideal self, mother, father, average man, average woman, neurotic man, neurotic woman, insane woman, old man, old woman, psychiatrist, and psychologist; Kogan and Wallach (1961) measured attitude toward family life, baby, older people, foreigner, my mother, my father, myself, and the ideal person; Nunnally (1961) measured attitude toward psychiatrist and mental patient; and Nickols and Shaw (1964) measured attitude toward college professors.

An approach used by Rickard, Triandis, and Patterson (1963) to measure prejudice toward disabled applicants is also essentially generalized in nature. This is a multifactor stimuli method which was introduced by Triandis and Triandis (1960). The purpose is to determine the effects of specific variables, with other variables held constant. As applied to disabled applicants, four characteristics of job applicants (disability, sex, competence, and sociability) were used. Disabilities were as follows: deaf, confined to a wheelchair, epileptic, discharged from a mental institution, discharged from a prison, discharged from a tuberculosis sanatorium, and no physical defect. Only two variations were used for the other three characteristics: male and female, barely competent and highly competent, sociable and unsociable. Thus there were $7 \times 2 \times 2 \times 2$ possible combinations; all combinations were used to form 56 items, such as "deaf, male, highly competent, unsociable." The respondents (personnel directors and school administrators) rated the applicant described on a seven-point scale ranging from "strongly recommend" to "strongly oppose." The scale is generalized in the sense that any job title may be used for the ratings. No evidence of reliability or validity was presented; hence, much work remains to be done before this device can be recommended as a satisfactory measure of attitude.

An attitude scale for measuring attitude toward any teacher *EXHIBIT 9-26*

Description. This scale was developed by Hoshaw (1936) under Remmers' supervision by the usual Thurstone procedure. Two forms of the scale were developed, each consisting of 45 items. In constructing the scale, 500 items were written from which 200 were selected for further analysis. These 200 items were then sent to five professors of education at Purdue University who rated them on a four-point scale. On the basis of these ratings the number was reduced to 157. The final selection was made by the sorting procedure developed by Thurstone. The Q values in the final scales ranged from 1.0 to 2.9.

Subjects. The subjects used in scale construction were 110 high school pupils and 60 Purdue University students. For obtaining reliability and validity data, the subjects were 875 students in a number of high schools in north central Indiana.

Response Mode. The subjects check each item with which they agree.

Scoring. The attitude score is the median of the scale values of those items with which the subject agrees.

Reliability. For the most part, scales were administered by the high school principals, although some were given by Hoshaw. For all schools ($N = 875$) the two-forms reliability was found to be .706; for those administered by Hoshaw ($N = 245$) the reliability was .738.

Validity. Only limited evidence of validity was presented by the author. Teachers' ratings of ability correlated .423 with attitude scores on Form A and .506 with scores on Form B. If one assumes that the teacher's perception of the student is influenced by the student's attitude toward the teacher, these results may be taken as evidence of the validity of the scale. However, the correlation between the students' grades and attitude was near 0.

Comments. This scale is subject to the same criticisms as other generalized scales. In addition, evidence of validity is quite limited, although the method of selecting items suggests consensual validity. Since this scale was developed some thirty years ago, the prospective user is advised to obtain new scale values from judges drawn from the target population.

EXHIBIT 9-26

AN ATTITUDE SCALE FOR MEASURING ATTITUDE TOWARD ANY TEACHER

Please indicate your agreement or disagreement with each of the following statements by marking them as follows:

(✓) Mark with a check mark if you agree that the statement applies to this teacher.
(X) Mark with an X if you disagree that the statement applies to this teacher.

Form A

Scale Value		
10.8	1	Is perfect in every way.
10.0	2	Makes the subject matter interesting.
10.0	3	Grades papers fairly.
10.0	4	Is an aid in developing high ideals.
9.9	5	Is always polite.
9.7	6	Is always pleasant.
9.7	7	Is one of the best citizens in the community.
9.7	8	Is brilliant.
9.4	9	Can talk well on many subjects.
9.3	10	Is progressive.
9.3	11	Is interested in the school activities.
9.3	12	Inspires respect on the part of the students.
9.1	13	Is natural and unaffected.
9.1	14	Has the moral support of the community.
9.0	15	Has a reason back of every request.
9.0	16	Is energetic.
8.9	17	Will admit an error if convinced.
8.8	18	Dresses well.
8.1	19	Is improving.
8.1	20	Is methodical.
6.4	21	Frequently publicly praises the student for good work.
4.5	22	Is too idealistic.
4.3	23	Tests too frequently.
3.9	24	Frequently uses gestures which are meaningless.
3.9	25	Is too serious.
3.8	26	Is too retiring.
3.4	27	Talks too little.
3.1	28	Has passed the period of usefulness.
3.1	29	Is annoyed in the presence of classroom visitors.
2.8	30	Makes decisions too hastily.
2.5	31	Often seems tired of the job.
2.3	32	Is isolated from the world.
2.3	33	Often lets the slackers get by.
2.1	34	Commands very little respect from the students.
2.1	35	Is disliked by many.
1.9	36	Does nothing to interest the student.
1.8	37	Gives carelessly worded tests.
1.7	38	Does not understand young people.
1.6	39	Shows partiality.
1.5	40	Never admits an error.
1.3	41	Exerts an influence for wrong.
1.3	42	Has more bad points than any teacher I know.
1.1	43	Has an ungovernable temper.
.9	44	Does not know the subject.
.8	45	Is a failure as a classroom teacher.

Form B

Scale Value		
10.9	**1**	Knows the subject.
10.2	**2**	Grades fairly.
10.0	**3**	Uses good English.
9.9	**4**	Makes cheating seem undesirable to the student.
9.8	**5**	Gives individual help willingly.
9.8	**6**	Can see a question from the pupil's point of view.
9.7	**7**	Gives test questions which are clearly understood.
9.6	**8**	Understands young people.
9.5	**9**	Is a natural leader.
9.4	**10**	Is uniformly well liked.
9.3	**11**	Uses a vocabulary best suited to the average student.
9.2	**12**	Can talk well on many subjects.
9.1	**13**	Has a keen sense of humor.
9.0	**14**	Weighs facts before making decisions.
9.0	**15**	Inspires students with confidence in their own abilities.
8.9	**16**	Recognizes the right to difference of opinion.
8.9	**17**	Seems never to tire of teaching.
8.7	**18**	Is a good entertainer outside of class.
8.1	**19**	Satisfies only the dull students.
7.8	**20**	Uses meaningful gestures.
6.0	**21**	Exalts accuracy with no regard for speed.
4.7	**22**	Has no hobby in life.
4.2	**23**	Uses personal illustrations too often.
4.0	**24**	Does not follow the text book closely enough.
3.8	**25**	Is too lenient.
3.7	**26**	Is not serious enough.
3.5	**27**	Depends too much on text books.
3.1	**28**	Is too reluctant to change.
3.0	**29**	Is frequently impatient.
2.9	**30**	Becomes greatly concerned over petty disturbances.
2.4	**31**	Frequently makes unreasonable requests.
2.4	**32**	Causes the student to feel inferior.
2.3	**33**	Frequently shows lack of preparation.
2.1	**34**	Makes vague assignments.
2.0	**35**	Does nothing to correct the poor study habits of the students.
2.0	**36**	Fails to teach students how to study.
1.7	**37**	Is a poor sport.
1.7	**38**	Is a bore.
1.6	**39**	Is not interested in the subject taught.
1.5	**40**	Does nothing to interest the student.
1.3	**41**	Frequently seeks to embarrass the slow student because of his lack of ability.
1.3	**42**	Becomes angry if anyone differs with him/her.
.9	**43**	Is frequently "two-faced."
.9	**44**	Is a disgrace to the community.
.9	**45**	Grades unfairly.

SUMMARY

In the summary statement of preceding chapters, we have noted that evidence of reliability is satisfactory for most scales, but that little evidence of validity is available. The same statement must be made regarding the scales included in this chapter, with the notable exception of the Acceptance of Self and Others Scale (Berger, 1952).

The coverage provided by these scales is perhaps less adequate than for most categories. Scales to measure attitude toward significant others in the family are adequate, but if the researcher is interested in attitudes toward significant others occupying particular status positions, the available scales are very limited. The same is true for attitudes toward significant others related to education. Additional scales in these categories are badly needed.

CHAPTER **10**

social institutions

In the process of development of social organization, there evolve a number of abstract entities that may be designated institutions. In this chapter, the institutions referred to are agencies and corporate bodies which are available to or are organized for public use. Such bodies are usually endowed with a degree of authority, as testified to by their ability to sanction, and come to function as agents of social control. They enforce, directly or indirectly, the existing social norms and possess a degree of control over what further norms will evolve. In this manner, they provide the continuity of the life of the social group across generations or changes in membership. Their effectiveness, and thereby the continued existence of the group, is conditioned by the attitudes of persons they serve and control.

ATTITUDES RELATED TO EDUCATIONAL INSTITUTIONS

In this section have been included scales for measuring attitudes toward educational institutions—attitudes toward high schools and colleges. The Remmers scale for measuring attitude toward any high school has been placed in the last section of this chapter.

Semantic distance questionnaire EXHIBIT 10-1

Description. This is a 36-item scale, developed by Weaver (1959). Construction of the scale was by a highly modified Thurstone procedure. Scale values for items are given in Exhibit 10-1. It measures attitudes toward the following referents: teachers, classroom, study hall, study, high school, and school rules. Items were selected by asking 147 students in the twelfth grade to write statements of attitudes, standards, rules of conduct, fashions, etc., which they believed their groups held toward 12 aspects of the educative process (teachers, classroom, study hall, etc.); 2,100 statements were obtained and given to 20 faculty members, who rated them on a seven-point continuum of "good" attitude to "bad" attitude. Since each teacher scaled about half of these items, the *N* for each item would be about 10 judges. Six dimensions (attitude objects) showed a consistent set of ratings. The 10 items which showed the greatest scale distances between students' responses and teachers' ratings were selected for each of the six dimensions and made into a test. A split-half reliability coefficient was computed for this 60-item test and found to be less than satisfactory. Six items were selected from the six dimensions (creating a test of 36 items) and the split-half reliability coefficient of .92 was obtained (*N* unknown). This form is presented in Exhibit 10-1. Weaver (1959) provides profiles on the six attitudinal objects, obtained upon 437 students and 16 teachers, which may be used for the purpose of comparison.

Subjects. The sample consisted of 16 high school teachers from two schools and 437 high school students from two different schools.

Response Mode. Subjects respond to each item by writing a number from 1 to 7 corresponding to the following continuum: strongly disagree, 1; neutral, 4; and strongly agree, 7. No verbal anchors were given to the numbers 2, 3, 5, or 6.

Scoring. For research purposes, Weaver (1959) took the subject's score as the mean of the numbers given the items by the subject, after reversing the weights for the negative items. In view of the fact that there are no items possessing extreme scale values, it would seem advisable to use a summated rating procedure for scoring. For this purpose one could use a standard Likert-type response continuum. Positive items would be weighted from 5 (strongly agree) to 1 (strongly disagree). Weights for negative items would be reversed, and the subject's score would be the sum of the weighted alternatives endorsed by him. If this procedure is used, it would be valuable to perform an item analysis to select the most discriminating items.

Reliability. The only evidence of reliability for this scale is the split-half reliability reported earlier and used as a criterion for item selection. This coefficient was $.92 \pm .06$ of a scale interval of a seven-point scale.

Validity. The items have good content validity for the six attitudinal referents toward which they are directed. Content validity would also seem to be assured on the basis of the source of, and number of, statements obtained in the original sample of statements. If the number of judges had been larger than 10, the value of the modified Thurstone procedure used would have been enhanced; Shaw et al. (1963) suggest that reliable Q values may be obtained with as few as 20 judges. Fewer than 20 judges will result in reliable values only in some instances. In this case, the difference in scale values obtained with the two samples of teachers (Exhibit 10-1) is relatively large for a number of items and seems to indicate a lack of stability. Weaver (1959) reports that the attitudes, as measured by this instrument, were found to be related to the achievement scores of students. This finding may be taken as further evidence of the validity of the scale, in that more positive attitudes toward education should reflect better motivation and would, therefore, be expected to be related to academic achievement.

Comments. With regard to both reliability and validity, the scale seems satisfactory for measurement of a general attitude toward the school situation and referents related to the school. Weaver presents some normative data which also should be valuable for the purpose of comparison of population samples. In view of the fact that the scale values for these items all fall between 2.6 and 6.0 on a seven-point scale, it does not seem feasible to use it as a Thurstone scale. It would appear preferable to use a Likert response continuum, to perform an item analysis, and to treat it as a Likert-type scale.

EXHIBIT 10-1

SEMANTIC DISTANCE QUESTIONNAIRE

Directions

1. Please print your name in the blank space above. You may be sure that in spite of this your answers on this paper will be kept confidential.

2. On the back of the *last page* of this questionnaire, please write the names of your best friends, the members of your "gang." You may write as many or as few names as you like.

3. There are 36 statements in this questionnaire, all written by high-school students. Please indicate *your own personal opinion* of each statement by writing a number from 1 to 7 in the blank before it, as follows:

Strongly disagree			Neutral			Strongly agree
1	2	3	4	5	6	7

Thus, if you strongly agree with a statement write a number 7 in the blank; if you strongly disagree write a number 1 in the blank. If you don't care either way, write a number 4 in the blank. If you agree or disagree less strongly, use the numbers 2, 3, 5, or 6.

Please do not write what you *ought* to believe or what other people (teachers, parents, etc.) want you to believe. Try to indicate what you really think about these statements.

Work fast. Do not puzzle too long over any statement. Write your first impulse.

Do not leave any blanks empty. Write a number in every one.

REMEMBER: You need not fear that your opinions will be exposed. No one in this school will ever see your paper. Your teachers will be given only general summaries of group answers. When you finish, hand your paper to me.

Table A: Thirty-six Item Test

Scale Values: Mount Pleasant Teachers	Scale Values: Bay City Teachers		Item
5.80	4.50	*1	Classrooms are dull places.
5.60	5.38	2	I enjoy going to class.
6.20	5.62	*3	A classroom is a place to put in your time.
5.70	5.00	*4	When I am in class I think of what is going on tonight.
5.60	4.87	*5	Classrooms are okay if you have friends there.
5.80	4.62	*6	There is too much applepolishing in classrooms.
6.80	5.89	*7	Rules make school seem like a prison.
6.80	5.00	8	We should always follow the rules with courtesy.
5.70	5.33	*9	Some rules were practically made to be broken.
6.10	4.56	*10	Some rules are stupid and unreasonable.
5.50	3.56	*11	I don't think too highly of having so many rules.
5.60	4.78	12	We should help make others obey the rules.
5.70	5.50	*13	Teachers think they're martyrs.
5.20	5.20	*14	Teachers often favor.
6.30	2.60	*15	Some teachers are lazy.
5.50	3.50	*16	Sometimes teachers' rules are just a little strict and stupid.
5.60	3.20	*17	Some teachers are unreasonable.
5.70	4.80	*18	Some teachers should be in the student's chair and the student should be teaching.
6.00	5.00	19	I enjoy school.
5.90	4.56	20	I think it's a privilege to attend high school.
5.90	4.67	*21	I think high school is boring.
5.70	5.44	22	I study hard.
5.90	3.89	*23	I think there are better things to do than going to school.
6.10	5.44	*24	I like school closed.
6.00	4.87	*25	I dislike studying.
5.60	3.25	*26	Studying interferes with some of my other plans and activities.
6.20	4.62	*27	There isn't any fun in studying.
6.00	4.13	28	I put study above most other things.
5.60	4.50	29	I think I should give up going places for studying.

* These items are negative and their weights must be reversed for purposes of scoring.

Scale Values Mount Pleasant Teachers	Bay City Teachers		Item
6.70	5.50	*30	Study is a bother.
5.50	5.22	*31	Study hall is a place to see your friends.
5.90	4.89	32	I think I should be quiet in study hall so others can work.
5.90	5.00	*33	Study hall is a place to talk over the happenings of the day.
5.60	5.00	*34	There aren't enough privileges in study halls.
6.10	6.44	*35	Study hall is our leisure time during the school day.
5.80	4.37	*36	Study hall is boring most of the time.

Faculty morale scale for institutional improvement EXHIBIT 10-2

Description. This scale was developed by an anonymous local chapter of the American Association of University Professors (1963) and is published by Psychometric Affiliates. It is a 34-item scale measuring attitudes toward "34 important considerations about the institution of employment" (AAUP, 1963). Thus, the scale is restricted in its use to the measurement of attitudes of faculty members. The publishers of the scale provide norms based upon random samples of faculty members of institutions in the United States.

Subjects. The sample was composed of 97 faculty members, 76 from one institution and 21 from a national sample of institutions.

Response Mode. Subjects check a space beside each item for one of five alternatives: very good, good, average, poor, very poor.

Scoring. The response alternatives are weighted from 5 (very good) to 1 (very poor). The score is the sum of the weighted alternatives chosen. There are no negative items to be reversed. High scores reflect positive attitudes.

Reliability. The publishers of the scale report a split-half reliability (corrected) of .94 based on an N of 97.

Validity. The scale appears to possess fair content validity judging from the appearance of its items. Otherwise, a positive correlation of .15 was found (as hypothesized by the authors of the scale) between academic rank and faculty morale, indicating that it was not just measuring satisfaction with success in academic endeavor.

Comments. This scale measures a larger content domain than attitude toward the institution. However, those other referents toward which attitude is also being assessed seem closely related to attitude toward the institution. The reliability estimate reported is quite good. But, since all the points questioned by the items are positive, the item form may exploit response sets and reduce validity. It would be a more valuable scale if the phrasing of some of the items were negative in nature.

EXHIBIT 10-2

FACULTY MORALE SCALE FOR INSTITUTIONAL IMPROVEMENT

	Check (√) One				
	Very Good	Good	Average	Poor	Very Poor
Academic Requirements					
1 Adequacy of salaries	____	____	____	____	____
2 Fairness of process for giving increases	____	____	____	____	____
3 Adequacy of faculty office space	____	____	____	____	____
4 Fair allocation of offices	____	____	____	____	____
5 Adequacy of class rooms	____	____	____	____	____
6 Fair allocation of class rooms	____	____	____	____	____
7 Adequacy of laboratories	____	____	____	____	____
8 Fair allocation of laboratories	____	____	____	____	____
9 Fair allocation of secretarial assistance	____	____	____	____	____
10 Fair assignment of assistants and clerks	____	____	____	____	____
11 Faculty voice in administrative selections	____	____	____	____	____
Administrative Encouragement of					
12 Subsidized research	____	____	____	____	____
13 Spontaneous research	____	____	____	____	____
14 Fundamental scholarly achievement	____	____	____	____	____
15 Good teaching	____	____	____	____	____
16 Good faculty-student relations	____	____	____	____	____
17 Community activities by faculty	____	____	____	____	____
18 Scholarly writing	____	____	____	____	____
19 Fairness of promotion policy	____	____	____	____	____
20 Sabbatical policy	____	____	____	____	____
21 Equal treatment of departments	____	____	____	____	____
22 Textbook choice freedom	____	____	____	____	____
23 General academic freedom	____	____	____	____	____
24 Freedom of communication and appeal	____	____	____	____	____

	Check (√) One				
	Very Good	Good	Average	Poor	Very Poor
Administrative Encouragement of					
25 Student freedom of choice of courses	____	____	____	____	____
26 Fair curriculum-making procedures	____	____	____	____	____
27 Faculty attitude toward teaching	____	____	____	____	____
Effectiveness of					
28 Faculty voice in policy-making	____	____	____	____	____
29 Academic administration	____	____	____	____	____
30 Student social program	____	____	____	____	____
31 Intramural athletic program	____	____	____	____	____
32 Intercollegiate athletic program	____	____	____	____	____
33 Student government program	____	____	____	____	____
34 Public relations activities	____	____	____	____	____

Attitude toward college fraternities *EXHIBIT 10-3*

Description. This is a 20-item scale developed by Banta (1961) using the unfolded partial rank order (UPRO) method. It measures attitudes toward the merit of the college fraternity as a social institution. The items were originally assembled by Segall (1957), who used them in a Thurstone scaling procedure. Banta (1961) states that such items are readily transferable to a UPRO response format. Both the UPRO and the Thurstone scale values are included in Exhibit 10-3, for the sake of comparison and to allow a choice of usage. These scale values were derived by giving each subject the same items with three different formats (Likert, Thurstone, and UPRO) on three different days, in a counterbalanced fashion.

Subjects. Twenty-five introductory psychology summer students from Columbia University composed the sample.

Response Mode. The response mode for subject-judges in a UPRO procedure is a 5-point scale (as compared with a Thurstone 11-point scale) with the middle point on the continuum being identified as the subject's own feelings. The other four points are labelled "too favorable (unfavorable) for me" and "much too favorable (unfavorable) for me"; see instructions for scale in Exhibit 10-3. A noncommittal response alternative of "?" is also provided. Although excluded from the exhibit, the symbols for these alternatives (— —, —, 0, +, ++, and ?) are placed at the left of each item.

Scoring. For research purposes, Banta (1961) derived the following three scores for the UPRO response format: the number agree score (the number of agreement responses made by *S*), a UPRO latitude of acceptance score (the difference between scale values of the most and least favorable items agreed to by *S*), and a number of valid answers score (the number of items in the scale minus the number of response omissions and use of the "?" category). A fourth score, the appropriate one for measurement of attitudes with this scale, is the median of the scale value of the items endorsed by subjects as "my feeling." High scores reflect positive attitudes.

Reliability. No reliability estimates are provided for this scale. However, in view of the striking correlation between the Thurstone and UPRO scale values, the reliability estimate for the scale should be approximately the same as that for Thurstone scales. Generally, Thurstone scales possess adequate reliability for group testing.

Validity. Banta (1961) reports an average intercorrelation of .87 between measurements of attitude toward college fraternities, using the Thurstone, Likert, and UPRO procedures. Also, the UPRO and Thurstone procedures yielded quite comparable means and standard deviations (on a sample of 25 persons).

Comments. Although the UPRO method of construction is similar to the Thurstone method, the UPRO procedure provides a partial rank order of favorability toward the referent. Also, this rank ordering is anchored by the person's own attitude, rather than by a neutral point or by end points of the attitude continuum. More research is required to determine the effects of this change in anchoring of the reference scale in sorting and responding. At present, the scale needs estimates of reliability and further validational studies.

EXHIBIT 10-3

ATTITUDE TOWARD COLLEGE FRATERNITIES

Read carefully

Some of the following statements may reflect your own views, while others may not. Of these statements that do not reflect your own views, there are likely to be some that are too favorable toward the issue; on the other hand, there are also likely to be some that are too unfavorable toward the issue to represent your own views.

Please read each statement carefully and indicate your reaction to it in accordance with the following rules.

Circle

−−	−	(0)	+	++	?	If the statement expresses your own feelings regarding the issue.
−−	−	0	(+)	++	?	If the statement is somewhat too favorable toward the issue in question to represent your own views.

Reference: T. J. Banta. Social attitudes and response styles. *Educ. psychol. Measmt,* 1961, 21, 543–557. Items obtained from author and published with his permission.

Circle

−−	−	0	+	(++)	?	If the statement is much too favorable to represent your own views.
−−	(−)	0	+	++	?	If the statement is too unfavorable to represent your own views.
(−−)	−	0	+	++	?	If the statement is very definitely too unfavorable to represent your own views.
−−	−	0	+	++	(?)	If the statement is not one that expresses your own feelings but you can't determine whether it is too favorable or too unfavorable toward the issue in question.

Scale Value UPRO	Thurstone		
3.33	3.68	*1	It is difficult to understand how anyone can take an unqualified stand on the question of fraternities. −− − 0 + ++ ?
3.32	3.73	2	Fraternities are fine for certain types of people.
1.78	1.88	3	All in all, there is more wrong than right about the fraternity system.
1.30	1.18	4	The sooner college fraternities cease to exist the better.
3.93	3.98	5	The non-fraternity student is missing one of the most important aspects of college training.
4.03	3.73	6	College fraternities are among the finest institutions yet devised by Western man.
1.70	1.48	7	Fraternities do far more harm than good.
3.17	3.50	8	Much can be said both in favor and against college fraternities.
1.79	1.75	9	Fraternity membership usually results in severe limitations on originality and productivity.
3.50	3.75	10	A large part of the opposition to fraternities is the result of jealousy and ignorance on the part of those who failed to gain admission to a fraternity.
3.42	3.65	11	College fraternities provide healthful experiences for many people.
3.78	3.85	12	It would be a calamity if fraternities didn't exist.
2.08	2.10	13	The question of whether college fraternities are a good thing or not is petty and unimportant.
1.18	1.18	14	Fraternities are loafer's clubs.
3.03	2.90	15	It is so hard to decide whether fraternities are good or not.
1.13	1.05	16	Fraternities are absolutely terrible.
3.83	3.70	17	Fraternities help to mold the college man into a well adjusted and productive member of society.
4.16	4.05	18	An employer would be wise to give preference to a fraternity man.
2.03	2.18	19	There is so much to find fault with in the institution of college fraternities.
2.26	2.23	20	Fraternities may be all right, but a lot of changes are necessary before they can be given wholehearted approval.

* The same response alternatives are used with all items.

ATTITUDES TOWARD HEALTH-RELATED INSTITUTIONS

Scales contained in this section measure attitudes toward mental health institutions. They include the following referents: mental hospitals, state hospitals, and counseling centers. Interested readers will also wish to see a number of attitude scales contained in Chapter 3, Social Practices, measuring institutional ideologies or orientations reflected in different treatment approaches to mental patients. For a projective technique to be used in measuring these attitudes, see Brady, Reznikoff, and Zeller (1960).

Attitudes toward mental hospitals EXHIBIT 10-4

Description. This 36-item, Thurstone-type scale was developed by Souelem (1955) to measure the attitudes of mental patients toward mental hospitals. However, the items are so phrased as to be useful with both patient and nonpatient samples. The items in Exhibit 10-4 are from two equivalent forms of the scale.

Subjects. The samples included 95 males from four wards at Rosebury (Oregon) VA Hospital and 103 males from four wards at Salem (Oregon) State Hospital.

Response Mode. Subjects underline "agree" for those items with which they agree and underline the phrase "do not agree" when they disagree with the item. These alternatives, which have been eliminated from Exhibit 10-4, are placed beside each item.

Scoring. The person's score is the median of the scale values of all items which he endorsed. Low scores indicate positive attitudes.

Reliability. The author reports the equivalent-forms reliability of the two scales to range from .795 to .866, based upon the above samples. Toomey, Reznikoff, Brady, and Schumann (1961) reported that mean scores of 93 nursing students changed less than .02 percent of a scale unit, over a three-month period.

Validity. The forms were validated by the author (Souelem, 1955) against an 11-item sentence-completion test which had been scored as favorable, unfavorable, or neutral by three clinical psychologists. The scale was further validated by Klopfer, Wylie, and Hillson (1956), who reported it to differentiate between known groups. These groups were state hospital psychiatric aides, state hospital clerical and administrative employees, state hospital ward charges, members of a community service organization, high school seniors, and state hospital inpatients. Klopfer, Wylie, and Hillson (1956) provided a discussion of the individual items and their discriminatory ability. Toomey, Reznikoff, Brady, and Schumann (1961) found that the scale did not discriminate between nursing students and psychiatric inpatients, although differences were in the expected direction.

Comments. This is a rather good scale, carefully constructed, and its functional characteristics are known. The scale has had general use, and the information in the articles by Klopfer, Wylie, and Hillson (1956) and Toomey, Reznikoff, Brady, and Schumann (1961) will serve as estimates of norms for various kinds of populations. The interested reader may also wish to see Imre and Wolf (1962).

EXHIBIT 10-4

ATTITUDES TOWARD MENTAL HOSPITALS

On the following pages you will find many statements people sometimes make about mental hospitals. Read each statement and show whether you agree with the statement or not. If you agree with the statement, underline the word "agree" beside the statement. If you do not agree, underline the words "do not agree" beside the statement.

Form A

Scale Value		
10.3	1	Mental hospitals are evil and sinful.
5.5	2	Being in a mental hospital is neither good nor bad.
7.6	3	I would hate to work in a mental hospital.
9.5	4	Mental hospitals are nauseating.
2.2	5	Mental hospitals perform a useful service in our society.
8.8	6	Mental hospitals bring unnecessary misery to the patient.
6.8	7	There are too many things to do in a mental hospital; a patient gets tired.
5.1	8	Mental hospitals are neither to be enjoyed nor to be feared, they are to be accepted.
10.4	9	Mental hospitals are houses of "living" death.
0.6	10	Mental hospitals are perfect in every way.
3.3	11	Recreation in mental hospitals is very entertaining.
2.6	12	Mental hospitals are improving every year.
8.5	13	A normal person could not stand being locked up in a mental hospital.
1.0	14	Mental hospitals are a great benefit to mankind.
9.9	15	We would be better off if no one had ever thought of mental hospitals.
6.5	16	Many patients won't want to be in a mental hospital against their will.
8.9	17	Most of those who enter mental hospitals might as well give up hope.
1.9	18	Mental hospitals give real help in meeting social problems.
5.5	19	Mental hospitals inspire no definite likes or dislikes in me.
4.0	20	A mental hospital is a place to rest.
7.4	21	In mental hospitals they prevent a person from doing what he wants.
4.1	22	Being in a mental hospital is a sort of vacation for a person.
2.6	23	Most patients really want to be in mental hospitals.
4.4	24	I guess the mental hospital is the right place for a patient.
9.9	25	A person going into a mental hospital should expect the worst.
4.7	26	While a person is in the mental hospital he should do what they tell him to do.

Scale Value		
3.1	**27**	Mental hospitals are quite nice and restful.
6.9	**28**	I don't like the idea of not being able to go where one wants to go, and to do what one wants to do, in a mental hospital.
5.7	**29**	I don't care whether mental hospitals are good or bad.
3.3	**30**	I think that mental illness can be helped in a mental hospital.
3.0	**31**	A mental hospital is probably the best place for a mentally sick person.
1.7	**32**	The mental hospital is a great help to the mentally sick.
7.8	**33**	It is better for a mentally sick person to be treated at home rather than in a mental hospital.
7.1	**34**	I would dislike being forced to go to movies and dances and ball games while in a mental hospital.
1.3	**35**	The men who started the first mental hospitals were great contributors to humanity.
8.1	**36**	Mental hospitals are frightening.

Form B

0.7	**37**	Mental hospitals are the most admirable of institutions.
5.6	**38**	Both the evils and benefits of mental hospitals are greatly exaggerated.
2.9	**39**	Being in a mental hospital does not make a person feel he is so different after all.
7.6	**40**	The money spent on mental hospitals could be much better spent on schools.
9.7	**41**	Mental hospitals are basically immoral.
8.3	**42**	Most mental hospitals give patients a feeling of unrest and anxiety.
3.7	**43**	I think the mental hospital is doing most patients some good.
1.3	**44**	Basically mental hospitals are a wonderful thing.
5.4	**45**	I don't know what to think about mental hospitals.
0.8	**46**	Mental hospitals are a blessing to mankind.
4.2	**47**	There is nothing unusual about being in a mental hospital.
8.9	**48**	Families of mental patients should be ashamed of sending them to the hospital.
9.8	**49**	Mental hospitals have not changed much since the time when they chained patients and beat them.
4.7	**50**	Some patients like it in a mental hospital—Three meals a day, no worry.
7.3	**51**	You'd think there would be more practical ways of handling patients than mental hospitals.
7.7	**52**	The hospital people don't pay enough attention to individuals and how different everyone is from everyone else.
10.4	**53**	Mental hospitals are as bad as concentration camps.
6.6	**54**	If they would just let patients do what they want to do in the mental hospitals, they would all get to feeling much better.
1.9	**55**	A patient is definitely being helped in a mental hospital.
8.8	**56**	Anyone who goes to a mental hospital should be ashamed.
2.2	**57**	The number of patients cured in mental hospitals is rising rapidly.
1.4	**58**	Mental hospitals are concerned with the welfare of every patient.
9.9	**59**	Mental hospitals are a disgrace.
8.2	**60**	Mental hospitals are so poorly planned that patients hate them.
10.3	**61**	Mental hospitals are snake pits.
6.8	**62**	In the mental hospitals they try to get the patients to talk about themselves too much.

Scale Value		
3.2	63	Although all patients do not improve in mental hospitals, most of them are helped.
2.3	64	A mental hospital is a place where the patient is relieved and comforted.
5.5	65	Mental hospitals are neither good nor bad.
4.3	66	Mental hospitals are alright, after all.
3.5	67	Improvements are being made in mental hospitals.
5.6	68	One hears so many different ideas about mental hospitals that it is hard to decide whether they are good or bad.
6.9	69	There is too much time in a mental hospital with nothing to do.
7.3	70	In the mental hospital, patients don't get any chance to use their own abilities to the best advantage.
3.3	71	There is a growing need for mental hospitals.
2.9	72	In mental hospitals they have very interesting things for the patients to do.

Attitudes relating to the state hospital EXHIBIT 10-5

Description. This is a 57-item scale developed by Pratt, Giannitrapani, and Khanna (1960). Nine staff psychologists at a large state psychiatric hospital wrote a pool of 200 items intended to measure attitudes in the following five content areas: clinical (acceptance of staff clinical services, and the hospital perceived as a treatment facility), social (assigning valence to the staff in terms of sociometric hierarchy and ingroup versus outgroup membership in the community), economic (perception of the economic potential of the hospital for the community), political (exclusion-inclusion of staff in civic and political community activities), criminally insane (differential perception of this subgroup of the hospital community's patient population). A key for the categorization of the items is provided in Exhibit 10-5. Of the 200 items written, 57 were selected by group consensus as best suited for assessment of relevant attitudes. Many of the items are specific to the locale (Larned, Kansas) and the hospital which served as the referent, or to practices in that area. They would, therefore, have to be assessed carefully and changed or dropped when the situation required. Furthermore, some items are more informational than attitudinal.

Subjects. The sample was composed of 400 adult residents of a small, typically Midwestern community (including the senior high school class). More than 13 percent of the total population was included in the sample.

Response Mode. The response mode is of two forms: "yes," "no," or "don't know" for 50 items and multiple-choice alternatives (a phrase, sentence, or noun) for 7 items.

Scoring. Responses to the items are scored according to their positive, negative, or neutral value. The direction of the items is indicated in Exhibit 10-5 and was established on the basis of the validity of the items in the judgment of nine clinical psychologists. The three alternatives for

50 of the items are weighted from 2 (yes) to 0 (no), for positive items; weights for negative items must be reversed. For items whose alternatives are rank-ordered with regard to favorability, the person's score on the item is the most favorable item chosen by him. For items possessing both positive and negative alternatives, the person's score is the algebraic sum of the alternatives endorsed, each alternative being scored as +1 or −1. Scores for each of the content areas are computed separately, and these scores are added to give a total scale score. High scores reflect positive attitudes.

Reliability. No evidence of reliability was reported.

Validity. Different subtests of the scale were reported to discriminate between known groups. Of 56 tests of significance by chi squares, 15 were found significant at the .02 level or better, and 1 was significant at the .05 level. These groups were known on the basis of certain demographic characteristics (age, sex, marital status, occupation, etc.). The content validity of the scale seems below average at best.

Comments. A good deal of work would be required in order to use the scale with confidence. Evidence of reliability is lacking; evidence of validity is unimpressive; and no equivalent form is available. It would seem better to treat this as a battery of five separate attitude scales and to use some standard procedure to assess the value of the individual items. Several of the items in the multiple-choice section (items 3, 6, and 7) are informational rather than attitudinal. The fact that the last four items in the test are only for businessmen and merchants reduces the generality of use for that section of the scale. Finally, the scoring procedure changes from one type of item to the next, making combination of the scores difficult or impossible and calling into question the meaning of the scores derived. The principal reason for including this scale was to make available the item pool.

EXHIBIT 10-5

ATTITUDES RELATING TO THE STATE HOSPITAL

Please read each item very carefully. Answer by circling either *yes, no,* or *don't know* (dk). Try to always answer with *yes* or *no,* even if you have to guess. Only when you absolutely cannot say *yes* or *no,* circle *don't know* (dk). Check very carefully to be sure you have answered *every* item. Unless *every* item is answered, we will be unable to use the questionnaire.

S †1 When you have visitors, do you ever take them out and show them the State Hospital?
yes no dk

† The same response alternatives are used with all items.

Reference: S. Pratt, D. Giannitrapani, and P. Khanna. Attitudes toward the mental hospital and selected population characteristics. *J. clin. Psychol.,* **1960, 16, 214–218. Items obtained from the authors and published with their permission.**

E	*2	Do you feel that Hospital people buy a lot of merchandise out of town?
P	3	Do Hospital employees take sufficient interest in community politics and affairs?
C	*4	As a resident of this area, do you wish that Larned didn't have a state mental hospital on its outskirts?
S	*5	Do you dislike the fact that the State Hospital employs many foreigners?
E	6	Do you feel that in general local businesses should offer charge account service to the lower paid employees at the State Hospital?
P	7	Should the people who work at the Hospital have use of the city auditorium, swimming pool, and other municipal facilities just as townspeople do?
C	8	Should the Hospital staff spend some of their time and energy in giving their services to the schools of Larned?
S	*9	Do you think most of the people who work at the State Hospital took the job because it was a soft touch?
IE	10	Assuming that you were going to hire someone for a job or to do some work, would you hire a qualified patient even though he had a "criminal charge" against him?
P	11	Should Hospital people be allowed to serve on the city council?
C	12	In time of emergency or epidemic, if the city hospitals were full, would you be in favor of sending patients out to the State Hospital rather than to a general hospital in another city?
S	*13	Do you think people who work at the mental hospital are more likely to become a little "odd" or mentally ill?
E	*14	If you had rental property would you rather rent to a person who did not work at the Hospital instead of someone who did work at the Hospital?
P	15	Do you think the townspeople have enough to say about how the Hospital is run?
C	*16	Should the name of **Larned** State Hospital be changed simply to State Hospital?
S	*17	Do you think some Hospital people look down on Larned and the people of Larned?
E	*18	Do you feel that the Hospital provides its employees with facilities or services that they should be purchasing in town?
C	19	Do you think the Hospital should provide more opportunity for townspeople to visit the Hospital?
C	*20	Do people in Larned hear too much about mental illness?
E	*21	Do you think that if there were someone whom no one in Larned would consider hiring, he could always get a job at the State Hospital?
C	22	Would you be interested in attending movies on mental health that are shown at the Hospital if these were open to the public?
C	23	Would you be interested in joining a community mental health association?
C	24	Should the State Hospital take care of the aged rather than have a county "old folks home" take them?
E	25	Do you feel that in general local businesses should offer charge account services to the professional people who work at the State Hospital?

* These items are negative and their weights must be reversed for purposes of scoring.

C, I, S, P, E: These letters indicate that the item in question pertains to the following attitudes: C—Clinical Attitudes, I—Attitudes toward Criminally Insane Patients, S—Social Attitudes, P—Political Attitudes, E—Economic Attitudes. Thus, scores for all C items should be summed, etc.

P	26	Do you think employees who live at the Hospital should be allowed to vote in local elections?
C	27	Should more of the staff at the Hospital give lectures on mental health in the community?
S	28	Do you think the foreign staff members should do more to tell townspeople about the countries from which they come?
E	29	Do you think that qualified patients should be paid the same wage that anyone else would receive for work that they do in town?
P	30	Should the police force of Larned have jurisdiction and authority at the State Hospital?
C	31	Should outpatient services for children and adults be available **in town** rather than at the Hospital?
P	32	Do most Hospital people consider Larned to be "their town" and take enough interest in it?
E	33	In hiring employees, should the State Hospital give preference to local people as opposed to outsiders if both are equally qualified?
P	34	Do you think that in general the new labor union at the State Hospital is a good thing?
C	*35	Has the State Hospital given the town a bad name?
S	36	Would you welcome more Hospital employees as members of your club?
S	*37	Do you think the Hospital hires too many non-white people? (South American, Indian, Chinese, Negro, etc.)
I	*38	Would you prefer to have the "criminally insane" kept at some other State Hospital?
C	*39	Should the people of the town be alerted when **any** patient escapes?
S	40	Do you think townspeople should be encouraged to attend employees' dances and social activities at the Hospital?
E	41	Do you feel that the Hospital bus should also pick up townspeople?
I	*42	Should a loud siren be blown in town when a "criminally insane" patient escapes?
E	43	Should the Hospital hire people who do poorly on psychological tests?
C	44	Should the local newspaper have a regular column which informs townspeople of what is happening at the State Hospital?
SE	*45	Have you ever had any unpleasant social experiences with Hospital employees?
C	46	Should local people who are suffering from mental illness be given priority over outsiders in accepting them as patients at the Hospital?

PLEASE ANSWER THE FOLLOWING SEVEN QUESTIONS BY *CHECKING*, AS INDICATED FOR EACH ITEM. NOTICE THAT SOME ARE TO BE ANSWERED WITH ONLY *ONE* CHECK, OTHERS MAY BE *AS MANY* CHECKS AS YOU WISH. ANSWERS WILL SELDOM BE EXACT. GUESS OR CHOOSE WHAT "FITS BEST," BUT ALWAYS ANSWER.

1 How do you feel if a "criminally insane" patient escapes? Check only **one**:

(3) Slightly anxious	(1) Doesn't bother me
(5) Afraid for my children	(7) Terrified
(4) That I should lock all doors	(2) Curious
(6) Very worried	

( ) Number in parentheses beside the item alternatives indicates the rank order of favorability of the alternatives, 1 always being most favorable.

2 In general, what do you think the people who work at the Hospital are like? Check as **many** of the following as apply:

*Screwballs
Friendly
*Undesirable neighbors
Just plain folks
*Uncouth
Good neighbors
*Poorly dressed
Cheerful
*Irreligious
*Untrustworthy
Polite
*Drink too much
Hard working
*Bargain hunters
*Unfriendly
Intelligent
*Neurotic

S 3 Of the people working at the Hospital, I would most want to be friends with: Check **as many** as apply.

Secretaries_______
Doctors_______
Attendants or aides_______
Psychologists_______
Plumbers and carpenters____
Bookkeepers_______
Nurses_______
Occupational therapists_______
Cooks_______
Top administrative personnel_______
Laundry workers_______
Social workers_______

E 4 What do you think about working at the State Hospital? Check **as many** as apply:

*Wouldn't want to work there_______
Often thought about working there_______
*Rather be caught dead____
Fine if I could get a good paying job_______
*If no other job is available_______
Good as an additional job_______

CE 5 For which of the following would you hire a qualified patient? Check **as many** as apply:

(1) Baby sitting_______
(4) Housework_______
(5) Garden & yard work____
(9) Only for work that could be done at the hospital
(3) Cooking_______
(2) Practical nurse_______
(6) Auto repair_______
(8) Farm work_______
(7) Watch repair_______
(10) None of these_______

E 6 Of all the people living in Larned who are gainfully employed, what percentage of them would you estimate (or guess) are employed at the State Hospital? Check only **one**.

75% 5% 50% 10% 30%
20%

E 7 Which of the following amounts would you estimate (or guess) is the closest to the total **yearly** payroll at the State Hospital? Check only **one.**

Six million dollars_______
One million_______
One hundred thousand____
Two million_______
Three million_______
Five hundred thousand_______

THESE FOUR ITEMS TO BE ANSWERED BY MERCHANTS AND BUSINESSMEN ONLY

E *1 Have you had more unfortunate business experiences with State Hospital employees than with other people? YES NO DK (Answer by circling)

E 2 Do you feel that you are getting a good share of the trade with Hospital employees? YES NO DK

E 3 If the State of Kansas were to move Larned State Hospital out of this territory, would this seriously affect your business? YES NO DK

E 4 If a patient were fully qualified for work, would you employ him in your establishment? YES NO DK

Counseling attitude scale EXHIBIT 10-6

Description. This 22-item scale was developed by Form (1955), using Edwards and Kilpatrick's scale discrimination method. In the construction of the scale, 120 items were sorted by 80 judges, and items having Q values of more than 1.71 (the median Q value of the 120 items) were rejected. Items were then given to 200 students, using a Likert response continuum, and an item analysis was performed. The 22 items with the highest phi coefficients were selected for the test.

Subjects. The samples included 80 unidentified judges and 200 unidentified students.

Response Mode. Subjects respond by circling one of five alternatives for each item: strongly agree, agree, undecided, disagree, and strongly disagree.

Scoring. Response alternatives are weighted from 5 (strongly agree) to 1 (strongly disagree) for positive items. Weights are reversed for negative items. The person's score is the sum of the weighted alternatives endorsed. High scores reflect positive attitudes. Direction of the items is shown in Exhibit 10-6.

Reliability. The authors report a split-half reliability of .94, based upon a third sample of 544 students selected by a stratified random-sampling technique. These 544 students represent 90 percent of the original 605 students to whom the scale was mailed.

Validity. The scale was submitted to a Guttman procedure, scoring 0 for the responses "agree," "strongly agree," and "uncertain," and 1 for "disagree" and "strongly disagree." A coefficient of reproducibility of .87 was derived, making it a quasi-scale. The theoretical range of scores is 0 to 22. The intensity function for the scale indicates that the 0 range is between 7 and 8 when scored in this way.

Comments. There are a number of theoretical bases on which to expect that combination of the Thurstone and Likert procedures (as in the scale discrimination technique) is unfeasible. One expected result of such combination is that the nonmonotonic items which would be selected by a Thurstone scaling procedure would not correlate well with total score. This expectation seems to have been fulfilled by the somewhat low phi coefficients obtained in the item analysis on these items. Nevertheless, the authors have expended a great deal of energy in the construction of the scale and have provided much more information regarding it than is usually provided in reports of scale construction. In view of this, it would seem valuable as a research instrument. Users of the scale should not expect that it will necessarily discriminate in the middle range.

EXHIBIT 10-6

COUNSELING ATTITUDE SCALE

We are interested in your feelings about the following statements concerning the Counseling Center at __________. Read each statement carefully and decide how you feel about it. *PLEASE respond to each item whether or not you have had direct experience with the Counseling Center.*

If you strongly agree, encircle **SA**
If you agree, encircle **A**
If you are undecided or uncertain, encircle **?**
If you disagree, encircle **D**
If you strongly disagree, encircle **SD**

†1 I think the Counseling Center is a great asset to __________ College.

SA A ? D SD

*2 I feel the Counseling Center is highly inadequate to solve any kind of problem.
3 Sometimes the reassurance and guidance offered to wavering students by the Counseling Center is helpful in straightening them out.
*4 The Counseling Center's efforts to help students are impractical and inefficient.
5 I believe the Counseling Center is helpful in assisting students with their problems.
6 Talks with counselors at the Center are tension releasing if nothing else.
*7 It is a complete waste of time to go to the Counseling Center.
8 I feel the Counseling Center can be helpful to students needing counseling if they properly use its service.
9 I regard the Counseling Center a very efficient and necessary part of the college.
*10 I feel that I can **not** trust anyone at the Counseling Center to help me.

† The same response alternatives are used with all items.
* These items are negative and their weights must be reversed for purposes of scoring.

11 I regard the Counseling Center a purposeful organization that is serving people with problems of adjustment.
*12 The Counseling Center is **not** effective in helping No-Preference students.
*13 I believe the Counseling Center does **not** adequately interpret test results.
*14 The Counseling Center is a poor excuse for a clinic where students may take their problems.
15 I believe the Counseling Center is a good device for advising students with their problems.
*16 The Counseling Center is of **no** direct help to students. One finds nothing he didn't already know by going there.
17 I think more students should take advantage of the services the Counseling Center offers.
18 I believe the tests used by the Counseling Center are worthwhile taking.
*19 I believe the Counseling Center is simply **not** interested in students or their problems.
20 I recommend the services of the Counseling Center to all who need help.
21 I feel that our Counseling Center does enough good work to warrant its existence.
*22 There is a complete lack of organization at the Counseling Center—one always gets the run around.

ATTITUDES TOWARD LEGAL INSTITUTIONS

There is only one scale in this section, and it measures attitudes toward legal agencies. These include attitudes toward detention homes, the Boys' Industrial School, and the juvenile court. Some of these referents border upon being social issues. Persons interested in these referents from that point of view should see Chapter 4.

Attitudes toward legal agencies *EXHIBIT 10-7*

Description. This is a Likert-type test developed by Chapman (1960) to measure attitudes toward various legal agencies. It might best be considered a set of scales to measure attitudes toward the following referents: attitudes toward the juvenile court (17 items), toward detention (16 items), and toward the Boys' Industrial School (16 items). Scales in this battery measuring attitudes toward the police and probation officers may be found in Chapter 9. Items are grouped in Exhibit 10-7 according to their referents, but the original number of the item in the scale is retained.

Subjects. The sample consisted of 133 delinquent Caucasian boys (on probation) and 133 nondelinquent Caucasian boys. The two groups were matched for age, number of years completed in school, intelligence, occupation of father, and residence. Subjects ranged from ages 13 to 18, with an average age of approximately 15 years.

Response Mode. Subjects respond by checking one of five alternatives to each item: strongly agree, agree, undecided, disagree, and strongly disagree.

Scoring. The scale is scored by summing the weighted responses for the items; the most socially acceptable or favorable response is weighted 5, and the most unacceptable response is weighted 1. Direction of the items is indicated in Exhibit 10-7. High scores reflect favorable attitudes.

Reliability. The author reports the following test-retest reliability coefficients: .85 for the juvenile court scale, .98 for the detention scale. He also reports split-half reliabilities (corrected) ranging from .92 for the probation scale to .98 for the detention scale. The reliability for the entire test is reported by him as being .91.

Validity. The fact that the items were selected from a total item pool of 250 items should provide a degree of content validity. The author selected only those items having critical ratios of 2.0 or more, indicating that they will discriminate between high and low scorers. Furthermore, that they were found to differentiate between nondelinquents and delinquents who had been to a boys' industrial school.

Comments. This is a satisfactorily valid and reliable set of scales measuring attitudes toward a number of legal agencies handling juvenile delinquents. Although developed using a sample of boys, most of the items are so phrased that they could be used with adult samples as well. This scale should function well as a research instrument.

EXHIBIT 10-7

ATTITUDES TOWARD LEGAL AGENCIES

The following pages contain a number of statements about which all boys don't feel the same way. Boys differ a great deal in the way they feel about each statement. There is no such thing as right and wrong answers. We would like to have your honest opinion about each of the statements. They will help many boys in the United States.

Read each statement carefully and then place an *X* in the space which expresses the way you feel about the statement. Wherever possible, let the things which have happened to you help you make a choice. Be sure to answer each statement.

Items Referring to the Juvenile Court

†2 The Juvenile Court Judge is just like a father to boys.
Strongly Agree Agree Undecided Disagree Strongly Disagree

7 Boys would rather do what the Juvenile Court Judge says more than anyone else they know.

*12 There is little chance of fair treatment in the juvenile court unless you have pull.

*17 It's hard for a boy to get a square deal in the juvenile court.

† The same response alternatives are used with all items.

* Agreement with these items is considered socially less acceptable and the weights must be reversed for purposes of scoring.

Reference: A. W. Chapman. Attitudes toward legal agencies of authority for juveniles. A comparative study of one-hundred-thirty-three delinquent and one-hundred-thirty-three nondelinquent boys in Dayton, Ohio. *Dissert. Abstr.*, 1960, 20, No. 7. Items obtained from author and published with his permission.

*22 The juvenile court is too hard on boys for little things.
*27 Older boys would rather go to the criminal court than to the juvenile court.
32 The Juvenile Court Judge gives a boy better advice than preachers.
37 If a boy tells the truth in the juvenile court the Judge won't be too hard on him.
42 Poor boys are treated the same as other boys in the juvenile court.
47 The adult workers in the juvenile court are very kind.
52 The juvenile court is very helpful in showing a boy the right way to act.
*57 Boys don't believe that the juvenile court should make them pay for stolen goods.
62 Bad boys ought to be sent to the criminal courts rather than the juvenile court.
67 Many boys would like to go to the juvenile court to see what goes on.
*72 Almost anything can be fixed in the juvenile court.
*82 The juvenile court sends boys to the Boys' Industrial School for little things.
*85 The judge in the juvenile court has too much power over boys.

Items Referring to Detention

4 Boys believe that the detention home can do a lot to change them.
9 The detention home is a good place for boys.
*14 Boys would rather stay in school for a year than to spend a few days in the detention home.
*19 Boys who go to the detention home don't have a chance to make good in life.
24 The detention home is just like the home of a large family.
*29 Older boys would rather go to jail than to the detention home.
*34 The detention home is a place for tough boys.
*39 The adults in the detention home put too many boys in the same room.
*44 Most boys are afraid of going to the detention home.
49 The detention home is just like a playground.
*54 Boys will do anything to stay out of the detention home.
*59 The detention home is just like a jail.
*64 The detention home is a place for "sissy boys."
*69 The detention home should be done away with.
*74 The adults in charge of the detention home are too soft on boys.
79 A boy learns a lot of good things while in the detention home.

Items Referring to the Boys' Industrial School

*5 Most boys are afraid of being sent to the Boys' Industrial School.
*10 Boys don't believe that the Boys' Industrial School can do anything to change them.
*15 Boys believe that there is little good in the Boys' Industrial School.
*20 Going to the Boys' Industrial School makes you a "big shot" among boys.
*25 Boys wouldn't mind going to the Boys' Industrial School if other boys didn't know about it.
30 Parole officers should visit boys more after they return from the Boys' Industrial School.
35 Boys don't believe that the Boys' Industrial School will do a boy any harm.
40 The Boys' Industrial School is just like the school to which I go.
45 Boys are much better when they return from the Boys' Industrial School.
50 Boys who have been to the Boys' Industrial School will stay out of trouble.
55 A boy who has been to the Boys' Industrial School knows how to make a living.
*60 Most of the adults in the Boys' Industrial School are mean to boys.

*65 Many boys believe that the Boys' Industrial School is the worst place in the world.
*70 Many boys would rather go to the work house than to the Boys' Industrial School.
*75 Boys who have been to the Boys' Industrial School are the worst boys in town.
*80 Boys who have been to the Boys' Industrial School usually continue in crime.

ATTITUDES RELATED TO ECONOMIC INSTITUTIONS

This section contains those scales measuring attitudes which have as their referents such economic institutions as unions, labor, management, and the company. One scale measuring attitude toward newspapers was included in this section for want of a better place to put it.

Attitude toward labor scale *EXHIBIT 10-8*

Description. This 16-item scale was developed by Newcomb (1939) to measure attitudes toward labor. The items are composed of pairs of statements relevant to the topic issue. Newcomb rejected the Likert and Thurstone procedures for scaling on the basis that they were inappropriate for the purposes of his study. It is to be noted that items 6, 8, and 12 are somewhat, although probably not seriously, dated. However, item 15 is seriously dated and probably should be discarded.

Subjects. Samples consisted of 680 members of the CIO and AFL, and nonaffiliated painters, longshoremen, and similar groups.

Response Mode. Subjects mark an X beside the statement with which they agree in each pair of statements. They mark a double X if they strongly agree (XX). No neutral alternative is provided.

Scoring. That item in each pair which conforms most closely to the central theme of workers as a potentially dominant class is scored 1 if marked with a single X, and 0 if marked with a double X. The other alternative is scored 3 for a single X, and 4 for a double X. The score is the sum of the weights of the alternatives endorsed. High scores reflect unfavorable attitudes toward the general notion of workers as a potentially dominant class.

Reliability. Newcomb (1939) reported split-half correlations (corrected) ranging from .55 to .94 for various samples, the average correlation being .906.

Validity. Proshansky (1943) reported correlations of .87 and .67 between scores on this test and scores on projective techniques, based upon a sample of 35 students chosen because of their strong feelings concerning labor. Newcomb (1939) stated that the scale differentiated between known groups. An internal consistency check was run to ensure that items were discriminating in the direction in which they were being scored.

Comments. The scale is somewhat dated but seems satisfactory for measuring attitudes toward labor if item 15 is dropped. However, there are other scales available in this chapter which might be preferred for general use.

EXHIBIT 10-8

ATTITUDE TOWARD LABOR SCALE

Everyone is interested these days in the question of labor unions. But no one is sure just what union members themselves think about some of their problems. This is an attempt to find out what you think about some of them. You will enjoy the experience.

There aren't any right or wrong answers to these questions. In fact, there aren't any questions to be answered. Below you will find some statements, and you will probably AGREE with some of them and DISAGREE with some of them.

DIRECTIONS: The statements are arranged in PAIRS. All you are asked to do is to CHOOSE ONE statement of each pair. CHOOSE THE ONE THAT YOU AGREE WITH MOST CLOSELY, AND PUT A CROSS-MARK IN FRONT OF IT. If you STRONGLY AGREE with it, then put TWO cross-marks in front of it. You may not entirely agree with either of them, but be sure to put at least one cross-mark in front of ONE statement out of each pair. Don't omit any.

(1) a. Labor unions should be concerned only with such matters as wages, working conditions, hiring and firing, etc.
*b. Labor unions can't get and keep good wages and working conditions unless they help elect public officials who are sympathetic to them.

(2) a. Anyone who is smart enough to become wealthy should be allowed to enjoy his wealth himself.
*b. People who are very wealthy are almost sure to use their power in ways which will keep working people down.

(3) *a. The main reason why workers are not better off is that labor unions don't have as much influence in political circles as employers and businessmen do.
b. On the whole, national, state, and city governments are run for the best interests of every group of people represented.

(4) a. It is the workers' business to work in a plant, and the owners' business to manage it, and both sides should stick to their business.
*b. Workers are affected more directly than owners are by what happens in a plant and so workers should try to become powerful enough to help decide how the plant should be managed.

* Score these alternatives 0 or 1 when the subject marks them as XX or X respectively. The other alternatives are scored 3 or 4 when marked as X or XX respectively.

(5) *a. I believe in the idea of majority rule. Workers are a majority in this country, and so if they all would join unions they would have the right to have control of the government.

b. If workers are fair in their demands, their unions can get a fair deal for them without the trouble of trying to use their influence in government.

(6) *a. If union demands can be won without bloodshed by sit-down strikes, as in the case of the General Motors strike in 1937, then I can't see much objection to the sit-down.

b. Unions can get farther in the long run if they don't use methods like the sit-down strike which are probably illegal.

(7) a. Talk about the working class as opposed to the owning class is foolish, because both classes suffer or prosper together.

*b. People who talk about workers and owners really having the same interests are usually afraid that labor unions will become strong enough to cut down the owners' profits.

(8) *a. A good many strikes are broken because police and militia are controlled by officials who sympathize with employers more than they do with labor unions.

b. When police or militia interfere in strikes, it is usually in the public interest and not because officials want to favor employers.

(9) *a. The majority of people in this country would be better off if we had a strong Farmer-Labor party to compete with the other political parties.

b. Workers can get all the political representation they need by electing Republicans or Democrats who favor labor unions.

(10) a. Skilled workers can get along better by playing ball with employers than they can by tying themselves up with unions which include ignorant, unskilled workers.

*b. The main reason why labor unions haven't got farther in this country is that skilled workers considered themselves above unskilled workers, and so unions remained small and powerless.

(11) *a. A worker's right to his job should be considered more important than an investor's right to his profits, because a worker usually has nothing else but his job to fall back upon.

b. Labor unions might as well admit that an employer's first responsibility is to the owners, and do the best they can on that basis.

(12) *a. The Wagner Act (concerning labor relations) was intended to favor labor unions, because it was recognized that unions didn't have a fair chance before that.

b. Labor unions would get more respect from the public if they admitted that the Wagner Act is unfair to employers and tried to get it changed.

(13) a. Almost any one who has brains and is willing to work hard can expect to rise to a position of moderate wealth and influence.

*b. Intelligence and hard work won't get you very far nowadays unless you have the backing of a powerful group.

(14) *a. It's hard to see how organized labor can have much influence on government if it doesn't include the millions of unskilled workers.
b. Labor unions can put all the pressure on government that they need to by clever lobbying, and so they don't need to include millions of unskilled workers.

(15) *a. Labor unions should welcome Republicans, Democrats, Socialists, and Communists alike, if they are honestly trying to do all they can for the union.
b. Labor unions should throw out all Communists, no matter how much they are helping, because they give the union the reputation of being radical.

(16) a. Most people disapprove of sit-down strikes because no one ever has a right to take control of other people's property.
*b. Most people who object to sit-down strikes don't like them just because they have been very useful in helping workers to win their rights.

IRC (Industrial Relations Center) union attitude questionnaire EXHIBIT 10-9

Description. This 77-item scale was developed by the University of Minnesota Industrial Relations Center and reported by Uphoff and Dunnette (1956). It measures attitudes in the following areas: unionism in general (items 1 through 20), local union in general (items 21 through 27), local union policies and practices (items 28 through 36), local union officers (items 37 through 48), local union administration (items 49 through 56), and national union (items 57 through 64). Items 65 through 77 are referred to as diagnostic items. To construct the scale, 121 items were given to 821 union members belonging to nine union groups. These data were used to perform item analyses which resulted in revision of the scale. The items of the scale were then regrouped into seven subscales on the basis of expert judgment: 10 IRC staff members sorted the items into one of seven categories on the basis of face validity, and a consensus of seven judges was accepted as evidence of proper placement on the item. Items on which six or fewer judges agreed were placed in an indeterminate category. The authors then subjected the items to an item analysis using the scale value difference technique. On the basis of this latter analysis, 64 items were assigned to six categories, and 13 items were retained as diagnostic items, even though they did not meet the requirements of the scale value difference technique. The resulting 77 items are shown in Exhibit 10-9.

Subjects. Samples included 821 members of nine union groups and 1,251 union members from 13 union groups (these groups representing about 14,000 union workers).

Response Mode. Subjects respond by choosing one of five alternative responses to each item: strongly agree, agree, undecided, disagree, and strongly disagree.

Scoring. The authors used two methods for scoring: The first was the standard Likert procedure whereby for positive statements responses are given the weights 0 (strongly disagree) through 4 (strongly agree), and the score is the sum of the weighted responses to the items. In this procedure, the weighting is reversed for negative items which are indicated in Exhibit 10-9. The second procedure used by the authors was that of assessing the percentage of union members giving favorable, undecided, and unfavorable responses to each item. The authors provide norms for the individual items in terms of percentage of endorsement.

Reliability. Uphoff and Dunnette (1956) reported the following split-half reliability coefficients (corrected) for the several subscales: unionism in general, .89; local union in general, .75; local union policies and practices, .75; local union officers, .90; local union administration, .79; national union, .84. Reliability coefficients for the six subscales using the Hoyt method are as follows: unionism in general, .87; local union in general, .71; local union policies and practices, .72; local union officers, .88; local union administration, .83; national union, .85. The split-half and Hoyt reliabilities for the six scales combined are .96 and .96, respectively.

Validity. The validity of the scale was assessed in two ways: First, the items have content validity, and, second, scores on the scale and on the subscales were found to discriminate known groups. The groups compared in the validational study included union members versus nonmembers, persons giving different reasons for joining the union, persons attending more or fewer union meetings, and present officers of the union versus past officers versus nonofficers. On the basis of these analyses (Uphoff and Dunnette, 1956, pp. 13–17), the scale and its subscales were considered valid.

Comments. This is a relatively valid and reliable instrument for assessing the attitudes of union members toward various facets of unions. However, the phrasing of the questions restricts its use to samples of union members; one should not expect to use it with samples from the general population.

EXHIBIT 10-9

IRC (Industrial Relations Center) UNION ATTITUDE QUESTIONNAIRE*

1 If it were not for unions, we'd have little protection against favoritism on the job.

Strongly agree   Agree   Undecided   Disagree   Strongly Disagree

†2 I think the best man should be kept on the job regardless of seniority.
†3 Unions impose too many restrictions on employers.
4 Charges of "racketeering" in unions are greatly exaggerated.
5 Employees of a firm have better wages and working conditions when all of them belong to unions.

* No specific instructions were used by the authors. However, Likert-type instructions and response mode should work satisfactorily with the scale. The same response alternatives are used with all items.
† These are negative items and their weights must be reversed for purposes of scoring.

6 Unions should have something to say about whom the employer hires.
7 A nonunion shop usually pays lower wages than a union shop.
†8 Union rules often interfere with the efficient running of the employer's business.
9 Every worker should be expected to join the union where he works.
†10 We need more laws to limit the power of labor unions.
†11 Labor unions hold back progress.
†12 The high wage demands of unions reduce chances for employment.
13 The growth of unions has made our democracy stronger.
14 The selfishness of employers can be fought only by strong unions.
†15 Workers should not have to join a union in order to hold a job.
†16 Labor unions should be regulated to a greater extent by the federal government.
†17 Every labor union should be required to take out a license from the U.S. government.
18 In a factory where there is a union, workers who are not members should be required to pay the regular union fees if they are getting union rates of pay.
†19 Most unions gain their membership by forcing workers to join by threats of violence.
20 If the majority of workers in a plant vote to have a union, the others should be required to join.
21 There isn't a better union than the one I belong to.
22 In case of a strike, I'm sure we'd stick together.
23 Every union member should attend at least two out of three of his local union meetings.
24 My union makes new members feel that it is worth while for them to belong.
25 My union is quick to defend any member who doesn't get a fair deal from his boss.
†26 The initiation fees for my local are too high.
†27 My union is not spending enough time telling members about what it is doing.
†28 My union is of no help when it comes to job transfer.
29 My union sees to it that overtime is given out fairly.
30 My union looks after labor's interests in the city council and the state legislature.
31 Our union dues are too low.
†32 There is not much "rhyme or reason" to the way our union votes to contribute to the various appeals for money that come to it.
†33 We give our delegates too much money to spend when they go to conventions.
34 My union doesn't show favoritism between members when it comes to settling grievances.
35 Nearly everyone in our union knows what to do when he has a grievance complaint.
36 Fines should be levied for not attending union meetings.
37 The local officers of my union are doing a good job.
38 Our officers are up-to-date on bargaining on fringe issues such as pensions, health plans, etc.
39 I feel free to discuss my personal problems with my union committeeman (or steward).
40 I like the way my business agent handles our union affairs.
41 My steward (or business agent) is firm in dealing with management.
42 My union officers see to it that all reported grievances are promptly settled.
43 Our officers usually welcome suggestions from members.
44 Officers of my union are chosen because they are real leaders.

45 Our union officers know how to get the members to do things for the union.
†46 I think the president of my union is too easy going when it comes to keeping order at meetings.
47 Our union officers keep us informed about what they are doing.
48 Our union officers get word to us promptly when something important comes up.
49 Our union meetings are run in an efficient manner.
50 Our union meetings are over at a reasonable time.
51 There is enough discussion on motions to show what the membership really thinks.
†52 Our union meetings are dull and uninteresting.
53 We have a well-planned "order of business" at our meetings.
†54 Our union president lets a few who like to talk take too much time at meetings.
55 A member who attends our union meetings gets the feeling that he is free to speak on any issue.
56 We have enough chance to give our ideas before the bargaining committee begins negotiations with the employer.
†57 The officers of my national union are paid too much.
†58 So much of our union policy is set by our national union that there is not much point in going to our local union meetings.
†59 It is practically impossible to elect different officers in our national union.
†60 Our national union exercises too much control over the affairs of our local.
†61 Our national union takes its share of our dues but gives us very little help.
†62 Our national union interferes too much in our local affairs.
†63 We don't get enough help for our union educational program from the national union.
64 Our national union provides the necessary facts and helps at negotiation time.
65 The paid officers of my local are worth the money we pay them.
66 I regard my union dues as a good investment.
67 My union got a "good deal" for me when the last contract was signed.
†68 My union does not keep careful enough records of all money taken in and spent.
†69 My union spends too much time and money on political action.
†70 My union officers spend too much time on things that are of no concern to my union.
71 If you read it in the union paper, you know you are getting the facts.
†72 Our union paper gives us only one side of an issue.
†73 My union does not teach us enough labor history.
†74 I feel that too many things are already decided before the union meetings are held.
75 Stewards and committeemen in my union are the choice of the rank-and-file members.
†76 If you don't agree with the officers of our union, you might as well stay home.
†77 Labor unions should be required by law to make annual public reports of the money they collect and spend.

Scale for management attitude toward union EXHIBIT 10-10

Description. This 11-item, Guttman-type scale, along with the scale in Exhibit 10-11, was developed by Stagner, Chalmers, and Derber

(1958) to study the relations between attitudes of union personnel toward management personnel, and vice versa. Scale construction was carried out through presentation of items in interview rather than in written form.

Subjects. The sample consisted of 79 executives in 41 business establishments.

Response Mode. Subjects respond by checking one of four alternatives to each item. The nature of the alternatives varies from item to item, but includes such continua as "very reasonable" through "extremely unreasonable" and "not too much" through "far too much."

Scoring. The individual's score is derived by counting the number of favorable responses endorsed by him. The cutoff point for favorable responses is indicated in parentheses beside each item in Exhibit 10-10. The range of possible scores is 0 to 10. High scores indicate positive attitudes.

Reliability. No estimates of reliability are reported. However, the coefficient of reproducibility (.915) is high enough to allow for good split-half reliability.

Validity. The scale has content validity, although the content domain of Guttman scales is usually considered to be restricted. The coefficient of reproducibility of the scale is reported by the authors as being .915, indicating a true scale.

Comments. Because of the relativity of scales to the time and population for which they are constructed, items which did not scale in the study by Stagner et al. (1958) have been included in Exhibit 10-10. It is possible that they would be scalable items in a sample of management representatives other than those used in the present study. The use of this scale is largely restricted to samples of executives and management-level people. It is presently in need of reliability estimates and further studies of validity.

EXHIBIT 10-10

*SCALE FOR MANAGEMENT ATTITUDE TOWARD UNION**

1 Are the union officers effective leaders of their organization?
- (1) Very much so
- (2) Pretty good
- (3) Mediocre
- (4) Very Poor (2.5)†

* Derber (private communication, 1965) states that the main instructions were by example and oral discussion rather than in writing. However, instructions from any Guttman-type scale should suffice for this scale.

† Numbers in parentheses indicate the cutoff point for favorable responses. If the alternative number chosen is as small or smaller than the number in parentheses, the person receives one point credit for its endorsement. Please note that item 10 is to be combined with item 11; if the total of alternatives endorsed for them is equal to 3 or less, the person receives one point credit.

2 Is the union generally reasonable or not in its claims?
(1) Very reasonable
(2) Reasonable most of the time
(3) Frequently unreasonable
(4) Extremely unreasonable (2.5)†

3 Does the union interfere seriously with how the company is managed, or does the management have a reasonably free hand in running the plant?
(1) Union is no problem
(2) It interferes a little but not seriously
(3) It interferes quite often
(4) It seriously interferes with management (2.0)†

4 Are the union officers interested in the welfare of the rank-and-file workers?
(1) Very much so
(2) Pretty much
(3) Slightly
(4) Very little (2.0)†

5 Does the union cooperate with management on production matters or not?
(1) They are extremely cooperative
(2) They will go along but not positively support
(3) They do not interfere seriously but sometimes are obstructionist
(4) They restrict production improvements quite often (2.5)†

6 In general, how do you personally feel about your company's relations with the union?
(1) Very satisfied
(2) Moderately satisfied
(3) Moderately dissatisfied
(4) Very dissatisfied (2.0)†

7 Has the union tended to weaken employee discipline, or has it cooperated with management on disciplinary matters?
(1) Cooperative and helpful
(2) Sometimes helps but not always
(3) Sometimes interferes with discipline
(4) Has created some serious disciplinary problems (2.5)†

8 Does the union have too much power in your establishment?
(1) Not too much
(2) Too much in a few respects
(3) Too much in many respects
(4) Far too much (1.5)†

9 Does the union have the support of the workers?
(1) Most of the workers are strongly behind it
(2) Only a few really active people but most workers go along
(3) Not too much feeling either way
(4) A lot of the workers are hostile (1.0)†

10 How do you feel about using the union as the main channel of communication to the workers on company policies?
(1) Strongly favor
(2) Moderately favor

(3) Moderately oppose
(4) Strongly oppose (Combine with 11)†

11 Are the local union officers skillful bargainers?
(1) Very much so
(2) Pretty good
(3) Mediocre
(4) Very poor (Favorable if 10 + 11 = 3 or less)†

The following items did not scale:

Are the international union representatives skillful bargainers?
(1) Very much so
(2) Pretty good
(3) Mediocre
(4) Very poor
(5) None are involved

Do the international union officers create any serious problems or not?
(1) They are generally responsible and helpful
(2) They are more helpful than troublesome
(3) They are more troublesome than helpful
(4) They generally stir up trouble
(5) None are involved

Does the union try to live up to its agreements?
(1) Always
(2) Usually
(3) Frequently does not
(4) Rarely

Scale for union attitude toward management *EXHIBIT 10-11*

Description. This nine-item, Guttman-type scale is the second of the two scales developed by Stagner et al. (1958). The first scale (Scale for Management Attitude Toward Union) is given in the paragraph above. This scale was constructed in the same manner as the above scale.

Subjects. The sample consisted of 81 union officials in 41 business establishments.

Response Mode. Subjects respond by checking one of four alternatives to each item. The nature of the alternatives varies from item to item, but includes such continua as "always" through "rarely," and "very satisfied" through "very dissatisfied."

Scoring. The individual's score is derived by counting the number of favorable responses endorsed by him. High scores indicate positive attitudes. The cutoff point for favorable responses is indicated in parentheses beside each item in Exhibit 10-11. The range of possible scores is from 0 to 9.

Reliability. No estimates of reliability are available for this scale.

Validity. Regarding content validity, Guttman scales are considered to be restricted in sampling of the content domain; this criticism seems to apply to this scale also. The authors report a reproducibility coefficient of .905, indicating a true scale and reflecting unidimensionality in the scale.

Comments. Just as the previous scale (Exhibit 10-10) was restricted in use to samples of management personnel, this scale is restricted to samples of union officials. Also, items which did not scale in the study cited (Stagner et al., 1958) have been included in Exhibit 10-11. Because of the relativity of the scalability of any pool of items, it is possible that these items would scale in use with a different sample of union officials. This seems a valid and unidimensional scale, but its value would be enhanced by some estimates of reliability.

EXHIBIT 10-11

*SCALE FOR UNION ATTITUDE TOWARD MANAGEMENT**

1 Are the top management officials effective executives of the establishment?
(1) very much so
(2) pretty good
(3) mediocre
(4) very poor (2.0)†

2 What is the top management attitude toward the union?
(1) strongly favorable
(2) moderately favorable
(3) moderately unfavorable
(4) strongly unfavorable (2.0)†

3 Does the company try to live up to its agreements?
(1) always
(2) usually
(3) frequently does not
(4) rarely (2.0)†

4 Does the company abuse its power in this establishment?
(1) rarely
(2) occasionally
(3) frequently
(4) very often (1.5)†

* Derber (private communication, 1965) states that the main instructions were by example and oral discussion rather than in writing. However, instructions from any Guttman-type scale should suffice for this scale.

† Numbers in parentheses indicate the cutoff point for favorable responses. If the alternative number chosen is as small or smaller than the number in parentheses, the person receives one point credit for its endorsement.

5 In general, how do you personally feel about your union's relations with the company?
(1) very satisfied
(2) moderately satisfied
(3) moderately dissatisfied
(4) very dissatisfied (2.0)†

6 Has the management shown any understanding of your problems as a union officer?
(1) very understanding
(2) understands the union situation pretty well
(3) understanding of union problems is limited
(4) little or no understanding of union problems (2.0)†

7 Has the management tried to undermine the union position through direct dealings with the workers, or has it been careful to safeguard the union position in such contacts?
(1) is always careful not to hurt union
(2) is usually careful not to hurt union
(3) occasionally tries to weaken union
(4) frequently tries to weaken union (2.0)†

8 Is the top management generally reasonable or not when it comes to discussing union claims?
(1) very reasonable
(2) reasonable most of the time
(3) frequently unreasonable
(4) extremely unreasonable (1.5)†

9 Are the top management officials interested in the welfare of the workers?
(1) very much so
(2) pretty much
(3) slightly
(4) very little (1.5)†

The following items did not scale:

Do the foremen, in general, act toward the union in the same way as top management?

(1) the foremen are very much easier to get along with
(2) the foremen are somewhat easier to get along with
(3) the foremen are about the same as top management
(4) the foremen are somewhat more difficult to get along with
(5) the foremen are much more difficult to get along with

Does middle management, in general, act toward the union in the same way as top management?

(1) the middle management are very much easier to get along with
(2) they are somewhat easier to get along with
(3) they are about the same as top management
(4) they are somewhat more difficult to get along with
(5) they are much more difficult to get along with

Are the top management officials skillful bargainers?

(1) very much so
(2) pretty good
(3) mediocre
(4) very poor

(If a multi-plant company with a home office outside this establishment) Are the company representatives from the home office skillful bargainers?

(1) very much so
(2) pretty good
(3) mediocre
(4) very poor
(5) not involved

(If a multi-plant company with a home office outside this establishment) Do company representatives from the home office create serious problems or not?

(1) they are generally responsible and helpful
(2) they are more helpful than troublesome
(3) they are more troublesome than helpful
(4) they generally stir up trouble
(5) not involved

About your company *EXHIBIT 10-12*

Description. This 20-item scale was originally a 33-item scale developed by Lawshe and refined by Storey (1955). These 20 dichotomously scored items were those remaining after two internal-consistency item analyses were made during the development of the scale. The first of these analyses was a Likert-type analysis for internal consistency based upon data from eight industrial plants (Storey, 1955). The second (King, 1960) was an analysis which was designed to select items which were internally consistent for both male and female respondents, based on 10 industrial plants. King (private communication, 1965) reported that the items were screened for communicability, maximum range of difficulty, brevity, and face validity. The 18 items shown in Exhibit 10-12 are those which survived both item analyses, and were reported by King (1960).

Subjects. The 33-item scale was mailed to 700 employees in 8 industrial plants (Storey, 1955). The median percent of usable returns was 45.5. The sample for the second analysis was 735 production employees in 10 industrial plants in 7 central Indiana cities (King, 1960). These persons varied in level of skilled occupation and type of industry in which they were employed (communications, electrical equipment manufacture, metal work, and ceramic work). Of the sample, 25 percent were women.

Response Mode. Persons respond to each item by marking one of two alternatives: yes or no.

Scoring. The score is the sum of the responses endorsed which reflect a positive orientation toward the company (i.e., the sum of the positive responses endorsed by "yes" and the negative items endorsed as "no." A high score reflects a favorable attitude toward the company.

Reliability. The split-half reliability (corrected) for the questionnaire is reported by Storey (1955) to be .92.

Validity. The items were screened for face validity, brevity, communicability, and maximum range of difficulty. The author also performed an internal-consistency check. Further, King (1960) reports that the items are all heavily loaded on a general factor which he interprets as representing the employees' general attitude or bias toward their company. They varied on their loadings on two other group factors of "respect for personal rights" and "opportunity for self-improvement."

Comments. This scale seems a valid and reliable method of assessing employee attitudes. Test-retest reliability estimates would enhance its value, as would equivalent forms. It also needs further validational studies. King (1960) reports the factor loadings of the specific items for those who are interested.

EXHIBIT 10-12

*ABOUT YOUR COMPANY**

†1 Would you say that the company is usually hardboiled and tough with its employees?

Yes No

2 Do you like to have your friends know where you work?

3 Considering everything about the company, are you fairly well satisfied with it?

†5 Do you think your company has more dissatisfied employees than most companies?

†8 Is there any other company around here where you would rather work?

10 If you were starting over again, would you probably go to work here?

12 Is there a friendly feeling in your company between the employees and management?

20 Would you say that your company is a better place to work than most around here?

†4 Does the company sometimes interfere with your personal rights?

†15 Does the company ever take advantage of the employees?

* No specific instructions were provided for this scale. However, any instructions which require the subject to indicate yes or no and to answer all questions should suffice.

† These items are negative; the person receives one point if he responds No to them. For all other items, the person receives one point if he answers Yes. The same response alternatives are used with all items.

Reprinted with permission from King, D. C. A multiplant factor analysis of employees' attitudes toward their company. *J. appl. Psychol.*, 1960, 44, 241–243. Copyright 1960 by The American Psychological Association, Washington, D.C.

6 Do the top people respect your rights as a person?
7 If you were in real trouble would you probably get a square deal from the people at the top?
9 Do you feel that the top men in the company are trying to do the right thing?
11 Do you have confidence in the business judgment of top management?
19 Do the people at the top pay enough attention to ambition and effort?
13 Do you think the company is really trying to improve relations with its employees?
14 Does management usually keep you informed about the things you want to know?
17 Does your company offer enough chance for self-improvement and learning?
16 Is your company a good one for a person trying to get ahead?
†18 Do employees usually have to fight for what they get in your company?

Scales to measure attitudes toward the company, its policies and its community contributions *EXHIBIT 10-13*

Description. This is a battery of three Guttman-type scales designed to measure general attitude toward the company (6 items), attitude toward the community contributions of the company (4 items), and attitude of the community toward the employee relations policies of the company (7 items). They were developed by Riland (1959) to study the attitudes of the members of a community toward a medium-sized local company.

Subjects. The sample consisted of 388 residents of a Pennsylvania community.

Response Mode. Persons check one of a set of alternative responses (either four or six alternatives) for each item. The content of these alternatives varies, but is of the order of "very good" to "very poor" and "strongly agree" to "strongly disagree."

Scoring. The alternatives for each item are treated as dichotomies and are weighted either 0 (negative replies) or 1 (positive replies) for Guttman-type scoring. For Likert-type scoring, the proper weight for each alternative is indicated beside the alternative in parentheses. In either case, the person's score is the sum of the weighted alternatives endorsed by him. A high score indicates a favorable attitude.

Reliability. No reliability estimates are reported by the author.

Validity. The author reports the following coefficients of reproducibility for the three scales: general attitude toward the company, .88 (a quasi-scale); attitude toward the community contributions of the company, .91 (a true scale); and attitude of the community toward the employee relations of the company, .92 (a true scale). The coefficients were all obtained upon the same 388 subjects, and are a reflection of the scale's unidimensionality or internal consistency. The content domain of the scales may be considered somewhat restricted.

Comments. These are useful scales which require further evidence regarding reliability and validity. The use of these scales requires the assumption that the items contained therein would be unidimensionally scalable for other populations as well as the one on which they were constructed, but this is the type of assumption generally demanded by an instrument developed and standardized on a population other than the one on which one intends to use it.

EXHIBIT 10-13

*SCALES TO MEASURE ATTITUDES TOWARD THE COMPANY, ITS POLICIES AND ITS COMMUNITY CONTRIBUTIONS**

General Attitude toward the Company:

1 How do you feel about employment at ____________Company in the future? Do you feel that:

(1) Considerably fewer people will probably be employed there.
(2) Somewhat fewer people will probably be employed there.
(3) Employment will probably remain the same.
†(4) A few more people will probably be employed there.
†(5) Quite a few more people will probably be employed there.
(0) Don't know.

2 If you were going to invest some money in a local company would you consider the ____________Company:

(1) A very poor investment
(2) A fairly poor investment
†(3) An average investment
†(4) A fairly good investment
†(5) A very good investment
(0) Don't know

3 How do you feel about this statement? "There are few companies in (the city) managed more successfully than the ____________Company." Do you:

†(5) Strongly agree
†(4) Agree
(2) Disagree
(1) Strongly disagree
†(3) Undecided
(0) Don't know

* No specific instructions were provided for this scale, as it was read to the respondents in a public opinion survey. However, instructions from any Guttman-type scale should prove feasible if the items are scored as dichotomies. If scored in a summated rating fashion, instructions of a Likert type should be used.

† These response alternatives are given a weight of 1 when endorsed. All other alternatives receive a weight of 0 when endorsed. The number in parentheses beside the response alternatives indicates the original Likert-type weight assigned the alternative.

Reference: L. H. Riland. Relationship of the Guttman components of attitude intensity and personal involvement. *J. appl. Psychol.*, 1959, 43, 279–284. Items obtained from author and published with his permission.

4 If you were telling a stranger about industries around here, would you mention the ____________Company in the first three best companies?

†(5) Yes
(1) No
†(3) Undecided
(0) Don't know

5 As companies go, do you feel that the ____________Company has kept up with other companies in **(the city)?** Do you feel they have:

†(5) Definitely kept up
†(4) Generally kept up
(2) Generally not kept up
(1) Definitely not kept up
†(3) Undecided
(0) Don't know

6 In your estimation, do you think the ____________Company is going downhill as a company? Would you say they are:

(1) Definitely going downhill
(2) Probably going downhill
†(4) Probably not going downhill
†(5) Definitely not going downhill
(3) Undecided
(0) Don't know

Attitude toward the Community Contributions of the Company:

1 Would you say that quite a few people at the ____________Company serve the community as leaders in school, church and other community affairs?

†(5) Yes
(1) No
†(3) Undecided
(0) Don't know

2 On the whole and compared to other companies of their size in (the city), how do you feel about the ____________Company's contributions to the community? Do you feel that they are:

(1) Much less than other companies here
(2) Somewhat less than other companies here
†(3) About the same as other companies here
†(4) Somewhat more than other companies here
†(5) Much more than other companies here
(0) Don't know

3 Do you agree or disagree with this statement? "(the Company)'s contributions as a company of money and time to schools, charities, and other community projects are better than average for a local company of its size."

†(5) Strongly agree
†(4) Agree
(2) Disagree
(1) Strongly disagree
†(3) Undecided
(0) Don't know

4 How active do you feel the individuals working at the ____________ Company are in community affairs?
(1) Not at all active
(2) Not too active
†(4) Fairly active
†(5) Very active
(3) Undecided
(0) Don't know

Attitude of the Community toward the Employee Relations Policies of the Company:

1 If someone looking for a job asked you about the ____________ Company as a good place to work, would you:
†(5) Recommend ____________ strongly
†(4) Recommend ____________, but with reservations
(2) Probably not recommend ____________
(1) Definitely not recommend ____________
†(3) Undecided
(0) Don't know

2 Do you believe that on the whole the employees at the ____________ Company are satisfied? Would you say they are:
†(5) Very satisfied
†(4) Generally satisfied
(2) Somewhat dissatisfied
(1) Very dissatisfied
†(3) Undecided
(0) Don't know

3 Which of the following terms comes closest to your opinion of the relations between the ____________ Company and its employees?
†(5) Excellent
†(4) Good
†(3) Average
(2) Poor
(1) Very poor
(0) Don't know

4 How do you feel the people who work at the ____________ Company are treated compared to other companies in (the city)?
†(5) Much better
†(4) Somewhat better
†(3) About the same
(2) Somewhat worse
(1) Much worse
(0) Don't know

5 In getting a promotion at the ____________ Company, do you feel that the workers' ability to do the job well is considered? Would you say that ability to do the job well is:
(1) Not really considered at all
(2) Not considered enough
†(4) Usually considered
†(5) Always considered
†(3) Undecided
(0) Don't know

6 On the whole, do you feel the ______________ Company has one of the highest pay scales of any company in (the city)?
†(5) Yes
(1) No
(3) Undecided
(0) Don't know

7 Generally speaking, what do you think of the ______________ Company as a place to work in (the city)? Would you say it is:
(1) A very poor place to work
(2) A poor place to work
(3) An average place to work
†(4) A good place to work
†(5) A very good place to work
(0) Don't know

Attitude toward newspapers EXHIBIT 10-14

Description. This is an eight-item, Guttman-type scale developed by Rogers (1955) in a study of prospective teachers' attitudes. He originally used it in conjunction with a scale measuring attitudes toward freedom of information, which is also an eight-item, Guttman-type scale (see Exhibit 6-18). The Freedom of Information Scale has as its content the freedom of newspapers to publish and of reporters to inquire, etc. The present scale, the Attitude toward Newspapers Scale, has as its content the effect of newspapers as a mass medium of communication. These scales were originally developed upon two samples of undergraduate and graduate students, whose responses were subjected to a scale analysis. After revision of the items, the scale was given to a new sample of students, upon which the characteristics of the scale were ascertained.

Subjects. Samples included 92 undergraduate and graduate students in secondary education and 686 undergraduates in seven state-supported, teacher-training institutions for white students in Texas.

Response Mode. The subject responds by checking one of five alternatives. For the first four items these alternatives are as follows: strongly agree, agree, undecided, disagree, and strongly disagree; for the second set of four items: always, usually, occasionally, hardly ever, and never. For all eight items, the subject is required to mark a second response indicating how hard it was for him to choose one of these alternatives: very hard, hard, and not at all hard. This latter is apparently a control device and is not used for formal scoring purposes.

Scoring. For items that are favorable to newspapers, response alternatives are weighted from 5 (strongly agree or always) to 1 (strongly disagree or never). Weights are reversed for negative items. The subject's score is the sum of the weighted alternatives endorsed by him. High scores reflect favorable attitudes toward newspapers.

Reliability. No estimates of reliability are provided by the author, but the reproducibility coefficient for this scale is sufficiently high to allow for good split-half reliability estimates.

Validity. The author reports a reproducibility coefficient of .81, based on 92 persons. The scale seems to have content validity for the question of whether newspapers are fair and accurate in their coverage of the news on several topic issues. As with other Guttman scales, however, the content domain seems restricted.

Comments. One item in the scale (item number 6) regarding the Eisenhower and Stevenson presidential election is somewhat dated for younger samples of subjects, and should be altered or excluded. Such alteration would require reestablishing the functional characteristics of the scale. The scale seems otherwise adequate, and a good deal of work has been put into it. However, evidence of reliability is lacking, and further studies of validity are desirable. The author reported that his approximation of the true zero point on this scale was at the 50.68 percentile. Thus the respondents were approximately evenly divided in their attitudes toward daily papers. He also points out that at least a third of the group of prospective teachers held strongly negative attitudes toward daily newspapers.

EXHIBIT 10-14

ATTITUDE TOWARD NEWSPAPERS

Read each of the statements or questions that follow. First check one of the answers to the question in the left-hand column. Then mark an X in the right-hand column to indicate how hard it was for you to make this choice.

*1 The daily newspaper weakens the reader's critical powers by doing his political and economic thinking for him.

______ strongly agree	How hard was it for you to make this choice?
______ agree	
______ undecided	______ very hard
______ disagree	______ hard
______ strongly disagree	______ not hard at all

*2 Monopoly conditions in the newspaper industry have led to an irresponsible use of power.

______ strongly agree	How hard was it for you to make this choice?
______ agree	
______ undecided	______ very hard
______ disagree	______ hard
______ strongly disagree	______ not hard at all

* These items are negative and their weights must be reversed for purposes of scoring.

*3 The economic interests of the daily newspaper are usually different from those of most of its readers.

________ strongly agree
________ agree
________ undecided
________ disagree
________ strongly disagree

How hard was it for you to make this choice?

________ very hard
________ hard
________ not hard at all

4 Newspapers are edited in the best interests of the general public.

________ strongly agree
________ agree
________ undecided
________ disagree
________ strongly disagree

How hard was it for you to make this choice?

________ very hard
________ hard
________ not hard at all

*5 Do the newspapers you read place too much emphasis on news of conflicts?

________ always
________ usually
________ occasionally
________ hardly ever
________ never

How strongly do you feel about your answer?

________ very strongly
________ strongly
________ not strongly at all

6 Were the news stories you read in the 1952 campaign fair to both Eisenhower and Stevenson?

________ always
________ usually
________ occasionally
________ hardly ever
________ never

How strongly do you feel about your answer?

________ very strongly
________ strongly
________ not strongly at all

7 Do you think that the daily newspaper is the best place to get news accurately?

________ always
________ usually
________ occasionally
________ hardly ever
________ never

How strongly do you feel about your answer?

________ very strongly
________ strongly
________ not strongly at all

8 Do you believe that daily newspapers give fair and unprejudiced news about stories involving Negroes?

________ always
________ usually
________ occasionally
________ hardly ever
________ never

How strongly do you feel about your answer?

________ very strongly
________ strongly
________ not strongly at all

ATTITUDES TOWARD RELIGIOUS INSTITUTIONS

Scales in this section have been designed to measure attitudes toward religious institutions (i.e., the church). Scales measuring attitudes toward other religious referents must be sought in other chapters (attitudes toward God are included in Chapter 6, attitudes toward Sunday observance and religious practices in Chapter 3, attitudes related to religious and philosophical issues are contained in Chapter 4). Persons interested in a scale for hostility toward the church should see Funk's battery of scales in Chapter 7.

Attitude toward the church *EXHIBIT 10-15*

Description. This is a 24-item scale developed by Thurstone and Chave (1929). It has been used extensively since that time. The items are not at all dated. The content of the scale deals with the social, personal, and moral significance of the church. Unfortunately, there are no equivalent forms for the scale, and the Q values for the items could not be located.

Subjects. The sample on which the scale was originally constructed is unknown, but it is assumed to have been University of Chicago undergraduate students.

Response Mode. Persons respond by placing a check mark beside those items with which they agree and a cross beside those with which they disagree; they place a question mark beside the items about which they are undecided.

Scoring. The person's score is the median of the scale values of the items which he endorses as "agree." A high score indicates an unfavorable attitude toward the church.

Reliability. Nelson (1956) reports a good degree of consistency on a test-retest type of study of changes in attitudes of ex-college students over a period of fifteen years (1936 to 1950), based upon N of 893. In his study, he reports that 51 percent of the subjects showed no shift in attitude. Of the remaining 49 percent, 35 percent shifted toward a more favorable attitude toward the church, and 14 percent shifted against the church. The two distributions of scores for the 1936 and 1950 testings of this sample are impressively similar.

Validity. Nickols and Shaw (1964) have found this scale to correlate .39 (a high saliency group) and .76 (a low saliency group) with the semantic differential measurement of attitude toward the church. Diggory (1953) reports the following correlations of this scale with the Thurstone scale measuring attitude toward God, based upon a sample of 75 men and 103 women: males, .78; females, .90. This finding would seem to show a high degree of construct validity. Osgood et al. (1957) report correlations ranging from .74 to .84 between Thurstone and semantic differential measurements of attitudes toward this and other referents.

Comments. This scale seems a relatively valid measuring instrument for purposes of group testing and has been widely used. Evidence is available on which to infer reliability, but further estimates of its reliability are required. For another study using this scale, see Telford (1934).

EXHIBIT 10-15

ATTITUDE TOWARD THE CHURCH

This is a study of attitudes toward the church. On the following page you will find twenty-four statements expressing different attitudes toward the church. Put a check mark (✓) if you agree with the statement. Put a cross (×) if you disagree with the statement. If you cannot decide about a statement, you may mark it with a question mark. This is not an examination. People differ in their opinions about what is right and wrong on this question. Please indicate *your own attitude* by a check mark when you agree and by a cross when you disagree.

Scale Value		
3.3	1	I enjoy my church because there is a spirit of friendliness there.
5.1	2	I like the ceremonies of my church but do not miss them much when I stay away.
8.8	3	I respect any church-member's beliefs but I think it is all "bunk."
6.1	4	I feel the need for religion but do not find what I want in any one church.
8.3	5	I think the teaching of the church is altogether too superficial to have much social significance.
11.0	6	I think the church is a parasite on society.
6.7	7	I believe in sincerity and goodness without any church ceremonies.
3.1	8	I do not understand the dogmas or creeds of the church but I find that the church helps me to be more honest and creditable.
9.6	9	I think the church is a hindrance to religion for it still depends upon magic, superstition, and myth.
9.2	10	I think the church seeks to impose a lot of worn-out dogmas and medieval superstitions.
4.0	11	When I go to church I enjoy a fine ritual service with good music.
0.8	12	I feel the church perpetuates the values which man puts highest in his philosophy of life.
5.6	13	Sometimes I feel that the church and religion are necessary and sometimes I doubt it.
7.5	14	I think too much money is being spent on the church for the benefit that is being derived.

Scale Value		
10.7	15	I think the organized church is an enemy of science and truth.
2.2	16	I like to go to church for I get something worth while to think about and it keeps my mind filled with right thoughts.
1.2	17	I believe the church is a powerful agency for promoting both individual and social righteousness.
7.2	18	I believe the churches are too much divided by factions and denominations to be a strong force for righteousness.
4.5	19	I believe in what the church teaches but with mental reservations.
0.2	20	I believe the church is the greatest institution in America today.
4.7	21	I am careless about religion and church relationships but I would not like to see my attitude become general.
10.4	22	The church represents shallowness, hypocrisy, and prejudice.
1.7	23	I feel the church services give me inspiration and help me to live up to my best during the following week.
2.6	24	I think the church keeps business and politics up to a higher standard than they would otherwise tend to maintain.

Attitudes and beliefs of LDS Church members toward their church and religion EXHIBIT 10-16

Description. This 25-item, Thurstone-type scale was developed by Hardy (1949) to measure attitudes toward the Latter-Day Saints Church (on the part of LDS Church members). In its original form, it was followed by 50 more Thurstone items, but, since these did not pass tests for ambiguity, these latter are not included in Exhibit 10-16. The referents of the items in this scale include the church, its activities, programs, policies, and (to some extent) its beliefs. Each item actually constitutes a separate five-item Thurstone scale. The result is a battery of Thurstone scales measuring highly specific attitudes toward policy, etc. Although some items are specific attitudes toward Latter-Day Saints Church programs and policies, many others could be used to measure attitudes toward other churches. To increase the generality of usage, however, it would be necessary to obtain new scale values and dispersion measures for the items. The author describes the item selection for this scale in the following manner: "Five statements representing various positions along the continuum of a given issue were constructed and typed onto separate cards. All of the cards were shuffled together and the judges asked to evaluate each statement according to the favorability or unfavorability of the statement toward the LDS Church. Wherever all five statements met Thurstone's requirements for unambiguity and were evaluated at various points along the attitude continuum, the statements were regrouped in a five alternative multiple-choice form . . ." (Hardy, private communication, 1963).

Subjects. The sample consisted of 162 LDS church members.

Response Mode. Subjects check that alternative of the five alternative statements in the item which best expresses their own attitude.

Scoring. The score is the median of the scale values of the items endorsed. A high score reflects an unfavorable attitude.

Reliability. The author reports the split-half reliability coefficient (corrected), based upon 162 cases, as .95.

Validity. The scale was validated against a composite criterion of religious activities. The correlation ratio (the regression line was significantly nonlinear) was .79, $N = 162$.

Comments. This scale has restricted usage in its present form (LDS Church member samples). However, it may be worthwhile to obtain sorts on these same items for use with churches other than the LDS in some instances. There are items which are too specific to allow such extension, but many items would serve quite well. For most purposes, the scale by Thurstone (Exhibit 10-15) would serve as well and would save the time required for rescaling items. However, this use by Hardy is quite interesting in its own right, as his scale is the equivalent of giving a set of 25 Thurstone scales to a subject. It should have quite high reliability, and the method deserves investigation as one possibly feasible manner of combining Thurstone and Likert procedures.

EXHIBIT 10-16

ATTITUDES AND BELIEFS OF LDS CHURCH MEMBERS TOWARD THEIR CHURCH AND RELIGION

This questionnaire is composed of two sections: one consisting of multiple-choice items, the other made up of single statements. In the first section, read carefully each of the five statements in the item, then check (✓) the statement which best expresses your own attitude. Then go on to the next item. If none of the statements in an item expresses your attitude fairly well, you may leave the item blank, but choose one statement whenever possible.

Scale Value		
2.7	1	I believe that God hears prayers and may at times act upon them.
10.7		Prayer is a demonstration of one's ignorance and helplessness.
6.4		I'm not sure that God answers prayers but praying does a person good.
1.1		I know that God hears and responds to prayers.
10.2		Prayer is probably just a waste of effort and time.
8.4	2	I feel that the Church provides only little opportunity for unselfish activity.
2.2		I feel that the Church provides many excellent opportunities for unselfish activity.

Reference: K. R. Hardy. Construction and validation of a scale measuring attitudes toward the L.D.S. Church. Unpublished master's thesis, Univer. of Utah, 1949. Items obtained from author and published with his permission.

Scale Value		
2.6		I feel that the Church provides some fine opportunities for unselfish activity.
5.6		I feel that the Church provides a few good opportunities for unselfish activity.
9.7		I feel that the Church provides no opportunities for unselfish activity.
5.1	3	I believe the MIA program is good in general but there are some weak areas.
8.0		I believe the MIA program is failing to influence and appeal in many respects.
10.4		I believe the MIA program is a complete waste of time and energy.
9.1		I believe the MIA program is "on the rocks" and needs a complete revision.
1.7		I believe the MIA program is excellent at all age levels.
1.4	4	I believe strongly in personal immortality: the continued existence of the individual as a separate, distinct being.
9.4		I have grave doubts about the possibility of personal immortality.
7.8		I am frequently beset with doubts about personal immortality.
7.0		I am at times beset with doubt about personal immortality.
10.7		I do not believe in immortality.
5.6	5	I believe that missionary work is primarily an opportunity to develop the missionary.
2.5		I believe that missionary work affords a good opportunity to engage in unselfish activity.
10.0		I believe that missionary work is largely a waste of time.
9.7		I believe that missionary work is not much more than an opportunity to travel and meet people.
1.3		I believe that missionary work is a choice opportunity to serve God and help others.
10.1	6	I believe that LDS Church members are much poorer neighbors because of the Church's influence.
9.9		I believe that LDS Church members are poorer neighbors because of the Church's influence.
2.3		I believe that LDS Church members are much better neighbors because of the Church's influence.
3.7		I believe that LDS Church members are somewhat better neighbors because of the Church's influence.
7.8		I believe that LDS Church members are no better neighbors because of the Church's influence.
2.3	7	When other people criticize the Church, I generally strongly defend it.
6.7		When other people criticize the Church, I generally remain silent.
8.0		When other people criticize the Church, I generally passively agree.
9.7		When other people criticize the Church, I generally join with them in criticism.
5.3		When other people criticize the Church, I generally mildly defend it.
9.8	8	The good done by the Church is not worth the money and energy spent on it.

Scale Value		
5.9		There is much energy and money wasted in the Church, but the good done probably compensates for it.
10.1		Time and money spent in the Church are a nearly complete waste.
1.4		Time and money are nowhere better spent than in the Church.
3.7		The time and money invested in the Church are probably well spent.
6.1	**9**	I feel that the Relief Society is probably a good thing but I am not impressed with it.
2.0		I feel that the Relief Society is a splendid organization.
9.3		I feel that the Relief Society is one organization which has little usefulness.
3.2		I feel that the Relief Society is one of the better auxiliary organizations.
9.9		I feel that the Relief Society is just a scheme to keep the women from getting dissatisfied with the Church.
9.6	**10**	The Word of Wisdom is of little if any practical value.
6.5		Some of the parts of the Word of Wisdom are good advice, but it certainly is not to be considered a commandment.
1.2		I believe the Church is absolutely correct in its teachings about the Word of Wisdom.
5.9		The Word of Wisdom is probably a good thing, but many other things are more important.
5.3		I believe in the Word of Wisdom, but I think the Church leaders stress it too much.
4.4	**11**	I think that the MIA is probably a good thing to have to keep the young people off the streets.
2.6		I think that the MIA is a Church auxiliary and therefore all those eligible should attend its meetings.
3.9		I think that the MIA is a fine auxiliary program for those interested in attending.
9.7		I think that the MIA is something to be disregarded.
9.7		I think that the MIA is not much better than nothing at all.
5.4	**12**	I believe that a few of our present leaders are occasionally inspired by God.
6.5		I believe that our leaders today are generally good men who are directing the affairs of the Church without supernatural aid.
9.6		I believe that Church leaders were inspired in Joseph Smith's day but are not any more because of unworthiness.
1.2		I believe that the Church remains under inspired leadership today.
10.8		I believe that the Church has never been under inspired leadership.
	13	In cases where the findings of science seem to conflict with the teachings of the Church, I generally tend to:
3.8		favor the Church over scientific findings.
9.8		defend strongly the findings of science.
2.4		defend strongly the Church's position.
6.1		favor neither the Church nor science to any extent.
8.8		favor the scientific findings over the Church's position.

Scale Value		
8.1	14	I feel that I only rarely benefit when I attend Church meetings.
3.5		I feel that I usually benefit when I attend Church meetings.
5.2		I feel that I benefit occasionally when I attend Church meetings.
9.8		I feel that I never benefit when I attend Church meetings.
2.0		I feel that I benefit greatly whenever I attend Church meetings.
1.5	15	I believe that the Church's method of selecting leaders is excellent.
5.4		I believe that the Church's method of selecting leaders is good but could be improved.
9.7		I believe that the Church's method of selecting leaders should be entirely revised and a good system substituted for it.
9.8		I believe that the Church's method of selecting leaders is unscientific and unfair.
6.1		I believe that the teachings of the Church have helped me tremendously in enjoying life.
6.3	16	I believe that the teachings of the Church have neither helped nor hindered me to any extent in enjoying life.
9.7		I believe that the teachings of the Church have hindered me to an appreciable extent from enjoying life.
2.7		I believe that the teachings of the Church have helped me to an appreciable extent in enjoying life.
1.7		I believe that the teachings of the Church have helped me tremendously in enjoying life.
10.7	17	On the whole, I believe the missionary program is a stupid waste of time and money.
1.9		On the whole, I believe the missionary program is excellently conceived and carried out.
5.4		On the whole, I believe the missionary program is falling down in spots but is generally progressing well.
8.1		On the whole, I believe the missionary program is not doing nearly as well as it should.
9.9		On the whole, I believe the missionary program is largely wasted effort.
8.1	18	My attitude toward the Church is passive, with some tendency to disfavor it.
10.9		I have little but contempt for the Church.
6.4		The Church is probably a good thing, but I'm not able to get interested in it.
1.1		I believe that the Church is the most important organization in the world.
2.9		I believe that the Church is one of our more important organizations.
1.8	19	I continually receive inspiration from our Church leaders to lead a better daily life.
2.3		I often am inspired to improve my daily behavior by the messages of our Church leaders.
8.4		I feel that the leaders of the Church do not deal with the practical problems of life.

Scale Value		
8.0		I feel that the Church authorities deal too infrequently with life's practical problems.
6.4		I feel that the Church leaders should spend a greater part of their time dealing with life's practical problems.
9.2	**20**	I believe that the Church wastes much of its money.
6.7		I believe that the Church makes only fair use of its money.
2.1		I believe that the Church makes excellent use of its money.
3.7		I believe that the Church generally makes good use of its money.
10.0		I believe that the Church wastes most of its money.
1.9	**21**	I feel that the Church has an excellent program for satisfying the needs of its members.
6.6		I feel that the Church has only a fair program for satisfying the needs of its members.
3.0		I feel that the Church in general satisfies well the needs of its members.
9.8		I feel that the Church has a very poor program for satisfying the needs of its members.
4.2		I feel that the Church has a fairly good program for satisfying the needs of its members.
10.4	**22**	When other people argue favorably for the Church, I usually strongly disagree.
5.4		When other people argue favorably for the Church, I usually passively agree with them.
6.3		When other people argue favorably for the Church, I usually remain silent.
3.3		When other people argue favorably for the Church, I usually join actively with them.
8.2		When other people argue favorably for the Church, I usually mildly disagree.
6.0	**23**	I feel that the tolerance and love fostered by the Church probably balances the intolerance fostered.
10.4		I feel that the Church greatly fosters intolerance and bigotry on the part of the members.
2.2		I feel that the Church greatly fosters an attitude of love and good will toward non-members.
8.8		I feel that the tolerance and love fostered by the Church is outweighed by the intolerance and bigotry fostered.
6.5		I feel that the Church on the whole fosters tolerance and love, but at times fosters intolerance and bigotry.
9.7	**24**	I have strong doubts about the reality of the pre-existence.
10.1		The reality of the pre-existence seems impossible.
4.5		I believe strongly in the reality of the pre-existence but occasionally have doubts.
9.8		The reality of the pre-existence seems highly improbable to me.
1.2		I believe wholeheartedly in the reality of the pre-existence.

Scale Value		
8.6	25	I feel that the Church is greatly declining in influence upon its membership.
2.4		I feel that the Church is gaining greatly in influence upon its membership.
8.6		I feel that the Church is measurably declining in influence upon its membership.
6.2		I feel that the Church is not measurably gaining or declining in influence on its membership.
4.2		I feel that the Church is gaining in influence on its membership to a certain degree.

GENERALIZED SCALES TO MEASURE ATTITUDES TOWARD INSTITUTIONS

The scales included in this section are designed to measure attitudes toward any one of a general class of referents (in this case, toward any social institution). The Osgood semantic differential is a device which may also be used in this manner. It has been used to measure attitudes toward the church (Osgood et al., 1957), and was discussed in Chapter 2.

Attitude toward any institution EXHIBIT 10-17

Description. This 45-item, Thurstone-type scale was developed by Kelley (1934). The author has provided equivalent forms, A and B. It was on the basis of this scale that Remmers (1960*a*) later developed his shorter (17-item) scale measuring the same attitude. While the Remmers scale is shorter, it is to be expected that this scale, by Kelley, is a more reliable measuring instrument. Items used by Remmers to create his scale are indicated in Exhibit 10-17 by an asterisk. This is a generalized scale which is intended to be applicable to any social or other institution. The Q values for all items are smaller than 3.0.

Subjects. The populations sampled in the development of the scale include 100 factory workers, 80 students at Purdue University, and 222 Seventh Day Adventists, Methodists, Baptists, and United Brethren.

Response Mode. Subjects respond by marking a plus (+) beside the items with which they agree.

Scoring. The score is the median of the scale values of the items with which the subject agrees. High scores indicate favorable attitudes toward the institution in question.

Reliability. The following equivalent-forms reliabilities have been reported by Kelley, applying the scale to the institution listed: communism, .89; war, .77; Sunday observance, .98; marriage, .71; divorce, .81.

Validity. Regarding concurrent validity, the following correlations have been obtained by the author (Kelley, 1934) between this generalized scale and specific Thurstone-type scales: .816 with attitude toward communism, using a sample of 100 factory workers;—.149 with attitude toward war on a sample of 80 students at Purdue University; .78 with attitude toward Sunday observance ($N = 222$). The Thurstone construction procedure should provide a degree of content validity.

Comments. It is noteworthy that both the reliability and validity of this scale were established on the basis of topics which have been considered in this book to be social issues and practices. Thus, it is to be expected that the scale could be used along with or instead of the generalized scales in Chapter 3 (the Attitude toward Any Practice Scale, Bues, 1934) and Chapter 4 (the Attitude toward Any Proposed Social Action Scale, Silance and Remmers, 1934). The scale for Attitude toward any Institution was included in this chapter of the book because most of the items have enough content validity to allow it to be used in measuring attitudes toward institutions as we have used the term. This use is allowed not only because of the content validity of the items and the highly general manner in which they are phrased, but also because, in measuring attitudes toward institutions, an issue has been raised in effect. However, if the scale is used in the manner proposed, it will be necessary to collect information regarding its functional characteristics when applied to these new topics.

EXHIBIT 10-17

ATTITUDE TOWARD ANY INSTITUTION

Following is a list of statements about institutions. Place a plus sign (+) before each statement with which you agree about the institution or institutions listed at the left of the statements. The person in charge will tell you the institution or institutions to write in at the head of the columns to the left of the statements. Your score will in no way affect your grade in any course.

Form A

Scale Value		
11.2	1	Is perfect in every way.
11.1	2	Is the most admirable of institutions.
11.1	3	Is necessary to the very existence of civilization.
11.0	4	Is the most beloved of institutions.
10.8	5	Represents the best thought in modern life.
10.5	6	Grew up in answer to a felt need and is serving that need perfectly.
*10.3	7	Exerts a strong influence for good government and right living.

* These items are the ones used by Remmers (1960) to create his shorter 17 item form of this scale.

Reprinted with permission from Kelley, I. B. Construction and validation of a scale to measure attitude toward any institution. *Purdue Univ. Study High. Educ.*, 1934, 35, 18–36. Copyright 1960 by the Purdue Research Foundation, LaFayette, Ind. Copies of the short form of the scale may be purchased from the Purdue University Bookstore, LaFayette, Ind.

Scale Value		
10.2	8	Has more pleasant things connected with it than any other institution.
10.2	9	Is a strong influence for right living.
10.2	10	Gives real help in meeting moral problems.
10.1	11	Gives real help in meeting social problems.
9.8	12	Is valuable in creating ideals.
9.8	13	Is necessary to the very existence of society.
9.7	14	Encourages social improvement.
*9.5	15	Serves society as a whole well.
9.3	16	Aids the individual in wise use of leisure time.
*9.1	17	Is necessary to society as organized.
*8.9	18	Adjusts itself to changing conditions.
*8.8	19	Is improving with the years.
*8.2	20	Does more good than harm.
*7.4	21	Will not harm anybody.
*6.4	22	Inspires no definite likes or dislikes.
*6.1	23	Is necessary only until a better can be found.
*5.4	24	Is too liberal in its policies.
5.3	25	Is too conservative for a changing civilization.
4.9	26	Does not consider individual differences.
*4.8	27	Is losing ground as education advances.
4.5	28	Gives too little service.
4.4	29	Represents outgrown beliefs.
4.2	30	Gives no opportunity for self-expression.
*3.5	31	Promotes false beliefs and much wishful thinking.
3.3	32	Is too selfish to benefit society.
*3.1	33	Does more harm than good.
3.0	34	Is cordially hated by the majority for its smugness and snobbishness.
2.9	35	Satisfies only the most stupid with its services.
2.8	36	Is hopelessly out of date.
*2.7	37	No one any longer has faith in this institution.
2.3	38	Is entirely unnecessary.
*2.2	39	Is detrimental to society and the individual.
2.1	40	The world would be better off without this institution.
2.0	41	Is in a hopeless condition.
1.9	42	Will destroy civilization if it is not radically changed.
1.8	43	Never was any good.
*1.7	44	Benefits no one.
*1.6	45	Has positively no value.

Form B

11.2	1	The world could not exist without this institution.
11.1	2	Is an ideal institution.
11.1	3	Has done more for society than any other institution.
11.0	4	Benefits everybody.
10.8	5	Has more good points than any other institution.
10.7	6	Appeals to man's highest nature.
*10.4	7	Develops good character.
10.2	8	Furthers the most lasting satisfactions in life.
10.2	9	Has a long useful life before it.
10.2	10	Is a powerful agency for promoting individual and social efficiency.

Scale Value		
10.1	**11**	Is of real value to the civilized individual.
9.9	**12**	Gives real help in meeting economic problems.
9.8	**13**	Encourages moral improvement.
9.7	**14**	Is fundamentally sound.
*9.6	**15**	Is retained in the civilized world because of its value to mankind.
9.4	**16**	Offers opportunity for individual initiative.
*9.2	**17**	Is increasing in its value to society.
*9.0	**18**	Is necessary as a means of controlling society.
*8.9	**19**	Is improving in its service to mankind.
*8.2	**20**	Is in the process of changing and will come out a fit instrument.
*7.5	**21**	Is not sufficiently appreciated by the general public.
*6.6	**22**	Its good and bad points balance each other.
*6.1	**23**	Has not yet proved itself indispensable to society.
*5.4	**24**	Is too conservative.
5.3	**25**	Is retained in the civilized world because of sentiment.
4.9	**26**	Is decreasing in its value to society.
*4.8	**27**	Is too changeable in its policies.
4.6	**28**	Regulates the individual's life too minutely.
4.4	**29**	Grew up in frontier days and does not fit our industrial civilization.
4.2	**30**	Is too radical in its views and actions.
*3.6	**31**	Is unfair to the individual.
3.3	**32**	Is a tool of the mercenary.
*3.1	**33**	Is disgraced by its past.
3.0	**34**	Is a tool of the unscrupulous.
2.9	**35**	Is developing into a racket.
2.8	**36**	Is fundamentally unsound.
*2.7	**37**	Is out of control of society and is running wild.
2.3	**38**	Appeals to man's lowest nature.
*2.2	**39**	Is an enemy of truth.
2.1	**40**	Has always cheated society.
1.9	**41**	Thrives on the avarice, jealousy, hatred, and greed in man.
1.9	**42**	Must be discarded immediately.
1.8	**43**	Has more bad points than any other institution.
*1.7	**44**	Is the most despicable of institutions.
*1.6	**45**	Is the most hateful of institutions.

High school attitude scale **EXHIBIT 10-18**

Description. This 17-item, Thurstone-type scale, developed by Remmers (1960*a*) to measure attitudes toward any high school, was first reported upon by Gillespie (1936). In addition to the usual 17 items on a Remmers generalized scale, this scale possesses one validating item on which the subject reports his attitude toward school on an 11-point continuum. Alternative forms of the scale are provided in Exhibit 10-18.

Subjects. The sample used to develop this scale is unknown, but samples used in developing Remmers' scales have included a wide range of subjects from sixth grade pupils to graduate students.

Response Mode. Subjects check those items with which they most agree by marking them with a plus.

Scoring. The score is the median of the scale values of all items endorsed by the subject. High scores reflect favorable attitudes.

Reliability. Although no specific information is available for this scale, the equivalent-forms reliability for Remmers scales is reported to range from .71 to .92 for a variety of samples ranging from sixth grade pupils to advanced graduate students (Purdue University Bookstore, 1961). Specific reliability estimates are unknown for this scale.

Validity. Specific information regarding validity is missing. However, the method of construction should provide content validity.

Comments. More than any of the other Remmers scales, this scale is an unknown quantity. However, it is expected that the method of construction should ensure to some extent the adequacy of the scale for purposes of group comparisons.

EXHIBIT 10-18

HIGH SCHOOL ATTITUDE SCALE

Below is a list of seventeen statements about school. Place a check mark before each statement with which you agree, and leave unmarked those with which you disagree. This test will in no way affect your standing in school.

Form A

Scale Value		
10.3	1	A high school education is worth a million dollars to any young person.
9.6	2	High school develops self-reliance.
9.2	3	A high school education will help one to be a good citizen.
8.9	4	It helps one to get a job if he has a high school diploma.
8.5	5	I like to do school work.
8.1	6	I would rather go to high school than to stay at home.
7.7	7	I don't like to associate with people who haven't a high school education.
6.5	8	High school has its drawbacks, but I like to go.
6.0	9	I don't care about high school, but I think one ought to.
5.5	10	High school is all right, but I don't like it.
4.7	11	High school may be all right, but I don't think it does any good.
3.6	12	There are too many rules and regulations in schools.
3.1	13	My classes are very uninteresting.
2.6	14	I can learn more working on a job than in high school.

Reprinted with permission from Remmers, H. H. *Manual for the Purdue Master Attitude Scales.* Lafayette, Ind.: Purdue Research Foundation, 1960. Copies of the scale may be purchased from the Purdue University Bookstore, Lafayette, Ind.

Scale Value		
2.2	**15**	A high school graduate is often worse off morally than he was before going to high school.
1.6	**16**	In high school, pupils learn to disrespect everything of high idealistic character.
1.0	**17**	High school teachers are parasites on the community.
		Form B
10.3	**1**	America could not stand as a nation if it were not for our high schools.
9.6	**2**	High school develops loyalty.
9.2	**3**	High school training develops personality.
8.9	**4**	The high schools lift the plane of sportsmanship in a community.
8.5	**5**	All the better class of people have high school educations.
8.1	**6**	My teachers always treat me fairly.
7.7	**7**	I like to go to school to be with other people.
6.5	**8**	I have a lot of fun in school.
6.0	**9**	Some things about high school are all right.
5.5	**10**	If one has plenty of money it may be all right to go to high school.
4.7	**11**	I haven't any definite like or dislike for high school.
3.6	**12**	The kindest and best people I know don't have high school educations.
3.1	**13**	Too much money is being spent on the high schools for the benefit received.
2.6	**14**	The high school teaches mostly old and useless information.
2.2	**15**	I hate most school work.
1.6	**16**	High school cramps and dwarfs one's personality.
1.0	**17**	Our high schools teach immorality and indecency.

SUMMARY

It is noteworthy that there are very few scales to measure attitudes toward specific educational and legal institutions, despite the importance of these institutions in a complex, highly organized society such as ours. Further, scales measuring attitudes toward health-related institutions seem largely restricted to those pertaining to mental health. Scales are lacking for measurement of attitudes toward institutions dealing with physical illness. But it should be quite interesting to obtain information about the attitudes of the public toward clinics and hospitals for the physically ill, especially regarding such frequently criticized practices as admissions, isolation, and handling of children's wards. Also lacking are scales to measure attitudes toward economic institutions other than management, labor, and unions. The government as an economic institution should be an interesting referent for a scale, as would be small business. Other scales which would seem to be especially relevant today include those measuring attitudes toward the military establishments and toward agencies of the Federal government.

It is interesting to note that there are a number of Guttman-type scales developed in the more applied interest areas. It would be helpful if the item marginals were reported along with the coefficient of reproducibility for these scales.

In this chapter, the authors found themselves particularly afflicted by the failure of researchers to report the instructions used with their scale and with failure to report items and item values. As a consequence, it was necessary in many instances to suggest possible instructions.

Finally, what has been dealt with as an institution in some instances (e.g., in Kelley's and Remmers' scales) would not meet the definition of institution advanced in this chapter. They would often be better classified as social practices or issues. Nonetheless, the scales seem valuable as methods of assessing attitudes toward institutions.

CHAPTER **11**

comments and conclusions

The survey of the literature upon which this volume is based leads to several inevitable conclusions. First, there seem to have been few major advances or breakthroughs in techniques of scale construction since the Thurstone and Likert methods were developed. Guttman scales represent a different approach and have some advantages but also some serious disadvantages relative to the Thurstone and/or Likert techniques. Techniques such as those proposed by Lazarsfeld, Coombs, and others show promise but have not been fully developed. Also, little progress has been made toward the measurement of structural characteristics of attitudes and attitudinal systems, despite theoretical formulations directed toward this aspect of attitude.

The second conclusion is related to the first: In the majority of researches reported in recent years the measures of attitude that are used are not developed according to the best procedures available. All too frequently the investigator simply asks a few unstandardized (unevaluated) questions and assumes that the attitude has been reliably and validly measured.

Third, attitude scales that purportedly are developed by one of the formal procedures, such as the Thurstone or Likert methods, often are only partially evaluated. Scale constructors often seem to ignore the assumptions underlying the scaling method employed, and evidence of reliability and validity is frequently lacking and almost always incomplete.

Fourth, the coverage of attitude population is spotty and uneven. For example, many scales are available for the measurement of attitudes toward child-rearing practices, toward ethnic groups, and toward liberalism-conservatism, but scales for measuring attitudes toward abstract concepts such as life, education, time, and freedom are few in number. Scales to measure attitudes toward international issues, to point out another example, are limited to attitudes toward war, the tariff, and nationalistic attitudes (see Chapter 5).

Finally, as a result of the shortcomings mentioned above, we believe that few of the attitude scales presented in this book are adequate for the assessment of individual attitude, although most are adequate for research purposes.

In this chapter we attempt a general evaluation of the scales included in this volume and the research in which such scales may be used. We also attempt to indicate areas in which new attitude scales are needed and to offer some suggestions for improving attitude measurement and research.

THE METHODS OF SCALE CONSTRUCTION

The overwhelming majority of scales has been developed by either the Thurstone or the Likert technique. This is in accord with the above observation that few advances have been made in scaling methods since the formulation of these techniques. A few scales were developed by the Guttman technique, even fewer by variations of Coombs's unfolding technique or by Hammond's error-choice technique, and none by Lazarsfeld's latent distance procedure or the method of graded dichotomies. This is probably a result of the greater complexity of the newer procedures. Several scales were developed by special procedures which differed from those of any of the formal methods and by variations of one or more of the formal methods. An example of the latter is the scale discrimination technique which incorporates parts of the Thurstone, Likert, and Guttman methods. As noted in Chapter 2, this procedure violates some of the assumptions underlying the parent methods.

There is little evidence in the literature that authors of attitude scales have given serious consideration to the assumptions underlying the procedures used to construct their scales. In some cases, little can be done to ensure that the assumption has been met. For example, it is assumed by the method of equal-appearing intervals that judges, in the aggregate, can accurately evaluate item validity; that is, that there is no systematic error of judgment (Thurstone, 1929). This assumption has been questioned, especially with reference to the judges' own attitudes upon their judgments of the favorability of items. Early studies by Hinckley (1932), Beyle (1932), Ferguson (1935), and Pintner and Forlano (1937) supported the Thurstone assumption that favorableness judgments are independent of the judges' own attitudes, since correlations between scale values obtained from different groups ranged from .93 to .99. More recently, Hovland and Sherif (1952) have shown that judges make finer discriminations among items near their own position than among items more distant from their own position on the attitude continuum. They concluded that the judges' own attitude may bias their judgments, and other investigators using similar methods have tended to support Hovland and Sherif. However, it seems to the present authors that persons representing the two sides of the controversy have been asking different questions. On the one hand, those supporting the Thurstone assumption (Beyle, 1932; Ferguson, 1935; Hinckley, 1932, 1963; Pintner and Forlano, 1937) have asked whether the judges' own attitudes bias the scale values assigned to the attitude statements in the final scale, whereas those disputing the Thurstone assumption (Ager and Dawes, 1965; Hovland and Sherif, 1952; Prothro, 1955, 1957; Sherif and Hovland, 1953; Zavalloni and Cook, 1965) have asked whether the judges' own attitudes influence in any way their judgments of item favorability. The answer to the latter question is clearly in the affirmative, but the evidence also indicates that this fact does not mean that valid scale values cannot be obtained by the method of equal-appearing intervals. On the contrary, we agree with Upshaw's (1965) conclusion that the evidence supports the validity of scale construction by equal-appearing intervals.

Another assumption that is commonly ignored by scale constructors concerns the type of item that is assumed by the various scaling methods. As explained in Chapter 2, the method of equal-appearing intervals assumes nonmonotone items (i.e., items that are acceptable to persons whose attitudes correspond to the point on the underlying attitude continuum represented by said items, but which are unacceptable to persons holding both more favorable and more unfavorable attitudes), whereas both the Likert and the Guttman techniques assume monotone items (i.e., items that are acceptable to all persons holding attitudes as favorable or more favorable than that represented by the items in question.) With the exception of Thurstone and his associates, failure to meet this assumption is most noticeable among authors of Thurstone-type scales, although it is sometimes violated by authors using other procedures. One consequence of this is that discrimination in the middle ranges is reduced. (At the extremes the trace lines for monotone and nonmonotone items are similar.) More will be said about this effect in the next section.

CHARACTERISTICS OF THE SCALES

In Chapter 2 it was suggested that, ideally, an attitude scale should be reliable, valid, unidimensional, and should have equal units and a zero point. The scales in this book vary widely in the degree to which these characteristics have been determined and reported. However, several general statements are in order.

Reliability

Almost all the scales included in this volume have been shown to have at least minimal reliability. The most commonly used estimate of reliability is internal consistency, determined by the split-half method. An estimate of this form of reliability is reported for 54.5 percent of the scales. This estimate indicates the degree to which items "hang together" or measure the same thing; it does not reveal the degree to which the scale yields consistent scores through time. Test-retest reliability (stated as a coefficient of stability) is reported for 28.4 percent of the scales. The coefficient of equivalence, based upon the correspondence between two forms of the same scale, is reported for only 18.2 percent of the scales. All too often, only one form of the scale is available. Authors of Guttman-type scales usually report only the coefficient of reproducibility (Rep), which is not an estimate of reliability in the usual sense of the word. Since Rep is influenced by several factors other than consistency of response (see Chapter 2), it would be helpful if authors reported item marginals as well as the value of Rep. Similarly, for some Thurstone scales only estimates of reliability of the scale values, stated in terms of probable error, are reported.

Ideally, all three forms of reliability estimates should be determined for each scale. This is rarely done, possibly because of the amount of effort required. Fortunately, the various procedures usually yield similar estimates of reliability.

Validity

Effective measurement of attitudes demands that the scales be valid, but this is one of the most difficult characteristics to establish and probably represents the greatest deficiency of the scales in this book. Methods of evaluating the validity of scales have been described in Chapter 2. These include content validity, predictive validity, concurrent validity, and construct validity (APA Committee, 1954).

Content validity is by far the most common method used by authors of scales in this volume. In fact, all scales described herein may be said to have some degree of content validity, in the sense that the items are drawn from the attitude content domain. However, many authors fail to consider the degree to which the items sample the total range of the attitude dimension. In one sense, content validity is specified by the procedure used in constructing Thurstone-type scales. Items are selected on the basis of agreement among judges regarding their content validity. However, as indicated earlier, failure to satisfy the assumption of nonmonotone items weakens this evidence. For example, if an item having a scale value of 5.0 is in fact a monotone item, it will be agreed to by persons with attitudes corresponding to a value of 5.0 *and* by all persons having more favorable (or more unfavorable) attitudes. Since the scoring procedure is based upon the assumption that items are nonmonotone, a systematic error is introduced into the attitude score. To some extent, this error will be reflected by large Q values and so can be minimized by selecting only items with small Q values. A similar error would be introduced if nonmonotone items were used in Likert and Guttman scaling, although item analysis and scale analysis usually eliminate this type of item.

Concurrent validity is the second most commonly used estimate of validity. Forty-five percent of the authors report validity estimates based upon this procedure. The known-groups variation of this method seems to be the most common technique used by scale constructors. Its adequacy, of course, depends upon how accurately the known groups have been identified. This procedure should not be confused with the extreme-groups procedure of item analysis.

Very few scales have been validated by the predictive method. Using a very broad criterion of predictive validity, including, for example, the effect of an experimental treatment upon attitude score, only 15.3 percent of scale authors provided any evidence of predictive validity. It is possible that this is because of the relatively large amount of work required to estimate predictive validity. It is also possible, however, that predictive validity is not regarded as important for many kinds of investigations. Predictive validity seems to be most important when one wishes to relate attitudes to actions. In attitude research we are often more interested in relating attitudes to such variables as education, socioeconomic status, and other attitudes (Green, 1954) than in predicting future actions. Nevertheless, evidence of predictive validity strengthens a scale, and lack of such evidence must be considered a weakness of the scales described in this book.

The construct validity of scales is seldom evaluated completely. However, if we consider the pattern of correlations between attitude scale scores and other measures of personality as evidence of construct validity (Campbell and Fiske, 1959), 23.9 percent of the authors provide such evidence. Although this is a relatively low percentage, it must be remembered that many of the scales in this volume were constructed before the notion of construct validity was explicitly stated.

In summary, problems of scale validation are not easy to solve, and the scales we have examined leave much to be desired in this respect. Except for content validity, many authors provide no evidence of validity, and many that do so provide only incomplete data.

Unidimensionality

No scale presented in this volume has been shown to be completely unidimensional. The degree to which a scale is unidimensional is largely a function of the technique used in its construction, and, as Green (1954) points out, each technique has its own definition of unidimensionality. The item-analysis procedure used in the Likert method of scale construction represents one attempt to insure unidimensionality, as does the judging procedure employed in the method of equal-appearing intervals. Various other procedures have been designed for the same purpose, e.g., Guttman's scale analysis. But the moderately high correlations among scales designed to measure different attitudes, coupled with the less-than-perfect correlations among scales designed to measure the same attitude, indicate that perfect unidimensionality has not been attained. [The alert reader will have noticed a marked similarity between this statement and statements made in connection with construct validity. A scale that is homogeneous in the sense that all items measure the same thing is usually reliable, and a scale that is homogeneous and reliable is valid for some purpose (see Green, 1954).]

Some writers (see Torgerson, 1958) have suggested that perhaps multidimensional scales might be more useful than unidimensional scales. However, the multidimensional attitude scales reported in the literature turn out to be merely several quasi-unidimensional scales combined into a single battery. For the most part, interpretation is based upon individual scale scores rather than the composite score. Models for combining subscale scores into a composite score are badly needed.

Equality of Units

Equal units of measurement permit several desirable operations, such as averaging the attitude scores for a given individual on different attitude scales or comparing the magnitude of attitude change by two individuals at different points on the attitude continuum (see Chapter 2). Thurstone's method of equal-appearing intervals is the only well-established technique that attempts to achieve equality of units. [Wilson's (1962) latent trend method also attempts to attain equality of units, but his procedure has not been developed sufficiently to permit adequate evaluation.] It is probably safe to say that Thurstone scales approximate judged equality of intervals, but it is questionable whether judges are able to accurately evaluate this characteristic of scales.

In general, we believe there is no good reason to assume that the scales in this book have established equality of units; hence it is recommended that attitude scores be treated accordingly. That is, we recommend that attitude scales be treated as ordinal scales (Stevens, 1951). Although this limits the permissible operations that can be performed upon the scores, it is still possible to make many useful comparisons. For example, we can order individuals along the attitude continuum, average the scale scores of groups of individuals for the purpose of group comparisons, evaluate changes in individual attitudes as a function of experimental treatments, relate attitudes to other variables, and perform similar operations upon attitude scores. (See Krech and Crutchfield, 1948, for a more extensive discussion of the equality-of-units question.)

The Zero Point of Scales

The scales in this book do not have clearly established zero points. The method of equal-appearing intervals includes a neutral category, so that the middle scale value may be considered to approximate the zero point. Again, this hinges upon the capabilities of the judges to validly estimate scale values; hence the psychological meaningfulness of this zero point may be questioned. Furthermore, Riker (1944) has shown that persons who attain a neutral score on Thurstone-type scales do not necessarily consider themselves neutral toward the attitude object.

Guttman and Suchman (1947) have attempted to determine a zero point for Guttman-type scales by relating attitude scores and measures of intensity. When attitude scores are plotted as a function of intensity, a U-shaped curve results, with intensities being lowest in the middle range of attitude scores and highest at the extremes. The zero point is taken as the inflection point of the intensity curve. The fact that the intensity of the attitude is low, however, does not guarantee that there is no positive or negative feeling toward the attitude object.

The Likert technique and other methods provide even less evidence of a zero point. Although the response categories provided by Likert-type scales include a neutral response to each item, the identification of a zero attitude score is highly ambiguous. The most obvious procedure would be to accept as the zero point the score that would be attained if an individual responded to all items with the neutral response category; however, this same score could be attained by an individual who responds with "strongly agree" to some items and "strongly disagree" to others. Few would consider this latter score a psychologically meaningful zero point.

In general, the Thurstone and Guttman techniques most nearly approximate a zero point, but many questions still remain unanswered.

SCALES AND RESEARCH

Research versus Individual Assessment

In a preceding section of this chapter we noted that the scales in this book are adequate for research purposes but not necessarily for the assessment of individual attitude. This point needs clarification. In most experimental investigations comparisons are made between attitudes held by groups of individuals. Errors of measurement may be assumed to be randomly distributed about the mean, so that with a sizable number of subjects in each group the obtained mean attitude score approximates the true mean of the population. Consequently, an attitude scale that measures individual attitude imperfectly may yield a reliable and valid measure of the mean attitude held by members of a group. Additionally, one of the most common methods of evaluating scale validity, other than content validity, is by the known-groups technique. When this is done, established validity means only that the scale is adequate for discriminating among groups holding different attitudes toward the attitude object. Generally speaking, then, the attitude scales we have reviewed have been shown to be satisfactory for most research purposes.

But the problem of individual assessment of attitude is quite different. Here we are concerned with measuring the attitude of a given individual toward a given attitude object. In such cases there is little opportunity for randomization of errors of measurement. If the scale is only moderately reliable and valid, the most likely outcome is that the obtained attitude score will be either larger or smaller than the true value for the individual. Since most of the scales presented here fall into this moderate category, we believe that their use for individual measurement is questionable.

Selection of Scales

We also noted that in much of the published research, attitudes were not measured by the best scales available. It can be argued that attitude scales developed by formal scaling procedures are satisfactory for research purposes if certain assumptions can be made about error distribution. But implicit in this argument is the further assumption that error is relatively small, and certainly less than 100 percent. Yet many investigators formulate a very small number of questions or items for the purpose of measuring a particular attitude, with no attempt whatsoever to determine the reliability or the validity of the set of items as a measure of the attitude in question. Beyond the mere fact that the content of the questions seems related to the attitude, there is no reason to believe that the error of measurement is not 100 percent; in short, that the set of items measures the attitude at all.

The reasons for this state of affairs are not clear. It may be that scales for the attitudes in question are nonexistent or not readily available to the investigator. Even so, the investigator could evaluate the reliability and validity of his new instruments. Failure to do this is probably due to the fact that the investigator is not primarily interested in the attitude and, hence, is unwilling to expend the effort required for adequate evaluation. Whether this saving of effort justifies the risk of obtaining inaccurate answers to the questions that *are* of primary concern is hardly an open question.

SUGGESTIONS FOR IMPROVEMENT

In accordance with the above-mentioned considerations, improvements in the measurement of attitudes may be made in techniques of scale construction, in the implementation of techniques (i.e., in the process of scale construction), in the selection of scales for measuring attitudes, and/or in the modification or evaluation of selected scales. Suggestions for the improvement of techniques of scale construction are beyond the scope of this book, although we might suggest that advances are most likely to be made along the lines proposed by Coombs (1950; 1953). However, we believe that much improvement can be made by careful implementation of existing methods, by judicious selection of scales for measuring attitudes, and, where needed, further evaluation of selected scales.

Implementation of Methods of Scale Construction

The first step in the construction of a scale is a decision concerning the technique to be used. This decision will often hinge upon the purposes of the investigator, but in many cases it will be merely a matter of personal preference. In Chapter 2 we have outlined the procedures for the various techniques and some of the advantages and disadvantages of each. Therefore we will not elaborate further on this point.

The second step is the formulation of items. This is often a critical step, since the success or failure of the attempt to develop a scale may depend upon the collection of items with which one begins. Numerous authors have detailed the general considerations involved in item writing (Edwards, 1957; Likert, 1932; Thurstone and Chave, 1929; Wang, 1932). Briefly, items should be stated in as simple and clear language as possible, should contain a single idea, and should be unambiguous. One should avoid the use of items that are factual, irrelevant to the attitude object or nondiscriminatory (i.e., items that are likely to be answered the same way by persons having both favorable and unfavorable attitudes).

We wish to point to another aspect of item writing that is often neglected. This is the type of item that is formulated. As we have pointed out several times, the method of scale construction that one adopts specifies the kind of item that is appropriate. The Thurstone method, for example, requires nonmonotone items, whereas both the Likert and Guttman methods assume monotone items; the error-choice technique requires a multiple-response item; and so on (see Green, 1954; Torgerson, 1958). The point we wish to make is that the scale constructor should give careful consideration to the question of item type required by the technique that he is using to ensure that assumptions are not being violated. We believe this alone would improve the validity of many scales.

The question of validity has reared its ugly head repeatedly in our presentation and description of scales. It is our opinion that it is incumbent upon both the scale constructor and the user of the scale to demonstrate that the scale validly measures the attitude in question. In Chapter 2 and in an earlier section of this chapter, four kinds of validity were described. Ideally, evidence concerning all kinds is desirable, but this is often not feasible, and, depending upon the purposes of the user, may be unnecessary. That is to say, the kind of validating evidence that is most important may depend upon the goal of the investigator. If the experimenter is interested in discriminating among groups, then concurrent validity is most relevant. If he wishes to predict some future behavior, however, then predictive validity becomes the crucial issue. Similarly, if the purpose is to interrelate attitude with other aspects of the personality, to integrate and organize behavior, construct validity must be considered. Content validity is useful as a preliminary screening device or similar purpose, but does not appear to be as closely related to purpose as other types of validity. The point we wish to emphasize here is that the investigator must be sure that the scale he uses is at least minimally valid for the purpose for which he is using it. That this minimum requirement is rarely met is amply demonstrated by the experimental literature.

Finally, we have noted a limitation in what is measured by attitude scales. Although attitudes have several dimensions (see Chapter 1), direction and intensity seem to be the only ones tapped by the scales in this book. With the exception of the work by Guttman and Suchman (1947), there is little attempt to separate these two aspects of attitude. Scales or techniques for measuring other aspects of attitude such as specificity, multiplexity, interconnectedness, centrality, and consistency are badly needed. Triandis (1964) conceptualized attitudes as consisting of evaluations and intentions and suggested that both aspects could be measured by the semantic differential. This is in accord with our suggestion, but we have some reservations concerning the semantic differential as a measure of attitude (see below).

Selection of Scales

It would appear to be an obvious point that the investigator should use the best scale available in his research work. As we have pointed out earlier, however, this all too often is not the case. The reasons for this are not clear, but a good guess is that the effort involved in searching the literature or developing a scale is responsible for this state of affairs. However, we would like to suggest once again that the avoidance of effort is meager compensation for the risk involved: An inadequate measuring instrument has nullified many research efforts.

One attempt to overcome the considerable work involved in scale construction is the use of generalized scales. Remmers' efforts in this direction are well known, and there is reasonable evidence that this type of generalized scale may be as acceptable as specific scales developed by the same method (Campbell, 1950; Grice, 1934; Remmers, 1954).

A more recent approach to generalized scales is the semantic differential. The major advantage of this approach is that the same instrument may be used to measure attitude toward any object. The evidence concerning the reliability and validity of the semantic differential is impressive (see Chapter 2). Nevertheless, a word of caution is in order. The validity of the semantic differential as a measure of attitude has been demonstrated primarily by correlating semantic differential scores with scores on standard Thurstone or Likert-type scales. Such correlations usually compare favorably with the reliabilities of these scales. However, Nickols and Shaw (1964) found low correlations (.29 to .39) between semantic differential scores and scores on Thurstone scales when the attitude in question was particularly salient for the respondents. The usual moderately high correlations (.71 to .76) were obtained with the same scales when the attitude was not especially salient for the respondents. Which scale is the more valid one is not clear from this study, but it is clear that the semantic differential and Thurstone-type scales cannot be treated as equivalent measures when high saliency obtains.

Special Recommendations

There are some special characteristics of scales developed by standard techniques that suggest certain precautions when scales developed by these methods are selected for us. In many cases the precautions may prove to have been unnecessary, but it is usually difficult, if not impossible, to determine in advance whether they are required. The following precautions are suggested to the careful investigator.

Thurstone Scale Values. Many of the Thurstone-type scales were developed twenty to thirty years ago. Since that time there have been many changes in norms, moral judgments, and evaluations of outcomes. It seems reasonable to suppose that these changes may result in changes in the meaning of items for attitude structure. If so, the scale values of such items will have changed with the changing social values. There is some evidence that this change is not as great as might be anticipated. Edwards and Kenney (1946) found that scale values for Thurstone's church scale correlated .95 with scale values derived from the judgments of college students in 1946. The only noticeable change was that the extreme values changed in the direction of the mean. Hinckley (1963) also reports little change after a thirty-year interval for items of his Attitude toward the Negro Scale. Nevertheless, we believe that the cautious researcher will want to recheck the scale values of older Thurstone scales before using them in other than exploratory research. We recommend such a check if the scales are more than a few years old or if the target population differs markedly from that originally used for scaling. This is not overly burdensome since reliable scale values can be obtained with as few as 15 or 20 judges (Webb, 1955).

Rechecking is generally recommended for any scale with scoring weights derived from subjects' judgments or responses.

Guttman Scales. It is well known that items of Guttman-type scales may not scale for populations different from that used in their development. Therefore, the scalability of such items should be checked for each new population. Only a few scales of the Guttman type are included in this book, in part because many of the scales in the literature are specific to a given population.

Cross Validation. In most cases, scales for which items were selected by some form of item analysis have not been cross validated. Since some items will be selected initially which are not really discriminative, the items of scales that have not been cross validated should be reevaluated before the scale is used.

The Semantic Differential Scales. Osgood et al. (1957) noted that the factor structure of meaning varies with the concept being evaluated. This means that the particular scales which are loaded on the evaluative factor vary with the concept being evaluated. Consequently, the set of bipolar scales which is appropriate for the measurement of attitude may be expected to vary with the attitude object. This renders the semantic differential less generally useful than it appears to be at first thought. Unfortunately, short of a full-scale factor or cluster analysis, there is no means of ensuring that the scales selected are loaded on the evaluative factor for the attitude in question. The best recommendation that we can make is that the potential user be alert to this possibility and take whatever precautions he can devise to guard against the use of inappropriate scales.

SUMMARY

This volume has attempted to present, describe, and to some extent evaluate scales for the measurement of attitudes. In the preceding pages of this chapter, we have stated some of the strong and weak points of these scales and have made certain recommendations concerning their use in research. These attempts may be summarized as follows:

(1) The scales in this book are recommended for *experimental use only*. Most of the scales have been developed sufficiently for research work, but the evidence is frequently inadequate for recommending their use for individual assessment. We do not mean to suggest that no scale in this volume is adequate for individual assessment; we only wish to indicate the need for caution in this regard.

(2) Most of the scales we have described are moderately reliable, having reliability coefficients ranging upwards from .75. On the other hand, few of the scales have been adequately validated. That is, many of the authors of scales rely solely upon content validity, and few provide more evidence than significant differences between mean scores of known groups.

(3) Many investigators do not use the best scales available. The reasons for this are not clear, but we believe more careful measurement would materially improve the quality of research. Recomputing scale values for items of Thurstone-type scales, rechecking the scalability of Guttman items, cross validation of scales derived from item analyses, and special attention to the stability of semantic structure when using the semantic differential are suggested techniques for improving the scales that are selected for use.

(4) Considerable attention has been given to the study of the direction of the attitude, but little attention has been devoted to the measurement of other aspects of attitude. We believe that much may be gained by measuring the structural characteristics of attitude, independent of content. This is especially critical when the question of attitude modifiability is being studied (see Harvey et al., 1961).

(5) In general, the measurement of attitude may be improved in at least four ways: by improving the techniques of scale construction, by careful construction of attitude scales according to the best procedures known, by selecting the best scales available, and/or by modifying or reevaluating the scales that are selected for use.

Much progress has been made in the scientific study of attitudes, but much remains to be done. It is hoped that this work will contribute in some small way to the advancement of our understanding of attitudes and their role in human behavior.

references

Ackerley, L. A. The information and attitudes regarding child development possessed by parents of elementary school children. *Univer. Iowa Stud. child Welf.*, 1934, **10**, 115–167.

Adorno, T. W., Frenkel-Brunswik, E., Levinson, D. J., and Sanford, R. N. *The authoritarian personality*. New York: Harper & Row, 1950.

Ager, J. W., and Dawes, R. M. The effect of judges' attitude on judgment. *J. pers. soc. Psychol.*, 1965, **1**, 533–538.

Aiken, E. G. Alternate forms of a semantic differential for measurement of changes in self-description. *Psychol. Rep.*, 1965, **16**, 177–178.

Aiken, L. R., Jr. Personality correlates of attitude toward mathematics. *J. educ. Res.*, 1963, **56**, 476–480.

Aiken, L. R., Jr., and Dreger, R. M. The effect of attitudes on performance in mathematics. *J. educ. Psychol.*, 1961, **52**, 19–24.

Alberts, W. E. Ministers' attitudes toward juvenile delinquency. *Res. Monogr., Div. Temperance gen. Welf.*, 1962.

Alberts, W. E. Personality and attitudes toward juvenile delinquency: A study of Protestant ministers. *J. soc. Psychol.*, 1963, **60**, 71–83.

Albright, L. E., Kirsch, A. D., Lawshe, C. H., and Remmers, H. H. A longitudinal comparison of student attitudes toward minorities. *J. educ. Psychol.*, 1956, **47**, 372–379.

Allen, L. B. Religious attitudes of a selected group of Negro college students. *J. Negro Educ.*, 1947, **16**, 142–147.

Allman, R. W. A study of the social attitudes of college students. *J. soc. Psychol.*, 1961, **53**, 33–51.

Allport, G. W. *Personality: A psychological interpretation*. New York: Holt, 1937.

Allport, G. W. The historical background of modern social psychology. In G. Lindzey (Ed.), *Handbook of social psychology*. Vol. I. Cambridge, Mass.: Addison-Wesley, 1954. Pp. 3–56.

Alpert, R., and Sargent, S. S. Conservatism-radicalism measured by immediate emotional reactions. *J. soc. Psychol.*, 1941, **14**, 181–186.

Altman, I., and McGinnies, E. Interpersonal perception and communication in discussion groups of varied attitudinal composition. *J. abnorm. soc. Psychol.*, 1960, **60**, 390–395.

Altrocchi, J., and Eisdorfer, C. Changes in attitudes toward mental illness. *Ment. Hygiene*, 1961, **45**, 563–570.

American Association of University Professors. *Faculty Morale Scale for Institutional Improvement manual*. Chicago: Psychometric Affiliates, 1963.

American Civil Liberties Union, Academic Freedom Committee, Illinois Division. *Academic freedom survey*. Chicago: Psychometric Affiliates, 1954.

American Psychological Association Committee. Technical recommendations for psychological tests and diagnostic techniques. *Psychol. Bull. Suppl.*, 1954, **51** (2), 1–38, Part 2.

Anderson, L. R., and Fishbein, M. Prediction of attitude from number, strength, and evaluative aspect of beliefs about the attitude object: A comparison of summation and congruity theories. *J. pers. soc. Psychol.,* 1965, **2,** 437–443.

Anderson, T. W. On estimation of parameters in latent structure analysis. *Psychometrika,* 1954, **19,** 1–11.

Ash, P. The development of a scale to measure anti-Negro prejudice. *J. soc. Psychol.,* 1954, **39,** 187–199.

Asher, J. J., and Evans, R. I. An investigation of some aspects of the social psychological impact of an educational television program. *J. appl. Psychol.,* 1959, **43,** 166–169.

Attneave, F. A method of graded dichotomies for the scaling of judgments. *Psychol. Rev.,* 1949, **56,** 334–340.

Ausubel, D. P., and Schpoont, S. H. Prediction of group opinion as a function of extremeness of predictor attitudes. *J. soc. Psychol.,* 1957, **46,** 19–29.

Axelrod, S., and Eisdorfer, C. Attitudes toward old people: An empirical analysis of the stimulus-group validity of the Tuckman-Lorge questionnaire. *J. Geront.,* 1961, **16,** 75–80.

Ayad, J. M., and Farnsworth, P. R. Shifts in the values of opinion items: Further data. *J. Psychol.,* 1953, **36,** 295–298.

Ballin, M. R., and Farnsworth, P. R. A graphic rating method for determining the scale values of statements in measuring social attitudes. *J. soc. Psychol.,* 1941, **13,** 323–327.

Balogh, J., and Mueller, M. A. A scaling technique for measuring social attitudes toward capital punishment. *Sociol. soc. Res.,* 1960, **45,** 24–26.

Banta, T. J. Social attitudes and response styles. *Educ. psychol. Measmt,* 1961, **21,** 543–557.

Bardis, P. D. A familism scale. *Marriage Fam. Living,* 1959*a,* **21,** 340–341.

Bardis, P. D. Attitudes toward the family among college students and their parents. *Sociol. soc. Res.,* 1959*b,* **43,** 352–358.

Bardis, P. D. A religion scale. *Soc. Sci.,* 1961, **36,** 120–123.

Bardis, P. D. A dating scale. A technique for the quantitative measurement of liberalism concerning selected aspects of dating. *Soc. Sci.,* 1962, **37,** 44–47.

Barkley, K. L. Relative influence of commercial and liberal arts curricula upon changes in students' attitudes. *J. soc. Psychol.,* 1942, **15,** 129–144.

Barron, F. Some personality correlates of independence of judgment. *J. Pers.,* 1952, **21,** 287–297.

Bartlett, C. J., Quay, L. C., and Wrightsman, L. S., Jr. A comparison of two methods of attitude measurement: Likert-type and forced-choice. *Educ. psychol. Measmt,* 1960, **20,** 699–704.

Bateman, R. M. The construction and evaluation of a scale to measure attitude toward any educational program. *J. educ. Res.,* 1943, **36,** 502–506.

Baumgartner, H. W. Measuring Negro self-respect. *J. Negro Educ.,* 1935, **4,** 490–499.

Berger, E. The relation between expressed acceptance of self and expressed acceptance of others. *J. abnorm. soc. Psychol.,* 1952, **47,** 778–782.

Beyle, H. C. A scale for the measurement of attitude toward candidates for elective governmental office. *Amer. pol. sci. Rev.,* 1932, **26,** 527–544.

Bills, R., Vance, E., and McLean, A. An index of adjustment and values. *J. consult. Psychol.,* 1951, **15,** 257–261.

Bogardus, E. S. Measuring social distance. *J. appl. Sociol.,* 1925, **9,** 299–308.

Bogardus, E. S. *Immigration and race attitudes.* Boston: Heath, 1928.

Bogardus, E. S. Social distance scale. *Sociol. soc. Res.,* 1933, **17,** 265–271.

Bolton, E. B. Effect of knowledge upon attitudes toward the Negro. *Psychol. Bull.,* 1933, **30,** 719.

Bolton, E. B. Effect of knowledge upon attitudes toward the Negro. *J. soc. Psychol.*, 1935, **6**, 68–90.

Bolton, E. B. The measurement of attitudes toward mathematics. *Psychol. Monogr.*, 1938, **50**, 155–182.

Brady, J. P., Reznikoff, M., and Zeller, W. W. The relationship of expectation of improvement to actual improvement of hospitalized psychiatric patients. *J. nerv. ment. Dis.*, 1960, **130**, 41–44.

Brady, J. P., Zeller, W. W., and Reznikoff, M. Attitudinal factors influencing outcome of treatment of hospitalized psychiatric patients. *J. clin. exp. Psychopath. quart. Rev. Psychiat. Neurol.*, 1959, **20**, 326–334.

Brim, O. G., Jr., and Hoff, D. B. Individual and situational differences in desire for certainty. *J. abnorm. soc. Psychol.*, 1957, **54**, 225–229.

Brown, J. F. A modification of the Rosenzweig picture-frustration test to study hostile interracial attitudes. *J. Psychol.*, 1947, **24**, 247–272.

Brown, W. Some experimental results in the correlation of mental abilities. *Brit. J. Psychol.*, 1910, **3**, 296–322.

Brownfain, J. J. Stability of the self-concept as a dimension of personality. *J. abnorm. soc. Psychol.*, 1952, **47**, 597–606.

Bues, H. W. The construction and validation of a scale to measure attitude toward any practice. *Purdue Univer. Stud. high. Educ., XXVI*, 1934, **35**, 64–67.

Burchinal, L. G. Parents' attitudes and adjustment of children. *J. genet. Psychol.*, 1958, **92**, 69–79.

Burwen, L. S., Campbell, D. T., and Kidd, J. The use of a sentence completion test in measuring attitudes toward superiors and subordinates. *J. appl. Psychol.*, 1956, **40**, 248–250.

Campbell, D. T. The indirect assessment of social attitudes. *Psychol. Bull.*, 1950, **47**, 15–38.

Campbell, D. T., and Damarin, F. L. Measuring leadership attitudes through an information test. *J. soc. Psychol.*, 1961, **55**, 159–176.

Campbell, D. T., and Fiske, D. W. Convergent and discriminant validation by the multitrait-multimethod matrix. *Psychol. Bull.*, 1959, **56**, 81–105.

Campbell, D. W., and Stover, G. F. Teaching international-mindedness in the social studies. *J. educ. Sociol.*, 1933, **7**, 244–248.

Campbell, N. R., et al. Final report. *Advanc. Sci.*, 1940, 2, 331–349.

Cardno, J. A. The notion of attitude: An historical note. *Psychol. Rep.*, 1955, **1**, 345–352.

Carey, G. L. Sex differences in problem-solving performance as a function of attitude differences. *J. abnorm. soc. Psychol.*, 1958, **56**, 256–260.

Carey, S. M. Changes in the opinions of female students after one year at a university. *J. soc. Psychol.*, 1940, **11**, 341–351.

Carlson, H. B. Intelligence and students' attitudes. *Psychol. Bull.*, 1933, **30**, 578.

Carlson, H. B. Attitudes of undergraduate students. *J. soc. Psychol.*, 1934, **5**, 202–213.

Case, H. M. Guttman scaling applied to Centers' Conservatism-Radicalism Battery. *Amer. J. Soc.*, 1953, **58**, 556–563.

Cattell, R. B. *Handbook for the IPAT anxiety scale.* Urbana, Ill.: Institute for Personality and Ability Testing, 1957.

Centers, R. *The psychology of social classes.* New Jersey: Princeton Univer. Press, 1949.

Chansky, N. M. The attitudes students assign to their teacher. *J. educ. Psychol.*, 1958, **49**, 13–16.

Chapman, A. W. Attitudes toward legal agencies of authority for juveniles: A comparative study of one hundred thirty-three delinquent and one hundred thirty-three non-delinquent boys in Dayton, Ohio. *Dissert. Abstr.*, 1960, **20**, No. 7.

Chapman, L. J., and Campbell, D. T. An attempt to predict the performance of three-man teams from attitude measures. *J. soc. Psychol.,* 1957, **46,** 277–286.

Chase, W. P. Attitudes of North Carolina college students (women) toward the Negro. *Psychol. Bull.,* 1939, **36,** 617.

Chase, W. P. Attitudes of North Carolina college students (women) toward the Negro. *J. soc. Psychol.,* 1940, **12,** 367–378.

Chase, W. P. Measurement of attitudes toward counseling. *Educ. Psychol. Measmt,* 1946, **6,** 467-473.

Chein, I. Behavior theory and the behavior of attitudes. Some critical comments. *Psychol. Rev.,* 1948, **55,** 174–188.

Cherrington, B. M., and Miller, L. W. Changes in attitude as the result of a lecture and reading similar materials. *J. soc. Psychol.,* 1933, **4,** 479–484.

Christensen, H. T., and Carpenter, G. R. Value-behavior discrepancies regarding premarital coitus in three Western cultures. *Amer. sociol. Rev.,* 1962, **27,** 66–74.

Christiansen, B. *Attitudes toward foreign affairs as a function of personality.* Oslo: Oslo Univer. Press, 1959.

Christie, R. The "Likertization" of Machiavelli. Unpublished manuscript. Columbia Univer., 1956.

Cohen, J. A scale for the measurement of attitude toward the aesthetic value. *J. Psychol.,* 1941, **12,** 75–79.

Cohen, J., and Struening, E. L. Factors underlying opinions about mental illness in the personnel of a large mental hospital. *Amer. Psychol.,* 1959, **14,** 339.

Cohen, J., and Struening, E. L. Opinions about mental illness in the personnel of two large mental hospitals. *J. abnorm. soc. Psychol.,* 1962, **64,** 349–360.

Cohen, J., and Struening, E. L. Opinions about mental illness: Mental hospital occupational profiles and profile clusters. *Psychol. Rep.,* 1963, **12,** 111–124.

Cohen, J., and Struening, E. L. Opinions about mental illness: Hospital social atmosphere profiles and their relevance to effectiveness. *J. consult. Psychol.,* 1964, **28,** 291–298.

Cook, L. A. *Intergroup relations in teacher education.* Vol. II. *College study in intergroup relations,* Washington, D.C.: American Council on Education, 1950.

Cook, W. W., Leeds, C. H., and Callis, R. *Minnesota teacher attitude inventory.* New York: Psychological Corporation, 1951.

Coombs, C. H. Psychological scaling without a unit of measurement. *Psychol. Rev.,* 1950, **57,** 145–158.

Coombs, C. H. The theory and methods of social measurement. In L. Festinger and D. Katz (Eds.), *Research methods in the behavioral sciences.* New York: Dryden Press, 1953. Pp. 471–535.

Costin, F. Attitudinal outcomes of child psychology courses having different orientations. *J. Psychol.,* 1961, **51,** 113–119.

Costin, F. The knowledge about psychology test. *J. exp. Educ.,* 1963, **31,** 395–400.

Costin, F., and Kerr, W. D. The effects of an abnormal psychology course on students' attitudes toward mental illness. *J. educ. Psychol.,* 1962, **53,** 214–218.

Cowen, E. L., Underberg, R. P., and Verrillo, R. T. The development and testing of an attitude to blindness scale. *J. soc. Psychol.,* 1958, **48,** 297–304.

Cronbach, L. J., and Meehl, P. E. Construct validity in psychological tests. *Psychol. Bull.,* 1955, **52,** 281–302.

Crowne, D., and Stephens, M. Self-acceptance and self-evaluative behavior: a critique of methodology. *Psychol. Bull.,* 1961, **58,** 104–121.

Crowne, D., Stephens, M., and Kelly, R. Validity and equivalence of tests of self-acceptance. *J. Psychol.,* 1961, **51,** 101–112.

Darley, J. G. Changes in measured attitudes and adjustment. *J soc. Psychol.,* 1938, **9,** 189–199.

Day, D. D., and Quackenbush, O. F. Attitudes toward defensive, cooperative, and aggressive war. *J. soc. Psychol.*, 1942, **16**, 11–20.

Day, H. P. Attitude changes of beginning teachers after initial teaching experience. *J. teacher Educ.*, 1959, **10**, 326–328.

Diab, L. N. Some limitations of existing scales in the measurement of social attitudes. Paper presented at Second Conf. Exp. Soc. Psychol. Europe, Frascati, Italy, December 11, 1964.

Diggory, J. C. Sex differences in the organization of attitudes. *J. Pers.*, 1953, **22**, 89–200.

Diggory, J. C., and Rothman, D. Z. Values destroyed by death. *J. abnorm. soc. Psychol.*, 1961, **63**, 205–210.

Di Vesta, F. J., and Merwin, J. C. The effects of need-oriented communications on attitude change. *J. abnorm. soc. Psychol.*, 1960, **60**, 80–85.

Dodd, S. C. A social distance test in the Near East. *Amer. J. Sociol.*, 1935, **41**, 194–204.

Dodd, S. C., and Griffiths, K. S. The logarithmic relation of social distance and intensity. *J. soc. Psychol.*, 1958, **48**, 91–101.

Doob, L. W. The behavior of attitudes. *Psychol. Rev.*, 1947, **54**, 135–156.

Drake, J. T. Some factors influencing students' attitudes toward older people. *Soc. Forces*, 1957, **35**, 266–271.

Dreger, R. M. Expressed attitudes and needs of religious persons compared with those determined by projective techniques. *J. gen. Psychol.*, 1958, **58**, 217–224.

Drinkwater, B. L. Development of an attitude inventory to measure the attitude of high school girls toward physical education as a career for women. *Res. Quart.*, 1960, **31**, 575–580.

Droba, D. D. A scale of militarism-pacifism. *J. educ. Psychol.*, 1931*a*, **22**, 96–111.

Droba, D. D. Effect of various factors on militarism-pacifism. *J. abnorm. soc. Psychol.*, 1931*b*, **26**, 141–153.

Droba, D. D. Churches and war attitudes. *Sociol. soc. Res.*, 1931*c*, **16**, 547–552.

Droba, D. D. Education and Negro attitudes. *Sociol. soc. Res.*, 1932, **17**, 137–141.

Droba, D. D. Political parties and war attitudes. *J. abnorm. soc. Psychol.*, 1934, **28**, 468–472.

Dudycha, G. J. The religious beliefs of college freshmen. *Sch. and Soc.*, 1930*a*, **31**, 206–208.

Dudycha, G. J. The moral and popular beliefs of college freshmen. *Sch. and Soc.*, 1930*b*, **32**, 69–72.

Dudycha, G. J. The beliefs of college students concerning the athlete and the scholar. *Sch. and Soc.*, 1932, **36**, 1–6.

Dudycha, G. J. The moral beliefs of college students. *Int. J. Eth.*, 1933*a*, **43**, 194–204.

Dudycha, G. J. The superstitious beliefs of college students. *J. abnorm. soc. Psychol.*, 1933*b*, **27**, 457–464.

Dudycha, G. J. The beliefs of college students concerning evolution. *J. appl. Psychol.*, 1934, **18**, 85–96.

Dudycha, G. J. A scale for measuring attitudes toward dependability. *J. soc. Psychol.*, 1941, **13**, 59–69.

Dudycha, G. J. The attitude of college students toward war. *J. soc. Psychol.*, 1942*a*, **15**, 75–89.

Dudycha, G. J. Attitudes toward war. *Psychol. Bull.*, 1942*b*, **39**, 846–860.

Dudycha, G. J. The attitudes of college students toward war and the Germans before and during the second World War. *J. soc. Psychol.*, 1942, **15**, 317–324.

Dudycha, G. J. The superstitious beliefs of college freshmen in 1939 and 1949. *Sch. and Soc.*, 1950, **72**, 376–379.

Dudycha, G. J. Race attitude and esthetic preference. *J. soc. Psychol.,* 1953, **37,** 61–68.

Duffy, E. Attitudes of parents and daughters toward war and toward treatment of criminals. *Psychol. Rec.,* 1941, **4,** 366–372.

Dynes, R. R. Church-sect typology and socio-economic status. *Amer. sociol. Rev.,* 1955, **20,** 555–560.

Edwards, A. L. Unlabelled fascist attitudes. *J. abnorm. soc. Psychol.,* 1941, **36,** 575–582.

Edwards, A. L. The scaling of stimuli by the method of successive intervals. *J. appl. Psychol.,* 1952, **36,** 118–122.

Edwards, A. L. *Techniques of attitude scale construction.* New York: Appleton-Century-Crofts, 1957.

Edwards, A. L., and Kenney, K. C. A comparison of the Thurstone and Likert techniques of attitude scale construction. *J. appl. Psychol.,* 1946, **30,** 72–83.

Edwards, A. L., and Kilpatrick, F. P. A technique for the construction of attitude scales. *J. appl. Psychol.,* 1948*a,* **32,** 374–384.

Edwards, A. L., and Kilpatrick, F. P. Scale analysis and the measurement of social attitudes. *Psychometrika,* 1948*b,* **13,** 99–114.

Eisdorfer, C., and Altrocchi, J. A comparison of attitudes toward old age and mental illness. *J. Geront.,* 1961, **16,** 340–343.

Engle, T. L. Attitudes toward war as expressed by Amish and non-Amish children. *J. educ. Psychol.,* 1944, **35,** 211–219.

English, H. B., and English, A. C. *A comprehensive dictionary of psychological and psychoanalytic terms: A guide to usage.* New York: McKay, 1958.

Ericksen, S. C. A skeptical note on the use of attitude scales toward war: I. In 1940, 1941. *J. soc. Psychol.,* 1942, **16,** 229–242.

Ewing, T. Changes in attitude during counseling. *J. counsel. Psychol.,* 1954, **1,** 232–239.

Eysenck, H. J. Primary Social Attitudes: 1. The organization and measurement of social attitudes. *Int. J. opin. attit. Res.,* 1947, **1,** 49–84.

Eysenck, H. J., and Crown, S. An experimental study in opinion-attitude methodology. *Int. J. opin. attit. Res.,* 1949, **3,** 48–86.

Fay, P. J., and Middleton, W. C. Certain factors related to liberal and conservative attitudes of college students; sex classification, fraternity membership, major subject. *J. educ. Psychol.,* 1939, **30,** 378–390.

Fay, P. J., and Middleton, W. C. Certain factors related to liberal and conservative attitudes of college students: Father's occupation, size of home town. *J. soc. Psychol.,* 1940*a,* **11,** 91–105.

Fay, P. J., and Middleton, W. C. Certain factors related to liberal and conservative attitudes of college students: Parental membership in certain organizations. *J. soc. Psychol.,* 1940*b,* **12,** 55–69.

Fehrer, E. Shifts in scale values of attitude statements as a function of the composition of the scale. *J. exp. Psychol.,* 1952, **44,** 179–188.

Ferguson, L. W. The influence of individual attitudes on construction of an attitude scale. *J. soc. Psychol.,* 1935, **6,** 115–117.

Ferguson, L. W. An item analysis of Peterson's "war" scale. *Psychol. Bull.,* 1938, **35,** 521.

Ferguson, L. W. Primary social attitudes. *J. Psychol.,* 1939, **8,** 217–223.

Ferguson, L. W. Comparison of scale values from the method of equal appearing intervals and paired comparisons method. *J. gen. Psychol.,* 1940*a,* **23,** 431–435.

Ferguson, L. W. The measurement of primary social attitudes. *J. Psychol.,* 1940*b,* **10,** 199–205.

Ferguson, L. W. A study of the Likert technique of attitude scale construction. *J. soc. Psychol.,* 1941, **13,** 51–57.

Ferguson, L. W. The isolation and measurement of nationalism. *J. soc. Psychol.,* 1942, **16,** 215–228.

Ferguson, L. W. A revision of the primary social attitude scales. *J. Psychol.,* 1944*a,* **17,** 229–241.

Ferguson, L. W. Socio-psychological correlates of primary attitude scales; I. Religionism, II. Humanitarianism. *J. soc. Psychol.,* 1944*b,* **19,** 18–98.

Ferguson, L. W. Analysis of sex temperaments in terms of Thurstone-type attitude items. *J. genet. Psychol.,* 1945, **66,** 233–238.

Ferguson, L. W. The sociological validity of Primary Social Attitude Scale No. I: Religionism. *J. soc. Psychol.,* 1946, **23,** 197–204.

Ferguson, L. W. *Personality measurement.* New York: McGraw-Hill, 1952.

Ferguson, L. W., and Lawrence, W. R. An appraisal of the validity of the factor loadings employed in the construction of the primary social attitudes scales. *Psychometrika,* 1942, **7,** 135–138.

Festinger, L. The treatment of qualitative data by "scale analysis." *Psychol. Bull.,* 1947, **44,** 149–161.

Festinger, L. *A theory of cognitive dissonance.* New York: Harper & Row, 1957.

Fitting, E. *Evaluation of adjustment to blindness.* New York: American Foundation for the Blind, Res. Ser. 2, 1954.

Ford, R. N. Scaling experience by a multiple-response technique: A study of white-Negro contacts. *Amer. sociol. Rev.,* 1941, **6,** 9–23.

Form, A. L. The construction of a scale on attitudes toward counseling. *J. counsel. Psychol.,* 1955, **2,** 96–102.

Forsyth, F. H. Social crises and social attitudes toward relief. *J. soc. Psychol.,* 1943, **18,** 55–69.

Freeman, H. E., and Haer, J. L. An empirical examination of the concept of clarity of attitude. *Int. J. opin. attit. Res.,* 1951, **5,** 465–474.

Fromme, A. On the use of certain qualitative methods of attitude research: A study of opinions on the methods of preventing war. *J. soc. Psychol.,* 1941, **13,** 425–459.

Frymier, J. R. Young people's attitudes toward Russia. *J. soc. Psychol.,* 1961, **53,** 127–131.

Funk, R. A. Experimental scales used in a study of religious attitudes as related to manifest anxiety. *Psychol. Newsltr,* 1958, **9,** 238–244.

Gallenbech, C., and Smith, K. U. Systematic formulation and experimental analysis of the phenomena of thinking and belief. *J. exp. Psychol.,* 1950, **40,** 74–80.

Gardiner, I. C. Effect of a group of social stimuli upon attitudes. *J. educ. Psychol.,* 1935, **26,** 471–479.

Garner, W. R., and Hake, H. W. The amount of information in absolute judgments. *Psychol. Rev.,* 1951, **58,** 445–459.

Garrison, K. C. Worldminded attitudes of college students in a Southern university. *J. soc. Psychol.,* 1961, **54,** 147–153.

Garrison, K. C. The relationship of certain variables to church-sect typology among college students. *J. soc. Psychol.,* 1962, **56,** 29–32.

Garrison, K. C., and Burch, U. S. A study of racial attitudes of college students. *J. soc. Psychol.,* 1933, **4,** 230–235.

Getzels, J. W., and Walsh, J. J. The method of paired direct and projective questionnaires in the study of attitude structure and specialization. *Psychol. Monogr.,* 1958, **72,** No. 1 (Whole No. 454).

Ghiselli, E. E. *Theory of psychological measurement.* New York: McGraw-Hill, 1964.

Gilbert, D. C., and Levinson, D. J. Ideology, personality, and institutional policy in the mental hospital. *J. abnorm. soc. Psychol.,* 1956, **53,** 263–271.

Gilbert, D. C., and Levinson, D. J. "Custodialism" and "Humanism" in mental hospital structure and in staff ideology. In M. Greenblatt, D. J. Levinson, and R. H. Williams (Eds.), *The patient and the mental hospital.* Glencoe, Ill.: Free Press, 1957. Pp. 20–35.

Gillespie, F. A. *High school attitude scale.* Purdue Univer., Personnel Evaluation Research Service, 1936.

Gladstone, R., Deal, R., and Drevdahl, J. E. An exploratory study of remedial Math. *Proc. Okla. Acad. Sci.,* 1960, **40,** 81–85.

Glasner, D. M. Factor analytic investigations of the components of attitude structure. Unpublished doctoral dissertation, Purdue Univer., 1963.

Glassey, W. The attitude of grammar school pupils and their parents to education, religion and sport. *Brit. J. educ. Psychol.,* 1945, **15,** 101–104.

Goodstein, L. W. Intellectual rigidity and social attitudes. *J. abnorm. soc. Psychol.,* 1953, **48,** 345–353.

Gorham, D. R., and Lasky, J. J. Do the attitudes depressed patients have toward chemotherapy affect their treatment response? *Amer. Psychologist,* 1962, **17,** 323.

Gorham, D. R., and Sherman, L. J. The relation of attitude toward medication to treatment outcomes in chemotherapy. *Amer. J. Psychiat.,* 1961, **117,** 830–832.

Grafton, T. H. An attitude scale on accepting Negro students. *Soc. Forces,* 1964, **43,** 38–41.

Gragg, D. B. Religious attitudes of denominational college students. *J. soc. Psychol.,* 1942, **15,** 245–254.

Graham, M. D. The effectiveness of photographs as a projective device in an international attitudes survey: I. Responses of 680 Britons to 10 photographs of American types. *J. soc. Psychol.,* 1954, **40,** 93–120.

Green, B. F. A general solution for the latent class model of structure analysis. *Psychometrika,* 1951, **16,** 151–168.

Green, B. F. Attitude measurement. In G. Lindsey (Ed.), *Handbook of social psychology.* Cambridge, Mass.: Addison-Wesley, 1954. Pp. 335–369.

Greenberg, H. M. The development of an integration attitude scale. *J. soc. Psychol.,* 1961, **54,** 103–109.

Greenberg, H., Chase, A. L., and Cannon, T. M., Jr. Attitudes of white and Negro high school students in a West Texas town toward school integration. *J. appl. Psychol.,* 1957, **41,** 27–31.

Greenberg, H., and Hutto, D. The attitudes of West Texas college students toward integration. *J. appl. Psychol.,* 1958, **42,** 301–304.

Greenblatt, M., Levinson, D. J., and Williams, R. H. (Eds.) *The patient and the mental hospital.* Glencoe, Ill.: Free Press, 1957.

Gregory, W. S. Ideology and affect regarding "law" and their relation to law-abidingness. Part I. *Charact. Pers.,* 1939, **7,** 265–284.

Grice, H. H. The construction and validation of a generalized scale designed to measure attitudes toward defined groups. *Bull. Purdue Univer.,* 1934, **25,** 37–46.

Gristle, M. The construction of a scale for measuring attitude toward militarism-pacifism. *J. soc. Psychol.,* 1940, **11,** 383–391.

Guilford, J. P. The phi coefficient and chi square as indices of item validity. *Psychometrika,* 1941, **6,** 11–19.

Guion, R. M., and Robins, J. E. A note on the Nagle attitude scale. *J. appl. Psychol.,* 1964, **48,** 29–30.

Guttman, L. A basis for scaling qualitative data. *Amer. sociol. Rev.,* 1944, **9,** 139–150.

Guttman, L. The Cornell technique for scale and intensity analysis. *Educ. psychol. Measmt,* 1947, **7,** 247–280.

Guttman, L. The principal components of scalable attitudes. In P. F. Lazarsfeld (Ed.), *Mathematical thinking in the social sciences.* Glencoe, Ill.: Free Press, 1954.

Guttman, L., and Suchman, E. A. Intensity and a zero point for attitude analysis. *Amer. sociol. Rev.*, 1947, **12**, 57–67.

Hall, O. M. Attitudes and unemployment, a comparison of the attitudes of employed and unemployed men. *Arch. Psychol.*, 1934, No. 165. P. 65.

Hammond, K. R. Measuring attitudes by error-choice: An indirect method. *J. abnorm. soc. Psychol.*, 1948, **43**, 38.

Hand, J. A method of weighting attitude scale items from subject responses. *J. clin. Psychol.*, 1953, **9**, 37–39.

Handy, U., and Lentz, T. F. Item value and test reliability. *J. educ. Psychol.*, 1934, **25**, 703–708.

Hardy, K. R. Construction and validation of a scale measuring attitudes toward the L.D.S. Church. Unpublished master's thesis, Univer. of Utah, 1949.

Hardy, K. R. Determinants of conformity and attitude change. *J. abnorm. soc. Psychol.*, 1957, **54**, 289–294.

Harlan, H. H. Some factors affecting attitude toward Jews. *Amer. sociol. Rev.*, 1942, **7**, 816–827.

Hartman, G. W., and Newcomb, T. M. (Eds.) *Industrial conflict*. New York: Cordon, 1939.

Harvey, O. J., Hunt, D. E., and Schroder, H. M. *Conceptual systems and personality organization*. New York: Wiley, 1961.

Hathaway, S. R., and McKinley, J. C. *Minnesota multiphasic personality inventory*. (Rev. ed.) New York: Psychological Corporation, 1951.

Havron, M. D., Nordlie, P. G., and Cofer, C. Measurement of attitudes by a simple word association technique. *J. soc. Psychol.*, 1957, **46**, 81–89.

Hays, D. G., and Borgatta, E. P. An empirical comparison of restricted and general latent distance analysis. *Psychometrika*, 1954, **19**, 271–279.

Heider, F. *The psychology of interpersonal relations*. New York: Wiley, 1958.

Heilbrun, A. B., Jr. Note on acquiescence set in endorsed attitudes of mothers of schizophrenics and normals. *J. clin. Psychol.*, 1960*a*, **16**, 104–105.

Heilbrun, A. B., Jr. Perceptual distortion and schizophrenia. *Amer. J. Orthopsychiat.*, 1960*b*, **30**, 412–418.

Helfant, K. Parents' attitudes vs. adolescent hostility in the determination of adolescent socio-political attitudes. *Psychol. Monogr.*, 1952, **66**, 1–23.

Helson, H. An experimental investigation of the effectiveness of the "big lie" in shifting attitudes. *J. soc. Psychol.*, 1958, **43**, 51–60.

Hevner, K. An empirical study of three psychophysical methods. *J. gen. Psychol.*, 1930, **4**, 191–212.

Hinckley, E. D. The influence of individual opinion on construction of an attitude scale. *J. soc. Psychol.*, 1932, **3**, 283–296.

Hinckley, E. D. *The influence of individual opinion on construction of an attitude scale*. Chicago: Univer. of Chicago Library, 1932.

Hinckley, E. D. A follow-up study on the influence of individual opinion on the construction of an attitude scale. *J. abnorm. soc. Psychol.*, 1963, **67**, 290–292.

Hinckley, E. D., and Hinckley, M. B. Attitude scales for measuring the influence of the work relief program. *J. soc. Psychol.*, 1939, **8**, 115–124.

Hines, V. A. Development and factor analysis of a scale of liberalism-conservatism. Mimeograph Rep., University of Florida.

Hirschberg, G., and Gilliland, A. R. Parent-child relationships in attitude. *J. abnorm. soc. Psychol.*, 1942, **37**, 125–130.

Horne, E. P., and Stender, W. H. Student attitudes toward religious practices. *J. soc. Psychol.*, 1945, **22**, 215–217.

Horowitz, R. E. Racial aspects of self-identification in nursery school children. *J. Psychol.*, 1939, **7**, 91–99.

Hoshaw, L. D. The construction and evaluation of a scale for measuring attitude toward any teacher. *Bull. Purdue Univer.*, 1936, **37**, 238–251.

Hovland, C. I., Harvey, O. J., and Sherif, M. Assimilation and contrast effects in reactions to communication and attitude change. *J. abnorm. soc. Psychol.*, 1957, **55**, 244–252.

Hovland, C. I., Janis, I. L., and Kelley, H. H. *Communication and persuasion.* New Haven: Yale Univer. Press, 1953.

Hovland, C. I., and Sherif, M. Judgmental phenomena and scales of attitude measurement: Item displacement in Thurstone scales. *J. abnorm. soc. Psychol.*, 1952, **47**, 822–832.

Imre, P., and Wolf, S. Attitudes of patients and personnel toward mental hospitals. *J. clin. Psychol.*, 1962, **18**, 232–234.

Itkin, W. Some relationships between intra-family attitudes and preparental attitudes toward children. *J. genet. Psychol.*, 1952, **80**, 221–252.

Itkin, W. Relationships between attitudes toward parents and parents' attitudes toward children. *J. genet. Psychol.*, 1955, **86**, 339–352.

Janis, I. L., and King, B. T. The influence of role playing upon opinion change. *J. abnorm soc. Psychol.*, 1954, **49**, 236–241.

Jarrett, R. F., and Sherriffs, A. C. Propaganda, debate, and impartial presentation as determiners of attitude change. *J. abnorm. soc. Psychol.*, 1953, **48**, 33–41.

Jenkins, J. J., Russell, W. A., and Suci, G. J. An atlas of semantic profiles for 360 words. In *Studies on the role of language in behavior.* Tech. Rep. No. 15. Minneapolis: Univer. of Minnesota, 1957.

Johnson, D. M. Confidence and the expression of opinion. *J. soc. Psychol.*, 1940, **12**, 213–220.

Johnson, G. B. An experimental projective technique for the analysis of racial attitudes. *J. educ. Psychol.*, 1950, **45**, 257–278.

Jones, V. Attitudes toward peace and war. *J. higher Educ.*, 1942*a*, **13**, 5–13.

Jones, V. The nature of changes in attitudes of college students toward war over an eleven year period. *J. educ. Psychol.*, 1942*b*, **33**, 481–494.

Jourard, S. M. Identification, parent-cathexis and self-esteem. *J. consult. Psychol.*, 1957, **21**, 375–380.

Kalish, R. A. Some variables in death attitudes. *J. soc. Psychol.*, 1963, **59**, 137–145.

Kasheiva, Y. L., and Smith, M. E. A study of the attitudes of some children of Japanese descent toward the Chinese and Japanese. *J. soc. Psychol.*, 1943, **18**, 149–153.

Katz, M. R. A hypothesis on anti-Negro prejudice. *Amer. J. Sociol.*, 1947, **53**, 100–104.

Kellar, B. The construction and validation of a scale to measure attitude toward any homemaking activity. *Purdue Univer. Stud. high. Educ., XXVI*, 1934, **35**, 47–63.

Kelley, I. B. Construction and validation of a scale to measure attitude toward any institution. *Purdue Univer. Stud. high. Educ.*, 1934, **35**, 18–36.

Kelley, I. B. An investigation of teacher's knowledge of and attitudes toward child and adolescent behavior in everyday school situation. *Further Stud. Attit.*, Ser. IV, Purdue Univer., June, 1941.

Kelley, J. G., Ferson, J. E., and Holtzman, W. H. The measurement of attitudes toward the Negro in the South. *J. soc. Psychol.*, 1958, **48**, 305–317.

Kelly, G. A. *The psychology of personal constructs.* New York: Norton, 1955. 2 vols.

Kerlinger, F. N., and Kaya, E. The construction and factor analytic validation of scales to measure attitudes toward education. *Educ. psychol. Measmt*, 1959*a*, **19**, 13–29.

Kerlinger, F. N., and Kaya, E. The predictive validity of scales constructed to measure attitudes toward education. *Educ. psychol. Measmt,* 1959*b,* **19,** 305–317.

Kerr, M. An experimental investigation of national stereotypes. *Sociol. Rev.,* 1943, **35,** 37–43.

Kerr, W. A. *Tulane factors of liberalism-conservatism: manual of instructions.* Chicago: Psychometric Affiliates, 1946.

Kerr, W. A. Untangling the liberalism-conservatism continuum. *J. soc. Psychol.,* 1952, **35,** 111–125.

Khanna, J. L., Pratt, S., and Gardiner, G. Attitudes of psychiatric aides toward "criminally insane" patients. *J. crim. Law, Criminol., police Sci.,* 1962, **53,** 55–60.

Kimbrough, R. B., and Hines, V. A. *The Florida scale of civic beliefs.* Gainesville, Fla.: Univer. of Florida, College of Education, 1963.

Kimbrough, W. W., and Cofer, C. N. Attitudes and stimuli as determiners of response. *Psychol. Rep.,* 1958, **4,** 61.

King, D. C. A multiplant factor analysis of employees' attitudes toward their company. *J. appl. Psychol.,* 1960, **44,** 241–243.

Kirchner, W. K. The attitudes of special groups toward the employment of older persons. *J. Geront.,* 1957, **12,** 216–220.

Kirchner, W. K., and Dunnette, M. D. Attitudes toward older workers. *Personnel Psychol.,* 1954, **7,** 257–265.

Kirchner, W. K., Lindbom, T., and Paterson, D. G. Attitudes toward employment of older people. *J. appl. Psychol.,* 1952, **36,** 154–156.

Kirkpatrick, C. An experimental study of the modification of social attitudes. *Amer. J. Sociol.,* 1936*a,* **41,** 649–656.

Kirkpatrick, C. The construction of a belief pattern scale for measuring attitudes toward feminism. *J. soc. Psychol.,* 1936*b,* **7,** 421–427.

Kirkpatrick, C. Religion and humanitarianism. A study of institutional implications. *Psychol. Monogr.,* 1949, **63,** No. 9 (Whole No. 304).

Kirkpatrick, C., and Stone, S. Attitude measurement and the comparison of generations. *J. appl. Psychol.,* 1935, **19,** 564–582.

Kitano, H. Differential child-rearing attitudes between first and second generation Japanese in the United States. *J. soc. Psychol.,* 1961, **53,** 13–19.

Klopfer, W. G., Wylie, A. A., and Hillson, J. S. Attitudes toward mental hospitals. *J. clin. Psychol.,* 1956, **12,** 361–365.

Knapp, R. H. A study of the metaphor. *J. proj. Techniques,* 1960, **24,** 389–395.

Knight, W. R., and Hall, J. F. Use of a cartoon-type projective technique in measuring attitudes toward psychology. *Percept. mtr. Skills,* 1957, **7,** 25–28.

Knode, J. C. Attitudes on state university campuses. *Amer. Sociol. Rev.,* 1943, **8,** 666–673.

Koch, H. L., Dentler, M., Dysart, B., and Streit, H. A scale for measuring attitudes toward the question of children's freedom. *Child Developm.,* 1934, **5,** 253–266.

Kogan, N. Attitudes toward old people: The development of a scale and an examination of correlates. *J. abnorm. soc. Psychol.,* 1961*a,* **62,** 44–54.

Kogan, N. Attitudes toward old people in an older sample. *J. abnorm. soc. Psychol.,* 1961*b,* **62,** 616–622.

Kogan, N., and Downey, J. F. Scaling norm conflicts in the area of prejudice and discrimination. *J. abnorm. soc. Psychol.,* 1956, **53,** 292–295.

Kogan, N., and Wallach, M. A. Age changes in values and attitudes. *J. Geront.,* 1961, **16,** 272–280.

Krech, D., and Crutchfield, R. S. *Theory and problems of social psychology.* New York: McGraw-Hill, 1948.

Krech, D., Crutchfield, R. S., and Ballachey, E. L. *Individual in society.* New York: McGraw-Hill, 1962.

Kruskal, J. B. Multidimensional scaling by optimizing goodness of fit to a nonmetric hypothesis. *Psychometrika,* 1964*a,* **29,** 1–27.

Kruskal, J. B. Nonmetric multidimensional scaling: A numerical method. *Psychometrika,* 1964*b,* **29,** 115–129.

Kuder, G. F., and Richardson, M. W. The theory of estimation of test reliability. *Psychometrika,* 1937, **2,** 151–160.

Kulp, D. H., II, and Davidson, H. H. Sibling resemblance in social attitudes. *J. educ. Sociol.,* 1933, **7,** 133–140.

Lakie, W. L. Expressed attitudes of various groups of athletes toward athletic competition. *Res. Quart.,* 1964, **35,** 497–503.

Lana, R. E. Pretest-treatment interaction effects in attitudinal studies. *Psychol. Bull.,* 1959, **56,** 293–300.

Lawshe, C. H., and Nagle, B. F. Productivity and attitude toward supervisor. *J. appl. Psychol.,* 1953, **37,** 159–162.

Lawson, E. D. Development of patriotism in children—a second look. *J. Psychol.,* 1963, **55,** 279–286.

Lazarsfeld, P. F. The logic and mathematical foundation of latent structure analysis. In S. A. Stouffer, L. Guttman, E. A. Schuman, P. F. Lazarsfeld, S. A. Star, and J. A. Clausen, *Measurement and prediction.* Princeton, N.J.: Princeton Univer. Press, 1950. Pp. 362–412.

Lazarsfeld, P. F. A conceptual introduction to latent structure analysis. In P. F. Lazarsfeld (Ed.), *Mathematical thinking in the social sciences.* Glencoe, Ill.: Free Press, 1954.

Lazarsfeld, P. F. Latent structure analysis. In S. Koch (Ed.), *Psychology: a study of science,* Vol. 3. New York: McGraw-Hill, 1959. Pp. 476–543.

Lentz, T. F., Jr. Utilizing opinion for character measurement. *J. soc. Psychol.,* 1930, **1,** 536–542.

Lentz, T. F., Jr. Reliability of opinionnaire technique, studied by retest method. *J. soc. Psychol.,* 1934, **5,** 338–364.

Lentz, T. F., Jr., and Colleagues. *Manual for C-R opinionnaire.* St. Louis: Washington Univer., Character Research Institute, 1935.

Levinson, D. J. An approach to the theory and measurement of ethnocentric ideology. *J. Psychol.,* 1949, **28,** 19–39.

Levinson, D. J. Authoritarian personality and foreign policy. *J. conflict Resolut.,* 1957, **1,** 37–47.

Levinson, D. J., and Huffman, P. E. Traditional family ideology and its relation to personality. *J. Pers.,* 1955, **23,** 251–273.

Levinson, D. J., and Sanford, R. N. A scale for the measurement of anti-Semitism. *J. Psychol.,* 1944, **17,** 339–370.

Libo, L. M. Authoritarianism and attitudes toward socialized medicine among senior medical students. *J. soc. Psychol.,* 1957, **46,** 133–136.

Likert, R. A technique for the measurement of attitudes. *Arch. Psychol.,* 1932, No. 140. Pp. 1–55.

Likert, R., Roslow, S., and Murphy, G. A simple and reliable method of scoring the Thurstone attitude scales. *J. soc. Psychol.,* 1934, **5,** 228–238.

Lilly, R. Psychodynamics of the attitudes of ex-service men toward feminism. *Amer. Psychol.,* 1947, **2,** 413. (Abstract)

Lindgren, H. C. Correlates of attitudes toward child-centered practices in education. *Psychol. Rep.,* 1961, **9,** 440.

Lindgren, H. C. Authoritarianism, independence, and child-centered practices in education: A study of attitudes. *Psychol. Rep.,* 1962, **10,** 747–750.

Lindgren, H. C., and Patton, G. M. Attitudes of high school and other teachers toward children and current educational methodology. *Calif. J. educ. Res.,* 1958, **9,** 80–85.

Loevinger, J., Gleser, G. C., and DuBois, P. M. Maximizing the discriminating power of a multiple-score test. *Psychometrika,* 1953, **18,** 309–317.

Lorge, I. The Thurstone attitude scales: I. Reliability and consistency of rejection and acceptance. *J. soc. Psychol.,* 1939, **10,** 187–198.

McCue, B. F. Constructing an instrument for evaluating attitudes toward intensive competition in team games. *Res. Quart.,* 1953, **24,** 205–209.

McGee, R. Comparison of attitudes toward intensive competition for high school girls. *Res. Quart.,* 1956, **27,** 60–73.

McGinnies, E., and Altman, I. Discussion as a function of attitudes and content of a persuasive communication. *J. appl. Psychol.,* 1959, **43,** 53–59.

McGrath, J. E. *Social psychology: A brief introduction.* New York: Holt, 1964.

McHugh, G., and Wasser, J. K. Application of the Thurstone-Chave attitude rating technique to attitudes toward menstruation. *Psychol. Rep.,* 1959, **5,** 677–682.

McKeachie, W. J. Individual conformity to attitudes of classroom groups. *J. abnorm. soc. Psychol.,* 1954, **49,** 282–289.

Maher, R. A., Watt, N., and Campbell, D. T. Comparative validity of two projective and two structured attitude tests in a prison population. *J. appl. Psychol.,* 1960, **44,** 284–288.

Mahler, I. Attitudes toward socialized medicine. *J. soc. Psychol.,* 1953, **38,** 273–282.

Manry, J. C. World citizenship. *Univer. Iowa Stud.: Stud. Charact.,* 1927, **1,** No. 1. Pp. 1–67.

Martin, C., and Nichols, R. C. Personality and religious belief. *J. soc. Psychol.,* 1962, **56,** 3–8.

Merwin, J. C., and Di Vesta, F. J. A study of need theory and career choice. *J. counsel. Psychol.,* 1959, **6,** 302–308.

Middleton, W. C., and Wright, R. R. A comparison of a group of ninth and tenth grade delinquent and nondelinquent boys and girls on certain attitude scales. *J. genet. Psychol.,* 1941, **58,** 139–150.

Miller, F. D. The validation of a generalized attitude scaling technique. Construction of an attitude scale toward teaching. *Purdue Univer. Stud. high. Educ. XXVI,* 1934, **35,** No. 4. Pp. 98–110.

Miller, H. E. The construction and evaluation of a scale of attitudes toward occupations. *Purdue Univer. Stud. high. Educ., XXVI,* 1934, **35,** 68–76.

Miller, K. M., and Biggs, J. B. Attitude change through undirected group discussion. *J. educ. Psychol.,* 1958, **49,** 224–228.

Miller, L. W. A critical analysis of the Peterson-Thurstone war attitude scale. *J. educ. Psychol.,* 1934, **25,** 662–668.

Mitchell, C. Do scales for measuring attitudes have any significance? *J. educ. Res.,* 1941, **34,** 444–452.

Mitnick, L. L., and McGinnies, E. Influencing ethnocentrism in small groups through a film communication. *J. abnorm. soc. Psychol.,* 1958, **56,** 82–90.

Molnar, A. The effects of styles, speakers, and arguments on the attitudes and perceptions of a listening audience. Unpublished master's thesis, Univer. of Maryland, 1955.

Murray, H. A., and Morgan, C. D. A clinical study of sentiments. *Genet. psychol. Monogr.,* 1945, **32,** 3–149.

Myster, A. M. Further validation of the Wert-Myster farming attitude scale. *Rural Sociol.,* 1944, **9,** 226–232.

Nadler, E. B., and Morrow, W. R. Authoritarian attitudes toward women and their correlates. *J. soc. Psychol.,* 1959, **49,** 113–123.

Nagle, B. F. Productivity, employee attitude, and supervisor sensitivity. Unpublished master's thesis, Purdue Univer., 1953.

Nelson, E. Radicalism-conservatism in student attitudes. *Psychol. Monogr.*, 1938, **50,** No. 4 (Whole No. 224).

Nelson, E. Fathers' vocation and certain student attitudes. *J. abnorm. soc. Psychol.*, 1939, **34,** 275–279.

Nelson, E. Student attitudes toward religion. *Genet. psychol. Monogr.*, 1940, **22,** 325–423.

Nelson, E., and Nelson, N. Student attitudes and vocational choices. *J. abnorm. soc. Psychol.*, 1940, **35,** 279–282.

Nelson, E. N. P. Persistence of attitudes of college students fourteen years later. *Psychol. Monogr.*, 1954, **68,** No. 2 (Whole No. 373).

Nelson, E. N. P. Patterns of religious attitude shifts from college to fourteen years later. *Psychol. Monogr.*, 1956, **70,** No. 17 (Whole No. 424).

Newcomb, T. M. Labor unions as seen by their members: An attempt to measure attitudes. In Hartman, G. W., and Newcomb, T. M. (Eds.), *Industrial conflict.* New York: Cordon Press, 1939. Pp. 313–338.

Newcomb, T. M. *Personality and social change: Attitude formation in a student community.* New York: Dryden Press, 1943.

Newcomb, T. M. *Social psychology.* New York: Holt, 1950.

Newcomb, T. M., and Svehla, G. Intrafamily relationships in attitudes. *Sociometry,* 1938, **1,** 180–205.

Newcomb, T. M., Turner, R. H., and Converse, P. E. *Social psychology: The study of human interaction.* New York: Holt, 1965.

Nichols, R. C. A factor analysis of parental attitudes of fathers. *Child Develpm.*, 1962, **33,** 791–802.

Nickols, S. A., and Shaw, M. E. Saliency and two measures of attitude. *Psychol. Rep.*, 1964, **14,** 273–274.

Nunnally, J. C. The communication of mental health information: A comparison of opinions of experts and public with mass media presentation. *Behav. Sci.*, 1957, **2,** 222–230.

Nunnally, J. C. *Tests and measurements: Assessment and prediction.* New York: McGraw-Hill, 1959.

Nunnally, J. C. *Popular conceptions of mental health.* New York: Holt, 1961.

Ojemann, R. H. The measurement of attitude toward self-reliance. *Univer. Iowa Stud. Child Welf.*, 1934, **10,** 101–111.

O'Reilly, C. T., and O'Reilly, E. J. Religious beliefs of Catholic college students and their attitudes toward minorities. *J. abnorm. soc. Psychol.*, 1954, **49,** 378–380.

Osgood, C. E. Cognitive dynamics in the conduct of human affairs. *Publ. Opin. Quart.*, 1960, **24,** 341–365.

Osgood, C. E., and Suci, G. J. Factor analysis of meaning. *J. exp. Psychol.*, 1955, **50,** 325–338.

Osgood, C. E., Suci, G. J., and Tannenbaum, P. H. *The measurement of meaning.* Urbana, Ill.: Univer. of Illinois Press, 1957.

Peak, H., Morrison, H. W., Spivak, M., and Zinnes, J. L. Some factors in resistance to attitude change. I. Personal factors. Tech. Rep. No. 1. Office of Naval Research, August 15, 1956.

Peak, H., and Morrison, H. W. The acceptance of information into attitude structure. *J. abnorm. soc. Psychol.*, 1958, **57,** 127–135.

Peckham, D. R. High school seniors' opinion of teaching. *Calif. J. educ. Res.*, 1962, **13,** 17–30.

Perricone, P. J. Doctor-patient interaction: Formulation of a hypothesis and development of a test for measuring attitudes toward physicians. Unpublished master's thesis, Univer. of Florida, December, 1964.

Peterson, R. C., and Thurstone, L. L. *The effect of motion pictures on the social attitudes of high school children.* Chicago: Univer. of Chicago Bookstore, 1933.

Pettigrew, T. F. Personality and sociocultural factors in intergroup attitudes. A cross-national comparison. *J. Conflict Resolut.*, 1958, **2**, 29.

Pettigrew, T. F. Social distance attitudes of South African Students. *Soc. Forces,* 1960, **38**, 246–253.

Phillips, E. L. Attitudes toward self and others: A brief questionnaire report. *J. consult. Psychol.,* 1951, **15**, 79–81.

Pintner, R., and Forlano, G. The influence of attitude upon scaling of attitude items. *J. soc. Psychol.,* 1937, **8**, 39–45.

Pratt, S., Giannitrapani, D., and Khanna, P. Attitudes toward the mental hospital and selected population characteristics. *J. clin. Psychol.,* 1960, **16**, 214–218.

Prentice, N. M. Critique and notes: The comparability of positive and negative items in scales of ethnic prejudice. *J. abnorm. soc. Psychol.,* 1956, **52**, 420–421.

Prentice, N. M. The influence of ethnic attitudes on reasoning about ethnic groups. *J. abnorm. soc. Psychol.,* 1957, **55**, 270–272.

Proshansky, H. M. A projective method for the study of attitudes. *J. abnorm. soc. Psychol.,* 1943, **38**, 393–395.

Prothro, E. T. The effect of strong negative attitudes on the placement of items in a Thurstone scale. *J. soc. Psychol.,* 1955, **41**, 11–17.

Prothro, E. T. Personal involvement and item displacement on Thurstone scales. *J. soc. Psychol.,* 1957, **45**, 191–196.

Pulos, L., and Spilka, B. Perceptual selectivity, memory, and anti-Semitism. *J. abnorm. soc. Psychol.,* 1961, **62**, 690–692.

Purdue University Bookstore. *Purdue measurement and evaluation instruments; tests and scales.* 1961–62 Catalog. Purdue Univer.: West Layfayette, Indiana, 1961.

Putney, S., and Middleton, R. Dimensions and correlates of religious ideologies. *Soc. Forces,* 1961, **39**, 285–290.

Quay, L. C., Bartlett, C. J., Wrightsman, L. S., Jr., and Catron, D. Attitude change in attendant employees. *J. soc. Psychol.,* 1961, **55**, 27–31.

Ramsey, C. E., and Nelson, L. Change in values and attitudes toward the family. *Amer. sociol. Rev.,* 1956, **21**, 605–609.

Remmers, H. H. Generalized attitudes scales—studies in social-psychological measurements. *Bull. Purdue Univer.,* 1934*a*, **25**, 7–17

Remmers, H. H. (Ed.) *Studies in Higher Education, XXVI, XXXI,* and *XXXIV.* Layfayette, Ind.: Purdue Univer., 1934*b*, 1936, 1938.

Remmers, H. H. Attitudes toward Germans, Japanese, Jews, and Nazis as affected by the war. *Sch. and Soc.,* 1943, **57**, 138–140.

Remmers, H. H. Changes in attitudes toward Germans, Japanese, Jews and Nazis as affected by the war. *Sch. and Soc.,* 1946, **63**, 118–119.

Remmers, H. H. Changes in attitude toward Germans, Japanese, Jews, and Nazis. *Sch. and Soc.,* 1947, **65**, 484–487.

Remmers, H. H. *Manual for the Purdue Master Attitude Scales.* Layfayette, Indiana: Purdue Research Foundation, 1960*a*.

Remmers, H. H. (Ed.) *A scale to measure attitude toward any school subject.* Layfayette, Ind.: Purdue Research Foundation, 1960*b*.

Remmers, H. H. (Ed.) Studies in attitudes; a contribution to social psychological research methods. *Stud. high. Educ.,* 1934, **35**.

Remmers, H. H., and Silance, E. B. Generalized attitude scales. *J. soc. Psychol.,* 1934, **5**, 298–312.

Reznikoff, M., Brady, J. P., and Zeller, W. W. The psychiatric attitudes battery: A procedure for assessing attitudes toward psychiatric treatment and hospitals. *J. clin. Psychol.,* 1959, **15**, 260–265.

Reznikoff, M., Brady, J. P., Zeller, W. W., and Toomey, L. C. Attitudinal change in hospitalized psychiatric patients. *J clin. exp. Psychopath. quart. Rev. Psychiat. Neurol.,* 1960, **21**, 309–314.

Rhine, R. J. A concept formation approach to attitude acquisition. *Psychol. Rev.*, 1958, **65**, 362–370.

Richardson, C. E. A sentence completion health attitudes test for college students. *J. Sch. Hlth*, 1960*a*, **30**, 32–35.

Richardson, C. E. Thurstone scales for measuring attitudes of college students toward physical fitness and exercise. *Res. Quart.*, 1960*b*, **31**, 638–643.

Riegel, K. F., and Riegel, R. M. Analysis of differences in test and item difficulty between young and old adults. *J. Geront.*, 1962, **17**, 97–105.

Rikard, T. E., Triandis, H. C., and Patterson, C. H. Indices of employer prejudice toward disabled applicants. *J. appl. Psychol.*, 1963, **47**, 52–55.

Riker, B. L. A comparison of the methods used in attitude research. *J. abnorm. soc. Psychol.*, 1944, **39**, 24–42.

Riland, L. H. Relationship of the Guttman components of attitude intensity and personal involvement. *J. appl. Psychol.*, 1959, **43**, 279–284.

Ritt, L. W. The development of a scale for measuring attitudes toward Negroes, based on a stochastic model. Unpublished master's thesis. Univer. of Florida, April, 1964.

Robinson, K. F. An experimental study of the effects of group discussion upon the social attitudes of college students. *Speech Monogr.*, 1941, **8**, 34–57.

Rogers, J. L. Prospective teachers' attitudes toward freedom of information. *Journ. Quart.*, 1955, **32**, 169–176.

Rokeach, M. *The open and closed mind.* New York: Basic Books, 1960.

Rosander, A. C. An attitude scale based upon behavior situations. *J. soc. Psychol.*, 1937, **8**, 3–16.

Rosander, A. C., and Thurstone, L. L. Attitude toward the Constitution of the United States: Scale No. 12, Forms A and B. In Thurstone, L. L. (Ed.), *The measurement of social attitudes.* Chicago: Univer. of Chicago Press, 1931.

Rosander, A. C., and Thurstone, L. L. Scale of Attitude toward Censorship: Scale No. 28. In Thurstone, L. L. (Ed.), *The measurement of social attitudes.* Chicago: Univer. of Chicago Press, 1931.

Rosenbaum, M. E., and Zimmerman, I. M. The effect of external commitment on response to an attempt to change opinions. *Pub. Opin. Quart.*, 1959, **23**, 247–254.

Rosenberg, N. J. The experimental investigation of a value-theory of attitude structure. *Dissert. Abstr.*, 1953, **13**, 899–900.

Rundquist, E. A., and Sletto, R. F. *Scoring instructions for the Minnesota scale for the Survey of Opinions.* Minneapolis: Univer. of Minneapolis Press, 1934.

Rundquist, E. A., and Sletto, R. F. *Personality in the depression.* Minneapolis: Univer. of Minnesota Press, 1936.

Saffir, M. A. A comparative study of scales constructed by three psychophysical methods. *Psychometrika*, 1937, **2**, 179–198.

Sampson, D. L., and Smith, H. P. A scale to measure worldminded attitudes. *J. soc. Psychol.*, 1957, **45**, 99–106.

Sanai, M. A. An experimental study of politico-economic attitudes. *Int. J. opin. Res.*, 1950*a*, **4**, 563–577.

Sanai, M. A. A factorial study of social attitudes. *J. soc. Psychol.*, 1950*b*, **31**, 167–182.

Sanai, M. A. The relation between social attitudes and characteristics of personality. *J. soc. Psychol.*, 1952, **36**, 3–13.

Sappenfield, B. R. The attitudes and attitude estimates of Catholics, Protestants, and Jewish students. *J. soc. Psychol.*, 1942, **16**, 173–197.

Sarnoff, I., and Katz, D. The motivational bases of attitude change. *J. abnorm. soc. Psychol.*, 1954, **49**, 115–124.

Schaefer, E. S., and Bell, R. Q. Patterns of attitudes toward child rearing and the family. *J. abnorm. soc. Psychol.*, 1957, **54**, 391–395.

Schaefer, E. S., and Bell, R. Q. Development of a parental attitude research instrument. *Child Develpm.*, 1958, **29**, 339–362.

Schmid, J., Jr., Morsh, J. E., and Detter, H. M. Analysis of job satisfaction. In *Thirteenth Yearb. nat. Council Measmt Used Educ.*, 1956, pp. 45–52. (Distributed separately as *Research Report* AFPTRC-TN-57-30, March, 1957, ASTIA Document No. 098935.)

Schuessler, K. F. A note on statistical significance of scalogram. *Sociometry*, 1961, **24**, 312–318.

Secord, P. F., and Backman, C. W. *Social psychology*. New York: McGraw-Hill, 1964.

Seeleman, V. The influence of attitude upon the remembering of pictorial material. *Arch. Psychol.*, 1940, No. 258. P. 69.

Segall, M. H. The effect of attitude and experience on judgments of controversial statements. *J. abnorm. soc. Psychol.*, 1959, **58**, 61–68.

Sewell, W. R., and Amend, E. E. The influence of size of home community on attitudes and personality traits. *Amer. sociol. Rev.*, **8**, 180–184.

Sharaf, M. R., and Levinson, D. J. Patterns of ideology and role definition among psychiatric residents. In M. Greenblatt, D. J. Levinson, and R. H. Williams (Eds.), *The patient and the mental hospital*. Glencoe, Ill.: Free Press, 1957. Pp. 263–285.

Shaw, M. E. Some correlates of social acquiescence. *J. soc. Psychol.*, 1961, **55**, 133–141.

Shaw, M. E., Worthy, M., and Blum, J. M. Effects of number of judges upon scale values in the analysis of small group tasks. Tech. Rep. No. 2. Office of Naval Research Contract NR 170-266, Nonr-580(11), Gainesville, Univer. of Florida, October, 1963.

Shepard, R. N. The analysis of proximities: Multidimensional scaling with an unknown distance function. I. *Psychometrika*, 1962*a*, **27**, 125–140.

Shepard, R. N. The analysis of proximities: Multidimensional scaling with an unknown distance function. II. *Psychometrika*, 1962*b*, **27**, 219–246.

Sherif, M., and Cantril, H. The psychology of attitudes: Part I. *Psychol. Rev.*, 1945, **52**, 295–319.

Sherif, M., and Hovland, C. I. Judgmental phenomena and scales of attitude measurement: Placement of items with individual choice of number of categories. *J. abnorm. soc. Psychol.*, 1953, **48**, 135–141.

Sherif, M., and Sherif, C. W. *An outline of social psychology*. (Rev. ed.) New York: Harper & Row, 1956.

Sherman, L. J. Mental patients' attitudes toward tranquilizing drugs: Test development. *Psychol. Rep.*, 1960, **7**, 167–170.

Shoben, E. J., Jr. The assessment of parental attitudes in relation to child adjustment. *Genet. psychol. Monogr.*, 1949, **39**, 101–148.

Siebrecht, E. B. *The Siebrecht Attitude Scale: manual of directions*. New York: New York Univer., Division of General Education, Center for Safety Education, 1941.

Siegel, A. E., and Siegel, S. Reference groups, membership groups, and attitude change. *J. abnorm. soc. Psychol.*, 1957, **55**, 360–364.

Sigerfoos, C. C. The validation and application of a scale of attitude toward any vocation. *Bull. Purdue Univer., further Stud. Attitudes, Ser. II*, 1936, 177–191.

Silance, E. B., and Remmers, H. H. An experimental generalized master scale: A scale to measure attitudes toward any school subject. *Purdue Univ. Stud. high. Educ., XXVI*, 1934, **35**, 84–88.

Sims, V. M., and Patrick, J. R. Attitude toward the Negro of Northern and Southern college students. *J. soc. Psychol.*, 1936, **7**, 192–204.

Smith, G. M. *Motivation research in advertising and marketing*. New York: McGraw-Hill, 1954.

Smith, H. P. Do intercultural experiences affect attitudes? *J. abnorm. soc. Psychol.*, 1955, **51**, 469–477.

Smith, M. A study of change of attitudes toward the Negro. *J. Negro Educ.*, 1939*a*, **8**, 64–70.

Smith, M. A note on attitude patterning among protagonists of war and capital punishment. *J. soc. Psychol.*, 1939*b*, **10**, 553–558.

Smith, M. Attitude homogeneity and length of group association. *J. abnorm. soc. Psychol.*, 1940*a*, **35**, 573–578.

Smith, M. Spontaneous change of attitude toward communism. *Sch. and Soc.*, 1940*b*, **51**, 684–688.

Smith, M. Change of attitude with reference to birth control. *Sch. and Soc.*, 1942, **56**, 25–28.

Smith, M. Attitudes toward war and capital punishment as to size of community. *Sch. and Soc.*, 1943, **58**, 220–222.

Smith, M. Change of attitude toward the law. *Sch. and Soc.*, 1944, **60**, 286–287.

Smith, M. Change of attitude toward punishment of criminals. *Sch. and Soc.*, 1945*a*, **61**, 236–238.

Smith, M. Increase in homogeneity of attitude during a sociology course. *Sch. and Soc.*, 1945*b*, **62**, 14–15.

Smith, M. On the increase in homogeneity of attitudes during a sociology course: Second report. *Sch. and Soc.*, 1946, **64**, 223–225.

Smith, M. H. Attitude toward Soviet Russia: I. The standardization of a scale and some distributions of scores. *J. soc. Psychol.*, 1946, **23**, 3–16.

Souelem, O. Mental patients' attitudes toward mental hospitals. *J. clin. Psychol.*, 1955, **11**, 181–185.

Spearman, C. Correlation calculated from faulty data. *Brit. J. Psychol.*, 1910, **3**, 271–295.

Stagner, R. Some factors related to attitude toward war, 1938. *J. soc. Psychol.*, 1942, **16**, 131–142.

Stagner, R. Studies of aggressive attitudes: I. Measurement and interrelation of selected attitudes. *J. soc. Psychol.*, 1944*a*, **20**, 109–130.

Stagner, R. Studies of aggressive attitudes: II. Changes from peace to war. *J. soc. Psychol.*, 1944*b*, **20**, 121–128.

Stagner, R. Studies of aggressive attitudes: III. The role of personal and family scores. *J. soc. Psychol.*, 1944*c*, **20**, 129–140.

Stagner, R., Brown, J. F., Gundlach, R. H., and White, R. K. A survey of public opinion on the prevention of war. *J. soc. Psychol., SPSSI Bull.*, 1942, **16**, 109–130.

Stagner, R., Chalmers, W. E., and Derber, M. Guttman-type scales for Union and Management attitudes toward each other. *J. appl. Psychol.*, 1958, **42**, 293–300.

Steckler, G. Authoritarian ideology in Negro college students. *J. abnorm. soc. psychol.*, 1957, **54**, 396–399.

Steiner, I. D., and Field, W. L. Role assignment and interpersonal influence. *J. abnorm. soc. Psychol.*, 1960, **61**, 239–245.

Steingisser, E. R. The influence of set upon attitudes toward the blind as related to self-concept. Unpublished master's thesis, Univer. of New Hampshire, 1954.

Stephenson, C. M. The relation between the attitudes toward Negroes of seniors in a school of education and their major subject. *J. educ. Res.*, 1955, **49**, 113–128.

Stevens, S. S. Mathematics, measurement, and psychophysics. In S. S. Stevens (Ed.), *Handbook of experimental psychology*. New York: Wiley, 1951. Pp. 1–49.

Storey, W. D. Standardization of an employee opinion survey. Unpublished master's thesis, Purdue Univer., 1955.

Stott, L. H. Parental attitudes of farm, town, and city parents in relation to certain personality adjustments in their children. *J. soc. Psychol.*, 1940, **11**, 325–339.

Strong, E. K., Jr. *Vocational interests of men and women*. Stanford, California: Stanford Univer. Press, 1943.

Strunk, O., Jr. Attitude toward psychology as a factor in the judgment of the readability of a psychology textbook. *Proc. W. Va. Acad. Sci.,* 1957–58, **29,** 175–179.

Stump, N. F., and Lewis, A. What some ministers think about war; some findings from a brief statistical study of ministers' responses toward war. *Religious Educ.,* 1935, **30,** 135–137.

Swenson, W. M. A study of death attitudes in the grontic population and their relationship to certain measurable physical and social characteristics. *Dissert. Abstr.,* 1958, **19.**

Swenson, W. M. Attitudes toward death in an aged population. *J. Geront.,* 1961*a,* **16,** 49–52.

Swenson, W. M. Structured personality testing in the aged: An MMPI study of the gerontic population. *J. clin. Psychol.,* 1961*b,* **17,** 302–304.

Telford, C. W. An experimental study of some factors influencing the social attitudes of college students. *J. soc. Psychol.,* 1934, **5,** 421–428.

Thistlethwaite, D. L. Attitude and structure as factors in the distortion of reasoning. *J. abnorm. soc. Psychol.,* 1950, **45,** 442–458.

Thomson, G. N. *The factorial analysis of human ability.* New York: Houghton Mifflin, 1939.

Thurstone, L. L. Psychophysical analysis. *Amer. J. Psychol.,* 1927, **38,** 368–389.

Thurstone, L. L. Theory of attitude measurement. *Psychol. Bull.,* 1929, **36,** 222–241.

Thurstone, L. L. (Ed.) *The measurement of social attitudes.* Chicago: Univer. of Chicago Press, 1929–34.

Thurstone, L. L. A scale for measuring attitude toward the movies. *J. educ. Res.,* 1930, **22,** 89–94.

Thurstone, L. L. The measurement of social attitudes. *J. abnorm. soc. Psychol.,* 1931*a,* **26,** 249–269.

Thurstone, L. L. (Ed.) *Scales for the measurement of social attitudes.* Chicago: Univer. of Chicago Press, 1931*b*.

Thurstone, L. L. (Ed.) *The measurement of social attitudes.* Chicago: Univer. of Chicago Press, 1932*a*.

Thurstone, L. L. *Motion pictures and attitudes of children.* Chicago: Univer. of Chicago Press, 1932*b*.

Thurstone, L. L. *The measurement of values.* Chicago: Univer. of Chicago Press, 1959.

Thurstone, L. L., and Chave, E. J. *The measurement of attitude.* Chicago: Univer. of Chicago Press, 1929.

Toomey, L. C., Reznikoff, M., Brady, J. P., and Schumann, D. W. Attitudes of nursing students toward psychiatric treatment and hospitals. *Ment. Hygiene,* 1961*a,* **45,** 589–602.

Toomey, L. C., Reznikoff, M., Brady, J. P., and Schumann, D. W. Some relationships between the attitudes of nursing students toward psychiatry and success in psychiatric affiliation. *Nursing Res.,* 1961*b,* **10,** 165–169.

Torgerson, W. S. *Theory and methods of scaling.* New York: Wiley, 1958.

Torgerson, W. S. Multidimensional scaling: I. Theory and method. *Psychometrika,* 1952, **17,** 401–419.

Traxler, A. E. Evaluation of scores of the high-school pupils on Droba-Thurstone attitude toward war scale. *J. educ. Psychol.,* 1935, **26,** 616–622.

Triandis, H. C. Cultural influences upon cognitive processes. In L. Berkowitz (Ed.), *Advances in experimental social psychology.* Vol. 1. New York: Academic Press, 1964*a*. Pp. 1–48.

Triandis, H. C. Exploratory factor analyses of the behavioral component of social attitudes. *J. abnorm. soc. Psychol.,* 1964*b,* **68,** 420–430.

Triandis, H. C., and Triandis, M. Race, social class, religion, and nationality as determinants of social distance. *J. abnorm. soc. Psychol.,* 1960, **61,** 110–118.

Trumbo, D. A. Individual and group correlates of attitudes toward work-related change. *J. appl. Psychol.*, 1961, **45**, 338–344.

Tuckman, J., and Lorge, I. The effect of institutionalization on attitudes toward old people. *J. abnorm. soc. Psychol.*, 1952*a*, **47**, 337–344.

Tuckman, J., and Lorge, I. Attitudes toward older workers. *J. appl. Psychol.*, 1952*b*, **36**, 149–153.

Tuckman, J., and Lorge, I. Experts' biases about the older worker. *Science*, 1952*c*, **115**, 685–687.

Tuckman, J., and Lorge, I. The attitudes of the aged toward the older worker; for institutionalized and noninstitutionalized adults. *J. Geront.*, 1952*d*, **7**, 559–564.

Tuckman, J., and Lorge, I. The influence of a course on the psychology of the adult on attitudes toward old people and older workers. *J. educ. Psychol.*, 1952*e*, **43**, 400–407.

Tuckman, J., and Lorge, I. Attitudes toward old people. *J. soc. Psychol.*, 1953*a*, **37**, 249–260.

Tuckman, J., and Lorge, I. The effect of changed directions on the attitudes about old people and the older worker. *Educ. psychol. Measmt*, 1953*b*, **13**, 607–613.

Tuckman, J., and Lorge, I. When aging begins and stereotypes about aging. *J. Geront.*, 1953*c*, **8**, 489–492.

Tuckman, J., and Lorge, I. The effects of changed directions on stereotypes about aging: Before and after instruction. *Educ. psychol. Measmt*, 1954, **14**, 128–132.

Tuckman, J., and Lorge, I. Attitudes toward aging of individuals with experience with the aged. *J. genet. Psychol.*, 1958*a*, **92**, 199–204.

Tuckman, J., and Lorge, I. The projection of personal symptom into stereotype about aging. *J. Geront.*, 1958*b*, **13**, 70–73.

Tuckman, J., Lorge, I., and Spooner, G. A. The effect of family environment on attitudes toward old people and the older worker. *J. soc. Psychol.*, 1953, **38**, 207–218.

Uphoff, W. H., and Dunnette, M. D. *Understanding the union member.* Minneapolis: Univer. of Minnesota Press, 1956.

Upshaw, H. S. Own attitude as an anchor in equal appearing intervals. *J. abnorm. soc. Psychol.*, 1962, **64**, 85–96.

Upshaw, H. S. The effect of variable perspectives on judgments of opinion statements for Thurstone scales: Equal appearing intervals, *J. pers. soc. Psychol.*, 1965, **2**, 60–69.

Vaughan, G. M., and Thompson, H. T. New Zealand children's attitudes toward Maoris. *J. abnorm. soc. Psychol.*, 1961, **62**, 701–704.

Voor, J. J. The relationship between the religious attitude and the conservative radical attitude among seminarians studying for the Catholic priesthood. Unpublished master's thesis, Catholic Univer. of America, Washington, D.C., February, 1953.

Walter, O. M. The improvement of attitude research. *J soc. Psychol.*, 1951, **31**, 143–146.

Walters, J. The effects of an introductory course in child development on the attitudes of college women toward child guidance. *J. exp. Educ.*, 1959, **27**, 311–321.

Walters, J., and Bridges, B. Attitudes of single men toward child guidance. *J. home Econ.*, 1956, **48**, 109–113.

Walters, J., and Fisher, C. Changes in the attitudes of young women toward child guidance over a two-year period. *J. educ. Res.*, 1958, **52**, 115–118.

Wang, C. K. A. Suggested criteria for writing attitude statements. *J. soc. Psychol.*, 1932, **3**, 367–373.

Wang, C. K. A., and Thurstone, L. L. Scale of attitude toward birth control: Scale

No. 21. In Thurstone, L. L. (Ed.), *The measurement of social attitudes.* Chicago: Univer. of Chicago Press, 1931.

Watt, N., and Maher, B. A. Prisoners' attitudes toward home and the judicial system. *J. crim. Law, Criminol., Police Sci.*, 1958, **49**, 327–330.

Wear, C. L. Construction of equivalent forms of an attitude scale. *Res. Quart. Amer. Assoc. Hlth Phys. Educ.*, 1955, **26**, 113–119.

Weatherley, D. Anti-Semitism and the expression of fantasy aggression. *J. abnorm. and soc. Psychol.*, 1961, **62**, 454–457.

Weatherley, D. Maternal response to childhood aggression and subsequent anti-Semitism. *J. abnorm. and soc. Psychol.*, 1963, **66**, 183–185.

Weaver, C. H. Semantic distance between students and teachers and its effect upon learning. *Speech Monogr.*, 1959, **26**, 273–281.

Webb, N. J., and Kobler, F. J. Clinical-empirical techniques for assessing the attitudes of religious toward psychiatry. *J. soc. Psychol.*, 1961, **55**, 245–251.

Webb, S. C. Scaling of attitudes by the method of equal-appearing intervals: a review. *J. soc. Psychol.*, 1955, **42**, 215–239.

Weitz, J., and Nuckols, R. C. The validity of direct and indirect questions in measuring job satisfaction. *Personnel Psychol.*, 1953, **6**, 487–494.

Weschler, I. R. An investigation of attitudes toward labor and management by means of the error-choice method: I. *J. soc. Psychol.*, 1950*a*, **32**, 51–62.

Weschler, I. R. A follow-up study on the measurement of attitudes toward labor and management by the error-choice method: II. *J. soc. Psychol.*, 1950*b*, **32**, 63–69.

Wheeler, D. K. The educational temper of a teaching source. *J. educ. Sociol.*, 1960, **34**, 160–171.

Wiley, J. H. A scale to measure parental attitudes. *J. Speech Hearing Disorders*, 1955, **20**, 284–290.

Wilke, W. H. An experimental comparison of the speech, the radio, and the printed page as propaganda devices. *Arch. Psychol.*, 1934, No. 169.

Williams, J. H. Attitudes of college students toward motion pictures. *Sch. and Soc.*, 1933, **38**, 222–224.

Wilson, D. T. Attitudes and their measurement. Mimeograph Rep., University of Florida, 1962.

Woodruff, A. D., and Di Vesta, F. J. The relationship between values, concepts, and attitudes. *Educ. Psychol. Measmt*, 1948, **8**, 645–659.

Wylie, R. C. *The self-concept. A critical survey of pertinent research literature.* Lincoln: Univer. of Nebraska Press, 1961.

Young, R. K., Benson, W. M., and Holtzman, W. H. Change in attitude toward the Negro in a Southern university. *J. abnorm. soc. Psychol.*, 1960, **60**, 131–133.

Yuker, H. E., Block, J. R., and Campbell, W. J. *A scale to measure attitudes toward disabled persons.* Study No. 5. Albertson, N.Y.: Human Resources Foundation, 1960.

Zavalloni, M., and Cook, S. W. Influence of judges' attitudes on ratings of favorableness of statements about a social group. *J. pers. soc. Psychol.*, 1965, **1**, 43–54.

Zeligs, R. Racial attitudes of children as expressed by their concepts of races. *Sociol. soc. Res.*, 1937, **21**, 361–371.

Zeligs, R. Children's intergroup concepts and stereotypes. *J. educ. Sociol.*, 1947, **21**, 113–126.

Zeligs, R. Children's intergroup attitudes. *J. genet. Psychol.*, 1948, **72**, 101–110.

Zeligs, R. Children's concepts and stereotypes of Turk, Portuguese, Roumanian, Chinese, French Canadian, Mulatto, South American, Hawaiian, and Australian. *J. genet. Psychol.*, 1953, **83**, 171–178.

Zeligs, R., and Hendrickson, G. Racial attitudes of two hundred sixth-grade children. *Sociol. soc. Res.*, 1933, **18**, 26–36.

Zubin, J., and Gristle, M. An empirical scale for measuring militarism-pacifism. *Psychol. Rec.*, 1937, **1**, 27–32.

Zuckerman, M. Reversed scales to control acquiescence response set in the parental attitude research instrument. *Child Develpm*, 1959, **30**, 523–532.

Zuckerman, M., Norton, J., and Sprague, D. S. Acquiescence and extreme sets and their role in tests of authoritarianism and parental attitudes. *Psychiatric Res. Rep.*, 1958, **10**, 28–45.

Zuckerman, M., Ribback, B. B., Monashkin, I., and Norton, J. A. Normative data and factor analysis of the parental attitude research instrument. *J. consult. Psychol.*, 1958, **22**, 165–171.

name index

subject index